A history of International Relations theory

MANCHESTER
1824
Manchester University Press

A history of International Relations theory

Third Edition

TORBJØRN L. KNUTSEN

Manchester University Press

Published by Manchester University Press
Altrincham Street, Manchester M1 7JA
www.manchesteruniversitypress.co.uk

British Library Cataloguing-in-Publication Data
A catalogue record for this book is available from the British Library

Library of Congress Cataloging-in-Publication Data applied for

ISBN   978 0 7190 9581 8 *paperback*

First published 2016

Typeset in Monotype Ehrhardt by
Koinonia, Manchester
Printed and bound in Great Britain by
Bell & Bain Ltd, Glasgow

To HAK who explained to me the love of power;
And to JLB who showed to me the power of love.

Contents

List of figures and tables   *page* viii
Preface to the third edition   ix

Introduction: Why a history of International Relations theory?   1

Part I Preludes
 1 Gods, sinners and preludes of International Relations theory   15
 2 Renaissance politics: the roots of the modern ages   45

Part II Philosophies of war and peace
 3 Reformation politics: guns, ships and printing presses   71
 4 Absolutist politics: kings, wars and an interstate system   97
 5 Enlightenment politics: the revolutionary rise of popular sovereignty   128
 6 Ideological politics: the nineteenth century and the rise of
    mass participation   169

Part III The classic age of International Relations
 7 Intermezzo: becoming contemporary   203
 8 The Great War, the big League and the twenty years' crisis   242
 9 World War II, the UN and the postwar order   278
10 Rivals, realists and Cold War   313
11 The thaw and the Third World: the Cold War after Stalin   336
12 Arms races and revolutions: systems and structures in an age
    of upheaval   364
13 The turn: the coming of the neo-liberal world   395

Part IV A future history of International Relations
14 Unipolar world?   427
15 Global politics: the end of International Relations?   456

Bibliography   493
Index   522

Figures and tables

Figures

1.1	Islam, Byzantium and the Far West, *c.* 1025	20
2.1	Italy at the end of the fifteenth century	48
3.1	State religions in Europe, *c.* 1560	76
3.2	Some sixteenth-century authors and their works	91
4.1	Europe in 1648	102
4.2	Some seventeenth-century authors and their works	119
5.1	Some eighteenth-century authors and their works	154
6.1	Some nineteenth-century authors and their works	191
13.1	The price of crude oil during the 1970s and 1980s	403
14.1	Trends of war in the world system, 1950–2005	438
14.2	Trends of war and regime types in the world system, 1950–2005	439
15.1	Four basic types of social theory	482
15.2	A simple wheel of basic IR theories	486

Tables

7.1	Colonial possessions of three European powers	215
7.2	World output of principal tropical commodities, 1880–1910	215
10.1	US national security expenditures, 1945–55	328
11.1	Wight's three traditions	352
11.2	Waltz's three images/levels of analysis	355
12.1	Number and type of wars in the first half of the Cold War, by decade	369
12.2	Numbers of US and Soviet nuclear launchers and warheads, 1962–80	372
12.3	The three main traditions of International Relations, *c.* 1975	383
14.1	The ten largest defence budgets in the world, 1993	443
14.2	The thirty largest economic entities in the world, in the mid-1990s	445
14.3	The ten largest economic entities in the world, 2014	452

Preface to the third edition

Research for the first edition of this book involved much travelling to libraries in several countries. With kind co-operation from countless librarians I tracked down old books on diplomacy, war and political thought. The original manuscript was completed during the summer of 1991 and mailed off in a thick envelope in mid-August. The envelope had scarcely left Norway before a coup took place in Moscow. Before it reached Manchester University Press, the Moscow coup had failed and the foundations of the Soviet Communist Party had cracked beyond repair. I called my editor in Manchester, told him that the world was about to change, and asked for a month's extension to rewrite my concluding chapter. He flatly rejected the request. 'You're not the only one who has called this week, you know', he remarked.

His answer underscored the truism that the world turns and things change. That politics plays itself out in the medium of time. That writing books about international relations is a reasonably hopeless task because its object will never stand still. In this regard it's much like painting flocks of birds in flight.

The object here scrutinized has not been the only thing in flux; the medium through which the object has been observed has been remarkably transformed. Many of the sources that I found in libraries then are electronically available now. They are easily downloadable from JSTOR, Project Gutenberg, Internet Archive and many other sites. I have found more texts through my desktop PC than I ever did walking around in great libraries on two continents. This new richness in sources is undoubtedly the reason why this third edition of the book is twice as thick as the first – and why it took twice as long to write.

Also, the eyes that have observed the events have changed as well. The first six chapters of the book have been edited for the new edition. The next four chapters have been entirely rewritten. The final five chapters are wholly new. The new chapters include more historical events than the old ones. One reason for this is to show how events affect theorizing – how international events shape the questions that are asked and the answers that are provided; how International Relations theory, in short, is shaped and channelled by its context.

Another reason for including more events is simply to remind the reader of some of the major changes in international history. The command of such events, together with the ability to discuss their consequences and to assess them as historical turning points, are part and parcel of studying International Relations. My impression of recent years is that incoming students often struggle with getting a decent grasp on the past and that International Relations teachers can no longer take for granted that everyone has a necessary knowledge of historical events. This is not to say that students of earlier years know more history. My impression is rather that historical knowledge has become more unevenly distributed – perhaps because many students suffer the illusion that it is unnecessary to carry historical information around in their heads since a suitable understanding of the past can now be electronically downloaded the moment the need arises.

There are times I miss the old ways – frustratingly inefficient though they often were. It was then generally assumed that the historical knowledge you carried around in your head provided raw material for political reasoning. It was also assumed that International Relations research involved travelling somewhere to find sources. Travel also means change of scene. But more importantly, travels mean change of perspective. Digital communication technology has largely conquered distance and time. Research has become incredibly more efficient. But it has also become more like office work, which rarely brings about changes in parallax.

There are many reasons for visiting libraries. And I owe many librarians deep debts. Wherever I visit – the University Libraries in Trondheim, the Library of Congress in Washington DC, the British Library in London, the Bibliothèque nationale in Paris – I am met with professionalism and patience. I owe a particular debt to the Nobel Institute in Oslo and the librarians there who have often helped me navigate through their unique collection of sources.

Many of the new chapters have been drafted in Odense, Denmark. I am much indebted to the University of Southern Denmark and its Political Science Department for inviting me for a semester and providing me with office space and time to think and write.

Various arguments in this revised edition have been inflicted upon students at the Norwegian University for Science and Technology (NTNU) and cadets at the Royal Norwegian Air Force Academy. I have benefited from seminars and discussions with colleagues at both institutions. I have been encouraged by their praise and sobered by their criticisms. And the text presented here has undoubtedly profited from both. Several chapters have also benefited from critical scrutiny by Sabrina Ramet, Christine Hassenstab, Paul Midford, Mikhail Gradovski, Pricilla Ringrose, Thomas Berker and other members of the Trondheim writers' circle.

The greatest thanks I owe to Jennifer L. Bailey – colleague, critic and unfailing supporter. I dedicate this book to her.

Torbjørn L. Knutsen
Trondheim, April 2015

Introduction:
Why a history of International Relations theory?

Why? The first short answer is: because the past has shaped the present. In order to understand the present states of world affairs, we need to know about the past events that shaped the nations, the states and the international system that we live in. The second short answer is: because the past has shaped the way we think and talk about the present. Thus, we also need to know how past events have shaped our perceptions. For the concepts we use, the theories we employ echo with experiences from the past. A reasonable grasp on the past is necessary to understand not only present international relations but also the way we have come to think and talk and theorize about these relations.

This double truism raises a double question: how, precisely, do we talk, think and theorize about the past? And what is it that distinguishes International Relations scholars from anybody else who talks and thinks about international politics? Briefly put, International Relations scholars are, first, active members of an academic community. Second, they obey a scientific methodology. Third, they are self-conscious about theory and about their place in a long theoretical tradition. This book is about this third distinction; it discusses the theoretical tradition that International Relations scholars self-consciously draw on. It argues that it goes quite far back. Also, it argues that theories are always shaped by the events of their times.

This book assumes a generous definition of the academic International Relations community. It assumes that this community of scholars is not limited to its present members. It also includes traders, soldiers, scholars and statesmen of the past. These were people who studied wealth, war, peace and power, who reported their assessments of international interaction, and who identified patterns and regularities in human interaction on the grand scale.[1]

It is an assumption of the book that these authors discussed international issues in order to better understand the events of their own time. Their theories tend to reflect questions and concerns of their own age. During the 1950s, US scholars were concerned about the Soviet build-up of nuclear missiles and developed game theory and theories of nuclear deterrence. During the 1960s, when politicians and activists were concerned with decolonization and with the fate of the increasing

1

number of newly independent states, they constructed theories to explain the poverty of these new states and to assess their chances of economic and political development.

Another assumption of the book is that scholars who address the concerns of their times tend to formulate their arguments in concepts and terms they have inherited from the past – whether they know it or not. John Maynard Keynes famously noted that knowledge about past debates is the hallmark of scholarship. Practical men, he noted famously, who care little about theories and old debates and 'who believe themselves to be exempt from any intellectual influence, are usually the slaves to some defunct economist. Madmen in authority, who hear voices in the air, are distilling their frenzy from some academic scribbler of a few years back' (Keynes 1936, p. 383).

It is often said that even the most original theorist stands on the shoulders of others. There are people who disagree and who think that they are under no one's influence and who renounce all traditions. Such people, Keynes suggests, are no true theorists, and their insistence will simply reveal ignorance about whose shoulders they stand on. And if they do, in fact, stand on no shoulders at all, they are unlikely to see very far and unlikely to contribute much to their chosen field. Writers who are independent of any 'republic of letters' and unconnected to its conversations are unlikely to add anything of scientific value.

This book reports on conversations of the past. Most of the people discussed here are long dead. Some of them may be defunct. But most of them have raised issues which have contributed to the way we talk and think and write about international relations today. Take the example of the nineteenth-century Scottish lawyer James Lorimer who argued some 150 years ago that any system composed of sovereign states is 'anarchical' in nature. 'Anarchy', however, must not be confused with chaos, continued Lorimer (1877). For anarchic systems tend to develop ordering mechanisms. In the case of the international anarchy, one such mechanism is the 'balance of power'. Another is that of 'interdependence'. These two mechanisms curtail the sovereignty of states and harness the anarchy of the system. To make the world even more orderly – to curtail the sovereignty of states even more – Lorimer proposed a third mechanism: namely, institutions of law which would regulate state behaviour through norms and generally accepted rules. Lorimer, in other words, formulated some of the most basic arguments of modern International Relations. He would have been a celebrated member of the International Relations Hall of Fame – if his arguments had not been so totally forgotten. No one cites Lorimer today. Yet, his insights are central to International Relations theory. They are, however, regularly attributed to other scholars who have waxed more recently on concepts like 'interstate system', 'anarchy', 'balance of power', 'interdependence' and 'institutions of order'.

IR, in other words, is not among those academic fields which are distinguished by a steady accumulation of knowledge. James Lorimer has, like many other International Relations authors of the past, relapsed into total darkness. Then there are International Relations authors who are not entirely forgotten but who have slid into partial oblivion. They live the life of the undead. Their texts are twilight classics, whose arguments are surrounded by myth and misunderstanding. One of these is Norman Angell, who warned against the threat of impending catastrophe on the eve of World War I. He began his most famous book, *The Great Illusion* [1910], with a warning: namely, that growing tension among Europe's Great Powers made war likely. And if war should break out, Angell continued, the result would be an unprecedented nightmare of slaughter and mass starvation. Four years later the Great War broke out. Proving Angell right.

The Great Illusion was built around the idea of interdependence – although Angell did not seem to recognize that his argument rested on the reinvention of Lorimer's idea. Angell's argument, published in 1910, is part of mainstream International Relations theory today – although Angell's name is rarely noted. The concept of interdependence was revived or reinvented by others more than half a century later. Today, if Angell is recalled at all, he is often ridiculed for having been wrong; his original message is regularly twisted into its opposite and confused with somebody else's claim that war had become impossible (Knutsen 2012).

IR history is replete with such oversights and misinterpretations. Instead of building on old insights and continuing old conversations, International Relations scholars have too often followed fads and fashions. Easy prey to the pressures of current events, International Relations has too often leaped at new questions, dropping old issues and leaving them behind to fade into oblivion – only to reinvent them decades later when new questions demand new approaches. Jean Bodin [1566] is not much invoked today; yet his discussion of the nature of 'sovereignty' still echoes through International Relations discussions.[2] Benedict Spinoza [1670] is rarely referred to, yet it was he (not Thomas Hobbes) who developed the concept of the 'state of nature' into a theory of interstate relations. William Robertson [1769] had a big impact in his time but is not much noted today, although he developed the modern 'balance-of-power' theory which is still used by International Relations Realists.

This book will recall some of these authors – pulling some of them out of the twilight of oblivion and adding a small measure of accumulation to counteract the attention-deficit disorder of the discipline. It will seek to recall these authors in their proper context. For International Relations theories, as suggested above, tend to emerge as responses to pressing questions asked in troubled times. When times change – when the troubles settle (or, more likely, when they are replaced by others) – and the questions are no longer pressing, the old responses may fade away. Or they may live their own life and shape perceptions and theories of some diligent author.

On 'Theory'

What is a 'theory'? It is hard to find a straight definition of the term. Here a 'theory' is seen as a conjectural answer to a question. A good theory is a well-reasoned and speculative explanation for a particular phenomenon. Theories bring enlightenment and understanding to an issue. To theorize is to imagine with an intention to understand. International Relations theories are mental constructs which help us make some sense out of the apparently disjointed events on the world scene.

Scholars have written about wars for hundreds of years in an effort to account for their origins, understand their nature and gauge their outcomes. Efforts to explain the outbreak of war (and also to identify the preconditions of peace) constitute a thick, red thread in the history of International Relations.

Some theories explain; they account for events and circumstances. Others prescribe; they produce guidelines for moral action. The focus of this book is on explanatory theories.

In principle there is a clear line of distinction between explanatory theory and prescriptive theory.[2] On the one hand are theories which are anchored in empirical knowledge about the past and which, through the mustering of factual, publicly available evidence, account for the way the world works. On the other are theories which are informed by value judgements and which prescribe how the world ought to be (and often add a discussion on how we ought to behave in order to move the world closer to the way it ought to be).

In practice it is hard to keep the two types of judgement apart. The 'law of supply and demand' is a powerful economic theory; the sweeping claim that the free market is the most efficient allocator of scarce resources is an ideological proposition. The distinction between theory and ideology is not always clear.

On 'International Relations'

It has been observed that speculation about the state goes back to antiquity, whereas speculation about relations among states goes back little further than to World War I. This book disputes this observation. It argues that scholars, soldiers and statesmen have, in fact, speculated about the relations among states since the modern state emerged four or five centuries ago.

The scientific study of international relations is relatively recent – indeed the very word 'international' appeared only in the late eighteenth century.[3] No long, clear and obvious tradition of international enquiry and speculation can be discerned before that, 'except dimly and obscured' (Wight 1991, p. 1). The first parts of this book seek to bring these speculations out of obscurity. They identify the major concepts and themes of these speculations, note when they emerged and how they were defined. These early phases of the tradition of International Relations are located in that part of Western history which is bracketed by the Renaissance and the Italian Wars on one side and by World War I on the other. These phases have been shaken and shaped by largescale war – by the Italian wars, the wars of Louis XIV, the Napoleonic Wars and World War I. Especially by World War I: for whereas previous wars triggered discussions on war, peace and international relations, only World War I produced 'the science of international politics' (Carr 2001). It gave the tradition a major jolt, a new emphasis, a higher popular profile, a new selfconsciousness, a mission and new institutions to help carry out that mission. It shaped the modern science of International Relations.

Where can we find the most salient speculations about relations among states? Most immediately, we find them in the tradition of political theory. For, while speculating about the state, many political theorists have also speculated about relations among states. Sometimes these speculations have been brief 'asides' – as in Hobbes's remark about how sovereign rulers are 'in the state and posture of Gladiators; having their weapons pointing and their eyes fixed upon one another' (Hobbes 1951, pp. 187f). At other times they have been spelled out in great length – as in Machiavelli's *History of Florence*, in Rousseau's discussion of 'Perpetual Peace', and in Hume's treatise on 'the Balance of Power'. Observation of and speculation about international politics are found in other places, as well: diplomatic missives, advice to heads of state, autobiographies of statesmen and stateswomen, letters of soldiers, deliberations of theologians, and texts on international law – especially texts on international law – are rich sources for a historical reconstruction of International Relations theory.[4]

The chief problem of this study is not that there are too few sources, but that there are too many. To simplify the selection and the analysis of the sources, and to facilitate the presentation of the argument, this book reduces the sources to manageable proportions in several ways. Most importantly, it provides a narrow definition of its object – that is, the tradition of International Relations theory. Also, its primary focus is on the sovereign state. Although economic theories are sometimes discussed to complete the account, the main focus is trained on interactions among sovereign states. Concerns about war and military capabilities of states are emphasized.

This restriction of focus has a high cost: it limits the study in time and space. It makes the 'state' the primary object of the discussion and 'sovereignty' the primary concept. The two are intimately intertwined through modern history. By the 'state' is meant the territorial state – an independent political community 'which possesses a government and asserts sovereignty in relation to a particular portion of the earth's surface and a particular segment of the human population' (Bull 1977, p. 8). This 'state' emerged out of the tumultuous interaction in Western Europe, which gives the present study a geographical limitation: it is inordinately preoccupied with Western events and with European theorists.

By 'sovereignty' is understood the ultimate source of legitimate authority over the state. This understanding of sovereignty has constituted the core concern in the long tradition of political science. Whereas economics has been organized around the problematic of 'wealth', philology around 'language' and medicine around the 'health' of the body, political science has been organized around the problematic of 'sovereignty'.

On International Relations theory

International Relations deals with human behaviour in the largest of all social groups: the international society. This society has two characteristic features which distinguish it from other human groups. First – most obviously but also most overlooked – membership in the international society is obligatory. Most other human societies offer, in principle at least, voluntary membership; individual members can leave if they want to, and the ultimate sanction which can be applied to individuals who refuse to obey the rules of sociability is expulsion. It is a peculiar nature of international society that membership in it is compulsory. No state can alter its geographic location; no territory can be made to go away.

Second, international society is governed by no ultimate authority. Many proposals have been made to organize a world government, yet no true world legislature exists which makes rules and laws that emphasize the solidaric and sociable side of human interaction. Although there exists an elaborate body of international law, there is neither a global legislator nor an executive power authorized to enforce these laws. In domestic society, laws and sanctions are devised and applied by political institutions which act in the name of society – domestic society has legislative and executive institutions, represented by a prime minister, a president or a king. International society has no such supreme institution (Lorimer 1877). Theories about international society distinguish themselves from other political theories by being preoccupied with human behaviour in a 'state of nature' or in an *anarchical* society (Bull 1977).

The evolution of International Relations theory

The absence of a supreme authority does not mean that human sociability is removed from international society altogether, as some authors maintain. Rather, it means that the sociable nature of humanity is deemphasized and that allowances are made for a larger share of egotistical, unilateral behaviour. The traditional way to justify this greater allowance of egotism is to emphasize the concept of sovereignty. Modern International Relations has been dominated by the twin notion of the presence and the absence of sovereignty. Applied to relations *within* states, this involves the belief that there is a final and absolute authority in society. Applied to relations *among* states, it expresses the antithesis of this belief – that is, the principle that internationally, over and above a collection of societies, no supreme authority exists. With the concept of sovereignty as its fulcrum, International Relations has traditionally been preoccupied with the dichotomies of 'war', and 'peace', 'anarchy' and 'order'.

When did scholars and statesmen and stateswomen begin to speculate about sovereign states and about the nature of their interaction? It is useful to distinguish between two phases in the development of International Relations theory. The first phase involves the emergence of the basic terms of the discourse – such as the modern concept of the 'state' and notions of an interstate 'system' and of a 'balance of power'. Part I of the book is entitled 'Preludes'. It covers this early, pre-theoretical phase in two chapters. Chapter 1 discusses the growth of states and the unique political system in Western Europe during the course of the Middle Ages. Several observers noted this development and wrote about it. Most of them were theologians – like Thomas Aquinas, Pierre Dubois and Marsiglio of Padua. In these early phases it is hard to assess the quality of their analysis. It is for example hard to say when empirical observations end and theological speculation begins.

Chapter 2 covers Europe in the 'long sixteenth century'. It presents a more secular age in which Renaissance discoveries in space (the Americas) and rediscoveries in time (the past cultures of ancient Greece and Rome) altered the traditional precepts of geography, history and social order. This chapter notes how these discoveries challenged the medieval outlook. It argues that it was during this crowded and tumultuous era that the key concepts of International Relations theorizing like 'state' and 'sovereignty' found their first secular definitions. Major contributors to this formative first phase were Iberian lawyers like Vitoria and Italian civil servants like Machiavelli and Guicciardini.

Part II of the book is entitled 'Philosophies of war and peace'. It covers the second main phase in the development of International Relations theory – which stretches from the Renaissance and the Reformation on the one hand to the Second Industrial Revolution and World War I on the other. This phase is covered in four chapters. They present the continued discussion of concepts like 'state' and 'sovereignty' and their inclusion in larger, explanatory frameworks of order.

Chapter 3 begins with the scientific innovations of the sixteenth and seventeenth centuries and the evolution of modern, rational approaches to the world. Speculations about international relations were now included in larger, secular systems of thought. Jean Bodin made an important contribution by clarifying the central concept of 'sovereignty'. Also, he initiated a discussion about the interaction between sovereign actors that was continued by later thinkers – like Gentili and Hobbes.

Chapter 4 covers the seventeenth century. It is a long and dense chapter and saturated with conceptual innovations we recognize as modern. It begins with the Thirty Years War which sees the growth of the modern European states and the concepts and theories of modern politics. The chapter discusses international relations in the age of absolutism. At its centre stands a portrait of Thomas Hobbes. He was hardly the first theorist to apply the concept of a social contract to describe relations between sovereign princes; but he was the first to use the modern concept of a precontractual state of nature as an analogy to interstate relations. The chapter then shows how Benedict Spinoza elaborated on Hobbes's concept of the state of nature and applied it to relations among sovereign states in a lawless world.

Other authors were taken aback by the bleak image drawn by Hobbes and Spinoza. The chapter shows how Émeric Crucé protested their pessimistic vision of international politics as red in tooth and claw and how he painted a more optimistic picture of international interaction that emphasized co-operation and harmony among rational individuals. Still other seventeenth-century theorists struck a middle position between the pessimism of Hobbes and the optimism of Crucé. The chapter singles out Hugo Grotius among them. He recognized that international interaction takes place in a lawless environment but argued that order could be much improved if rulers could agree on a common codex of international law derived from human reason, common interest and past habits of peaceful interaction.

This seventeenth-century optimism also informs Chapter 5, which presents the theories of the European Enlightenment. Its main visions of international interaction were built around a basic, mechanical view of human society. This view was inspired by the celestial model of Isaac Newton and found its typical expression in the early balanceofpower theories. This chapter begins with a discussion of John Locke. It continues with Émeric Vattel who expanded on Locke's theory and applied it to international relations. It devotes several pages to the social philosophy of Jean-Jacques Rousseau, a complex character who is rich in contrasts and whose theories of perpetual peace have inspired generations of subsequent International Relations thinkers. The chapter ends with discussions of how Enlightenment theories of peace and order were received in Europe (by Hume, Smith, Bentham and Kant) and in America (by Paine, Franklin, Hamilton and Madison) where they evolved into the theory of a peaceful federation of states.

If eighteenth-century theories were built around a mechanical vision of self-equilibrium, then nineteenth-century theories introduced an organic image of 'progress' or 'evolution'. Chapter 6 first shows how international interaction was altered by the economic innovations of England's Industrial Revolution and by the political ideals of the American and French Revolutions. The Enlightenment universalism of the revolutionaries triggered local and particularist reactions on the Continent. They fired up the modern idea of nationalism and of entire systems of political thought – most prominent among them were the ideologies of liberalism and radicalism and, after the excesses of the French Revolution, conservatism. The ways in which these impulses altered political thought and International Relations theory is here conveyed through the ideas of Georg Wilhelm Friedrich Hegel.

Part III, entitled 'The classic age of International Relations', discusses a more mature phase in which International Relations is established as a 'science of international politics' (Carr 2001 [1939], p. 3). The transition from a 'philosophy of war and peace' to a 'science of international politics' was not marked by a sudden rupture but by evolution over time; much like the material evolution, in fact, from modern history to contemporary history. This transition took place during the course of the nineteenth century and involved two 'industrial revolutions'. It also involved the development of new social sciences and new social theories. Chapter 7 shows how the growth of industrialism made the West richer and more powerful than the rest of the world. A widening gap of wealth and power opened up between the West and the rest – which, interacting with nationalism, paved the way for a wave of Western imperialist expansion towards century's end. The International Relations theories which emerged during the final decades of the nineteenth century were deeply marked by these developments – and by Darwin's theories of evolution.

Chapter 8 shows how a 'science of international politics', which had been prepared for centuries, finally emerged under the impact of World War I. The birth of International Relations was induced by academics who looked for ways to establish a lasting peace and by diplomats who prepared for a major conference to establish a robust, new world order. The new discipline was at first dominated by the mental furniture of the nineteenth century; in particular by the liberal internationalism of the Anglo–American peace movement, expressed by members of the British Foreign Office and by the US President Woodrow Wilson. But these theories were soon challenged by arguments formulated by strong, illiberal leaders on the Continent, such as Vladimir Lenin and, later, Adolf Hitler. This chapter ends with a discussion of Hitler and the ways in which he reorganized the German state, seduced the German nation and launched a war of imperial expansion.

Chapter 9 emphasizes the importance of individual statesmen. It begins with a description of Hitler and his bio-nationalist programme of racial purity. It continues with the ways in which Churchill, Roosevelt and Stalin worked to contain Hitler and destroy his *Reich*. The chapter then shows how their vast effort to stop Nazi Germany exhausted Europe and its old interstate system. In the wake of the war, the USA emerged as the wealthiest and the most powerful state in the world, with a monopoly of the atomic bomb and with dominance over the political and financial institutions of the world. These events – Hitler's rise and the war to defeat him – shaped the International Relations scholarship of the age, as indicated by the dominance of Realist theories. This chapter singles out the influential work of Hans Morgenthau for special attention.

Chapter 10 begins with America's success in establishing a new order on the Western world. It then moves into a discussion of the limits of America's postwar influence by noting how the USA was counterbalanced by the Soviet Union. The US–Soviet rivalry over central Europe grew tense and then spread to all of Europe. Then it spread to the Middle East and to Asia. By 1950 an intense Great-Power rivalry encompassed most regions of the world, rendering the international system bipolar and affecting its workings for the next half-century. The chapter makes the point that theories of liberal internationalism evolved to explain relations among Western states, whereas Realist approaches dominated the discussions of super-power relations. The chapter also notes that in this period, when US observers knew little about the inner workings of the USSR, the field of strategic studies emerged – a specialized sub-field in International Relations, which sprang out of Realism and was nourished by rational-actor models and game theory.

Chapter 11 opens with the changes that followed the outbreak of the Korean War and the death of Stalin. Both events affected the nature of the Cold War and influenced International Relations theory. The chapter discusses the beginning integration of Western Europe and the revival of liberal theories of interdepend-ence. It also touches upon the new wars of liberation that broke out in the 'Third World' and the attending rise of radical theories of dependency. The chapter ends with an examination of two scholars who tried to systematize the expanding debates in scholarly International Relations. In London, Martin Wight organized Inter-national Relations literature in terms of three approaches. In New York, Kenneth N. Waltz developed the notion of three levels of analysis. The conceptual schemes developed by Wight and Waltz greatly influenced International Relations for over a generation.

Chapter 12 opens with the Cuban Missile Crisis. It demonstrated the dangerous nature of the unregulated superpower rivalry and convinced American and Soviet leaders of the necessity to harness the nuclear arms race. At the same time, a new aspect of the Cold War opened up when rebels challenged Western colonial powers and demanded independence. The USSR began to systematically support Third World independence movements, whose anti-colonial struggles had an electric effect on students and scholars in the West. Many academics sympathized with the rebel cause and their sympathies were reflected in the rise of radical political theories.

Radical theories, sparked by Third World rebellions, made a deep mark on International Relations theories from the late 1960s on – as discussed in Chapter 12. Chapter 13 shows how the International Relations theories then changed; how revolutionary politics lost appeal whereas a revived brand of liberalism gained popularity. The change began in the West – first in Britain and then in the USA – and then quickly spread around the world. The economic logic of neo-liberalism affected International Relations theorizing deeply. Among other things, it provided a new, structural foundation for the Realist approach. This was the result of the work done, more than anyone, by Kenneth Waltz. This chapter discusses the structural approaches and pays special attention to the emergence of 'structural realism' or 'neorealism' during the 1970s.

Part IV of the book – 'A future history of International Relations' – discusses the end of the Cold War and reviews some of the scholarly efforts to theorize about the post-Cold War world. Chapter 14 first recalls some of the events that led up to the collapse of the USSR in 1991. It then discusses the sentiment of triumph which washed across the West in the wake of the Soviet collapse. Post-Cold War International Relations was coloured by the Western view that the USSR had been defeated and that the West had emerged victorious with its liberal ideals vindicated. A wave of Neo-idealism swept across the Western world. It coloured the rhetoric of statesmen and stateswomen and affected the theories of scholars. It instilled in the West neo-liberal ideals of human rights, free trade, democratic rule and international law. The theory of 'democratic peace' resurfaced and rose to pre-eminence in the wake of the Soviet collapse, challenging the premises of structural realism.

Chapter 15 brings the history of International Relations theory up to the twenty-first century. It focuses in particular on the ideational aspects of globalization, on the neo-idealism of the post-Cold War age, the emergence of digital communications technology and its impact on ideologies and perceptions. The post-men and women – scholars who discussed post-structural theory, post-positivist methodology and the postmodern condition – are presented and discussed. A special point is made, first, of the ways in which philosophical investigations have been brought back into the discussions and, second, of a renewed interest in the history of International Relations as a discipline – of which this present book is an example.

The purpose of the study

This book discusses the theoretical tradition of International Relations. It argues that contributors to this tradition constitute a 'community of scholars' and that the tradition goes far back in time. It includes traders, soldiers, scholars and statesmen of the past who have studied wealth, war, peace and power over the long haul. The tradition may stretch as far back as to antiquity. and among its earliest contributors are authors like Kautilya and Thucydides.

Aristotle may also be counted among its early authors. He laid the foundation for a systematic study of politics with the proposition that the human being is by nature a political animal – a *zoon politikon*. Aristotle argued that attempts to derive knowledge about politics from the endowments and behaviour of human-beingsini-solation are misguided. Human beings, Aristotle emphasized, cannot exist outside of a social context: 'he who is unable to live in society, or who has no need because he is sufficient for himself, must be either a beast or a god'.

Political theorists ever since have adopted Aristotle's argument that political actors are influenced by the social context they inhabit. Increasingly, they have also accepted that the same maxim applies to political theorists: they, too, are affected by their time, shaped by their landscape and coloured by their culture. Their discourse is affected by the imagery and the mythology which surround them and which form their perceptions, their experience and their knowledge. As this social context changes – from one historical epoch to the next or from one culture to another – theorists are moulded in different forms and their speculations are given different modes and flavours.

International Relations theory varies across space and time. And to trace the history of a subject matter which constantly undergoes mutations and transformations, as this book tries to do, is much like hunting chameleons. When Robert Heilbroner set out to write a brief history of capitalism, he faced this problem of the constant transformation of his subject matter. 'It is helpful', he observed,

> to approach this daunting task by reminding ourselves that understanding, explanation and prediction are universal attributes of human experience, not achievements of social science – never complete, but rarely completely inadequate. They are attained in varying degrees in different social circumstances. Thus the problem for our consideration is not whether we can understand, explain or predict, at all ... but the limits of our capacity to do so. (Heilbroner 1986, p. 180)

This book on the history of International Relations theory takes Heilbroner's advice *ad notam*. International Relations (like other social-scientific disciplines) does not 'evolve' in the sense that it progresses by steadily accumulating new knowledge to a field of constantly confined subject matter. Consequently, the purpose of a survey cannot be to depict the evolution of International Relations Theory from its palaeological past and arrive at a mature, complete set of explanatory principles. Rather, the task is to engage with the vast 'republic of letters' and report on some of the ways in which past observers have sought to understand the nature and logic of international politics.

Notes

1 A more extensive discussion of these features is found in e.g. Moses and Knutsen (2012, pp. 183ff). The idea of a vast virtual community of scholars blazes through modern philosophy of knowledge from Pierre Bayle's notion of a 'republic of letters' to Karl Popper's (1979) idea of a 'world 3'.

2 Niccolò Machiavelli (1961, p. 90) was among the first authors to draw this distinction; although David Hume (1955, pp. 26ff) may be the most famous. Hume's sharp distinction has later been elaborated by others (see e.g. Popper 1963), and the debates which have regularly attended these elaborations have been extremely useful in defining the scientific core of social investigations.

3 The word 'international' made its first appearance in Jeremy Bentham's *Principles of Morals and Legislation* [1789]. Bentham was a great innovator of words; however most of his neologisms fell still born from the presses – words like *phthanao-paronomic* (which referred to the abuse of an officer of the law) or *polemo-tamieutic* (which denoted sabotage of war materiel) never caught on. The word *international*, however, was a huge hit. And Bentham must have sensed the promise of the term, for he provides a footnote to explicitly mark its arrival. 'The word *international*, it must be acknowledged, is a new one', he boasts (Bentham 1948, p. 326).

4 Wight (1991, p. 1) recognized that the discipline of law carries a long and sustained tradition of International Relations theory. So did Bentham. He had no sooner invented the term 'international' than he sensed that it bore all the hallmarks of an instant hit, and defined it – in legal terms. The new term, he wrote, 'is calculated to express, in a more significant way, the branch of law which goes commonly under the name of the *law of nations*' (Bentham 1948, p. 326).

Part I
Preludes

1

Gods, sinners and preludes of International Relations theory

Where should we look for the origins of an International Relations theory tradition?[1] On the one hand are authors who claim that we should begin with World War I. This is too late. Long before World War I, a large body of literature existed which discussed issues of war, wealth, peace and power in international relations – as this book seeks to show. On the other hand are authors who argue that we should begin with the dawn of recorded history. But this is too early. No sustained connection exists between the famous discussions of Xenophon, Thucydides and other classical authors with the arguments of modern theorists.

There are many reasons why discussions about the genealogy of International Relations theory are littered with disagreements. One reason is that such discussions are clouded by an unclear idea of what 'tradition' means. It is therefore useful to distinguish at the outset between a 'historical tradition' and an 'analytic tradition' (Gunnell 1978; Schmidt 1998, pp. 24, 61ff). This book will emphasize the latter.

A *historical tradition* is commonly defined as a self-constituted pattern of conventional practice. A historical tradition of International Relations may be traced back to antiquity – to Xenophon, Thucydides, Herodotus, Livy, Plutarch and other ancient authors who discussed the causes of war, described practices of containment and counterbalance and claimed that kings and princes will always try to divide in order to conquer and form alliances in order to defend. However, one cannot safely assume that political practices indicate the existence of political theories. It can be argued that political practice in fact preceded political theorizing, and that a historic tradition of International Relations existed long before an analytic tradition. This is the argument of David Hume (1985c, p. 337), for whom the balance of power is inherent in politics; it follows naturally from political interaction as one fencer's parry follows another's thrust. By this view, ancient accounts convey little more than the existence of 'common sense and obvious reasoning' (Hume 1985c, p. 337).

An *analytic tradition* refers to an inherited pattern of thought or a sustained intellectual connection through time along which scholars stipulate certain concepts, themes and texts as functionally similar. As an analytic tradition the study of International Relations can hardly be traced back more than a few centuries. Thucydides may testify to the existence of balance-of-power practices in ancient Greece, but his account does not demonstrate the existence of a sustained intellectual tradition originating in ancient times – in this case lasting some 2500 years. Indeed, Thucydides and other classics faded from Western scholarship when Greece fell to Macedon and Rome. And when Rome collapsed, they slipped out of view altogether.

Yet, it is precisely the collapse of Rome which marks the beginning of the present study. On the face of it, it seems unlikely that the beginnings of a sustained intellectual connection along International-Relations themes and concepts could emerge from the primitive, rough and turbulent era which followed the collapse of Rome. But several authors of the 'Dark Ages' touched on some of the broader issues of international affairs. Cassiodorus (490–583) briefly discussed issues war in his *History of the Goths*; Gregory of Tours (538–94) touched on issues of diplomacy in his *History of the Franks*; and Paul the Deacon (720–99) noted both themes in his *History of the Lombards*. Pope Gregory the Great (590–604) wrote about the experiences of his youth when he was Rome's ambassador to Byzantium and negotiator with the Lombards.

This chapter will sketch the distant adumbrations of a few terms and notions that are central to International Relations theory – rudimentary concepts of states and state interactions, early notions of the value of peace and the necessity to achieve it by establishing rules for war. It will begin by briefly sketching the fall of Rome and the chaos that followed in its wake. It will then discuss the slow emergence of feudal institutions which reintroduced some order in the West. Finally it will point out that discussions about the nature of these institutions, and of the order they sustained, were steeped in religion – as is evident in the writings of Christian authors like Augustine and Gelasius and in Muslim authors like al-Shaybani. Political discussions were much enriched by the rediscovery of classical thought – especially Aristotle – which reverberate through the works of thinkers like Aquinas, Dubois and Marsiglio.

The fall and rise of the Far West

Rome had imposed unity and order upon Europe, Asia Minor, the Middle East and the northern coast of Africa from about 500 BC. By the fourth century AD, the politics of the Empire was riddled by corruption and paralysis. Armies gained influence; generals fought each other; they recruited bands of barbarians to serve under them; they seated and unseated emperors. Roman cities faltered; industry and commerce decayed. Since the eastern regions of the Empire remained stronger, wealthier and more unified, Emperor Constantine moved the imperial capital to Byzantium (Constantinople) in AD 330. Soon the great Roman Empire split into a Western and an Eastern half.

In this weakened state, the Empire faced a sudden wave of great migrations (380–450). It was mortally challenged by the Goths who came from south Russia, threatened Constantinople about AD 380, tore through Greece in 396 and sacked Rome in 410. The entire Empire shook. Its western half collapsed under this added burden. The tribes which overran the old Roman provinces did not have a sturdy political organization at more than a local level. Security and order all but disappeared; the old, gigantic Empire split into local, self-sufficient, impoverished fragments. More precisely put, it split in two: into a consolidated eastern half and a fragmented western half.[2]

The eastern part of the Roman Empire survived the great migrations. It clung to its Roman traditions under the onslaught of the barbarians. From its splendid capital in Byzantium, the East Roman Empire managed to ensure the traditional unity of Orthodox religion and authoritarian politics. It secured the survival of the empire partly by repelling the barbarian onslaught by armed force, and partly by deflecting them by diplomacy – in 489, for example, Emperor Zeno gave Theodoric, the leader of the Ostrogoths, permission to conquer Italy[3] and rule in the emperor's name. Byzantium remained the major European city. But the Byzantine Empire closed itself defensively off from the rest of the world, and took no leadership in European events.

It is the western part of the Roman Empire that will most concern us here. It unravelled under the impact of the great migrations. Communications ground to a halt. Production and trade choked. Two centuries afterwards, the area had unravelled into a great jumble of tribes, military raiders, villages, manors, monasteries and trading towns. Kingdoms rose under exceptionally strong rulers, but fell apart again under weaker ones.

The early Church; the early Empire

Various institutions emerged during these centuries to provide some measure of unity and order on the Far West. The most important of these was the Church. It maintained, against all odds, the rudiments of a common Western identity through the Dark Ages. It kept the Christian religion alive; it conserved the remnants of the Roman civilization; it provided a reservoir of literacy. It also spread the light of religion, learning and literacy to the north-western peripheries.

The Church became an important force partly because it offered the only ordering structure of central administration in these chaotic times, and partly because conversions of more barbarians contributed to its growing might. Such conversions were actively promoted by missionaries and were often sponsored by the pope. They extended Catholic Christendom northwards and steeped the Far West in a common culture. The conversion of the Anglo-Saxons in the seventh century and the Germans in the eighth were important milestones in medieval history. The Catholic religion and the Latin language provided, together with the memories of Roman law and various remnants of imperial institutions, some measure of cultural unity to the fragmented Continent.

Another important force for unity was the German and Frankish kingdoms which rose – often with support from the pope – and fell during the early Middle Ages. One of these was established by Clovis (466–511).[4] Another by *Carolus Magnus* or Charlemagne (768–814). Both were supported by the Church. Charlemagne was even crowned emperor of the West by the pope in 800. He became so powerful in the end that he became a competitor to the pope and prepared the grounds for a secular conflict between pope and emperor concerning power and authority over vast, Western territories. However, the Carolingian Empire (like the Merovingian Empire before it) did not long survive its founder. It disintegrated in all but name soon after Charlemagne's death.

The demise of the Carolingian Empire was quickened by new waves of destructive migrations. Magyar, Viking and Arab assaults threatened to bring chaos to the Far West in the eighth and ninth centuries – as the Goths had done half a millennium earlier. But the Carolingian Empire lacked a strong imperial centre. Although Charlemagne had developed a formidable cavalry force, it was slow, cumbersome and ineffective when faced by warriors who emphasized swiftness – like the Magyars on their light steppe ponies or the Vikings who harassed the Carolingian coasts in the their fast ships.

The recovery of the West

Magyar tribes emerged from the Hungarians plains and attacked northern Italy and Germany. Vikings descended upon the coasts and rivers of the British Isles and the Continent's Atlantic rim. Saracens attacked the Mediterranean coasts of Italy and France. Arab armies, flying the flag of the new religion of Islam, conquered all of Iberia during the first half of the eighth century and launched incursions into the heart of the Rhône valley. These onslaughts destroyed the order which Charlemagne had imposed upon the Far West. But in some places the onslaughts also spurred constructive actions which stimulated the growth of military tactics and organization.

The most consequential of these developments concerned the evolution of knightly cavalry tactics. These had evolved in the Carolingian Empire. But since it was immensely expensive to equip armoured knights, they were for a long time considered too costly to maintain. However, frequent Viking and Magyar attacks in the ninth century made some Frankish regions realize that it was better to make heavy, regular payments to local knights who remained in residence and on call than to periodically be exposed to devastating barbarian raids. Counts and other administrators enfeoffed knights who promised military service in return for rights to collect income from one or more villages. In one sense, then, these barbarian invasions triggered a reaction which in some places produced stable order on the local level. The origins of feudal society, in short, lie with the heavy cavalry which evolved within the Carolingian Empire.

The evolution of cavalry – which amounted to a military revolution in its day – produced the trunk of the feudal order: a supreme class of specialized warriors ('vassals') who received large land grants ('fiefs') in exchange for armed service. When the Carolingian Empire collapsed, the warrior class remained a distinguishing feature of the post-imperial order. But without the Empire to contain it, it was not harnessed by any clear political purpose. Legally, its members were liegemen or vassals of kings (of whom Charlemagne had been the greatest). But in practice they could ignore royal orders; the new monarchs had neither the fiscal base nor the military power to enforce their claims. Europe thus fell under the rule of armoured lords who assumed authority to govern all those who lived on their fiefdom. They administered justice, collected taxes and agricultural produce, claimed labour service and military service from the residents. And in the process they evolved from a military elite to a social elite. Its members called themselves *nobiles* in the Roman fashion and appropriated various late imperial titles such as *comes* (count) and *dux* (duke).

It may be argued, as a crude simplification, that early feudal society was an elaborate supply system which ensured that mounted knights were equipped and maintained. Mounted warfare was specialized, costly and exclusive and gave feudal society its armorial bearing and its knightly code of chivalry. However, even at the height of their power, a military aristocrat could never do precisely as he liked. He inhabited a 'heteronomous' political framework. His own authority was circumscribed by that of others. His freedom of action was limited by a web of allegiances and obligations.

The word 'feudal' is derived from *feudum* ('fief') which in essence was land which a lord bestowed upon his vassal by investiture in return for services. This etymology suggests a crucial point: that the entire feudal structure rested on entitlement to land. When this is said, another crucial point must be added: that a fief was not simply defined by drawing clear 'boundaries' around it and giving it as 'property' to an individual owner. No, a fief was an amalgam of conditional property and private authority – property was conditional in that it carried with it explicit social obligations which limited a lord's freedom of action; authority was private in that the rights of jurisdiction over the inhabitants of a fiefdom resided personally in its ruler. The system was rendered more complicated still by the prevailing concept of usufructure which meant that different lords could have different titles to the same landed property. As a result, the medieval system of rule reflected a patchwork of overlapping and incomplete rights of government (Strayer 1970); a lattice-like web in which 'different juridical instances were geographically interwoven and stratified, and plural allegiances, asymmetrical suzerainties and anomalous enclaves abounded' (Anderson 1979, pp. 37f). Medieval politics was a heteronomous system in which even the highest lord found himself circumscribed. His actions were restricted by other high lords – by popes (who were able to modify, if not control, the behaviour of clerics and noblemen) or by monarchs (like those which developed in England, France, Germany and the Iberian Peninsula before 1000)[5]. He was limited by towns and structures of trade which gradually revived at the turn of the millennium and stimulated the rise of walled cities and powerful city-states in Italy, the Rhineland and the Low Countries.

States existed, but they did not reign supreme. Medieval Europe was not really a state system; it was a shifting kaleidoscope of political arrangements among monarchs, nobles, clerics and towns (Spruyt 1994).

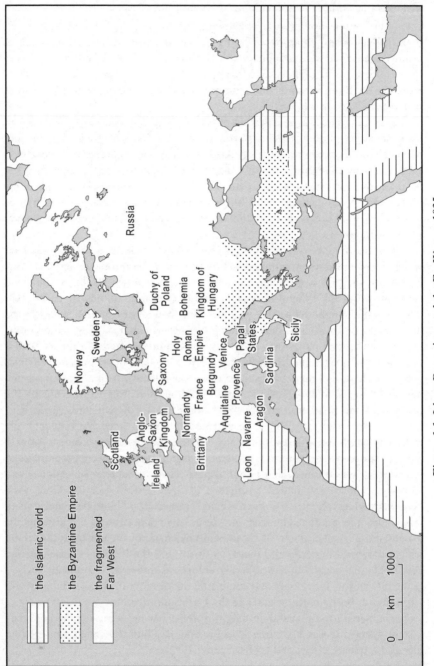

Figure 1.1 Islam, Byzantium and the Far West, *c.* 1025

the Islamic world

the Byzantine Empire

the fragmented
Far West

0   km   1000

Russia

Norway

Sweden

Duchy of
Poland

Bohemia

Kingdom of
Hungary

Saxony

Holy
Roman
Empire

Venice

Papal
States

Scotland

Anglo-
Saxon
Kingdom

Ireland

Normandy

France

Burgundy

Provence

Sardinia

Sicily

Brittany

Aquitaine

Leon

Navarre

Aragon

The three medieval civilizations

By AD 950 three distinct civilizations existed in the Western world, confronting each other around the Mediterranean: the Byzantine, the Arabic and the 'barbarian' civilizations.

Byzantium

The first civilization of the High Middle Ages was the Byzantine Empire. It was contained within the Eastern Roman Empire which had survived the onslaught of the Great Migrations. It included Asia Minor, the Balkan peninsula and scattered parts of Italy. Byzantium was Christian in religion and Greek in language and culture. Geographically, it guarded the Straits of the Bosporus; spiritually, it guarded the Graeco-Roman tradition in its orthodox, Christian version. Commerce and navigation were continued on much the same level as in ancient times. Byzantine scholarship was not as creative and flexible as in the classical age, but it was still an advanced civilization. For most Christians, the Byzantine emperor represented the world's supreme ruler; and Constantinople, which had about a million inhabitants by the tenth century and was the largest city of the known world at the time, was the world's pre-eminent city.

The rulers of Byzantium constantly faced the threat of invasion. In dealing with it, they developed the arts of war and diplomacy. To better combat the barbarians, the early Empire built an efficient field army, small but with great mobility and personally attached to the emperor. In response to changes in barbarian tactics, the armoured cavalry gained steadily in importance after the sixth century. These developments are treated in the *Peri Polemon* (or 'The Wars') – eight books on the long struggle of Emperors Justin I (518–27) and Justinian I (527–65) against the Persians, the Vandals and the Goths. The books were written by Procopius of Caesarea (*c.* 500–70?), and reflect his ambition to emulate Thucydides.

Procopius was not unique in having studied ancient texts on history and warfare. Such texts were collected and copied in schools, universities and libraries. Byzantine libraries were richly stocked with classical literature – including many important works which have since disappeared. The inhabitants were highly aware of the long civilizational heritage they represented. Byzantine scholars drew upon these classic texts to compile handbooks, anthologies and commentaries on all subjects, including diplomacy and warfare. One of the most famous manuals on warfare was the *Strategicon*. Written under Emperor Leo III (717–41), this military manual showed a rare degree of independence in that it subjected old military maxims to a critical review in the light of recent experience; among its recommendations were more flexible lines of battle, defence in depth and carefully rehearsed manoeuvres. Another study was the *Tactica*, written under the auspices of Emperor Leo VI (886–912) – but apparently derived from an older manual (which was also entitled *Strategicon*) written under Emperor Maurice (582–602).

The internal resources of the Byzantine Empire could not sustain a permanently successful military response to the threatening invaders. They also had to rely on the arts of negotiation, counterbalance and containment. One principal method employed in Byzantine diplomacy was to weaken enemies by fomenting strife and rivalries between them. A second diplomatic method consisted in winning the friendship of neighbouring nations by bribes and flattery. A third method was to convert their heathen neighbours to the Christian faith. A final method, used during the tenth and eleventh centuries when states' finances were low, was to marry off Byzantine princesses to foreign potentates (Hamilton and Langhorne 1995, pp. 17f). By the concurrent employment of such methods, Byzantine emperors managed to extend their influence over the Sudan, Arabia and Abyssinia and to keep at bay the tribes of the Black Sea and the Caucasus (Nicolson 1988, p. 10).

Activities of war and diplomacy were practices which may be construed as furnishing elements to a historic tradition of international relations. Can they also be said to contribute to an analytic tradition of international relations? Were the practices informed by theory? In light of the definition used here, it is hard to see Byzantine warfare and diplomacy in the early Middle Ages as theoretically informed activities. Rather, both warfare and diplomacy were religiously informed. Religion penetrated the whole of Byzantine life. Civil and religious institutions were so intertwined that one cannot understand one without the other. The head of the Church in Constantinople was a patriarch who was appointed by the emperor and could be dismissed by him; the emperor was the representative of God and was the head of the Church as well as the state.

The emperor's court had a large staff of diplomats and interpreters, but its members performed foreign-service functions rather than tasks of analysis and theorizing.[6] Universities entertained educators and scholars and their libraries were stocked with a wealth of Greek and Roman literature. But Byzantine scholarship occurred within the joint frame of Church and state. The scholars had a thorough knowledge of the whole range of classical learning, but they were hampered by an authoritarian Church/state structure and by an overwhelming reverence for the ancients. They commented ceaselessly on texts inherited from the past, but they rarely doubted them and never subjected them to critical review. They composed endless streams of commentaries, compendiums, abridgements and anthologies, but they produced few contributions of lasting scholarly importance. 'Age after age, innumerable pens moved, lakes of ink were exhausted, but no literary work remains which can claim a place among the memorable books of the world' (Artz 1967, p. 112). International practices existed in the Byzantine Empire, but they were informed by little or no theory.

The Islamic world

The second medieval civilization was inscribed by the political-religious institutions of the Caliphate. It stretched from the Iberian peninsula across North Africa, through the Middle East and Persia and far into India; it was the geographically most extensive of the civilizations, and the intellectually most advanced. Islam was its religion. Arabic was its language.

The Arab civilization was built by tough and ruthless means. The Muslims were at the outset cavalry warriors – indeed Muhammad was a strategist and military leader; and the remarkable expansion of Islam after his death shows that his successors, too, were shrewd strategists. They possessed the ability to observe their enemies, attack their weak points, emulate the strong and learn and adapt militarily to changing circumstances. In their encounters with Byzantine cavalry, the Saracens organized a heavy cavalry of their own. And, most astonishingly, these former desert dwellers built warships in great numbers and launched two great land-and-sea invasions on Constantinople in the late seventh century.

The early caliphal empire, governed by the Umayyad dynasty (661–750), retained the original Arab manners. But when the Umayyad dynasty was toppled (750), the new 'Abbasid dynasty reformed government procedures and moved the seat of empire to Baghdad. This implied a turning away from the empire's Arab roots and its Bedouin sentiment and an embrace of a sedentary, urban culture. Baghdad lay on the intersection of Middle Eastern trade routes. As the capital of a growing empire, the city grew rapidly in wealth, power and size – counting some 800,000 inhabitants by the tenth century (and was then, after Constantinople, the second largest city in the known world). Its political culture was marked by merchants and professional classes. A complex network of communications intersected in Baghdad. The city lay on the central routes of the caravans. They were encouraged by trade and by pilgrimage and helped reinforce the unity of the Islamic world. Merchandise moved along these routes. So did ideas and arguments – in the tangible form of documents, books and letters, or in the human form of teachers, students, preachers and pilgrims.[7] No city could compare with al-Rashid's Baghdad. Not even the court of Charlemagne could rival that of the caliph in splendour, sophistication and scholarship.

The 'Abbasids valued education and learning. Schools were systematically built, usually in connection to mosques. By 900 nearly every mosque had an elementary school.[8] 'Abbasid scholars studied the translated works of the Graeco-Roman tradition. Many of them were influenced by Aristotle. Others were informed by non-Western impulses – especially by a distinctly Persian genre of political commentaries known as the 'mirror of Princes'.[9] But in the final account, political scholarship was informed by Islam. The 'Abbasids publically professed to base their rule on the religion of Islam, and acknowledged the embryonic Islamic law as the legal basis of their society. 'Abbasid foreign policy was based on the notion that history was moving inexorably towards global peace and order conferred by the only true faith. Until Islam emerged victorious, however, the world was divided between one area which was Islamic (*dar al-Islam* or the Abode of Islam) and one area which was not (*dar al-Harb* or the Abode of War). Between the two there was a state of war of some kind – either in full flood in the form of Holy War (*jihad*), or else a temporary armistice.

Did Islamic writings on foreign affairs introduce an analytic tradition of International Relations? The traditional Western view is that it did not: that warfare and diplomacy were, in Baghdad as in Byzantium, religiously informed. That 'Abbasid state was, in essence, a theocracy. Its discussions on politics and law were anchored in faith and divine command and not in the free pursuit of theoretical argument.

This is reflected in the Muslim view of the world as a single entity, unified under one, true God; 'Abbasid texts did not depict a world of multiple states, and could therefore not conceive of interstate relations.

The traditional view is not untrue, but it is un-nuanced. 'Abbasid texts were deeply theological; yet 'Abbasid practice was quite pragmatic. Scholars discussed the permanent condition of war that was advocated by Islamic doctrine, but this did not prevent peaceful relations and cultural and commercial exchanges between the Islamic and the Christian worlds. Indeed, it was not uncommon for caliph and emperor to exchange poets or scholars as gifts or on loan; and it was possible for non-Muslims to take up residence in Muslim territory and engage in commerce there. Clearly, in practice the 'Abbasids did not view the world as fully united – the world was divided at least into two camps. Also, this division was more than a simple case of permanent hostility; Muslim practice indicated that the 'Abbasids entertained a more complex view of macro-politics than a simple two-camp doctrine of 'cold war'.[10]

The complexity is revealed in discussions of Islamic law conducted in Baghdad at the time of Caliph Harun al-Rashid, especially by the book *al-Siyar al-Kibir* ('The Islamic Law of Nations' [*c*. 800]). Its author was Muhammad ibn al-Hasan al-Shaybani, a judge and an adviser to al-Rashid. The book discusses the conditions for war (*jihad*) and peace, and it lays out principles for military action and diplomacy.[11] It begins by establishing the traditional distinction between the peaceful *dar al-Islam* and the conflictual *dar al-Harb*, but it does not dwell on their theological difference. Instead of making a theological point, al-Shaybani makes a geographical one: he establishes that Muslims and Christians inhabit different parts of the earth's geography, and then makes this territorial segregation the vantage point for his subsequent discussions of the relationships between them.

A first notable thing about al-Shaybani's book, then, is that it discusses the political relationship between territorial entities.[12] A second notable thing is that it presents a systematic study of the law that regulates the relationship between these territorial entities. He recognizes that people who inhabit different territories also obey different legal principles; from this he infers that whenever a Muslim resides in a non-Muslim territory, local law must be accepted as binding – and vice versa: if a non-Muslim (a *harbi*) enters the area of *dar al-Islam*, he must obey Islamic law (Khadduri 1966, pp. 174ff). He also infers, from his basic principle of territoriality, a principle of reciprocity – which guides his discussions of mercantile relationships, diplomatic emissaries and the exchange of prisoners (Khadduri 1966, pp. 170f). When, in the middle of the book, he discusses war and peace, he repeats that the world is divided between a peaceful Islamic area (*dar al-Islam*) and a conflictual *dar al-Harb*, and that a war of some kind exists between the two. However, he elaborates on the concept of war and explains that war can be fought against four different types of enemies: infidels, apostates, rebels and bandits. Only the first two – war against infidels and apostates – count as *jihad*.

By implication, *jihad* is a religious obligation, and it is the instrument by the means of which the Muslims will expand the *dar al-Islam*, transform the *dar al-Harb* and establish a just, orderly and peaceful world. There is, then, a religious teleology in al-Shaybani's argument. But it is hardly more pronounced than the teleology expressed by contemporary Christian writers. Muslims and Christians alike embraced the Graeco-Roman heritage. Both translated and commented on the old texts and stored them for posterity to recover. Some Muslim scholars, however, did more than simply translate and comment; to a greater degree than their colleagues in Constantinople, some Muslim scholars apparently went beyond the letter of the texts; they probed their meaning and drew inferences from their arguments. Thus, it is conceivable that the Muslims spurred an analytic tradition of International Relations – a tradition which builds on ancient authors (some from the Graeco-Roman world, some from Persia) and which continued through medieval Islamic scholarship. This is a possibility that few Western scholars have seriously explored.

The Far West
Compared to the Caliphate and the Byzantine Empire, the western regions of Europe hardly deserve to be called a 'civilization'. These regions, which the Caliphate had been unable to conquer and Byzantium unwilling to hold, were filled with busy, barbarian kings who did their best to maintain a semblance of order on their savage turfs. The political unity imposed by Rome had long collapsed. The spiritual concord impressed by the Church had been unravelled by migration and occupation and reverted to heathen tribalism. Most religions were an intricate folklore of myths and stories reverberating with echoes of a Christian past. There was no sense of loyalty to embracing and supreme institutions like a state (Wallace-Hadrill 1956). The old Roman roads had fallen into neglect; their flat stones were often removed and used as convenient building blocks. Travel was rendered dangerous by brigandage and highway bandits.

The Church was a lingering centre of power and a source of some order. Trade had died down, but some relations continued to exist between Rome and the rest of the West. The pope presided over a chancery which collected diplomatic records in specialized archives under the direction of and authority of the 'masters of the rolls'. Charlemagne's court at Aix-la-Chapelle (or Aachen) also had a chancery – a large and elaborate office which operated under the charge of a 'chancellor'. Such archives reveal that the envoys of Constantinople, Rome and Aachen did not merely represent the interests of their respective masters; they also furnished reports on the internal situation in foreign courts and on the relations of those courts towards each other. These early medieval envoys, then, were sent to foreign courts for other reasons than their gifts of eloquent oration, they also sent for their trained powers of observation and the soundness of their judgement. In the education of envoys, then – in the routines used by the medieval chanceries to train their powers of observation and develop the soundness of their judgement – lie important precursors to the systematic study of International Relations.

Charlemagne created an empire, he created a powerful competitor to the pope. This prepared the grounds for a secular conflict between pope and emperor and was a political watershed in Western history. When he also established a scholarly and an administrative centre for his growing empire, he made an intellectual watershed as well. He created a splendid court at Aachen to which he summoned prominent scholars from all parts of Europe. He exchanged cultural gifts with Caliph Harun al-Rashid and Empress Irene. He established a court library which included a collection of ancient authors. He initiated a campaign to establish schools and teach literacy near the cathedrals and in the monasteries of his realm.

When Charlemagne died in 814, the Carolingian Empire unravelled. And it set in motion an evolution which would take Western civilization in a unique direction. First, the unravelling of the empire lead to multiple centres of power in the West, which was never reconstituted as a single, unified empire again. Rather, the West remained a politically heterogeneous area which, during the ninth and tenth centuries, evolved a peculiar plurality of power centres in the form of independent territorial states. These states were justified by doctrines drawn from Christian theology. And although the Church retained a virtual monopoly on Western scholarship, no standardized theology entirely overwhelmed European values and norms. Ancient, local legal codes were, for example, never entirely extinguished. Instead, they made their imprint on local political institutions and processes. As the feudal system was shocked by the advent of trade and urban centres in the late Middle Ages, a plurality of peculiar social formations emerged in the Far West (Spruyt 1994) – city-states evolved in northern Italy, city leagues emerged in the German Empire and the Baltic, monarchic states matured in England, France and Spain.

Second, the unravelling of the Charlemagne's empire did not end the conflict between pope and emperor. Rather, it stimulated questions which had been discussed at the Carolingian court – questions about the nature of power and the division of political authority between religious and secular actors. If the pope's authority came from God, where did the emperor's authority come from? From the pope (as the pope maintained)? From God (as the emperor argued)? Or from men (as the seven German princes who elected the emperor claimed)? These questions drove high-pitched struggles in European politics for centuries after the collapse of the Carolingian Empire and were at the core of the so-called Investiture Contest of medieval Europe.

The most public battle of this contest began in 1073, with the election of a brilliant and pugnacious monk by the name of Hildebrand as Pope Gregory VII. The new pope was a firebrand who insisted on the dominance of papal authority within Western Christendom and on the independence of the Church from any lay authority. In 1075 Gregory VII forbade any layman to appoint clerics to ecclesiastical offices. When the counsellors of the Holy Roman Empire protested the decision, the pope excommunicated them. When Emperor Henry IV protested, the pope excommunicated him as well. This put the emperor in an awkward predicament. He faced powerful German enemies who were now supported by the pope. Also, since he was excommunicated, he wanted to avoid trial before the German bishops because they were presided over by Gregory. So Henry decided to appeal directly to the pope. In mid-winter he made a strenuous journey across the

Alps and reached the pope's fortress at Canossa in Northern Italy on 25 January 1077. Henry IV approached the fortress gate in penitence, barefoot and wearing the simple clothing of a monk. The pope refused him entry at first. The emperor waited for three days before the snowy gates until Pope Gregory VII relented and received his penance. The episode did not cause much of a stir at the time. In time, however, the standoff at Canossa would turn out to be one of the most dramatic of all confrontations between lay and spiritual authority. And events did not turn out to Gregory's advantage. Henry IV had shrewdly outflanked the pope. He had revealed the pope's position to be extreme; that the pope asserted a revolutionary doctrine which held kings to be little more than officers who could be removed by the will of the pope. This doctrine was unacceptable to the kings of Europe. The effect of Gregory's reforms was, in fact, to differentiate more sharply between clerics and laymen, between Church and state.

This gave the state greater autonomy. Together with the political diversity which emerged in the West, opportunities were opened up for independent intellectuals to manoeuvre.

For centuries scholars have observed the exceptionalism of the West and fiercely discussed its origins. Some authors have located the uniqueness of the West in the Renaissance, other authors point to the Reformation or the Enlightenment or the Industrial Revolution as the turning point. Tom Holland (2008) argues that the defining characteristic of the Western civilization is the division between Church and state, and directs attention to the Investiture Contest. 'Of Islam', he writes, 'it is often said that it has never had a Reformation – but more to the point might be to say that it has never had a Canossa' (p. xxii).

Sources of Western political theorizing

While the lights of Byzantine and Islamic culture burned most brightly, the Far West was, by comparison, illuminated by a dim twilight. 'Culturally Latin Christendom, like a ruined family that could no longer maintain its old dwelling, came to live in a few rooms of the cellar' (Artz 1967, pp. 179f). Some achievements in political theory were accomplished around the time of the collapse of Rome – as evinced in the works of Ambrose, Bede and others. Among these authors, two men stand out because they had an extraordinary influence on subsequent scholarship of the Western world: Capella and Augustine. The former exerted a defining influence on the form of Western scholarship; the latter exercised a decisive influence on its content.

Religion and the seven liberal arts

Capella and Augustine both lived in fifth-century Carthage; one of the richest cities of the Roman Empire. Both men observed with great concern the barbarian onslaught on the Empire's peripheral provinces and feared for the fate of the imperial order. Both reacted with horror to news that Rome was sacked (410) at the hands of Alaric the Goth. But they reacted in very different ways.

Martianus Capella was a Roman proconsul and reacted to the events in practical and pragmatic ways. He feared that the Roman way of life would be gone for good, and resolved to do what he could to conserve it. If the central authority of the Empire unravelled, the Roman world would be fragmented into smaller units, provinces, states and cities would have to exist autonomously. To assist these units and to preserve the key elements of the Roman civilization, Capella began to condense and systematize the knowledge and scholarship of Rome. After several years of painstaking work, he had condensed the imperial school curriculum into nine books. The first of them contained the rules for teaching the three main subjects of the early Empire: rhetoric, grammar and logic. These had been the three staple subjects (*trivium*) in an expanding Roman republic with a need to win over conquered tribes with oratory, Latin language and complex legislation. To these early subjects Capella added four more from the Empire's later years: arithmetic, music, geometry and astronomy (*quadrivium*). Capella considered them more practical subjects, relevant to the sophisticated urban life. Taken together, the *trivium* and the *quadrivium* amounted to what Capella called the seven liberal arts. Capella's books, published in one volume under the title *De nuptiis philologiæ et Mercurii* ('The marriage of Philology and Mercury') would remain a standard reference for education for the subsequent six centuries.[13] It is one of the most influential handbooks ever published.

Augustine (354–430) was a theologian and a bishop. As a man of the Church he reacted to the events of the age by turning to the Bible. It provided the basic, ultimate explanatory authority of the later Empire. It was *the* source of wisdom. It provided answers to all questions, and Augustine turned to it for an appropriate response to the earth-shattering events of the age. In order to appreciate Augustin's reaction to the crisis of fifth-century Rome, it is necessary to recall the biblical claims that the world had been created in six days by God for an ultimate if inscrutable purpose. Although created perfect, man had fallen from grace into sin and error, thereby incurring the penalty of eternal damnation. However, God had, in his infinite benevolence, provided a way of atonement and salvation through a propitiatory sacrifice of his only son. Helpless in himself, man could still be permitted, through God's mercy and by humility and obedience of his will, to obtain pardon for sin and error. Life on earth was just a temporary probation, a means to a greater end. In God's appointed time, this world would come to an end. The earthly city would be swallowed up in flames, and good and evil men would be separated.

When Alaric the Goth sacked Rome in 410, Augustine decided that the whole, gigantic, bureaucracy of the Roman Empire was destined to unravel. Driven by his apocalyptic expectations he wrote furiously. His manuscript grew to gigantic proportions, but allowed Augustine to reason his way towards an escape. He entitled the result *City of God*. With Christian dualism as his vantage point, Augustine argues that man inhabits two parallel realities: this world of violence, war, hunger and misery on the one hand, and the Kingdom of God on the other. Augustine argued that social life is divinely ordained. However, because of Adam's original sin which man inherits, the human race has been condemned in its first origin.

'Life itself, if life it is to be called, bears witness by the host of cruel ills with which it is filled', he writes (Augustine 1954, p. 474). Because of his sinful and corrupt nature, man requires government and coercive laws. And as an act of mercy, God has created laws to impose some order upon the sinful and corrupt human society. He has also created monarchs and princes and given them authority to enforce the laws and maintain civil order. God has, according to Augustine, given kings and princes a just reason to use violent means to preserve the safety of the state! A good citizen should therefore obey his government. This secures the order and peace which man so obviously cannot keep on his own. Man is always at risk, unless aided by the Church. This medieval worldview was not challenged for several hundred years. It infused all social theorising until the High Middle Ages.

The *City of God* delivered the premises for all medieval social studies. All political theories were deduced from its theological axioms and tended to reflect Augustine's pessimistic assumptions about the corrupt and sinful nature of man. Scholars of the Church may have denounced the excesses of cruel tyrants and the conquests of strong rulers, but they argued that such behaviour was a natural consequence of man's wicked and sinful nature. They may have condemned war, but they did no condemn it on principle; they maintained, with Augustine, that certain wars were just. Defensive wars, for example, waged to maintain traditional order against the onslaught of barbarian marauders, were considered just. So were wars waged on God's behalf against the infidels.

Rome's struggle against the invading barbarians was, according to Augustine, an example of a just war. It was a case where Christian defenders of order sought to combat an enemy of both faith and order.[14] The example showed that the moral qualities of men like Cicero had made the empire great. They had been devoted to the common good and their devotion had been enforced by imperial authority and power. Yet, these men had been misguided in glorifying Rome rather than God, argued Augustine. They had insisted on allegiance to temporal affairs rather than the natural and eternal values of the Christian faith. They had glorified the City of Man (*civitas terrena*) rather than the City of God (*civitas dei*). This duality between the two realms of human existence was also discussed by Pope Gelasius I (492–6). He, too, drew a sharp distinction between state and Church, but, unlike Augustine, he argued that *both* institutions reflect the will of God; thus both are equally 'natural' and equally just. However, the state and the Church have different tasks to perform, Gelasius claimed. The state, represented by the emperor, should concern itself with temporal issues, whereas the Church, represented by the pope, should deal with mankind's spiritual needs (Momigliano 1963).

Augustine and Gelasius introduced to medieval Europe a political doctrine which benefited the Christian Church and, ultimately, the pope. It explained that all monarchs and princes of Europe had their authorities from God. And since the pope was God's representative on earth, the kings and emperors owed obedience and submission to Rome. This doctrine sanctioned the notion that there exists a universal community of man, under God, represented by the Christian Church. No temporal body, neither civilian nor military, could assume absolute authority over it. When the Roman Empire caved in, and the political structure it had imposed upon Europe unravelled, the visions of Augustine remained. They were guarded and managed by a network of bishops and priests and overseen from Rome by the authority of the pope who imposed some measure of mental unity on the Far West.

After the fall of Rome, all scholarly activities in the Far West were dominated by the Christian clergy. They were embraced Augustin's notions of a worldly city, a human community (*humanitas*) to which all inhabitants of the world belonged. This community consisted of all peoples and all races. It was unified under God, and transcended the smaller communities of the village, the town or the state. This notion of 'humanity' unified the human species under a supreme principle, 'so that there is no room for distinction between Greek and Jew, between circumcised and uncircumcised, or between barbarian and Scythian, slave and free man. There is only Christ: he is everything and he is in everything' (Colossians 3:11).

Throughout the Middle Ages, the intellectuals of the Far West thought of themselves as belonging to this large human community. There were wars and quarrels, uprisings, doctrinal disputes, the great schism between pope and emperor. But through it all, there was a belief in the actual unity of Christendom, however variously felt and expressed. This belief was a fundamental condition of all medieval political thought and activity. It reverberated through late medieval visions of a peaceful world. John of Paris expressed it in his plea for a government of Christendom (*De potstate regia et papali* or 'On Royal and Papal Power' [*c.* 1302]). And Dante Alighieri called for the establishment of Christian world state in his *De monarchia* ('On Monarchy' [*c.* 1313]). Dante's ideal monarch should be an all-powerful ruler who was as unselfish as he was omnipotent and could end all conflicts, suppress all tyrannies and bring about universal peace.

Religion and law
The scholarship of the medieval Church allowed no essential difference between the various branches of knowledge. It derived its concepts from theology and drew no clear distinction between knowledge about nature and knowledge about humanity. The one, conspicuous issue of international politics of the age, the political debate between pope and emperor, was maintained within a theological discourse.

The Church exercised a solid dominance over medieval scholarship. But it was not the exclusive font of Western political argument. Another important source was 'custom' or 'customary law'. Although the Middle Ages was rife with conflict and violence, medieval society attached a great respect to customary law. And although disputes were regularly settled by force (especially when kings were disputants), medieval Europeans were as busily engaged in litigation as they were in battle. Every great estate was hung about with lawsuits. Rights, titles and privileges were constantly granted, revoked and reaffirmed. By the High Middle Ages, legally demonstrable privileges had become the universal cement of European society.

In contrast to Byzantium, whose jurisprudence drew directly upon the legal heritage from Rome, Western scholars drew upon two legal traditions: canon law and customary law. Canon law was developed by Church leaders and informed by

Christian theology, but it was anchored in Roman law. Customary law, by contrast, represented a codification of customary behaviour. It had its origins centuries back among barbarian chieftains and kings (Keen 1963).

The stubborn persistence of customary law is an important factor in the development of political theory in the Far West. It was local in caption and was primarily concerned with local relations – as such it was a conservative force and tended to perpetuate local privileges.[15] However, there were aspects of customary law which pertained to war. Warfare was not really subject to any control during the Middle Ages; Germanic tribesmen entertained no clear idea that war was wrong – let alone illegal. Yet, they entertained some rudimentary notions of fair conduct – including the chivalrous treatment of imprisoned soldiers and heralds. These notions, as reflected in customary law on war and diplomacy, may be considered an early source for rules on state conduct and hence relevant for International Relations theory.

Religion, law and foreign policy
Canon law and customary law can be considered early sources of International Relations scholarship. Influenced by the codes of Christian morality, Western scribes and scholars lamented the destruction wrought by war and pitied the innocent victims. And from this lamentation rise important medieval efforts to regulate war through ecclesiastical and royal legislation. A concept of the Peace of God (*pax ecclesia*) arose in the 990s from the Church synods as an effort to forbid, under threat of excommunication, acts of warfare and violence against ecclesiastical property, against innocent persons (clerics, pilgrims, women, merchants and peasants). A concept of the Truce of God (*treuga dei*) emerged in the eleventh century from the Church as an attempt to forbid fighting on certain days of the week and during certain seasons and Church festivals. It was expressed by many bishops in the second quarter of the century. It was repeated by Pope Urban II at the Council of Clermont (1095), and this served as a reminder which renewed and generalized the concept. Subsequent condemnations of wars and warfare met with considerable popular support and evolved into veritable anti-war movements. Several European localities proclaimed a Peace of God or a Truce of God.

These concepts of peace were steeped in Christian morality and in the universal vision of a human community (*humanitas*). And, like all universal visions, it had a downside. In some interpretations the idea of humanity implied a duty to defend Christianity. In others it implied a Christian duty to convert heathen peoples – an interpretation that was bolstered by Christ's command to go out and 'make disciples of all nations' (Matthew 28:19). Both interpretations fuelled the Western expansionism which began on the eve of the twelfth century and was expressed by the Crusades.

It is a testimony to the two-sided nature of the Christian concept of peace that Pope Urban II, who spoke in favour of regulations within Christendom at the Council of Clermont, proposed on the same occasion (1095) the First Crusade against Islam. The pope recalled that the land of the Holy Sepulchre was under Muslim domination, and he promised full remission of sins to everyone who joined an expedition to liberate Jerusalem. People from all over the Far West answered his call. Driven by religious ardour, adventurism, greed or other motives they joined the Crusaders who followed the old Byzantine main road across Asia Minor. Their capture of the Seljuk capital of Nicaea (1096) and the Syrian city of Antioch (1097) opened the way to the Holy Land. They conquered Jerusalem in 1099 and founded a number of Christian principalities in its immediate vicinity (Runciman 1992). These small settlements, outposts of Christendom, were constantly threatened by adjacent Muslim societies. Several Western expeditions were equipped to assist them and to consolidate the Christian presence in Palestine. None of them was infused by the zeal of the First Crusade and none was as successful.

Crusades, states and interstate relations

The Crusades were armed expeditions. They involved issues of logistics and strategy which were discussed and decided by military commanders. But the Crusades were also religious ventures. They were pilgrimages in need of theological justifications, and these were provided by the Church. Ultimately, it was the pope who sanctioned each crusading initiative and, formally at least, financed them. Also, it was the pope who provided the justification. This he found in the just-war theory of Augustine. Urban II justified the Crusades as assistance to the Orthodox Christians in the East who were besieged by the Muslims. Later popes portrayed the Crusades as defences of Western Christians who had settled in the Holy Land. During the twelfth century, the theme of the Holy Land was increasingly stressed, suggesting that the holy places (the Holy Sepulchre and Jerusalem) were indispensable to Christians who had been expelled by the Muslims. Ultimately, when the pope argued that the final purpose of the Crusade was to defend Christianity, this meant in practice an effort to liberate the Holy Land. This became the main, justifying goal of the Crusades.

The Crusades involved the clash of two very different political worlds, the Christian West and the Islamic East, and they had important effects on both of them. In the East, the Crusades helped unify and militarize the Muslim world. They caused the Muslims to co-ordinate their armies and to invest more of their resources into military forces. Towards the end of the twelfth century they fielded bigger armies, recaptured Jerusalem (1182) and left the Muslims both stronger and more hostile. When the Muslim world later found leaders such as Saladin, the Crusader states in Palestine and Syria were doomed and Byzantium was threatened.

In the West, the Crusades helped developed more co-ordinated, powerful and confident states. First, they were big. Earlier warfare had been amateurish and small-scale, but the Crusades were vast ventures. They reflected a veritable revolution in organizational ability. They show that, at the threshold of the twelfth century, the Far West was wealthy, powerful, confident and co-ordinated enough to stage vast assaults on the world outside (Ganshof 1995, pp. 82f).

Second, the Crusades were intercontinental operations. Early medieval warfare had been small-scale, local affairs. But the Crusades created, for the first time since the Roman Empire, armies which operated according to intercontinental strategies.

They reflected a broadening of the strategic visions of the Westerners, a kind of world strategy which had the papacy in the centre. The pope was, ultimately, the paymaster of the ventures, and he was able to direct funds to whatever theatre of war he felt needed it most at the time. Compared with a situation in the tenth and eleventh centuries, when warfare in Europe was almost local, the twelfth century witnessed the eruption of intercontinental operations.

Third, the Crusades were sustained expeditions. Early medieval warfare had involved short, explosive campaigns. So the Crusades imposed new, heavy demands on traditional systems of mobilization. In fact, the old feudal system of raising armies could no longer cope with the demands imposed by lengthy periods of campaigning abroad. It became clear around 1300 that the old system would no longer do. New ways of raising and maintaining armed forces were needed. Ways which could evolve only when powerful kings emerged as independent actors on the political scene. Monarchs had emerged at the centre of a new form of web or organization, and the nobility was increasingly given the role of recruiters (Strayer 1955, pp. 163ff). The monarch drove the nobility out to recruit soldiers. And he promised those who were willing to serve that in return for their services they would be paid a certain sum of money per day or per week.

Two intertwined developments mark these changes in military and political organization. The first was the transition from an old-type feudal army, essentially based upon obligation, to a new-type army based on payment for service. The second development concerned the beginning of centralization of economic and political power in the hands of the monarch. It affected politics and society because it altered the royal relationship with important domestic groups: It eroded the position of the landed aristocracy – beginning in the thirteenth century and continuing through the fourteenth. This erosion was expressed in a steady decline in the role of the noble horseman in war. Heavy cavalry was repeatedly defeated by lighter adversaries as the fourteenth century progressed – the battles of Lake Copaïs (1311), Crécy (1346), Poitiers (1356), Nájera (1367) and Aljubarrota being cases in point. By the time of Tannenberg (1411) and Agincourt (1415) the functions of the noble knights had largely been reduced to ceremonial displays of style, splendour and opulence. Their traditional warfare role of the noble horseman had been undermined by well-trained, well-organized infantry armies. The king no longer depended exclusively on the military services of the nobility. Their declining military importance was reflected in their social and political demise.

At the same time other groups were on the rise. As the warfare role of the cavalry declined, that of the infantry mushroomed. Since they demanded to be paid in ready money, this development presented the king with a desperate need for cash. To cover these expenses, he began to cultivate good relationships with the moneyed groups in society. Most particularly, he upgraded his relationship with urban commercial classes, merchants and bankers. In order to tax these wealthy groups more easily, the king brought them in as participants in the new institutions of royal decision-making. During the thirteenth century the new and wealthy classes were included in royal deliberations over matters of national expenditures. By the fourteenth, this practice was common enough to be formalized. And the formalization altered the nature of the Western state. It foreshadowed the growth of parliamentary politics in England, Spain, France and other emerging territorial states of the Far West. It stimulated the growth and the consolidation of territorial states.[16] This evolution, which took place in several adjacent states simultaneously, would bring into being an interstate system along the North Atlantic rim of Western Europe.

The (r)evolution of medieval knowledge

During the Dark Ages, faith had been the major source and support of scholarly speculation. 'Let us believe in order that we may know,' insisted Augustine, who had applied reason in order to fortify faith. In the High Middle Ages, however, reason began to supplant faith as the chief support of Christian thought. This upgrading of reason was sustained by a variety of cultural, economic and political factors. It may have its preconditions in peculiar features of Judaeo-Christian thought – such as the linear notion of time and of salvation as the outcome of an effort in and through history (Niebuhr 1949, pp. 15ff). It was conditioned by the growth of cities and by a 'higher artisanate' which found access to the company of educated scholars in the late Middle Ages – a development which stimulated the rise of a group of free entrepreneurs, craftsmen-inventors and quasi-intellectuals who belonged neither to the Church nor to the state. In effect, this development gave rise to a group of independent intellectuals, who were constantly in search of princely patronage and who were therefore cosmopolitan, who had a nose for novelties and who tended to exploit the opportunities such novelties afforded (Needham 1969, p. 193).

The rediscovery of the past

The upgrading of reason and the development of political theorising was stimulated by the discovery and dissemination of pre-Christian texts on economics, politics and logic. Manuscripts were discovered in the Far West. Some were found in the old, great Western cities like Athens or Rome. For example, a digest of the *Corpus juris civilis* – the voluminous collection of laws compiled by Emperor Justinian I (527–65) – was discovered in Ravenna in 1071 and triggered a revolution in legal and political thought. Although the Dark Ages descended upon the Far West for seven or eight centuries, classic, non-Christian scholarship was not entirely lost.

Much of it was preserved in the West itself by a type of religious institution which emerged rapidly during the fifth and sixth centuries and grafted itself on to the ancient infrastructure of the Church: the monasteries. Serious and sensitive persons all over the Far West could reject the barbarian world around them and retire into the calmer communities enclosed by the monastery wall. These religious communities were self-sufficient and usually left unmolested by rough neighbours who held them in religious awe. As the monastic communities spread northwards during the seventh century, they also disseminated ancient writs. In a world of violence, these were islands of calm which copied and kept the knowledge of Graeco-Roman scholarship.

Much scholarship was discovered outside the West. Some were found in the universities and libraries of Byzantium where large collections of ancient texts had been compiled and preserved through the Dark Ages. But the largest discoveries were made in the Arab world. When Christian soldiers broke through Arab defences of Al-Andalus in the eleventh century, they did more than reconquer Iberian territory; they also captured the products of the sophisticated Arab civilization – the houses, the mosques, the public baths, the bookshops and the libraries. Such discoveries sparked an intellectual revolution in Europe. Northern scholars came across the Pyrenees and around the Provençal coast to study and steal the greatest book collections the West had ever seen. They immediately encountered a major problem: most of the books were written in Arabic, which the Western scholars could not read. So they got the Arab texts translated – often by Toledan Jews – into Spanish. Then Christian scholars would convert the Spanish translations into Latin for the rest of Europe. And during the process they soon realized that the Arab texts were themselves translations – many of them from ancient Greek and Roman manuscripts that had long been given up for lost after the fall of Rome. From the late eleventh century onwards, all kinds of texts flooded across the Spanish mountain passes with their old/new knowledge. Architecture, astronomy, biology, botany, chemistry, engineering, pharmacology, geometry, mathematics, medicine, optics, philosophy, physics, zoology. The job took 150 years, and it profoundly altered Western civilization.

One early problem with all this new knowledge was that it arrived in a confusing mass. Another problem was that it competed with the religious orthodoxy of the Church. Soon, however, a solution was discovered to both problems: Aristotle. Among the newly translated texts Western scholars found Aristotelian texts that arranged all human knowledge in a comprehensive system. In the *Organon*, for example, Aristotle had first divided all knowledge into three kinds (practical, productive and theoretical), then he had subdivided these into a vast array of specializations. Aristotle had put everything into place. And Aristotle was known and trusted. The Church had long known of him. Indeed, it had already incorporated some of his arguments into its theology. Church scholars could therefore neither ignore nor reject Aristotle's newly discovered writings which were now made available. Some of the Christian scholastics even suggested that Aristotle might assist them in deducing an exhaustive, solid and consistently rational defensc of Christianity. One of them was Thomas Aquinas (1225–74).

The work of St Thomas
Thomas Aquinas was Italian by birth. He studied and taught in Paris, Cologne, Naples and Rome. On his many travels, he noted the political and economic changes which occurred all over Europe. He observed the rise of 'new monarchies' in France, Spain and England; he witnessed the re-emergence of city-states in Catalonia and northern Italy; he noted the growth of manufacture, trade and communication and the advent of new merchant classes; and he read the recently discovered philosophy of Plato, Aristotle and other early advocates of reason. He

was particularly impressed by Aristotle. Aquinas believed, that, if he could understand the principles of Aristotle's rules of logic, then he could use it to develop a firm, logical basis for Christian theology. For the rest of his life he systematically applied Aristotle's philosophy to Catholic doctrine in an effort to produce one, perfectly rational system.

The fruit of his labours was the *Summa theologica*. It held that the world was created by God in seven days as an organized whole in which each constituent item had a prescribed place and obeyed rules specific to its position. Each rock, plant, animal, human and angel had its specific position in the great order of things. When a rock fell to earth, it obeyed the rule which said that lifeless objects seek to lie still on the surface of the earth. And when a man acted, he obeyed the rule of reason. God was the embodiment of perfect reason, and the more rational a man was, the nearer he was to God.

Aquinas's argument had important consequences for political theory. First, it modified Augustine's claim that man was corrupted by original sin. In Aquinas's view, man's physical and mental abilities were vitiated but not destroyed. Thus, Aquinas introduced a new faith in human reason.[17]

Second, it revived Aristotle's claim that man is by nature a political being. His argument that politics is the interaction of rational men acting out their God-given nature sharply contradicted Augustine's view that political authority is merely a compensation for the corrupt and sinful nature of man.

Third, Aquinas made politics part of the God-given, rule-bound order of the universe. Politics became 'participation in the eternal law by a rational creature'. This 'eternal law' was partly revealed in the Bible – Aquinas identified the Ten Commandments and the Sermon on the Mount as its most authoritative expression. Also, the eternal law could be partly grasped by human reason. The part of God's law which could be uncovered by human reason, Aquinas called 'natural law'. The discovery of natural law was not a prerogative of Christian men (Aquinas 1947, p. 1011). It helps all men to separate right from wrong and direct their actions towards the good and just. Since just actions lead to happiness, natural law tells man to act justly and it promises happiness in return for man as well as society – including international society.

Aquinas argued that the supreme purpose of political authorities was to maintain order and peace.[18] Therefore he deplores war. He recommends its avoidance as far as possible, for war 'produces little good and it wastes much more than it produces'. At the same time, he accepts Augustine's argument that man has a right to wage war under certain circumstances. War is justified if it is waged on the authority of the sovereign, for a just cause and with the right intention of preventing injustice. In Aquinas's famous words:

> In order for a war to be just, three things are necessary. First, the authority of the sovereign by whose command the war is to be waged. For it is not the business of a private person to declare war, because he can seek for redress of his rights from the tribunal of his superior ...

Secondly, a just cause is required, namely that those who are attacked should be attacked because they deserve it on account of some fault. Therefore Augustine says ...: 'A just war is usually described as one that avenges wrongs, when a nation or state has to be punished, for refusing to make amends for the wrongs inflicted by its subjects, or to restore what it has seized unjustly'.

Thirdly, it is necessary that the belligerents should have a right intention, so that they intend the advancement of good, or the avoidance of evil. Hence, Augustine says ...: 'True religion does not look upon as sinful those wars that are waged not for motives of aggrandizement, or cruelty, but with the object of securing peace, of punishing evildoers, and of uplifting the good'. For it may happen that the war is declared by the legitimate authority, and for a just cause, and yet be rendered unlawful through a wicked intention. (Aquinas 1947, pp. 1359–60)

The peculiar Western context

An account of the origins of International Relations theory must begin with the intellectual and political development of the medieval Far West. It must discuss at least three things: law, theology and the public sphere.

First, it must include a discussion of medieval law. This must include both canon law (as expressed in the early attempts to limit warfare such as the 'Peace of God' and the 'Truce of God') and the customary law which dovetailed with it. It must include Church doctrines (most notably the *lex mercatoria*) as well as the emerging codes of conduct among chieftains and kings.

Second, it must include a discussion of the evolution of medieval theology. One reason for this is that in the medieval world theology encompassed all other scholarly pursuits. When medieval scholars struggled to grasp the nature of the world – including the emergent social formations and their interaction – their discussions were maintained within the theological discourse of the age. There is also another reason why theology is important here: namely, because theological discussions provided a scholarly unity to a continent that was riven and split into smaller regions by geography – by mountain ranges and broad rivers. It is, in other words, not the content of the religious doctrine that is of primary interest in this connection, but rather that the Church was a Europe-wide institution that provided a common forum and unifying language for discussion and dissemination of concepts, ideas and arguments.

This leads into the third and final point, namely, that an account of early International Relations theory must consider the role of a nascent public sphere. For the scholars who discussed the changing social and political affairs of the High Middle Ages this constituted an emerging academic network. It was largely Church-sponsored. But it relied on an openly available (albeit often selective) tradition of ancient authorities. Medieval scholars discussed each other's interpretations and arguments: And they sometimes disagreed openly on important issues – including issues concerning war, peace and world order.

Dubois and nascent disagreements
Thomas Aquinas made major contributors to medieval discussions on politics. His political thought leans heavily on Aristotle and Augustine. By relying on Augustine's discussions of war and peace, Aquinas elaborated on the ancient idea of a God-given natural law. By combining Augustine's idea of natural law with an Aristotelian notion of man as 'by nature a social and political being', Aquinas established a connection across time that has proved to be one of the most solid lines in the intellectual tradition of the West. By relying on Aristotle, Aquinas drew connections backwards, thus forging theoretical links between Christian theology and the political thought of Europe's classical past. By elaborating upon the classical connection between the state and man's moral life, he drew connections forwards: he reintroduced a natural-law theory of the state which would blaze through the political thought of the West until far into the eighteenth century.

Another important contributor to the early development of International Relations theory was Pierre Dubois (1233–1322). He had attended Aquinas's last lectures at the University of Paris. Around 1306 he wrote *De recuperatione Terre Sancte* ('The Recovery of the Holy Land'). The title indicates that Dubois was arguing the necessity for launching a new crusade to wrest Palestine out of Muslim hands. But he also discussed how it was possible to obtain peace and stability in Europe. Dubois opposed the establishment of a world state. He criticized this idea – which most of his contemporaries entertained – of a universal, Christian empire. Instead he advocated a federation of Christian states. The premise of this proposal is noteworthy. For at the end of the Middle Ages Dubois recognized the rise of territorial states in Europe. Also, he observed that they tended to behave in independent or egotistical ways, and he feared that any effort to harness them or unify them under some common purpose, or seek some revival of the Roman Empire, would lead to wars and disaster. He proposed instead the establishment of a council of states designed to decide all state quarrels by arbitration.[19]

De recuperatione includes several clues to why political theorizing emerged in the West rather than in Byzantium or in the Islamic world. The first clue lies in his explicit disagreement with the traditional world-state argument. Dubois did not only disagree with the Church's position; he published an alternative argument. This suggests some diversity in the intellectual climate around 1300. And in this respect, the medieval West differed from Byzantium and the Caliphate. Along the North Atlantic rim lands there emerged a plurality of polities as well as a diversity of political opinions. Dubois's *De recuperatione* reflects the evolution of several early social formations in the western regions of Europe. Also it indicates that these formations add up to a unique macro-phenomenon: that they formed the early beginnings of a distinct interstate system.

A nascent diversity
It was in this unique context of the simultaneous evolution of adjacent polities along the north Atlantic rim that Dubois applied theological codes of conduct to issues of war and peace and diplomatic interaction. In the Byzantine and Islamic

civilizations, such codes and norms were also studied, but in an imperial context. Here, scholars were bound by the values of church and mosque and by the concerns of empire. Here, scholarship was an integral part of the imperial state whose primary objective was to keep law and order. Here, speculations on world affairs tended to be universalist extensions of the order of empire. In the Far West, however, emerged a multi-state alternative to empire. And its emergence is a first unique factor of the development of the Far West and it helps illuminate the region's early discussions on international relations.

Dubois's *De recuperatione* is an important work. Not only because it reflects the evolution of a multi-state system along the North Atlantic rim. But also because this system was altering political theorizing in fundamental ways. For its emergence did not merely give early scholars something new to theorize about; it also provided a social environment within which they were permitted to theorize with imagination and independence. The evolution of several independent states involved the evolution of several courts and of local interpretations of Church doctrines.

The growth of the multi-state system in the Far West hardly ushered in any mature public sphere, within which scholars could freely disseminate and discuss their ideas. Yet, it did assist in the growth of a multi-centred environment of scholarship within which independent and diverse political theorizing was allowed to occur. The rise of a multi-state system in Europe was attended by the emergence of intellectuals who were independent of Church authority. Pierre Dubois was one of them. He was employed not by the Church, but by Philippe le Bel – an ambitious French monarch who treated the papacy with suspicion and disrespect. Another independent scholar was Marsiglio of Padua (*c*. 1275–1343). Marsiglio was first employed by the University of Paris and later by several secular rulers. He, too, understood that important political changes were wrought by the rise of the modern state and a European state system. He struggled to identify the quality which expressed the essence of the modern state. His *Defensor pacis* ('Defender of the Peace' [1324]) 'manipulates phrases and struggles to express the idea of state sovereignty', comments Artz (1967, p. 299).

Marsiglio struggled but did not succeed. However, his struggle is impressive enough to warrant a comment: Marsiglio portrays the state as independent of God. In the first part of his treatise, he sees the law of the state as independent of any higher law; for him, the essence of law lies in its enforceability. The right to make law is backed by coercive force, and the force lies with the more substantial citizens, argues Marsiglio. He recommends that these citizens should meet in an assembly and delegate the direction of government to a single ruler. At the end of this first part Marsiglio has established that absolute authority belongs to the state, and that no superior power exists above the state. Then he drops the point. He has reached the limits of his argument. His limited concepts will not bring him further, and he is quickly recaptured by medieval concerns. Yet, for a brief moment he is clearly grappling with a phenomenon which later scholars grasped by the concept of 'sovereignty' – a concept which was beyond the range of his Latin vocabulary.[20] Marsiglio's effort is noteworthy because he formulates a theory of the state which foreshadows later theorists – such as Bodin.

Aquinas, Dubois, Marsiglio and others sensed how the evolution of the modern state wrought momentous changes in European politics. Their efforts to grasp these changes stretched established political conceptions and foreshadowed central notions of International Relations theory. Their efforts occurred within the discursive tradition of the Church and were informed by Christian themes and precepts. They also reflect an evolution of a wide community of scholars – first within the Church, but later independent of Church authorities. This was a unique feature in the development of the Far West (Needham 1969). This uniqueness helps explain why International Relations theorizing originated in the ascendant multi-state context of Western Europe rather than in the old empires of the Near or the Middle East.

Nowhere did this multi-state ascendancy create a more intense political environment than in Renaissance Italy. To which it is natural to turn next.

Notes

1 I capitalize 'International Relations' whenever it refers to the academic discipline. This is to distinguish it from the lower-case 'international relations' which I consider a more general term that denotes diplomatic events or 'world politics'. In Part IV of the book I use 'IR', following usual practice in the discipline today.
2 A most famous description of these events are found in Gibbon (1994a, pp. 1048ff; 1994b, 121ff, 196ff).
3 Terms like 'Europe', 'Italy', 'England', 'France' are anachronisms. Strictly speaking, it is not justified to use these modern labels when discussing the early Middle Ages, for there existed no cultural or political entities of such coherence or duration that they could fill the terms with any meaningful content. However, the alternative is worse: more appropriate designations would involve such elliptic descriptions that the few points covered in this hurried overview might easily be lost in ponderous prose.
4 Clovis was a Germanic king who conquered most of Western Europe and unified it into a vast kingdom. Although this kingdom fell apart shortly after his death, Clovis made three important contributions which drove the Continent towards greater unity. First, many of the quarrelling Germanic kings were depicted as descendants of Clovis and his grandfather Meroveus – from which the great variety of subsequent rulers derive their common label 'Merovingians'. Second, Clovis embraced the Catholic faith; he became the only Catholic ruler among the German kings and got what no Germanic other ruler had: the support of the Church. Third, he inspired other kings to try to repeat the feat. Carolus Magnus, a Frankish king, did, some 250 years later.
5 In England, Alfred the Great (871–99) organized a successful defence against the Viking invasions and won the allegiance of all Anglo-Saxons. In Germany, local counts and dukes repulsed the infringements of foreign attackers in the late 800s and managed to rebuild political stability from the local level. In the early 900s they elected themselves a king, Henry I (919–36). His son, Otto I, allied with the Church,

repressed domestic rebellions, defeated the Magyars once and for all (955) and made good his claim to be king of Italy (962). Such ties were also evident in France where political stability was similarly rebuilt in the early 900s from the local level by counts and dukes. In the late 900s the great lords of France chose Hugh Capet (987–96) as their king, and became his vassals. Hugh seized the old Carolingian crown, gave it to his own family and thus founded the Capetian dynasty.

6 More research is needed on this point. This staff was attached to the imperial post office (or the *drome*), one part of which was called the *Scrinium Barbarorum* (the Office of the Barbarians). The official in charge of this office was the *logothete* of the *drome*, who was responsible for the imperial post. As diplomatic relations evolved during the ninth and tenth centuries, the tasks of the *logothete* came to include the reception of foreign envoys, their formal introduction to the Emperor and his court and the internal security of the Empire. In practice it involved the constant gathering of intelligence pertaining to domestic security as well as to external relations with neighbouring societies, the frequent (often daily) interviews with the Emperor and the entertainment of visiting envoys – foreign visitors were treated lavishly, but also confined in special quarters and subject to constant surveillance.

The duties of the *logothete* also involved the collection of diplomatic information; not only from professional envoys, but also from merchants, missionaries, military men and foreign prisoners. In addition, information was collected from renegades – for example from Muslims like the eunuch Samonas who entered the service of Byzantium around 900. Such intelligence was systematically stored in special archives. Here they could be retrieved upon request and inform the decisions of generals, ambassadors or emperors.

7 The caravans sustained a postal system which enabled Arab scholars to exchange books and commentaries over thousands of miles between different parts of the empire. The postal system also served as a diplomatic infrastructure. The caliph wrote letters of state to Constantinople, Rome and Aachen. He sent out special missions. He also received visiting envoys who were treated with great grandeur in Baghdad. The caliphs of Baghdad, like the emperors of Constantinople, loved to dazzle foreign ambassadors. But visitors to Baghdad were, like emissaries to Constantinople, carefully watched and isolated from ordinary civilians. Access to the caliph was controlled by the *hâjib* (or 'doorkeeper'); power was delegated to a chief minister (*wazir* or 'helper') who was placed at the head of a hierarchical central administration (*diwan* or 'chancery') which included representatives from the army, the office of finance and the postal system (including the intelligence services). The Muslims understood that foreigners might be sent on other errands than mere deliveries of messages. They understood this well, because they themselves sent agents abroad to observe and gather information – as is explicitly described in writings of Arab geographers (Canard 1966, p. 734) and implicitly noted in some of the tales from the *Arabian Nights*. The reign of Harun al-Rashid (786–809) marked a zenith of political power, economic prosperity and cultural efflorescence.

8 In 830 the Caliph al-Ma'mun founded the *Bayt al-Hikmah* ('the House of Wisdom') in Baghdad. It contained several astronomical observatories with scientific equipment, a translation bureau and a vast library – which by the eleventh century claimed to have over a million volumes on its shelves. The translations of classical works represented

a significant incentive to learning. Through the munificence of rulers and princes, large private and public libraries and schools were built. Caliph al-Hakim built the *Dar al-Hikmah* ('the hall of wisdom') in Cairo. The tenth-century library of al-Hakim in Córdova boasted more than four hundred thousand books. In 1065 a great university was founded in Baghdad. Soon after, universities were also built in Damascus, Jerusalem and Cairo. Córdova, the capital of Arab Andalusia, quickly merged as a great centre of learning. Its public library, completed around 970, contained nearly half a million books; and it was merely one of seventy libraries in the city. Hroswitha, a tenth-century German observer, described the parks, palaces and paved roads of Córdova and pronounced it 'the jewel of the world'.

9 The 'Mirror-of-Princes' genre include texts written in the form of advise to new rulers. The genre was introduced from Persian into Arabic as early as the eighth century, but it did not produce its most celebrated texts until the Caliphate found its final definition in the eleventh century. The most famous Islamic example of the 'Mirror-of-Princes' genre in the Caliphate is probably the *Seyasat-nameh* ('Book of Government') written by Nizam al-Mulk (1018–92). Other famous examples include texts by prince 'Onsor ol-Ma'ali Keykavus (1021–98) and the mystic al-Ghazali (1058–1111). The genre emerged in Western Europe in the middle of the twelfth century (Berges 1938).

10 The term 'Cold War' – or *guerra fria* – was applied to this tense coexistence between Islam and Christendom by the thirteenth-century Spanish scholar Don Juan Manuel, who defined it as a tacit 'agreement to conduct their relations on the basis of equality and mutual interest'.

11 Al-Shaybani's book contains eleven chapters that fall into four separate parts. The first and introductory part (chapter I) spells out the theoretical or religious foundation of the book. The second part (chapters II–VIII) is a systematic study of the law that regulates the relationship between states. The third part (chapter IX) is a brief discussion on royal prerogatives; while the fourth and final part ideals with taxation – and is strictly speaking not an integral part of the work. Clearly, it is the first and the second part of Shaybani's *Siyar* which are of greatest interest.

The second part of Shaybani's *Siyar* is a systematic study of the law that regulates the relationship between territorial entities – nations or states. Shaybani's territorial vantage point shapes all his arguments. One of them is that people who inhabit different territories also obey different legal principles, and that, whenever a Muslim resides in a non-Muslim territory, local law must be accepted as binding – and vice versa: if a non-Muslim (a *harbi*) enters the area of *dar al-Islam*, he must obey Islamic law (Khadduri 1966, pp. 174ff). Upon the basic principle of territoriality, Shaybani introduces a principle of reciprocity – which guides his discussions of mercantile relationships, diplomatic emissaries and the exchange of prisoners (Khadduri 1966, pp. 170f). It also informs his discussions of war and peace.

12 It is worth recalling that these territories are of course not seen as states but as far rougher units. The 'territorial state' evolved in the West after the end of the Middle Ages – as described in subsequent chapters of this book. In the Muslim world, the *dar al-Islam* consists of those territories where the law of Islam prevails (i.e., broadly, the Muslim Empire. The *dar al-Harb* refers to the territories which lie outside of this Empire, i.e., the rest of the world.

13 Capella's title refers to the union between learning (Philology) and eloquence (Mercury). The original manuscript would strike the modern reader as bizarre: a curious medley of prose and verse that told a romantic story. Mercury has grown weary of celibacy, but has been successively refused by Wisdom, Divination and the Soul. Apollo then appears and speaks favourably of a charming young maiden named Philologia. They are (after a complicated process of courting and preparation) married. Among the wedding gifts are a number of young women who will be Philologia's slaves: Rhetoric, Grammar, Logic, Arithmetic, Harmony, Geometry and Astronomy. The first and second book of *De nuptiis* set up the allegory. Each of the remaining seven books treats one of the young female slaves. See, e.g., Stahl (1977).

14 When Augustine observed that even the Roman Empire, that bastion of constancy and civility, was collapsing, he was forced to conclude that no earthly state can eternally ensure security from internal and external attack. Everything on earth is temporal. And although temporal rulers are ordained by God, they will always be victims of fear, envy, greed, vanity and ignorance. Because no earthly ruler can be permanently sheltered from such human frailties, there will always be wars, and there will always be an end to every earthly kingdom. Rome was no exception.

15 It protected local privileges and immunities determined by inherited status that characterized the feudal order. It is often portrayed as benefiting the ruling elites. However, customary law also included a unique, perhaps even a proto-democratic, element of popular involvement (Szücs 1990, pp. 27ff). It was derived ultimately from the people who, at least tacitly, had given it their consent; and it applied to vassals and lords alike. It had 'percolated up from below' as Ferguson and Mansbach (1988, p. 53) put it, and applied to individuals by virtue of their membership in a tribe or local group.

16 The formalization of civic representation in the king's council furnished the origins of the Parliament in England, the Cortes in Spain, the Reichstag in Germany, the Estates-General in France. This development not only consolidated the territorial state in state, it also laid the foundations for the distinct form of the *Ständestaat* – a late medieval regime type in which the monarch and the court emerged as the strong centre of political gravity but where key decision-making bodies included representatives from the main estates of the country (Poggi 1978) – and, later, the absolute monarchy (Anderson 1979).

17 This represented a turn away from the dark pessimism of Augustine. Aquinas's attitude, together with the claim that the crucifixion of Christ involved a restoration of man's original status, provided a more optimistic analysis of the human condition. Since man was rational, he had the capacity to follow the law of God consciously. He could, through his own will and devotion, improve his faculties of reason and thus approach God.

18 Aquinas explains that peace is the first aim of government and that God's laws must be obeyed over those of man. Furthermore, he acknowledges the importance of economic activities in human society. His proposition that basic, material needs for food, shelter and clothing must be satisfied before man can be expected to engage in spiritual pursuits shows that he recognized the important role played by production. He also recognizes the realm of exchange, but he betrays a pronounced scepticism

towards mercantile affairs. He associated these with profit-making and with 'artificial wealth' which he suspected because the lust for it know no limits. Aquinas emphasizes that all exchange must be guided by a concern for justice, and is careful to specify that the just price of a commodity must be calculated by adding the costs of production to a reasonable payment to the producer in proportion to their social status (Aquinas 1947, pp. 1513–22). Financial activities, however, are reserved a harsh judgement in the *Summa*, where usury is abhorred in no uncertain terms. However, Aquinas does not expand upon issues of production, exchange or finance. He mostly repeated the strong scepticism towards mercantile affairs entertained by his contemporaries and by Aristotle.

19 Pierre Dubois is hailed by some as the man who first proposed an international council or court of arbitration. But he did more. He also urged the council members to break associations with any states that initiate war and advocated concerted action against the offensive state – thus foreshadowing Woodrow Wilson's doctrine of collective security by about six hundred years.

It is hard to gauge the influence of *De recuperatione Terre Sancte* (which did not appear in print until 1611). But it seems to have been known to George Podebrad and Marini who, in the 1460s, proposed a scheme for an international body of arbitration which would settle disputes among kings (ter Meulen 1917). Dubois was clearly known to Erasmus and Suarez.

20 It should be added that, more surprisingly, the concept of the 'state' was not really within the range of the late medieval vocabulary either. The ancients had used terms like *polis* or *imperium* to denote independent territorial associations. And when Dubois and Marsiglio display, towards the end of the Middle Ages, a gradual awareness that a new kind of political association was emerging in Europe, the idea of 'the state' came into being. The term emerged slowly and in many local variations (*status, stato, el estado, l'État, der Staat* ...). It was at first used with little clarity. And the resulting ambiguities reflected the complexity of the new experience and of the factors which gave rise to it. It was only by the fifteenth century that the term began to acquire a clearer political usage as reference to a specific form of polity. Only after the Dutch proclamation of Independence (1581) was *status* frequently invested with a republican tone which contrasted a 'popular' or 'republican' association with a monarchic one (Dyson 1980, pp. 25ff; Vincent 1987, pp. 16ff).

2

Renaissance politics:
the roots of the modern ages

The seeds of International Relations theorizing were sown in the fragmented and rural High Middle Ages and they took centuries to grow. Their growth was spurred by the evolution of the modern state. By the fifteenth century, the evolution was not as far developed as is often believed. Renaissance authors are often presented as important contributors to modern international theory. Yet, their speculations tended to reverberate with antique and medieval echoes, and to be more preoccupied with state affairs than with interstate relations.

Machiavelli, one of the most famous political theorists of the Renaissance, is an example. When he discussed politics in terms of *virtue* and *fortune* he drew on established, medieval terms. When he discussed affairs of state, he had the city-state foremost in mind. There is no doubt that Machiavelli was a pioneer of political analysis. However, his contributions to International Relations are surprisingly modest. His younger contemporary, Francesco Guicciardini, offered a more elaborate International Relations argument and will here be deemed to be the more important theorist.

This chapter will begin with a discussion of some of the medieval themes that marked the political discussions of the early Renaissance. It will present the Italian city-states, focusing on Florence with its distinct splendour, its social fashions and its humanist thinkers like Leonardo Bruni and Lorenzo Valla. The chapter will briefly discuss the Italian wars which destroyed this splendour, and caused Niccolò Machiavelli, Francesco Guicciardini and other scholars to analyse the nature of war, peace and politics in distinctly modern ways.

A great transformation

'In the history of the world, no civilization has appeared to be more completely rural than that of the Middle Ages,' writes Georges Duby (1968, p. xi) about the sparsely populated, heavily forested Far West of the tenth and eleventh centuries. In spite of powerful, centralized institutions like the Holy Roman Empire and the papacy, medieval Europe was fragmented. It was plagued by invasions and shifting personalized rule. Under these conditions, life and property were precarious. Social and economic relationships were organized in highly localized networks of production and protection.

These conditions changed dramatically after 1000. Especially in northern Italy. Here, within the confines of massive walls or hemmed in by water, the heavy bustle of politics first appeared in the eleventh century. It emerged among groups of urban residents as they snatched more and more power from traditional authorities – from local bishops and kings, and from foreign lords and emperors – until nothing less than self-rule could satisfy them. The process was slow and gradual. By the end of the fourteenth century it had produced a cluster of city-states and a veritable city-state system. Without it Machiavelli would not have written his *Prince*. Without it, Guicciardini would never have remarked that never to have held political office was almost not to have been a man. Without it, theories of international relations might have looked very different indeed.

The medieval sentiment

Renaissance theorizing emerged from an environment which was steeped in Christian theology. Medieval education and discussion took place within Church institutions. These acknowledged no essential difference between the various branches of knowledge. They drew no distinction between knowledge about nature and knowledge about humanity. In the final instance, they subordinated all existence to participation in a dramatic morality play, dominated by the four themes of God, Nature, Prescription and Obedience.

God was the dominant theme. He was conceived as an omnipotent and omniscient intelligence; a master dramatist who has planned an infinitely complex, cosmic drama in the smallest detail. Finished in idea before it was enacted in fact, God had, even before the world begun, written the last syllable of recorded time. And his drama was unalterable (Becker 1932, p. 7). Man must accept God's drama, because he could not alter it. His fate was to play the role he was assigned. In order for him to play his role according to the divine text, the authorities of Church and state – deriving their just powers from the will of God – were instituted among men to dispose them into submission and to instruct them in their proper lines.

Nature was a second major theme of medieval speculation. Nature was seen as perfect, good and eternal simply because it was created by God who *is* Perfection, Goodness and Eternity. All things made by man, by contrast, were clumsy and temporal infringements upon God's perfect work. There was therefore no distinction between 'natural' and 'good' in medieval thought. And the two core questions of political theory – 'Why should man obey the state?' and 'What is the good state?' – had no meaning. The state was part of God's great plan; created by God for the benefit of man, it was natural and therefore good by definition.

Prescription and *obedience* were two final themes of the medieval, Christian drama. The two were intimately intertwined. Man could use his intelligence and identify the laws which God had invested in the universe. These laws were natural and good, and, since man was imperfect, he would be wise to emulate them. If man could live according to God's laws, he would live a good and natural life, and he might receive forgiveness from God on the day of final judgement. He might save his soul and attain an afterlife of eternal bliss. In the medieval mind, human reason was subordinate to a larger theological purpose. The function of intelligence was therefore to demonstrate the truth of revealed knowledge, to reconcile diverse and pragmatic experience with the rational pattern of the world as given in faith.

In the High Middle Ages, the function of science was to scrutinize God's two primary creations: the World and the Bible. God had left clues in both creations, and he had equipped man with intelligence and reason to find these clues and read in them God's intentions. The primary duty of scholars was to compare the clues found in nature with the clues found in the Bible, identify God's intentions as clearly as possible and then create rules and prescriptions for all human activities. Only by obeying these prescriptions could man hope to attain salvation.

Emergence of modern notions

The evolution of the feudal order brought a marked improvement of social stability in the core areas of Europe. During the eleventh century it described an accelerating tendency to concentrate political power and centralize command in the hands of monarchs and courts. This development was remarkably quick along Europe's Atlantic rim where a rudimentary system of monarchic states evolved rapidly – before 990 it did not exist; by 1100 a complex macro-political structure consisting of territorial states was being consolidated (Tilly 1994).

This rise of territorial states altered the social processes in Europe. From a long-term, large-scale perspective, this development improved the social stability in core areas of Europe. Travel became safer. People ventured further away from their village or local fortress-town to cultivate new land or to exchange their products. Horses were effectively harnessed and shod for heavier work. Iron ploughs made possible new techniques of agriculture, such as crop rotation which produced higher yields. Watermills and windmills were more frequently built and used to grind corn, press oil, saw lumber and, by the fourteenth century, make paper. Such innovations encouraged the evolution of new, more productive systems of social organization (White 1972).

Gradually, life was transformed. Commercial networks branched across Europe, stimulated by the Crusades, which offered great opportunities to entrepreneurial individuals –principally the merchants of northern Italy who were so conveniently located both across the Crusaders' path and on the thriving trade routes to the eastern Mediterranean and Asia (Pirenne 1937). This transit trade was a great stimulus for the city-states in northern Italy. Many Italian rulers saw the need for interstate agreements to encourage the smooth flow of trade. Slowly, treaties between these city-states produced the basis for diplomatic interaction and swept away traditional webs of cumbersome feudal laws. Merchants met regularly at the fairs and markets which spread across the map of Europe like shoots of climbing ivy: Saint-Denis, Foggia, Champagne, Lyon and others. By one estimate, trade increased as much as twenty times during the eleventh and the twelfth centuries (Southern 1953, p. 44).

The most astounding developments occurred in the northern regions of the Italian peninsula. By the year 1400, Italy was a kaleidoscope of social formations. In the south, where the High Middle Ages witnessed several changes of dynasty – Muslim, Viking, Angevin and Aragonese chieftains succeeded one another as rulers – lay Naples and Sicily. In the centre, the Papal States stretched across the Apennines from Rome to Ravenna. In the north were the wealthy merchant cities of Milan, Venice, Genoa and Florence. Here, strong city governments controlled not only their own immediate vicinity but hundreds of square miles of rural territory as well. The city-states had developed vast territorial domains around themselves.

In the late fifteenth century, five major city-states dominated peninsular politics: the republics of Venice and Florence, the Papal States and the principalities of Milan and Naples. Some of these states were controlled by a prince or despot, like Milan. Others governed themselves as republics – like Florence; the only republic in the Western world before the seventeenth century and a city which allowed its inhabitants great freedom to pursue their own interests, undisturbed by popes and monarchs.

Each of the five major city-states differed from the others in their histories as well as by the nature of the institutions. Yet, they interacted regularly and their interaction established a complex system of states (Franke 1968; Baron 1952). The emergence of what is generally considered to be the first modern example of a family or a system of states was intimately related to the decline of the two dominant medieval institutions of the papacy and the Holy Roman Empire. Both institutions embodied

Figure 2.1 Italy at the end of the fifteenth century

the medieval conception of a universal community. The decline of this conception and its replacement with alternative views of political organization opened up the floodgates of power politics within the Italian city-states and produced a political environment in which the concept of a reason of state – *ragione di stato* – became a predominant principle. This evolution was paralleled by the establishment of a diplomatic system – a network of permanent embassies with accredited diplomats, foreign policy analysts and advisers in addition to an elaborate structure for the rapid transport and the safe storage of diplomatic dispatches (Nicolson 1954, pp. 27–31; Elton 1981).

These developments are significant. They mark the end of the medieval notion that the order of the state reflects the natural harmony of a divine universe. The principles of government were no longer derived from a theologically defined, God-given order. Rather, they reflect an emerging view of the state and of state interaction as embodying an autonomous rationality. The principles of government are seen as immanent, as they flow from the nature of the state itself. To know how to govern, one must know the innate workings of the state. Thus, the development of the concept of the reason of state signals the starting point of modern political theorizing.

Trade and humanism in Renaissance Florence

Most of the city-states of northern Italy had grown wealthy from trade and finance. Already in the High Middle Ages, merchants and bankers from Italy had played central roles at the fairs of Champagne and Lyon and at the permanent markets which succeeded them in Paris, Bruges and London. By the year 1300, the network of Italian banking spanned all the major market centres of Europe – the Peruzzi of Florence, for example, were represented by partners and salaried employees in fifteen locations all across western and northern Europe (Roover 1965, pp. 80, 85).

Commerce, communication and lay concerns
This growth of commerce changed the social conditions of Europe. It created new patterns of social relations, caused new problems and triggered new attitudes to them. The rise of financial and entrepreneurial elites in core areas of Europe altered the social structures and changed social attitudes. First of all, it fuelled the growth of a new transnational class of people who saw business facts in a new light and from different angles; 'a class, in short, that was *in* business, and therefore could never look at its problems with the aloofness of the schoolman' (Schumpeter 1954, p. 78). This new class accumulated and controlled wealth. It attained an increased social presence as well as power to assert its own interests.

Second, the growth of commerce was attended by new systems of knowledge and communication. The development of new professions, estates, social groups and classes established horizontal networks of producers, traders and financiers, all of whom were dependent upon current knowledge about markets, prices and power relations (Braudel 1982). The evolution of their networks may be glimpsed as early as the 1450s in the form of regularized meetings or institutionalized correspondence. Trading partners would exchange letters across city-walls and state boundaries. As the decades passed, and as their systems of communication became regular and institutionalized, business dispatches would increasingly include assessments of safety and comments on traffic and social order; sometimes they would incorporate comments on social issues, including views on politics and literature.

The invention of movable typeface (around 1450) greatly stimulated this development – as is evident in a swelling debate about lifestyles, beliefs, ideas, social and political conditions and the literary arts.[1] The subsequent growth in communication and knowledge fed the emergence of a peculiarly social sphere, within which scholars produced texts for a reading public – a predominantly urban, educated *publicum*. This public sphere emerged outside of the state and beyond the control of the Church. It sustained authors who defied the views of traditional elites. It constituted a decisively important medium for the dissemination of social and political ideas. It helped nourish the growing social weight of the culture and business values.

As the businessman's social weight increased, he imparted to society an increasing dose of his mind. The particular mental habits generated by the work in the business office, the schema of values that emanated from it, and the attitude to public and private life that was characteristic of it, slowly spread in *all* classes and over all fields of human thought and action. Starting from their professional needs and problems, craftspeople, bankers, merchants, rulers and artists began to develop funds of tools and knowledge – mechanics, credit, navigation, chains of economic command and a social division of labour. This initially practical reservoir of knowledge evolved in the public sphere, outside of the universities which were dominated by the Church. It gave rise to a body of secular or lay concerns.

Lay scholars had long existed in the West (Needham 1969). In late fifteenth-century Italy they began to outnumber the scholars of the Church. The new urban elite in the wealthy city-states like Venice and Florence grew obsessed with the secular aspects of human history and philosophy. They were concerned with moral and civic questions. The rediscovery of Greek and Roman artefacts mushroomed towards obsessive proportions among the *nouveau riches*.

The lay, classical scholars were professionally concerned with ancient affairs and became known as *humanists*. They evolved within the expanding public sphere of the age, and were in high demand at Italian universities and with the better families. They had studied Greek and could teach it to others. They read and interpreted the classical texts – as did Marcilio Ficino, who translated all of Plato's works into Latin. They edited and wrote commentaries on the classic texts. They devised new methods of historical investigation that enabled them to position old manuscripts in time and distinguish originals from copies and forgeries. The humanists were something new in European society: lay scholars who made a living from their knowledge in secular affairs. They rediscovered what classical writers like Martianus Capella (Stahl 1977) had meant by the 'liberal arts': the study of great literature and philosophy which had a liberating effect on mind and imagination.

The humanists broke the Church monopoly of learning and initiated a revolution in education and scholarship. They challenged Church authority – when Lorenzo Valla in the 1440s demonstrated errors in authoritative Church documents, he created a major controversy.[2] The humanists brought a new spirit of courage and independence to Renaissance scholarship. Even the Bible was subjected to critical analysis – and shown to contain errors of translation. They also brought with them a new individualism, a fascination with classical culture and a unique historical self-consciousness.

Ancient virtue, new social fashions

The independence and individualism are reflected in the Renaissance preoccupation with heroes and hero-worship, and with the central concept of *virtù*. The fifteenth-century hero possessed elements of both traditional feudal-chivalric values and new urban-cultural attributes. The Renaissance gentleman was the great individual who shaped his own destiny by skill and insight.[3]

The enthusiasm for classical culture is apparent in the eagerness with which the humanists searched for ancient texts and manuscripts. In them the found echoes of ancient societies which were curiously like their own. These ancient texts alluded to urban environments comparable to their own city-states. They made it evident that ancient Greece and Rome had been places where a person of means was looked up to – which were just what the *nouveaux riches* of Florence and Milan wanted to hear. In authors like Thucydides and Tacitus they found descriptions of individuals who reasoned, took calculated risks, gambled, conquered difficulties or who were vanquished by their obstacles.

Enterprising individuals were quick to respond to the public demand for ancient culture. They scurried all over southern Europe for artefacts and manuscripts and discovered an astonishing amount of texts and fragments covering a variety of topics – agriculture, astronomy, etiquette, ethics, geometry, good living, history, philosophy, poetry, politics, post-prandial speaking, rhetoric. Leading citizens were fascinated by such findings. They were insatiable. Some merchants organized regular package tours to Athens and Rome – the more expensive tours even included humanist scholars who would guide the *nouveau-riche* urbanites of Florence and Venice in their search for ancient, valuable items. And like all adventurous and wealthy tourists, they bought everything in sight, carried their souvenirs home, showed them off to their friends and told them about the trip.

Leading families wanted to know more about their high-cultured ancestors. They recruited humanist scholars to find out more, to write histories. The copyist Francesco Poggio allowed himself to be hired by princes, merchants and bankers to track down classical manuscripts and return with copies.[4] Palla Strozzi, one of the richest men in Florence, paid agents to retrieve old manuscripts, and procured from Greece Plutarch's *Lives*, Aristotle's' *Politics* and Ptolemy's *Cosmography*. In 1423, Giovanni Aurispa arrived in Italy with 238 manuscripts from Greece. Among these was Thucydides' *Peloponnesian War*, which was translated from Greek by Lorenzo Valla in 1485 and had an immediate impact on Renaissance humanism.

The intensely sought-after Greek and Roman manuscripts provided fledgling political theorists with sustained and systematic discussions of political theory. Some complete works of the classical period had been known and studied before the fifteenth century. Euclid and selections from Aristotle and Plato and others had been accessible since the High Middle Ages but through often inexact Arabic translations. Immense horizons were opened by the sudden influx of classical masterpieces in the 1420s and 1430s:

> The *Iliad* and *Odyssey*, the tragedies of Aeschylus, Sophocles and Euripides, the comedies of Aristophanes, the odes of Pindar, the eclogues of Theocritus, the histories of Herodotus, Thucydides and Xenophon, the character studies of Theophrastus, the speeches of Demosthenes, the dialogues of Plato, the writings of Cynics, Stoics and Neo-Platonists, the speculations of the Ionian philosophers, the medical writings of Hippocrates and Galen, the geography of Ptolemy and Strabo – it was as if these masterpieces had been written all at once and suddenly given to Florence. (Cronin 1967, p. 51)

Wars and *virtù*

The influx of classical texts did more than trigger new fads and social fashions among the leading lights of Florence. It revolutionized their knowledge and altered their worldview. The classical texts were pre-Christian. The educated Renaissance person identified more easily with the classical accounts of complex human beings who faced complex human problems than with the Church's predictable, one-dimensional stories of saints who were saved and sinners who were punished. The ancient texts had none of the moralism and none of the wealth- and fun-denying properties of the Church doctrines. They conveyed new knowledge. They introduced new ideals and set new cultural standards.

Leonardo Bruni (1369–1444) was one of a new generation of humanists who sought to live up to the ideals and emulate the standards. He sought to trace the historical evolution of Florence. In *The History of the Florentine People* Bruni attributed the power and wealth of Florence to its republican government. It was the source of its beauty of style, courage, industriousness, strength and other instances of Renaissance *virtù*. Other authors invoked a similar argument. Among them was Niccolò Machiavelli, who largely repeats Bruni's thesis in his *Histories of Florence*.

Niccolò de Bernardo Machiavelli (1469–1527) contributed greatly to political theory. His contribution to International Relations theory is also significant, but it is indirect and often overestimated. One of his younger contemporaries, Francesco Guicciardini (1483–1540), may be a more important contributor in this respect. For whereas Machiavelli focused on politics within states, Guicciardini discussed politics among states as well. In order to grasp their concerns and appreciate their arguments, it is necessary to understand that they addressed the specific problems of an uncertain age, marked by the high stakes and the ruthlessness of the Italian Wars.

The Italian Wars

When Machiavelli and Guicciardini were young men, Lorenzo de' Medici ruled Florence. Strong and cunning, he maintained order not only in Florence; his imaginative diplomacy helped preserve order among the five central Italian states (Florence itself, Venice, Milan, Naples and the Papacy). When Lorenzo died in 1492 (aged forty-four), his diplomacy unravelled. His son Piero took over, but he had none of his father's qualities. When Charles VIII of France invaded Italy in 1492, Piero surrendered. The citizens of Florence rose up in anger. They considered it a cowardly act. They revolted, expelled Piero and, under the influence of the religious leader Savonarola, declared Florence a republic with Christ as its only ruler.

The Florentine rebellion received support from Spain. Spanish rulers had long been wary of French expansionism; the French house of Valois and the Spanish house of Habsburg were rivals. And when a Valois king invaded Italy in 1494, the Spanish Habsburgs reacted swiftly with an invasion of their own. France was the stronger power in fifteenth-century Europe, commanding some forty thousand soldiers in 1470. But Spain developed faster – boosted by the unification of Catalonia and Aragon in 1469 and, later, by the *conquista* and by influx of bullion from the Americas. France could not in the long run hold on to the territories it had occupied in Italy. Spain slowly gained the upper hand. And in the meantime, the two countries fought each other in Italy.

The Italian wars spelled disaster for Italy. They ruined the trade and the ordering institutions upon which its splendour rested. It squeezed the Italian city-states helplessly between the two, much larger states. It forced Italian rulers to submit to foreign rule (Machiavelli 1961, pp. 133ff). In 1498, the pope took France's side in the war. He turned against Spain and Florence, captured Savonarola, tried him for heresy and burned him at the stake. However the Florentine Republic survived under the leadership of Piero Soderini. He employed Machiavelli as a secretary and, later, sent Guicciardini as ambassador to Spain.

Machiavelli: between virtù and self-interest

Machiavelli's sinister reputation rests almost entirely on one short, extreme, epigrammatic book, *The Prince*. He wrote it during the last six months of 1513, but it was published posthumously twenty years later in 1532 (five years after the author's death). It reflects Machiavelli's experiences as a civil servant in Soderini's Florence, most particularly as secretary for the Council of Ten which sent him on diplomatic missions to Tuscany, Rome and, later, to Spain and France.

Machiavelli worked with Leonardo da Vinci (Masters 1996). On his diplomatic travels he negotiated with Pandulfo Petrucci, tyrant of Siena. He met several of the important foreign statesmen of his day – Louis XII of France, Ferdinand of Aragon, Habsburg Emperor Maximilian and Pope Alexander VI. He visited Pope Alexander's son, Cesare Borgia, for whom he developed a high admiration (Machiavelli 1961, pp. 54ff). He was a systematic observer. He wrote reports and assessments and sent them back to Florence to inform Soderini's government. From these reports –

and from the interviews, observations, concerns and practical assessments that went into them – Machiavelli distilled his famous little book, *The Prince*.

The book belonged to a tradition of books: the 'mirror of princes'.[5] It consists of twenty-six short chapters, which can be grouped into four parts according to subject matter: Part one (chapters 1–9) deals with principalities. Part two (chapters 10–14) deals with the state and the power that undergirds it. Part three (chapters 15–23) deals with the prince and the qualities which will secure his rule. Part four (chapters 24–6) deals with the political situation in Italy in the 1520s.[6]

The book's first part begins by listing up various types of principalities and by explaining the means by which they are acquired and maintained. Then they introduce the key conceptual terms of the book: that is, the old, conceptual pair of *fortuna* and *virtù*. Translators agree about the first term, *fortuna*, and translate it as 'fortune'. The term is derived from the goddess Fortuna who had been worshipped in Italy from the earliest times and always portrayed as a controller of destinies. Originally, Fortuna was the goddess of prosperity; later she became the goddess of chance (and thus identified with the Greek Tyche, a capricious dispenser of good and ill luck). Machiavelli largely uses the term 'fortune' in a secularized and descriptive sense. Rather as a synonym for 'event' or 'chance occurrence', but with a dramatic edge to it – in one context Machiavelli compares fortune to a violent river; in another to a sudden storm.

Translators disagree about the second term, *virtù*. Some translate it as 'virtue' (which is misleadingly wide), others as 'prowess' (which may be too narrow, but closer to the mark). *Virtù* is derived from the word *vír* which means 'man'; and it is obvious from Machiavelli's usage that the term reverberate with the masculine ideal of the Renaissance gentleman. Castiglione (1959, p. 295) saw this ideal as involving both genius and determination; properties that made for greatness in literature and artistic creativity as well as in statesmanship and war. The 'strength of a lion' and the 'cunning of a fox' are political virtues for Machiavelli, because possession would increase the chances of a prince to master the twists and turns of fortune. He 'must be a fox in order to recognize traps, and a lion to frighten off wolves. Those who simply act like lions are stupid. So it follows that a prudent ruler cannot, and must not honour his word when it places him at a disadvantage' (Machiavelli 1961, pp. 99f). He must *appear* to be trustworthy, truthful, honest and good, but be careful not to go too far. For 'if he has these qualities and always behaves accordingly, he will find them harmful'. However, if he only pretends to have them, then will be of great political service. The prince 'should appear to be compassionate, faithful to his word, kind, guileless, and devout. And indeed, he should be so. But his disposition should be such that, if he needs to be the opposite, he knows how' (p. 100). Machiavelli, then, loaded his understanding of *virtù* with qualities of cunning, leadership, command and other abilities which would enable a ruler to master the twists of 'fortune' and to ride off the frequent storms of Italian politics. His explanations are rife with sexual overtones. *Virtù* can harness *fortuna* 'because fortune is a woman and if she is to be submissive it is necessary to beat and coerce her' (p. 133; Pitkin 1984).

In addition to the conceptual pair of *fortuna* and *virtù*, Machiavelli also develops a more typically modern concept to explain political action: self-interest. This principle is evident in the second part of *The Prince*, which discusses military power as the foundation of the state. It is most notable in Machiavelli's discussion of the several types of armed force. Indeed, the principle first appears when Machiavelli explains the behaviour of soldiers: armies can be composed of mercenary, auxiliary or national troops, or of a mixture of the three. Mercenary troops are always dangerous, for there is 'no loyalty or inducement to keep them on the field apart from the little they are paid, and this is not enough to make them want to die for you' (p. 77). Auxiliary troops (i.e. troops who are supplied by another state to assist your own) are even more dangerous, for they obey the orders of another ruler, and 'you are left in a lurch if they are defeated, and in their power if they are victorious' (p. 83). National troops are the best. These are the only troops a prince can depend on, for they live with their families on the very territory they are set to defend and they depend upon a victory for continued survival.

Machiavelli's explanation is distinctly modern: it makes good sense for mercenaries and auxiliary troops to desert when war break out: bravery in war entails a risk which is higher than the salary can compensate for. The national soldier, by contrast, fights neither for a salary nor for his prince, but for himself. Thus, it makes good sense for the national solder, who is a subject and a citizen with a family and a property to defend, to fight for the survival of the state in which he has concrete stakes. The explanatory principle to which Machiavelli appeals in this second part of *The Prince* is, in short, the self-interest of the modern, rational individual.

In the third part of the book, Machiavelli uses this notion of self-interest to explain the behaviour of successful princes. Also, he draws no distinction between the interests of the Prince and those of the state. The two converge. The Prince fully represents the state and embodies its interests. It is therefore in the interest of the state that a prince should feel free to break his word whenever he deems it necessary. By same token, the Prince should not feel obliged to keep his promises if he thinks this would be counter to state interests; the prince must learn 'to be a great liar and deceiver' but he must also learn to conceal this important skill. Princes must always act according to the best interests of the state, they do not answer to ordinary moral rules. In politics, and most particularly in interstate politics, there exists a different morality; it is governed by the self-interest and the security of the prince or state (Machiavelli 1997, p. 394f; Meinecke 1957; Ferrari 1860).[7]

The fourth and final part of *The Prince* deals with the political situation in Italy in Machiavelli's own time. Its analysis is guided by the old conceptual pair of *fortuna* and *virtù*. Here he argues that fortune is the arbiter of only half of man's actions. The remaining half is governed by man's own will and his *virtù*. This claim, which implies than man is largely the maker of his own fate, reverberates with Renaissance individualism and represents a resounding break with the medieval belief that man's faith is authored by God. Distinctly modern is Machiavelli's final chapter – which many readers consider the key to the entire book. Here Machiavelli expresses the hope that Italy can unify, grow strong and cast off the curse of foreign intervention which is threatening to grind the country to pieces.

Some commentators see a modern reasoning in this argument. They argue that, when Machiavelli proposed to unify the city-states of Italy against strong enemies, he invoked a balance-of-power theory. Machiavelli, however, never used the term 'balance of power'.[8] The chapter is significant, but for other reasons than this. First, it amounts to a plea, not to a benevolent God, but to a prince who possesses the secular virtues that Machiavelli has introduced in previous chapters – will, cunning, strength and rational self-interest. Second, the chapter introduces patriotic intent as a motivating force in political action. It is Machiavelli's hope that a virtuous prince will raise a national army, unify Italy, chase the foreign invaders off Italian soil and restore the country to independence and glory.

This plea invokes nothing less than Europe's first doctrine of national liberation.

Guicciardini: chronicler of power

Machiavelli shows some influence from Thucydides – he was for example affected by the ancient historian's psychological portrayal of political leaders. However, Machiavelli adopted neither Thucydides' method nor his balance-of-power theory. But others did. One of the most significant of these – at least from an International Relations perspective – is Francesco Guicciardini (1483–1540). Whereas Machiavelli seems to have treated *The Peloponnesian War* 'as only a reservoir of stories from which he selected a few' (Bondanella 1973, p. 17), Guicciardini found in Thucydides' book instructive elements towards a deeper understanding of interstate relations.

Although Guicciardini drew theoretical insights from antique authors, most of his discussions concern the uncertain and ruthless issues of his own day. But more explicitly than Machiavelli, Guicciardini portrayed Lorenzo 'the Magnificent' as the last, brilliant statesman of the age.

Guicciardini's life

Guicciardini was born in 1483 into one of the oldest and most important families of the Florentine aristocracy. In 1498 he enrolled as a student of law at the University of Florence. After three years he transferred to the University of Ferrara – largely because his father wished to have a member of the family (and a share of the family fortune) in a more secure city in the event of political upheavals. He received the doctorate in civil law in 1505, and began to write. He first wrote a history of his family. Then he began a more ambitious study of the history of Florence.

Guicciardini's writing was interrupted in 1509 because he became entangled in high-stakes political games. He was elected to minor posts in the Florentine Republic. Then he was appointed as Soderini's ambassador to the court of King Ferdinand of Aragon. Finally, he married Maria Salvati – an act which had dire consequences because the marriage represented an open declaration of political sympathies: the Salvatis strongly opposed the powerful Medici family. So, in 1512 when the Medici family overthrew Soderini's government and took power, Guicciardini's goose was cooked. He was forced to give up his ambassadorship in Spain, return to Florence and open up a law practice there. In his spare time, he wrote.

He entered the service of the papacy in 1516. He showed himself as an efficient administrator and was rapidly promoted.[9] During the height of the Italian wars – the complex struggle over Italy between the kings of France and Spain – Guicciardini became Pope Clement VII's trusted foreign-policy adviser. He counselled the Pope to manoeuvre delicately between the rival rulers of France and Spain while maintaining control over Italy. On Guicciardini's advice, the Pope first supported Charles V of Spain in the fighting which ended in the battle of Pavia (February 1525) during which King Francis I was defeated. In a clear balance-of-power move, the Pope then joined France's Francis I and helped establish the League of Cognac whose aim was to contain the ambitions of Charles V.

Guicciardini retired from politics in 1538. During the final years of his life he worked on his most ambitious work, *The History of Italy*. It covers Italian politics between 1494 and 1534, the most chaotic and formative period of the Italian wars. He was working on the final revision of this book when he died in May 1540.

Guicciardini's contributions

In spite of a busy career as a diplomat and papal adviser, Guicciardini was a prolific author. While ambassador in Spain, he wrote a book on Spanish politics and a collection of essays. After the death of Pope Leo X he began a work on Florentine politics. During a difficult few years after 1527 he composed several biographical works.[10] In addition, through a period of eighteen active years, he wrote a series of observations and thoughts on a variety of subjects. He incessantly revised and rewrote this collection, which is known as his *Ricordi*. This collection of maxims or aphorisms represents the harvest of an active and turbulent life.

Some of Guicciardini's *Ricordi* were rules that instructed his family on how to maintain their status and reputation. Others were comments on political events. But all of them reflect the author's experiences in Renaissance Italy. They leave an impression of cruel and corrupt rulers, driven by ambition and vice. The *Ricordi* are infused with a bleak and cynical view of the human condition. They attribute the sufferings of humanity to human failings. They warn against trusting individual rulers because they follow their desires rather than their reason (Gilbert 1965, p. 288; Ferrari 1860, pp. 277ff). Guicciardini puts little faith in the wisdom of the popular masses – which he likens to a 'mad animal, full of a thousand errors, of a thousand confusions, lacking in taste, in discernment, in stability'. He refers to the clergy as 'bands of ruffians' among whom he had seen nothing but ambition, avarice and sensuality (C-28).[11]

Guicciardini argues, like Machiavelli, that political behaviour cannot be understood in terms of moral arguments; rather it must be understood in terms of interest. 'Princes will often do what they please or what they know, and not what they should' (C-128). His reasoning behind this is suggested by a passage in *Dialogue on the Government of Florence* [1524], in which Guicciardini discusses what Florence should do with a group of prisoners whom the city has captured in a war with Pisa. Here, he lets his alter ego, Bernardo del Nero, propose that the prisoners be promptly killed. When his interlocutors think that this is excessively cruel and that it violates all Christian principles and counters common conscience, Bernardo defends his proposal. 'The Pisans are our inveterate enemies', he says. If the Florentines were to act according to what is their Christian duty and moral right, they should release them. But the prisoners would then return to Pisa, rejoin the Pisan army and make everyone there laugh at the short-sighted leniency of the Florentine government. To release the prisoners, then, would only increase the number and the strength of Florence's enemies, and make them all less fearful of Florentine capture.

> You see the position to which someone who wanted to govern states strictly according to conscience would be reduced. Therefore when I talk of murdering or sparing the Pisans imprisoned, I didn't talk as a Christian: I talked according to the reason and practice of states. (Guicciardini 1994, p. 159)

With this notion of the 'reason of state', Guicciardini took Machiavelli's notion of self-interest and applied it to the state. This application broke resoundingly with orthodox political thinking. It marked a transition in social theorizing between medieval Christendom and the modern age. For where the medieval outlook was dominated by concerns about God, Machiavelli and Guicciardini concerned themselves with the state, and they attributed motivating properties to the impersonal institutions of the state.

This idea that the state can be seen as an actor in its own right is also apparent in Guicciardini's masterpiece, his *History of Italy*. This book has exerted a lasting influence because of its description of the relations among the Italian city-states. Tracing the welter of alliances, wars and diplomatic moves that shaped Italian politics in the late fifteenth century, Guicciardini draws an image of a self-regulating city-state system. The image which posterity has inherited of Renaissance Italy relies to a great degree on Guicciardini's account. And there is no question that his account embodies balance-of-power arguments. He writes about Lorenzo (the Magnificent) de' Medici (1448–92):

> Realizing that it would be most perilous to the Florentine Republic and to himself if any of the major powers should extend their area of domination, he carefully saw to it that the Italian situation should be maintained in a state of balance, not leaning more toward one side than the other. (Guicciardini 1969, pp. 4f)

Several questions are raised by this description. One question concerns the representative nature of Lorenzo's policies: was Lorenzo a politician of exceptional skill or was his approach to politics a common one among Italian rulers? The most probable answer is that Lorenzo was unique. Lorenzo was a humanist, a poet and a sponsor of the arts. Also he was, by all accounts, a master of affairs of state – including foreign affairs. And it is evident from Guicciardini's own account that Lorenzo approached the ideal of a Renaissance gentleman to an uncommon degree; a soldier and a scholar who possessed 'all the signs and indications of virtues that are apparent and of value in civic life'. Lorenzo was such an important force in Italian politics, Guicciardini explains, that, when he died in 1492, the stability of Florence ended – indeed, the entire Italian city-state system unravelled. Clearly, Lorenzo was no ordinary politician, and his political skills ought not be considered representative of all Renaissance rulers.

Another question concerns Guicciardini's description of Lorenzo's policies: did this unique ruler entertain a balance-of-power theory? The most probable answer is that he did not. For in the letters that Lorenzo wrote, no clear and consistent balance-of-power logic guides his foreign-policy arguments. Lorenzo might, indeed, have been more skilful than most. However, like other tyrants of his day, he conducted his foreign policies on a pragmatic, *ad-hoc* basis and not according to any master model. The balance-of-power arguments which are found in Guicciardini's *History*, then, are likely to be creations of its author rather than the guiding star of its protagonist.

It is unlikely that Lorenzo acted on any self-conscious balance-of-power theory. But it is likely that Guicciardini portrayed him as if he did. Like other Renaissance rulers, Lorenzo strove to obtain short-term gains and not to establish lasting, interstate relationships. His decisions were quick, his moves were sudden. Gradual creation of trust, confidence and goodwill were unknown values in Renaissance politics which was guided by opportunism rather than planning. For the Renaissance rulers, interstate affairs was games of hazard for high and immediate stakes; 'it was conducted in an atmosphere of excitement and with that combination of cunning, recklessness and ruthlessness which they lauded as *virtù*' (Nicolson 1954, p. 31). But Guicciardini used balance-of-power arguments to explain the actions of Lorenzo. Thus it is *he*, rather than Lorenzo, who deserves a place among the earliest modern International Relations theoreticians.

Rediscovering Thucydides
Since Guicciardini was an experienced diplomat, scholars have often assumed that his descriptions of Italian statecraft reflect common diplomatic practices. This is hardly the case. Guicciardini extracted the notion of a balance-of-power principle not from the diplomatic discussions of his day but from the historic accounts of classical authors which he then applied to contemporary practices. Most likely, he found the notion of a balance of power in Thucydides' *Peloponnesian War*.

Thucydides discusses the causes and the nature of the war between the ever-active, innovating sea power of Athens and the slower-moving, more cautious land power of Sparta. Throughout his long narrative, Thucydides kept rigidly to his theme: a chronicle of battles and sieges, of alliances made and broken and, most important, of the effect of war on peoples – of the inevitable 'corrosion of the human spirit'. He discusses the character and influence of the most outstanding political leaders of the age. Guicciardini and other Renaissance authors saw the obvious parallels in the destructive wars between Greece and Sparta and those between France and Spain of his own time. Thucydides' studies of character had a pervasive influence on the Renaissance humanists, and many sought to emulate his style.

Thucydides depicts a condition in which power yields the ultimate authority in relations among states. Thus, 'the strong do what they have the power to do and the weak accept what they have to accept' (Thucydides 1972, p. 402). The implication that a strong, ambitious state can be contained by an alliance of smaller states was to influence International Relations theory in subsequent centuries.

Italian humanists used Thucydides' discussion of alliance politics and warfare among ancient Greek city-states to shine an explanatory light on the wars of their own day. When Guicciardini adopted Thucydides' balance-of-power vision, the Greek historian was reconnected to Western political theory, after a millennium of neglect. Thucydides' impact on subsequent International Relations theory cannot be fully appreciated unless he is considered a citizen of two distinct ages: ancient Greece as well as Renaissance Italy.

Towards a modern sentiment

Renaissance Florence was populated by artists and academics (*humanists*) whose activities were increasingly independent of traditional authorities like the state and the Church. Many of them cultivated a high public profile. Some of them were surrounded by controversy. One example is Lorenzo Valla, who demonstrated, by a new method of textual criticism, that the Donation of Constantine was a forgery. Another example is Niccolò Machiavelli. He wrote political analyses in the form of secret briefs for Soderini's Chancery or the Council of Ten. But he also wrote texts – poems and plays – for a growing, literate public. And whereas the secret briefs were written in longhand, the public texts were often printed.

Machiavelli's play *Mandragola* was printed within a year of its completion [1518] and publicly performed. *The Art of War* [1521], *The Histories of Florence* [1525], *The Discourses* and *The Prince* were written for a larger and scholarly audience; and although the latter two were printed only posthumously, both books were read and discussed in the author's lifetime – sometimes with the author present, for Machiavelli was much in demand as a wit and storyteller.[12]

Books cannot be judged by their cover, and Renaissance books least of all. For during the early sixteenth century, books were expensive and a book was an object which took on a certain meaning from the context of social practices within which it appeared. More often than not, a sixteenth-century book was a costly gift rather than a commodity for the mass market. As a costly article it was a part of the court culture of the age. It was enmeshed in conventions of status recognition, reciprocity and reward and other traditional practices. A book on political theory was not a simple commodity; it was a symbol-laden part of a larger social system. It was subject to the conventions which surrounded the scientific and philosophical disputes of the age. Its meaning was a product not only of the text which was bound between its covers but also of the authority to which it was first presented, the channels through which it was distributed, the patron with which it was identified.[13]

A public sphere hardly existed in the early sixteenth century. Yet, the situation was rapidly changing. Commercial print-shops emerged like mushrooms after rain in urban centres all over Europe. Printing was becoming a rapidly expanding business in northern Italy during this period. Many humanists nourished the ambition of getting their texts printed, thereby enhancing the power of their writing and securing it better for posterity. The alliance between ambitious humanist scholars and commercially minded printers represented an important stimulus for the advent of the modern public sphere – as would be most evident during the Reformation a few years later.[14]

As time passed and Machiavelli's *Prince* was printed, it was met with shock, fear and anger. A century after his death, Machiavelli was reviled as the spokesman of diabolical, treacherous, villainous, cruel practices – during the seventeenth century it was commonly held that *The Prince* was inspired by the Devil; and in Elizabethan England, Niccolò Machiavelli was identified with Old Nick, and Satan was at times unflatteringly referred to as 'Machiavellian'.

It is odd, then, that Guicciardini should escape the attention of angry moralists, for his political writings are sharper and more cynical than Machiavelli's. However, if Guicciardini has been spared vilification, it may be because Machiavelli was the first public figure who broke so resoundingly with the God-centred, medieval worldview. It was Machiavelli who first expressed publicly that the medieval dream of a politically united Christendom was a meaningless pipedream. This was a shocking claim to people whose whole intellectual background was based on Christian theology. Machiavelli was a humanist. Like Guicciardini he believed that scholarship based on analysis of historical events could shape policy. Such analysis ought not to be confused with ethical and moral concerns, he claimed. He saw his task as describing things as they really happen and not to speculate on things as they might be. What really happens, Machiavelli insisted, was that effective rulers exclusively act in their own political interest. Guicciardini agreed – indeed, he extended this principle to all political actors; even 'those who preach liberty so convincingly have as their objective their own personal interest' (C-66).

With such claims Machiavelli and Guicciardini expressed a transition from medieval Christendom to the modern age. It is this transition which makes them so important. They deviated from a medieval orthodoxy which was dominated by concerns about God, and they concerned themselves with the state. Where the medieval philosophers saw nature as a divine creation which encompassed human society, Machiavelli and Guicciardini took nature as a given and considered it separate from society (which they saw as fashioned by the individual). Where medieval thinkers sought to prescribe divine rules by which people could live a virtuous life and save their souls, they sought to describe human behaviour in order to infer lessons about the conditions for individual freedoms.

From God to the Prince

Machiavelli and Guicciardini removed God from scholarly attention. They did not do this explicitly by denying God's existence. They did it implicitly by quietly directing the attention elsewhere; away from the salvation of the soul towards the security of the state. Disregarding theological concerns, they argue that there exist two moral realms, each with its specific interests and its specific code of ethics. On the one hand is the code which emphasizes justice, honesty, compassion and other virtues of traditional Christianity. On the other is the code which applies to the interest of the state.

Machiavelli (1997, p. 28) is quite explicit in this regard. In politics, 'one must take it for granted that all men are evil and that they will always act according to the wickedness of their nature whenever they have an opportunity'. Guicciardini added that, in politics among states, God is no longer the legitimizing, moral authority; the prince is. And princes obey a moral code entirely their own. A prudent prince cannot, and must not, honour his word if this places him and his state at a disadvantage (Machiavelli 1961, p. 90).

Guicciardini describes Renaissance politics as a turbulent and dangerous game played by men who are 'false insidious, deceitful and cunning' (C-157). The prince, he avers, must remain constantly alert to challenges which threaten to unravel his state and to opportunities which may serve to strengthen it. To assert himself, the prince must always be guided by self-interest (C-218); he must simulate and hide his intentions (C-49, 104), exaggerate his power (C-86) and cover up his weaknesses (C-196). To safeguard his state, the prince must disregard the individual virtues of civil society and instead consider the collective interests of state – thus, although it is humanly desirable to discuss things openly, it is politically prudent never to reveal one's own affairs (C-184); although lying is morally reprehensible, it is politically expedient and the prince must learn to practice it well (C-37). Guicciardini's prince inhabits a ruthless world in which revenge is not only sweet but necessary (C-72, 74) and security means that your enemies are unable to harm you, although they would certainly wish to do so!

From nature to society
Unlike the medieval philosophers who were concerned with the relationship between the state and God, Machiavelli and Guicciardini focused on the state as a self-sufficient entity – as ancient theorists had done. However, they pushed the classical perspective one logical step further: they conceived of the state as a self-sufficient actor which continually interacted with other states, and they vested in it a legitimizing authority for political acts. The prince was the personification of the state. Machiavelli turns the attention inward and focus on the prince; he portrays the prince as a self-sufficient, self-reliant actor who must seek to make himself as independent as possible of other actors. Including God. Guicciardini also turns his attention outwards; he sees the state as part of a larger, interstate context. Both argue that the state needs to concern itself with its own security, with armies and with leadership. Guicciardini, however, has a richer portrayal of the larger political environment within which the individual state exists.

Where medieval philosophers saw society as part of a great, God-given, natural order of things, Machiavelli and Guicciardini saw society as man-made. They saw the state as an artificial, temporal creation which must be ceaselessly monitored and tended to by men. Thus, by replacing God with the state, they also replaced Nature with society. Again, they pushed the argument as far as it would go: nothing, they reiterated, is superior to the state. No consideration of justice or cruelty, praise or shame is to interfere with the necessary task of maintaining the state and of preserving the prince's freedom of action. Guicciardini took the last, extreme, step explicitly. He self-consciously removed God from political considerations altogether. And in the place of God-given, Christian values he put 'the reason and practice of states' (Guicciardini 1994, p. 159).

From prescription to description

Machiavelli and Guicciardini replaced the prescriptive concerns of medieval thought with descriptive analysis. Machiavelli was a practical man and his *Prince* a practical book. And 'since my intention is to say something that will prove of practical use to the enquirer,' he notes, 'I have thought it proper to represent things as they are in real truth, rather than as they are imagined' (p. 90). Guicciardini agreed.

This attitude 'was a sword which was plunged into the flank of the body politic of Western humanity, causing it to shriek and rear up' (Meinecke 1957, p. 49). Machiavelli and Guicciardini did not concern themselves with how princes ought to behave; rather, they sought to explain how successful princes in the past have, in fact, behaved. Machiavelli's exposition of the amoral code of princes enraged many humanists. To them, Machiavelli explained – with echoes of Thucydides (1972, pp. 404f) – that he has not invented this code, he has simply observed it and faithfully described something which already existed. Successful princes have always distinguished between private morality and the interests of the state. They all know that they 'cannot observe all those things which give men a reputation for virtue, because in order to maintain his state he is often forced to act in defiance of good faith, of charity, of kindness, or religion' (Machiavelli 1961, p. 101).

This flagrant disregard for traditional ethics enraged the Christians. They believed that Machiavelli not only accepted man's sinful nature but that he considered it a positive virtue. This position was worse than wicked: it disregarded the day of judgement on which all injustice would be punished. In response to the Christians, Machiavelli said nothing. His silence was eloquent, indeed epoch-making; 'it echoed around Christian Europe, at first eliciting a stunned silence in return, and then, a howl of execration that has never finally died away' (Skinner 1981, p. 38). Machiavelli's silence represents a resounding rupture with medieval preoccupations.

Guicciardini had the same, clinical and descriptive approach to politics as Machiavelli, he escaped the criticism which humanists and Christians levied against it. Machiavelli became the favourite *Prügelknabe* of the moralists. Guicciardini became the first of the Machiavellians.

Reason, free will and determinism

By making men masters of their own destiny, Renaissance humanists ushered in a distinctively modern political outlook. By portraying man as his own master, and denying that God or nature impose limits on human action, they made a resounding rupture with the medieval worldview. Whereas medieval scholars found man's distinctive characteristic in 'reason' tempered by 'faith', Renaissance authors found it in the power of man's 'free will'.

This does not mean that the Renaissance men denied human rationality; it means that they changed it. Machiavelli, for example, reduced it to a matter of calculation. For the medieval scholars 'reason' meant the ability to distinguish just from unjust acts; for Machiavelli 'reason' became the ability to compute ways to realize one's will. As the Aristotelians (like Aquinas) celebrated man's wisdom, Machiavellians celebrated man's freedom. This is obvious in the final part of *The Prince* where Machiavelli, wondering whether *fortuna* or *virtù* is the most determining principle in the life of a man, stresses the importance of the latter to an unprecedented degree: 'So as not to rule out our free will, I believe that it is probably true that fortune is the arbiter of half the things we do, leaving the other half or so to be controlled by ourselves', writes Machiavelli (1961, p. 130).

On this point Machiavelli and Guicciardini diverge. In the great debate on the respective role of *virtù* and *fortuna*, Machiavelli stresses the former and Guicciardini the latter. '[Y]ou cannot deny that Fortune has great power over human affairs', Guicciardini writes in maxim C-30. 'We see that these affairs constantly are being affected by fortuitous circumstances that men could neither foresee nor avoid. Although cleverness and care may accomplish many things, they are nevertheless not enough.' Guicciardini, then, seems more pessimistic about the human condition than Machiavelli. He is more conscious of the limits of human reason. He is more sceptical of man's ability to learn from history and from observing political events (C-114). This leads him to counter Machiavelli's faith in reason and free will. He writes in maxim C-128:

> In affairs of state, you should guide yourself not so much by what reason demonstrates a prince ought to do, as by what he will most likely do, according to his nature and his habits. Princes will often do what they please or what they know, and not what they should. If you guide yourself by any rule other than this, you will get into very great trouble. (Guicciardini 1970, p. 73)

This observation strikes at the very foundations of Machiavelli's *Prince* as a guide to political action. At the same time, it consolidates a key principle in modern International Relations analysis: in order to understand the actions of politicians, it is not enough to understand their rational calculations; it is also necessary to understand the history and the interests of the state which they represent.

Final remarks

Political theory was revolutionised during the Renaissance. During a few busy decades of the early 1500s, the Western worldview was irreversibly altered as the old, theological discussions yielded to a new, expansive, modern discourse. It focused on states, not on God; it presented the state as a human-made thing and saw politics as a ceaseless activity necessary to sustain the state. Renaissance theories yielded new and lasting insights into politics within states. Theories about politics *among* states made small progress by comparison.

Renaissance manuals on war and on diplomacy, the two types of commonly written texts in which one would expect to find theoretical approaches to international politics, are fairly pedestrian. The military manuals of the age demonstrated one thing clearly: that the nature of warfare changed dramatically. The formative event was the Italian wars. Charles VIII had hardly invaded Italy with French troops, in 1494, before Robert de Balsac noted the changes. His *Nef des Princes et des Batailles* [1502] describes the deployment in the field of new French and Spanish weapons systems such as light artillery and handguns. Machiavelli, too, notes the introduction of new, destructive weapons systems in his *Art of War* [1521]. Battista della Valle goes one step further in his *Libro continente appertenentie ad Capitanii* [1528]; he includes field guns into his diagrams of efficient battle formations. But all these books concentrate on technical aspects of war – handling horses, provisioning armies, setting up and guarding camp, devising marching formations and battle tactics (Hale 1981, pp. 276f). Few books discussed relations among states. And the few which did expressed little theory.

During the final quarter of the century, however, International Relations theorizing began to gain momentum. Suddenly, several authors begin to use the notion of a 'reason of state' in a big way. Guicciardini was apparently the first author to use the term. By the final quarter of the sixteenth century it was already a fashionable catch-word. It proliferated in diplomatic manuals and even found its way into the title of several late-sixteenth century books. Etienne Thuau notes about the age:

> point of departure for political speculation is no longer the Creation in its entirety, but the sovereign state. Reason of state seems to have perverted the old order of values ... Born of the calculation and ruse of men, a knowing machine, a work of reason, the state encompasses a whole heretical substrate ... Set above human and religious considerations, the state is thus subject to a particular necessity ... Obeying its own laws, *raison d'état* appears as a scandalous and all-powerful reality, whose nature escapes the intelligence and constitutes a mystery. (quoted in Gordon 1991, p. 9)

These words suggest a more self-conscious attitude to the ends and means of diplomacy and interstate politics. However, it did not notably advance the understanding of international relations. Guicciardini was among the first authors to use the notion of balance-of-power and the term 'reason of state' as explanatory principles to analyse the interaction of states. It suggested a more self-conscious attitude to the ends and means of interstate politics. However, it took some time before these conceptions made their mark on International Relations theorizing. This, however, is part of another story which is more appropriately told in the next chapter.

Notes

1 The social and political consequences of printing is also touched on at the beginning of Chapter 3. But see also Mandrou (1978) and Eisenstein (1993).

2 Lorenzo Valla ignited a major controversy in the 1440s when he applied a new method of textual criticism to the Donation of Constantine – a three-thousand-word document allegedly from Emperor Constantine to Pope Sylvester I, on which the papacy based its temporal claims – and showed that it was a clever forgery.

3 The ideal of the virtuous gentleman is identified in Castiglione's best-selling *Book of the Courtier* [1528], a handbook of etiquette which portrays the ideal courtier in terms of the old chivalric virtues (physical dexterity, courage, skill in combat, courtesy) as well as the new urban ones (knowledge of classical philosophy, appreciation of art, eloquence and good taste). This ideal of the virtuous gentlemen reflects a new emphasis on individualism as a value in its own right. Also, Pico della Mirandola's most famous *Oration on the Dignity of Man* [1486] expresses this new emphasis on the individual as a private person. This emphasis on the private and the individual is also strikingly apparent in the fresh development of a literary form which was rare in the Middle Ages, the biography – and most characteristically, in the autobiography, the most noteworthy instances of which were written by Cellini (1936) and Cardano (1930).

4 Francesco Poggio Braccioline (1380–1459) was one of many entrepreneurs in classical humanist culture. Dissatisfied with the low salaries he earned as a copyist for notaries and diplomats, he went into business for himself, tracking down and copying classical manuscripts. On his many expeditions all over Europe, Poggio found several important works which he copied. The originals were often neglected by their owners, and were lost or destroyed; Poggio's copies were preserved in Florence. In effect, copies like Poggio's are often the oldest testimonies extant about life in ancient Greece and Rome.

5 See note 9 in Chapter 1 for a comment on this genre of political literature.

6 Most commentaries emphasize the third part of Machiavelli's book. In most anthologies it is the third part's most wicked chapters 17 and 18 which are most commonly reproduced. From the point of view of International Relations theory, the third part is not necessarily the most interesting. Rather, the short part two of *The Prince* is more revealing, for it is here that Machiavelli formulates his insights about the nature of the state and touches briefly upon relations among states in the form of war. Machiavelli also discusses war and relations of states in his *History of Florence* – especially in books 5 and 6 (Knutsen 2012).

7 Many despots have found in Machiavelli's book good excuses for doing anything they felt necessary to keep themselves in power. Through this principle, Machiavelli has greatly influenced rulers – such as Henry IV of France who is said to have had a copy of *The Prince* in his pocket when he was assassinated.

8 Machiavelli does not explicitly invoke the balance-of-power concept to account for the political dispositions of statesmen. This observation goes against much received wisdom of International Relations theory, which often assumes that, because Machiavelli was a key contributor to the realist tradition of politics, he was also was a balance-of-power analyst. This is too simple. Even a cursory glance at his writings suggests that Machiavelli's preoccupation was with domestic not with international politics. He

frequently discusses affairs of security, defence and foreign policy. However, he rarely produces a sustained discussion of interstate relations. *The Prince* does not contain the modern phrase 'balance of power'. (Although there is a brief allusion to it in chapter 11, where Machiavelli discusses the motives of Italian rulers, and, more clearly, in chapter 20 where he refers to relations among Italy's states as 'a sort of balance' ('uno certo modo bilanciata'). Some English-language editions have translated this into 'a balance of power' (Machiavelli 1961, pp. 74, 116.) However, the word 'balance' might here simply indicate 'harmony' or 'health' – as when medieval doctors argued that the health of the body was determined by the balance of the humours. Machiavelli rarely reflected on the rationale of the statesmen who forged (and broke) alliances. In a rare case where he did, he recommended a statesman to help the *stronger* side in a war in order to share in the prestige of victory – an idea which flies in the face of any balance-of-power argument. There is no doubt that Machiavelli is an important power theorist; but it would be an exaggeration to call him a *balance*-of-power theorist.

When that is said: Machiavelli's most probing and direct discussion of international issues is found neither in *The Prince*, *The Discourses* nor *The Art of War*; it is found in the dispatches he sent to Florence when he was on diplomatic missions on behalf of its ruling Council of Ten. It is possible that a systematic study of these dispatches will weaken the claim presented here and furnish the established view with a more convincing foundation.

9 Pope Leo X (1513–21) appointed Guicciardini governor of Modena and Reggio and, later, commissioner of the papal armies. Pope Adrian VI (1522–23) demoted him. But Pope Clement VII (1523—34) made him president of the province of Romagna, the northernmost papal province (Quatela 1991).

10 While ambassador to Spain (1512), Guicciardini found the time to write *Relazione de Spagna* and *Discorsa di Logrogno*. His book on Florentine politics, which is called *The Dialogue on the Government of Florence*, was begun in 1521 and completed three years later. In 1530 he wrote a long commentary entitled *Considerations on the 'Discourses' of Machiavelli*. Guicciardini's biographical works include *The Consolatoria* (which discusses the merits of religion and philosophy), *Oratio Accusatoria* and *Oratio Defensoria* (Guicciardini 1994, pp. vii–xxxi; Quatala 1991).

11 C-28 refers to 'maxim' 28 in the compilation that Guicciardini himself made of his *Ricordi*: the so-called 'C-collection'. Guicciardini wrote several versions of his *Ricordi*. The first two were written during his ambassadorship in Spain (1512) and were little more than a collection of brief jottings (and are usually denoted as quartos 1 and 2, respectively – or Q^1 and Q^2). After his return to Florence, Guicciardini apparently wrote another collection which has subsequently been lost, but which has been denoted the A-collection. In 1528, he rewrote his maxims, added some new ones and produced a collection of 181 *Ricordi* (the B-collection). In 1530, he completed his final compilation of 221 *Ricordi* (the C-collection).

12 This raises an interesting question: Did there in Machiavelli's time exist a public sphere within which modern, academic theorizing could take place? Hardly. Machiavelli's books were neither written for nor read by an anonymous mass audience; they were read by a fairly constant and closed circle of friends who met regularly as an informal discussion group for literary and political topics in the Oricellari gardens (Hale 1960, pp. 149ff).

13 In this light it becomes significant that Machiavelli dedicated *The Prince* to Lorenzo de' Medici (the grandson of Lorenzo 'the Magnificent'), whereas he dedicated his *Discourses* to Zanobi Buondelmati (a former anti-Medici conspirator) and Cosimo Rucellai (the host of the discussions at the Oricellari gardens).

14 It is an interesting biographical fact that Machiavelli appreciated the free and learned conversation among friends. It is an interesting political-theory fact that he saw the intellectual and political value of such conversations. He touches on the point in *The Prince*. When Machiavelli (1961, p. 90) has stated that empirical observation is a means towards knowledge, he adds that free discussion among scholars contributes to the dissemination of knowledge. (He advises 'the shrewd prince' to choose wise men for his council and allow them to speak freely and truthfully. Indeed, Machiavelli (1961, p. 126) recommends that the prince's 'attitude towards his councils and towards each one of his advisers should be such that they will recognize that the more freely they speak out the more acceptable they will be'.) In *The Prince* Machiavelli leaves the impression that such free speech must occur only 'in private' – within the closed and controlled environment of the prince's entourage: 'in public', such free speech on political issues must remain forbidden, because it will only serve to undermine political stability and social order. Machiavelli (1997, pp. 30f) also touches on this point in *The Discourses*; but here he develops a far more complex argument which leaves the impression that free speech in fact serves the interests of the self-governed republic of free citizens.

Part II
Philosophies of war and peace

3

Reformation politics:
guns, ships and printing presses

International Relations theory appeared in the sixteenth century. It emerged alongside the painful twin-birth of the modern state system and the modern world economy. Its growth was part of a process which eroded old institutions and overthrew traditional truths, but which did not replace the old conceptions with new certainties. It was a central part of the intellectual anxiety of that sprawling, tumultuous epoch which marked the transition from the medieval to the modern world. It was an age torn between the beliefs of the medieval mind and the concerns of the modern age.

The sixteenth century began as an age of vicious warfare between competing universal truths. It ended as an age of anxious relativism. The interminable warfare of the age failed to provide solutions to any of the fundamental questions over which the wars were fought. The failure to produce a healing peace forced forth new investigations of the causes and justifications for war, and the construction of new sets of rules to regulate relations among the powerful monarchs.

The emergence of the modern world can be captured through analysis of three key inventions which appeared in Western Europe in the long sixteenth century: firearms, the compass and the printing press. This chapter begins with a brief discussion of these inventions and the social changes that followed in their wake – how they altered the relative ability of different social groups to punish and reward, how they altered European society, how they affected the nature of Europe's states and altered their international interaction. The chapter will pay special attention to Italy and Spain, two of the dominant powers of the age. It will introduce writers like the Italian diplomat Alberico Gentili and the Spanish lawyer Francisco de Vitoria. But it will emphasize the writings of the French scholar Jean Bodin who formulated the modern concept of 'sovereignty' and exerted a formative influence on the subsequent scholarship of interstate relations.

Social innovations, economic changes and political power

No one knows who invented gunpowder. The ancient Chinese certainly possessed it. It came via the Islamic empire to Europe. The Europeans put it to purposeful military use in the late 1400s, and thereby altered the distribution of political power among the emerging states. Monarchs who acquired guns vastly enhanced their military power. This made their neighbours insecure and compelled them to acquire similar weapons. The arrival of gunpowder, then, stimulated the growth of the modern state. Guns made battles more destructive and warfare more costly. And the rising costs of warfare pressured kings and princes to invent new ways of raising revenues. This, in turn, stimulated the growth of the modern state and the state system.

Taxation was one way of raising revenues. Long-distance trade was another. But such trade was a fairly recent option: it was made possible by new ship models and improved means of navigation. Such maritime innovations also made possible expeditions of discovery and adventure. Later, when cannons were fitted to the new ships, the Europeans were enabled to pillage and colonize America, Africa and Asia. Colonization, then, attended trade as a way in which the states of Western Europe could raise much-needed revenues. And with these new sources of revenues the new European monarchs could build larger armies and equip them with more guns. Trade and colonialism stimulated the growth of trade routes between Europe and other regions; they fuelled an international network of communications and transport which would provide the scaffolding of the modern world economy.

The printing press spread the culture of the Renaissance, with its enthusiasm for ancient texts, its knowledge and its entrepreneurial spirit, to the rest of Europe. It also fuelled the dissent within the Church and hastened the religious fragmentation which we call 'the Reformation'.

The gunpowder revolution and political change
The feudal organization of society sustained a class of noble landowners and trained them as warriors. The advent of gunpowder destroyed this class. The mounted warriors became easy targets for the new handguns and cannons. And when it became obvious that an untrained foot soldier equipped with an arquebus could kill a nobleman from a safe distance, the *cavalry* lost its leading role in warfare; the warrior-noblemen were rendered obsolete in war, and the cavaliers saw their position in civil society eroded as well. The *infantry* became the important branch of the armed forces of the Renaissance. The cost of a foot soldier with a gun was a fraction of the cost of a nobleman with horse and entourage, and encouraged the monarchs of Europe to invest in infantry. Army sizes expanded rapidly as a result. Also, the introduction of field guns during the Italian Wars gave rise to a third, distinctly modern, branch of the armed forces: the *artillery*. The introduction of new weapons systems and the changes in military organization eroded some of the restraints imposed on warfare by medieval custom and Christian argument. War became a more deadly affair.

As armies grew in size and complexity during the Italian wars, the costs of equipping an army skyrocketed. Even the wealthiest aristocrat could no longer afford to raise large armies of professional soldiers. Only the monarch could afford the expenses of modern warfare – 'the man who had at his disposal the taxes of an entire country was in position to hire more warriors than any other' (Braudel 1972, p. 657).

In this way, the military revolution of the fifteenth and sixteenth centuries furthered the rise of 'the new monarchies' in Europe (Tilly 1994). Larger armies meant soaring military expenditures. This stimulated rulers to find more efficient ways to collect and manage taxes. And these efforts, in turn, stimulated the creation of the modern state. They consolidated the power of the monarch, thus contributing to the early absolutist form of European states; they made the king less dependent on the landed aristocracy, but upgraded his relations with the commercial classes in the expanding towns, thus encouraging the rise of the multifaceted, estate-based *Ständestaat* (Poggi 1978, pp. 36ff) and preparing the grounds for the systems of popular representation of West European politics. The fiscal apparatus was, in short, 'the institution which pulled the other institutions in its wake' (Schumpeter 1976, p. 141).

Evolution in transport, revolution in commerce
Politics within states were altered by the intense royal efforts to extort funds from their populations. Politics among states also changed, as monarchs searched for ways to extort revenues from the extra-European regions. Long-distance travel was made possible by new Iberian ship models which improved the speed and comfort of sea travel. It was also stimulated by new developments in mathematics, astronomy and map-making which enhanced the accuracy of navigation. With the improvement of the compass and the innovation of the astrolabe, seafarers no longer found it necessary to scurry along the crowded coasts of Europe, navigating from one island to the next. They boldly struck out into the open oceans of the globe.

Throughout the fifteenth century, ocean traders grew more prominent in coastal towns of southern Europe. The evolution was notably brisk in Iberian cities such as Lisbon and Oporto, where trade mushroomed both in luxuries and in bulk goods. This growth of trade stimulated an emancipation of the mercantile strata of society from traditional controls.

It is easy to exaggerate the rise of the mercantile classes, for the greatest merchant of all was the Crown. The most famous of all the royal merchants was Henrique Infante de Portugal, better known as Prince Henry the Navigator. Henrique's historical fame rests on his founding of a naval academy, a veritable 'think tank', to which he brought some of the best mapmakers and astronomers of Europe. He was among the first monarchs systematically to finance his activities with income from colonial exploits – from the import of dyes and sugar into Portugal from West Africa and the Atlantic islands, and from the capture and sale of African slaves.

Henrique inaugurated an age of expansion (sometimes referred to as an 'Age of Discovery'). His success demonstrated to other monarchs the wealth and power which awaited them in overseas expansion. Thus, 'discovery' was attended by a fever of competitive colonization and war. The improved military capabilities which characterized the competition among monarchs at home also provided superior forces to conquer new lands abroad. Guns mounted on ships enabled the seafaring nations of Europe to rapidly expand along the Mediterranean, African, Asian and American coasts.

Henrique Infante also exemplifies a more subtle and psychological effect of overseas expansion: it stimulated a new entrepreneurial spirit among people who understood that overseas expansion opened up substantial opportunities for gain and fame. The discovery of the New World created an awareness of new opportunities, and this awareness in itself provided a stimulus to further change.

Movable type, revolution in thought

The advent of print altered the way in which human thought was expressed, disseminated and preserved (Eisenstein 1993). Once introduced, the new technology of the movable typeface was quickly propagated throughout Europe. Around 1450 Johann Gutenberg completed his first set of printed Bibles; by 1470, printing shops had appeared in Cologne, Basle, Rome and Venice. After fifty years, an estimated eight million books had been printed (Mandrou 1978, pp. 27ff).

The first printed texts were Bibles, prayer books, sermons and breviaries. Then followed all kinds of entertaining texts – stories, fables of varying quality and the spectacularly successful chivalric romances (Leonard 1949). Among the sixteenth-century best-sellers were also a wide variety of handbooks and manuals. How-to books of all kinds – agriculture, building, design, fashion, pottery, tool-handling, surveying – together with maps, calendars and tables for weights and measures were among the most popular printed products. Last but not least, Greek and Latin classics were printed – a practice which undoubtedly saved several ancient texts written on animal skins that had grown mouldy or brittle with advancing age.

Printing spread texts and theories beyond the narrow scholarly elite. The immediate result was to bring dissent and confusion to established bodies of knowledge. This was, for example, quite apparent in the emerging disciplines of geography and cartography. Geographers described the various countries in the world – their inhabitants, their climate, their resources – and provided important information for traders and buccaneers. Cartographers drew maps. They identified places where trade and pillage were most promising, and determined the quickest and safest routes to those places. It did not take long for descriptions and maps to provoke conflicts between lay scholars and traders on the one hand and Church authorities on the other. The scholars noted that new knowledge about the world flatly contradicted traditional, Bible-based contentions about the division of land and water and about the inhabitants of the earth. The new cartographic representation of a round earth, turning both upon itself and around a fixed sun, contradicted the official vision of the Church: a flat earth in the centre of a universe arranged around Palestine.

Furthermore, printing exacerbated dissensions within the Church. As religious texts were printed and spread, it became obvious that the Church was not unified, but that its members entertained a diverse array of ideas and interpretations. Sermons and tracts spread to every corner of Europe with the advent of print, and revealed that churchmen in different regions had widely different interpretations of even the most basic doctrines of the faith. The theologians of Spain had quite different views from their colleagues in Rome – not to mention how different they were from the theologians of France, Poland, Denmark and the many German principalities.

The heterogeneity of the Church, revealed by the art of printing, triggered a flood of demands for Church reform. The last straw was added to centuries of accumulated dissatisfaction when Church authorities allowed entrepreneurial clerics to raise revenues by mass-printing letters of indulgence – documents given to the faithful in return for prayer, penitence, pilgrimage or, most shockingly, hard cash. Demands for Church reform had been voiced since the Middle Ages. However, these demands did not constitute any unified reform movement, for they, too, assumed different forms in different social and geographical locations. Printed matter changed the nature of the protest. It spread the consciousness of diversity within Christian Europe; but it also spread certain unifying key ideas and the names of key authors who symbolized different schools of interpretations.

One of these key ideas was the claim that religious faith was a private matter. This notion was formulated by several authors; the most famous were Martin Luther and Jean Calvin. Luther formulated the first, more obedient and passive challenge to the established doctrine that religious faith was demonstrated in acts – generally by participation in public ceremonies and sacraments. Since sacraments could not be properly administered without the clergy, salvation could not be achieved without the Church hierarchy. Luther denied the clergy their indispensable role. He (and Calvin) claimed that individual intentions were a better indicator of faith than collective rituals; that faith was 'nothing else but the truth of the heart'.

This theory was revolutionary. It captured a sentiment of individuality and privacy which appealed to the merchants and the rising middle-class artisans of the age. The way in which the theory was disseminated was also revolutionary: in 1517, Luther formulated his argument in the form of ninety-five points of trenchant criticism of corrupt Church practices and nailed them up on a church door. His expectations of a scholarly discussion of his grievances were rudely shattered when his friends printed up the *Ninety-five Theses* and distributed them. Within a fortnight, they were discussed all over Germany; within a month, all over Europe (Eisenstein 1993, pp. 151ff),

Events quickly spiralled out of control. The explosive political potential of the new teachings was most immediately realized where the merchant and middle classes were most numerous and found a ready ally in the ruler. In Holland, in states and free cities in the Holy Roman Empire and in England, revolutions were fomented by demands for religious freedoms. The clamour for religious reform was often embraced by statesmen and monarchs to further their own political interests. In the predominantly rural, relatively poor areas of north-western Europe – in northern Germany, England and Scandinavia – Protestant reform was particularly successful, because it was championed by monarchs who sought to strengthen royal power at the expense of the established Church.

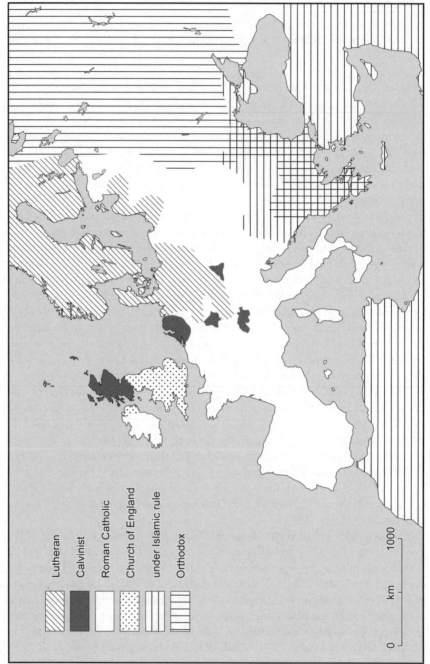

Figure 3.1 State religions in Europe, *c.* 1560

Lutheran

Calvinist

Roman Catholic

Church of England

under Islamic rule

Orthodox

1000

km

0

A time out of joint

A key question of political theory emerged from this turbulence: what is the relationship between religion and war? On the one hand, many spokesmen of the established Church maintained the right to wage war against infidels and heretics – Spanish jurists in particular argued that heretics should be punished by war and that infidels, who set themselves outside the law of God and nature, have no true jurisdiction. On the other hand were jurists and philosophers who disagreed with Church doctrine and claimed that many soldiers and statesmen exploited religion to justify their own political aims. One of these critics was Erasmus.

Desiderius Erasmus (1469–1536) was a Dutch theologian; a Christian humanist and religious reformer. He claimed that human beings are made not for contests and war but for companionship and co-operation. His essay *Dulce bellum inexpertis* ('war is sweet to those who have not tried it') begins by stating that Nature has endowed all creatures with their own weapons – the bull with horns, the lion with claws and the snake with a poisonous bite. She fortified some with a protective shell and others with shielding scales. But man is an exception. 'Only man was produced naked, weak, tender, unarmed, with a very soft flesh and smooth skin. Among his members nothing would seem to have been intended for fighting and violence' (Erasmus 1964 [*c*. 1515], p. 311). So why did war seem to be everywhere? Erasmus asks.

Why does man fight? Why has he fashioned himself with horns of iron? Teeth of steel? Death-dealing darts? Plates of armour and scaly cuirass? Because, argues Erasmus, man has been gradually corrupted by his effort to safeguard and secure himself. First, against wild animals; later against his fellow men. And as ferocity increased by being exercised, anger rose, ambition grew hotter. Ingenuity provided weapons for defence and for destruction. Soon war was everywhere.

'This was clearly madness', comments Erasmus. Yet, he sees some valour in early warfare. He calls it '*bellum*' and notes that it was considered courageous and valiant 'if anyone risked his own life to defend his children, his wife, his flocks and his dwelling from the attacks of an enemy'. And although the activity was cruel in itself, Erasmus notes that there remained traces of humanity in its conduct – as when opponents sent priests to argue their cause, called gods to witness, and skirmished with words before they came to blows. Over time, however, Erasmus observes a gradual estrangement from the pacific ideals of Christ. As cities, kingdoms and empires were built, old contests of bravery and honour were corrupted by lust for killing and quest for loot and power.

> [Over time], there have been continual changes and chances of war, as one thrusts the other from the seat of empire and seizes it himself. After all this, as the supreme power had come into the hands of the worst rogues, anybody and everybody was attacked at will, and it began to be not the evildoers but the wealthy who were in most danger from the perils of war; the whole aim of fighting was not glory now but base profit, or something even more discreditable than that ...
>
> [Today] we are continually at war, city against city, kingdom against kingdom, prince against prince ...; finally, a thing which in my opinion is worse than these,

Christians fight against men; … and, this is the very worst of all, Christians fight Christians. And, O blindness of the human mind! No one is astonished, no one is horrified. There are those who applaud this thing, greet it with cheers and call it holy when it is worse than hellish … We heard warlike sermons of this sort from monks, theologians, bishops. All go to war. The decrepit, the priest, the monk, and we mix up Christ with a thing so diabolical! Two armies m arch against each other each carrying the standard of the Cross. (Erasmus 1964 [*c*. 1515], p. 321f)

Erasmus's *Dulce bellum inexpertis* has often been read as a criticism of the Thomist doctrine of just war. As the sixteenth century proceeded, theologians and jurists argued that kings often justified their adventurism with religious arguments. Vitoria was among the first Spanish jurists to warn against the dangers of making religion a cause for war. He observed that, if religious doctrine could legitimize war, then every prince would always declare his own war a holy one. Gentili agreed, arguing that religious claims are often 'said to be inventions of the most greedy of men and to be cloaks for their dishonesty'. Religion is a relationship between man and God, he maintained. It is divine in origin, and 'since the laws of religion do not properly exist between man and man, therefore no man's right is violated by a difference in religion, nor is it lawful to make war because of religion', he argued. 'A man cannot complain of being wronged because others differ from him in religion' (Gentili 1964).

The argument that religion is not a sufficient justification for war supports a distinctly modern understanding of religious faith as a personal concern and an individual right. The case for religious tolerance was fuelled by political stale-mate. It increased as the religious wars dragged on with no clear victor in sight. In 1555 the concept of tolerance was advanced in the Treaty of Augsburg, which proposed a compromise solution to the religious strife between various German principalities. The treaty proclaimed that it ought to be up to the individual prince to determine the religion of his realm. Although this position was diplomatically expedient, it remained intellectually unsatisfying. The time was not yet ripe for the tolerance of the religious authority of princes; this position would have to wait for another century to be generally accepted as the principle of *cuius regio, eius religio*. The Treaty of Augsburg did, however, inaugurate a period of intense debate about princely authority in war and religion. The debate did not end until the Treaty of Westphalia in 1648 more clearly expressed the terms on which the new international order was to be based. The long interval between the two treaties of Augsburg and Westphalia marked a steady increase in the pitch of the religious war in a divided Europe. It also marked one of the most formative periods in the history of International Relations theory.

Contradictions of the age
The mounting pace of social change divided social philosophers. Several political thinkers struggled to re-establish the old intellectual certainties in the face of turbu-lent times and uncertain futures (Ferrari 1860, pp. 298ff). But all were torn between the comfortable certainties of traditional knowledge and the intellectually engaging

emerging spirit of tolerance; between the ethical and the pragmatic; between Aquinas and Machiavelli. Innocent Gentillet defended traditional doctrines in his *Anti-Machiavel*. Francis Bacon put in a good word for Machiavelli in his *Essays*.

The struggle with the changing times is evident in the writings of Justus Lipsius (1517–1606). He repudiated Machiavelli and sought to resurrect the traditional concept of virtue as a quality marked by rigorous morality, wisdom, justice, courage and temperance – virtues which accord with the Greek and Roman classics as well as with established Christian values. In the first chapters of his *Politics* of 1589 Lipsius elaborates a classical definition of *virtù* and laboriously establishes it as the moral basis for princely rule. But then he abruptly raises the question of whether the prince can, in fact, be expected to measure up to such high ethical standards. After all, he remarks, we do not live in Plato's *Republic*, but in a world where men are known to be duplicitous, if not downright evil. Accordingly, we would be exceedingly naive if we did not realize that princes often use both deception and fraud to further their political objectives (Leira 2008).

A similar struggle is apparent in the works of Tommaso Campanella (1568–1639), a Dominican monk, a passionate philosopher poet and a political revolutionary. A prominent transition figure, Campanella sought to reconcile Catholic theology with Renaissance science. His books contain both some of the most retrograde astrological superstitions and religious fanaticisms and some of the most progressive notions of his day.[1] He identified Machiavelli as the primary theorist of the earth, and castigated him for having reduced religion to a political tool and destroyed the spiritual community of man with a nefarious doctrine of egotistic reasoning and individual interest. He saw his own teachings as an antidote to the Renaissance humanists, and spelled them out in *La città del sole* ('The City of the Sun') of 1602.

Campanella taught that the world had two centres: one associated with the earth and marked by darkness, cold and hatred; another associated with the sun, and marked by brightness, warmth and love. The book is a political dialogue in the tradition of Plato's *Republic* and More's *Utopia*, proposing an ideal state governed by reason, love and social solidarity. But it also contains shrewd comments on contemporary politics. This duality is even more apparent in his *Discorsi politici ai principi d'Italia* ('Political Discourses to the Princes of Italy') (159?). Here Campanella portrays European affairs as formed by a double tension: a contest between Turk and Habsburg on the one hand and between Habsburg and Valois on the other. In effect, Campanella opposes Renaissance humanism one moment, and borrows from it the next. In one place he angrily opposes the notion of a 'reason of state'; in another he uses it. He even employs the balance-of-power principle: he notes that Italian rulers assist France in order to contain Spain, and adds that this policy would be reversed if Spain were to decline and France to become the greater power. Such contradictions express the paradox of the age: even the fiercest opponents to Machiavelli borrow from him and finish by emulating him. What in fact happened to Campanella 'was that the evil enemy of Machiavellism, against which he was bitterly struggling, gained and held possession over him himself from the very first' (Meinecke 1957, p. 102).

Comparable contradictions are evident in the works of Giovanni Botero (1540–1617). On the first pages of his *Reason of State* (1956 [1589]) Botero declares himself an opponent of Machiavelli; he insists, like Lipsius and Campanella, that justice and integrity are qualities requisite in a ruler. Yet, by the time he draws his conclusions, Botero has adopted many of Machiavelli's arguments. For example, he recommends that a ruler appear virtuous not because such conduct is good in itself, but because it earns him goodwill and prestige (Botero 1956, p. 96). He agrees that self-interest lies at the core of all political action – 'that in the decisions made by princes interest will always override every other argument' (p. 41). He even repeats Machiavelli's claim that the self-interest of the prince is identical to the interest of the state – that 'in the last resort *ragione di stato* is little else but *ragione d'interesse*' (quoted in Meinecke 1957, p. 69).

The first five books of Botero's *Reason of State* address the same themes as Machiavelli's Prince – the nature of the state, the necessary skills of the ruler, the different classes of people and how to best treat them, and so on. The sixth book marks a transition from internal to external concerns; from domestic affairs to foreign policies and international relations. Like most sixteenth-century authors, Botero lists the accepted facts of practical affairs – the raising of armies, the building of fortresses and the maintenance of garrisons. But he also displays a much wider scope and a more fertile imagination than his contemporaries. Some of his observations are brilliant – as when he explains how Italy and Germany have been kept at peace because their powers have been 'equally balanced' (Botero 1956, p. 125). Others are odd – as when he argues that some rivers of the world are well suited for trade and navigation because their waters are particularly thick and slimy.

In book 7 appears one of the most original aspects of Botero's international analysis: his emphasis on economic factors. Whereas Machiavelli and Guicciardini argued that armed force is the ultimate basis of the state, Botero adds that production and international trade are also crucial, for such activities create wealth by the means of which a prince can purchase means of force. Botero also explains (in book 8) that, to be powerful, a country must possess a numerous population, because many citizens provide many soldiers, more taxes and a greater economic efficiency. However, it is crucial that the population does not grow to exceed the country's resource base. For if this should happen, it would cause scarcity, misery, disease and jealousies, and would erode the unity and strength of the state.[2] Unless the prince conducts an active policy of colonialism and exports the surplus population to foreign lands – 'like swarms of bees leaving the hive when they would die from disease or overcrowding if they remained' (p. 156).

Two sixteenth-century traditions: Spain and Italy

In 1492, Columbus first sighted the New World. His discovery was followed by fifteen years of coastal expeditions which established the existence of an enormous American land-mass. After 1508, the pattern of discovery changed. Spain began to establish permanent bases on the Greater Antilles to serve as bases for future expeditions. The first probings were completed in 1518. Over the following two decades, Spanish soldiers undertook a full-scale conquest of the entire American interior. Hernan Cortes conquered the Aztec empire of Mexico in 1519; Francisco Pizarro destroyed the great Inca empire of the Andes in 1533. From the hearts of the two fallen native empires, the conquistadors fanned out over South America in the pursuit of El Dorado. By 1540, after only about twenty-five years of intense effort, the great age of the *conquista* was over. The new age that opened up offered boundless opportunities for persons seeking adventure and profit; it also offered conceptual turbulence and legal and ethical dilemmas.

Politics and empire: the Iberian tradition
Cortés and Pizarro conquered the Americas with a brilliance and daring which fired the imagination of future generations. In their wake came colonists, whose cupidity drove them to commit unspeakable cruelties against the natives. Their actions were condoned by a substantial body of legal and religious sophisms. The influential Juan Ginés de Sepulveda (1490–1573), Charles V's priest and Philip II's educator, for example, defended this policy of pillage and extermination. Bartolomeo de Las Casas (1474–1566), on the other hand, gained fame as an indefatigable champion of the rights of the 'Indians' (Alker 1992). In an age in which travel to the New World was physically demanding and dangerous, he crossed the Atlantic fourteen times to plead with the King of Spain for just and humane treatment of the natives. The debate reached its apex when, in 1550, Sepulveda and Las Casas held their famous dispute before a committee of theologians and jurists at Valladolid (Hanke 1974). Las Casas won this duel of minds. But it was a victory in a debate on legal theory and moral philosophy; in the real world the cruel treatment of Indians continued unabated. The population of Spanish America declined from an estimated fifty million in the early sixteenth century to only four million in the seventeenth (Stavrianos 1981, p. 80).

The moral and legal aspects of the wars against the Indians remained under discussion in Spain, and the continuing debate had the effect of enlarging the conception of international relations. Authors such as Francisco de Vitoria (1480–1549) and Domingo Soto (1494–1560) extended the scope of international law, giving maritime matters a more systematic treatment. The debate was particularly intense at the famous university in Salamanca, home of the illustrious 'primo professor', Vitoria. In 1532, he issued *De Indis noviter inventis* ('On the Indians Recently Discovered'), which discusses whether Spain was entitled to rule the new peoples that the conquistadors had discovered in the new world. This treatise was followed by *De jure belli Hispaniorum in barbaros* ('On the Right of the Spanish to Wage War against the Barbarians') (153?), which discusses the circumstances under which Spain's war against the Indians may be justified. These two brief treatises complement each other. The first discusses the preconditions for peace; the second the reasons or justifications for war. Together they constitute one of the first sustained expositions in Western thought on the law of peace and war.

In his first treatise, *De Indis*, Vitoria does not make any big issue of the conquistadors' presence in the New World. All people have a natural right to travel, he argues. Thus, 'the Spaniards have a right to travel into the lands in question and to sojourn there, provided they do no harm to the natives, and the natives may not prevent them' (Vitoria 1934a, p. xxxvi). He does, however, make an issue of the fact that, when the Spaniards arrived, the Indians were clearly in peaceful possession of property, both publicly and privately. But since the Indians were infidels, could their possession amount to true ownership? The conquistadors had answered this question in the negative, arguing that Christian people for that reason were entitled to seize the goods and the land of heretical Indians. Vitoria emphatically rejects this position. For him, the Indians 'had true dominion in both public and private matters, just like Christians, and that neither their princes nor private persons could be despoiled of their property on the ground of their not being true owners' (p. xiii).

In his second treatise, *De jure belli*, Vitoria discusses the legality of the war which the Spanish conquistadors fought against the Indians of the New World. This treatise focuses more on Spanish politics than on the Americas, for it involves the complex question of who has the right to declare war. Vitoria's argument begins with St Augustine's proposition that any private person has a right to defend himself and his property with armed force if necessary. But Vitoria soon transcends Augustine's analogy between private persons and states. He claims that whereas persons can lawfully resort to violent defence only in the moment of danger, states can use armed force for certain offensive purposes as well. States, for example, have the right to avenge themselves and to exact reparations for wrongs suffered in the recent past. In a war between states, then, 'everything is lawful which the defence of the common weal requires. This is notorious, for the end and aim of war is the defence and preservation of the State' (Vitoria 1934b, p. lv). A state's authority to wage war rests with the prince, Vitoria continues, for 'he is its representative and wields its authority; and where there are already lawful princes in a State, all authority is in their hands and without them nothing of a public nature can be done either in war or in peace' (p. iii).

Vitoria acknowledges that, although the prince is the pre-eminent representative of the authority of the state, limits must be imposed upon princely action in matters of war. To define those limits, he again relies on Augustine's claim that war is lawful only if it has a just cause. Thus, he is forced to address the question 'What may be a reason and cause of just war?' To answer this question, Vitoria immediately rejects differences in religion, extension of empire and the prince's personal gain as causes of just war. There is only one just cause of an offensive war, he argues, 'namely a wrong received'. An offensive war is just, then, when it is a punishment for the violation of right. However, he warns, war is a most extreme punishment, and not every violation of a right justifies war, any more than every crime in civil society justifies the most extreme punishment of the wrongdoer. When contemplating an offensive war, the prince must seek to balance the defence of the state against the public welfare; he must always be concerned with making the punishment correspond to the measure of the offence and with furthering the cause of justice (p. liv).

Vitoria recognizes that state security, public welfare and justice do not always coincide. Consequently, the prince is often torn between contradictory concerns.

The final pages of the *De jure belli* address these various concerns and relate them to the conquistadors' war against the Indians. Vitoria recognizes that religion is used by Christian rulers to extend their empires and amass personal gain and glory. He proposes that the prince consult his advisers before he commits troops in an offensive action. This, he says, will restrain zealous rulers – that is, princes who are concerned not with private gain as much as with God. He explains that actions of crusading rulers should be limited in order to prevent hasty and frivolous wars.

Vitoria concludes that, although there are conditions under which Christian soldiers can lawfully engage in offensive war, religion alone is not among them. Did conditions exist in the New World around 1500 that could justify the wars against the American Indians? In defending themselves, could the Spanish lawfully execute and enslave the Indians? Vitoria's answers are ambiguous. On the one hand, he denies that it is lawful in itself to kill innocent men, women and children. On the other, he acknowledges that innocent bystanders are often casualties of military action and that this cannot be helped – he even admits that civilians may be deliberately killed if sparing them would imperil the success of military operations. Vitoria's argument is complicated by his acknowledgement that, if an enemy refuses to restore things wrongfully seized, the injured party may recoup losses from innocent as well as from guilty persons. This recognition opens up the way for endless reprisals, as one party and then another each seeks to recoup its losses from civilian populations.

Only one clear point emerges from this final discussion: a sharp distinction drawn between two types of war: war between Christians and pagans on the one hand and war among Christian nations on the other. The enslavement of non-combatants is lawful only in the first type of war, but not in the second. It is a received rule of Christendom that Christians do not become slaves according to the law of war; this enslaving is not lawful in a war between Christians, Vitoria explains (pp. lxiv–lxv).

Politics and counterpoise: the Italian tradition

Vitoria's defence of the Indians is, in some ways, quite modern. For example, his discussion includes assertions of the rights to private property, to travel and to trade. In other aspects, the treatise is rife with medieval concerns; the discussions of war and peace, for example, rely on Aristotle, Augustine and Aquinas and their assumptions on divine, natural law. Vitoria's view of politics was dominated by individual decision-makers – by princes and soldiers and, the choices they faced, and by the nature and the moral and legal implications of their acts.

Vitoria's non-Iberian contemporaries tended to pay less attention to individuals and to ethics. Italian theorists in particular emphasized relations between institutions. The Italians tended to view international relations not in terms of ethical choices but in terms of interaction between *states*.

Vitoria wrote in Spain, one of the most religiously orthodox regions of Atlantic Europe and the leading force behind the Counter-Reformation. Botero, Gentili and several others wrote in late-Renaissance Italy, the most pragmatic and vibrant region of Europe. Furthermore, whereas Vitoria was a citizen of an expanding empire, and was concerned with the moral problems of imperial expansion, his Italian counterparts were inhabitants of threatened city-states, and preoccupied with issues of order and security. Such differences in cultural and political context help explain why sixteenth-century Iberian authors formulated the foundations for modern international law, whereas their Italian counterparts developed theories of balance of power. The Italian awareness of interstate relations and state power are obvious in authors like Belli, Paruta, Boccalini and others.[3]

Alberico Gentili (1552–1608) reflected the principles and perspectives of the Italians particularly well. He identifies states, not individuals, as the basic units of international politics, but he also recognizes that there is a need for a legal codex to regulate the interaction between states. Gentili's most famous work, *De jure belli libri tres* ('The Three Books on the Law of War', 1598), is remarkably free of many of his contemporaries' myopic preoccupations with the shape of fortresses, soldiers' discipline and municipal defence. The first of the books deals with war in general; what it is, who may make it and what motives or causes justify it. The second book establishes a legal framework for conducting belligerent operations. The third book discusses the conclusions of war. By Gentili's definition, war is a violent conflict between public authorities. In contrast, operations against piracy, for example, cannot be regarded as war. The contending parties in wars must be independent sovereigns or peoples subject to no higher jurisdiction; and pirates obey no sovereign authority.

Princes represent the highest authority of the state, Gentili writes. Because states are subject to no higher jurisdiction, disputes between them will routinely arise. Because the primary duty of the prince is to maintain the security and the well-being of his citizens, such disputes will often erupt in war. This vision of interstate relations echoes Guicciardini's idea of a reason of state. Gentili has little to add to Vitoria or Botero on the nature of war. He does, however, formulate several important insights about negotiated settlement between states. Part lawyer, part politician and part practising diplomat, Gentili drew on his varied experience to define rules which could regulate the conduct between states and minimize war.

For Gentili, disputes between states are unavoidable. When such disputes arise, they can be settled either by negotiation or by force. He accentuates the desirability of negotiated settlements, and proposes that princes submit their differences to third parties for arbitration. Negotiation, however, will be an option only when both (or all) disputing princes voluntarily agree to negotiate. Because there is no higher authority to compel independent princes to negotiate, it follows that if one of them refuses to do so, then only war will settle the dispute.

Although Gentili sees war as part and parcel of interstate interaction, he does not argue that war is the natural condition of humankind. He sees the human species as essentially sociable and gregarious (1964, pp. 53f). All men are unified by relations of kin and by reciprocal needs, and they owe one another mutual aid. Gentili then extends this reasoning to states by drawing an analogy from his vision of a society of men and applying it to that of a society of states (pp. 67f). On the basis of this parallel, Gentili argues that, subject to the exercise of sovereignty, both the earth and the oceans belong to all. All states have the right to undisturbed maritime navigation, to carry on commercial intercourse and to secure shelter in foreign ports. No state can legitimately deny anyone innocent passage over its territory. These are natural rights of all men, or what Gentili calls 'privileges of nature', and they constitute the fundamental principles of the society of states. For the purpose of defending these fundamental principles, war may be justly declared. In Gentili's words, 'a war will be called natural, if it is undertaken because of some privilege of nature is denied to us by man. For example, if a right of way is refused to us, or if we are excluded from harbours or kept from provisions, commerce and trade' (p. 86).

Denial of the privileges of nature is not only an unlawful injury to the party directly hurt by it; it is also an offence against human society at large. In order to protect and defend these privileges of nature upon which this society depends, other states should rally to the defence of the injured party. It is commonly accepted in civil society, he argues, than an honest man is bound by his honour and his conscience to come to the aid of a fellow man who is injured or endangered. 'We are bound by a natural law ... to aid one another', he writes, and continues:

> And if these things are true in the case of private individuals, how much truer they will be of sovereigns, who call one another kindred, cousins, brothers. They will be so much the more true of princes because, if one private citizen does not defend another, there is a magistrate who can avenge the wrongs of private individuals and make good their losses; but there is no one to mend the wrongs and losses of princes, unless it be that same prince, who would prefer to apply a remedy to an evil afterwards, rather than prevent the evil from being done in the beginning. (pp. 70f)

Similar attitudes mark Gentili's *De legationibus* ('On Legations') of 1584, which examines the principle of the inviolability of envoys.

Gentili's argument reverberates with the now familiar distinction between domestic and interstate affairs. Domestic politics occur under the watchful eye of a civil magistrate, whereas international politics mean interaction between sovereign states subject to no higher earthly authority. In Gentili's view, the principal reality of international politics is that it concerns states rather than individual human beings. To this distinction Gentili adds that the interaction between states expresses neither complete conflict of interest nor complete identity of interest; it is a complex balance of conflict and co-operation. In their dealings with one another, all states are bound by the rudimentary rules and institutions of the society they form. This argument informs Gentili's less-known, posthumously published book *Hispanica advocatio* of 1613. This book contains notes on the cases that Gentili prepared as counsel for Spain against the Netherlands. Even in this partisan setting, Gentili argues a succinct case for a doctrine of territorial sovereignty as the basic principle underlying the rights and obligations of belligerent as well as neutral states.

Jean Bodin: conceptualizing sovereignty

In Gentili's society of states, war is not a natural condition. It is, however, a common enough occurrence. It should be fought only for a just cause, by just means and only by those with the proper authority. But Gentili is unclear on the question of who should be considered a 'proper authority'. He approaches the modern notion that only public authorities are entitled to wage war and that only states can be considered such authorities. Through a discussion of the rights and the duties of the prince, Gentili sketches a distinctly modern outline of interstate relations as an anarchical society. However, the seminal clarification of these issues is found not in Alberico Gentili but in Jean Bodin (1530–95), whose clarification rests on two contributions to International Relations theory: on his lasting definition of 'sovereignty' and on his formulation of the principle of *pacta sunt servanda* – the insistence that sovereign rulers must keep their commitments.

The life of Jean Bodin is, like the century he lived in, only imperfectly known. But we know that he was, like Europe itself, torn between the religious theories which proliferated in the wake of the Reformation. He was brought up Catholic, but he studied the Lutheran arguments – indeed, he read them so seriously that he apparently spent some time in prison on charges of expressing Protestant views.

Like many other thinkers of this turbulent age, Bodin was influenced by the methods and theories of Renaissance scholarship. He attended school first in Paris before he transferred to the university in Toulouse. It was a centre of international and humanist learning, visited by scholars from Germany, Italy and Switzerland. About 1550, Bodin embarked upon the study of law. He was a humanist. He did not approach law through the study of cases and arguments; he thought that an understanding of legal principles was best ascertained through the study of history.

Around 1560 Bodin left Toulouse. Disappointed in his ambitions and worried that religious wars would soon engulf the city, Bodin left for Paris. Here he abandoned the teaching of law for its practice. But he found time to integrate his many notes from Toulouse into a pedagogical system, *Method for the Easy Comprehension of History* (1945 [1566]).[4] He interpreted the term 'history' broadly to include the diverse issues of 'the customs of peoples and the beginnings, growth, conditions, changes and decline of all states'. These issues have their analytic origins in Bodin's pedagogical system. However, they also have a historical genesis in a deep religious crisis which confounded sixteenth-century European politics – a crisis which very nearly tore France asunder before Bodin's eyes. Attempts to stem the rapid progress of Calvinism by force sparked sustained resistance. Riots erupted in 1562, and ignited a veritable civil war which lasted for over a generation.

Keenly aware of the political potential of religious doctrines, Bodin echoed a key claim of Vitoria, Gentili and others: that religion is not a sufficient cause for war. His position was based neither on religious doctrine nor on philosophical argument, but on a pragmatic concern for civil order founded in law. Bodin's *Six Books on the Commonwealth* (1967 [1576]) discuss the salient properties of 'the best and most enduring forms of law'. Readers often find the first book dry and confusing, because it contains a wealth of legal definitions and has a tendency to raise theoretical questions only to discuss them in legal and in practical terms. Despite the fact that Bodin never actually identifies the 'best and most enduring forms of law', Bodin's first book is quite readable once two things are understood: first, that its primary purpose is actually not to provide a description of the ideal constitution, but to define the key terms applied throughout the rest of the books; and second, that Bodin's primary concern is a practical one: to identify the best workable regime type for his age.

'Book Two' approaches a description of the good state. It contains a lengthy comparison of three different types of commonwealths: monarchic, aristocratic and democratic. Superficially read, it may appear that Bodin has derived his argument from the similar scheme found in Aristotle's *Politics*. More closely perused, it is evident that Bodin's *Six Books* is intended as a rebuttal to Aristotle; Bodin merely uses Aristotle as a convenient vantage point for his own purposes. Indeed, Bodin appears positively annoyed with Aristotle's accounts, and repeatedly points out the philosopher's shortcomings – a bold, iconoclastic streak for a Catholic educator, but one which was not untypical of the day.

'Book Three' complements Bodin's discussion of various forms of state with a lengthy examination of the essential structures of a just and effective government. His meticulous treatment of actual states reveals his ultimate, practical purpose: he wants to find the most orderly and stable commonwealth in a world whose traditional order is rapidly waning.

This purpose is also evident in the next two books. 'Book Four' is devoted to historical change: it is largely a comparison of the rise and fall of good and powerful states. Bodin singles out civil war and revolutions as special issues of concern. 'Book Five' discusses continuity and order. Again, Bodin raises the issue of revolution, but this time in the context of raising and maintaining armies. In the sixth and final book, Bodin returns to the question of the best form of government. True to his habit of providing pragmatic answers to normative questions, he extols the powerful monarch; and it is unclear whether he held that monarchic rule was conducive to virtue or whether he felt that it could best guarantee social order and political stability.

Bodin's *Six Books on the Commonwealth* are largely devoted to politics within states. Bodin is nevertheless counted among the most important contributors to International Relations theory, primarily because of the conceptual discussions of the dry and elusive 'Book One', notably his discussions of the concept of 'sovereignty'. Bodin realized that, although this concept is central to the study of all politics, 'no jurist or political philosopher has in fact attempted to define it' (Bodin 1967, p. 25). He decided to be the first man to do so.

Bodin defines sovereignty as 'that absolute and perpetual power vested in a commonwealth' (1967, p. 25). This brief definition hinges on three decisive postulates. First of all, it implies that sovereignty does not really pertain to individuals, but to states; sovereignty is not a property owned by any one individual, it is a quality ultimately vested in a commonwealth. Its precise locus depends upon the type of commonwealth. Bodin explains: 'A state is called a monarchy when sovereignty is vested in one person, and the rest have only to obey. Democracy, or the popular state, is one in which all the people, or a majority among them, exercise sovereign power collectively. A state is an aristocracy when a minority collectively enjoy sovereign power and impose law on the rest' (pp. 51ff).

Bodin's second message is that sovereignty is perpetual; it remains vested in the commonwealth, and is in principle unaffected by the comings and goings of individuals. Individual rulers represent the commonwealth as a communal and historical organism, and are given sovereignty only in temporary trust (alone or in a group, according to rules specified by the type of commonwealth). These rulers 'cannot properly be regarded as sovereign rulers, but only as the lieutenants and agents of the sovereign ruler, till the moment comes when it pleases the prince or the people to revoke the gift' (p. 25).

Third, sovereignty is absolute. It is unconditional and irrevocable; and it is the source of all power and authority inside the commonwealth. 'It is the distinguishing mark of the sovereign that he cannot in any way be subject to the commands of another, for it is he who makes law for the subject, abrogates law already made, and amends obsolete law' (p. 28). This does not mean that a sovereign ruler is entirely exempt from law.

Bodin identifies three limits to sovereign power: divine or natural law, regime type and covenants. First of all, a prince is bound by divine or natural law. Although his authority is absolute in relation to other elements of the state, the source of his authority lies in a higher law and his power is limited by the requirements of justice as specified by this higher law. 'There is no prince in the world who can be regarded as sovereign, since all the princes on earth are subject to the laws of God and of nature', Bodin admonishes. 'All the princes of the earth are subject to them, and cannot contravene them without treason and rebellion against God. His yoke is upon them, and they must bow their heads in fear and reverence before His divine majesty. The absolute power of princes and sovereign lords does not extend to the laws of God and nature' (pp. 28f).

Several corollaries follow from this conception that sovereignty is not the personal property of the prince, but rather the incarnation of a principle which could not have a will at variance with the interests of the state. One corollary of great importance is that sovereignty is indivisible. This interpretation challenges the medieval theory of the *Ständestaat*, that is a state in which supreme authority was shared among the prince, an aristocracy and representatives of the people. There can be monarchies, aristocracies and democracies, argued Bodin, but never a stable mixed state. In this sense Bodin marks a rupture with medieval political theory.

A second limit is imposed upon sovereign power by what Bodin calls 'the constitutional laws of the realm'. Any lawful ruler is constrained by the type of commonwealth he rules – or, as Bodin phrases it at one point, 'the true sovereign is always seized of his power'. To clarify this point, Bodin defines several attributes of sovereignty, the principal of which is to make the laws of the realm. However, there are certain laws that even the most sovereign of princes can neither make nor unmake. Those are the laws that define the basic rules of operation of the regime type – 'the constitutional laws of the realm'. These laws are given by nature and 'cannot be infringed by the prince. Should he do so, his successor can always annul any act prejudicial to the traditional form of the monarchy, since on it is founded and sustained his very claim to sovereign majesty' (p. 31). An absolute prince, then, cannot transform his monarchy into an aristocracy or a democracy; such a transformation would be tantamount to revolution.

This argument captures a position which was emerging in north-western Europe at the time – most notably around the trade centres on both sides of the British Channel. In the 1560s it was advanced in the Spanish Netherlands, where the northernmost Dutch Provinces rebelled against Philip II of Spain. This argument foreshadows a position which would emerge fully fledged in the English Civil War nearly a century later: that the monarch is bound by certain basic laws of the constitution of the land. Bodin's discussions on the limits of sovereign princes strongly foreshadow the principle of the constitutional monarchy.

Finally, princely powers are limited by covenants. 'A law and a covenant must not be confused', Bodin writes. A law is a command made freely by a ruler in the exercise of his sovereign powers – which means that he can make or unmake them at will. A covenant is a mutual undertaking and is equally binding on all parties involved. Even the most absolute king is 'bound by the just covenants and the promises he has made'.

Bodin distinguishes between two types of covenants: on the one hand are those which a prince makes with his subjects. Such agreements are not laws, and a prince does not draw on his sovereign powers in entering into them; thus his covenants are no different from those of other private individuals. He is therefore obligated, like any other private individual, to honour the contracts, oaths and promises he has made. Also, like any other private person, a prince can be released from such covenants only under specific conditions – a commitment can be invalidated if, for example, it is deemed 'unjust or unreasonable, or beyond his competence to fulfil, or extracted from him by misrepresentations or fraud'. Bodin, then, sees no difference between the covenants entered into by the prince and his citizens and those which his citizens enter into among themselves. In either case, a covenant is a contract between rational, responsible, private individuals (p. 29).

On the other hand are covenants which a prince makes with other princes. These covenants Bodin calls 'treaties'. He argues that treaties are not 'of the same order as contracts and agreements between private citizens'. For, when princes engage in covenants, they make them on behalf of their commonwealths, thus making them in the exercise of their sovereign powers. Since treaties are covenants made between sovereign actors, and no supreme authority exists above these actors, no legal agent can intervene to arbitrate in contests between them. The absence of any supreme authority above the commonwealth emerges from Bodin's discussion as the key characteristic of interstate relations.

The law which regulates the interactions of citizens within commonwealths does not apply to interaction between sovereign princes – on this broad principle Bodin agrees with Machiavelli: in relations between states the power of the sovereign prince is limited only by the power of other sovereign princes. However, Bodin's recognition that princely interaction is not limited by civil law does not mean that interstate relations are conducted in an environment of lawlessness. Rather, it drives Bodin into an argument of how imperative it is that the interaction of sovereign princes be guided by principles of rational and moral conduct. By merit of his acknowledgement of this restriction on state behaviour and in the effort to identify rational principles of interstate conduct, scholars have identified Bodin as a founder of modern international law.

Since interaction between sovereign states is not sanctioned by any supreme authority, there exist only two principles of order in interstate relations: force and faith. Bodin devotes the entire chapter 5 of book five to the ordering effects of force, but his discussion covers little new ground. He draws on Machiavelli's *Art of War* and focuses on issues of order and revolution within states. On one occasion, however, Bodin saddles 'the most powerful of princes' with particular responsibilities for maintaining international order, for 'to him falls the honour of being judge and arbiter' (1967, p. 177). Bodin's comments on international order fall short, however, of the modern notion of collective security. He writes that the sovereign has 'no promise more binding than the undertaking to defend the goals, the life, and the honour of the weak against the strong, the poor against the rich, or the innocent threatened by violence of wicked men' (p. 22). However, he nowhere suggests that peaceful sovereigns owe it to themselves to ally and contain warlike princes. Rather, if a powerful sovereign intervenes to stop quarrels between lesser princes, he does it for reasons of honour. According to Bodin, the primary moral obligation of princes lies not with interstate order but with the laws of nature and the divine principles of decency and justice.

It is the second principle of international order which Bodin makes his major focus: faith in justice. Non-violent, social interaction – among states as well as among individuals – can take place only on the basis of agreements. These will be made only if it is generally believed that they will be upheld once they are entered into. In civil society, systems of justice, sanctioned by the supreme authority of a sovereign power, exist to ensure that the sanctity of agreements is respected. In the interstate arena, however, sovereign princes interact with no supreme authority to arbitrate their conflicts; here agreements are made on the basis of faith alone: 'Since faith is the sole foundation and prop of that justice on which all commonwealths, alliances, and associations of men whatsoever is founded, it should be preserved sacred and inviolable in all cases where no injustice is contemplated' (p. 177).

Agreements between princes are the ultimate basis for interstate interaction, and it is essential that princes can rightly assume that such agreements will be kept once they are entered into. It is only short-sighted princes who make promises they have no intention of keeping, Bodin argues quite pragmatically. For, by breaking his word, a ruler will undermine the faith others will have in him. If a sovereign prince is not sure that he can keep his promise, he should not give it (p. 178). Indeed, even when dealing with scoundrels and the enemies of faith, a wise prince should

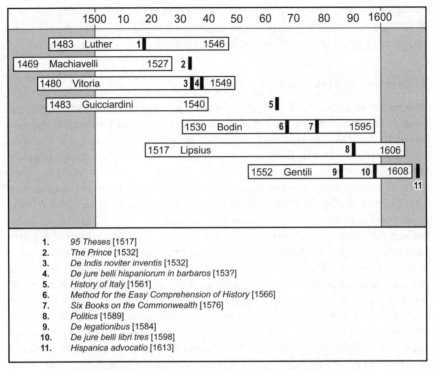

Figure 3.2 Some sixteenth-century authors and their works

consider himself bound by his word (p. 180). Bodin's insistence that princes must keep all covenants they make is in international law referred to as the principle of *pacta sunt servanda*. It is Bodin's second major contribution to International Relations theory.

The argument which leads up to this principle deserves two brief comments. First, for Bodin a covenant is an agreement entered into by rational, responsible, private individuals – he repeatedly uses the term 'contract' interchangeably with it. In his *Six Books on the Commonwealth*, Bodin formulates several arguments which would later be elaborated by the contract theorists of the seventeenth and eighteenth centuries – by Thomas Hobbes, John Locke and Adam Smith most famously. These elaborations still constitute the key building-blocks of the liberal political tradition. Bodin was not the only social philosopher to reason in terms of contract, so this was hardly an original contribution on his part.

Second, Bodin's account contains an early distinction between two levels of human interaction. On one level is the society among men; this is the level of the commonwealth. On another is the society of commonwealths. This vision contrasts sharply with the medieval notion that the international society, too, was a society among men. For Bodin, international interaction constitutes a society among sovereign states. His major insight is that, in spite of the constant threat of anomy, this interstate society, too, is governed by identifiable principles of order. The corollary of this insight is that, if humanity can identify, strengthen and obey these principles, it can regulate interstate interaction and reduce, and perhaps abolish, war.

The sentiment of the century

The sixteenth century was an era of transition between the Middle Ages and modern history. It saw the advent of more efficient means of production and new modes of exchange; it witnessed the rise of new means of destruction and new modes of political power. In this era a few countries on the Atlantic rim began to conquer the rest of the globe with capital and with arms.

On the one hand, the century began to tie large sections of the world together on a truly global scale. On the other, it began to divide the world in unprecedented ways. Differences had always existed between the militarily powerful and the powerless nations; now these differences were accentuated by new, European, gunpowder-based weapons systems. Similarly, differences had always existed between rich and poor regions; now these differences were exacerbated by the advent in Europe of new forms of agriculture, of manufactories, long-distance trade and systems of finance.

Also, in the sixteenth century the Catholic Church lost its exclusive domination over the mind of European peoples. The old division between Christians and pagans was replaced by a new division within Europe itself between Catholics and Protestants. Partly because of this new division, Europe turned away from its enduring preoccupation with the Muslim threat. Instead of unifying against the challenge of the infidel Turk, European princes turned against each other. From 1530 on, Europe plunged into a protracted era of internecine destruction intensified by colonial rivalries, religious doctrine, new weapons and new-found wealth. By 1600, the fever of wars had escaped the rational political control of kings and emperors. It degenerated into anarchy and self-perpetuating violence, which reached a climax of brutality and pointlessness in the Thirty Years War (1618–48).

Variations in sixteenth-century theorizing

The sixteenth century was marked by socio-economic change and violent conflict. It was also an age of political theorizing – an activity which both generated conflict and drew momentum from the warfare between competing universal truths. It was an age in which traditional truths were challenged and overthrown before new certainties could be established.

The essence of the century's mentality is hard to pin down. The sixteenth century does not have the clear themes that the fifteenth century had before it and that the seventeenth century would display after it. It was torn between medieval and modern concerns. By the middle of the century, two dimensions had appeared in political thought. One dimension was the conflict between the Catholic and the Protestant interpretation of the Christian heritage; the other was a conflict between a religious and a secular conception of social authority.

The religious dimension spanned the mental distance between the Catholic tradition of Augustine on the one hand and the new, Protestant opposition of Luther and Calvin on the other. The Protestant message appealed to the mercantile and manufacturing middle classes which were slowly emerging along the Atlantic rim. It flourished in countries where monarchs broke with Catholic doctrines. Between 1530 and 1560, kings in Scandinavia, England and Germany broke with the Catholic Church – many of them tempted by the possibility offered by conversion to seize the lands of the Church and include them in the royal household. The pope, fearing an unravelling of his authority, reacted to these defections by summoning a group of eminent churchmen to a Council in Trent to give the old Church a thorough facelift. As a result, the churches in Europe were filled with better music, brighter paintings, more opulent spectacles – in a word, with Baroque art. Also, the defections made the fanatic King Philip II of Spain (1556–98) take it upon himself to head a far-flung Catholic counteroffensive. But the religious reactions of the pope and Philip II produced little new theorizing about International Relations.

The secular dimension of sixteenth-century thought was fuelled by a greater belief in human rationality and by more insistent demands for privacy and individual freedom. The ever-increasing trend of secularization of thought is evident in the many major innovations which appeared in the age: gunpowder, compass, printing press. The printing press, most particularly, was a decisive disseminator of intellectual innovations: of new religious interpretations (Luther, Calvin), new versions of old classics (Plato, Aristotle, Ptolemy ...), new theories about the universe (Copernicus) and, not least, the innumerable charts, calendars and handbooks which spread among European scholars and politicians like wildfire.

The sixteenth century was the age of scientific awakening, and the growth of scientific thought was a strong secularizing force. In International Relations theory, the secularizing trend was reflected in the sudden embrace of the concept of a 'reason of state'. In Italy most particularly, a spate of texts on politics and diplomacy emerge. Girolamo Frachetta advertises by his very titles – *Il Principe*, *Discorsi di stato e di guerra* and *Ragione di stato* – that he pursues the secular, humanist themes of Machiavelli and Guicciardini into the seventeenth century. And he is not alone. Scipione Ammirato, Ciro Spontone, Antonio Palazzo, Pietro Canonhiero, Ludovico Zuccoli, Federico Bonaventura, Gabriel Zinano, Lodovico Settala, Scipione Chiaramonti and others were all informed by the secular concepts of state power and state interests. Even in doctrinaire Spain, the notion strikes root. When Don Quixote was convalescent, he passed the time discussing with the priest and barber 'that which is called the reason of state'.

The emergence of secular theorizing
The emphasis on rationality, individualism and freedom had long been prepared by the Renaissance humanists. Their emphasis on history and classical learning flowered in the fifteenth-century societies of the Italian city-states. However, by the early sixteenth century the Italian Renaissance was near collapse, shattered by the ruinous Italian wars. At this time, the Italian Renaissance had made little impact

on the rest of Europe. North and west of the Alps, the vast majority of scholars still accepted medieval authorities as a matter of course. The conceptual context of the new monarchs and their primary advisers was still provided by the traditional teachings of the Church. But, with the advent of printing, the concerns of the Italian humanists spread to other regions of Europe, notably to the dynamic trading centres on the Atlantic coast which experienced an awakening of individualism and concern for privacy. The resulting preoccupation with individuality and the greater interest in the concepts of liberty and private property became evident in both religious and juridical treatises. Bodin, Luther and others argued that faith is essentially a private concern. Bodin insisted that the task of political philosophy is to strike the right balance between the realms of the public and the private (Chartier 1987). Luther argued that salvation could not be achieved through public rituals, but that each individual had to consult their own heart to determine if their acts were motivated by a pure faith in God.

The sixteenth century was not yet a secular age (Febvre 1942; Bloch 1961). In Spain most particularly, religion still played a decisive role in intellectual life; here the Counter-Reformation imposed a uniformity of thought which was fortified with the persuasive power of the Inquisition. In the German principalities and in the northern Dutch Provinces the Reformation produced its own firebrand Protestant doctrines. All across Europe, in fact, social thinkers were still steeped in religious concerns. Yet during the course of the century religious debates were complicated by secular issues. Protestant demands for religious freedom, for example, were always attended by political considerations. In the Dutch Provinces, a campaign for freedom of religion soon broadened to include demands for individual rights more generally, and then to protests against Spanish taxation. In 1576, broad anti-Spanish sentiments prevailed over narrow religious demands when representatives from all seventeen Dutch Provinces formed a political union to liberate their territory from Spanish occupation. Religious demands had become political struggle.

At the same time, new elements of pragmatism and tolerance intruded upon the religious debates. After warfare had failed to restore the religious unity of the Christian world, scholars argued that religion alone could not be a just cause of war. Increasingly, princes agreed to disagree on the religious issue. As a result, a consensus of religious tolerance slowly emerged – as evinced in Bodin's propensity to prefer pragmatic solutions to political problems. Indeed, the new tolerance went so far that, if excessive religious intensity constituted a major source of political problems at the beginning of the century, then excessive relativism was a cause of trouble towards its end. New knowledge about peoples and customs of the non-European world was collected by soldiers, traders and adventurers and disseminated through the new medium of print. Some information was of a high standard. Much of it was nonsense. Fantastic travellers' tales, mystical forecasts, religious scares and witchcraft panics swept across the West.

The late sixteenth century was an age of great diversity. The optimism and life-affirming attitudes of the Renaissance continued; but the age also witnessed the growth of pessimism and introvert reactions. Proud, conspicuous castles were built in this age; but so were sombre, hidden monasteries. *Carpe diem* ('seize the day') was a popular motto of the age; but so was *memento mori* ('remember you are mortal'). It was an age of intellectual uncertainty. And when new knowledge about the extra-European world arrived, it contributed to the chaotic relativism which rapidly emerged – a view that beliefs and customs vary with time and place and that there are no absolute standards for evaluating human values and conduct. This point of view is illustrated by the French essayist Montaigne, who wrote that one should not judge too harshly a tropical people's habit of eating human flesh. 'I find that there is nothing barbarous and savage in this nation, as far as I have been informed, except that everyone calls barbarian that which is not his own usage', writes Montaigne (1935, p. 18), with tongue only half in cheek.

By the seventeenth century, Europe stood at the brink of political and cultural exhaustion. It was by no means clear which way Europe was going to develop – it might conceivably have fallen into the same kind of chaos as India did at about this time. People were ready to grasp at any certain belief, and this readiness provided a fertile environment for visionaries and charlatans like Nostradamus, Paracelsus and innumerable others. However, this sorry state also provided the womb for modern science. With superstition went doubt. And when doubt was systematized – by thinkers like Bacon and Descartes – new critical methods of thought and knowledge offered promises of a new certitude which, in time, provided Europe with a new epistemological foundation and a new faith in itself. The roots of modern science lie in the confusion of the late sixteenth century. 'The rise of science in the seventeenth century possibly saved European civilization from petering out in a long post-medieval afterglow, or from wandering off into the diverse paths of a genial scepticism, intellectual philosophizing, desultory magic, or mad fear of the unknown' (Palmer 1951, p. 233).

Notes

1 Campanella wrote in his *Philosophia sensibus demonstrata* ('Philosophy Demonstrated by the Senses') of 1591 that philosophy must be based on methodic doubt (as later systematized by Descartes) and on self-conscious, human experience (as was later elaborated by Bacon). This book was interpreted as a critique of Scholastic Aristotelianism; its author was seized by the Inquisition and imprisoned for heresy. Campanella spent over twenty-five years in prison. And although he was subjected to deprivation and torture, he managed to write prolifically. In addition to *Philosophia*, a list of his books must include: *De monarchia Christianorum* ('On Christian Monarchy') of 1593; *Dialogo politico contra Luterani, Calvinisti ed altri eretici* ('Political Dialogue against Lutherans, Calvinists and Other Heretics') of 1595; *La città del sole* ('The City of the Sun') of 1602; *Apologia pro Galilaeo* ('Apology for Galileo') of 1616; and *Atheismus triumphatus* ('Atheism Led in Triumph') [c. 1606].

2 Botero's 'principle of population' is unmistakable in his *Reason of State* (book 8, chapter 4). However, it is restated with greater clarity and force in his *Treatise Concerning the Causes of the Magnificence and Greatness of Cities* (1956 [1606]). In an account which foreshadows Malthus's *Essay on Population* by nearly two hundred

years, Botero claims that populations strive to increase to the full extent made possible by human fecundity (or humankind's *virtus generativa*); however, since any society offers only limited means of subsistence (*virtus nutritiva*), unlimited population growth is always checked by limited resources. This limit asserts itself through want and misery, squalor and disease. It may also assert itself in wars, Botero intimates.

3 Pierino Belli (1502–75) offered thorough discussions of strategy and international law in his *De re militari et de bello* (1936 [1563]). Paolo Paruta (1540–98) discussed the balance of power among the Italian city-states in his *Discorsi politici* of 1599. Traiano Boccalini (1556–1613) portrayed the cynicism of statesmen in his influential satire *Ragguagli di Parnaso* ('Reports from Parnassus') of 1612 and discussed the European balance of power in his disillusioned commentaries upon Tacitus, *Osservazioni politiche sopra I Sei Libhri degli Annali di Cornelio Tacita* of 1678.

4 Bodin's Method divides human knowledge into three main branches: divine history, natural history and human history. In modern parlance these three branches would roughly cover theology, natural sciences and history/social sciences respectively (Bodin 1945, p. 2). That that division provided a lasting vantage point for Bodin's scholarship is evident from his treatment of each of the three branches separately in his three major works: his *Dialogue of Seven Wise Men* of 1593 is an exposition of the world's religions; *The Theatre of Nature* of 1596 is a treatise on the physical properties of the world; *The Six Books on the Commonwealth* of 1576 discusses human history and universal law.

4

Absolutist politics:
kings, wars and an interstate system

The long sixteenth century saw the evolution of the basic elements of modern international politics – territorial states, sovereign rulers, military structures and overseas ventures. It also witnessed the first stirrings of theoretical considerations about the nature and the operation of these new phenomena. Seventeenth-century thinkers integrated these elements into the vision of a recognizable state system. They forged it on the anvil of the Thirty Years War (1618–48).

The Thirty Years War was the climax of an escalating religious conflict that had begun with the Reformation nearly a century earlier. It erupted in Europe's middle regions, where it was at first fought by princes who hired military entrepreneurs to provide the Crown with soldiers and weapons. But the war rapidly evolved into a struggle between the entrepreneurs themselves. Soon they lost control. The armies they had created developed into vast, predatory formations which roamed the central parts of Europe in pursuit of the basic necessities of life. They swarmed into villages. They devoured resources and moved on like an enormous pack of starving wolves. The villages were left destitute behind. Many of the inhabitants chose to join the predatory pack, living parasitically off its wake. An army of thirty thousand men could be followed by twice as many starving men, women and children who supplied a thievish tail to the soldiers' rougher plundering. Armies and camp-followers constituted gigantic, ambulatory slums a hundred thousand strong, their itineraries directed less by goals of war than by concerns for immediate survival.

The central regions of Europe were economically devastated and politically fragmented by this warfare. Here emerged a class of military adventurers, landless, homeless, pitiless, without religion or scruple, without knowledge of any trade but war and incapable of anything but destruction. Here emerged no centralizing state structures. By 1648, when the Peace of Westphalia was signed, these adventurers had worked up a vested interest in war. Many of the armies mutinied when they heard that a peace treaty was signed. Demobilization drew out for years, as leaderless armies roamed aimlessly across the central regions of Europe in search of food and loot. Many mercenaries were never integrated into civil society; they retained, as bandits, pimps or professional assassins, the parasitic character they had acquired during the long years of warfare.

North-western Europe, by contrast, saw the evolution of steadily more efficient and powerful state structures. Historians have often asked why these state structures evolved so rapidly during the seventeenth century. Some find the answer in the Reformation. Distinctly modern state structures evolved in England and Sweden, where monarchs had rejected Catholicism, confiscated Church lands, seized large landed properties and gained unprecedented economic influence. This argument hardly provides the whole answer. For the evolution of a strong state was particularly marked in France, which remained a staunchly Catholic country and where no confiscation of Church lands occurred.

Other authors propose that the evolution of strong states was a function of the increased power of monarchs, Protestant as well as Catholic. In the late sixteenth and early seventeenth centuries, the kings of Europe became commanders-in-chief of their countries' armed forces. This put them in a position to expand their power over their civil societies. Although this explanation may be closer to the mark, it cannot account for the evolution of state structures in the United Provinces, which were not a monarchy at all, but a rather loose confederation of states.

There is one feature which the United Provinces, France, England and Sweden had in common, and which helps explain the seventeenth-century evolution of their state institutions: they all participated in the Thirty Years War, but only intermittently. They all unified their territories and enhanced the political power of their central institutions in the shadow of war, but without bearing its terrible cost in full.

This chapter opens with a discussion of the Thirty Years War and the political differentiation that evolved in Europe between the Atlantic sea powers in the west and the land powers in the centre and the east. It emphasizes the consolidation of efficient and powerful state structures in the west and the constitution of a new state system. The chapter then presents social philosophers who observed the changes of the age and who contributed to the political theory of absolutism and the associated economic doctrines of mercantilism. The political philosophers of the age tried to capture the key features of the new, Western state. The major international philosophers of the age – Crucé, Filmer, Grotius, Hobbes, Leibniz, Mun, Spinoza and many others – were in particular preoccupied with the concept of sovereignty. The chapter will touch them all, but will single out Hobbes for special attention and seek to place his ideas in historical context.

Troops, tolerance, taxes and the Thirty Years War

During the religious wars, an old division grew increasingly visible in Europe between a western and an eastern half – between a 'Latin' and an 'Orthodox' civilization (Szücs 1990). A rough dividing line can be drawn from the Baltic in the north, down along the Elbe River and the Bohemian mountains to the head of the Adriatic Sea. This line divided Europe's trade-oriented western seaboard from its agricultural eastern regions.

A second line can be added: a wavy line drawn from Brussels in the west via Stuttgart and Prague to Warsaw in the east. This second line roughly divides the Protestant northern half from the Catholic southern half of Europe. It crosses the first line in the heart of the Holy Roman Empire, and the intersection coincides closely with the major battlefields of the Thirty Years War. When the war ended in 1648 with the Treaty of Westphalia, territorial states had emerged both in the east and the west. The unruly central regions of the Continent, by contrast, emerged hopelessly fragmented.

Territorial states in a dividing Europe

The Treaty of Westphalia gave sovereignty to the small states in the heart of Europe. Thus it rendered the Holy Roman Emperor politically impotent. According to the Treaty, the Emperor could no longer recruit soldiers, make laws, levy taxes, declare war or ratify peace terms without the consent of representatives from all the states. Since such consent was a practical impossibility, the central region of Europe remained fragmented. During the next two hundred years it was a vast, unruly territory which separated the large, trade-oriented, progressive states of western Europe from the agricultural, reactionary states of the eastern interior.

The countries situated to the east of the fragmented middle were largely landlocked. Only a few of them possessed merchant fleets and navies. They participated marginally in long-distance trade. No significant mercantile class emerged to match the wealth, to challenge the power and to threaten the entrenched social position of the landed aristocracy.

The countries to the west developed differently. Along the Atlantic coast of Europe, political and religious authority also gathered in the hands of the monarch and his court of ministers and advisers. But this development occurred within a unique political setting. Its characteristic features, the most important of which were the representative assemblies, provided the predispositions for participatory institutions – market-centred economic institutions as well as political structures which allowed for popular involvement.

The monarchs of Western Europe drew two lessons from the Thirty Years War. First, they agreed that the religious conflicts which had fomented a century of rivalries and destruction had to be stopped. So when the war was brought to an end (1648), the monarchs agreed to disagree on the issue of whether Catholicism or Protestantism was the one true doctrine. They agreed to give the individual king the authority to choose a version of Christianity and impose it upon his country. This agreement (referred to in the peace treaty as *cuius regio eius religio*) meant that the monarchs of Europe should respect each other's choice of religion. It also meant that the king was the supreme religious authority in his own country; that the king (and not the Church) was granted spiritual authority over the inhabitants of his kingdom, and no outside actor had the right to challenge this authority within his realm. This agreement confirmed that *territory* was the key requirement for participation in modern international politics. It consolidated the concept of the territorial state, which thus gained common acceptance in Europe. But it also undermined the influence of rulers who had wielded great political power in the past by virtue of a transcendent principle of authority – a religious or a philosophical belief. The powers of the pope and the emperor, then, were drastically reduced by the agreement which was expressed in the Treaty of Westphalia.

A second lesson which the European kings drew from the Thirty Years War was that hired troops were dangerous. After Westphalia, the kings strove to establish their own, national armies. They reserved for themselves the role of commanders-in-chief. Emulating the New Model Armies of Sweden and the United Provinces, officers and men were paid, clothed and equipped by the Crown and commanded by the king or his trusted lieutenants. New military institutions and ancillary services emerged all across the Continent as part of the evolution of modern state structures. Military treasuries, camps, hospitals and judicial and secretarial institutions proliferated, as did quartermaster and victualling arrangements (Parker 1978). The soldiers' days were increasingly organized by physical training – by ceaseless drill, by marching and by exercises in siegecraft.

This introduction of permanent forces required new military infrastructures to accommodate the men and to produce, store and maintain their military materiel. Barracks, depots, payment plans and administrators were developed by all states of Europe. The pioneer was France, where Michel and François-Michel le Tellier created a civil bureaucracy to administer the new forces. Their system was, in turn, copied by other European states.

This build-up of such new institutions solved the problems which the military entrepreneurs represented. It was an extraordinarily expensive process (Finer 1975). It raised urgent new questions of state finances. How should the new forces and institutions be paid for? Kings and royal councillors provided two answers: revenues should be raised by two separate methods: taxation and colonialism.

Different monarchs handled their financial problems in different ways. Their choices of financial strategies depended on the physical size of the nation, its resource base and the historical experiences of its people. Also, it depended on geographic position. Countries along the Atlantic seaboard had the opportunity to increase their national wealth through maritime trade and colonial exploits. Land-locked countries in eastern Europe were forced to raise money in other ways – through taxation, through increasing repression at home or through foreign war and the conquest of neighbouring territories. The different ways in which the countries of Europe raised new revenues reflected and reinforced a growing division of Europe between an Atlantic and a Continental region.

The necessity for the European kings to cover military costs stimulated the development of more efficient structures and routines of national finance. Finance involves payment services. Financial systems mobilize money and allocate credit. They limit, price, pool and trade risks. In the seventeenth century, the large-scale handling of money and credit was complicated by soaring military costs which weighed down national budgets. Taxes constituted the basic financial resource of the seventeenth-century state (Ardant 1975, p. 165). All over Europe, the fiscal screws were tightened. The monarchs increased old taxes and invented new ones.

They also intervened heavily in civil society to stimulate economic development in order to tax it.

After the Thirty Years War, Europe was dominated by six nations: Austria, Russia, Prussia, England, France and the United Provinces. The eastern region was dominated by Austria, Russia and Prussia. These three states grew rapidly after 1648, conquering the territories of their immediate neighbours – overrunning the decaying Holy Roman Empire, the Ottoman Empire and the Kingdom of Poland – until their borders met. These areas east of the fragmented Germanys saw little of the commercial revolution and the market expansion which occurred along Europe's Atlantic seaboard. In contrast to the west, where the seventeenth century saw the emergence of a wealthy bourgeoisie and a free mobile labour force, eastern Europe experienced a 'manorial reaction' and a 'refeudalization' of society. After the Thirty Years War the entire region slid back into conditions reminiscent of medieval Europe. The chief socio-economic unit in the east remained the agricultural estate, run by an omnipotent landlord with uncompensated compulsory labour furnished by tenants and serfs. The landlords constituted the only significant political class. They concentrated their military energies on the armies, dominated by noble officers. They developed no significant navies; they took no part in the race for overseas possessions, and developed few mercantile interests (Anderson 1988, pp. 46ff).

The western regions of Europe were dominated by England, France and the United Provinces. Here private enterprise was encouraged by new commercial laws, subsidies and tax exemptions. In England and France, privileges were introduced to expand manufacture. Massive state projects were implemented to improve the roads and canals of the nations. Both countries encouraged the export of domestic manufactures to maximize import earning; both levied heavy taxes on imported goods to discourage money from leaving the country. They established chartered companies, stressed the need for new colonies and built up their navies.

The rise of the Western world
The western nations' new emphasis on naval forces markedly affected their socio-economic structures. The building of ships took time – several years for a good man-of-war. It required an infrastructure of dockyards, shipwrights, pilots and cartographers. Also, ship-building was very expensive. The building of strong, permanent navies accentuated the financial problems of the age. However, the navies also promised a solution: the king could enhance his revenues by supporting ventures of colonialism and long-distance trade. The most important example of this was the chartered company. The Crown would issue a charter which included a private company in the realm of royal sovereignty. This would ensure the company a monopoly on a specific trade in a specific area; furthermore, it would enable it to negotiate with foreign rulers, purchase arms, raise armies and fleets, establish garrisons abroad and even declare war and peace.

The first chartered companies had been formed by the Dutch in the second half of the sixteenth century. In the early decades of the seventeenth, England and

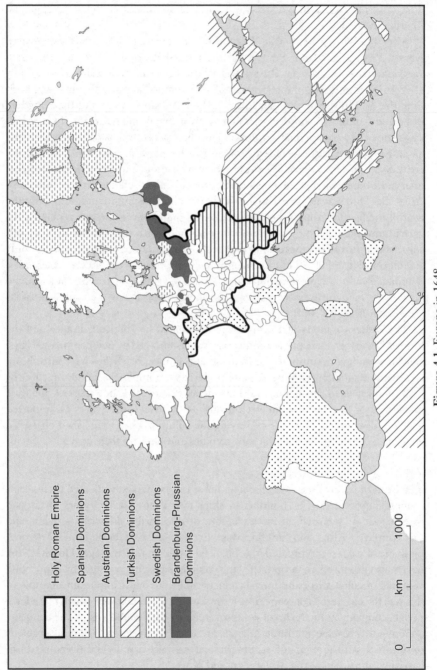

Figure 4.1 Europe in 1648

Holy Roman Empire

Spanish Dominions

Austrian Dominions

Turkish Dominions

Swedish Dominions

Brandenburg-Prussian Dominions

0   km   1000

France followed suit. The English East India Company was created in 1600, the Virginia Company in 1606, the English Amazon Company in 1619–23, and the Massachusetts Bay Company in 1629. Still later, in 1660, came the Royal Adventurers, who pioneered trade in Africa and were replaced a dozen years later by the more tightly organized Royal African Company. The French were not far behind. The powerful ministers Richelieu (1585–1642) and Colbert (1619–83), both of whom effected an unprecedented centralization and concentration of the political and economic power in the person of the king, applied mercantilist measures to increase the wealth of France and make the country a self-sufficing economic unit.

The mercantilist measures were economic means designed to serve military ends. They added economic power to the religious and the military authorities of the monarchs, strengthened the state structures of western Europe, and blurred the distinctions between trade and war, economics and politics. In eastern Europe, by contrast, societies increasingly exported raw materials and imported West European consumer goods – foreshadowing the imperialist dependencies (and the anti-imperialist theorizing) of the nineteenth and twentieth centuries.

To put it boldly: along the Atlantic rim, the absolutist state marked a break with the old, feudal order. It emerged in the wake of a disintegrating feudal order; it was 'a compensation for the disappearance of serfdom in the context of an increasingly urban economy' which the political apparatus did not completely control and to which it had to adapt. In the eastern regions of the continent, by contrast, the absolutist state was the repressive continuation of the feudal order. It was 'a device for the consolidation of serfdom, in a landscape scoured by autonomous urban life or resistance' (Anderson 1979, p. 195).[1]

The territorial state

The changes which occurred during the religious struggles of the early seventeenth century were expressed in the recognizably modern features of the territorial state. First, the state became defined in territorial terms, occupying a specific area of the earth's surface and surrounding itself with an inviolate boundary.

Second, this territory was governed by a set of institutions loyal to the monarch and staffed with professional bureaucrats, divided into subservient and increasingly specialized departments. These departments, at first devoted to the maintenance of military and fiscal functions, increasingly assisted the monarch in making rational policy decisions, and in implementing and enforcing the decisions made.

Third, the territory contained a population whose identity was partly a product of its monarchs' century-long efforts to inculcate a shared set of myths and symbols of nationhood.

Finally, the state was infused with a new notion of sovereignty. A clarification of the nature of this new notion was made by the mathematician, hobby-statesman and versatile genius Gottfried Wilhelm Leibniz (1646–1716). In his *Caesarinus fürstenerius* of 1677 Leibniz tries to prove that his employer (the Duke of Hanover) has a right of legation, and in the process he develops a new notion of sovereignty. At the outset he defines the Duke's primary problem: the Treaty of Westphalia conferred sovereignty upon all those German rulers who had formerly been included in the Holy Roman Empire; however, it had not abolished the traditional, essentially feudal, structure of the Empire itself. Local German rulers were therefore still enmeshed in old webs of traditional duties, allegiances and jurisdictions. In which sense, Leibniz asked, could the many German princes be said to be sovereign?

Instead of answering the question in legal terms, Leibniz first defines the concept of 'sovereignty' in terms of 'what actually happens in the world today' (Leibniz 1963, p. 340). In his mind, the first condition for sovereignty is a minimum size of territory (pp. 304ff). The smallest principalities – quite abundant at the time as Germany was divided into well over three hundred states – could not claim to be treated as equals of the largest in respect of war, alliances and the general affairs of Europe. Smaller territories, not possessing sufficient territory, could 'at best, with their garrisons, only maintain *internal* order'.

A second condition for sovereignty, Leibniz continues, is 'majesty' (pp. 307ff). By this he means the authority that enables a ruler to demand obedience from his people. Majesty is not the same as sovereignty. Majesty involves normative and moral authority, whereas sovereignty means the 'actual and present power to constrain' subjects on their own territories.

In this lies Leibniz's third criterion for sovereignty: the actual control of one's territory by virtue of one's military power (pp. 304ff). Bodin addressed the internal aspects of sovereignty; Leibniz places these internal aspects into a larger, practical, interstate context. He argues that, among the many nominally sovereign princes of the former Empire, only those princes are sovereign who actually possess the ability to constrain their subjects without in turn being constrained by a superior power. The decisive criterion thus is actual control of one's 'estates' by one's military power, which excludes any other power within and without. Among the over three hundred princes who claimed sovereignty in Germany, Leibniz counts as truly sovereign only those princes who had the ability to render their territories impermeable to foreign influence. As for the Holy Roman Emperor, whose sovereignty had been vastly reduced by the Treaty of Westphalia, he could enforce his authority or rights only by applying military force (p. 313). The Treaty of Westphalia had made him no different from any other sovereign.

From Leibniz's notion of impermeability emerges the concept of external sovereignty. With its implicit recognition of this concept, the Treaty of Westphalia laid the legal basis for the modern territorial state. Upon its foundation was erected a new system of international interaction and a new system of concepts and theories by which this interaction could be understood. The Treaty's recognition of the principle of external sovereignty represents the formal recognition and the legal consolidation of the modern interstate system: that is, a system of political interaction between legally equal territorial states, whose monarchs exercise their authority (their 'internal sovereignty') within well-defined, geographical frontiers, their inhabitants subject to no higher authority. The Treaty of Westphalia marks a decisive shift from a view of international law *above* the states to a law *among* states;

the vision of international law as divine in inspiration was replaced by the argument that international law is a codified set of customs or conventions – rules of conduct created and prescribed by the states themselves for the purpose of facilitating inter-state interaction.

Absolutism

The two key concerns of seventeenth-century international politics were 'order' and 'wealth'. They were embodied in the twin terms 'absolutism' and 'mercantilism'. The two must be seen as political and economic aspects of the development of the state and of the interstate relations of the age.

The term 'absolutism' entered the language of politics during the decade after the revolution in 1789. The phenomenon to which the term refers was, of course, much older. During the fourteenth and fifteenth centuries, monarchic power was developing toward monopoly. During the long sixteenth century, kings indulged themselves in international politics. They used marriages and military manoeuvres as their primary diplomatic tools – and kept the Continent in a fever of wars and their courts permanently short of moneys. The central idea of absolutism is that the justice and power of a state should be monopolized by the monarch. The reason most typically given was theological: the king was said to possess a divine right to make political dispositions. Jean Bodin (1530–96) foreshadowed this argument. But the first explicit doctrine of the divine right of kings may have been formulated by Pierre de Belloy (1540–1612) who argued, in his *De l'autorité du roi* of 1588, that the monarch was instituted by God and responsible to God alone.

The most famous argument for absolutism may have been formulated by Robert Filmer (1588–1653). In *Patriarcha* (1991 [1680]),[2] Filmer begins his argument by insisting that human society originated with Adam. Kings rule by divine right because God granted all social power to Adam, who became his direct heir. Adam then passed it on to his many descendants through the history of humankind, Filmer continues. This argument has several implications. It implies, first, that humankind constitutes one large family which descends from one single male individual. Since God had fashioned Eve out of Adam's rib and explicitly subjected her to Adam, woman is always inferior to man. And since God created Adam first, and gave him authority over all men who came after him, all men were born subjects to their fathers and inferior to their elders. Men were, in a word, born unfree and unequal, and first-born sons were superior to younger brothers.

Filmer's argument also implies that no society ever began with free and equal individuals! Because God gave Adam possession of the whole world and because Adam's oldest son was subject to his father's will, Adam's son enjoyed only as much property as Adam had voluntarily given him. And after Adam's death, his son inherited his father's entire property and all his authority and power. After the death of Adam's son, Adam's property and authority was in turn inherited by a line of first-born sons down to Noah. With Noah, the process of patriarchal inheritance changed. Noah, whose family was all that was left of the human race after the flood, made a momentous political decision: instead of keeping to himself the governance of the whole world, he divided it up into four parts. His three sons, Shem, Ham and Japheth, each received a part; and for himself Noah retained that territory which was to belong to the Chosen People. In Filmer's opinion, then, Noah founded the states of the world.[3] And after Noah the authority of father and political patriarch was inherited by a direct line of succeeding first-born sons. With this argument, Filmer provided a theoretical basis for the principle of primogeniture. According to this principle, the heads of the seventeenth-century states of Europe all derived their kingdom, their power and their political authority from their succession to one or other 'of the sons or nephews of Noah' (Filmer 1991, p. 7).

Filmer's argument was not unique. The idea that the justice and power of a state should be monopolized by the monarch was also justified by the English monarchs James I (1603–25) and Charles I (1625–49). Both of them anchored their claims in the Bible. They argued that they were personally chosen by God to govern their people. A most influential spokesman of absolutist theory was the French bishop Jacques-Bénigne Bossuet (1627–1704). Like Filmer in England, Bossuet in France formulated an argument for the Divine Right of Kings, hinging it on the proposition that the monarch is chosen by God and responsible to him alone; kings were God's vice-regents in political affairs on earth. But Bossuet was more explicit on one important point: Divine Right may give the king absolute authority in political affairs, but it does not give him the right to arbitrary rule. Bossuet was careful to explain that, as citizens are bound by the rules defined by their king, so the king is bound by the rules defined by God. Royal rule must be reasonable and just, like the will of God which it reflects. Thus, a king is sovereign so long as he conforms to the will of God. With this argument – which carries strong echoes of Jean Bodin – Bossuet distinguished sharply between absolutism and arbitrariness (1824, pp. 103–267).

Mercantilism

The central idea of mercantilism is that economic activities should be subordinate to the goal of state-building and the interests of the state. It is largely a theory of statecraft, and must be understood against the background of rivalry of the great powers of seventeenth-century Europe: the United Provinces, England and France. The decisive developments of the age were England's successful challenge of the strongest commercial power of the age in Europe, the United Provinces. The rise of mercantilist thought parallels the rise of England as a global power and a world empire.

The 'balance of trade' is a key notion of mercantilism. This idea reverberates through the writings of Walter Raleigh (1554–1618) and John Selden (1584–1641). It is no coincidence that one of the earliest expositors of this notion was Francis Bacon (1561–1626), an early formulator of England's balance-of-power policy. For Bacon, wealth and military capabilities were mutually reinforcing dimensions of national power. There is, as he put it, an unbroken chain 'from shipping to Indies, from Indies to treasure, and from treasure to greatness' (Bacon 1852, p. 201). According to Bacon, a favourable balance of trade should be an important foreign-policy goal. This goal can be achieved by establishing colonies that will export raw materials (particularly precious metals) to the mother country and buy manufactured goods from her.

One of the most popular mercantile arguments was presented by Thomas Mun (1571–1641). His main work, *England's Treasure by Forraign Trade, or the Ballance of our Forraign Trade is the Rule of our Treasure*, was published posthumously in 1664. It was very influential and went into several editions. Mun associated the balance of trade with the 'ballance of greatness'. The association between the balance and power and the balance of wealth became obvious during the Protectorate: the military republic of Oliver Cromwell. It devised the Navigation Act (1651) with the explicit purpose of protecting English shipping from foreign competition.

Underlying the mercantilist thought of Bacon, Selden, Mun and others was the notion that wealth could be translated into naval power, and naval power would protect trade, which would engender more wealth, which, in turn, would strengthen the nation's naval power ... and so on in a beneficial cycle (Heckscher 1935).

Anarchy, reason, contract and order

Absolutism and mercantilism both addressed the issues of human co-operation, wealth and order. The theme of 'order' was a key concern for the trading nations which had experienced first-hand the destructive effects of the Thirty Years War. International Relations theory in the mid-seventeenth century was dominated by a quest for a set of regulatory principles which could impose order upon a chaos of competing and self-contained states.

The problem of order was first discussed at the level of individuals rather than the level of states. The discussions began with the Reformation and with the interest it created in the relationship between God, human reason and religious freedom. Several sixteenth-century thinkers agreed that religion is a private concern; that, in matters of faith, individuals should be granted freedom of conscience. During the religious wars, social thinkers began to investigate conflicts and war in the light of human reason and individual freedom. During the Thirty Years War, many of them argued that individual freedom was gained at the cost of social order. They speculated that, if all individuals were perfectly free, then interaction would produce the most chaotic and violent condition imaginable.

In a 'state of nature' where man is endowed with total freedom, man will have a right to everything – 'men live without a common power to keep them all in awe, they are in that condition which is called warre; and such a warre, as is of every man, against every man', wrote Thomas Hobbes in 1651. In the state of nature, he continued, 'the life of man [is] solitary, poore, nasty, brutish and short' (1951, pp. 185f). Benedict de Spinoza agreed. In a sketch from 1670, Spinoza explains that in the state of nature neither reason nor morality can exist; thus, each man 'looks to his own interest, according to his own view and acts at his own advantage, and endeavours to preserve that which he loves and to destroy that which he hates' (Spinoza 1951b, p. 211).

This image of the lawless state of nature became a central concept in seventeenth-century political thought. It drove many thinkers to conclude that the state is necessary to maintain social order. In the state of nature, most authors agreed, man is driven by passion and by egotism. However, since man possesses the faculty of *reason*, he will sooner or later realize that his individual interests are better served by order than by chaos. Therefore he will band together with his fellow men and form institutions which can impose order upon human interaction. This logic developed into two different arguments. At the one extreme were authors like Hobbes and Spinoza, who, intrigued by the apparent paradox of the logic, concluded that man can exercise true reason and true freedom only within the confines of the state. Spinoza, for example, maintained that 'man, who is guided by reason, is more free in a State, where he lives under a general system of law, than in solitude, where he is independent' (1951b, p. 235). This argument rapidly evolved into a secular justification for absolutism.

At the other extreme were authors like John Amos Comenius and Émeric Crucé. Comenius (1592–1670) stressed the importance of reason and education. In a brief proposal entitled *The Angel of Peace* [*c*. 1628], he claimed that, in order to make a peaceful Europe, it was essential to introduce children to rational thought and expose them to a common European culture steeped in Christian values. Crucé entertained similar ideas. If man is only granted fuller freedom by his rulers, Crucé writes, he will, guided by reason and by Christian values of 'devotion, sweetness and charity', create a new Europe. Here men could go here and there freely, and mix together without any hindrance of country, ceremonies, or other such like differences as if the earth were, as it really is, a city common to all (Crucé 1972, p. 36).

During the seventeenth century, then, there evolved a tension between two approaches to international order. One was based on the notion that human nature was egotistical and self-serving and is well represented by Hobbes and Spinoza – both of whom will be presented in greater detail below. The other was based on the notion that humans were social beings endowed with reason and the ability to learn from experience. An example of the latter was Émeric Crucé.

Émeric Crucé (1590–1648)

Crucé recognizes that Christianity had been used by princes for political purposes. In *The New Cyneas* (1972 [1623]),[4] Crucé writes that the many wars in his age 'are undertaken either for honour or profit, or for the reparation of some wrong, or else from exercise. One could add religion if experience had not made known that this serves most often as a pretext' (Crucé 1972, p. 8). This idea expresses a key lesson of the Thirty Years War.

Crucé also articulates another lesson: that soldiers are necessary in times of war, but that they constitute a dangerous problem in times of peace. He sees soldiers, thieves and savages as the three primary obstacles to the establishment of a unified and peaceful Europe. It is, however, quite possible that, if they were shunned by society, 'even they would think of their own conscience'. Crucé's reasoning foreshadows an important point in social-contract theory:

If they should prefer to continue to live in their own savage fashion, they would not be sufficiently strong to resist so many people who are bound closely by common consent. These good people would descend upon them, hem them in, attack, and kill them like miserable beasts in their lair. War will always be a just measure against them if they cannot be brought to reason. (p. 29)

In the interest of social order, wise princes should assist these poor people, and help them find new employment. Soldiers are dangerous because they possess ambition and means of violence, and therefore represent a threat both to the power of their prince and to the general order of society. In order both to secure his own position and to maintain social order, a wise ruler would give soldiers something to do 'with honour without murder'. Some soldiers could be employed by a police force, or a constabulary, he suggests; others should be encouraged to go into trades which contribute to the wealth and well-being of society, such as agriculture or business (pp. 25f).

About one-third of the way into *The New Cyneas*, the argument changes pace as the author changes topic from conflict and order within states to war and peace among states. Crucé argues that men are rational and equal, and that they understand very well how their interests are better served by trade and co-operation than by war and conflict. Crucé dreams of a new Europe in which men travel freely from one country to the next, for there are, he insists, no major differences between people of different countries. 'Why should I, a Frenchman, wish to harm an Englishman, a Spaniard, or an Indian?' he asks. 'I cannot, when I consider that they are men like I am, and that, just as they, I am subject to error and sin, and that all nations are joined by a natural and therefore insoluble bond' (p. 36).

Crucé acknowledges that Europe is divided between several sovereign states. He is pragmatic enough to avoid any proposal to dismantle them. However, he does suggest that these sovereign states join together as members of a world organization. He proposes that some neutral, centrally located city be selected as the headquarters of a 'general assembly' to which all the states of Europe should send ambassadors. When differences arise between the states, the ambassadors would assemble and pass judgement after hearing the arguments of the representatives of the contending nations. Crucé's fame rests upon this proposal. Subsequent scholars have seen in it a blueprint for a League of Nations.[5]

Crucé's argument deserves attention for another reason as well: his is the first elaborate peace proposal which assumes that merchants have a vested interest in peace. For Crucé, the basic unit of analysis is the rational individual rather than the state; it is the citizen rather than the prince. He claims that interaction between enlightened economic actors leads to interdependent interaction and to peace. Crucé foreshadows nineteenth- and twentieth-century idealism when he awards the merchants and the manufacturers important roles in preserving interstate order. No occupations can compare with these in social utility, Crucé argues. The merchant 'nourishes a state' and the manufacturer 'enriches it'. And if princes saw to it that their subjects were employed in trade and production, they would never again seek amusement in war.

Benedict (Baruch) de Spinoza (1632–77)

Spinoza relies on some of the same axioms as Crucé, but he arrives at very different conclusions about war and peace in seventeenth-century Europe. Where Crucé selects the rational individual as his main unit of analysis, Spinoza selected the territorial state. His discussion is complex, yet stunningly streamlined; it is a vast deductive edifice in which the state has its distinct place in a larger metaphysical system.

It may be unfair to select another entry into Spinoza's system than his own theological axioms. But, in the interest of brevity, Spinoza's discussion of human nature provides a convenient short cut to his political observations. Human beings, Spinoza asserts, are always torn between reason and passion; and the greater their freedom, the more passion dominates. In the state of nature, passion is near-indomitable. Spinoza uses the Latin term *conatus* to describe human passion as a vital, self-protective, self-aggrandizing *élan*. Through *conatus* people seek to avoid injury, resist threats of injury and, if injured, restore themselves out of an inherent principle of self-recovery – unless the injury is so serious as to destroy this *élan* altogether. In the state of nature, people's actions are dominated by *conatus*; by their constant efforts to protect their lives and their belongings.

Reason exists in the state of nature, but in the service of *conatus*. It does not engender any collective agreement as to criteria for right or wrong, good or bad. In the state of nature there is no moral consensus, no politics and no law for people to obey. In the state of nature, every human individual is sovereign. They can do precisely as they please, for 'by sovereign natural right every man judges what is good and what is bad' (Spinoza 1951b, p. 211). In this state of total freedom, the only thing that can stop people in a state of nature from taking from another what they want to satisfy their pleasures is the knowledge that the other is stronger. Only the certainty that their actions will be rewarded by injury and pain will persuade them to refrain from fulfilling their desires.

At some point, Spinoza argues, humans will discover that their existence is better preserved and their pleasures best pursued by co-operation with other people. At that point, people will enter into social agreements. They will pass from the contending disorder of the state of nature to civil society. They will create a 'commonwealth' which is built on mutual assistance and designed to enhance humanity's self-preservation and improve its wealth and pleasures (pp. 201f). In the act of creating the commonwealth, they also make themselves citizens and subjects – 'Citizens, as far as they enjoy by the civil law all the advantages of the Commonwealth, and Subjects, as far as they are bound to obey its ordinances or laws' (Spinoza 1951c, p. 301).

Spinoza's political philosophy is guided by two major insights. First, that the creation of the commonwealth does not alter human nature. In civil society, the end of every human act is the self-preservation of the actor. 'The natural right of every man does not cease in the civil state. For man, alike in the natural and in the civil state, acts according to the laws of his own nature and consults his own interest' (p. 302). The commonwealth does, however, alter people's behaviour, because it constrains by law the means through which they are allowed to pursue their pleasures. It forces people to seek their interest within the law. The law represents reason: it is an elaboration made by enlightened, self-interested humans who seek to preserve social order. It forces the multitudes, whose reason is assumed to remain comparatively undeveloped, to behave according to reason. Thus, the law made by the few becomes a substitute for the imperfect reason of the many.

Second, Spinoza recognizes that the commonwealth does not solve the problem of order. It solves the problem on the level of sovereign individuals; however, it recreates a state of nature in the lawless interaction among sovereign states. Two commonwealths, Spinoza writes, 'stand towards each other in the same relation as do two men in the state of nature'. All commonwealths are sovereign, and have the right to act precisely as they will. This state of nature among commonwealths is exacerbated by the internal order and the division of tasks of the commonwealths. People in the state of nature must divide their attentions between many tasks to keep themselves alive; at times they will be overcome 'by sleep, by disease or mental instability, and in the end by old age'. A commonwealth, by contrast, is a timeless organism where a social division of tasks makes some people soldiers and others providers of food and arms. People who are tired and hungry are relieved by those who are rested and fed; those who are old and tired are replaced by those who are young and eager.

Unlike the individual person, the state is constantly alert. Whereas individuals compete intermittently in the state of nature, states struggle ceaselessly. Whereas war erupts as soon as one state wills it, peace occurs only when several states agree that it is to their mutual advantage – and then it is unlikely to last:

> This 'contract' remains so long unmoved as the motive for entering into it, that is fear of hurt or hope of gain, subsists. But take away from either commonwealth this hope or fear, and it is left independent, and the link, whereby the commonwealths were mutually bound, breaks itself. And therefore every commonwealth has the right to break its contract, whenever it chooses, and cannot be said to act treacherously or perfidiously in breaking its word, as soon as the motive of hope or fear is removed. (Spinoza 1951c, p. 307)

Hugo Grotius (1583–1645)

Between the extreme positions of Spinoza and Crucé existed more moderate arguments. The most influential of these was formulated by Hugo Grotius. According to Spinoza, the states of Europe have guarded their sovereign rights jealously, and history has shown no progress towards a society of states. Politics among states has always been, and given the limits of human reason is likely to remain, power politics. Grotius shared Spinoza's bleak view of contemporary affairs. In his major work *De jure belli ac pacis* ('On the Law of War and Peace', 1853 [1625]), Grotius observes that the glamour which had attended interstate relations a hundred years earlier had disappeared with the fragmentation of Christendom. In his own time, Grotius observed 'a licence in making war of which even barbarous nations would have been ashamed; recourse was had to arms for slight reasons, or for no reason; and when arms were once taken up, all reverence for divine and human law was thrown away' (Grotius 1853, I, p. lix).

Grotius shared some of Crucé's optimism about the rational and pragmatic nature of international interaction. On the very first pages of the 'Prolegomena' to his *De jure belli ac pacis*, Grotius criticizes the power-focused, state-centred view of politics. He acknowledges that the human is a creature that, like other animals, is impelled by nature to seek its own gratification. But he immediately notes that man is an animal of a quite peculiar kind: man has a unique desire for society – 'that is, a desire for a life spent in common with fellow men, and not merely spent somehow, but spent tranquilly and in a manner corresponding to the character of his intellect'. Then Grotius adds that humans are equipped with language and reason, and that this gives them 'a faculty of knowing and acting according to general principles; and such tendencies as agree with this faculty do not belong to all animals, but are peculiar attributes of human nature'. These peculiar attributes, in turn, drive humans to devise general principles which will guarantee peaceful interaction among sovereign states and thus serve people's desire for a human society. Such general principles will benefit all the actors involved. And as soon as the rulers of Europe realize this, they will begin to devise rules and legal institutions to arbitrate in their conflicts.

De jure belli ac pacis was Grotius's own effort to construct a set of principles and rules designed to regulate international interaction. It helped establish international law as an independent branch of learning. Although Grotius had several precursors, none of them had considered the subject of international law in its entirety. Some of them, such as Vitoria, had studied the law of war. Others, like Bodin and Leibniz, had investigated the concept of state sovereignty. Still others, like Gentili, had pursued the rules of diplomatic interaction. Grotius's main accomplishment was to bring together already existing *disjecta membra* into one masterful synthesis, and to breathe life into it. This constituted a gigantic contribution to the study of International Relations.

Grotius expressed the interests of the United Provinces, the pre-eminent trading nation of his day. His first work, *De jure praedae* ('The Law of Prize and Booty' of 1609),[6] set out his famous doctrine of *mare liberum*: the claim that the open seas are free to all. Grotius's argument is clad in the quasi-religious discourse of the age. It begins with theological claims that God had created all nations different, and that he had provided no nation with all the necessities of life, but distributed the world's bounty unevenly, so that humanity would be forced to trade and exchange. However, the continuation of the argument is pragmatic. It hinges on an appeal to natural law, which Grotius considered to be a product not of divine creation but of human reason and of customary practices.

Grotius's conception of natural law hinges on two theoretical constructs. First, it is sustained by the assumption that each state is founded on a social contract which had, at one point, been established by its citizens. A comparable contract – vaguer, less authoritative, but equally informed by self-interest – could be created among sovereign states. As soon as the rulers of Europe realized that they would all benefit from such a contract, they would devise rules and legal institutions to arbitrate in conflicts between states, Grotius argued. The second basis for a natural law Grotius found in the principle of *pacta sunt servanda* – the respect for promises given and treaties signed. Grotius uses the same pragmatic argument as Bodin to explain that rational actors in an anarchic world soon learn that their best long-term interest is served by keeping the promises they make and by making promises only when they intend to keep them.

Grotius witnessed the destructive effects of the Thirty Years War and the evolution of the various new kingdoms, dukedoms, principalities and cities that emerged from the debris. He acknowledged that there was no prospect of re-establishing the traditional authority which had been exercised in the past by popes and emperors. Neither was there any hope of abolishing or banning war. But Grotius also realized that there was an urgent need to furnish international relations with some new code of behaviour. And he understood that there was a need to humanize the conduct of war, even within modest limits.

Following Bodin, Grotius created a conception of International Relations as political interaction in a *society of states*. He called for the establishment of a set of laws to regulate interstate conduct, and argued that states must accept these laws as binding. These arguments together with his proposal for an exhaustive set of laws, are spelled out his *De jure belli ac pacis*. Since he was a practical and pragmatic man, he did not conceive of this law as created by God. More explicitly than Bodin, Grotius anchored this natural law firmly in human reason and in customary practices. For Grotius, too, then, human reason promised a solution to the problem of international conflict and war (Grotius 1853; Bull 1977, pp. 28–36).

Thomas Hobbes: 'twin of fear'

The major themes of seventeenth-century social thought that reverberate through the international speculations of Crucé, Grotius and Spinoza attain a famous expression in the works of Thomas Hobbes (1588–1679). He was born in the same year that the Spanish Armada launched its ill-fated attack on England. News of the approaching Armada seized the country; and, when it reached Hobbes's mother, she was so gripped with fear that she gave premature birth. This, at least, is how Thomas Hobbes writes about his entrance into this miserable world. With reference to this anecdote, he saw himself as 'the twin of fear'. He suggests by this that his fear, insecurity and introspection were major sources of inspiration for his bleak vision of society.

The Spanish Armada was not the only source of Hobbes's fear and insecurity. His uncertain childhood may also have contributed to his depressed visions. His father, a vicar with taste for card games and drink, abandoned wife and children after a violent brawl outside his own church door. Thomas was raised by an uncle and sent away to school in 1592 – the uncle assumed that, at the age of four, Thomas could take reasonably good care of himself.

A third source of Hobbes's pessimistic outlook may be traced to an intellectual crisis which brought his entire body of knowledge and understanding to collapse when he was still young and impressionable. Upon his graduation from Oxford (1608), Hobbes became the tutor of a young nobleman, whom he escorted on visits to France and Italy. Here, a veritable scientific revolution was challenging the established truths of the Church and the Aristotelian tradition of Western philosophy. Hobbes found that the Aristotelian philosophy that he had been taught at Oxford was crumbling before the discoveries of Johannes Kepler, Galileo Galilei and other members of the new scientific movement.

On returning home, Hobbes felt spiritually bewildered. Bereft of his old intellectual moorings, he began to search for new sources of knowledge and insight. He voraciously studied the writings of classical thinkers other than the authoritative Aristotle, among them Euclid and Thucydides, whose works greatly influenced him. Euclid's *Elements* was for Hobbes what the revelation on the road to Damascus had been for Paul. In Euclid, Hobbes learned to perceive the world through a cool geometric logic, and to trace proofs back through proposition after proposition until he was demonstratively convinced of their true and axiomatic nature. Thucydides' *Peloponnesian War* opened his eyes to politics and gave him a new vision of the workings of international politics. In Thucydides Hobbes found an ambitious attempt to identify regularities in human society, to establish laws which regulated human behaviour. In Thucydides' discussion of the war between Athens and Sparta he found a historian's struggle to engender, from observations of social events, conclusions about general forces which shape human behaviour. 'My work is not a piece of writing designed to meet the taste of an immediate public, but was done to last for ever', Thucydides had explained. His aim had not been to entertain, but to be 'judged useful by those who want to understand clearly the events which happened in the past and which (human nature being what it is) will, at some time or other and in much the same ways, be repeated in the future' (Thucydides, 1972, p. 48). Hobbes read Thucydides' ambitious purpose in the light of the scientific revolution of the seventeenth century, and saw in it an effort to establish the very axioms of human interaction. By 1629 Hobbes had, as a fruit of his intense studies of Thucydides, produced the first English translation of the *Peloponnesian War*.

The final, and undoubtedly the most important source of Hobbes's preoccupation with fear and insecurity was political. During the 1620s, he had occasion to observe a conflict as bitter and momentous as the one Thucydides had observed two thousand years before. At home, he experienced the English Civil Wars; on the Continent, he witnessed the ravages of the Thirty Years War. Like Crucé, Grotius and Spinoza, Hobbes was marked by its atmosphere of violence, insecurity and fear. Like Thucydides and Guicciardini, both of whom also wrote in the shadow of destructive warfare, Hobbes entertained a pessimistic view of human nature. He held war to be a natural state of affairs in human society, and argued that the only way to put an end to war is to trust human reason to form a commonwealth – either by common agreement or by force of arms. This commonwealth must be led by a sovereign monarch who demands absolute obedience from citizens. He wrote in his masterpiece, *Leviathan* (1951 [1651]): 'There must be some coercive power to compel men equally to the performance of their covenants, by the terror of some punishment, greater than the benefit they expect by the breach of their covenant.'

Hobbes's state of nature

Hobbes sketched a state of nature with the intent of showing what a society would be like without a supreme authority. He describes a condition of violent anarchy or war – 'a Warre, as is of every man, against every man'. International Relations theorists who define interstate relations in terms of an absence of supreme authority and therefore see interstate politics as interaction in an anarchical society, often refer to Hobbes's state of nature as the key analogy of the interstate system.

The logic of proof which underlies this analogy articulates the geometric logic of the century. Its axioms are clearly expressed in Hobbes's theory of perception and communication. Like prisoners locked up in solitary confinement, who can communicate only by tapping signals on their walls, human beings are shut off from each other by the very medium they depend upon to send their signals. Alone, separated from the world and isolated from one another, individuals can only be aware of their own feelings.

From this solipsistic perspective, Hobbes explains that 'good' is simply the name which each individual gives to a 'fancy' which attracts them; 'evil' is the name they give to unpleasant things. 'Fear' is the 'opinion of Hurt' engendered by the appearance of things which repel him. 'Courage' is the same, with the hope of avoiding that fear by resistance (Hobbes 1951, pp. 118ff). Such notions make a common guiding moral for humanity impossible. They sustain the view that the world is composed of self-absorbed egotists who are constantly in search of felicity and present enjoyment. Since they are all endowed with reason, they all seek to store up means to secure their future content. Hobbes uses the term 'power' to signify these means. He assumes as a 'generall inclination of all mankind, a perpetuall and restlesse desire for Power after Power that ceaseth only in Death' (pp. 150–60).

In the state of nature, in which no government exists and where individuals exercise unlimited liberty, everyone's perpetual search for power results in a constant struggle. If Hobbes's thought does not include any supreme good (any *Summum Bonum*), it does include a supreme evil (a *Summum Malum*): namely the constant fear of a violent death at the hands of others. This supreme evil constitutes a cornerstone in Hobbes's political thought, and its description as a 'time of Warre, where every man is Enemy to every other man' has, by theorists ever since, been considered a forceful analogy to international society. In such a state of nature, 'the notions of Right and Wrong, Justice and Injustice have there no place', for 'where there is no common Power, there is no Law: where there is no Law, no Injustice. Force and Fraud, are in warre the two Cardinall virtues.' In the state of nature, there can be no notion of property, 'no *Mine and Thine* distinct; but onely that to be every mans that he can get; and for so long as he can keep it' (p. 188). In the state of nature, then, all have the same right to all things. Hobbes maintains in a most celebrated passage:

men live without other security, than what their own strength, and their own invention shall furnish them withall. In such condition there is no place for Industry; because the fruit thereof is uncertain: and consequently no Culture of the Earth; no Navigation or use of the commodities that may be imported by Sea; no commodious Building; no Instruments of moving, and removing such things as require much force; no Knowledge of the face of the Earth; no account of Time; no Arts; no Letters; no Society; and which is worst of all, the life of man, solitary, poore, nasty, brutish, and short. (p. 186)

The notion of a supreme evil is important for Hobbes, because natural man will perceive it with his reason, This perception motivates him to enlighten himself and to discover the one basic dictate of reason: 'to look to the preservation and safeguard to ourselves'. Self-preservation, then, becomes the primary axiom in Hobbes's political system. In the state of nature, there exists no other moral code than the law of self-preservation. This Hobbes refers to as the 'Right of Nature'. No rule is valid in the state of nature, except the rule of self-preservation; no right exists except the right of the strongest. From this one rule and this one right, Hobbes effects a revolution in Western thought. He makes the 'Right of Nature' his political law of gravity, a scientific axiom upon which he builds his entire political system – aided by the method of geometry, the bricks of Natural Law and the clay of fear and reason.

A second axiom of Hobbes's is that all men are equal in the faculties of mind and body. This equality perpetuates the struggle and war which, in turn, leads to the fear of a violent death:

For as to the strength of body, the weakest has strength enough to kill the strongest, either by secret machination, or by confederacy with others, that are in the same danger with himselfe.

And as to the faculties of the mind ... I find yet a greater equality amongst men ... From this equality of ability, ariseth equality of hope in the attaining of our Ends. And therefore if any two men desire the same thing, which neverthelesse they cannot both enjoy, they become enemies; and in the way to their End ... endeavour to destroy, or subdue one an other ... Hereby it is manifest, that during the time men live without a common Power to keep them all in awe, they are in that condition which is called Warre; and such a warre, as is of every man, against every man. (pp. 183–5)

In the state of nature, where everyone enjoys full freedom, everyone also lives in perpetual fear of a sudden death at the jealous hands of others. Acting in accordance with the principle of self-preservation, people deduce that, in order to remove that paralysing fear, they must remove its cause: that is, that must remove everyone's natural right to everything. This can be achieved only if everyone agrees to give up their natural right to everything: each and everyone must, on a solemn promise of good behaviour, give up their right to everything. In order to guarantee that this promise is kept, people must create a strong central power. This is done by everyone's promising everyone else that they will obey whatever command some central power shall consider necessary for the peace and defence of all. By giving this unreserved vow of obedience, people create a power strong enough to deter everyone else from breaking their promises.

Hobbes defined 'freedom' as the absence of restraint. He held that absolute freedom is an intolerable condition, and that people must sacrifice some freedom if they are to enjoy any freedom at all. Therefore they build a state designed to provide some restraint and to ensure them the security collectively that they cannot find individually. They create a *Leviathan*, an omnipotent power which can exercise absolute power *within* the state. However, by putting an end to the state of nature between individuals, they have re-established another state of nature *among* individual states. In Hobbes's words:

> in all times, Kings and Persons of Soveraigne authority, of their Independency, are in continuall jealousies, and in the state and posture of Gladiators; having their weapons pointing and their eyes fixed upon one another; that is, their Forts, Garrisons, and Guns upon the Frontiers of their Kingdomes; and continual Spyes upon their neighbours; which is a posture of War. (pp. 187f)

Sovereignty and power

Like Bodin and Grotius, Hobbes made the concept of sovereignty the fulcrum of his vision of interstate relations. However, whereas Bodin and Grotius associated sovereignty with law, Hobbes associated it with a ruler's absolute and unrestricted force. In *Leviathan* Hobbes argues that, within the state, rulers can demand unreserved obedience from their citizens. The rulers *are* the state; their interests are the state's interests and their will the state's will. The ruler is sovereign, and therefore represents the state in relations with other states.

These rulers are sovereign individuals. Because they are *sovereign* individuals, their freedom is restricted by no one. They have not surrendered their Right of Nature. They are hindered by no one in their ceaseless search for felicity and present enjoyment and in their constant quest to store up means to secure their future content, that is, to accumulate 'power'.

Because rulers of states are sovereign *individuals*, they are essentially equal in body and mind. In their perpetual pursuit of 'Power after Power', some states will inevitably become physically stronger or more wealthy than others. But in the intelligence of their rulers, states are unlikely to differ substantially; and, when all factors of power are taken into account, the difference between states is not considerable. Although strength and wealth are primary manifestations of power, they are by no means the decisive sources of power. For Hobbes, knowledge is power – and through knowledge, science is power, because science is 'the knowledge of consequence and dependence of one fact upon another'. Furthermore, 'worth, dignity, honour and worthiness' are power. And 'eloquence, liberality, nobility' are power. Indeed, 'reputation of power, is Power, because it draweth with it the adherence of those that need protection' (p. 150). And most importantly, friends are power, and through confederacy with friends – 'with others who are in the same danger' – even the weakest sovereign can harm the strongest, either by the overt use of force or by covert machination.

Hobbes presents a complex and sophisticated concept of political power. And his discussion of self-interested rulers' pursuit of 'Power after Power' provides an elaborate justification for the balance-of-power policy which England conducted at the end of the seventeenth century. It also provides support for the term 'balance of power' – the general use of the term emerged in Europe during the 1660s, just as Hobbes's *Leviathan* attracted the attention of European scholars.

Power politics and *pacta sunt servanda*

Hobbes's discussions of the many facets of power and of the calculated use of alliances to contain expansionist monarchs was entirely in tune with the foreign policies of Elizabeth I, who repeatedly intervened to support weaker Continental powers against the might of Spain or France. It also supports the observations of Hobbes's elder contemporary, Francis Bacon, man of letters and Lord Chancellor of England. In a pamphlet 'Considerations Touching a War with Spain' [1623], Bacon estimates whether it is possible for England and its allies to contain the forces of Spain. 'The balancing of the forces of these kingdoms and their allies with Spain and their allies', he writes, is a 'great and weighty consideration' for England (Bacon 1852, p. 200).

Towards the end of Hobbes's life, it was no longer Spain but France that represented a threat to England. Under the leadership of Louis XIV (1661–1715), France sought to establish a universal monarchy over Europe and subordinate all other countries in Europe. The response levelled against this expansionist policy was a balance-of-power policy. The efforts to contain French ambitions were chiefly the work of Holland – the small country in which both Spinoza and Hobbes sought refuge from civil war and persecution in their own countries. When France made aggressive moves on the Spanish Netherlands in 1667, William III of Orange immediately dropped all quarrels with England – with which he had just fought two large mercantile wars (1652–54 and 1665–67) – and signed an Anglo–Dutch alliance designed to contain French expansion. When Sweden became the third member of this anti–French alliance (1668), King Louis XIV found himself overpowered, and withdrew from the Spanish Netherlands. The French withdrawal was immediately followed by the collapse of the Triple Alliance; indeed, Louis XIV had no sooner sued for peace than a secret treaty was signed between England and France (1670) according to which the two great powers divided Holland between them two years later.

These events, in which rulers sign secret treaties one moment and violate them the next, are quite in tune with Hobbes's and Spinoza's understanding of the behaviour of sovereign actors. Both maintained that rulers, like other people, are driven by self-interest. Because rulers are sovereign, they are not constrained in their actions by any law. In effect, they enjoy the full Right of Nature, according to which might is the only right (Spinoza 1951b, p. 213; 1951c, p. 309). Hobbes and Spinoza accepted the implication that, if any rulers are free to act according to their own will and inclination, they are also free to renege on promises and break treaties whenever they decide this to be in their interest.

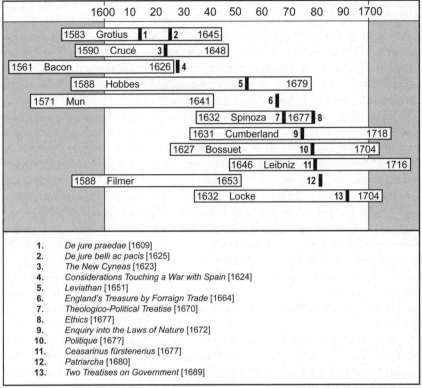

Figure 4.2 Some seventeenth-century authors and their works

In theory, then, any ruler is free to break treaties or violate alliances. In practice, it would be unwise for a ruler to abuse the privilege and routinely break treaties. This would quickly undermine their reputation and soon no one would trust them to keep their promises. Since trust is an essential asset in international politics, Hobbes and Spinoza strongly underscored that once treaties had been signed they must also be kept – advice they summarized in the principle of *pacta sunt servanda*. If a ruler has the intention of entering a treaty only to break it later, they should refrain from entering it in the first place, they argued.

Consequently, any treaty of peace or alliance can be trusted to remain in force as long as the motives for concluding it continues to hold good. Thus, when France withdrew from the Spanish Netherlands, the Triple Alliance lost its purpose and immediately collapsed. However, every time the expansionist Louis XIV launched an ambitious military offensive, anti-French alliances were organized by William III to resist his aggression – first in the War of Devolution (1667–68), then in the Dutch War (1672–78) and finally in the War of the Grand Alliance (1689–97).

The sentiment of the century

The seventeenth century opened in the name of God. It evolved through conflicts and wars that were fuelled by incompatible religious interpretations. The century closed in the name of the absolute monarch and with the secular argument that war could be kept at bay through a policy of counterpoise. During the course of this process, International Relations theory came of age.

This coming of age was indicated by a proliferation of books and treatises which discussed interstate relations. It was attended by a trend towards a more secularized view of political affairs. Social theorists increasingly saw the causes of war less as God's intention to punish people for their sins, and more in terms of properties of human nature and of the interplay of human interests. Hobbes, Crucé, Spinoza and Grotius, for example, all explained the causes of war in terms of human emotions such as greed and pride; and they all found new hopes for a peaceful social order in people's ability to calculate that human existence would be much improved if human reason could impose limits upon human passions. Also, all of them based their argument on a secular redefinition of the concept of 'natural law'.

This development is apparent in the works of Samuel Pufendorf (1632–94). He was keenly aware of the international changes which had occurred in his lifetime. He saw the Treaty of Westphalia (1648) as a watershed in international history, and distinguished sharply between the chaotic world of war and devastation which preceded Westphalia and the orderly world of self-governing equilibrium which emerged after it. He noted that, before Westphalia, authors like Grotius and Hobbes had been naturally predisposed by chaotic circumstances to ask how humans could establish an orderly society. And he realized that, once the Westphalian system of sovereign states was established, it was more natural to ask how one could ensure that sovereign actors would become useful contributors to an orderly Europe. To achieve this end, he argued, it was necessary to devise a new morality which could gain the consent of all Europeans. The essential constituents of this new morality, 'which would teach one how to conduct oneself to become a useful member of human society, are called natural laws' (Pufendorf 1991, p. 35).

Greater secularization: natural law and national interest

The tradition of natural law reaches back to the philosophies of ancient Greece and can be traced through Western social and religious thought. As a preliminary definition, it can be said that 'natural law' denotes a set of principles that transcend the laws of individual societies and of different epochs. Whereas the laws of a given society or a given epoch are transitory and changing phenomena, natural law is a supreme phenomenon which outlives the times and sanctions a supreme, unchanging moral order.[7]

Hobbes, Spinoza, Crucé, Grotius and Pufendorf all anchored their political theories in a secular understanding of natural law. Pufendorf, for example, argued explicitly that, if natural law were to furnish Europe with precepts for useful political conduct, then this could not be grounded in religion – for, as the Treaty of Westphalia recognized with its principle of *cujus regio eius religio*, Europe was still racked with religious quarrels. Thus, it became important for him to cleanse natural law of its grounding in Aristotelian and Thomistic theology. From the 1660s onwards, his project was to construct a comprehensive secular moral philosophy grounded in natural law and adapted to the conditions of post-Westphalian Europe – a set of universal principles of right deduced from two premises no person could reasonably doubt: a scientifically reconstructed condition common to all persons, the 'state of nature', and the empirically verifiable self-love or concern each person has with their own preservation. Pufendorf helped free International Relations theory from the fetters of theological thought. He sought in his analysis to trace political events back to the rational motives of the agent (Meinecke 1957, pp. 224f).

In this respect, Pufendorf was a representative voice of the times. Several authors of the third quarter of the seventeenth century developed theories of social interaction from speculations about human nature and from notions like 'reason', 'motives' and 'interests'. Most of them were driven by an attempt to replace the pessimistic argument of Thomas Hobbes with a more optimistic alternative – as in the case of John Bramhall's *Catching of Leviathan* [1658]. Like Bramhall, many of them were churchmen who were incensed by Hobbes's emphasizing necessity rather than liberty. They saw self-interest as a constant feature of human life. And they reasoned that, since self-interest was universal, it was also universally predictable, and would therefore provide a firm basis on which to build social theory. Some of them devised a theory around the claim that, when individuals are allowed to pursue their own interest, great benefits will accrue for society at large. Joseph Lee, for example, opened his argument with a defence of the 'undeniable maxime that everyone by the light of nature and reason will do what makes for his greatest advantage', and he closed it with the claim that 'the advancement of private persons will be the advantage of the publick' (quoted in Appleby, 1978, p. 62). Bishop Richard Cumberland agreed.

Cumberland's *De legibus naturae* ('A Treatise of the Laws of Nature', 1727 [1672]) was explicitly written as an attack on Hobbes. Cumberland argues that people are not only endowed with needs, wants and self-serving reason (which Hobbes had recognized); human beings also have a natural liking for each other and a capacity for benevolence. Cumberland sought to demonstrate that this benevolence did not depend on religious texts, legal authority or the threat of force. Rather, benevolent acts would occur naturally. In a world of rational humans, Cumberland claimed, there are sufficient 'contingent' sanctions in the form of natural rewards for virtue and of punishments for vice to make possible a peaceable and tolerable society even in the absence of civil force. 'I suppose everyone seeks his *own* Good, and that to act in *pursuit thereof*, adds to the *perfection* of his Nature,' he writes (1727, p. 215). In pursuit of his own good, each individual enters into 'Compacts' with others 'by which their mutual Happiness may be both secur'd and increas'd ... By *these Methods* the Powers of some will of necessity be counter poiz'd by others' (p. 297). Thus 'governed by the universal Benevolence of all rational Beings towards all, are the principal Causes of the publick Happiness of all' (p. 114).

When Bramhall's, Lee's and Cumberland's notion of self-interest was allowed to inform theories of individual interactions, they foreshadowed the doctrines of liberal moral philosophers like Adam Smith and Jeremy Bentham. When the concept of self-interest was applied to the interaction of princes and statesmen, it greatly enriched the old concepts *of raison d'état* and balance of power. This is apparent in the case of the French Duke of Rohan (1579–1638). He introduces his book *On the Interest of Princes and States of Christendom* (1673 [1638]) with the observation that 'Princes command their peoples, as they are themselves commanded by Interest ... The Prince may err. His councels may be corrupted. But the Interest alone can never fail; and in proportion to whether it is well or ill understood, it causes States to live or die' (Rohan 1673, p. 7).

Rohan's maxim that 'interest can never fail', was immediately embraced by British analysts. It informed Marchament Nedham's book *Interest will Not Lie, or a View of England's True Interest* (1659) and his newspaper *Mercurius Politicus* (Gunn 1969). By this maxim, any analysis of international relations must begin by defining the interests of states. But how are such interests best determined? Rohan proposed that the most appropriate vantage point is to assess each state's military strength and geographic situation. In addition, it is helpful to gauge each state's cohesive force of religion, its ability to negotiate and enter into alliances and, last but not least, its reputation and ambitions.

The new context of inquiry: the scientific revolution
The growing secularization of the century was attended by greater methodological self-awareness. Theorists increasingly speculated about state interaction in descriptive rather than in prescriptive terms. They still referred copiously to classical authorities; however, they did this with a greater independence than before. They displayed a greater propensity to question ancient wisdom.[8]

These attitudes reflect a larger tendency to question authorities – all authorities, secular (Aristotle, Plato) as well as religious ones (the Church, the pope and the Holy Roman Emperor). Such attitudes may be related to the incessant wars of the age, and to the powerlessness of priests, philosophers and politicians to deal with them, to the breakdown of traditional law and beliefs and to the emergence in Europe of a state of normative chaos. It made the matter worse that travellers and traders brought new information about peoples, manners and customs of distant new worlds into a violent Europe. In the prevalent state of normative vacuum, such new knowledge only contributed to the relativism of the age.

The way out of relativism was pioneered by scholars who sought to regain humanity's certainty of mind. Three contributors stand out in this respect as facilitators of the scientific revolution: Bacon, Galileo and Descartes. All three wrote their most influential works around the time of the Thirty Years War. They shared the doubts of the age. They asked how it is possible for anyone to gain reliable, truthful and usable knowledge. They rejected the methods advocated by the academic tradition of the universities founded in the Middle Ages, and provided alternative methods of knowledge acquisition.

Traditional science had been deductive. But Bacon, Galileo and Descartes argued that deduction alone could produce no new knowledge. For them, truth is not something one could postulate at the beginning of an exploration. It is something one discovers after a process of investigation. Appropriate methods of investigation had long been used by practical cartographers and astronomers. Map-makers did not draw their information from learned authorities and holy texts; rather, they took notes on what sailors and traders could tell about distant lands, systematized the tales, cross-checked the information, and compared notes and extant maps. Star-gazers charted the heavens by observing the skies at night and keeping meticulous logs of their nocturnal observations. Copernicus relied on pre-Christian observations of the paths of planets and stars, and found that their movements did not fit official, geocentric accounts. Brahe observed the skies regularly throughout a long lifetime. He left stacks of meticulous nocturnal notes to his assistant, Kepler, whose calculations replaced the complex orthodox vision with a simple heliocentric model. He summarized the planetary orbits in a few mathematical statements and presented them in this form as 'laws of nature'. Galileo drove the point home by depicting the planetary orbits and drawing individual planets as he had observed them with his own eyes through the lens of a telescope.

The fact that Galileo made his observations through a telescope has a symbolic significance: seventeenth-century science was profoundly optical in its orientation. It emphasized the single sense of human sight. Scientific observation meant selecting a few things from the confusing wealth of the universe, and being content with seeing these things systematically, measuring their apparent size and weight, describing their colour, shape and character, explaining their position in relation to each other and, if applicable, calculating their movement in space. The understanding which accompanied such optical observations was phrased in mechanical terms. The unchallenged exemplar of this scientific vision is Isaac Newton's *Mathematical Principles of Natural Philosophy* of 1687. It demonstrates that all bodies – whether they are located on earth or in the heavens – can be measured, that their motion can be timed and their movement captured in terms of laws described in mathematical formulae. All matter in the universe moves as if every particle attracted every other particle with a force proportional to the product of the two masses and inversely proportional to the square of the distance between them.

New modes of theorizing: interests, states and balance
Seventeenth-century scientific knowledge came to mean knowledge about visible differences between static objects. Botany and biology relied on taxonomic tables. The study of language was presented as a logical system in which each component part performed a specific function. The analysis of wealth examined the circulation of objects (like coins) that could be represented in a system of exchange (Foucault 1973). The study of history was purged of its propensity simply to retell past events. Historians increasingly relied on a meticulous examination of things themselves, and then transcribed the information they had gathered in neutralized and faithful words. The study of International Relations came to mean the study of

interrelations between impermeable territorial states. This obsession with matter in geometric motion informs one of the most mechanical visions in the social sciences: the theory of the balance of power.

Balance-of-power theories were not new in the seventeenth century. They were expressed earlier by Italian theorists like Guicciardini, Gentili and Botero. However, in the seventeenth century the imagery of equilibrium presented itself with unprecedented clarity – as is apparent in the theories of thinkers like Bacon, Mun, Spinoza, Pufendorf, Hobbes and Cumberland (and evident in the practices of William III of Orange, Frederick the Great and Charles II). Also, the phrase 'balance of power' came into general use. It denoted a policy in which one state allied with other states (preferably weaker than itself) against any state which threatened to dominate Europe. Through the balance-of-power principle a state could preserve or maximize its independence of action: by manipulating alliances states could create a counterpoise against any state whose ascendancy they feared. According to this notion, a balance-of-power policy allows a state to throw its weight where it is most needed in order to safeguard its own independence.

One important reason for this improved clarity in balance-of-power theories lies in the new scientific epistemology of the age. With the deductive approach of the orthodox schoolmen ridiculed, Bacon, Descartes and Galileo hastened the evolution of the scientific approach. The natural world was 'de-spiritualized' and 'de-animated'. Whereas the orthodox schoolmen had tended to impute purposes to natural phenomena, the seventeenth-century scientists imposed a mechanical model. The branch of science which had the greatest success was geometry, and its method and mechanical vision are evident in the writings of Descartes, Hobbes, Galileo, Leibniz, Newton and Spinoza. These authors described natural phenomena by identifying the presumably simple motions from which their behaviour could be derived. There was no longer any essential difference between bodies called stones and bodies called animals. Descartes and Hobbes agreed that the world can be reduced to matter in motion. Both conceived of animal bodies as complex machines. Even the spiritually oriented Leibniz recognized that every organic body of a living being is a sort of God-made machine, or natural robot, which infinitely excels all artificial robots. Indeed, few theorists reflected this *Zeitgeist* better in their conception of international interaction than Leibniz. His vision is very much informed by his overall, Teutonically complex image of states as discrete, impermeable, indestructible, animated organisms; all interacting with others, each distinguished from others by its self-consciousness.[9]

A second reason for the improved clarity is that the old notion of balance benefited from the new concept of 'interest'. Pufendorf (1991, p. 35) sensed this when he deemed the Treaty of Westphalia a watershed in international history. Gatien Courtilz de Sandras noted that a new preoccupation with 'interest' suddenly took precedence over dynastic squabbles and religious affinity in European diplomacy (Courtilz 1686, p. 3). The same notion is apparent in Rohan's discussion of European politics. In his words, the interest of a state always aims at the augmentation, or at least the conservation, of the State. To fulfil its aim, it adapts to the times. So in order to consider well the interest of contemporary Princes, it is not necessary to go very far; it is sufficient to analyse current affairs. Thus we can take as our vantage point the claim that there are at present in Christendom two Powers which represent the two poles from whence descend the influences of peace and war upon the other states: viz. the Houses of France and Spain. That of Spain finds itself suddenly augmented, and has not been able to conceal the ambition of making herself mistress and cause the Sun of a new Monarchy to rise in the West. That of France is forthwith carried to make a counterpoise. The other princes join the one or the other, according to their interest. But for as much as this interest, as it has been well or ill followed, has caused the ruin of some and the greatness of others, I have proposed to publish in this present Treatise: First, what was the true interest of these two mighty powers, and then of the others which seem in some manner to depend on their protection. Next of all I shall show how much has been the digression from this true interest, either because it was not well understood by the Prince or else because it was concealed from him by the corruption of his Ministers. (Rohan 1673, pp. 7f)

Rohan was much influenced by Renaissance scholars (notably by Machiavelli, Guicciardini, Boccalini and Bonaventura). But – as should be apparent from his portrayal above of mid-seventeenth-century European politics – Rohan identified the balance-of-power mechanism more keenly than his predecessors. The reason is that he has linked the old notion of counterpoise to the new concept of 'interest'. Indeed, he may be the first European theorist to make this link. The Duke of Rohan, Huguenot general and statesman, is an important contributor to modern International Relations theory. He drew on the Italian tradition of politics and counterpoise, and formulated a keen balance-of-power analysis which, in turn, greatly influenced English social theorists.

A final important reason for the improved clarity in the political theories of this age lies in a tighter grasp on the concept of the state. After the Peace of Westphalia, the kings of Europe replaced the old, volatile arrangements of military entrepreneurs with a new, centrally directed system of military command and control. The monarchs became commanders-in-chief of their countries' armed forces. By the same token they expanded their powers over their civil societies. The reins of political power were collected and concentrated in the hands of the monarch. Around the king evolved the characteristic features of the absolutist court. And around the court emerged the streamlined structures of the modern state. During the second half of the seventeenth century the states of (Western) Europe became conceived of as independent communities whose court-led government asserted full authority over a specific portion of the earth's surface. The territorial nature of statehood was clarified. The delineation of an 'internal' and an 'external' realm of politics – domestic politics versus foreign affairs – was emphasized. The state was individuated as a political actor and became a more clearly observed analytic unit. The classic concept of sovereignty was completed. The concept was also irreversibly removed from the realm of the divine and the universal and planted in the province of the secular and specific. As a result political actors like the pope and the emperor, whose authority rested on divine and universal principles, were eclipsed by the great monarchs of Europe (Herz 1957).

Notes

1 There is an enormous literature which seeks to explain the emergence of Western Europe and its modern institutions. Downing (1992, pp. 4ff) makes a useful division of this literature into five macro-historical schools: (1) the German sociological approach (inspired by Weber and Hinze); (2) the modernization theorists (represented by the US Committee on Comparative Politics which was set up by the Social Science Research Council and led by Gabriel Almond); (3) the 'bourgeois revolution' school (inspired by Adam Smith and Karl Marx); (4) the culturalist or idealist perspective (exemplified by Bendix); and (5) the Barrington Moore thesis.

2 When did Filmer write *Patriarcha*? He must have written it after 1635 but before 1640. The book was circulated in manuscript form before it was finally published posthumously in 1680. Long before it was printed, it had earned its author the reputation of an extreme supporter of royal prerogatives (Laslett 1960, p. 71). The main reason why Filmer has become such a famous representative for monarchic absolutism is less the sophistication of his argument and more the fact that he served as a whipping boy (*Prügelknabe*) in John Locke's landmark *First Treatise of Government* of 1688.

3 For Filmer this division of the world into states was greatly enhanced by the confusion of Babel, whence God scattered humanity 'over the whole face of the earth' (Genesis 11:8). 'It is a common opinion that at the confusion of tongues there were seventy-two distinct nations erected', writes Filmer (1991, p. 7). This continued fragmentation of the earth into several smaller political units occurred not only with God's blessing, but with his direct participation. It was God, after all, who had created the confusion of Babel in the first place (Filmer 1991, p. 7).

4 Cineas (or 'Cyneas') was a Thessalian diplomat employed by Pyrrhus of Epirus (celebrated for his 'pyrrhic victories') in his war with Rome. He is chiefly known for his observations that the Roman senate was 'an assembly of Kings' and that war with Rome was like fighting a many-headed hydra: hence presumably a type of figure for one who is well able to recognize unwelcome politico-strategic realities.

5 It is very tempting to trace a line of evolution from Crucé's vision of a 'general assembly' of states in *The New Cyneas* through the writings of the Duke of Sully, via William Penn and the internationalist ideas of the Society of Friends (the Quakers) to twentieth-century ideas like Woodrow Wilson's League of Nation and Franklin D. Roosevelt's United Nations.

6 *De jure praedae* was a report commissioned by the Dutch East India Company, which was involved in a hot legal contest with Portuguese companies about prizes. Grotius realized that, to prove that a Portuguese ship had been legally captured, he had to invalidate the claim that the Indian Ocean was Portugal's private property. He did this by relying on Vitoria's argument that all nations have a natural right to trade. This axiom furnished the basis for Grotius's famous claim that the open seas are free for all. When Grotius had completed his sizeable report (at the age

of twenty-six), its important twelfth chapter was published under the title *Mare liberum* in 1609. To appreciate fully John Selden's *Mare clausum* in 1635, it is important to note that he wrote this text as an effort to rebut Grotius's *Mare liberum* (Selden 1652, pp. 447ff). The full text of Grotius's report was not published until 1868.

7 There are two major explanations for why natural law is eternal – both of them discussed by Selden (1652, pp. 12f). The first is religious and medieval in origin. It was clearly expressed by Augustine, who formulated the doctrine that participation in God's thought is the moral and obligatory end of all intellectual pursuit. In the light of this explanation, natural law is but the formulation of a divinely inspired moral order. Natural law, in other words, is created by God.

The second explanation is secular and evolved during the sixteenth and seventeenth centuries. It is well represented by Thomas Hobbes, who held that the basic, permanent characteristic of human beings is their ability to reason. And since all humans are essentially alike, they are likely to reason in the same manner. The implication of this argument is that humans can use their reason to logically deduce universal and self-evident rules for human behaviour. Natural law, in other words, is created by humanity.

The tendency of the seventeenth century was towards rejecting the former explanation and accepting the latter. This conforms to the larger theme of the age: the mounting tendency on the part of scholars and statesmen to remove both political authority and responsibility from the realm of the divine and place it in the hands of rational individuals. Thomas Hobbes formulated a pessimistic variation on this theme of the age. Émeric Crucé formulated an optimistic one. Hugo Grotius took a middle position.

8 Thomas Hobbes exemplifies the rebellious spirit of the age. Hobbes admits freely he has 'neglected the Ornament of quoting ancient Poets, Orators and Philosophers contrary to the custom of late time'. Indeed, he disapproves of authors who, instead of explaining their thoughts as clearly as possible, 'stick their corrupt Doctrine with the Cloves of other men's Wit'. It is, he complains 'an argument of Indigestion, when Greek and Latin Sentences unchewed come up again, as they use to doe, unchanged' (Hobbes 1951, p. 727).

9 Leibniz saw the 'state' much in the same way that he saw his 'monads' (Ross 1984, pp. 89ff). And although he did not elaborate on how discrete, impenetrable, territorial states were organs in a larger interstate organism, his 'monadology' suggests a complex vision of the interstate system – a composite organism in which each member is a unique, self-conscious society which is, in turn, composed of many smaller, self-conscious societies and so on, down the several levels of the multi-layered system. On the face of it, Leibniz's speculations are dense and abstract to the point of absurdity. However, their basic imagery gains by close acquaintance, exuding a seductive intellectual force rivalled in its generality only by the system which Hegel formulated a century later – and which also relied on self-consciousness as the key attribute of the state.

5

Enlightenment politics:
the revolutionary rise of popular sovereignty

The eighteenth century has many names: the Age of the Old Regime, the Age of Enlightenment, the Age of Democratic Revolution, the Age of Cosmopolitanism … It is rarely called the Age of Upheaval, although it is an apt label: The eighteenth century began with a wave of great wars. These wars stimulated the emergence of the modern state. The growth of the state was one of the characteristic features of the century. Debates about the nature of states and about their interrelations mark the political thought of the age.

The evolving institutions of modern government became a means of securing order and safety at home. This included the raising, supporting and controlling of armies for use against other states. The use of these armies was increasingly regulated according to precise protocol by professional diplomats and scholars in international law. Wars were conducted according to well-defined rules by professional soldiers. Each state explicitly acknowledged the legitimacy of others' territories; none had the right to universalize its own regime or its own laws at the expense of others. The modern state concentrated political power and military command. But it also transformed the wolf-packs of the Thirty Years War into the trained Baroque poodles of the wars of Louis XIV.

Most European rulers were absolute sovereigns. France's Louis XIV was the most absolute and powerful of them all. His machinations kept Europe in a fever of wars (1672–1713). They exhausted France. In the last years of his reign, Louis's life work was undone. A grand alliance led by Britain defeated him. England emerged from the wars of Louis XIV as the greatest winner and, improbably, as the dominant actor in eighteenth-century international politics.

England stood apart from the states on the European continent in one important respect: the country was not an absolute monarchy. The Glorious Revolution (1688) had forced the English king to accept that Parliament imposed specific checks on his freedom of action – no citizen could be arrested and detained without legal process, no law could be suspended by the king alone, no taxes could be levied and no army maintained without Parliamentary consent. Thus, by the end of the wars of Louis XIV, European politics was torn between two different doctrines of sovereignty. On the one hand was the old doctrine of the Divine Right of Kings which supported the absolute regimes on the Continent. On the other was a new doctrine of popular sovereignty which had emerged in the wealthier, mercantile sea powers of the North Atlantic rim.

This difference brought about a political division in eighteenth-century Europe between the Continental states, with their absolutist regimes and centralized politics, and the trading states of the North Atlantic rim, with relatively weak state structures and growing market economies. This chapter will discuss the tension between these two regime types, and document the ways in which the Atlantic trading states increasingly challenged the Continental autocracies during the course of the eighteenth century.

The chapter begins by discussing the advent of a new anthropology – the view that humans are rational creatures endowed with individual rights. It then shows how this new view affected social theorists in Britain (Hume and Smith), France (Montesquieu and Voltaire), and the German lands (Friedrich II and Kant). During the course of the century, they increasingly portrayed social relations in terms of reason and natural harmony. One of its manifestations was the notion of a self-equilibrating market economy. Another was the idea of a self-adjusting balance among sovereign states. Modern balance-of-power theories emerged in France and Britain during the second half of the eighteenth century. At first, these theories were simple and mechanical. But soon thinkers like Hume and Robertson developed more complex theories of the balance of power, which they saw as peculiarly European in origin and a product of reasoned interaction by diplomats and statesmen. These theories were criticized by radical publicists in Europe (like Paine and Godwin) and by anti-monarchists in America. Here, on the other side of the Atlantic, authors like Hamilton and Madison sought to escape the balance-of-power politics of Europe by developing a uniquely American alternative in the form of a peaceful federation of states.

Changes in the use of power and in acquisition of wealth

England emerged as a formidable land power during the wars of Louis XIV, its superiority gained by virtue of technological pre-eminence and great wealth and by the country's immense sea power: the Royal Navy both protected English trade and projected the country's power wherever in the world it was deemed necessary.

In the international struggle for power and prestige the national navies played a decisive role in this busy age of growing global commerce and trade. The eighteenth century was the age of mature mercantilism, and it was in England that the mercantilist doctrines had been theoretically elaborated and most consciously applied: in order to discourage imports, certain foreign goods were prohibited or discouraged by heavy duties; in order to promote domestic production, the state intervened heavily to improve communication and to encourage private enterprise. The economic doctrine of mercantilism was attended by the political doctrine of absolutism. And the two continued to dominate European politics after the wars of Louis XIV. But the relationship between them changed during the course of the century. While they had been mutually supporting doctrines at its beginning, they became riddled by internal contradictions and mutual oppositions by its end.

Absolutism went through a marked evolution during the long reign of Louis XIV (1661–1715). On the Continent, the centralization of power evolved towards enlightened despotism. This evolution was spurred not so much by the monarch as by the ministerial entourage. Through the needs of recruitment and taxation, the royal bureaucracy expanded. From within absolutism itself emerged new structures and processes of production, procurement and allocation. At first, these structures represented the monarch and reflected the lustre and the authority of the Crown. Soon, they assumed authority in their own right. In the hands of the kings' powerful ministers, the absolute sovereignty of the monarch was incrementally superseded by its own institutional product. Absolutist theory was supplemented by doctrines of Divine Right, and the person of the monarch became such an intense focus of sovereignty that the monarch was rendered impersonal, abstract and half-divine – as exemplified by Louis XIV, 'the Sun King'. With much of the official work being done by a growing corps of administrators, the actual monarch became more and more a figurehead. The impersonality of the state was beginning to take over.

Mercantilism, too, changed during the eighteenth century. It was streamlined and perfected in regions where the development of manufacturers and industrial wealth was slow. But among the wealthiest industrializing sea powers of the North Atlantic rim, mercantilism and absolutism were, in fact, eroded from below. Here the growing merchant and manufacturing middle classes had challenged the key principles of absolutism as early as the end of the seventeenth century. In England, for example, mercantilism had enriched the nation, but it had also boosted the growth of citizens' wealth beneath and outside the royal entourage. It had fuelled the evolution of new and independent social groups and forces. First it had spurred the transformation of the country's landholding elite; then it had fuelled the growth of new entrepreneurial classes.

During the course of the eighteenth century England's landowning nobles consolidated their power over British society. More and more of the country's common pastures were enclosed into private landholdings. These enclosures hurt the smaller free-holding farmers, who depended on the commons to feed their animals; but they consolidated the economic and political base of a narrow landholding elite from which most government officials were recruited. England's wealthy landowners dominated Parliament, passed enclosure acts and conducted foreign policies which suited their interests. Unlike the nobility on the Continent, they did not depend upon the Crown for wealth or influence, and would therefore, at times, feel free to oppose their king if his proposals hurt their interests.

Hand in hand with the enclosure movement, British networks of communication and commerce were greatly expanded. Roads and canals were improved and extended. Transportation costs were greatly reduced. Markets expanded for bulk goods (foodstuffs as well as iron and coal) and finished products (agricultural and industrial, both). Such developments stimulated the growth of new, intermediate social groups – manufacturers, merchants, financiers, engineers. These were generally not represented in Parliament. But as the eighteenth century progressed, they clamoured for inclusion in the political process with mounting insistence.

The new groups tended to express an individualistic view of social life. They often argued that everyone was the architect of their own fortunes – which of course implied that those who held high office and great wealth held them because of personal talent, ingenuity, skill and diligence. They tended to resent the hereditary privileges of the old nobility, but they defended the right to inherit economic wealth – which obviously gave their own heirs great advantages. Their arguments tended to be rationalistic and optimistic. They were propagated through new channels of communications, notably the emerging popular press. During the eighteenth century, these groups began to oppose the prevailing mercantilist views. They claimed that a real increase in the wealth of the nation could be achieved if all hindrances to their rational self-interested plans were removed.

At first the members of these groups made no attempt to interfere with the king's prerogative to make foreign policy. However, they soon came to protest against the consequences of his foreign-policy entanglements. The entanglements meant war, which was expensive and disruptive for business. Wealthier groups objected to the consequences of war: heavy taxation, interference with trade and industry, arbitrary justice and control of consciences by the monarch. It was around such issues that the Dutch and, later, the English organized opposition against the institutions and principles of absolutism.

Symmetry, sovereignty and the cult of Reason

England emerged as a Great Power during the wars of Louis XIV. And as British wealth and force dominated interstate affairs in the postwar period, so British ideas influenced the study of international relations during this Age of Enlightenment.

The sentiment of the age was marked by a confidence in the powers of human reason and a firm conviction of the regularity of nature. It had emerged during the seventeenth century; by the eighteenth, it had matured into a pervasive vision. Scientists and philosophers sought to capture the symmetry and regularity of nature and to express it in intellectual terms – through flow-charts, taxonomies or mechanical models. This obsession with balance and symmetry unified the contributions to science and philosophy of the age. Its most famous representation is Isaac Newton's vision of the universe; his *Mathematical Principles of Natural Philosophy* of 1687 expressed perfectly the vision of repeated movement in space. Newton's orderly universe dovetailed nicely with the ordered psychology of John Locke (1632–1704); his *Essay Concerning Human Understanding* of 1690 portrayed the human mind as a blank slate inscribed by experience – experience, obviously, of the physical universe. Locke expressed a new philosophy of knowledge. He provided a theory of sense-impressions that countered Descartes's assumption of innate ideas. He also rendered knowledge subjective, as it was made relative to the perceptions of the individual.

By mid-eighteenth century, Locke's argument had become a commonplace epistemological companion to Newtonian physics. What Newton did for humanity's view of nature, John Locke did for humanity's view of itself. Newton and Locke, with their belief in reason, their visions of a law-abiding universe and their mechanistic approach to nature, provided the basis for an empiricist approach to knowledge. Locke also provided the basis for a doctrine of popular sovereignty which suited the emerging middle classes of the North Atlantic trading states. The British ideas would exercise a great influence on political theorizing in France – significantly mediated through the popular interpretations of Voltaire (1980, pp. 68ff).

The most famous expression of this new doctrine of politics was Locke's *Two Treatises of Government* (1960 [1689]). The topic of the first is clear from its title: *The False Principles and Foundation of Sir Robert Filmer, and his Followers, are Detected and Overthrown*. Its aim was to refute the 'false principle' which 'flatters princes with an Opinion, that they have a Divine Right to absolute Power' (Locke 1960, p. 176).

The aim of the second treatise was to formulate an alternative to the principle of the Divine Right of Kings. It was entitled *An Essay Concerning the True Originals, Extent, and End of Civil Government* and mollifies Hobbes's state of nature. Whereas Hobbes described the state of nature as the worst possible condition, Locke sees it as quite happy. The main reason for this happiness lies in Locke's description of humans as reasonable creatures who have a God-given law of nature to govern them. Locke's state of nature is governed by a law of nature which gives all humans certain Natural Rights: the rights to life, liberty and property. Since people are rational, most of them will obey the law of nature, argues Locke. They will be content to enjoy their own Natural Rights and will not violate the Rights of their fellows. Most people are reasonable. However, there are always some who are not. Some people disregard the law of nature and knowingly invade the Rights of others. They steal other people's property, enslave their liberty and destroy their lives.

Locke's state of nature appears benign when compared to Hobbes's ruthless scenario of 'perpetuall warre'.[1] However, Locke's state of nature, too, contains elements of conflict and war. The existence of a few people who knowingly violate the Rights of their fellows prods Locke to explore the necessity of self-defence. In Locke's view, any person has a right to protect his or her own Natural Rights in the state of nature. Locke's basic idea is the same as Crucé's (1972, p. 29). But the new notion of a state of nature and the new concept of Natural Rights greatly refined the old argument: anyone who violates the Natural Rights of others forfeits his or her own Natural Rights. By committing acts of theft, slavery or murder, people set themselves outside the realm of reason and law. They render themselves lawless. They declare war on others, and anyone has the right to pursue and punish them. Indeed, anyone has the right to hunt and destroy them, just as one would hunt and destroy a wolf or a lion: 'because such Men are not under the ties of the Common Law of Reason, have no rule, but that of Force and Violence, and so may be treated as Beasts of Prey' (Locke 1960, p. 321).

The main problem with the state of nature is that those who have had their rights violated are rarely fair and impartial in their pursuit of revenge. So, in order to prevent excessive revenge meted out in affect, people agree to set up a government to enforce the observance of the Natural Rights of all persons. The conflicts and wars which occur in the state of nature, then, drive rational people to establish government.

Did Locke understand the state of nature literally? Did it correspond to any actual social condition? Locke's discussion is far from clear on this point. However there is ample evidence in his *Second Treatise* to suggest that he would answer both questions in the affirmative. First of all, he suggests (in chapter 2) that the state of nature describes an actual condition in humankind's distant past. Second, he claims that the state of nature exists in two places in his contemporary world: among savages in other lands (for instance the natives in America), and among '*Princes* and Rulers of *Independent* Governments all through the World' (Locke 1960, p. 317). However, he does not elaborate on the point.

Locke acknowledges that a state of nature exists among the sovereign states of the world (and that there is an essential difference between politics within commonwealths and politics between them).[2] However, he never actually discusses international relations at length in the light of this analogy. But as the eighteenth century unfolded, other authors did. Jean Barbeyrac's *L'histoire des anciens traités* of 1739 was greatly influenced by Locke's doctrines of right. Christian Wolff's *Jus gentium* ('The Law of Nations', 1749) applied Locke's ideas to International Relations. But it was Wolff's gifted Swiss pupil, Émeric de Vattel (1714–67), who wrote the most influential Lockean analysis of international relations: the *Droit des gens* ('The Law of Nations' [1758]).

Vattel portrayed the relations among states as analogous to Locke's description of human beings in the state of nature. He acknowledged that each state is a sovereign actor, yet he did not believe that interstate relations exhibit the vicious Hobbesian scenario of a perpetual war of all against all. In Vattel's analysis, interstate relations are governed by a natural law which obligates all states to respect each other's Rights. 'From this indispensable obligation ... results the right of every state not to suffer any of her Rights to be taken away, or any thing which lawfully belongs to her' writes Vattel (1863, p. 160) in book II of his *Droit des Gens*. This right is fundamental; 'that is to say, it is accompanied with the right of using force in order to assert it'. And from this right arise two corollaries:

> First, the right of a just defence, which belongs to every nation – or the right of making use of force against whoever attacks her and her Rights. This is the foundation of defensive war. Secondly, the right to obtain justice by force, if we cannot obtain it otherwise, or to pursue our right by force of arms. This is the foundation of offensive war. (p. 161)

Vattel repeats an ancient proposition when he notes that states have a natural right to wage defensive war – that if one state should violate the Rights of another, then the offended state would have the right to protect itself by armed force. Also, he echoes an old argument when he claims that states, under certain circumstances have a right to wage an offensive war. But he gave this old 'just-war' argument an important (Lockean) formulation. By knowingly violating the Rights of another, an offensive state forfeits its own Rights. By 'trampling justice under foot', the offensive state sets itself outside the realm of natural law. In such cases, explains Vattel, any state may pursue and punish the offender. Then he adds, in an argument which amounts to nothing less than an early formulation of the idea of collective security:

> If there were a people who made open profession of trampling justice under foot, ... the interests of human society would authorize all the other nations to form a confederacy in order to humble and chastise the delinquents ... [I]f, by her constant maxims, and by the whole tenor of her conduct, a nation evidently proves herself to be actuated by that mischievous disposition, – if she regards no right sacred, – the safety of the human race requires that she should be repressed. To form and support an unjust pretension, is only doing an injury to the party whose interests are affected by that pretension; but, to despise justice in general, is doing an injury to all nations. (p. 161)

Speculation about interstate relations – national varieties

The basic unit of eighteenth-century international relations was the impenetrable, unitary, territorial state. States' interests, capabilities and power played as important a role for speculation about international relations as the concepts of velocity, mass and gravity played in Newtonian physics. And the conception of a natural balance between states of unequal capabilities provided the foundation for early eighteenth-century theories of international relations. This idea is present in the balance-of-power theories of the period. It is also evident in the century's theories of international economics, most of which were variations on the theme of a balance of trade.

Both political and economic speculations hinged on the mechanical assumption that power and wealth exist as fixed quantities: when one country increases its share, other countries suffer a corresponding loss. The Newtonian themes of mechanics and equilibrium dominated the century, and were extended to new levels of analysis. The empirical orientation – with its mechanical logic, its demand for parsimony, its vision of equilibrium and its individualist theories of sense perception – was soon applied to domestic and international politics alike. And as it was extended from political relations among states to economic relations within states, new arguments would emerge and undermine the old, dominant balance-of-power model. This development is apparent among British social theorists.

British theories – transparency and balance
In his struggle against the Louis XIV, the Dutch Prince William of Orange developed arguments of containment and balance. When he became King of England in 1689, concerns of equilibrium were discussed in British circles as well. Around 1700 Charles Davenant, a Tory Member of Parliament, wrote essays on both the 'balance of trade' and on the 'balance of power' (Davenant 1701). So did Daniel Defoe (1660–1731).

Although Defoe is best known for his fiction, he was also a businessman and an astute political essayist who published regular commentaries on world politics in his journal *Review* (Roosen 1986). In 1709 he discussed the war against Louis XIV in balance-of-power terms. He observed that, although the balance of power was 'something we have made much ado about in the World', it was still 'little understood' (Defoe 1938, p. 263). Later he would devote many pages of his *Review* to the European balance, but without producing convincing elucidation as to its basic principles.

When Louis XIV finally admitted defeat in 1713, the notion of equilibrium became an important issue at the peace negotiations and was also reflected in the peace Treaty of Utrecht, which specified that the new European order should be based on an equilibrium of power. Henry St John (later Viscount Bolingbroke, 1678–1751) had been Secretary of War under Queen Anne and chief architect of the Peace of Utrecht. When he retired and wrote his *Letters on the Study and Use of History* [1738], notions of equilibrium intrude upon his discussions of European affairs. But he, like Defoe, seemed to take the notion of equilibrium for granted; he made no attempt to account for the workings of the balance-of-power principle.

Among the most famous applications of the Newtonian principle of balance to international affairs were made by David Hume (1711–76) and Adam Smith (1723–90). In his essay 'Of the Balance of Power' [1752] Hume applied the Newtonian notion of equilibrium to interstate affairs. His formidable *History of England* [1754–62] includes references to how English monarchs relied on balance-of-power politics in their dealings with Continental powers. In his economic essays, such as 'Of the balance of trade', Hume applied the notion of equilibrium to questions of international trade. Hume's discussions influenced his good friend Adam Smith, who greatly expanded upon Hume's reflections in a much admired and most influential book: *The Wealth of Nations* [1776].

English radicals like Thomas Paine (1737–1809) and William Godwin (1756–1836) begged to differ. They criticized the notions of balance of power. Their writings reached a wide audience and were extremely influential. Their many essays, pamphlets, feuilletons, notes and letters discussed war, wealth, peace and power, and their various discussions add up to a progressive view of world affairs which differed sharply from the more established views of the age. Neither Paine nor Godwin invested any credence in the balance-of-power principle which other authors hailed as a guarantee for international order and stability. Paine (1908a) argued that royal manoeuvrings achieved little else than to extend 'the spirit of duelling' to an international scale. And Godwin very much doubted that there was any substance at all behind the notion of an interstate balance: 'The pretense of the balance of power has, in a multitude of instances, served as a veil to the intrigue of courts', he claims (Godwin 1985, p. 516).

Paine and Godwin both saw international politics largely as an activity of kings. They also saw royal activities as the key cause of international conflict and war. They claimed that the royal courts always 'opened a door to the foolish, the wicked, and the improper'. Kings surround themselves with a court of fawning ministers and secretaries – 'voluntary prostitutes' Godwin (1985, p. 435) called them. Members of the royal entourage play games of deception and power among themselves and against foreign rivals. And in the process they produce injustices, conflicts and wars for the whole world. The kings of Europe 'are like individuals in the state of nature', argued Paine (1908b, p. 236; Keane 1996, p. 230) in 'Letter to the Abbé Raynal'. And if people should have any hope of changing this sad predicament and establish peaceful relations among states, then the corrupt royal courts must be removed from the states of Europe and replaced with democratic systems of government (Paine 1969, p. 183).

Paine and Godwin also agreed on another point: that, whereas monarchies and aristocracies are aggressive and warlike by nature, democracies are peaceful. Thus, in order to solve the problems of international conflict and war, it is necessary to first wrest power from the many incompetent, self-seeking and capricious monarchs of the world, and establish democratic states in their stead. 'When all governments of Europe shall be established on the representative system, nations will become acquainted, and the animosities and prejudices fomented by the intrigue and artifice of courts, will cease', argued Paine (1995, p. 321). Social transparency and open enquiry in all matters are essential to democracy, he maintained. On the one hand, trade encourages peaceful relationships within and among nations – first, because trade increases understanding of foreign lands and peoples; and, second, as the value of international increases, so will the motivation to avoid wars that may disrupt them (Paine 1969, pp. 233ff). On the other, open enquiry in matters political and economic would make common people realize that they have little or nothing to gain by war. Kings and courtiers may believe that war is a glorious and profitable venture; however, common people know that wars bring death and destruction and that, ultimately, it is they who will have to pay their cost in blood and taxes, so they will strive to avoid it (Keane 1996, pp. 296ff). Godwin agreed that 'war will be foreign to the character of any people in proportion as their democracy becomes simple and unalloyed' (Godwin 1985, p. 507).

French theorists – mechanical equilibrium

The many brilliant theorists of Enlightenment Europe make it difficult to select a single writer to represent the International Relations theory of the age. Even the shortest list of authors who might be considered 'the voice of the eighteenth century' must include William Godwin. He was one of the most original and influential thinkers of the age. But Godwin stood on the shoulders of giants. Most of his heroes were French. France, too, applied balance-of-power theory to practical politics. It is quietly assumed in Louis XIV's *Memoirs for the Instruction of the Dauphin* [1668], in François de Callières's (1645–1717) famous text on *The Art of Diplomacy* [1716] and in Abbé de Mably's *Public Right of Europe* [1747], among others. It is explicitly evaluated by François Fénelon (1815, pp. 766ff), who sought to base it on principles of natural law. It is criticized by Baron Montesquieu (1689–1755) and others, who fear that stability may be purchased at the cost of an arms race – that as soon as one king augments his military forces in the name of peace and stability, 'the others suddenly increase, so that nothing is gained thereby but the public ruin' (Montesquieu 1990, p. 224).

Montesquieu made spectacular contributions to the political theories of the Enlightenment, and the twin themes of mechanics and equilibrium, which marked his age, are apparent in his famous *Spirit of the Laws* (1990 [1748]). Although Montesquieu does not explicitly address international politics, he made spectacular contributions to the study of International Relations. First, because other authors allowed his general arguments to illuminate their analyses of interstate relations. Antoine Pecquet is an important case in point. His *Spirit of Political Maxims* [1757] was an analysis of international politics pretentiously conceived as a sequel to Montesquieu's masterpiece. And although Pecquet falls short of this ultimate ambition, he nevertheless provides a masterful discussion of 'the Equilibrium of Europe' – chapter 12 (pp. 191–207) of Pecquet's 1757 book, for example, rivals any of the best analyses written in English.

Also, Montesquieu often drew learned connections between international issues and the study of law, government, economics, history and so on. One such connection is his claim that war is associated with regime type. 'The spirit of monarchy is war and expansion; the spirit of republics is peace and moderation', writes Montesquieu (1990, p. 132). His argument is that monarchies are driven to conquest by their very nature. Republics, on the other hand, are largely preoccupied with defending themselves. And if the republics are small, Montesquieu continues, they cannot defend themselves without alliances; and since monarchies are expansionist, small republics must seek protection through alliances with other republics (1990, pp. 60ff). This line of reasoning adumbrates a point which is later elaborated by others: that from relations among popularly governed states a peaceful international community can be constructed.

Montesquieu draws a related connection between republics, peace and commerce. 'The natural effect of commerce is to lead to peace', he submits on one occasion. (p. 338). 'Two nations that trade with each other become reciprocally dependent', he continues. The logic which underlies this claim is that commerce has an enlightening effect on those who engage in it. Commerce spreads knowledge. It deepens insight into other peoples' customs and mores. It increases understanding and diminishes fear of others. 'Commerce has spread knowledge of the mores of all nations everywhere; they have been compared to each other, and good things have resulted from this.' Commerce cultivates tolerance by diluting 'destructive prejudices', and this encourages peaceful international relations.[3]

A third connection is drawn by Montesquieu from monarchies and war to slavery and colonialism. He notes that the quest for security which drives monarchies towards expansion and conquest in Europe also applies to their behaviour in the extra-European world. He notes how the Spaniards arrived in the Americas, declared war on the natives and enslaved them. He also notes how the Europeans exterminated the native Americans but found new slaves in Africa so that they could clear land, establish plantations and supply Europe with sugar (p. 250).

137

This distinction between masters and slaves which is found in Montesquieu's political discussions is paralleled by a distinction between northern and southern nations which is drawn in his economic discussions: the nations of the North have 'many needs and few comforts of life', whereas those of the South have 'all sorts of comforts of life and very few needs'. Peoples of the North are obliged to work hard, lest 'they should lack everything and become barbarians'; peoples of the South, by contrast, have developed a lazy disposition, argues Montesquieu (1990, p. 355). These differences in industry have political consequences, for the nations of the South remain poor and weak and easily fall under the domination of the more entrepreneurial nations of the North. Montesquieu concludes with a sweeping, macro-historical claim:

> What has naturalized servitude among the southern peoples is that, as they can easily do without wealth, they can do even better without liberty. But the northern peoples need liberty, which procures for them more of the means of satisfying all the needs nature has given them. The northern peoples are, therefore, in a forced state unless they are either free or barbarians; almost all the southern peoples are, in some fashion, in a violent state unless they are slaves. (1990, p. 355)

Many of Montesquieu's ideas reverberated through French discussions of international politics for the remainder of the century.[4] The idea which associates monarchy with war was revolutionary in its implications: if monarchs cause war, then peace can be achieved by replacing monarchies with democratic republics. Voltaire (1694–1778) drew the revolutionary implications of the argument quite explicitly. He includes war, along with pestilence and famine, as among the worst scourges of humanity, and blames them on 'the imagination of three or four hundred persons scattered over the surface of the globe under the name of princes and ministers'. Voltaire, then, stripped the rhetoric of monarchs of pretence and patriotism and disclosed eighteenth-century wars for what they were: dynastic squabbles (Voltaire 1967). Voltaire's discussions on international politics constitute a tiny part of his prolific production. But his opinions on war and peace are unmistakable and firm, and reverberate with the revolutionary arguments of Montesquieu.

On the belligerency of autocracy and on democratic peace
Montesquieu's influence transcended France. He wrote within a long republican tradition with roots in classical thinkers like Aristotle and in Renaissance authors like Machiavelli. This tradition had long fed anti-monarchic and revolutionary arguments in Britain. Atlantic radicals like William Godwin and Thomas Paine grafted a new branch on to its trunk. First, they broke with the habit of Continental thinkers who retained old notion of 'Republic' when they discussed governments based on popular sovereignty: Paine and Godwin instead began to use the more radical and revolutionary term 'Democracy'. And they argued that democracies were peaceful states – in contrast to monarchies, which were warlike.

William Godwin distinguished himself in another respect as well. He observed the international scene carefully and noted that states which entertained a measure of popular sovereignty did not in fact seem to be less belligerent than monarchies. He pondered this observation carefully, and concluded by elaborating upon an argument which Paine had already foreshadowed (Paine 1908b, p. 219; 1969, p. 174): namely, that in practice it will be difficult to observe directly the peaceful nature of democracies, because democracies will be in regular conflict with non-democracies. Consequently, the peaceful nature of democracies would be apparent in cases where democratic states shared common boundaries. From this simple observation, Godwin derived two important implications. First, that the peaceful nature of democracies can be observed only in democracies' behaviour towards one another.[5] Second, that several adjacent democracies in the world would constitute a zone of peace in the international community.

German theorists – idealists and organizers
In Britain and France Enlightenment theories triggered social revolutions. In Germany they sparked elaborate speculations. The key ideas of the Enlightenment never struck root in Germany; they were discussed, but in a socio-political vacuum. Germany was fragmented into hundreds of tiny states and principalities. Apart from Prussia, which was ruled by the iron-fisted Frederick the Great, there existed no central government as in Paris or London; the middle class was small and powerless; political reform was unthinkable. The British extracted from the Enlightenment ideas, political agendas and practical hard-headed demands for social change. The Germans extracted from the Enlightenment abstract ideas and universal (or cosmopolitan) formulations. Theirs was an Enlightenment of the spirit only.

German International Relations theorizing reflects this stark duality: the discussions were either abstractly idealistic or highly practical. This duality is evident in a little book written by Crown Prince Frederick (later Frederick II) of Prussia: *Anti-Machiavel* (1981 [1740]). In this curious little volume on statesmanship, Frederick musters the major authorities of the Enlightenment to refute the pernicious doctrines set out in Machiavelli's *The Prince*. On one level, *Anti-Machiavel* is a seductively simple book; its intended message is clear, and its composition is straightforward. 'I dare come to the defense of humanity against this monster who would destroy it,' writes the young crown prince. 'I dare to oppose reason and justice to iniquity and crime, and I have ventured my reflections on Machiavelli's *Prince* following each chapter, so that the antidote may be found right next to the poison' (Frederick II 1981, p. 31).

On another level, *Anti-Machiavel* is a complex and enigmatic articulation of the contradictions which tormented Enlightenment statesmen. The author appears caught in a dilemma between the Enlightenment theories that he professes (but which he may not accept) and the Machiavellian practices that he despises (but may not yet fully understand). In the end, he 'falls into considerably greater contradictions than those he claims to find in his *bête noire*, and utterly misses the glaring similarity between Machiavelli and himself' (Sonnino 1981, p. 15). Frederick wrote his treatise in 1740, upon considerable encouragement from Voltaire – and Voltaire's Enlightenment ideals are very much present in its pages.

It is worth noting that, when Frederick succeeded to the Prussian throne in 1740, inheriting one of the most centralized states and one of the most disciplined armies in Europe, he suddenly displayed a very different image. As King Frederick II, he was an enlightened monarch – he liberalized laws regarding censorship, religion and torture. But he was hardly an Enlightenment monarch. He was an absolutist ruler, and soon emerged as one of the most astute and unscrupulous princes of the age. He threw Europe into turmoil for more than two decades, exploited the political confusion in a series of brilliantly conceived stratagems and greatly enlarged Prussia's territories. Crown Prince Frederick became King Frederick 'the Great', a *Machtmensch* who made Prussia the foremost military power in eighteenth-century Europe – paving the way for German unification and dealing Europe's traditional balance of power its first major blow (Airas 1978, pp. 14ff). When he again found the time to write a book on statecraft, it was entitled *Military Instructions of the King of Prussia for His Generals*. This little volume – replete with information about the treatment of weapons, the training of horses and the organization of armies – is in essential respects similar to Machiavelli's *Art of War*. Frederick's *Politisches Testament* of 1768, however, is more similar to *The Prince*. This little book, which was intended as a 'foreign-policy handbook' for Frederick's successor, opens with the following bald claim: 'In international politics you should have no special predilections for one people, nor aversion to another. You must follow the interests of the state blindly, allying yourself with the power whose interests at the time match the interests of Prussia' (Luard 1992, p. 162). It then proceeds to discuss Prussia's position in European politics – in terms which would have earned him the most profound admiration of Machiavelli and Guicciardini:

> The greatest error one can fall into is to believe that kings and ministers are inter-ested in our fate. These people only love themselves; their own self-interest is their god. Their manner becomes flattering and insinuating only in so far as they have need of you. They will swear, with shameless falsehood, that your interests are as dear to them as their own. But do not believe them; block your ears to their siren calls. (p. 162)

This odd juxtaposition of aloofness and hard-headed practicality was hardly more interestingly expressed than in the international-relations theories of Immanuel Kant. On the face of it, his description of interstate relations is pessimistic. Kant writes about the readiness with which states go to war and how this 'is exhibited without disguise in the unrestrained relations of the Nations to each other'. He notes how war requires 'no special motive', 'how it appears to be ingrafted in human nature' (Kant 1970b, pp. 220f). However, below the surface of Kant's argument, there are echoes of Paine's optimism and veins of rich ore from which Kant mines one of the most idealistic doctrines in the tradition of International Relations theory: humanity also possesses reason; and, as human rationality inevitably evolves, all people will increasingly recognize the evils of international strife, and will work to put an end to all wars.

Kant recognized that a balance-of-power principle existed in interstate relations. However, he did not believe that it was based on any natural, self-equilibrating properties. 'A lasting Universal Peace on the basis of the so-called Balance of Power in Europe is a mere chimera', he argued. 'It is like the house which was built by an architect so perfectly in accordance with all the laws of equilibrium, that when a sparrow lighted upon it, it immediately fell' (1970b, p. 92). Consequently, he refused to accept the widely popular argument that some natural balance-of-power principle could be trusted to produce peace automatically through interstate equilibrium. Peace among states could only be established through human reason and political will.

Such a will would inevitably emerge as history unfolded, Kant continued. It would emerge not as the outcome of reason but as the result of a fear-induced logic of self-preservation. The progress of science would drive humanity to discover new and steadily more bestial weapons and more efficient form of war. In the long run, Kant concluded, Eternal Peace is inevitable. Either it would come about because the evolution of steadily more destructive weapons systems would obliterate the human race in the end; this would produce the kind of perpetual peace one would find a graveyard (Kant 1970b, p. 200). Or peace would come about because the ever-increasing levels of destruction would force humanity to stop in time and accept the futility of war. Deterred by the growth of their own destructive capabilities, statesmen would realize the pressing need to abolish war and to establish a federation of republics in order to keep peace (Kant 1970a, p. 198).

A peaceful federation could be established from a common recognition that all nations share the same sense of justice, argued Kant.[6] When events in America produced such an actual federation, Kant followed the process with interest. However, he did not praise the final result.

American theorists – contract and federation

The American events were set in motion by a deteriorating relationship between England and her colonies along North America's east coast. The colonists felt unfairly treated and argued that they had always done their duty and paid taxes to the English king, whereas the king had not kept his part of the bargain; he had not consulted them before deciding on colonial matters. The king had, in short, violated the rights of English citizens in America.

It was, in essence, a contract-theoretical argument. Several American thinkers elaborated upon it. One of the more influential of the elaborators was Thomas Paine. He had left his native England in 1774 to seek his fortune in America. He arrived in Philadelphia just as the English government decided to clamp down on the American protests; a decision that caused the colonial unrest to flare up in open rebellion. Paine landed a job as assistant editor in the *Pennsylvania Magazine*. He contributed inflammatory essays and commentaries to the debate. The American colonies should not just revolt against taxes unjustly imposed, he argued; they should demand full independence. The English king had broken the terms of the colonial contract and the colonies should in return declare that their duties to the

English Crown had come to an end! Paine published his argument in January 1776 in a thick pamphlet entitled *Common Sense*. Within a few months it sold more than five hundred thousand copies and made its author famous.

Paine was not alone in formulating such a contractarian argument. Later that year it was embraced by the congress of delegates from all thirteen American colonies that had gathered in Philadelphia. Paine was, however, one of the few commentators who also explored the consequences of the argument. He explained that the British government was likely to refuse any demand of American independence. In fact, Britain was likely to respond with armed force. Consequently, the Americans would gain independence only by preparing a more powerful force and defeating the English in battle. This would be a tall order, he continued. It would require the Americans to make costly military preparations – the colonists would have to enrol as soldiers in a new, American army and pay taxes to finance it. Also, the Americans could not do this without assistance from England's enemies in Europe, in particular from France.[7]

In the summer of 1776 the congress of delegates met in Philadelphia and decided to declare all English colonies in America independent states. The congress selected Thomas Jefferson to formulate a 'Declaration of Independence'. The colonies 'are, and of Right ought to be, Free and Independent States', Jefferson began. The colonies, he continued,

> are Absolved from all Allegiance to the British Crown, and … all political connection between them and the State of Great Britain, is and ought to be totally dissolved; and … as Free and Independent States, they have full Power to levy War, conclude Peace, contract Alliances, establish Commerce, and to do all other Acts and Things which Independent States may of right do.

The British Parliament perceived the American declaration as an affront to the nation and the English king. They rejected it out of hand and sent soldiers to the colonies to impose the king's authority with military force – as Paine had predicted. The colonists, however, raised armies of their own. During the course of this effort, they developed institutions of finance, command and governance. They organized recruitment drives to provide soldiers, established fiscal institutions to finance them and erected organizations to co-ordinate all thirteen colonies in a common political effort. They sent diplomats abroad, like Benjamin Franklin, to solicit support with the royal courts of Europe. Under the leadership of George Washington, and with economic and military aid from France, the American army resisted the English imposition for four years of war. In 1781 they succeeded in defeating the English.

It is hard to win a war. It is harder still to build a nation. The United States of America did not flow effortlessly from victory in the War of Independence. When the English soldiers withdrew, the thirteen American colonies became, in fact, so many sovereign entities. Each adopted a republican constitutions and celebrated its independence. General Washington had mixed feeling about this and cautioned against excessive rejoicing. If each of the thirteen ex-colonies began to celebrate its independent status and cultivate its sovereignty, they could easily trigger jealousy and strife.

Alexander Hamilton, Washington's chief of staff, put the point in stronger words. He noted that Europe's imperial powers still had a strong presence in America – English troops were gathered in Canada, France owned enormous territories west of the Mississippi, Spain controlled vast lands along North America's Pacific coast. Hamilton summarized the strategic situation succinctly. The thirteen newly independent states – strung along America's eastern coast from Massachusetts in the north to Georgia in the south – were surrounded by European powers on three sides, in the north, the south and the west. It was imperative that the American states stick closely together.

Hamilton boosted his claim by invoking Thucydides' argument about how independent states tend to fear each other – either because each state seeks to ensure its own safety and thereby frighten others, or because of commercial rivalries, or else because their leaders are driven by petty passions. 'A man must be far gone in Utopian speculations', Hamilton (1987, p. 104) commented, if he can seriously believe that the newly independent American state is an exception to this general rule. If the ex-colonial states began to cultivate their own sovereignty, they would also begin to fear each other. They would take measures to defend themselves. Soon, they would have recreated a European-style system of interstate competition.

The ex-colonies would, in effect, have reconstituted the balance-of-power system of the Old World on the soil of the New. And since Europe's great colonial powers were located around its edges, they would be free to participate in this game of power. They would be ready to fuel any fear and to swoop in and pick up the pieces of any quarrel and then add them to their own respective empires. Under these conditions the Americans had no choice but to pull together. But, Hamilton concluded, they must not only form an alliance against a common European threat, they must avoid the old balance-of-power game altogether. They must form a permanent federation of states.

Hamilton's proposal triggered a huge debate. It was this debate, rather than the victory in the War of Independence, which marked the beginning of the real work of American nationbuilding. The victory created thirteen sovereign states and set in motion rivalries that began to pull them apart. The debate enabled four men of genius – Washington, Hamilton, Madison and Jay – to stem these centrifugal forces (Ellis 2015). In 1787, just as a new congress of state representatives gathered in Philadelphia, Hamilton together with James Madison and John Jay wrote a series of articles for various New York papers, arguing for a federation of American states. All three authors used the same pen-name, 'Publius'. Their articles, eighty-five in number, were quickly collected in a single volume and published as *The Federalist*. Theirs was a struggle against long odds, for mistrust of centralized authority was at the heart of the American Revolution. Yet, they triumphed in the end. They established a federation. And they forged a new nation out of an inchoate mass of immigrants.

The book has long been lauded as a classic in political theory. It also deserves to be hailed as an important contribution to International Relations theory. The basic assumption of *The Federalist* was that war broke down political order and society reverts to a state of nature. It would then be necessary to draw up a new social contract. The question which lay at the core of *The Federalist* was this: what kind of contract should the Americans establish after their War of Independence? The articles in *The Federalist* papers added up to a unique answer. Also, they offered an important contribution to the old discussion of the causes of war and, most particularly, of the preconditions for peace (Deudney 2007).

The diagnosis of *The Federalist* was old. And Alexander Hamilton relied on arguments that could have been taken from Hobbes or Spinoza. His analysis was dark and pessimistic and very different from the bright prewar optimism of Paine and Jefferson. The prognosis of *The Federalist* was also old. It found the main cause of war in the sovereign nature of states. And if sovereignty was the problem, then the solution was for each sovereign actor to give up its sovereignty and invest it in a common, central power.

The conversion of this general answer into political practice, however, was unprecedented and revolutionary. The details were specified first and foremost by James Madison. He was no utopian and saw an obvious danger in handing sovereignty over to a central power: it might create an all-powerful state – a Hobbesian *Leviathan*.[8] Madison tried to solve the problem by a complicated theory of multiple contracts. First, each sovereign actor gave up only some of its sovereignty – just enough for the state to be able to protect the rights of each individual. Second, the contract were to be applied to two levels of government – not only would every individual American hand over some of their sovereignty to a local government, each local government would also invest a portion of its sovereignty in a higher, federal power. Third, the federal power would be divided into three specialized branches – an executive, a legislative and a judicial branch – and each branch would be made to counterbalance the other two. The end result, accepted at a Constitutional Congress in 1787, was an intricate system of checks and balances.

The American Revolution met with mixed reactions from European observers. Some considered it a mad experiment and did not expect it to last long. The Americans had not understood the first thing about sovereignty, they argued; the American constitution was a flagrant violation of the most basic proposition that sovereignty is indivisible (Bodin 1967). Other Europeans received the American ideas with enthusiasm. They praised the anti-monarchic notion of equality in the *Declaration of Independence*. They applauded the republican principles of government inherent in the American Constitution. In England the American ideals of a government based on citizens' rights became riotously popular. Even MPs defended them openly – such as Edmund Burke. In France the American Revolution fuelled Parisian debates on human rights and criticism of the monarchy. In June 1789, radical members of the *parlement* in Paris broke out and set themselves up as a Constitutional Assembly for all of France. When popular masses of Paris took to arms, attacked the Bastille and released its prisoners, Thomas Paine travelled to

Paris to play a part in the events. He saw the French rebellion as a continuation of the American Revolution. And he wrote a book, *The Rights of Man* [1791], to argue the point.

Edmund Burke disagreed strongly with Paine. The American Revolution had been an uprising to defend traditional rights and English liberties, Burke maintained. He saw the French upheaval as very different: It was based on a deeply misguided political philosophy. It invoked universal principles which were little but 'cant and gibberish'. It wanted to abolish private property and the natural solidarity of the Christian kingdom of France. The result, Burke (1988 [1790]) predicted, would be mob rule and collapse of social order. Descent into further chaos could only be interrupted by the intervention of a strong ordering force, he continued – for example, with the rise of a general who could impose military rule on the wayward nation.

What was it that made Burke so upset? One irritant was the revolutionary romanticism of Thomas Paine. Another was the political philosophy of Jean-Jacques Rousseau – whom Burke mockingly referred to as 'the mad Socrates'. Thus, it is to Rousseau that we turn next. He provided central ideas which drove the French revolution in a radical direction. Also, Rousseau's arguments transcended France and affected the entire European Enlightenment. Few authors were more important champions of justice, rights and republicanism than him. And few thinkers have provided more penetrating analyses of the international situation. Rousseau can, in fact, be said to provide the main impulses behind a long and radical tradition in modern international analysis. He deserves a thorough exploration.

Rousseau: prophet and paradox

Jean-Jacques Rousseau (1712–78) is an apt representative of this rich and complex century. He wrote on astonishingly varied themes – including novels, operas and beautiful essays on botany. His analyses of international politics amount to only a minor part of his production. But what a part! He wrote on peace, justice and constitutional reform. He discussed colonialism and wars of liberation (Knutsen 1994). And always from a unique, sceptical perspective and with a penetration which singles him out as perhaps the major contributor to International Relations theory of this Age of Enlightenment.

Always a champion of individual freedom and self-reliance, Rousseau was a delinquent youth. He ran away from home several times, and periodically led the unsettled life of a penniless wanderer. He tramped around southern Europe and earned his living as a tutor of music, a copyist, a writer of operas, a confidence trickster and a secretary to the French ambassador in Venice. At the age of sixteen, he encountered Mme de Warens at Annecy in Savoy. She would play for him the role of the mother he had never had. She would also become his protector, his teacher and his mistress (Cranston 1991).

Rousseau's first major essay, *Discourse on the Arts and Sciences* [1749], won first prize in a competition announced by the Academy of Dijon. Much encouraged by the prize, Rousseau launched a career as a writer. Within a dozen years he had written most of his major works, including the *Discourse on the Origin and Basis of Inequality among Men* (1950a [1755]) and the *Social Contract* (1950b [1762]). During the 1750s, Rousseau established himself as one of the first of the modern intellectuals – one of the first modern radicals and 'angry young men'. His penetrating intellect and his considerable charm earned him admirers all over Europe. His unorthodox clothing and his calculated scandals made him an object of gossip and the darling of the Parisian salons.

Although he died a decade before the French Revolution, many contemporaries held him responsible for it – indeed, this was one of the few things on which Louis XVI and Robespierre agreed. During the Revolution, the National Convention voted to have his ashes transferred to the Panthéon. In the decades which followed this transfer, public opinion grew increasingly divided on his place in history. He attained the status of a saint to some, and favourite villain to others. To Shelley he was 'a sublime genius'. To Schiller he was 'a Christ-like soul for whom only Heaven's angels are fit company'. People who had met him usually begged to differ. Diderot, after long acquaintance, characterized him as 'vain as Satan, ungrateful, cruel, hypocritical and full of malice' (Crocker 1974, Vol. I, p. 356). But on one point has there been full agreement: Rousseau was a momentous contributor to International Relations theory.

Saint-Pierre and Rousseau and war and peace

To put Rousseau's International Relations analysis into perspective, it is necessary to begin with Charles Castel, Abbé de Saint-Pierre (1658–1743). Like other peace projects of the age, Saint-Pierre's *Project for Making Peace Perpetual in Europe* of 1713 is founded on the Enlightenment anthropology that men are endowed with reason. He had studied Hobbes, and he found in Hobbes's description of the state of nature a powerful analogy to the condition of war which existed among states. His solution to the problem of war was similar to Hobbes's – except that whereas Hobbes wrote about all humanity, Saint-Pierre only wrote about princes. The rulers of Europe will sooner or later be forced by reason to realize that their interests are better served by peace and order than by war, he argued. This realization would drive them into closer co-operation and, finally, into a 'confederal government' – a council or diet on which the ruling princes of all member states would be represented.

Saint-Pierre was, like Crucé, an advocate of the integration of the states of Europe into a confederate union. He devised a variety of bureaux which should handle different matters of common interest to the member states; thus, one important bureau should work out a code of commercial law to regulate trade among subjects of different states; another should standardize weights, measures and the currency of the member states. Saint-Pierre was, like Crucé (and also like Montesquieu and other Enlightenment authors), preoccupied with the characteristic Enlightenment belief that trade furthers peace (Perkins 1959; Russell 1936, p. 191).

Saint-Pierre's simple, appealing and important message was obstructed by his unattractively repetitious and rhapsodic style. After Saint-Pierre's death, his friends and family searched for a sympathetic scholar who could make the Abbé's voluminous writings on war and peace accessible to the princes and peoples of Europe. In 1754, they asked Jean-Jacques Rousseau to edit and abridge Saint-Pierre's grand Project. This request would spark one of the most unique and penetrating analyses in the history of International Relations theory – although not necessarily one which met with the approval of the Abbé's heirs. The work kept Rousseau busy for several years. But it was never completed. He only finished a long introduction to the planned work. This was issued separately in 1760 as the *Project for a Perpetual Peace* (Hoffmann and Fidler 1991, p. xxii).

Rousseau was too impatient and imaginative to reproduce faithfully the thoughts of another man. His *Project* is a brilliant essay. But it contains more of Rousseau than of Saint-Pierre. Indeed Rousseau could scarcely hide his opinion that the Abbé's argument was 'superficial' and 'impractical owing to one idea from which the author could never escape: that men are motivated by their intelligence rather than by their passions' (Rousseau 1978, p. 393). He ends this abridgement, with the remark that the Abbé's case rests on the unproven assumption that kings have enough reason to see what is useful for society at large (1964a). He then wrote a detailed criticism in a separate commentary, *Judgment on Perpetual Peace* (1964b [1782]) – which he did not dare to publish.[9]

Where Hobbes, Crucé, Grotius, Hume, Kant, Voltaire and Saint-Pierre sought to reduce the dynamics of international politics to human nature, Rousseau introduces other elements as well. There is nothing inherent in human nature that predisposes people to aggression, Rousseau (1964c) claimed. People become fighters and warriors only when they are moved from the state of nature to civil society. War is a *social* undertaking; it is a product of human civilization. It is the *citizen* who is most eager to become a soldier, not the human being in a state of nature. Armies and wars do not exist until societies exist with states which organize their citizens into armies and march them off to further the interest of their rulers. At this point Rousseau is at odds with all other contract thinkers: for them, the social contract ends conflict among people; but for Rousseau it creates the preconditions for war.

Rousseau argued (like Locke) that human beings are endowed with natural reason and with a natural right to freedom; but he also claimed that, in actuality, humanity is enslaved. This apparent paradox appears in several of Rousseau's writings – most famously in the opening line of his *Social Contract*: 'Man is born free; and everywhere he is in chains' (Rousseau 1950b, p. 3). His major social treatises all address this apparent paradox of liberty and rationality on the one hand and enslavement on the other.

If people are rational, why aren't they capable of seeing that they are enslaved and exploited by the existing social order? Rousseau's answer is that humanity has been corrupted by this order. Society is corrupt, and as individuals are born into this corrupt society they become corrupted in turn. People, then, are malleable. They are shaped by the society they inhabit. If they are born into a good society, they will develop their reason and become good people; if they are born into a corrupt society, their reason will be stunted and warped and their natural liberty will be replaced with vanity, contempt, shame and envy. In a corrupt society, in short, people will be alienated from their original liberty, happiness and innocence.

Two important corollaries flow from this line of reasoning. First, the corruption and alienation of humanity cannot be explained as an outcome of human nature; it must be explained as a result of an intolerable social situation. Second, humanity is rational, but only potentially so. People are not born with reason; they *develop* reason.

This raises another question: if people were originally free, good, happy and innocent, how did society come to be so corrupt? Rousseau's answer to this question hinges on two intimately intertwined components: a historical analysis and a theory of a division of labour.

Evolution of the state: the loss of natural innocence
Rousseau's account of the historical evolution of civil society provides a convenient entry into his International Relations theory. This account describes an evolution which has alienated people from their original free, happy and innocent selves. It is most clearly set out in *A Discourse on the Origin and Basis of Inequality among Men* (1950a [1755].) Like so many of his contemporaries, Rousseau, too, uses a state of nature as his vantage point. Before state and civil society existed, Rousseau claims, people lived in total freedom and innocence. He explains, with echoes of Erasmus (1964, pp. 311f): 'I see him satisfying his hunger at the first oak, and slaking his thirst at the first brook; finding his bed at the foot of the tree which afforded him a repast; and, with that, all his wants are supplied' (Rousseau 1950a, p. 200).

From this initial condition of innocence, human history has been driven forward by an emerging division of labour. This division first evolved in response to demographic and geographic circumstances, Rousseau argues, and it removed humanity from its happy state of nature through stages of historical evolution.

In the initial stages, co-operation among people stimulated the growth of reason and language. People accumulated knowledge, and, the more they were enlightened, the more they improved their efficiency of production. Then, as industry improved, people developed a sense of the advantages of mutual undertakings. Instructed by experience, they learnt that love of one's own well-being is the most powerful motive of human action. So an individual grew selfish; but also learnt to acknowledge the selfishness in others, and to identify situations 'in which mutual interest might justify him in relying upon the assistance of his fellows'. So 'he joined in the same herd with them, or at most in some kind of loose association'. This was no lasting union, Rousseau, explains; it was strictly an *ad hoc* affair, for these individuals

> were perfect strangers to foresight, and were so far from troubling themselves about the distant future, that they hardly thought of the morrow. If a deer was to be taken, every one saw that, in order to succeed, he must abide faithfully by his post: but if a hare happened to come within the reach of any one of them, it is not to be doubted that he pursued it without scruple, and, having seized his prey, cared very little, if by so doing he caused his companions to miss theirs. (1950, p. 238)

In later stages of human development, people were more permanently united by communalities which had evolved among many of them: language, customs, common ways of living and eating. And as co-operation became more systematic, the division of labour became more formalized and human relationships became more governed by laws or involved work and responsibilities. A decisive stage was reached in human evolution when metallurgy was introduced. This meant that some people had to specialize in the smelting and forging of iron; and others had to provide food for them as well as for themselves. Because no one could survive without the others, work became compulsory.

Rousseau realized that, on the one hand, a social division of labour meant increased efficiency in production and the creation of wealth which made life more abundant and comfortable. But on the other hand, the division of labour also meant the advent of compulsory labour, civil obligations and the dependence of each upon everyone. The more Rousseau considered the notion of interdependence, the more he grew convinced that a conflict existed between affluence and freedom; and that social wealth was purchased at the cost of human liberty. As long as people were content with their rustic huts and their primitive clothes made from animal skins, they were happy and free; 'but from the moment one man began to stand in need of the help of another ... work became indispensable, and vast forests became smiling fields which man had to water with the sweat of his brow, where slavery and misery were soon seen to germinate and grow up with the crops' (1950a, pp. 243f). Matters developed rapidly for the worse when private property was introduced:

> The first man who, having enclosed a piece of ground, bethought himself of saying 'This is mine,' and found people simple enough to believe him, was the real founder of civil society. From how many crimes, wars and murders, from how many horrors and misfortunes might not any one have saved mankind, by pulling up the stakes, or filling up the ditch, and crying to his fellows: 'Beware of listening to this impostor; you are undone if you once forget that the fruits of the earth belong to all of us, and the earth itself to nobody!' (1950a, pp. 234f)

On this paragraph, undergirded by a vision of historical evolution and a theory of a division of labour, hinges Rousseau's vision of international politics.

The international system: 'the law of the strongest'
The social division of labour enhanced the material well-being of humanity. However, it also created conflict and inequality. It robbed all the individual participants of their natural liberty. This signalled a fatal turn of events in human history. As humanity evolved, social interdependence was exacerbated by private property, which released an insatiable quest in humankind for selfish economic advantages. 'Those who have nothing have limited desires, those who do not rule have limited ambitions', Rousseau writes. However, as society evolves, it imposes upon humanity both property and responsibilities. Material possessions have their own needs, the satisfaction of which stimulates the quest for more possessions and awakens

the vanity and cupidity of humankind. 'The more one has, the more one wants. Whoever has much wants everything', writes Rousseau (1964c, p. 610).

Ever since the advent of private property, all human qualities have been tainted with a possessive element – infusing strength with a tinge of vanity, skill with competitiveness, love with jealousy. This development has robbed people of their ability to distinguish between good and evil, between real and apparent interest. History testifies to how the advent of property exacerbated the inequalities which nature had placed in humankind, rendering them more clearly seen and more deeply felt. It shows how the gap between the haves and the have-nots has widened. In the midst of growing misery and strife and the further weakening of the weak, humanity was driven to develop social hierarchies and orders (Rousseau 1950a, p. 244).

Finally, humanity developed political institutions backed by law. These institutions consolidated the principle of private property, sanctioned social inequality, protected the wealth and the power of the ruling elite, oppressed the poor majority of humankind and alienated them all in the process.

The foundation of the commonwealth marks the final stage of a long historical process. The commonwealth imposes order upon the anarchy among individuals. However, the same act which solves the problem of anarchy among individuals creates a condition of anarchy among states. In Rousseau's mind, humanity has left one state of nature, characterized by liberty and peace, and entered another state of nature, marked by oppression and war. It is not difficult to see

> that each of us is in the civil state with regard to our fellow citizens, but in the state of nature as regards the rest of the world; that we have taken all kinds of precautions against private wars only to kindle national wars which are a thousand times more terrible; that in joining a particular group of men, we have in reality become the enemy of mankind. (Rousseau 1964a, p. 654)

Out of his depiction of rulers' greed and citizens' misery and everyone's alienation, Rousseau formulates a vision whose nightmarish qualities rival even those of Hobbes's state of nature. The rulers are greedy and animated solely by two desires: to extend their territorial power and to achieve a more absolute rule over their subjects. The citizens are alienated, and enthusiastically contribute money and men to support wars of conquest and the subjection of conquered peoples; and they do not realize that they thereby deepen their own misery. Rulers' greed and citizens' alienation feed on each other.

> Anyone can understand that war and conquest without and the encroachments of despotism within give each other mutual support; that money and men are habitually taken at pleasure from a people of slaves, to bring others beneath the same yoke; and that conversely war furnishes a pretext for exactions of money and … for keeping large armies constantly on foot, to hold the people in awe. In a word, anyone can see that aggressive princes wage war at least as much on their subjects as on their enemies, and that the conquering nation is left no better off than the conquered. (Rousseau 1964b, p. 592)

Rousseau depicts domestic society in gloomy terms, but his vision of international society is far bleaker. For whereas civil society at least is regulated by law (albeit the law of the ruling elite), the society of states, in effect, obeys no law but 'the law of the strongest' (Rousseau 1964d, p. 1013). In his description of this 'law', Rousseau is true to the sentiment of the age: he describes it in explicit, balance-of-power terms, and he does this with a sophistication and a concreteness which was scarcely superseded by other eighteenth-century authors.

In his *Project for a Perpetual Peace* (1964a [1760]), Rousseau introduces a discussion of the European balance of power by a description of Europe's cultural geography. 'The powers of Europe constitute a kind of system, united by the same religion, international law and moral standards; by letters, by commerce and by a kind of equilibrium which is the inevitable outcome of all these ties' (1964a, p. 565). This equilibrium is in Rousseau's mind more a product of nature than the work of any human hand. 'The lie of the mountains, seas, and rivers which serve as frontiers for the various nations who inhabit it, seems to have fixed forever their number and their size' (p. 570). This equilibrium brings a semblance of order to the relations between European states, Rousseau explains. And although the rulers of individual states always act to extend their dominions, the balance still obtains. 'It is there; and men who do not feel themselves strong enough to break it conceal the selfishness of their designs under the pretext of preserving it' (p. 570). Rousseau articulates the sentiment of the age when he depicts the European balance of power as self-equilibrating:

> Whether we are aware of it or not, the equilibrium continues to support itself without the aid of any special intervention. If it breaks for a moment on one side, it soon restores itself on another; so that, if princes who are accused of aspiring to universal monarchy were in reality guilty of any such venture, they displayed more evidence of ambition than of genius. How could any man look such a project in the face without instantly perceiving its absurdity? without realizing that there is not a single potentate in Europe so much stronger than the others as ever to have a chance of making himself their master. (p. 570)

This self-sustaining balance prevents any one state from attaining mastery over all Europe. For whenever a ruler seeks to extend his country's territory by military means, other rulers will unite against him at every step. Every once in a while, a ruler may be lucky, and conquer an uncommonly large territory. However, Rousseau writes, even such lucky breaks are bound to fail over the longer haul: 'the resistance is in the long run as strong as the attack; and time soon repairs the sudden accidents of fortune, if not for each prince individually, at least for the general balance of the whole' (p. 571).

This self-regulating balance of power imposes a principle of order on the interaction between states. But it does not bring peace. Although the European balance of power blocks major conquests over the longer haul, in day-to-day politics it merely perpetuates instability and irritation. Indeed, Europe is plagued by perpetual conflict – quarrels, robberies, usurpations, revolts and wars 'which bring daily desolation to this venerable home of philosophy, this brilliant sanctuary of art and science' (p. 568).

The integration of the states of Europe has made the continent wealthier than other regions of the world and forged a historic 'fellowship far closer than is found elsewhere'. However, since their cruel conflicts occur not in spite of interdependence but *because* of it, tighter integration only renders these plagues and conflicts more frequent, more intense and more deadly. Explains Rousseau:

> The historic union of the nations of Europe has entangled their rights and interests in a thousand complications; they touch each other at so many points that the smallest movement of one of them gives a jolt to all the rest; their differences are all the more deadly, as their ties are more intimately woven; their frequent quarrels are almost as savage as civil wars.
>
> Let us admit then that the powers of Europe stand to each other strictly in a state of war, and that all the separate treaties between them are in the nature rather of a temporary truce than a real peace. (p. 568)

The origins and nature of the state system

The 'law of the strongest' only partly accounts for the relative order of the European interstate system; balance-of-power dynamics only explains the mechanical workings of the system. In order to understand the origins of European politics, Rousseau adds a historical argument: the stability of the system hinges on historically formed preconditions which allow the balance-of-power dynamics to operate. Europe's interstate system is a temporal arrangement. It had a beginning, which can be distinctly determined by the historical formation of the preconditions upon which it depends – and consequently, it is likely to meet its historical end once these preconditions are removed.

The most important of these historical preconditions is the complex 'German Body', the Holy Roman Empire. Rousseau identifies several unique attributes which contribute to the stabilizing role of the German Empire. First, its geographical position; the German Body 'lies nearly at the centre of Europe and holds all the other parts in their place'. Second, its size; Germany covers a vast area and appears as 'a body formidable to all by its size and by the number and valour of its component peoples'. Third, its fragmented nature; Germany consists of over three hundred states, and constitutes an exceptionally complex and stable balance-of-power system in its own right. The constitution of the Holy Roman Empire, which deprived it 'both of the means and the will to conquer, makes it a rock on which all schemes of conquest are doomed infallibly to falter'. What Rousseau refers to as the 'constitution' of the German Body was established at the Peace of Westphalia (1648). Concludes Rousseau:

> In spite of all its defects, it is certain that, so long as that constitution endures, the equilibrium of Europe will never be broken; that no potentate need fear to be cast from his throne by any of its rivals; and that the Treaty of Westphalia will perhaps forever remain the foundation of our international system. (p. 572)

By identifying the Treaty of Westphalia as 'the foundation of our international system', Rousseau pinpoints the fountainhead of Europe's interstate order: the general acceptance of the principle of the sovereignty of states. The Treaty of Westphalia recognized the right of princes to act solely on the calculus of their own interest. While the brute power of these rulers *within* states keeps in check greedy individuals, who are constantly at each other's throats in pursuit of their personal gains, the relations *among* states are characterized by permanent conflict, since there is no higher system to regulate their interaction.

If war is the product of interdependent relations among sovereign states, then war can be abolished by removing the states' sovereign attributes. Peace can be secured only if the states of Europe give up their sovereignty and invest it in a higher, federal body. War can be abolished if the states establish a social contract between them – that is, if they establish 'such a form of federal government as shall unite nations by bonds similar to those which already unite their individual members and place the one no less than the other under the authority of the law' (p. 564).

Virtually all social contract philosophers who have addressed questions of war and peace have arrived at this conclusion. Rousseau, however, is distinct in that he went further. Other Enlightenment thinkers built on the assumption that reason is a universal human property and that freedom and right are universal political values. Abbé Saint-Pierre, for example, argued that, since all possess the faculties of reason and all strive to realize their freedom and right, it should be possible to replicate the social contract established among individuals within a state and form another contract among states. Most particularly, this should be possible in Europe, whose states possess so many common traits in customs, religion, letters, language, laws and trade. This contract would remove the states from the bellicose state of nature in which they presently find themselves, and establish a world federation.

Rousseau did not disagree with this proposal. He did not doubt that, once it was implemented, the princes and peoples of Europe would immediately find its advantages 'immense, manifest, incontestable'. Realize 'this commonwealth of Europe for a single day', he wrote, 'and you may be sure that it will last forever; so fully would experience convince men that their own gain is to be found in the good of all' (1964b, p. 591). Rousseau did, however, protest at the proposal's basic assumption about human rationality. For him, humans are only *potentially* rational. *Actually* they are so alienated by the corrupt society they inhabit that they can no longer recognize their own best interests.

Saint-Pierre believed that, once the kings of Europe had considered his reasoned argument, they would agree to it. Rousseau doubts this – not because the Abbé's scheme is not good enough, but because it is so good and so sensible that alienated humanity 'will know no other way to react to it than with ridicule'. The Abbé's project will remain unrealized because the kings no longer know their true interest; they will not recognize a reasonable argument when they see one. Rather than follow the voice of reason, they will habitually act according to passion. In the corrupt environment of contemporary politics, alienation has robbed humanity of its ability to distinguish, 'in politics as in morals, between real and apparent

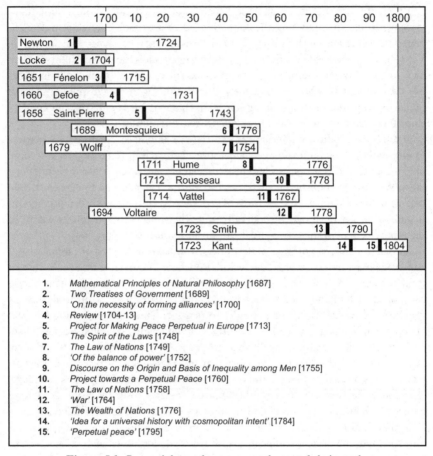

Figure 5.1 Some eighteenth-century authors and their works

interest' (p. 592). If the Abbé's project remains unrealized, 'it is not because it is utopian; it is because men are crazy, and to be sane in a world of madmen is itself a kind of madness' (1964a, p. 589).

In a world of alienated individuals, a federation of Europe would never come about through a spontaneous agreement. If it were to be established, this could be done only through force. A federation of Europe could be established only if one single state managed to conquer the entire continent militarily and rob all other important states of their sovereignty by the force of arms. Once this was achieved, the victor must replace these disparate sovereignties with a single, supranational legislative body with such immense powers that it could compel every other state to obey its common resolves.

To prove that this is not inconceivable, Rousseau recalls an earlier attempt to establish a lasting peace through a European federation. The French King Henry IV and his trusted minister, the Duc de Sully, had conceived of a plan for a Christian Commonwealth around the turn of the seventeenth century. They had made immense, protracted and detailed preparations to implement this plan when Henry IV was assassinated in 1610.

The Abbé de Saint-Pierre sought to revive the policy of Henry IV, and create a Christian Commonwealth through peaceful means, Rousseau argues. The Abbé, however, made two mistakes. First, he had no theory of alienation; he was therefore so naive as to believe that the kings of Europe would accept his proposal voluntarily. Second, he had no theory of history; he did not therefore realize that European politics has evolved since the times of Henry IV, and that the unification of Europe (admittedly through force), which was so close to success before Westphalia, would be met with failure after it.[10] Even if a strong ruler should emerge who understood the merits of the Abbé's proposal, who followed the example of Henry IV and who launched an effort to unify Europe through force, he would be defeated. He would be prevented by the balance-of-power principle which was consolidated at Westphalia in 1648. Instead of establishing a universal monarchy, he would – given the immensity of the force required to establish a federation of Europe and given the high likelihood of failure – launch a war of such unprecedented magnitude that Europe might be destroyed in the effort. Rousseau wonders, at the end 'whether the League of Europe is a thing more desired or feared? It would perhaps do more harm in the moment than it would guard against for ages' (1964b, p. 600).

The sentiment(s) of the century

During the seventeenth century, the natural world became an object systematically scrutinized by the human mind. Bacon, Galileo, Descartes, Hobbes and others had devised methods by which the world could be known and mastered. This 'scientific revolution' was the womb of the Enlightenment. The insights of seventeenth-century science were cultivated by eighteenth-century *philosophes*. They stressed the unlimited potentials of human reason (Kant 1949a). They were sceptical of tradition, confident in the powers of reason, convinced of the regularity of nature. They saw themselves no longer as servants and interpreters of the gods, but as challengers, even substitutes. Their heroes were Prometheus, who stole the celestial fire and brought it to earth, or Faust, who pursued knowledge, truth and power at the peril of his soul.

The spread of Enlightenment ideas was aided by technological and social innovations. New kinds of paper and advances in print technology, for example, made it easier and cheaper to produce books and pamphlets. Printed matter was produced at an increasing rate and spread all kinds of popular publications throughout society. Also, the age saw the advent of a new kind of author; the popular publicist who lived by his pen – Voltaire, Diderot and Rousseau in France; Swift, Defoe, Godwin and Hume in Britain. Some of them had big success and wielded great political impact, –like Thomas Paine, whose *Rights of Man* was an instant success. It was an immediate best-seller in England and America when it appeared in two parts in 1791 and 1792. Translations quickly appeared in French, German and Dutch

(Keane 1996, p. 305). Within its first year of publication hundreds of thousands of copies circulated throughout Europe in several languages (Walker 2000, p. 55).

The spread of Enlightenment ideas was also aided by the advent of new social institutions. In France, intellectuals and academics established the *salon* – an elitist forum for daring discussions, gossip and socializing. In Britain and the Netherlands there emerged pubs and clubs and coffee houses. In Scotland, there was a notable growth in scientific societies in the four ancient university towns of Glasgow, Aberdeen, St Andrews and Edinburgh. In contrast to Paris, where new ideas often sparked abstract quarrels and academic one-upmanship, Scotland provided an amiable and co-operative environment. New ideas were discussed in a pragmatic spirit. The discussions suited Scotland's religious tenor well. Newton's calculations of the heavenly bodies were not seen as a challenge to God; rather they were seen as confirming his wisdom and omnipotence. Thus, at the threshold to the eighteenth century, Scottish academics were studying Newton's *Principia mathematica* with reverence and gusto. They were also reading Locke's *Two Treatises of Government* and his *Essay Concerning Human Understanding*; all with a pragmatic eye towards how this could improve education, research and industry.

Scotland was deeply affected by the Enlightenment sentiment. During the second half of the eighteenth century Scottish universities excelled in the practical field of 'Natural Philosophy'. Also, they pioneered the discipline of 'Moral Philosophy' – which the influential Francis Hutcheson (1755) presented as a combination of ethics, jurisprudence, economics and politics.

Among Hutcheson's students at the University of Edinburg were David Hume and Adam Smith. They became close friends. They admired and affected one another and became influential representatives of 'the Scottish Enlightenment'. They admired French thinkers like Montesquieu and Voltaire. Hume had a high opinion of Rousseau. Smith was deeply influenced by Quesnay. Both were preoccupied with how a principle of equilibrium governed social relations wherever rational humans were allowed to act freely. However, the two authors left the actual mechanisms of equilibrium rather vague.

Smith, it is useful to recall, was professor in Moral Philosophy at the University of Glasgow and wrote two major books in the field. The first, *The Theory of Moral Sentiments* [1759], is an introduction to the subjects of ethics and jurisprudence and drew heavily on lectures from the first half of his Glasgow course on Moral Philosophy. The second, *The Wealth of Nations* [1776], is a discussion of economics and politics that greatly expanded upon the second part of his course. Both books present social order as the outcome of an 'invisible hand'. They must be read together. It wouldn't hurt if they were also read in combination with Hume's essays.

Hume was a publicist. He never held a teaching post but was an independent essayist and historian. He wrote essays which discussed the causes of social order, but never invoked God, natural law or an invisible hand. Rather, his arguments tend to be based on an idea of social evolution. He discussed the origin of government and of states, and the development of state relations. Inspired by Rousseau and Hutcheson, Hume argued that states are social formations which have evolved over time through human interaction. States maintain order among themselves. Diplomats regulate state interaction by developing rules of just conduct and by formalizing these rules into diplomatic codes and laws of nations. They also maintain order through policies based on the balance-of-power principle.[11]

Another Scottish contributor to late eighteenth-century international theory was the historian William Robertson (1721–93). He, too, considered the balance of power a peculiarly European institution. He located its origins in Italy. He saw it as a product of the Renaissance and its particular 'political science'. The Italians, he wrote,

> had discovered the method of preventing any monarch from rising to such a degree of power as was inconsistent with the general liberty, and had manifested the importance of attending to that great secret in modern policy, the preservation of a proper distribution of power among all the members of the system into which the states of Europe are formed. (Robertson 1896 [1769], p. 120)

Enlightenment visions in Europe

The scientists and theorists of the Enlightenment retained the seventeenth-century predilection for classificatory tables and taxonomies, the culminating expression of which was the mechanical universe of Isaac Newton. The eighteenth-century vision of symmetry permeated all sectors of art, thought and human knowledge. Their vision of symmetry was apparent in the architecture of the century's grand estates – in Louis XIV's Versailles as well as in Marlborough's Blenheim. It was visible in the splendid geometry of the estate gardens. It was audible in eighteenth-century music, in the fugues of Johann Sebastian Bach as well as in the sonatas of Joseph Haydn. It provided the organizing principle of the paintings of Reynolds, the novels of Defoe, Swift and Fielding. It blazed through the 'tree of knowledge' which organized the *Cyclopaedia* of Ephraim Chambers and the *Encyclopaedia* of Diderot and d'Alembert. It organized the binary taxonomies of the Swedish botanist Karl von Linnae.

In Britain, a notably influential argument for the natural harmony of free individual interaction was written at the outbreak of the wars of Louis XIV by Richard Cumberland. He argued that a society of rational individuals contains natural rewards for virtuous behaviour and that all citizens will consequently act with benevolence and tolerance towards each other. Another famous argument for the natural harmony of free interaction was written at the end of the wars by Bernard de Mandeville (1670–1733). In his *Fable of the Bees: or Private Vices, Publick Benefits* (1924 [1714]), Mandeville argued that the vices which were most despised in the older moral code would, if practised by all individuals, result in the greatest public good. Selfishness, individual greed and acquisitive behaviour were all properties which contributed to industriousness, to a thriving economy and to national wealth. Mandeville's point was that, in view of the new moral and economic philosophies of the age, these motives should no longer be considered vices.

Social thinkers on the Continent developed variations on this eighteenth-century theme. The vision of the harmony of free individual interaction is evident in the writings of the French economist François Quesnay (1694–1774). Jean-Baptiste Say (1767–1832) developed a theorem of market equilibrium, arguing that the very process of production creates a market for the commodities produced – that supply creates its own demand – and that any productive economy would remain in equilibrium. Adam Smith was greatly inspired by them when he worked out his classic vision of a self-harmonizing economy in the *Wealth of Nations* [1776]:

> As every individual endeavours as much as he can both to employ his capital in the support of domestick industry, and so to direct that industry that its produce may be of the greatest value; every individual necessarily labours to render the annual revenue of the society as great as he can. He generally, indeed, neither intends to promote the publick interest, nor knows how much he is promoting it … he intends only his own gain, and he is in this, as in many other cases, led by an invisible hand to promote an end which was no part of his intention. (Smith 1976, p. 456)

This vision of a natural harmony of free, individual interaction was not restricted to economics; it also made its imprint on discussions of politics. It is evident in Jean-Jacques Burlamaqui's argument for a separation of powers in government; an argument which is more famously elaborated in Montesquieu's *The Spirit of the Laws* (1990 [1748]). Montesquieu argued that, if a state intends to promote liberty, it ought to divide its supreme political authority into three branches of government: the legislative, the executive and the judiciary. If these three branches act independently of each other, then each one will act as a check upon the political authority of the others and thus guarantee the overall harmony of society and maximize the liberty of its citizens (Montesquieu 1990, pp. 68–75).

American variations – the Enlightenment torn between Calvin and Hobbes

America was unique. It was built not on conquest by powerful kings but by ordinary people who immigrated to the English colonies on the north-eastern coast of America, cleared steadily more land and expanded in all directions. Many of them were pulled to America by the promise of freedom and fortune. Others were pushed out of Europe by poverty and persecution.

During the final decades of the eighteenth century the colonists felt unfairly treated by the English Crown and rebelled. The English government responded with military repression. However, some Englishmen reacted to the rebellion with understanding. One of them was Edmund Burke. In the spring of 1775, as tensions increased between colonies and mother country, Burke made a speech in Parliament and warned his government against using force against the Americans. It would provoke an American rebellion, he argued. The British government must negotiate with the colonists, not repress them, Burke (1999) insisted. The Americans will resist repression because they cherish their rights and will rebel against any effort to curtail them. The result will be an uneven fight and costly for the

English Crown. It will be politically costly because the English will fight an unjust cause. It will be expensive in money because the English will rely on supply-lines that stretch half-way around the globe. The Americans will fight at home in a just defence of rights and liberties.

Nowhere on earth is the 'spirit of Liberty' stronger than in the American colonies, Burke told the Parliament. 'In the Character of the Americans, a love of Freedom is the predominant feature' (p. 221), he began. He then explained this 'fierce spirit of Liberty' with several reasons. First, the Americans are Englishmen, devoted to Liberty 'according to English ideas, and on English principles'. Second, they subscribe to the doctrine of popular sovereignty and are used to a great extent of self-rule. Third, they enjoy a high degree of literacy and education – they are especially schooled in the fields of law and theology, which have accustomed them to discussions of rights and rules. Fourth, in the South the value of freedom and independence is accentuated by the institution of slavery. Fifth, in the North the love of liberty is accentuated by religion in societies built by Protestant dissenters.

Burke was not alone in emphasizing the role of religion in American nation-building (Haselby 2015). Alexis de Tocqueville (1969, pp. 46f), the French aristo-crat who toured the American republic in 1831, observed how American society was sustained by a unique blend of puritanism and liberty. Other commentators, too, noted that the people who settled along the New England coast saw themselves as 'pilgrims' – travellers who had come from afar to a land promised by God. Their leaders, men like William Bradford and John Winthrop, had portrayed America as a 'promised land' and a 'New Jerusalem'. Cotton Mather had explained that the settlers had escaped a Europe that was marked by sin and corruption; that they were chosen by God to build a pure society in America and 'begin the world anew'. This society would be constructed according to the God-given right to liberty.

The spirit of liberty and rights dominate the preamble of the American *Declaration of Independence*. 'We hold these truths to be self-evident, that all men are created equal, that they are endowed by the Creator with unalienable Rights, that among these are life, Liberty and the pursuit of Happiness'. These few, famous words contained the seeds for an American philosophy of government. Humans are endowed with Rights. The purpose of government is to protect those Rights. And if the government will not do so, it violates its primary purpose. The contract between government and people could then be considered null and void. On this Lockean logic,[12] the *Declaration* legitimized the decision to break all ties with England. The government in London had not protected the Rights of the American colonists – it had, in fact actively violated them and thus broken the contract between colony and mother country. The implications were obvious, for whenever a government violates these God-given Rights to Life, Liberty and Happiness,

> whenever any Form of Government becomes destructive of these ends, it is the Right of the People to alter or to abolish it, and to institute a new Government, laying its foundation on such principles and organizing its powers in such form, as to them shall seem most likely to affect their Safety and Happiness.

The *Declaration of Independence* from 1776 expressed a simple argument based on an optimistic anthropology anchored in a doctrine of Rights and human reason. The American Constitution, written eleven year later, reflects darker and more pessimistic assumptions. In particular, it reflects the assumptions of James Madison. He had read several eighteenth-century projects of perpetual peace and rejected them as utopian (Madison 1906). If men were angels, no government would be necessary (Madison 1987). However, since human nature was sadly imperfect, it was necessary to establish a government to keep order and peace among people. The problem was that government involves power and that power always tempts those who execute it to abuse it. How, Madison asked, could a government be constructed that is strong enough to impose social order, yet weak enough to prevent abuse of power? Ethical forces alone could not control human ambition. However, a complex system of checks and balances could be constructed in which 'ambition would be made to counter ambition' (Madison 1987). This would limit government and preserve an equilibrium of power.

The 1776 *Declaration of Independence* is optimistic and revolutionary. The 1787 Constitution is pessimistic and conservative. It does not secure a good government as much as it seeks to avert the tyranny of a powerful state. What could explain the source of its pessimism? One possibility is the war between England and the colonies that followed the *Declaration of Independence*. It was a terrible and sobering experience. War with England and conflict among the American colonies brought disillusion to the American leaders.

Another possibility is in the impact of religion – or, more precisely, of the Puritan brand of Protestantism with its pessimistic view of human nature. Its doctrine of original sin introduced peculiar preoccupations and tensions to America's politics. The United States was conceived in a struggle for independence and informed by liberal theories of Rights and liberty. But the pessimistic anthropology of Puritanism added complications to the liberal argument.

The American colonists exhibit 'a fierce spirit of Liberty', argued Burke (1999 [1775], p. 239f). But to understand the American spirit fully, it is necessary to understand their religion, he continued: the colonists were dissenters. They were Puritans and Calvinists opposed to the Church of England as well as the Church of Rome. 'Their dissenting interests have sprung up in direct opposition to all the ordinary powers of the world; and could justify that opposition only on a strong claim to natural liberty'.

In order to appreciate the American Constitution, it is helpful to recall that it was the work of men who believed in original sin and that, although they wanted freedom for their people, they also wanted to make sure that they were not led into temptation and corruption. This, then was the Americans' dilemma: they wanted to maximize liberty, but they also feared what ambitious and sinful individuals might do with it. So they sought to limit it by constructing a government that checked the effects of that liberty. American politics, as James Bryce (1888, p. 299) once formulated it, is suspended between the theology of Calvin and the philosophy of Hobbes.

This makes the American notion of liberty different from that of the *philosophes* of Continental Europe. The roots of the American notion of liberty are very much defined by opposition to the Anglican Church and to the state that this Church served. It was weak on the reason-based secularism, the material equality and the collectivist solidarity exhibited by the Continental Enlightenment. Americans cultivated a freedom that was religious and individualist in orientation.

The political philosophy of the USA had European roots, but it developed in unique ways – affected by America's colonial experiences, among other things. Some of the resulting differences are brought out by a comparison between America's practically oriented *Federalist* and Immanuel Kant's theoretically abstract federation of perpetual peace. Where the American federation was informed by individualism, Kant's was perceived in terms of a solidaric community. Also, where the American understanding of 'liberty' and 'Right' was based on an individual rationality with religious overtones, Kant's understanding drew on a secular political philosophy that emphasized social interaction. America's colonial experience included memories of religious persecution, efforts to escape the power and authority of European state Churches and to establish Puritan havens in the New World.

Kant's political philosophy had a limited impact on the American view of relations among states. But another Continental thinker gained a great influence in America: the Swiss jurist Émeric de Vattel. His *Droit des gens* was published in 1758 and quickly reached American leaders like Franklin and Jefferson. The book was translated into English in 1760 as *The Law of Nations* and rapidly became the standard text on international law in America (Wiltse 1960). Its argument was based squarely on the John Locke's *Second Treatise of Government* and thus harmonized nicely with America's liberal approach to international affairs at a time when tensions with Britain forced American leaders to consult international law. After the American Revolution, Vattel's authority continued undiminished. His definitions of liberty and equality coincided with those of the American *Declaration of Independence*.[13]

Enlightenment International Relations theory
The themes of symmetry, balance and self-equilibrium are apparent in eighteenth-century speculations about international affairs. Defoe, Fénelon, Hamilton, Hume, Kant, Rousseau and others articulated this dominant sentiment of the age in their discussion. This is most evident in their discussion of the international balance of power.

This vision of social balance which characterizes eighteenth-century social thought, differs from that of earlier ages. In the previous century, the balance of power among states was seen as a policy which could benefit a particular country.[14] After 1700 social balance was seen not as particularist but as systemic. It was seen as a policy which benefited the whole international society. The balance of power was seen in terms of an entire self-equilibrating social system. When William Robertson expressed this view in the 1760s, he explained that, after the Italian wars, the balance-of-power practice grew 'to be fashionable and universal'. It then 'linked the powers of Europe … closely together'. In the early sixteenth century,

Robertson continued, the balance of power operated all over the West. Indeed, Robertson explains, 'uncommon lustre' is shed on the age by the simultaneous presence of five outstanding monarchs: Charles V, Henry VIII, Francis I, Pope Leo X and Suleiman the Magnificent.

> In every contest, great power as well as great abilities were set in opposition; the efforts of valour and conduct on one side, counterbalanced by an equal exertion of the same qualities on the other ... served to check the exorbitant progress of any one of those princes, and prevent their attaining such pre-eminence in power as would have been fatal to the liberty and happiness of mankind. (Robertson 1896 [1769], p. 121)

Robertson's book was immensely popular. It was widely read and admired.[15] It presented the balance of power as a phenomenon which benefited the entire system of states – and therefore also all the system's individual members. It portrayed the balance of power as a continuing practice (rather than an *ad hoc* response by individual states to particular situations). By this notion, the primary purpose of an eighteenth-century balance-of-power politics was not to preserve the sovereignty and independence of individual states – although it did accomplish this. Rather, it was to preserve the order of the interstate system itself. During the eighteenth century, Robertson's understanding became dominant. The international balance of power was seen as the essential stabilizing factor in the society of sovereign states. It became an end in itself.

This idea provided a popular underpinning for the late eighteenth-century understanding of Europe as a system of states. This system was seen as an outcome of an evolution through modern history and as a workable alternative to empire. In the age of Newton and mechanistic physics, Robertson's explanation had a seductive naturalness about it.

Order-in-space, progress-through-time and the Enlightenment paradox

Enlightenment contributions to International Relations theory included a shift in focus from the individual state to the state system. This implied a shift in level of analysis and in logic. It implied a general acceptance of – if not a profound faith in – a principle of natural harmony. And in this faith lies the major paradox of the Age of Enlightenment. This age, which emphasized so insistently the primacy of human reason, built its most characteristic social vision on an irrational, extra-human principle of self-adjustment.

Some authors sensed this paradox and wrestled with it. Rousseau, Hume and Kant, for example, took part in the century's characteristic discourse of self-adjustment; yet neither fully accepted the claim that self-regulation would be an automatic outcome of the free exercise of human reason. They discussed interstate relations in balance-of-power terms and they explored the idea that human societies are governed by immutable laws. Yet none of them was willing to derive these laws from the rational workings-together of individual minds. 'Individual human beings, each pursuing his own ends according to his inclination and often one against another (and even one entire people against another) rarely unintentionally promote, as if it were their guide, an end of nature which is unknown to them,' writes Kant (1949b, p. 117) – who did not seem to invest much trust in the workings of an invisible hand.

There is in authors like Rousseau, Hume and Kant a notion that reason alone cannot explain the regularities of human behaviour. Rousseau insists on this point, since he believes that humanity is potentially rational but actually alienated. If millions of people are given the liberty to pursue their individual interests while still in this alienated condition, they are likely to produce chaos and conflict rather than harmony. But if reason cannot explain human behaviour, what can? Rousseau's famous answer is that human beings, though their actions, produce social conditions that capture and imprison them and which shape their outlooks and mentalities. Rousseau explained how humans have evolved through time – from free-roaming individuals, through families and tribal societies to more highly evolved states. This evolution affected humans and alienated them. Alienated humans would in turn produce societies marked by exploitation and repression and trap their citizens in situations over which they had no control.

Hume pursued this argument and supplied some empirical content to Rousseau's theory of political evolution. From his vantage point Hume (1978) noted that human beings are social animals – not by inclination but by necessity. Humans are badly adapted to life in the wild and are pressed by necessity to develop some kind of society, argued Hume (1978; 1985b). He compared distant societies – ancient societies in antiquity and contemporary societies in Asia and America – and noted that the most primitive humans organize themselves in families. As families enter into competition with each other, they create alliances and evolve into tribes. Then competition and conflict among tribes produce larger and more complex societies.

Societies protect humans against enemies and bolster their safety. Also, societies allow individuals to develop special skills and enter into a social division of labour – which is greatly more productive than if every person were to work only for themselves. Finally, societies evolve institutions of government. The 'first rudiments of government', explains Hume (1978, pp. 540f) – who once again invokes competition and strife as an explanatory principle in politics – were established by the tribal leader during military campaigns. Tribal military camps, then, are the true mothers of governments. And human quest for security is a powerful force behind the evolution of states.

Hume differs from Rousseau in many respects. Yet, it is Rousseau's argument of historical evolution which provides the basis for Hume's theory of the state. It was very influential. It demolished older theories that saw the state as God's gift to humankind or as a product of human reason. It paved the way for a powerful criticism of the dominant contract theories of Hobbes and Locke. Social contracts are nothing but figments of philosophers' imagination, argued Hume. No such contract has ever actually existed. All governments begin with power, not with a contract. States are largely products of conquest by those who are strong and a quest for order and security by those who are weak.

Rousseau and Hume provided an alternative, historically based explanation to established theories of social contract. 'Man, born in a family, is compelled to maintain society from necessity, from natural inclination and from habit', argued Hume (1985b, pp. 37ff). From elementary kinship groups state structures evolve through historical stages – from tribes through chieftainships and monarchies to republics.

Immanuel Kant seems to agree with the thrust of Rousseau's and Hume's argument. He, too, saw man as a creature of 'unsocial sociability' and largely agreed with Hume that competition among clans, tribes and states led to conflict and war and that war in turn fuelled human progress (Kant 1949b). 'Man is an animal who, if he lives among others of his kind, *needs a master*, for man certainly misuses his freedom in regard to others of his kind ... Man therefore *needs* a master who can break man's will and compel him to obey a general will under which every man could be free', argues Kant (p. 122).

Social harmony cannot be an assured outcome of the free exercise of a reason which is warped and crooked. International peace cannot occur until human reason is transformed, educated, un-alienated, liberated by a good society and developed to its fullest potential. Rousseau and Kant explored ways in which reason might be so transformed. They did this in terms of political will and human history. Instead of embracing the faith in reason and self-equilibration, which was expressed by so many Atlantic authors, they stressed the role played by political will. This emphasis on the volitional side of human nature had long characterized Europe's humanist tradition. Rousseau re-emphasized it, elaborated it and expressed it in his doctrine of the General Will – which is what each individual would will if alienation were removed and people could see their real interests. This doctrine had a formative impact on Continental political philosophy (Talmon 1952; 1960).

Rousseau, Hume and Kant also stressed the effect of history on human society. They cast their discussions in evolutionary terms and foreshadowed a major new theme which would characterize social-scientific discussions of the nineteenth century. They held the notion that individual human beings are actors in a play whose plot they do not fully understand. Their discussions of reason, will and historical progress signalled a new conception of social order. They began the transition from the static eighteenth-century vision, according to which social order is depicted in terms of symmetry in space, to a dynamic nineteenth-century vision, where social order is captured through the notion of evolution through time. This emphasis on reason/will and history/progress would later provide a vantage point for Hegel's and Marx's philosophical systems.

Rousseau made historical investigation a key component of International Relations theory. Building on Rousseau, Hume and Kant broke with the mechanical, eighteenth-century vision of order-as-symmetry-in-space, and introduced an organic vision of order-as-progress-through-time. Both Rousseau and Kant saw this progress in terms of a dialectical relationship between man and nature: nature imposes afflictions and hardships upon man, who, in overcoming these, is gradually guided towards his moral destiny. This dialectic, which reverberates through

Rousseau's and Kant's conception of politics, would later inform Karl Marx, for whom politics involved transformation not only of society but of the political actors as well.

The belief that it is possible to discern in the course of human history some general scheme or design is very old. However, around 1800 there emerged a distinctly new version of historical evolution of which Rousseau provided an early foreshadowing. This 'new historiography' implied, first of all, a view of steady progress in human affairs. Second, it argued that this progress was a result of humanity's conquering the natural environment by means of human reason. Third, it divided the progress of human civilization into phases or ages. Rousseau, Hume and Kant are not the only representatives of this 'new historiography' – Adam Smith's account of the economic progress of humanity (1976 [1776]) divided human evolution into four historical phases; Condorcet's sketch of the progress of the human mind (1798 [1794]) divided human history into nine periods, each starting with some great invention; Fichte, Schlegel, Görres and, above all, George W. F. Hegel (1980) subsumed all human history under a reason-driven progress. But Rousseau and Kant were among the first thinkers who also allowed this vision to undergird their International Relations theories.

Notes

1 Locke's argument echoes Hobbes's in its claim that humanity created government through a social contract. However, Locke differed from Hobbes in several respects. First, whereas Hobbes saw natural rights as people's unlimited privilege to do anything they pleased, Locke saw natural rights as a set of specific rights limited by duties towards others. For example, Locke argued that human beings have a right to life, and defined this in terms of a property right. All individuals own their own bodies and no one could be born the property of someone else – no one, then, could be born a slave or a serf. From this axiom Locke deduced that human beings have the right to own the products of their own labour. When people work, they 'mix their labour' with objects of nature, which thereby became their property. To Locke, it was as if labour enclosed parts of the great common which was nature.

Second, whereas Hobbes envisioned the state of nature as a condition of war, Locke saw it as a state of peace. If free and largely happy individuals agreed to set up a government, this was only because a few deluded or evil individuals insisted on exceeding their natural rights and taking the lives and property of others. In order to have an efficient defence against such people, it was necessary for peace-loving property-owners to organize a government which could legislate in accordance with natural rights and enforce this legislation. Consequently, Locke's state emphasized the legislative and the judicial aspects of government over the executive functions. A good government, Locke implied, is that which restricts its functions as much as possible to refining and enforcing the law.

Third, in contrast to Hobbes, Locke's social contract is not unconditional; it imposes mutual obligations on individual citizens as well as on the government. The citizen must agree to act in accordance with reason (and the God-given natural law which represents reason); for, Locke adds with emphasis, only rational individuals can be free. The government, on its part, must respect the contract. If the government threatens citizens' rights (which it is its sole purpose to protect), then the citizens might consider the contract null and void. They may even as a last resort rebel against it.

2 This acknowledgement is quite explicit in chapter 12 of Locke's *Second Treatise*, where he discusses the three aspects of governmental power: legislative, executive and federative. He explains that, whereas the legislative and the executive powers pertain to domestic affairs, the federative power pertains to foreign relations – it encompasses 'the Power of War and Peace, Leagues and Alliances, and all the Transactions, with all Persons and Communities without the Commonwealth' (Locke 1960, p. 411).

3 This notion, that more knowledge (and especially more knowledge about other peoples) encourages tolerance and thus serves the cause of peace, is ancient. But few theorists have drawn such a clear connection between commerce and increased knowledge as Montesquieu. After him, this connection has been elaborated in several projects on perpetual peace. Most authors, especially liberal Englishmen – e.g. Bentham (1843a) and his Manchester followers (Blainey 1973) – have agreed that 'good things have resulted from this'. But some authors, notably German radicals – e.g. Herder (1829) and Fichte (1979a) – have argued that commerce corrupts mores and encourages conflicts and war.

4 Connections explored by Montesquieu are evident in de Forbonnais's entries on '*colonie*' and '*commerce*' in d'Alembert's famous *Encyclopedie*; they are noticeable in the Abbé Raynal's celebrated *Histoire de Deux Indes* (1804 [1770]). The writings of Diderot (1713–84) echo with Montesquieu's ideas – his contributions to Raynal's *Histoire* suggest a connection between monarchic rule and colonialism; and in *Observations sur le Nakaz* of 1767 Diderot (1992) claims that absolute monarchs foment conflict and war. De Jaucourt repeated this point in the article he wrote on '*guerre*' for the *Encyclopedie*. When d'Holbach (1773: II, pp. 137f) wrote that wealth which is not the fruit of labour is a source of corruption, his argument is satiated with doubts about the ways in which monarchs wage wars and acquire colonies. The same attitudes inform Condorcet's attacks on slavery and his claims that freedoms of industry and commerce will both favour the distribution of wealth and prevent the concentration of power in the hands of a few individuals (Condorcet 1970 [1795]).

5 To put it more modern terms, Godwin moves from the facile, nation-level claim that democracies do not start wars to the more sophisticated, dyadic claim that democracies do not fight each other. See e.g. Gates et al. (1996).

6 Kant argued that a peace among sovereign states could be ensured by a federation – a league or a union – established by a binding agreement or contract among republican states. He published a short digest of his argument in 1795 under the title *Perpetual Peace: A Philosophical Sketch*. This is a simple version of a more complicated argument – too complex to be handled well by subsequent theorists of war and peace. Some have emphasized the deterrence theory which underlies Kant's argument and claim him a Realist – among them Henry Kissinger, who argued that his policy of détente between the USA and the USSR 'was giving new

meaning to Kant's prediction' (Kissinger 1979, p. 70). For 'when nations are able to inflict tens of millions of casualties in a matter of hours', Kissinger continued, the 'peace has become a moral imperative'. Others have emphasized Kant's universalist moral philosophy and claim that Kant is an anti-realist. Among them is Martin Wight (1991), who allowed an idealist interpretation of Kant to inform his discussion of the 'Revolutionist tradition' in International Relations scholarship.

7 Paine seemed to revel in the irony of his ploy: the Americans would seek assistance from the very European monarchies they wished to destroy.

8 Madison had read several of the eighteen-century projects of perpetual peace and rejected them all (Madison 1906). His design owes much to the French Baron Montesquieu and his ingenious doctrine on the separation of powers.

9 Rousseau published neither his *Judgement* on Saint-Pierre nor his thoughts on colonialism. As a foreigner in France, he feared that government agents would identify him as a dangerous subversive, handle him 'roughly' and expel him (Rousseau 1978, p. 394; Cranston 1991, pp. 26ff; Starobinski 1988, pp. 201ff). The French government had good cause for concern. For in France, as in Britain and America, the Enlightenment celebration of human reason, individual liberty and the social contract drove demands for human liberation – through revolution if necessary.

10 Rousseau's argument has regularly been misunderstood. Most commentators have failed to connect Rousseau's theories of alienation and history to his theory of International Relations. One reason for this failure is that most interpretations have focused on the 'Project for a Perpetual Peace' and taken the text at face value. Most commentators have forgotten that this essay was originally intended as a presentation of Saint-Pierre's argument – which Rousseau found more 'superficial', 'impractical' and naive the more he read of it. Consequently, the commentators have often confused Rousseau's rendition of St Pierre's argument with Rousseau's own ideas. They have therefore tended to find the text unclear and contradictory, and to emerge confused from it. Thus James Madison (1906 [1792], p. 89) found the 'project of Rousseau ... preposterous and impotent'; Dickinson (1927, p. xxii) found it to contain the blueprint for 'an institution which, rightly used, should at last bring jarring races and warring nations into the calm and prosperous haven of perpetual peace'. Even Waltz (1959, p. 185) seems to think that Rousseau, when push comes to shove, is a proponent of a worldwide federation. A publication of the diplomatic dispatches which Rousseau wrote on behalf of the French ambassador to Venice (Cranston 1982, p. 173) may throw additional light on the development and nature of his argument.

11 David Hume's argument is scattered across many essays which add to a significant contribution to International Relations theory. His discussions of the causes of social order and the origin of government and of states are clearly argued cases of historical evolution. His approach foreshadows the so-called English School in many ways. See e.g. Hume 1978, part III; 1985a; 1985b; 1985c; 1985d.

12 John Locke's *Second Treatise of Government* is quite clear on this point. If a government threatens citizens' Rights (which it is its sole purpose to protect), then the citizens may, as a last resort, rebel against it. See Locke (1960) and this chapter's long note 1, above.

13 Vattel and Locke greatly affected the foreign policies of the United States. The Americans were attracted to Vattel's (and Locke's) proposition that human beings are born free and endowed with natural rights; that nations are 'composed of men naturally free and independent, and who before the establishment of civil societies lived together in the state of nature' (Vattel 1863, p. iv). The Americans embraced fondly Vattel's argument that in certain circumstances a part of a nation had a right to separate itself from the rest (pp. 96–8). The distinctive American approach to interstate relations is impressively presented in Deudney's (2007) discussion of the 'The Philadelphian system' (pp. 161ff).

14 When Francis Bacon recommended that Britain throw its weight where it was most needed, his aim was to protect England's own sovereignty and enhance its freedom of action. His assessment of the relative strengths of the European countries, conjures up the image of a pair of balancing scales. Bacon referred to this image as a policy of counterpoise, 'whose object is the security and well-being of a particular state'.

15 Both Gibbon and Voltaire claim to have been affected by it.

6

Ideological politics: the nineteenth century and the rise of mass participation

Two revolutions convulsed the Old Regime: the political revolution in France and the Industrial Revolution in England. They occurred with rough simultaneity. Together they created new conduits for political and economic mass participation: large-scale armies, mass parties, mass production of consumer goods and rapid growth of consumer markets.

The triumphant growth of industry and human power over the physical world gave nineteenth-century people new confidence in reason and science. Scholars applied novel scientific techniques and logic to society, feeding the rapid growth of the social sciences. The study of International Relations broke away from its narrow confines of diplomatic law and military science.

The Enlightenment had been populated with an astonishing number of men of genius. Ironically, as their emphasis on individual rights and liberties met with greater acceptance, individual theorists were increasingly overtaken by systems of thought – by schools, traditions, approaches and ideologies. Such new systems flourished in the post-Napoleonic age, which became an era of 'isms'. The word 'liberalism' appeared in the English language in 1819; 'radicalism' appeared in 1820, 'socialism' in 1832, 'conservatism' in 1835; in the 1830s came 'individualism' and 'constitutionalism'. The proliferation of systems of ideas at first overwhelmed the explorers of international relations; they were expelled from a garden carefully tended by a few legal and historical authorities into a new, uneven terrain of dense theoretical foliage.

Yet the spread of 'isms' did not always mean the dissemination of new ideas. Rather, the appearance of 'isms' marked the beginning of the systematic exploration, re-evaluation and arrangement of many existing ideas in the fresh context of a rapidly changing society. One of the most important novelties of this busy age, then, was not so much the discussion of the ideas themselves; rather it was their synthesizing into *systems* of ideas and the self-conscious placement of these systems in a social context. The early nineteenth century elaborated upon the Enlightenment discovery of 'society' as something which was both more than the mere sum of its constituent individuals and *different from* the state in which it was constituted. The political thinkers of the age began to search for the 'natural laws' which governed this new human arena. This search is reflected in the evolution of political economy, sociology, demography and other disciplines. Speculation about international political relations followed suit, and soon moved beyond the traditional domains of international law, political philosophy and diplomatic investigations of diplomats, generals and kings.

This chapter emphasizes the first half of the nineteenth century; the major changes wrought in the century's final decades are addressed more systematically in Chapter 7.

Revolutions in politics and economy

Earlier thinkers had viewed the state as an approximation to a divinely sanctioned order. The Enlightenment portrayed it as an artefact – as a mutually beneficial, voluntary arrangement created by free and rational human beings to protect their natural rights and self-interest. This idea that the state originated in a voluntary social contract clashed conspicuously with the rhetoric of absolutist monarchies of the Old Regime, and fuelled criticism of the status quo. John Locke – and later Sidney and Bentham in Britain, Voltaire, Montesquieu and Rousseau in France, Jefferson in America – contributed to the mounting critique of the absolutist state and to the advocacy of alternative reason-based forms of rule. In the final quarter of the eighteenth century, this evolution climaxed in sweeping reforms in England and in revolution in America (1776) and France (1789). The celebrations of abstract reason and the excesses of social revolution would, in turn, provoke reactions and mutations in conservatism and Romanticism.

The American and the French revolutions transformed politics *within* states. They removed sovereignty from the monarch and lodged it in institutions which claimed to represent the people. Countries throughout Europe were compelled to confront the intoxicating notion of popular sovereignty. Some statesmen (like Russia's Tsar Alexander I and Austria's Chancellor Metternich) sought to contain and combat the revolutionary ideal; others (like Britain's Lord Liverpool and Latin America's Bolivar) sought to adjust old political structures to new demands – to secularize, rationalize and reform existing institutions in the light of new democratic principles.

These changes which occurred within states would, in turn, alter the political relations among states. This is readily visible in the case of France. When foreign enemies threatened France in 1793, the revolutionary regime issued a general call to arms, a *levée en masse*, as an emergency measure to defend the new nation and its revolutionary ideals. This appeal to the patriotism of millions of free and equal citizens of France raised enough soldiers to fend off enemy assaults. Later, Napoleon transformed the revolutionary regime's last-resort appeal to popular sentiment into armies infused with such ardour that they conquered much of Continental Europe.

Other European states could not withstand France's armies without emulating their radically new organization. The novel emphasis on merit and mobility in the

French army mirrored the new moral equality and openness in French society; Napoleon's rational subdivision of the army into specialized branches reflected its new spirit of rational planning and political engineering. Popular ideological and patriotic passions whipped up by the French whirlwind had to be guided by techniques of propaganda and mass-mobilization. The language, rationale and style of politics were transformed.

Great changes also occurred in the economic realm. The productive forces of countries were harnessed to the engine of mass-mobilization and transformed into political power. Carried on a wave of unprecedented industrial expansion, Britain emerged from the Napoleonic Wars of 1792–1815 economically strengthened and socially changed. Industrial expansion vastly increased Britain's national wealth: between 1800 and 1850 the value of Britain's exports tripled and the value of imports more than quadrupled (Kennedy 1987).

The economic changes amounted to a veritable revolution in their own right. They altered the structures and relations within states.[1] They also changed the relations among states. In England, the rise of new middle and working classes eroded the old institutions of the great landowners who controlled Parliament. The rise of new occupations drove the new technology deep into the fabric of British society, and then outward into the rest of the world, stimulating trade and inter-action of unprecedented scope. Groups of industrialists, financiers, shippers and shopkeepers increasingly opposed the chief obstacles to their mercantile activities – Corn Laws, Navigation Acts and aristocratic privileges at home; the forces of feudal and monarchic reaction abroad. They soon universalized their position and claimed that policies which had brought them wealth would similarly benefit others: the free movement of labour, capital and commodities would contribute to the emergence of a fairer, wealthier and more peaceful world. The Holy Alliance of European emperors, which had united the traditional monarchies of Europe against the rising revolutionary tide, struck them as repugnant. The first among the victors of the Napoleonic Wars, Britain broke with the Alliance, pursuing instead a more independent policy of national interest tailored to suit its dynamic economy.

Along with new means of production came new means of destruction. Prussia was one of the first states to adapt its armed forces to the new industrial culture. The introduction of rifled barrels enhanced Prussian artillery; the packaging of ball and charge into standard cartridges increased the rate of fire; the construction of guns and cartridges out of lighter material improved military mobility. Also, railways moved Prussian troops rapidly across Europe; the telegraph produced a new, centralized system of instantaneous communication and military co-ordina-tion around which was built the famous German general-staff system. During the 1860s, these improvements were instrumental in unifying the divided German people through a string of quick, successful wars. Prussia's crowning achievement was its rapid mobilization of over a million soldiers in 1871 and its quick victory over France. This success led almost all other states in Europe to emulate Prussian military organization.

The application of science and technology to warfare tied the national security of states intimately to the nation's economic health and rate of development, setting the stage for a new phase of military history characterized by a self-reinforcing armaments spiral. Whereas past arms races had varied greatly in intensity and duration, they now became part and parcel of industrial nations' economic institutions.

Revolutions in systems of thought

The pre-revolutionary mind was permeated by visions of natural order – regimentation, symmetry and balance. Post-revolutionary thinkers were thrust into a disorderly world in which the dominant theme was not constancy but change. Despite the turbulence of the age, new scientific discoveries, applications and methods gave rise to robust confidence. Now scholars began to insist that scientific methods could be transferred from the study of nature to the study of society. Just as the political and economic revolutions coincided and intertwined at the very end of the eighteenth century, the growth of the new social sciences and the evolution of political ideologies converged and intertwined throughout the nineteenth.

The evolution of social thought displayed two contradictory tendencies: unification and differentiation. On the one hand, there was an optimistic drive towards grand theory, that is, a single, unified master science. Hegel, Comte and others argued that society was indivisible, and so likewise the study of society must be holistic and indivisible. On the other hand, there was a tendency towards greater differentiation and a deeper specialization of individual sciences.

Economics was the first to single itself out as a separate social science. 'Political economy', as it was called, addressed the key issues raised by the Industrial Revolution. Elaborating on old conceptions synthesized by Adam Smith and the physiocrats, the new science explored the creation of wealth and its social distribution in terms of a self-regulating process. Political economy analysed the social and economic aspects of the new methods of producing ever greater economic surplus, and it addressed the resulting critical question of its just distribution among society's various classes. 'The produce of the earth – all that is derived from its surface by the united application of labour, machinery, and capital, is divided among three classes of the community,' wrote David Ricardo – namely, the proprietor of land, the owner of the capital and the workers. 'To determine the laws which regulate this distribution is the principal problem in Political Economy' (Ricardo 1984, p. 3). Students of International Relations, notably diplomats and officers at first, came under the spell of the new science of political economy and the arguments of Ricardo and Malthus.

The application of scientific modes of thought to human affairs led scholars to search for some hidden principle which governed their apparent chaos. The two themes which dominated these efforts were 'competition' and 'progress'. Nineteenth-century theories understood competition as a natural feature of human society, but infused the term with at least three different meanings: First, there were the liberal authors, for whom competition was beneficial for society; it was society's dynamic and creative force. They adopted Adam Smith's position that people's competitive nature is regulated by some natural law which applies equally to civil society and to the society of nations.

Second, there were conservative authors, who conceived of competition as a mortal struggle. Theorists like Burke, Malthus, Metternich and Bismarck maintained that this struggle characterizes relations among individuals and states alike.

Finally, there were radical theorists, like Marx and Engels, who shared this position. However, whereas the conservatives saw the struggle as an unalterable outcome of human nature, the radicals viewed it as a curable illness, as a temporary human condition.

A large and varied panopticon of political economists maintained that the struggle for existence pertains to one type of political relations but not to others. Ricardo, for example, painted a gloomy picture of domestic society as a vicious struggle between social classes; yet he drew an optimistic sketch of interstate relations as a system of free competition harmonized by the law of 'comparative advantage'. More common was the argument proposed by Kant (1970b) and Hegel that domestic society is harmonious, whereas the interstate system is conflictual. Some thinkers refined this argument further. Mill and Mazzini claimed that only democratic society is harmonious. Godwin agreed, but added that democracies also behave peacefully on the international scene; that despotic regimes are belligerent by nature, whereas democracies do not initiate war – at least not on each other (Godwin 1985, pp. 506f, 529ff).

If nineteenth-century theorists differed as to the first theme (competition), they largely agreed about the second (progress). They reconceptualized the old vision of order-as-movement-in-space into a new vision of order-as-progress-through-time. They saw social change as the uni-directional improvement of human existence. They captured progress in terms like 'development' and 'history'.

Ideologies and world politics

Around the turn of the nineteenth century, the discussion of social change yielded three major secular systems of thought in the West. It fragmented the tradition of Western political thought into the three ideologies of liberalism, radicalism and conservatism. An 'ideology' is a systematic body of beliefs about the structures and processes of society; it includes a comprehensive theory of human nature that sustains a programme of practical politics. The liberal and the radical ideologies can be seen as continuations of the Enlightenment project; conservatism, by contrast, as a reaction against it. In practice, these three ideologies were never sharply demarcated; they interacted and overlapped. Especially in the early decades of the nineteenth century, it was often difficult to determine where radicalism ended and where liberalism or conservatism began. This section sketches the three ideologies as ideal types, distinguishing them with excessive clarity to isolate their distinctive cores.

Liberalism and the bliss of the world economy

Liberalism has its firmest foundations in the socio-political culture of the North Atlantic rim. The 'classic' version of liberal ideology is a continuation and elaboration of the major themes of the Enlightenment, nourished by changes wrought by the political and industrial revolutions and articulated by members of the emerging middle classes in the Atlantic world.

As the new industrial and commercial entrepreneurs hastened to build their mills and factories, they found their way blocked by the traditional privileges of the aristocracy, the institutions of the established Church and the state, and the restrictive mercantilist policies of the seventeenth and eighteenth centuries, These obstacles forced them to systematize their outlook as they struggled to construct institutions and policies more congenial to their needs.

The liberal outlook can be summed up in the four concepts of 'equality', 'rationality', 'liberty' and 'property'. Eighteenth-century *philosophes* reformulated the old idea of the moral equality of humanity into more abstract social, economic and human rights. This reformulation lies at the core of John Locke's political philosophy. It also informs the American *Declaration of Independence* (1776), which holds 'that all men are created equal, that they are endowed by their Creator with certain inalienable rights, that among these are life, liberty and the pursuit of happiness'. Equality of opportunity – not the equal distribution of material and social goods among all citizens – is the first cornerstone of nineteenth-century liberalism.

The second cornerstone is an optimistic view of man as able to satisfy his natural needs and wants in rational ways. Man is fully capable of comprehending and mastering the social and physical reality which surrounds him. He has the capacity for self-improvement and self-reliance and should therefore be given the opportunity to realize his right freely to pursue his happiness according to his own life-plan.

Liberalism's fundamental commitment is to the rational individual rather than to society. For the liberal, the proper goal of social policy is to maximize the autonomy and the freedom of the individual. The best society allows the rational individual the greatest liberty. The individual could be allowed great autonomy largely for reasons set forth by political economists like Adam Smith: their particular interests would fit together harmoniously, producing a wealthy, happy and peaceful society. In the context of the eighteenth and nineteenth centuries, liberty meant freedom from tradition, from hierarchical authority and from any concentration of political power. This demand for citizens' liberty to seek private ends is the third cornerstone of liberalism.

The fourth cornerstone is private property. Through private property, man can seek private ends and thus realize his individuality and his happiness. Property gives man an incentive to work; and through his labour, man will not only enrich himself, he will enrich society as well.

Of the many theorists who contributed to the development of nineteenth-century liberalism, few have exerted more influence than Jeremy Bentham (1748–1832). To the basic liberal themes of equality, rationality, liberty and property, Bentham adds the concepts of economic utility and harmony of interests. Bentham's confidence in an open society, the common man, the value of popular democracy and the general harmonizing effect of free trade stems from his identification of the ancient concept of 'the Good' with 'Happiness,' and the definition of Happiness as an outcome of man's habit of 'maximizing pleasure and minimizing pain'. As each man strives to obtain Happiness through this rational 'calculus of felicity', he automatically does the Good. The common man will 'infallibly conform to the moral law of nature once its content had been rationally determined' (Carr 2001, p. 23). If every man were free to maximize pleasure and minimize pain, 'the greatest happiness for the greatest number' would result.

Adam Smith postulated a connection between the self-interest of the individual and the Good of society. Bentham provided a simple and logical connection between the two – in a sense, Bentham laid bare the social mechanism which governed the operation of Smith's 'invisible hand'. By making Happiness the criterion for Goodness, the only requirement for separating good from bad was to understand where one's Happiness lay. This made Goodness 'not a matter of abstruse philosophical speculation, but of simple common sense' (p. 24).

Bentham also distinguishes between the realm of economics and the realm of politics. For Bentham, the economic order is the realm of private activities of production, procurement, distribution and consumption of goods and services. It is a realm of open access operating under natural laws and a fundamental harmony of nature. It allows human society to self-equilibrate and operates best and to the benefit of all when political authority interferes least with the system's automatic operation. In contrast, the political order is the realm of public decision-making, influence and the exercise of power. Politics does not obey natural laws: it is a closed realm in which social control is maintained through manipulation, corruption, conflict, strife and, occasionally, by forceful repression.[2]

The liberal view on international affairs undergirds Bentham's 'Plan for a Universal and Perpetual Peace' (1843a [*c.* 1794]).[3] It is largely an economic tract, and argues that colonialism is the major impediment to free trade and, therefore, to international stability and peace as well. Colonialism forces states to maintain strong navies in order to defend their colonies and to protect their trade. Since trade is limited by the amount of capital available at any given moment, the more national capital is tied up in naval forces, the less there is available for productive investments. If the nations of Europe divested themselves of their overseas possessions, they would reduce conflict at home as well as in their colonies. They could reduce the size of their military forces and government, freeing national capital for investment in domestic industries and overseas trade. In sum, a Europe without its overseas dependencies would be a more peaceful and richer Europe. Its colonies would similarly prosper (Bentham 1843b, pp. 546–9; Airas 1978, pp. 432ff).

The dismantlement of empires would restore European politics to its precolonial condition, argues Bentham. In the absence of colonial struggles, international conflict could easily be reduced to manageable proportions. Of the four basic causes of international conflict, feudalism is 'happily extinct everywhere'. Religious conflict and the passion for conquest are extinct 'almost everywhere', and, where they still persist, they might be easily managed by a Common Court of Judicature or a Congress of States. The uncertainties of succession are also largely removed from civilized politics, and, should they flare up, they, too, might be easily managed by a Congress of States, writes Bentham. Only the fourth cause of conflict, colonialism, remains. But if the colonial empires were dismantled, global peace would be within the realm of the possible for the first time in human history (Benthem 1843, p. 552).

The idea of a Congress of States is discussed by many earlier authors – by Dubois, Crucé, Sully, Saint-Pierre, to mention but a few. But Bentham adds a new dimension to the discussion. He claims that punitive force is dispensable in orderly interstate relations. His Congress of States would not 'be armed with any coercive powers', but would operate by the force of human reason alone. The most powerful instrument for the sanction of the Congress' resolutions was, he insisted, 'the tribunal of public opinion'. In order for the world's public to judge fairly and reasonably, the citizens of the world must have free and constant access to full information about disputes among states. Consequently, the Congress of States must not only report widely upon all matters presented before it, it must also operate under 'a clause guaranteeing the liberty of the Press in each State'.

This recognition of the key role which liberty of the press plays in the free workings of human reason and the sustaining of world peace leads Bentham to formulate his famous argument for the abolition of secret diplomacy. The veil of secrecy makes it possible for monarchs, ministers and military men to exploit foreign negotiations for their own enrichment, he argues. In the process, they corrupt the nation's politics and plunge the world into wars which serve only a minuscule elite. 'Under the present system of secrecy, ministers have … every seduction to lead them into misconduct, while they have no check to keep them out of it' (p. 556).

Bentham influenced the study of International Relations in important ways. First, he made an indelible mark upon its discourse. He coined the term 'international law', thus distinguishing between laws designed for government internal to states on the one hand, and those created for transactions of sovereigns on the other. This drew the boundaries of the study of 'international relations' – a term he was also the first to use.

Also, Bentham deeply affected the liberal view of international politics by distinguishing between politics and economics. In domestic society, the liberal wants government to stay out of economic affairs; he largely restricts the role of government to legislation, law enforcement and adjudication. In the society of states, by contrast, no over-arching government exists, nor is there an economic order to obey the self-equilibrating laws of nature. The countries of the world exist in a state of nature in which politics and economics have not yet evolved into differentiated activities. The liberal statesman, then, must *make* this differentiation. His task is to set up some kind of Court or Congress of States in which the functions of legislation, law enforcement and adjudication can be carried out on an international scale. The main function of this Congress is to promote the operation of the world economy according to the principles of natural law – in a word, to replace colonial and protectionist practices with free trade.

Radicalism and the global class struggle

Critics took issue with the liberal axiom that man is a rational creature. Both conservatives and radicals agreed that man is passionate as well as rational; that he is part of a larger society which shapes him in its image; that this society, in turn, is an organic product of a historical evolution.

Radicals generally perceived themselves to be members of an international movement and accordingly developed concepts and theories of international inter- action. They seized upon the need for revolution against the existing system of government to achieve the transformation of society required for the perfection of man. The French Revolution of 1789 swiftly became the signal modern event for left-wing radical theorists.

In France, radical ideas were formulated by authors like Saint-Simon and Fourier. In England, they were expressed by Godwin, Price, Owen and members of radical organizations like the Chartist movement. These early radicals developed the continuing theme that war is a function of the vast accumulation of private property, blaming the social and economic systems which made such accumulation possible. Radical internationalism was spurred by the Continental upheavals of 1830 and 1848. The age's most influential radical theorists, Karl Marx and Friedrich Engels, added and expanded upon Rousseau's insights, arguing that social inequality and human alienation are the outcomes of a social division of labour.

The Enlightenment was the fundamental source of radical ideology. The dual revolution in politics and economics boosted and redirected the energies of the Enlightenment project into an oppositional mode. The left-wing radicalism of the age is perhaps more correctly dubbed an 'insurgent creed' or an 'oppositional state of mind' than an ideology, although it does possess a clear philosophical core from which emerge distinct blueprints for 'the good society'. Radicalism's central aspects are: 'rationalism', 'critical analysis' of the status quo (including a hostile attitude towards private property), 'political activism' and a belief in 'historical progress'.

The first and most fundamental radical assumption is the Enlightenment premise that human beings are essentially good, that they are endowed with natural reason and accordingly have a natural right to freedom. Human beings have the ability to comprehend their social and material environment and the potential to construct a new, good and just society.

But if individuals are good and rational, what can account for the wretched condition in which humankind finds itself? Rousseau formulated the two essential elements in the radical response to this question in the 1750s, and they need to be noted before the second cornerstone of radicalism can be addressed. First, people are not endowed with fully developed powers of reason at birth; they have the potential for developing reason, but this development is dependent on the nature of the society in which they find themselves. Second, society is corrupt; and, when individuals are born into a corrupt society, their natural goodness is thwarted and the growth of their rational faculties is stunted. Radical theory singles out private property as the most insidious of society's corrupting influences. Rousseau (1950a, p. 279) claims that under the impact of property people's souls and passions 'gradually deteriorate until they can almost be said to have changed their nature'. Godwin (1985, p. 436) writes that the accumulation of property is always attended by abuse of power, capricious politics, personal convenience and pecuniary corruption. Marx and Engels argue that under the influence of private property, people become alienated from their true selves (Mészáros 1970). In sum, people are only potentially rational, and their potentialities for reason can be fully realized only within the context of a good society – that is a society in which the unlimited accumulation of private property is abolished.

The second cornerstone of left-wing radicalism flows from this logic: a critical analysis of the existing social order – an analysis which seeks to disclose the intimate relationship between relations of property and political power. The existing order serves the narrow property interests of a small, privileged elite at the expense of the interests of the vast majority of humanity. Existing socio-political institutions, broadly designed, support the elite while they enslave the majority and deny people the ability to develop to their full human potential.

Because the prevailing order is oppressive for most people, it must be changed if their lives are to improve. Political action is the third cornerstone of radicalism. Radicals are not satisfied with merely understanding the world; they want to better it. In its last instance, this argument becomes an advocacy for the overthrow of the existing regime – for revolution. It becomes a plea for 'the dissolution of political government, which has been the perennial cause of the vices of mankind' (Godwin 1985, p. 16). Marx and Engels advocated such a revolution on a global scale in the famous closing command of the *Communist Manifesto* (1974 [1848]):

> The Communists everywhere support every revolutionary movement against the existing social and political order of things. In all these movements they bring to the front, as the leading question of each, the property question ... They openly declare that their ends can be attained only by the forcible overthrow of all existing social conditions. Let the ruling classes tremble at a Communist revolution. The proletarians have nothing to lose but their chains. They have a world to win.

The fourth cornerstone of left-wing radicalism is the vision that history evolves in such a way that the material wealth of humanity improves over time. Nineteenth-century liberals nurtured a comparable claim, but the radical vision is distinctive in two ways. First, the radicals observe that material wealth is unequally and unfairly distributed among social classes. Although the wealthiest classes of society note considerable improvement over time, the poorest classes do not share in the improvement. Second, the radicals maintain that history is of decisive importance in the study of politics and society. Whether a specific event implies a betterment or a worsening of the condition of the working masses of the world depends upon the historical context of the event. It depends upon where in the *Stufengang*, or stage of historical evolution, the event occurs.

Marx and Engels furnished radicalism with a new, crisp, historically self-conscious formulation which spread across the West after 1850, replacing the 'utopian socialism' of the first half of the century with the 'scientific socialism' of the second.

The Communist Manifesto expresses a new, internationalist vision of politics. It holds that the exploitative and alienating regime of capitalism is challenged by a self-aware, defiant and global working class. It sees international politics in terms not of sovereign states but of global classes. It argues that the capitalist economy constitutes a new, truly international system, an essential aspect of which 'is the internationalization of communications and commerce, the development of a global division of labour and the emergence of a class struggle on a world scale' (Marx and Engels 1974, p. 73). It describes human society as sharply divided between rich and poor, between those who rule and those who are ruled. This division results in a perpetual struggle between two classes. This struggle is the force which drives the evolution of history (p. 67).

This vision of the historical evolution which undergirds 'scientific socialism' was built on the social theories of Rousseau and Hegel and fortified by the new political economy of Mill and Ricardo. The struggle between classes is a material, essentially economic, struggle; it inevitably ends in a revolution which destroys the old social order (or mode of production) and erects a new order in its place. 'At a certain stage of development, the material productive forces of society come into conflict with the existing relations of production', explains Marx. 'From forms of development of the productive forces these relations turn into their fetters. Then begins an era of social revolution' (Marx 1975b, pp. 425f).

Marx dubbed this vision of social evolution 'dialectical materialism'. He argued that the rapid development of productive forces which took place in the West in the modern ages inaugurated a new stage in history. As the new productive forces evolved, they destroyed the old industries and the traditional relationships of production which sustained them. In this light, the discoveries of the long sixteenth-century opened up fresh ground for a new entrepreneurial class, the bourgeoisie.

The East Indian and Chinese markets, the colonization of America, trade with the colonies, the increase in the means of exchange and in commodities generally, gave to commerce, to navigation, to industry, an impulse never before known. The feudal system of industry, under which industrial production was monopolized by guilds, now no longer sufficed for the growing wants of the new markets. The manufacturing system took its place.

> Thereupon, steam and machinery revolutionized industrial production. The place of manufacture was taken by the giant, modem industry, the place of the industrial middle class, by industrial millionaires, the leaders of whole industrial armies, the modem bourgeois. (Marx and Engels 1974, pp. 68f)

The bourgeoisie evolved during the seventeenth and eighteenth centuries, and accomplished several feats. First, it fuelled a string of social revolutions which marked the transition from the feudal age dominated by the old nobility to a capitalist age dominated by the new bourgeoisie. The first of these revolutions took place in the United Provinces, followed by the revolutions in England and France; the era which followed was marked by the rise of Dutch and British colonialism (Marx 1977, pp. 914–20). Second, the bourgeoisie instituted wage labour; separating the workers from the means of production, making labour a commodity and creating a property-less class or proletariat. Third, it conquered the governing institutions of the modern state – indeed, the 'executive of the modern state is but a committee for managing the common affairs of the whole bourgeoisie' (Marx and Engels 1974, p. 69).

Finally, the bourgeoisie, helped by the means of organization and oppression which the modern state put at its disposal, spread its capital, its political influence and its interests all over the world:

> The need for a constantly expanding market for its products chases the bourgeoisie over the whole surface of the globe. It must nestle everywhere, settle everywhere, establish connections everywhere ... The bourgeoisie, by the immensely facili-tated means of communication, draws all, even the most barbarian, nations into civilization ... It compels all nations, on pain of extinction, to adopt the bourgeois mode of production. (p. 71)

However, by creating the world in its own image, the new global capitalist class is also sowing the seeds of its own destruction. For by exporting the capitalist mode of production to all corners of the earth, the bourgeoisie also calls into exist-ence its own antithesis – an international class of wage labourers. For a time, the global proletarians 'do not fight their enemies, but the enemies of their enemies, the remnants of absolute monarchy, the landowners, the non-industrial bourgeois, the petty bourgeoisie' (p. 75). However, as the old classes decline in strength, and the proletariat increases in number, it becomes concentrated in greater masses, its strength and its political self-consciousness grow. Thus,

> the unceasing improvement of machinery, ever more rapidly developing, makes their livelihood more and more precarious; the collisions between individual workmen and individual bourgeois take more and more the character of collisions between two classes. Thereupon the workers begin to form combinations (trade unions) against the bourgeoisie. (Marx and Engels 1974, p. 75)

Marx and Engels understood all politics in the light of an expansionist, global economy characterized by a growing antagonism between a dominant (bourgeois) and a dominated (proletarian) class. These two classes are international in scope; they are both creations of a global economy.

Although classes and class struggles exist within individual states, the overriding struggle is that which exists between a global bourgeoisie and a global proletariat (p. 78). The nation is not the primary social actor for Marx and Engels, the class is; the primary social struggle is expressed not in war between states but in war between global classes.

Sooner or later, a global revolution will usher in a socialist mode of production: the working class will sweep away the remnants of bourgeois society – including the state, and the bourgeois ideology of nationalism – by means of a social revolution, for which the French Revolution was a prototype (pp. 85–7). The bourgeoisie will then dissolve as a class, and the traditional bourgeois mechanisms of oppression will 'be thrown in the dustbin of History'. The state itself will ultimately wither away. The Great Proletarian Revolution will first triumph in the most advanced capitalist countries. Then war will liberate those peoples who are still unjustly oppressed by their own ruling classes or by colonialist occupiers.

The early nineteenth-century radical view of world politics is little more than a magnified version of domestic politics. In this respect, radicalism and liberalism have much in common. Both envision peace and harmony as the natural state of properly managed human affairs; both maintain that conflict and war are caused by ruling classes who intervene to protect and further their vested interests. This similarity between the two Enlightenment traditions was most visible in the early decades of the century, when liberal democracy and utopian socialism stood shoulder to shoulder in opposition to the status quo. However, its utopian streak ran far into 'scientific socialism'. When the International Working Men's Association – the 'First International', founded by Karl Marx in 1864 – debated foreign policy, national defence and the causes of war, the recurring arguments tended to be as vague as they were simplistic: war was caused by capitalism; peace would come with socialism.

This initial naivety changed with the founding of the Second International (1889). This organization was intended as a kind of international parliament of socialist movements, rather than as the doctrinally pure organization that the First International sought to be. The German Social Democratic Party (SPD) dominated the Second International. The SPD provided, on the eve of World War I, a radical environment within which modern radicalism transcended both Rousseau and Marx and sponsored several sophisticated and influential radical discussions of international politics (Semmel 1981).

Conservatism and the defence of the old order
The conservative ideology arose in response to the rapid evolution of industrialists, entrepreneurs, merchants, labourers, mass movements and progressive authors. Conservatism repudiated the advocacy of the equal rights of man, and denounced the new faith in reason, science, and historical progress. In opposition to the concepts of equality and individual freedom, conservatives posed the primacy of community; against the rhetoric of improvement and change, they emphasized traditional social order and responsibility. The French Revolution, which so inspired the radicals, haunted the conservatives. They adopted a defensive mission: to provide the philosophical basis of opposition to the progress which liberals and radicals championed.

Edmund Burke (1729–97) laid the foundations for this mission in his *Reflections on the Revolution in France* (1988 [1790]). Its cornerstones are 'communalism and traditional authority', a 'pessimistic anthropology', 'hierarchy' and 'private property'. For Burke, the community is prior to and above the individual. On this claim Burke constructs a conception of the individual's proper relationship to the social order in staunch opposition to the rational individual of the Enlightenment project. A society is more than the mere sum of its constituent individuals, argues Burke. It is a network of social obligations, historical in origin, fashioned by generations of social interaction. From this argument emerges the first corner-stone of conservatism: a deep respect for tradition and established authority. Traditional authority governs the dynamic web of familiarity and respect, duty and allegiance that obviates the need for administrative bureaucracy, political repression and military force to maintain the well-ordered society. The conservative fear of progress rests on the belief that the Enlightenment project was unravelling traditional community and authority by stressing individualism and rationalizing economic and social relations. The destruction of accustomed points of social reference – the patriarchal family, the guild, the village and the church – left people bereft of direction, prey to their own whims and the manipulation of demagogues. 'A certain *quantum* of power must always exist in the community, in some hands, and under some appellation,' lest social order be irreparably undone by human frailty and vice, Burke (1988, p. 248) insists. To a member of the revolutionary National Assembly in France in 1791, Burke wrote:

> I doubt much, very much indeed, whether France is at all ripe for liberty at any standard. Men are qualified for civil liberty in exact proportion to their disposition to put moral chains upon their appetites ... Society cannot exist unless a controlling power upon will and appetite be placed somewhere, and the less of it there is within, the more there must be without. (Burke 1866, pp. 51f)

This grim estimate of human capabilities is the second cornerstone of the conservative tradition. Burke expressed a profound scepticism about the intellectual capabilities of humanity, and rejected the concept of the autonomous and rational individual. He distrusted the human intellect with 'all its defects, redundancies and errors', its pride, 'personal self-sufficiency and arrogance' (Burke 1988, p. 193). The study of history confirms the frailties, follies and infirmities of humankind, Burke maintained. 'History consists of the miseries brought upon the world by pride, ambition, avarice, revenge, lust, sedition, hypocrisy, ungoverned zeal, and all the train of disorderly appetites' (1988, p. 247). Religion, morals, laws and other supposedly universal principles upon which individuals claim to base their actions are in reality mere 'pretexts' or reflections of particular interests. The conflict of interests among competing groups constitutes the essence of human existence, which politics must master.

Burke's ideal society is founded on social hierarchy and differentiated status – the third conservative cornerstone. Conservatism distrusts the 'masses'. Burke displayed a paternalistic attitude towards them. He recommended that leadership be entrusted to those groups that have already demonstrated their ability to lead – that is, to the rich, the well-born, and the able. Only under such leaders can a people find the freedom to act and to live in accordance with their own traditions. Properly placed and held within the gravitational field of community and tradition (nation, Church and family), ordinary people are protected from their own vices and freed from fear and disorder.

The need for an elite within society leads to the final cornerstone of conservatism: private property. Ownership and management of property, primarily landed estates, have an ennobling effect on man, argues Burke. Ownership provides a unique social experience which instils responsibility, skill and practical reason, and which tempers man's passionate nature. It is among the largest property owners and the most successful managers of industry and institutions that the nation should recruit its leaders. The wealth and status of these men guarantee their dispassionate pursuit of the common good; their property allows them leisure, which is the prerequisite for knowledge and independence. Private property is therefore the necessary precondition for a good government, and the large-scale destruction of property is the most heinous of all crimes. Burke's attack on the French Revolution obsessively stresses its destruction of property (pp. 260ff).

Burke's outlook is summed up in his view that only a strong state can produce the social stability and political order necessary for human freedom (p. 196). Conservatives do not conceive of a 'strong state' in terms of forceful bureaucratic institutions. Rather, the state is an imagined corporation produced by distinct geography and shared historical experiences; it is a spiritual community founded as a partnership and seasoned by history. 'As the end of such a partnership cannot be obtained in many generations', Burke notes, 'it becomes a partnership not only between those who are living, but between those who are living, those who are dead and those who are to be born' (pp. 194f). A state is a collectivity, not a collection of individuals. It is the product of history. The movement of a people through time results in a collective memory and heritage which cannot be consciously altered or designed.

For conservative thinkers, the primary task of government is to maintain order. They do this best by resisting the natural tendency of humanity towards conflict and war. Around a central core of power, governments establish institutions which can defend the physical safety of the nation, the property rights of its citizens and the wealth and welfare of the population against external and internal enemies. As important as defending its territory against physical enemies is the preservation of the historical partnership, traditions and communal values. Such conservative maxims sustain Burke's *Reflections on the Revolution in France*. That they also inform his observations of foreign and international relations is apparent in his contributions to the Annual Register, a yearly survey of world affairs which he edited (unacknowledged) from 1758 to about 1776. For Burke, governments must help maintain international (as well as domestic) order. States must co-ordinate their capabilities and manage their interests. And always within a balance-of-power framework.

Burke praises the balance of power as the main stabilizing institution in international politics. He claims that the prudent management of Europe's balance of power preserves interstate order and international peace. This management is facilitated by several factors. One of these is the set of rules specified by international law – that 'great ligament of mankind'. Another decisive factor is the set of communal values which inform European states. These create an underlying sense of unity among the states of Europe and a collective commitment to maintaining order. Burke emphasizes the common factors which contribute to 'similitude' throughout

Europe – Christian religion, monarchical principles of government and a common Roman-law heritage foremost among them. At one point he even goes so far as to portray Europe as one great state whose unity is marred only by a few trifling diversities in provincial customs and local establishments. For Burke, Europe owes its relative order and superior wealth to a balance-of-power system which is regulated by the common norms, rules and law embedded in (European) society. While other civilizations have perished 'for want of any union or system of policy of this nature', the Western world has acquired an astonishing 'superiority over the rest of the globe'. Whereas other regions have been torn apart by strife or folded under the weight of excessive conquest, Europe has emerged pre-eminent in the world owing to the vigilant maintenance of the balance of power (Burke 1772, p. 2).

The conservative approach to International Relations is informed by the two modern notions of state interest and necessity – by *raison d'état* (the phrase that comprehends both). The conservative politician maintains, with Guicciardini and Rohan, that the interest of the state is the mainspring of political action; and agrees with Spinoza that the necessities of policy arise from the anarchical interstate context in which states are forced to operate. The theoretical implications which flow from these notions contradict the liberal doctrine of a general harmony of social interests. Rather, conflict of interest is the normal state of human affairs, and war is the normal condition of interstate relations. No universal principles exist on to which a new world order can be grafted. Each state – each culture, religion and nation – defines its own truth.

Conservative thinkers belittle the importance of theoretical blueprints. They are often pragmatists who stress experience over speculation. They treat politics as a practical activity, and react to events as they occur, rather than follow any long-term master plan. They treat international politics not as a science but as an art. And since they consciously adopt an atheoretical posture, it is difficult to find a clear exponent of a conservative International Relations theory. To the extent that conservative statesmen theorize, they examine the past with a pronounced empirical disposition, guided by an 'ear for history', and draw careful lessons from concrete events. Conservative theorizing is characteristically a carefully delineated, empirically based 'conversation with tradition'. It focuses on the complex interconnectedness of past events; the lasting properties of 'tradition' as well as the constellation of forces of a particular moment. Still, the challenges presented by liberalism and radicalism and the social and economic changes of the dual revolution forced conservative paladins consciously to defend their traditions and to justify that defence.

One of the most theoretically explicit conservative commentators of the age was Friedrich Gentz (1764–1832). As secretary and foreign policy adviser to the powerful Austrian statesman Klemens von Metternich (1773–1859), he was also one of the most influential. Gentz translated Burke's *Reflections* into German in 1793, and adopted many of Burke's ideas. A constant theme in his writings on international politics is the idea of a coalition of like-minded peoples to act as a stabilizing body in peace and war (Gentz 1953). He argued that an alliance between

Russia, Austria and Prussia was necessary to minimize the influence of radical French and English ideas and to contain the expansion of revolutionary French power (Gentz 1806).

Gentz placed his faith in the post-Napoleonic Holy Alliance as the coalition which would preserve the old order. As the Holy Alliance disintegrated, he championed the notion of a Continental Order, an idealized version of the eighteenth-century Concert, to defend against the unfolding of the nineteenth century. For Gentz, the balance of power was the international counterpart of domestic traditional authority, which preserved the social order. If the existing balance were disturbed, he maintained, then the challenging force must be blunted, co-opted and absorbed and a new but essentially similar status quo established. Whether commenting on the Greek rebellion against the Turks, the Spanish liberals' opposition to Bourbon absolutism, the Latin Americans' declaration of war on Spain or German students battling the Prussian police, Gentz invariably supported Metternich's policy of opposing the forces of liberalism and democratization and defending the old order.

Metternich, too, was an advocate of a balance-of-power system; he, too, excluded all illusory ethical considerations from the conduct of international politics. After Napoleon's fall, he opposed proposals from his more morally minded colleagues to punish France severely for its belligerence. If a stable order were to be imposed upon the Continent, France must be retained as one of the major actors in a balanced system. If too severely penalized, France would be weakened and Europe would find itself at the mercy of Russia. Europe could not have order without balance or justice without restraint.

Among the conservative International Relations theorists, Carl Philipp Gottlieb von Clausewitz (1780–1831) ranks among the most sophisticated. He once stated his view of international politics in a credo which summarizes the conservative sentiment well: 'never relax vigilance, expect nothing from the magnanimity of others; never abandon a purpose until it has become impossible, beyond doubt, to attain it; hold the honour of the state sacred' (Clausewitz 1962, p. 304).

Clausewitz experienced the Battle of Jena (1806), where Napoleon soundly defeated the Prussians, as an intellectual awakening. As an officer of Prussia's defeated army, Clausewitz grasped that the French victory stemmed from Napoleon's ability to mobilize the entire French nation for war and fire it with nationalist ardour (Clausewitz 1976, p. 593). He realized that the future would belong to spiritually unified nations (*Völker*). Napoleon showed him that armies which were not founded on a *Volk* would be destroyed.

In internment in France, Clausewitz brooded on the Prussian defeat and on the fate of the fragmented German nation. The task which faced Prussia, he resolved, was not just military reform, but also spiritual renewal. Confronted with the real danger of annihilation, it was essential that Prussia's ruling Hohenzollern dynasty articulate and cultivate a patriotic sentiment, place itself at the helm of a popular nationalist movement, and create what would in effect be a modern nation-state.[4]

Clausewitz saw humanity as naturally divided into nations (*Völker*), each of which has its own characteristics and qualities. He argued that a *Volk* forms a state in order to express its national identity and to maintain its freedom (Clausewitz 1922). This vision has a democratic aspect, because it acknowledges that state policies must somehow reflect the popular will. Yet Clausewitz's brand of democracy is quite different from the Enlightenment notion of popular participation. He was doubtful of the potential of human reason, which he saw as limited by passion and chance; he feared that a system based on broad participation would 'not allow citizens to sleep at night for worry of what the government did yesterday, does today and will do tomorrow' (Smith 1990, p. 43). His distrust in the democratic ideas of the Atlantic states fits perfectly the paternalistic vision of Continental conservatism.

Clausewitz developed a theory of war on the conservative premise that conflict of interest is inherent in human society. 'War is part of man's social existence. War is a clash between major interests, which is resolved in bloodshed – that is the only way in which it differs from other conflicts,' writes Clausewitz (1976, pp. 78ff). War is the supreme manifestation of human conflict; it is politics concentrated in a single point.

From this premise, Clausewitz develops the argument that war is embedded in society and history. War is never an isolated act. It occurs in a distinct social and historical context which affects the nature of its outbreak, its conduct and its outcome. War is shaped by the intentions of the belligerents, the nature of their military forces, the geography of the battlefield, the prewar relationship of the participants and the international environment. In the modern age, states are so closely integrated that 'no cannon could be fired in Europe without every government feeling its interest affected' (p. 590). Attuned to the natural propensity for people to feud and to the immense complexity of interstate interaction, Clausewitz does not harbour any illusions about humanity's ability to impose lasting order upon his social environment. He has little admiration for the intellect of the citizen; instead, he invests his faith in the genius of the exceptional leader – the skill of the general, the wisdom of the statesman – and in the historically sanctioned, collective reason of the *Volk*.

Although war is a natural feature in international relations, it cannot be separated from politics; it is part of politics, a mode of it, a continuation of political intercourse with the addition of other means. 'We deliberately use the phrase "with the addition of other means"', he explains,

> because we also want to make it clear that war in itself does not suspend political intercourse or change it into something entirely different ... War cannot be divorced from political life; and whenever this occurs in our thinking about war, the many links that connect the two elements are destroyed and we are left with something pointless and devoid of sense. (p. 605)

The overriding, formative concern of statesmen and strategists must be the political objectives specific to their own states. The political interests and objectives of sovereign nation-states constitute, at each moment in history, an intricate political field. They are fashioned by the character of the states, the perceptions of national leaders and their (usually limited) aims: territorial annexation, regional domination or maintenance of the existent relations of forces among states.

States monitor their position in this dynamic diplomatico-strategic field, and adapt to its incessantly changing matrix of interests (Aron 1966, pp. 4–16, 437–58; 1986). Emphasizing the role of force, Clausewitz repeats Thucydides' insight that law and justice play a role in international politics only in so far as the states involved are of equal power. Otherwise, the strong do what they will and the weak suffer what they must.

The purpose of the war is always 'to compel our enemy to do our will' (Clausewitz 1976, p. 75). In order to achieve this purpose, it is necessary either to destroy the enemy's armed forces so that he is rendered defenceless, or to place him in 'a position that is even more unpleasant than the sacrifice you call on him to make' (p. 77). Clausewitz devotes most of his book to various techniques by which a state can produce these outcomes, either of which will put the victorious state in a position to dictate the terms of peace. But it is not this exposition of the techniques of battle which is Clausewitz's main concern; it is the political purpose and the goals that they must serve.

Nation-states do not resort to war in their everyday efforts to secure or further their objectives. They are, however, always exposed to the risk of war and they always remain under arms. Their environment is one of change and uncertainty, in which no absolute equilibrium of force is possible. The strength of states continually waxes and wanes, causing the balance of forces to fluctuate. Consequently, long periods of peace between two armed, hostile states 'cannot be explained by the concept of balance. The only explanation is that both are waiting for a better time to act' (p. 82). Peace, then, has no higher meaning than the temporary absence of war.

Also, Clausewitz recognizes that war has a meaning beyond the strictly and obviously political. For some reason, states have tacitly agreed to accept limited war as at least a temporary arbiter in their clash of interests. He suggests two reasons for this. First, war is accepted because the use of physical force is a common occurrence among individuals or groups that have a clash of interests. Second, there are two factors which give war and battle a special quality: war is conducted in the name of the state and on behalf of the nation, infusing it with a larger political purpose; also, war transcends politics – it is a conflict of interest 'resolved by bloodshed' (p. 149).

When Clausewitz refers to 'bloodshed' in the very definition of war, he alludes to acts of universal significance. The shedding of blood has a deep symbolic meaning and a powerful mythic appeal in human affairs. A variety of myths and religions use blood as a symbol of both life and death in rites of atonement, purification and renewal – Christianity included. Blood is associated with a broad variety of social relationships and political objectives. References to battles, and blood as a symbol of the ultimate heroic sacrifice and as the ultimate signifier of ownership or membership, evoke powerful emotions. In Clausewitz's words:

> I believe and profess that a people never must value anything higher than the
> dignity and freedom of its existence; that it must defend these with the last drop
> of blood; ... that shame of a cowardly submission can never be wiped out; that
> the poison of submission in the bloodstream of a people will be transmitted to its

children, and paralyse and undermine the strength of later generations; ... that a bloody and honourable fight assures the rebirth of the people even if freedom were lost; and that such a struggle is the seed of life from which a new tree inevitably will blossom. (Clausewitz 1962, p. 301)

Hegel: The last great synthesizer

As the three ideological tendencies evolved and the nineteenth century span itself out, their development echoed the prevailing themes of the age – fragmentation and unity on the one hand, competition and progress on the other. As proponents of each tendency clarified their views, they produced universally applicable systems of thought.

In practical politics these competing systems of thought were not starkly delineated; adherents of the three ideologies of liberalism, radicalism and conservatism often formed expedient alliances in which a common interest would temporarily unify two ideologies against the third. In theory, however, while the three ideologies share some assumptions, they are, in their totality, fundamentally at odds with one another.[5] The liberal ideology was born of the struggle to throw off the confining social, political and economic institutions that conservatives understood to be the heart, soul, and connective tissue of society. Radicalism developed as a critique of both the comfortable world of the *ancien régime* and of self-congratulatory liberalism. Conservatism defined its essence in opposition to radicalism and liberalism. In terms of theory, the West fragmented into three competing political approaches.

At the heart of the conflict lay questions which radiated out from the notions of 'progress' and 'competition'. The states of the Atlantic rim which embraced liberalism also embraced industrialization, agrarian reform and political democratization. Their economies were dynamic and aggressive and they came to embody and define the idea of 'progress'. The peoples in Central and Eastern Europe perceived themselves as competing with the economic and political power of the West and as wrestling with the mesmerizing idea of progress. The Prussian philosopher Georg Wilhelm Friedrich Hegel (1770–1831) expressed this anti-liberal *Angst*. He also combined the most typical themes of his age into a complex and abstract system which has provided one of the richest ores of anti-liberal theorizing ever devised.

Hegel is a suitable representative for the sentiment (or the 'spirit') of the age. At the core of Hegel's political theory, the century's distinctive themes of progress and competition intertwine – it even embraces the two different views of competition: the harmonious as well as the conflictual. For Hegel, history is the progressive realization of the ultimate Truth or Idea. The Idea evolves through a dialectical struggle towards an Absolute End.

In the Hegelian approach, history must be understood in terms of ideas rather than events. History is the evolutionary process through which the Absolute Idea attains full consciousness of itself as spirit (*Geist*) and realizes itself in the form of a new world spirit (or *Weltgeist*) of Reason, Freedom and Equality. For Hegel, this process is not linear, but dialectical: a given thought will always contain inherent contradictory aspects and will produce its own negation. Thus, a given state of affairs (the 'thesis') will inevitably produce a conception of an opposite state of affairs (the 'antithesis'). The contest between the two will, in turn, be resolved in an *Aufhebung*: a reconciliation and a fusion (a 'synthesis') which includes the key elements of the original thesis as well as the antithesis, but which is more than and different from both.

Hegel first set out his system in *The Phenomenology of Spirit* in 1807. He saw in the French Revolution the irresistible rise of progressive values, and he saw in the Napoleonic Wars the triumphant dissemination of these values throughout the world. Like Clausewitz, he saw Napoleon as the agent of history, advancing its ultimate development by acting to universalize the progressive ideas of Freedom and Equality throughout Europe, by force when necessary.

After the fall of Napoleon and the triumph of reaction in Central and Eastern Europe, Hegel shifted his emphasis to the necessary competition and struggle which accompanies progress. His new analysis is set forth in Hegel's last, major work, *The Philosophy of Right* (1980 [1821]). It discusses how the *Geist* articulates itself through a rationally organized (and therefore genuinely free) nation or *Volk* and its state. The *Volk* is the basic spiritual unit in Hegel's later works. Each free *Volk* possesses its own proper spirit. This *Volksgeist* is the supra-individual Reason, or 'spirit objectified' of a nation, expressed in the institutions of its state. A people without a state is merely a vulnerable 'formless mass' (Hegel 1980, p. 183).

Politics internal to states is harmonious. Since the state is *Volksgeist* objectified, it invests in each individual a core identity. Thus, it is only as a citizen 'that the individual himself has objectivity, genuine individuality and an ethical life' (p. 156). Politics among states, by contrast, is marked by extreme conflict. In Hegel's earlier works, the *Volksgeist* is only a subordinate, historically specific part of the *Weltgeist* – ultimately, the *Weltgeist* will prevail and provide the final context within which the individual *Volksgeist* (and its state) will find self-consciousness and freedom. After the defeat of Napoleon, however, Hegel's long-term optimism dampened. The synthesis which promised to remove the contradiction between *Volksgeist* and *Weltgeist* fades from view; the violent competition between nation-states emerges as a permanent feature of international politics.

Hegel agreed with Clausewitz that a state articulates the sovereign will of a *Volk* and that 'if states disagree, and their particular wills cannot be harmonized, the matter can only be settled by war' (p. 214). Such 'war is not to be regarded as an absolute evil and as a purely external accident'. Rather, for Hegel, war has constructive, even progressive, functions. It promotes national unity. It stimulates the growth of states. It contributes to the progress of history. War also prevents established nation-states from deteriorating; peace makes people and states grow soft – 'corruption in nations would be the product of prolonged, let alone "perpetual" peace', writes Hegel (p. 209f). War keeps states fit and alert.

Hegel was enormously influential – partly because he included all the major early nineteenth-century themes in his vast synthesis; partly because his arguments were so abstract that adherents of all ideologies found some support in his works.

He provided philosophical support to the stage-theories of historic evolution which marked the age. This initially attracted liberals, who held the view that human history had passed from primitive tribal life to higher stages of evolution in which increasing differentiation meant social advance. However, it soon grew obvious that Hegel's definitions of 'liberty' and 'equality' and his elevation of a strong state were quite incompatible with the liberal outlook. When Darwin's theory of evolution offered an alternative (and, by liberal standards, a more 'scientific') vision of historical progress in the final decades of the century, Hegel's spell was broken in the liberal cultures around the Atlantic rim.[6]

On the Continent, however, Hegelian thought remained firm. It provided Continental conservatives with a set of concepts and a sense of purpose which allowed them to comprehend the dramatic social changes they couldn't prevent. Also, conservatives who were frustrated by the fragmented nature of German politics found in Hegel a conception of the nation-state as an 'imagined community' – as *Geist*, or a set of spiritual common values which had evolved historically and had articulated themselves through a people to form a consensual community and a nation. Hegel's arguments constituted a Teutonic counterpart to Burke's conservative view of the British state as an organic, historically created whole and a necessary precondition for social order and individual freedom.

Hegel also transfixed Continental radicals. He provided philosophical support particularly suited to their doctrines of progress and the dialectical method they favoured. When Hegel renovated the old, radical theme of human alienation in the light of the concept of human labour, he exerted an immediate impact on radical theorizing. From the early nineteenth century on, radical theorists placed the concept of 'labour' at the heart of their social critique (Marx 1975a).

After his death in 1831, Hegel's works remained popular, especially in Germany, whose traditional industries were under strain owing to a flood of inexpensive British imports. Anti-British and anti-liberal sentiments intertwined with economic patriotism and Romantic empathy for German artisans, and fuelled new applications of Hegel's arguments. Hegel's interpreters divided into two camps. The conservative right Hegelians emphasized the older, somewhat disillusioned Hegel. They argued that through the dialectical progress of history, the disunity of Germany would produce the idea of unity and *Volk* and would inevitably bring about the creation of a German state. Hegel's emphasis on *Volk*, war and history and his advocacy of monarchism as the best form of state endeared him to the Prussian state.

Radical left Hegelians saw in the early Hegelian dialectic a revolutionary international force. They claimed that history would soon transcend the Prussian state. Their analysis soon proceeded to study of the destiny of historical evolution and its necessary preconditions – as evinced in the works of Karl Marx.

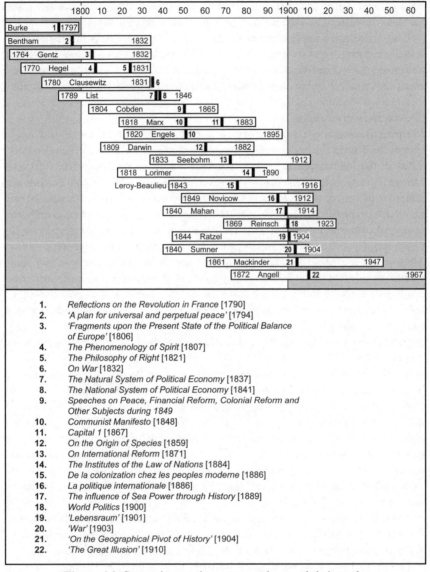

Figure 6.1 Some nineteenth-century authors and their works

1. Reflections on the Revolution in France [1790]
2. 'A plan for universal and perpetual peace' [1794]
3. 'Fragments upon the Present State of the Political Balance of Europe' [1806]
4. The Phenomenology of Spirit [1807]
5. The Philosophy of Right [1821]
6. On War [1832]
7. The Natural System of Political Economy [1837]
8. The National System of Political Economy [1841]
9. Speeches on Peace, Financial Reform, Colonial Reform and Other Subjects during 1849
10. Communist Manifesto [1848]
11. Capital 1 [1867]
12. On the Origin of Species [1859]
13. On International Reform [1871]
14. The Institutes of the Law of Nations [1884]
15. De la colonization chez les peoples moderne [1886]
16. La politique internationale [1886]
17. The influence of Sea Power through History [1889]
18. World Politics [1900]
19. 'Lebensraum' [1901]
20. 'War' [1903]
21. 'On the Geographical Pivot of History' [1904]
22. 'The Great Illusion' [1910]

The sentiment(s) of the century

The spread of industrialism, the increase in commercial interaction and the rise of democratic ideals of freedom and equality eroded the old order. The growth of the social sciences, too, were powerful solvents – the rapid growth of political economy, most notably, had a profound effect on nineteenth-century social speculation. These events contributed to the fragmentation of social theorizing in the

West. After Hegel's death, they boosted divisions among different ideologies and between the eastern and the western regions of the Western world.

The nineteenth century witnessed a rapid development of the political ideologies into distinct systems of social thought. These ideologies did not develop or take root uniformly throughout Western Europe, but separated into two distinctive political traditions, which roughly correspond to distinctive economic and social systems.

The two Western traditions

In the most general of terms the origins of this division can be traced back to the split of the Roman Empire. The split was reinforced in the Middle Ages and consolidated in the long sixteenth century – Western Europe evolved urban, seawards centres (Amsterdam, England and north-western France) which specialized in trade and manufacturing, whereas Eastern Europe specialized in rural production of raw materials. In the seventeenth and eighteenth centuries the division was accentuated as several countries in the West (the United Provinces, England, America, France) experienced political revolution, agrarian reform and the advent of wage labour. These countries spread their ideas along the North Atlantic rim. In the largely land-locked regions east of the Elbe River, by contrast, the old regimes retrenched their traditional social and political positions. By 1800, a politico-economic division of the Western world was drawn quite clearly between the market- and trade-oriented nation-states along the North Atlantic rim, which professed democratic, Enlightenment-derived political ideals, and the agriculturally based, authoritarian states east of the Elbe.

Liberal Enlightenment values had origins deep in British history. Notions of human rights and individual freedom were, for example, present in the Magna Carta (1215). In the rapid economic and political evolution in the eighteenth and nineteenth centuries, the expanding middle classes embraced the values of social equality, individual freedom and the right to unencumbered accumulation of private property. A rapid succession of political and constitutional Reform Bills passed during the 1830s transformed Britain into the most liberal country in Europe. By mid-century, most British thinkers had rejected mercantilist thought in favour of Bentham's vision of free trade.

In post-Napoleonic France, the liberal ideology was only reluctantly embraced – domestic politics were a tense tug-of-war between democrats of various hues and a counter-revolutionary reaction, which first gained the upper hand but then collapsed. In July 1830, workers, intellectuals and members of the bourgeoisie in Paris toppled the reactionary Charles X and replaced him with the progressive Louis-Philippe. The Paris parliament passed a series of reforms which liberalized the French political economy. Yet the conservative tendency (which in the French context became reactionary) remained an important presence in French politics. The radical tradition fired by Rousseau and the Revolution also remained a permanent fixture of French political life.

The social and political differences between the Atlantic rim and the Continent were accentuated by the policies of the conservative Austrian statesman Klemens von Metternich. After Napoleon's defeat, Metternich was the architect of the Congress of Vienna (1814–15), which provided Europe with a comprehensive peace treaty. His intention was to manage postwar policies through a system of regular congresses, later known as the Concert of Europe, which would facilitate the settlement of disputes between the European powers and work to repress revolution on the Continent.

Metternich's Concert of Europe was an effort to reconstruct the Europe of the Absolutist age. It rested on a pre-revolutionary vision of world politics and was supported by Europe's most autocratic regimes. Britain was a member of the Concert at the outset, but soon clashed with its conservative scheme. Britain wanted to preserve its ability to conduct free trade and to support the spread of liberal values to the rest of the world. In 1822 Britain left the Concert in a huff and proceeded to defend the South American nations in their revolt against Spain, and the Greek insurgents' struggle for independence from Turkey.

By leaving the Concert, England deflated Metternich's influence in western and in southern Europe. But by the same token, England also surrendered its opportunity to mitigate Metternich's anti-liberal policies in central and eastern Europe. In the absence of both British and French meddling, Metternich's scheme remained unchallenged there.

The purpose of the Concert was to contain liberalism. This policy was successful in the short run.[7] However, despite the best efforts of Metternich and the Holy Alliance, the Enlightenment project and its attendant visions of progress, industrialism and mass participation gradually emerged as the dominant vision of the century. In 1848, a wave of upheavals washed across the Continent and swept away both Metternich and his reactionary system. This collapse of the anti-Enlightenment bulwark of the reactionaries did not result in the clear victory of liberalism. Rather, it produced throughout Europe a fragmented political scene of kaleidoscopic complexity. On the Atlantic rim, liberalism broke up into a 'classic' and a 'revisionist' interpretation, as the key themes of equality, reason, freedom and property became subject to various interpretations. On the Continent, scholars and statesmen elaborated their ideological reactions to westcoast individualism into a variety of conservative and radical approaches.

Atlantic theories: Cobden and Mazzini

In France, the revolution of 1848 produced a half-way house between the Atlantic and the Continental traditions. The upheavals introduced more liberal measures in some areas (such as universal suffrage); at the same time they established a unique kind of mass–dictatorship under Emperor Louis Napoleon.[8]

In Britain, a split in liberalism became evident as Bentham's classic doctrines were challenged by new, reformist arguments. This mid-century split between a 'classic' and a 'reformist' interpretation of liberalism hinged on a debate about the proper function of the state. The classic doctrine distinguished sharply between politics and economics, and claimed that the economic sphere obeyed natural laws and that the state disturbed the natural, harmonious properties of social life if it intruded in the economic realm. Reformist liberals disagreed, and argued for an active role for the State in certain economic activities. Their argument hinged on a distinction drawn (for example by Mill 1866) between productive and distributive activities. The realm of production is subject to immutable natural laws which are fixed by nature and technology, it was argued. Distributive activities, by contrast, are socially determined and subject to human control. The reformist liberals argued that the laws of the free market can be trusted to stimulate the social division of labour and to enhance the efficiency of production. However, they cannot be trusted to allocate the goods produced in a fair and just manner. The state had an important role to play in the allocation of values in society, they claimed. State intervention was necessary to prevent social inequalities which would erode social justice and equality, and to provide conditions under which free economic competition could operate most efficiently.

The reformist argument influenced liberal approaches to international politics. A more active state in the domestic realm implied a more active role in foreign affairs as well. In domestic politics, the role of the state is to maintain justice and order in ways sanctioned by popular consensus through democratic channels. In the anarchical environment of international politics, by contrast, the state can maintain justice and order only if it can overcome the opposition of other states. When a democratic state assumes the role of judge and executor in the realm of international politics, it must be prepared to back its adjudications by force. The reformist liberal would agree with the conservative that war is the ultimate means of settling disputes among states. By this acknowledgement state intervention in domestic politics would find a functional equivalent of war in interstate relations. The British foreign minister Sir Edward Grey (1925, p. 286), reflecting in his memoirs upon the experiences of a liberal statesman, resolved that force must be available to uphold law among states as within states. Herbert Spencer put the point most succinctly: 'policemen are soldiers who act alone; soldiers are policemen who act in concert' (Spencer 1897, p. 118).

Bentham had argued that peace and order are best guaranteed by the principles of utility, free trade and non-intervention. His followers argued that the streams of goods and ideas which flowed unhindered across borders had peaceful effects on world affairs. Nations would grow richer through commerce than through conquest. According to Richard Cobden, humanity could best combat conflict and war by continuing to develop new means of communications which would, ultimately, spin humanity into a web of wealth and understanding – parliaments, international conferences, the popular press, compulsory education, the public reading room, the penny postage stamp, railways, submarine telegraphs, three-funnelled ocean liners and the Manchester cotton exchange were all forces for understanding, peace and harmony (Blainey 1973, pp. 18–32).

But how should democratic states behave towards assertive, intolerant and aggressive autocracies? Cobden was among the first liberal theorists to wrestle with the difficult question of whether a democratic state should tolerate states which rejected democratic principles. He noted that the lawless international environment 'corrupts [domestic] society; exhausts its wealth, raises up false gods for hero-worship, and fixes before the eyes of the rising generation a spurious if glittering standard of glory' (Morley 1881, p. 276). Faced with such contaminating international forces, should democratic societies retain their non-interventionist policies? Or should they actively combat despotism and the ignorance which sustains it?

In 1846, Cobden concluded that liberal democracies must not risk their ideals by exposing them to power politics. Democratic states should limit themselves to economic transactions and shun war. They should put their faith in free trade and in the steady progress of reason and freedom through history. Sooner or later, the inhabitants of autocracies, too, would realize that their true interests lie in Bentham's greatest happiness principle, in free trade, democracy and tolerance. The popular masses would then rise up, throw off the yoke of despotism and join the ranks of the open, enlightened and democratic societies (Cobden 1973).

The Italian patriot Giuseppe Mazzini disagreed. He countered Cobden's 'optimistic non-interventionism' with a doctrine of 'messianic interventionism' (Waltz 1959, p. 103). If democratic states do not contain despotic states, they will in effect allow those states to expand their influence, argued Mazzini. Such a passive stance would ultimately endanger the very existence of democracy. In 1853, Mazzini used this argument to convince the British government to support Turkish and Italian nationalists in a war to stop the westward expansion of autocratic Russia. He insisted that such a war would be unlike any war waged by despotic states; it would be a war for progress, peace, liberty and justice (Mazzini 1945, p. 91).[9]

Continental reaction: List and Bismarck

As Metternich's stable order eroded during the 1840s, several Continental states felt increasingly threatened by the political ideals of popular participation and by the increasing flood of low-cost British products. In the wake of the revolutionary upheavals of 1848, many states evolved their own ideological responses to the North Atlantic doctrines of social order.

Put on the political defensive, conservative rulers sought to stave off Atlantic influences through appeals to national communalism and the nation-state. Neither institution was fully established on the Continent; yet the concept of a *Staat* which articulated the will of a *Volk* was immensely seductive. Without it, as Clausewitz and Hegel had observed at Jena, the fragmented central region of Europe would easily become the prey to either the military power of France or the industrial power of England. During the Napoleonic Wars, German scholars had attacked the Enlightenment project's claim to universality and developed an alternative doctrine of cultural relativism. Herder, Hegel, Clausewitz and others argued that each people possessed not only a unique collective spirit but also an inherent right to preserve its identity and independence.

Fichte (1979a) developed an important, concrete foreign-policy theory which reflected these concerns. He delivered an emphatic attack on the free-market ideology of Britain and proposed a mercantilist policy based on a doctrine of strict protectionism as the obvious German response. Similar arguments were pursued by Friedrich List.[10] He denounced the liberal economic theory as 'pure ideology' – by which he meant the universalization of the special interests of a dominant state. Free trade was no universal doctrine; it was a body of ideas developed to suit a specific country at a certain stage in history. It was designed to make England the world's industrial centre by keeping other countries in the dependent role of suppliers of raw materials and food (List 1927).

Like Fichte, List emphasized the value of the national community. Individuals come and go; the nation has a continual life. The nation–state represents continuity, whereas individuals are its temporary inhabitants, and the concerns of the individual must be subordinated to those of the *Volk*, It is only 'right and proper that the individual should be ready to sacrifice his own interests for the benefit of the nation to which he belongs', writes List (1927, pp. 181–9).

The security and the stability of a nation–state must be judged in terms of the harmonious development of its three major productive sectors, List continues (1930): agriculture, industry and commerce. This sectoral division of the national economy provides him with a stage theory of history as well as a strategy for industrialization. The first and most primitive stage is based on agricultural production. In an agricultural society, people work the land for subsistence and remain isolated from the international economy. Here, 'the whole range of intellectual and moral powers is virtually non-existent and sheer physical strength is all that can be expected from those who work the land' (List 1927, pp. 239f; also 1930, p. 214).

The second stage of development introduces trade. Agriculture is complemented by trade and by some manufacturing, which 'promotes the growth of intellectual and moral forces of every kind' (List 1927, p. 243). Enterprising citizens emulate foreign means of production, elaborate domestic manufactures into fledgling industries. These budding domestic ventures will, however, inevitably reach a point at which further development is impossible, argues List. For when local entrepreneurs begin to master elementary industrial techniques, they will encounter competition from cheap, high-quality foreign imports and be undercut by them. Consequently, the nation's development will stall at a relatively low level of industrialization.

This stagnation can be overcome by state intervention. The state can bring a nation to the third stage of economic development by a policy of protectionism – the state can, in a manner of speaking, decouple the nation from the world economy and temporarily isolate it behind a tariff wall. Tariffs and state planning will 'revive the spirit of enterprise in a country' and propel the nation on to a higher, more competitive stage of economic development, argues List (1930, p. 357).

During this period of temporary isolation, the nation has an opportunity to combine the sectors of agriculture, industry and commerce into a mutually supporting, self-reliant whole (p. 257). When the domestic economy is harmonious and domestic industries strong enough to compete with foreign producers, the state must dismantle its protective tariff wall and re-enter the world economy. Now that it can participate in the international economic competition from a position of strength, a country has everything to gain from a free-trade world economy.

List did not provide a general theory of economic development. Only countries which possessed a certain '*völkish*' unity of spirit, an inordinate political discipline and a strong state could bear the temporary cost of a strategy which would sacrifice the gains and enjoyments of an entire generation of citizens (1927, pp. 181–9). It fell to Otto von Bismarck to provide Germany with the final prerequisite in List's strategy, a strong nation-state – thus ensuring the success of the Continental response to Atlantic liberalism.

It was not immediately apparent that Bismarck's aim was to contain liberalism. He first advocated German unity at a time when this idea was identified with the liberal cause of an all-German parliamentary democracy. But it soon became clear that, while Bismarck supported German unity, he did not support the cause of parliamentarism. Nor did he believe that democratic reform and greater economic co-operation would achieve German unification as German liberals argued. In Bismarck's view, Germany could be united only through war. 'It is not by speeches and resolutions that the great questions of the time are decided,' he insisted, 'but by iron and blood'. He saw international relations as a struggle between conflicting state interests. And he understood that, in the age of modern, powerful nation-states, Prussia's interests could be maintained either through a close association with Austria or through unification with other, smaller German states, thus building Prussia into a substantial nation-state in its own right.

Bismarck is a significant contributor to International Relations theory. But his fame rests not so much on his writings as on his example. It rests on his remarkable practice of balance-of-power politics – through which he managed to unify Germany (Bismarck 1898).[11] Once he had attained this goal, the old 'white revolutionary' suddenly distinguished himself by his moderation, insisting that Germany be content with the frontiers he had given her. Illustrating Goethe's words 'in der Beschränkung zeigt sich der Meister', Bismarck restrained German's power and limited national ambitions. He avoided acts which could upset Germany's neighbours and trigger a collective reaction among them; instead he invested his considerable acumen in a policy of reassurance and interstate stability. He became an honest broker for peace, and his shrewd system of alliances compelled every country on the Continent, whatever its will, to follow a peaceful course (Kissinger 1968; 2015, pp. 77f).

Beyond Europe

The upsurge of industrialism and democracy spread the new confidence in science and the new visions of society throughout Europe and beyond. The Western concepts of 'industrialism', 'nationalism', 'democracy', 'liberty' and 'equality' proved irresistible to extra-European areas. So did the interconnected, capitalist world economy which emerged from the Atlantic rim, and remained centred there. This involved a dual revolution 'of the economies and states in a particular geographical region of the world (part of Europe and a few patches of North America), whose centre was the neighbouring and rival states of Great Britain and France' (Hobsbawm 1962, pp. 17ff).

Western institutions, ideology and techniques thence spread across the world. The economic and military power displayed by the Western countries as they conquered other regions made their ideological visions extraordinarily potent far beyond their point of origin. These new ideologies appealed to mass audiences throughout the world and stirred them to action. Statesmen, soldiers and charlatans soon developed tools of mass propaganda and organization through which they could bring mass action to bear in their intra-elite quarrels or to mobilize societies to meet the economic, technological and military threats from the West.

The nineteenth-century Prussian response to the onslaught of investments, armies and Enlightenment doctrines from the West foreshadowed the twentieth-century dilemma which would face non-European areas: the assault from the West could be beaten only by adopting Western ideas and institutions. Prussia's response proved particularly attractive. Prussia adopted several Western ideas and institutions as it built a new, strong state. But, at the same time, it rejected the liberal ethos upon which these ideas and institutions were originally based. The Prussian example suggested that particular elements of the Western outlook could be successfully extracted from the Enlightenment package of liberal modernism and then turned against it. In particular, industrialism, the strong state and a mass-mobilizing political programme could be adopted with minimum threat to local elites (Barraclough 1976, pp. 153–99; Laue 1987).

It is vital to bear in mind the indigenous roots of the nationalism which drove extra-European societies towards independence in the twentieth century. However, it is also important to recall that the first successful defences against the free-market liberalism of the Atlantic rim were erected not in Asia or Africa but in the heart of Europe (Veblen 1939). Bismarck successfully contained the liberal influence from the West – informed by a nationalist doctrine expressed by Fichte and a centre–periphery theory developed by List, Bismarck provided the economic basis for a strong and viable state; he constructed a modern state bureaucracy, a rationalized military force, progressive voting laws and a social legislation which foreshadowed the twentieth-century welfare state. It appears paradoxical on the face of it, but the paternalist conservatism of nineteenth-century Prussians exerted a profound influence on radical twentieth-century national-liberation movements in the extra-European world.

Notes

1 Factories and shops created solidarity among workers subjected to the wearisome pace set by the new machines. In the industrial cities huddled a new, proletarianized working class, as well as a city mob of unemployed and dispossessed people. Since these two emerged together on the social scene, they raised the spectre of mass action and disorder for the established classes of society, whose members could not always distinguish between them.

2 Bentham, like Smith, recognized that politics is unavoidable because it provides necessary services for society: legislation, maintenance of civil order and national defence. Yet politics should not interfere with the natural properties of the economic order. All forms of government intervention involve some degree of interruption of this order; whatever the legislator does, it is bound to be 'felt in the shape of hardship and coercion somewhere' (Stark 1952–54, p. 311).

3 Bentham wrote three major essays on international affairs: 'Objects of international

law', 'War considered in respect of its causes and consequences' and 'A plan for a universal and perpetual peace'. These were all written in the late 1790s and are collected in a comparatively slim volume entitled *Principles of International Law* (which is included in Bentham's collected *Works* (1843), Vol. 2, pp. 531–61). A fourth essay, 'Emancipate your colonies', was issued separately (and is included in Bentham's *Works* (1843), Vol. 4, pp. 408–19).

4   Around 1800, Germany still consisted of some three hundred states, principalities and free cities, loosely linked together as the Holy Roman Empire under the leadership of Francis I of Austria. Napoleon abolished this thousand-year-old empire when he vanquished the Austrians at Ulm and Austerlitz (1805) and the Prussians at Jena (1806). Clausewitz was not the only observer present at Jena who realized the importance of the concept of *Volk* in history and in international politics; Hegel was there too.

5   The degree to which the three ideologies of liberalism, radicalism and conservatism appear similar or different depends upon the vantage point of the observer. From the narrowly Eurocentric perspective adopted in this discussion, the differences far outweigh the similarities. However, it must be borne in mind that these ideologies are all products of a Western-Christian political culture; thus, from a Buddhist or a Confucian perspective, the differences between them may appear rather minute.

6   Although Hegel continued to exert influence on the Anglo–American world through theorists like F. H. Bradley, J. E. McTaggert, T. H. Green, Josiah Royce and R. G. Collingwood.

7   Metternich grafted his worldview on to a balance-of-power argument. Devoted to the cause of Austria's national interest, Metternich saw in liberal democracy a challenge to Austrian power in south-central Europe. Liberal Germans, for example, argued for greater unity among the thirty-nine members of the German Confederation (*Bund*). If the members of the *Bund* could only remove the existing restrictions on transport, trade and travel and adopt democratic constitutions, then the forces of free exchange would stimulate the creation of wealth, binding the German states together in tight interdependence. Metternich saw that such integration would seriously impede Austria's policies in Hungary, Italy and the Balkans. He therefore sought to persuade the local German rulers that the liberals were working to undermine the established order in central Europe.

The landowning nobility east of the River Rhine also opposed the doctrines of Western-style reforms. Metternich skilfully exploited and accentuated the difference in socioeconomic structure and philosophical sentiment between the western and the central regions of Europe to his own benefit. By presenting Enlightenment ideals as an unwelcome intrusion on the part of Germany's expanding western neighbours, Metternich managed to foment a chauvinistic and xenophobic reaction which helped his cause and broadened the gap between the Atlantic and the Continental political traditions of Europe.

8   The sentiment surrounding these events is well represented by the texts of Alexis de Tocqueville.

9   This conflict within liberalism between 'optimistic non-interventionism' and 'messianic interventionism' – between a passive and an active state – has remained endemic, notably in US foreign policy.

10   List had studied political economy in the United States and carefully observed

how American politicians had built up the new nation's industries behind a wall of selective tariffs. List especially admired Alexander Hamilton's efforts to escape the influence of Europe's imperial economies. He embraced Hamilton's claims: that a strong economy is an invaluable basis for a country's defence; that a government can intervene in the domestic economy and greatly encourage its rate of development; that in the modern age such development must be based on the superiority of manufacturing over agriculture (Hamilton 1928).

11   The upheavals of 1848 swept Metternich's reactionary regime away. Austria was a multinational empire embracing at least ten major nationalities, and the revolutionary sentiment which had ousted Metternich from power had also fuelled demands for self-determination among various national groups and pushed the old Austrian empire close to fragmentation and political paralysis. In Germany, by contrast, the upheavals had stimulated the vision of a larger German *Volk*, and had strengthened the idea of a German Confederation (*Bund*).

In Bismarck's view, Prussia's old policy of a close alliance with Austria had become unviable. Prussia's interests could be served only by the establishment of a larger, Prussian-led German state. Such a policy would be resented by the smaller members of the German *Bund*, Bismarck realized: left to their own volition, the small states would seek to maximize their petty interests by striking a neutral position between the two major German actors, Austria and Prussia. If Prussia undertook to unify Germany, this would drive many minor states into Austria's embrace. Germany could be unified only through a war between Austria and Prussia. And if war was inevitable, Prussia should prepare for it sooner rather than later. His mind made up, Bismarck bided his time and waited for an opportunity to build up Prussia's military forces and for a constellation of forces in Europe which could allow Prussia to challenge Austria for the leadership of Germany.

Bismarck had his opportunity when Kaiser Wilhelm I appointed him Chancellor (1862). He immediately expanded Prussia's military forces, seeing this as the first, necessary step towards his goal of a unified Germany under Prussian leadership. His second step was to bring into the open the conflict of interest between Prussia and Austria: he allied with Austria in a war against Denmark over the duchies of Schleswig and Holstein (1864), and then he exploited the joint annexation of the duchies to trigger the conflict with Austria that he had so long sought. Through 1865, Bismarck allowed the animosities to deepen while he quietly discredited Austria in British, Russian and French eyes. When Austria was isolated diplomatically, he provoked Austria to declare war. Having prepared this war for four years, he crushed the Austrian army in seven weeks. He annexed both Schleswig and Holstein, together with the kingdom of Hanover, the duchies of Nassau and Hesse--Cassel and the free city of Frankfurt. These annexations dissolved the German *Bund*. In its place, Bismarck organized a North German Confederation (1867), which the newly enlarged Prussia joined with twenty-one other German states.

In 1870, Bismarck pursued his policy of violent unification by provoking war with France, relying on traditional German fears of France to drive the remaining German states into the new Confederation. Again, he was wildly successful: Prussia defeated France in nine months, and the small states of Germany were unified under Prussian leadership.

Part III

The classic age of International Relations

7

Intermezzo: becoming contemporary

In the spring of 1872, the Academy of Sciences in the city of Amiens admitted a new member to their circle; he was not really a scientist but a novelist with a keen interest in science. His name was Jules Verne. As it was customary for new affiliates to publicly substantiate their scholarly worth, Verne was expected to make a formal acceptance speech. He asked if he could read extracts from his forthcoming book. It dealt, he explained, with a 'sort of problem whose solution is geographically demonstrated' (Lottman 1997, p. 164). The Academy's governors agreed.

So on the day of his admission, Verne read a story about an unflappable Englishman, Mr Phileas Fogg. Mr Fogg read in the newspaper that a new section of the Great Indian Peninsular Railway had just been opened and pronounced that, according to his calculations, a journey around the world could now be made in eighty days. When some members of Mr Fogg's club protested, he made a bet with them that such a journey could indeed be made in eighty days. He packed his bags and left London – dramatically and by balloon. Accompanied by his faithful servant, Passepartout, the phlegmatic circumnavigator then tore around the globe in a race against time.

Around the World in Eighty Days was published in 1873 and was an instant success. One reason for this was the string of exciting adventures afforded by its plot. Another was the way in which Verne deftly spruced up the adventurous action with comedy, drama and suspense. A third reason for the book's success was its basic globetrotting concept. Verne larded his story with factual information about peoples and places and 'every possible means of conveyance – steamers, railways, carriages, yachts, trading ships, sledges, elephants' (Verne 1991 [1872]: 245). His audience was fascinated by the faraway places, the exotic settings, the unusual events – as well as the unexpected time twist in the last chapter.

The runaway success of Verne's book testifies to the enormous interest sparked by things international. This interest is the main concern of this chapter. The many ways in which this interest manifested itself will also be addressed – thus, it will be noted that international approaches were regularly shaped by an old confidence in the symmetry of the universe and the self-regulating properties of human action, and that this informed new, nineteenth-century views on the progress of history and the evolution of humankind.

Nineteenth-century international thought differed from that of earlier centuries in several respects. One of them concerns diversity. In the case of previous centuries, it is easier to identify a particular theme which characterized the age and a distinct 'voice' which expressed it. The nineteenth century is different. In some ways it resembles the sixteenth century in that it is hard to find a clear, unifying theme. The nineteenth century was torn between irreconcilable modes of thought. Instead of these thoughts being expressed by different individuals, they were reflected in different systems of thought – they were expressed in '-isms'. Their development began with the Enlightenment and continued with the late eighteenth-century evolution of the distinct ideologies of liberalism, radicalism and conservatism. But they were first torn and pummelled during the course of the Industrial Revolution and the Napoleonic Wars, and then by social and intellectual forces – by industrialism, imperialism and nationalism.

This chapter is devoted to these various -isms, to their interaction and to their effect on the international thinking of the age. It will open by a discussion of nationalism – a phenomenon which has long historical roots but which attained new forms and a greater significance during the course of the nineteenth century. It will introduce industrialism and imperialism before addressing theories that made an impression on virtually all political discussions towards the end the century, such as evolutionism. The chapter will conclude with discussing some of the forces that produced a significant interest in international affairs towards the end of the nineteenth century – and which paved the way for a new science of international politics by the beginning of the twentieth.

Nationalism

It is hard to determine when the idea of the 'nation' emerged. However, it is clear that it constituted a notable political force in the wake of the French Revolution. It spread to the Americas and, in the wake of the revolutionary upheavals of 1848, to central Europe. The 1860s saw the emergence of several new self-titled nation-states: a unified kingdom in Italy, a new empire in Germany, a dual monarchy in Austria–Hungary and a political reorganization in tsarist Russia. In the last decades of the century, it was additionally stimulated by the growth of modern industry, the expansion of international trade and the global expansion of Western interest and influence. By the end of the century, nationalism had spread beyond the West. To Asia, for example, where arose the new 'Westernized' nation of Japan.

The word 'nation' can be traced back to medieval universities, where it signified groups of students of a distinct, common origin. From the beginning of its modern usage, then, the word denoted a group of people, and it concerned their common geographical origin. Soon it would also denote their allegiance.

In medieval and early modern times people gave their allegiance to the city-state, the feudal fief, the town, the region or the religious group. The rise of nationalism implied an important change of allegiance: it forged strong bonds of loyalty between people and state.

At the core of the concept lies the idea that all citizens owe their supreme loyalty to the nation and its representative state institutions. Patriotism has long been present in the Western political tradition – as is evident in the concluding chapter of Machiavelli's (1961) *The Prince*. Nationalism is a more recent phenomenon.

Print vernaculars
The roots of modern nationalism can be traced to fifteenth-century Europe and to debates about belongingness, authority and identity that led up to the Reformation. One of the prompts of that debate was the rise of modern print technologies and the attending evolution of different print vernaculars. This development shattered the dominance of Church Latin as a universal language. It weakened the notion of a universal Christian community. It broke the unifying power of the pope. At the same time it stimulated to the rise of alternative identities.

Local languages and local identities evolved all over Europe, stimulated by the growth of markets for cheap editions of printed vernacular texts – bibles, practical handbooks, almanacs, novels, leaflets, pamphlets and news-sheets. The markets defined linguistic boundaries and contributed to the standardization of market-specific print-vernaculars. This development was encouraged by princes and kings, who standardized print-vernaculars further and relied on them as languages-of-state-power.[1]

The growth of vernacular texts provided a decisively important precondition for the emergence in Europe of national communities, each unified by a common language and by linguistically specific stories, myths and norms. In this sense, a nation is 'an imagined political community – and imagined as both inherently limited and sovereign' (Anderson 1983, p. 6).[2] There is, however, more to the story. A couple of centuries later, the advent of industrialism intensified the unifying impact of print-vernaculars in Western society. For hand in hand with the growth of industry and commerce went a new secularization of life, new urban centres, modern school systems and mass literacy.

In their wake of the reforms of primary education followed the rise, for the first time in history, of a truly mass readership and a popular literature within everybody's reach. This prompted a sudden emergence of a literate mass audience. New literary genres emerged that catered to a mass market. It also created a greater familiarity with Enlightenment ideas, such as the concept of popular sovereignty and of human rights. By the end of the nineteenth century these ideas had spread widely across the industrializing regions of Europe.

As industrialism, urbanization and literacy waxed, the legitimacy of the absolute monarchs waned. By the nineteenth century, the monarch embodied neither the nation nor the state; the state became a people's state, a national state, a *patrie* or a *Vaterland*. And with this rapid spread of the Enlightenment idea of the self-determination of the people and the general participation of all its members ('citzens') in the politics of the state, nationalism emerged as an irresistible political force. It ideas of self-determination and mass-participation boosted the basic claim that the policies of the state should reflect the will of the people.

Constitutional and cultural versions of nationalism

Nationalism is inconceivable without the idea of popular sovereignty. This basic idea was early articulated by Enlightenment authors like Jean-Jacques Rousseau and implemented by the French Revolution. Soon it was criticized and attacked – especially by academics who inhabited the lands conquered by Napoleon's armies. For as Napoleon expanded his rule and introduced his own *code Napoléon* on the newly conquered territories, the native populations protested. One notable important protest was articulated by Johann Gottfried Herder. His argument provided the foundation for a new kind of nationalism. By the time the Napoleonic Wars were over, there existed two conceptions of the nation and two different doctrines of nationalism in Europe.

On the one hand was the original conception, which was based on the ideas of Rousseau and spread by the French Revolution. Rousseau had wanted to restore the close togetherness of the ancient city-states. He followed the example of Sparta in regarding love of the *patrie* as the most heroic of human passions. However, whereas the Spartans praised the values of the urban, educated elite and the warrior noblemen, Rousseau extolled the virtues of the common person (Rousseau 1950b, 1964d). He sought to marry the notion of a popular togetherness with the idea of an active 'consent of the governed'. He devised the potent concept of the 'general will' to capture the tight unity of the people. The French revolutionaries included these notions in their idea of the nation as a *patrie*. They saw the nation as a contract. It was based on an agreement of basic political values and expressed in a constitution. The constitution would specify these values and delineate political institutions designed to defend and further them. The French ideologist Abbe Sieyès captured this contractarian concept well, when he (in 1789) defined a nation as 'a union of individuals governed by one law, and represented by the same law-giving assembly' (see also Renan n.d. [1882]).

On the other hand was the nationalism expressed by Herder. His concept of a nation was not based on a political contract but on a long, organic evolution of common cultural characteristics. Herder, too, expressed an admiration for the common people. But his arguments were steeped in a bucolic imagery that exceeded the Romanticism of even Rousseau. The authentic identity of a nation must rise from the native roots of the natural, rural masses, claimed Herder. He criticized the evils of pride and lust and bellicosity, which he attributed to the artificial, educated upper classes. But he glorified the unsullied virtues of the common *Volk*.

During the Napoleonic Wars, then, two different understandings of the 'nation' evolved in Europe. One saw the nation in terms of a vast contract, common laws and a set of social institutions. Its advocates would accept as citizen any individual who pledged allegiance to the laws of the land and the norms and values it represented. This was Napoleon's understanding. As he conquered new lands in central and eastern Europe, and imposed his own norms and laws on their populations, they protested and rebelled. Their rebellion consolidated another understanding of nation and nationhood. It was based on the vision, not of a contract among people, but of historical evolution of a *Volk*. It argued that a nation has evolved organically through time and expresses itself as a cultural unity through its language, folklore, religion and common historical understanding of a shard ancestry. Its advocates did not accept just anybody as a member of their nation; they would only admit those individuals who shared all the traits – language, faith and ethnic features – which characterized the communal culture.

This cultural understanding of nationhood, which was constructed in opposition to the Napoleonic expansion eastwards, became the dominant understanding in the central and eastern regions in Europe. Furthermore, opposition to Napoleon and to the political values of the French invaders, caused peoples to throw out more general Enlightenment values with the Napoleonic bathwater. Opposition to the French invaders led to rejection of Enlightenment values *tout court*, and drove the occupied peoples in the region deeper into Herder's Romanticism and identities forged in a mythic past.

In the eastern regions of Europe, then, anti-Westernism, Romanticism and nationalism became intertwined concepts. When Prussian scholars countered the universalist faith in human reason and popular participation which were inherent in the French Enlightenment, they drew upon Herder's particularist claim that each *Volk* possessed a unique collective spirit. The emphasis on language, history and culture was glorified and the concept of the *Volk* was idealized. The French brand of constitutional nationalism was rejected and replaced with a nationalism which stressed the unifying effect of common cultural norms – a common language, a common religion and a common past – organically evolved through a long (and often sad and heroic) history.

During the nineteenth century, Herder-type arguments gathered strength. They were picked up by counter-Enlightenment authors like Johann Georg Hamann (1730–88) and Johann Gottlieb Fichte (1762–1814), who whipped them into pitched intensity in Prussia, and made concepts like *Volksgeist* and *Volkstum* into explosive political ideas. In a self-conscious reaction against the threats of French militarism and British mercantilism, Hamann and Fichte emphasized the distinctive qualities of the German *Volksgeist*. They argued that Germans possessed greater spiritual depth – more music – than the materialist or cerebral imports from France or Britain. They argued that the servant, knowing both his own role and that of his master, is wiser than the master, who knows only his own.

Authors like Hegel and Clausewitz elaborated on these arguments and noted that, whereas eighteenth-century monarchs had found it hard to generate popular enthusiasm for diplomacy or war, nineteenth-century kings had discovered how to use the concept of the *Volk* to mobilize mass support. Clausewitz found it significant that whereas eighteenth-century armies had counted between ten thousand and seventy thousand men, Napoleon had managed to mobilize over a million soldiers. He observed that the mobilization of popular masses affected the traditional system of international politics.

During the course of the nineteenth century, the stakes of international politics transcended the limited concerns of dynastic diplomacy. Clausewitz (1976) argued already at the century's beginning that war 'became the business of the people'. He saw a break in the history of war and macro-politics. In the past, international interaction had largely been dynastic. The kings of Europe had traded territories with relative ease according to rules of marriage and war – the two most important tools of dynastic diplomacy – and had paid little attention to the inhabitants of the territories traded. From now on, however, the will of the inhabitants constituted the only acceptable criterion for drawing state boundaries. From now on, the outcome of wars would depend not only on the wealth of the monarch, but also on the will of the nation. From now on the people who belonged to the same distinct ethnic or linguistic group would inhabit the same territory. This way of seeing things would cause movements of national independence to spread throughout Europe and the Americas. These movements were driven, not by kings' concerns for territory, but by peoples' quest for self-determination.

Mass education

The observations on popular identity which Clausewitz noted during the Napole-onic Wars became steadily more visible after the conclusion of peace at Vienna. New education laws introduced elementary schools in most Western states. Mass education had a socializing effect on all Europeans. Reading, writing and religion were taught to children from all layers of society. Children from all regions of a country were introduced to a standardized print-language, shared cultural values and a common history.

European institutions of higher learning were also reformed. Chairs of 'national' literature and history were established at European universities. Dissertations were written in the vernacular rather than in Latin or Greek. This initiated a golden age for European philologists, grammarians, lexicographers and litterateurs. There was also the related effect of the expanding market for cheap, vernacular texts. Encouraged by growing literacy, cheap paper and the rotary press, commercial printed matter proliferated all over Europe and people were socialized into key national legends and myths through mass-produced texts. Elementary readers and patriotic history books were efficient means of socialization, by means of which each new generation of citizens was introduced into a collective imagination and identity.

Early nineteenth-century nationalism had a progressive character. The movement was built around the idea that all citizens owe their supreme secular loyalty to the nation and its representative institutions – often with an emphasis on the institutions. This idea implies, in turn, both the development of strong emotional attachments between citizens and a central state and the involvement of the citizens in the political life of the state. Late nineteenth-century nationalism, by contrast, was largely associated with conservatism if not reaction. This shift in nationalism from the political left to the right was more marked on the Continent than along the Atlantic rim.

Around the North Atlantic rim, a 'nation' was politically defined – often in liberal democratic terms – by reference to a constitution, a state and its representative institutions. Thus defined, the unity and identity of a nation would derive from political organization. Also, the state would be logically prior to the nation.

In the central regions of Europe, however, a nation tended to be defined in terms of culture. By this definition, the nation was logically prior to the state. Whereas the French revolutionaries saw the nation as a group of individuals unified by and subject to a single political order, the Germans saw nations as produced by history and distinguished from one another by God and nature. For the French *philosophes*, the nation was expressed through the state, for the Germans the nation was expressed through the *Volk*, which articulated a distinct *Geist* that was expressed in its language.

The liberal nationalists of the Atlantic tradition possessed no elaborate notion of how a world of nation-states would interact. They commonly entertained the simple faith that, if all nations established their own states, these states would become more similar. They would all be established on the reason of sensible people, humankind would become unified along rational lines and international conflict would cease to exist.

In the fragmented central regions of Europe, nationalist thinkers developed very different visions. They would tend to argue that as different *Völker* established their own states, these states would differ from each other. The world would become more culturally diverse. Some of them would claim, with Herder, that each *Volk* would contribute in its unique way to the vast variety and richness of human civilization. Each *Volk*, secure in its own identity, would respect the identity of all others. Thus, a world of many different *Völker* would produce a rich and harmonious humanity.

Others would argue that world harmony was a naive dream. They would claim, with Fichte, that the many different *Völker* of the world would vary wildly in wealth, power and level of material and cultural development. The nations of the world were not at all equal. Some were primitive whereas others were advanced. And those that were superior were destined to rule over those that were inferior.

Both of these multicultural arguments evolved during the nineteenth century. In large, multinational empires the visions fuelled wars of national liberation; here echoes from Herder would reverberate through the political rhetoric of the rebels. Among fragmented states, the visions fuelled wars of national unification; here variations of Fichte's chauvinism would appear. During the course of the century, it looked like chauvinism would win out. In the 1860s, Cavour united Italy in a series of remarkable military operations. Soon after, in the 1870s, Bismarck united Germany through a succession of masterfully contained wars. In both cases profound changes were produced in the nationalist movements. Fuelled by a sentimental mix of historical myths and Romantic philosophy and fortified by industrial expansionism, nationalism became a chauvinistic and right-wing cause.[3]

Industrialism

The spread of nationalism was boosted by the expansion of industry; not only by the new printing presses but also by railroads, steamships, telegraphs and the mass markets of mass-produced consumer goods. These products of industrialism made communication of ideas, exchange of goods and transport of people easier than ever before (Buzan and Lawson 2015, ch. 3). The last quarter of the nineteenth century marked a particularly intense and turbulent phase in the evolution of industrialism. It implied not just the expansion to the rest of the world of the industrializing process that had altered England so dramatically during the Napoleonic Wars (the 'first industrial revolution'). It was in many respects so different in nature and pace that it deserves to be seen as a phenomenon in its own right (the 'second industrial revolution'). For whereas the first industrial revolution had involved incremental change, the second was sudden. It was quicker in its pace and more immediately prodigious in its impact.[4]

Industrial expansion effected a rapid growth in the size of enterprises and necessitated new modes of economic and social organization. In all sectors of industry, factories were built in gigantic dimensions which required the co-operation of hundreds of workers. This meant that the old enterprises which employed a dozen workers were rendered anachronistic. The new factories hired armies of workers who came from far away to live in rapidly growing urban agglomerations.

Mobilizing the masses

The trends towards greater concentration of capital, growth in factory size and urbanization of labour gathered pace during the last quarter of the century. It was a period of unprecedented triumphs. It was also an age of spectacular failures. But most of all it was a period of rapid transformation. Change acted as a solvent of the old order and a catalyst of the new.

The rapid pace of industrialism upset the old, domestic order in the countries of the West. As it spread across Europe, it converted the rural labourers of the traditional village into the workers of the new industrial towns. Industrialism and urbanization fuelled the rise of new and powerful groups and classes. The development of modern business – of new kinds of corporations, banks and insurance companies – boosted the growth of financial elites in Britain, France, Germany and the United States. The second half of the nineteenth century saw the development of conglomerates and trusts with international reach.

Organizational transformation also took place in government. Western countries evolved more central and merit-based state bureaucracies. Politicians passed bills which sought to regulate business and allow governments to play more active roles in harnessing the economy and shaping civil society. They incrementally expanded voting rights, which stimulated the advent of modern political organizations – parties, interest groups and trade unions foremost among them.[5]

Such bills transformed the political systems of the industrializing countries of the West after 1850. They tended to increase the dominance of national assemblies over the political process and thus paved the way for Parliamentarism and a modern system of liberal democracy. Further away from the North Atlantic rim, reforms also cleared the way for anti-liberal mass movements – on both sides of the political spectrum. And as a rule, the more rapid the industrialization, the stronger the anti-liberal reaction (Bull 1948). The creation of new industrial societies encouraged the growth of workers' unions, labour parties, class consciousness and radical politics. Also, the destruction of the traditional social order stimulated the rise of conservative Romantic movements which resisted the new trends of urbanization and social *anomie*.

The pace of industrialization also upset the old order among states. The faster the nations industrialized, the more their capacities grew. When the nations of the West improved their school systems, they not only enhanced the quality of the workforce, they also improved the quality of their soldiers. When they improved the methods of steel production, they also increased their ability to build better weapons. When they improved their roads and railways, they also improved their ability to project their military power. When they replaced their wooden ships with steel vessels, they increased the speed and capacity of their navies and boosted their ability to transport vast numbers of people rapidly to any port or bay on the globe.

Uneven growth rates, uncertain relations
Different Western countries industrialized at different rates. This uneven industrial growth translated into uneven growth of nations' military potentials. During the final quarter of the nineteenth century, some medium-size states in Europe (like Germany) expanded their industrial capabilities and their military potentials at a breakneck rate. By contrast, some traditionally great powers (like Britain) grew at a slower rate, and were, by 1900, not as superior as before. The old interstate balance of power became unclear, and the hierarchies of military force and political prestige became unclear.

These developments created uncertainties in international affairs. First, the uneven growth of state capabilities tore apart the last remainders of the relatively stable Concert system. Second, Europe's own monopoly of modern production was broken by the dissemination of industrialism to other continents.[6] During the final quarter of the century, the mounting uncertainty of world politics was accentuated by great economic fluctuations. The first serious downswing occurred in 1873, when major US ventures defaulted on their bonds. This triggered a panic which immediately swept the capitals of Europe. Waves of booms and busts followed for the next twenty-odd years, earning the period 1873–96 the sobriquet 'the Great Depression'.

The depression triggered a panic. It increased the speed with which capital concentrated and centralized. The main casualty of the panic was the old small-scale family business. Small ventures, which had typically emerged during the first industrial revolution, were too narrowly based and too inefficiently run to withstand the birth-pains of the second. The more diversified and rationally run enterprises did better. The panic, in effect, favoured the large-scale concern. It stimulated diversification and combination, and encouraged the formation of trusts and cartels.

Germany and the United States were hardest hit. Both were new states. Both were thrown from domestic war and nation-building into financial panic. Both saw an inordinate amount of bankruptcies and small businesses going under, large ones growing larger, and capital concentrating in large combines. By 1900, the economies of Germany and the USA were dominated by a small number of huge combines. The credit requirements for these companies were gigantic, and the banks and credit institutions involved in their financing insisted on membership of their boards of directors in order to safeguard their loans and investments. In this way, great financiers came to exert a great influence on the management of the behemoths of business.

Britain and France, older and established nation-states, escaped more easily from the 1873 panic. In both countries the small-scale, family venture remained a common feature in the economic landscape. But here, too, the concentration of capital produced giant combines in steel and chemicals – in Britain, firms like Brunner-Mond and Vickers-Armstrong grew to giant proportions during the final quarter of the century, and in France the Schneider-Creusot company grew rapidly.

In 1880, Britain was the world's leading industrial power; twenty-five years later it was second to the United States, and was also challenged by Germany, which industrialized at a more rapid rate. Germany took the lead in the newer, more important industries of chemicals and machine tools. German engineers like Diesel, Daimler and Benz ignited a revolution in transportation when they, in the 1880s and 1890s, developed small, efficient engines which ran on the light, volatile fractions of petroleum.

The swift spread of the new engines sparked the creation of ventures for the exploration, drilling, transport and refinement of oil. Around the turn of the century, large oil companies were drilling in Europe, the United States, the Middle East and Asia. The quest for petroleum altered the political economies of the world. For although most European countries initially could find the oil they needed on their own territories, the largest reserves were found at great distances from the major consumer countries. Great discoveries in Pennsylvania, Texas and California made the United States self-sufficient in oil. Europe, however, realized that its future needs for petroleum could be secured only by safeguarding access to foreign wells.

At the turn of the century, this reliance on extra-European oil increased the geopolitical importance of the Near and the Middle East. This development intruded upon the concerns of Britain, whose leaders had long propped up the tottering Ottoman Empire so that it could serve to contain the interference of other European powers in the Near East, notably Russia – indeed, defeating Russian designs in Asia Minor was an obsessive goal of British officials. At first, concerns for oil supplies were minimal – although oil companies were scrambling for concessions in areas controlled by the drowsy and negligent Ottomans, it was not yet known that astonishing quantities of oil existed in the area. But by the end of World War I, when the Ottoman Empire had finally collapsed, Middle Eastern oil began to emerge as a complicating and divisive factor in the politics of the region.

The diffusion of modern instruments of industry and the worldwide quest for fossil fuels illustrate a final difference between the first industrial revolution and the second. Whereas the first revolution had largely concerned England and Europe near the Channel, the second involved the whole world.

Imperialism

This nineteenth-century wave of Western expansion was different from previous waves. To denote its unique character, many scholars refer to it as 'imperialism', so as to distinguish it from the 'colonialism' of earlier ages.

Old-style colonialism had evolved since the fifteenth century. During the sixteenth and seventeenth centuries it was formulated within a mercantilist framework. The old-style colonists simply bought what was brought to them by native merchants – or they took what they wanted by force. Precious metals, tropical products and slave labour were acquired through a kind of cash-and-carry mercantilism. By the late eighteenth century, however, this old-style colonial system was pushed out and replaced by a new-style imperialism.

Under the new system the Westerners were not content to just buy what native merchants provided. The Westerners wanted to direct the provisions. They moved into the interior of distant countries and organized the production, extraction and transport of the goods they needed. They penetrated entire regions in Africa and Asia and built up vast infrastructures designed to satisfy the needs of the industrializing economies of the West (Buzan and Lawson 2015). They built harbours, docks and warehouses. They sought out the resources in the interior. They built roads, railways, river steamship companies, mines, plantations, refineries, factories, offices, homes, banks and hotels.

Liberal and radical ideologies of imperialism
Colonialism and imperialism were two different things. Industrialism had changed the old needs and the trading patterns of Europe and dictated a shift in colonial policy. Spices, sugar and slaves diminished in relative importance; industrialism brought increasing demand for raw materials for Western factories and food for the swelling legions of Western factory workers. Also, the West was no longer just a buyer of colonial goods; industrialism made the West into an exporter of capital and a seller of machine-made products. Western countries which, in the past, had frequently been under strain to offer their colonies sufficient goods to balance out the products they imported, were now brimming with new products. And they were frantically searching for markets for them.

Liberals argued that free trade would serve all interests. Expanding on Ricardo's theory of comparative advantage, they argued that countries in the industrialized West would help poor and backward countries if they traded with them. If Western capital were allowed to work freely in poor countries, it would trigger processes of growth and evolution. Free trade, argued the liberals, was different from the colonialism of the past. They tended to associate colonialism with mercantilism, protectionism, blockades, rivalries and war. War, in turn, meant taxes and unprofitable depletion of a nation's capital. Free trade, on the other hand, was associated with progress and it meant the inclusion of all the world's peoples into the harmonizing embrace of an international division of labour marked by interdependent transactions, a self-regulating world order, and the development of knowledge and wealth. The liberal gospel has strong spokesmen in the British city of Manchester. It exported cotton and the philosophy of free trade to every corner of the world. All nations grew richer through commerce than through conquest, they argued. The welfare of countries was more enhanced by negotiations and rational discussion than by threats. Also, they added, relations among nations would be more peaceful and orderly the more trade expanded, because commercial relations increased knowledge, mutual understanding, confidence and trust.

Radicals tended to associate 'colonialism' with looting, enslavement and murder. Also, colonialism involved mercantile wars between colonial nations. It implied press gangs, forced conscription of sailors and the depletion of the labour force in the mother country. Although imperialism, too, was predatory and repressive, the radicals admitted that it nevertheless served a progressive function by pulling 'non-historical' and 'barbarian' societies out of their 'Asian mode of production' and into the cog-wheels of historical evolution. Karl Marx put this radical paradox succinctly: 'England has to fulfil a double mission in India: one destructive, the other regenerating – the annihilation of old Asiatic society, and the laying of the material foundations of Western society in Asia' (Marx 1972, p. 82; 1977, pp. 931–41).

Economic dimensions of change
During the nineteenth century, Western agents invested capital in various regions of the World. They took over the productive life of large regions of the world, and in doing so westernized them. They overhauled the existing land-claims and property arrangements – introducing the concept of private property to areas where it had not previously existed. They transformed large populations into wage employees, levied taxes upon them, introduced the market exchange of commodities and spread the use of money. They lent money to native rulers. The Khedive of Egypt, the Shah of Persia and the Emperor of China were all indebted to Western financiers. This established ties between Western actors and native elites. It also gave the West financial stakes in the continuation of the native regimes.

Western agents realized that they had a profound effect on non-European societies. But they did not consider this a bad thing. They saw the world in terms of the dominant nineteenth-century vision of historical progress. It was commonly held that the progressive nation-states in the West did the 'backward' nations of the world a favour by bringing them Christianity, education, wealth and the values of European civilization; by including them in the historical evolution of Reason and Freedom. Thus, imperialist practice went hand in hand with anti-colonial rhetoric.

Henry C. Morris (1900) discussed one aspect of this imperialist practice – the acquisition of new territories. His numbers, presented in Table 7.1 below, show that Britain increased its possessions at a rapid rate between 1860 and 1880, more than tripling the area it governed (from 2.5 to 7.7 million square miles) and nearly doubling the native populations it ruled over (from 145 to 268 million people). France and Germany experienced their greatest colonial expansion during the 1890s.

Table 7.1 Colonial possessions of three European powers
(millions of square miles, millions of people)

	Great Britain		France		Germany	
Year	*Area*	*Population*	*Area*	*Population*	*Area*	*Population*
1815/30	?	126.4	0.02	0.5	–	–
1860	2.5	145.1	0.20	3.4	–	–
1880	7.7	267.9	0.70	7.5	–	–
1899	9.3	309.0	3.70	56.4	1.0	14.7

Source: Morris (1900)

Historians commonly argue that a change took place in British foreign policy in 1872, when the Tory leader Benjamin Disraeli suddenly abandoned his earlier anti-colonial stance and adopted a policy of imperial expansion. The suddenness of Disraeli's conversion, and the willingness with which other statesmen in Europe followed suit, has been the subject of many books ever since. Most authors argue that the wave of overseas expansion that is indicated in Table 7.1 was fuelled by economic incentives which grew out of the second industrial revolution: that as European powers industrialized, they were driven abroad for raw materials and foodstuffs, developing new modes of communication and transport in the process. In the last quarter of the nineteenth century Western imports included growing amounts of raw materials for Europe's expanding industries (cotton, wool, timber, ore, hemp, jute, dyes, vegetable oils and, increasingly, petroleum) and important

Table 7.2 World output of principal tropical commodities, 1880–1910
(000 tons)

	1880	*1900*	*1910*
Bananas	30	300	1,800
Cocoa	60	102	227
Coffee	550	970	1,090
Cotton fibre	950	1,200	1,770
Jute	600	1,220	1,560
Raw sugar cane	1,850	3,340	6,320
Tea	175	290	360
Rubber	11	53	87

Source: Bairoch (1975, p. 15)

food staples (wheat and meat). This explanation is borne out by the trade figures presented in Table 7.2. They show the rapid increase in trade of commodities that were produced in tropical countries and transported to faraway markets between 1880 and 1910.

Political dimensions of change
When the Crimean War broke out in 1853, it interrupted some forty years of peace among Europe's Great Powers. When it ended in 1856, it was followed by Italian and German wars during the 1860s. In 1871, Prussia won a quick and unexpected victory over France. This victory created a deep-seated wish for revenge in the French nation. The French feelings were complicated by the rapid consolidation and industrialization of a new German state. This added fear and apprehension to French policies. Additional frustration was added by Bismarck's success in isolating France diplomatically and courting Russia – a brilliant diplomacy which prevented France from developing a rapprochement with Russia, Germany's other natural foe. During the final quarter of the century the international situation was additionally complicated by the rise of nationalism in the Balkans and by imperial tensions between French and British interests in Africa.

Colonial conflicts tied in with the uneven development of European industrialism. First, by the fact that different states industrialized at different rates – Germany, for example, industrialized at a faster rate than England and France. Second, industry evolved in fits and starts – the 1860s brought surges of new jobs in expanding industrial towns; however, a sudden US recession spread panic to Europe in 1873 and threw millions out of work on both sides of the Atlantic.

These changes deeply affected the spiritual climate of the age. People would enjoy the undoubted benefits of progress and industrialism; at the same time they would recoil from the civilization they had created (von Suttner 1891). A new international interconnectedness, in which blind forces of boom and slump determined the fortunes of the popular masses in many countries, produced *Angst* or obscure fears. Urban centres would seethe with poverty and mass frustration, crime and revolutionary danger. A wave of assassination and terrorism received great international attention and created fear during the 1890s. Some would project their fears on to imaginary enemies and invent theories of universal conspiracy, others would dream of a better order of things and work to implement blueprints of revolution or radical reform. Some reactions were purely spiritual.[7] Others were materialist and political. And there would be a good deal of hybrid responses in between..

The final decades of the century would be marked by domestic tensions and by new international power games. This affected the way people perceived their condition and thought about world events. It brought a change in political ideals and a political atmosphere in which the old, optimistic age of Reason was replaced by a new, pessimistic age of Will. This change in intellectual climate is the theme of the next section.

Darwin: evolution, anarchy and interdependence

Nationalism, industrialism and imperialism affected the behaviour of nineteenth-century states. Two additional factors also affected the behaviour of states – or rather, shaped the way statesmen and scholars perceived state relations: 'interdependence' and 'evolution'. Both factors made deep marks on late nineteenth-century International Relations theory. Also, they informed the first efforts to build a science of international politics and they cast long shadows over International Relations International Relations theorizing for many decades.

Interdependence
The basic idea, that states which trade with each other become dependent upon each other is old. It had been discussed by eighteenth-century authors like Montesquieu, Smith and Ricardo (who all agreed that such mutual dependency was a force for order and peace). It had been noted by Rousseau (who claimed that it was a source of insecurity and conflict).

During the nineteenth century the argument of Montesquieu, Smith and Ricardo was pursued in greater depth by activists like Richard Cobden. Free trade 'unites' nations, 'making each equally anxious for the prosperity and happiness of both', wrote Cobden (1973, p. 225), merchant of Manchester and citizen of the world. His arguments were shared by John Bright, William Gladstone, Robert Peel, John Stuart Mill and scores of English economists and literary figures. Nowhere was this more evident than at the opening of the Great Exhibition in London in 1851. The Exhibition, and the marvellous Crystal Palace which housed it, became a popular symbol of how science, technology and free trade worked together to produce prosperity, order and world peace.

Many scholars shared the sentiment expressed by the simple, basic deductive model. But some lawyers observed that the simple, Ricardian model did not correspond to international trade practice. Different countries had different property and trade laws and this often made international transactions difficult; exchanging valued goods across languages and legal systems was hampered by misunderstanding, complicated paperwork, slow financing and uncertain insurance – as the British lawyer John Westlake explained in his *Treatise on Private International Law* [1858]. Friction and frustration would be reduced if industrial states could establish some body with a mandate to co-ordinate and standardize their systems of law, he argued.

Tobias Asser and Gustave Rolin-Jaequemyns and other lawyers pursued the point. It was difficult to harmonize the laws of nations in an age that was marked by rising nationalism, they observed. It was necessary to counteract this rising spirit of nationalism by an 'international spirit', they continued. During the late 1860s, Westlake, Asser and Rolin-Jaequemyns gathered support from fellow lawyers all over the West to launch a new legal journal which would explore and encourage the new internationalism. The first issue of the *Revue de droit international et de legislation comparée* (*RDI*) was published in 1868. Its first editorial, written by Rolin-

Jaequemyns, advocated an ambitious programme of international legal reform. The establishment of a new, practical and positive international law would ease international transactions, increase international understanding, counteract interstate conflict and lower the chance of war, he argued.

The *RDI* quickly became an influential journal at a time when, in the words of Charles Vergé (1858, p. xxviii), new communications and increasing exchanges of goods, people and ideas drove international law to transform itself into a more practical and politically efficacious field. It became the centre of an international network of legal experts dedicated to a reform of international law. Its dynamic editor worked with John Westlake, Thomas Asser, Francis Lieber, James Lorimer and many others to organize an Institute of International Law, dedicated to a double purpose: to develop a new set of norms and rules which would promote peaceful conduct among states, and to make war more humane. Time was now ripe to fulfil both purposes, argued Frederic Seebohm in his book *On International Reform*. It was published in 1871, after the Franco-Prussian War had shaken European relations.

Industrialism and the rapid rise of new communications, modern finance and trade had altered international relations by making the industrial nations of the world 'interdependent', claimed Seebohm. The main cause of this interdependence was found 'not merely in human contrivance' but in 'certain laws of nature', explained Seebohm (1871, p. 5, 137). These laws would continue to operate and to deepen international interdependence over time.

The effect of interdependence was a steadily more fine-tuned division of international labour, which would increase productivity and wealth in the trading states of the world. This in turn would change in interstate relations. It would then would thrust aside old norms and rules that had traditionally governed the conduct of states – norms which Seebohm refers to as the old 'Lynch Laws' of sovereign states. A new and efficient system of Positive Law of Nations would replace them and guarantee international order and peace.

James Lorimer placed Seebohm's argument in a larger, elegant theoretical context. Lorimer was an incisive legal mind, a member of Rolin-Jaequemyns's network and a founding member of the Institute of International Law. He wrote an essay on the question: what is the most important problem in international law? His answer provided a brilliant simplification which reduced centuries of international theorizing to a few basic points. The states of the world compose a very peculiar society, Lorimer began. States are sovereign entities. They guard their sovereignty jealously and tend to reject any initiative which may erode their sovereign status and transfer political authority to any actor external to themselves. The sovereignty of states is, in other words, the greatest impediment to establish a legislative authority in the society of states. Since no such authority exists, the international society is, in a world, *'anarchic'*.

The term 'anarchic' is derived from Greek, Lorimer explained: it is a composite of the prefix *'an'* (which denotes the absence of something) and *'arkhein'* (which means rule or law). Anarchy quite literally means 'without leader or law'. The peculiar characteristic of international society is that it is lawless. In the international society, 'anarchy prevails today as a permanent condition', Lorimer (1877, p. 166) submitted. This claim, about the anarchic nature of international society, became the axiom of Lorimer's further reasoning.

When we consult contemporary history, Lorimer continued, we do not observe anything like Thomas Hobbes's war of all against all. On the contrary, we see that everyday relations among states are largely marked by order and regularity. War is not the rule in international relations, it is the exception. A condition of anarchy, in other words, is not the same as war and chaos. International lawlessness does not mean the absence of order. Clearly, order exists in a condition of anarchy. The question is why? What kind of mechanism maintains order in a condition of international anarchy?

Lorimer provided two answers: one was 'diplomatic', the other was 'economic'. The 'diplomatic' answer invoked balance-of-power theory. The mechanism of balance of power provides order in the anarchic society of states, Lorimer averred. This has been known for at least three hundred years – it was discussed at the Peace of Westphalia (1648) and was expressly mentioned in the Treaty of Utrecht (1713). The balance of power maintains order by preventing any single state from accumulating so much power that it can control the international society by itself. The balance-of-power mechanism in effect protects the sovereignty and the juridical independence of states. It works by sovereign states entering or leaving alliances. The conceptual vantage point of this mechanism was sketched by Thomas Hobbes in his notion of an original state of nature and later elaborated by others. Its long-term function has been to prevent the European state system from sliding into empire.

The 'economic' answer to the question of international order is more recent. It does not hinge on the balance of power but on the balance of trade. Its point is not to preserve the sovereignty and independence of states, but to establish an '*inter*dependence' among them. Its conceptual vantage point was sketched by Adam Smith and elaborated by others. It had found an articulate spokesman in Frederic Seebohm (1871), maintained Lorimer.

The international society is anarchic. Order is maintained by two mechanisms: balance of power and interdependence. However, they do not provide a robust or stable order. When we observe contemporary history, we will easily see that, although the emergence of interdependence may have complemented the balance of power and made international society a little more stable. But we will also see friction, conflict and quarrel. The two mechanisms of order have not prevented war from breaking out among Europe's Great Powers. There is much room for improvement in making the international order more robust.

To do this, it is not sufficient merely to address the anarchical nature of international society. It is necessary to address directly the precondition for that anarchy: namely, the sovereign status of states. It is required to break the ancient notion that sovereignty is the most valuable and most characteristic property of the state. Only when state sovereignty is weakened can the international anarchy be harnessed. But how can this be done?

Lorimer first formulated what he calls the 'idealistic answer' – an answer which hinged on religious norms and on education. Faith and education provide part of the answer, he continued. But they will have no impact by themselves. Lorimer then introduced 'the scientific answer'. It involved the building of a body of international law and the establishment of institutions which assume functions of jurisdiction, legislation and execution. International law and a body of international institutions will reduce the sovereignty of states and diminish the effects of the international anarchy. Increasing levels of interdependence among states will make this work more easily, Lorimer concluded.

Progress as evolution

History, change and progress were dominant themes in economic and political theorizing of the nineteenth century. Seebohm and Lorimer were liberal theorists who trusted the human ability to reason and to establish co-operative organs, and who entertained an optimistic notion of steady progress; it was driven by 'certain natural laws' and produced an irresistible historical 'current which seems to be bearing us onward', in the words of Seebohm (1871, p. 140). Such arguments were criticized by radical theorists who perceived reason to be twisted and man to be alienated. They invested their faith in the iron laws of history, in the stepwise evolution of humanity *Stufengang*, and in a final, liberating revolution. Conservative theorists were reluctant to embrace any doctrines of easy progress; however, they trusted that a close reading of history could produce lessons for statesmen.

The age was obsessed with the idea that lessons could be drawn from history. During the first half of the nineteenth century, this obsession found its most influential expression in the works of the German philosopher G. W. F. Hegel. In the second half, the most influential articulator of the obsession was the British naturalist Charles Darwin.

Darwin was, of course, immersed in a larger scholarly debate about the precise nature of evolution. He shared with others the organic *Zeitgeist* that marked the age.[8] His *Origin of Species* was only one of several books on evolution that was published around the middle of the nineteenth century.[9] *The Origin of Species*, however, combines the characteristic themes of the age with an image which has reverberated through International Relations theories since their earliest times: notions of interdependence and of evolution; and the idea that order emerges from an initially anarchic condition as a result of unrestrained competition between free agents (Crook, 1994).

Darwin's theory of evolution has its roots back in the early 1830s, in the experiences he had on a voyage to South America. The observations he made on the Galapagos Islands, 600 miles off the coast of Ecuador, particularly stimulated Darwin's curiosity and imagination. Here he discovered birds and animals which 'bear the unmistakable stamp of the American continent'. They had adapted to life on these isolated islands. Many of them had evolved so distinct characteristics that they could rank as separate species. Darwin found it strange that the Galapagos birds were unafraid of people, and that the iguana was less afraid of people than of the sea, where its natural predators lived. It struck Darwin that this anomalous behaviour could be the outcome of a long-term conditioning. The species had attained their characteristic attributes by adapting to their natural environment.

Why, he wondered, would some species adapt successfully to their environment whereas others did not? And would the successful adaptation of species to natural circumstances describes a teleological path – that is, was there a direction in the evolution of species? (Darwin 1962 [1839], ch. 13; 1958 [1869], ch. 27). Darwin could think of no general answer. It was only when, in 1838, he read Malthus's *Essay on the Principle of Population* [1798] that he found a general proposition which ordered his thought. Malthus argues that the human population always tends to increase at a higher rate than agricultural crops. Population would always outgrow food supply, and people are destined always to compete for scarce resources. Darwin reviewed his questions in the light of Malthus's argument. The guiding principle that governs the evolution of the species is a struggle for scarce resources, he resolved. In this struggle for survival only the cleverest and the most adaptable will make it. And they will in turn pass on their cleverness and adaptability to their children. Survival, Darwin contended, will always be a matter of constant competition for limited resources. 'A struggle for existence inevitably follows from the high rate at which all organic beings tend to increase. It is the doctrine of Malthus applied with manifold force to the whole animal and vegetable kingdoms,' he wrote (1958, p. 376).

In a universal struggle for existence, the most adaptable prevails. This principle, which Herbert Spencer (1864, pp. 444ff) summarized as the 'survival of the fittest', gave Darwin the answer to why some species were successful and others became extinct. Only those best equipped to command the available food supply would survive the struggle for existence.

Darwin published his theory in the *Origin of Species* [1859]. It hit the scholarly world like a bombshell. It unleashed a ferocious debate which closed the circle on Malthusian political economy and profoundly transformed the three political ideologies of liberalism, radicalism and conservatism.

Darwinian influences I: Marx and Marxism
Darwin provided the social sciences with a new term: 'adaptation'. Through adaptation living organisms fit themselves to the distinct features of their environment – partly by modifying their own behaviour, partly by labouring to change their environment. Those organisms which adapt well to their environment flourish; whereas those which do not might perish.

Marx recognized immediately that Darwin's argument could be used to identify 'the laws of capitalist production', and explain how these laws worked 'with iron necessity towards inevitable results' (Marx 1977, pp. 91f). Marx was writing *Capital* at the time Darwin published his *Origin of Species*, and he found that Darwin's concept of adaptation suited the major themes which guided his own research. It fitted perfectly with the claim that humankind transforms its natural environment through its labour and is, in turn, transformed by it. In addition, it echoed the

Hegelian claim that nothing was real but 'the whole' and that history was a series of advances from the less to the more perfect. Marx noted that although *The Origin of Species* was 'developed in the crude English style, this is the book which contains the basis in natural history for our view' (Marx 1964a, p. 131).

The nineteenth-century idea of progress-through-struggle, which reverberated through the theories of Hegel and Darwin, also guided the writings of Marx and Engels. The dialectical method, through which Marx sought to discover 'the natural laws' which drove history through successively more advanced stages of development, parallels Darwin's theory of evolution. In Marx's vision, humanity forges ahead towards a new society with the weight and momentum of all human history behind it. Society, like nature, progresses over time, driven by an inherent struggle among its members. Darwin's claim that evolution was general and inevitable echoes through Marx and Engels's notion of the inevitable victory of the new, proletarian society.

After Marx's death, some of his followers attempted to bring the doctrines of 'scientific socialism' into greater harmony with Darwinism. Such efforts were quite explicit in the writings of prominent socialist theorists like August Bebel (1893). Other Marxists, however, warned against too close an identification between Darwinism and Marxism. Darwin discussed the animal world, whereas Marx discussed human history, and, although humanity belongs to the animal world, it also transcends it, wrote Anton Pannekoek. In contrast to the rapacious animals which Darwin discusses, human beings are social animals. In human society, it is neither brute strength nor individual cleverness which determines an individual's survival; it is the size of the individual's property. 'The competitive struggle between men does not bring forth the best and the most qualified, but destroys many strong and healthy ones because of their poverty; while those who are rich, even if they are weak and sick, survive', writes Pannekoek (1912, p. 33).

Darwinian influences II: Spencer, Sumner and Social-Darwinism

From the early 1800s, liberal thinkers had sought to develop a theory of social evolution. Herbert Spencer made a celebrated effort in his *Principles of Biology* (1864). This book gave an influential definition of evolution as 'a change from an indefinite, incoherent heterogeneity, through continuous differentiations and integrations'. Such change, he wrote, came about through a struggle for survival in which only the fittest will survive. In the 1860s, Spencer applied his definition to issues of political economy and history. He saw the evolution of human civilization in terms of an increasing division of labour from primitive, undifferentiated tribes into complex civilizations, which allow for greater and greater individual freedom.

Darwin's theory assisted Spencer greatly. Where Darwin saw that a struggle for existence brought evolutionary change in plants and animals, Spencer argued that in human society, too, the struggle for existence was a progressive force. A principle of natural selection would weed out society's weaker members; the poor, the incapable, the imprudent, the stupid, the disease-ridden and the idle would succumb in the keen competition for survival. This would allow the healthiest and strongest members of society to mature and procreate. Spencer argued that this principle benefited the good of the greater community. Any effort to help the weakest members of society would only make everyone worse off in the longer haul. Any interference by the state to provide housing, education and poor-relief to society's poorest members would only stimulate their procreation, to the detriment of the community.

Such views informed authors who discussed the Franco-German War and explained its outcome in terms of the greater 'vitality' of the German peoples by comparison with the 'exhausted' Latins. Later, these views would support racist theories which submitted that the Nordic peoples possessed a natural superiority. They informed authors like Houston S. Chamberlain (1899) and Madison Grant (1916), who claimed that an Anglo-German alliance of white people would dominate the world in the twentieth century (Hobson 2012). They also affected statesmen, like the German Kaiser, who warned that a war was coming and that it would be 'a death struggle between Teutons and Slavs'.

More subtle echoes of Spencer are present in Walter Bagehot's sweeping attempt to explain the principles of human history in the light of a few general laws:

> First, in every particular state of the world, those nations which are strongest tend to prevail over the others; and in certain marked peculiarities the strongest tend to be the best.
>
> Secondly, within every particular nation the type or types of character then and there most attractive tend to prevail; and the most attractive, though with exceptions, is what we call the best character.
>
> Thirdly, neither of these competitions is in most historic conditions intensified by extrinsic forces; but in some conditions ... both are so intensified.
>
> These are the sort of doctrines with which, under the name of 'natural selection' in physical science, we have become familiar, (Bagehot 1889 [1872], pp. 457f)

Bagehot was an influential British journalist and editor. His *Physics and Politics* [1872] is an early, sustained discussion of nation-building. It explores at great length the 'first law of politics', explaining how civilization progresses through time because of the innate human propensity to emulate all behaviour which proves most advantageous in the 'competition between nation and nation'.

Bagehot's argument was echoed by Benjamin Kidd and William Sumner – American advocates of Spencer and writers on historical and international issues. Kidd builds a theory of human civilization, according to which 'states are cradled and nurtured in continuous war, and grow up by a kind of natural selection, having worsted and subordinated their competitors in the long-drawn-out rivalry through which they survive' (Kidd 1894, pp. 43f). Sumner agrees, but retains a more Malthusian attitude. Conflicts arise among people because there are not enough natural resources to satisfy everybody's demand, argues Sumner (1954; 1965). Resource scarcity drives people 'into rivalry and a collision of interest with each other'. In prehistoric times, people organized in groups in order to ensure their survival in an environment of scarcity; partly to divide social tasks and produce more effectively, and partly to defend themselves against other groups. With echoes of Bagehot and Kidd, Sumner writes:

> Such a group, therefore, has a common interest. It must have control over a certain area of land; here it comes into collision with every other group. The competition of life, therefore, arises between groups, not between individuals, and we see that the members of the in-group are allies and joint-partners in one interest while they are brought into antagonism of interest with all outsiders. It is the competition of life, therefore which makes war, and that is why war always has existed and always will. It is the condition of human existence. (Sumner 1965, p. 206)

As groups fought each another, they acquired greater discipline and efficiency inward; through war 'they were learning cooperation, perseverance, fortitude, and patience'. The more cohesive and efficient a group was within, the greater chances it had to emerge victorious in the struggle without. War is 'the iron spur of the nature process', for it is through war that human groups have evolved institutions of domestic order; laws and rights, political bodies, social classes, division of labour – even the nation-state itself and the economic base upon which its rests are products of war (pp. 229, 211, 225).

This did not mean that Sumner glorified war. Far from it. He argued that war is an evil. However, it is part of the human condition, and 'like other evils, it must be met when it is unavoidable, and such gain as can be got from it must be won' (p. 230). The struggle for survival, which had characterized world politics in the past, would in Sumner's mind also mark international relations in the future. On the threshold of a new century Sumner foreshadowed the coming of a new wave of disastrous wars. He observed how the Great Powers of his time were building ever-larger navies and carving up overseas territories into colonies. On the eve of World War I, he commented that as the Great Powers 'prepare for war they certainly will have war, and their methods of colonization and exploitation will destroy the aborigines. In this way the human race will be civilized – but by the extermination of the uncivilized' (p. 229).

The German general and military author Friedrich von Bernhardi agreed with the main tenets of Sumner's argument. But whereas Sumner was essentially an American liberal, who saw war as a frightful 'waste of life and waste of capital' (p. 230), von Bernhardi was a German reactionary who saw war as a force for the further evolution of humanity towards ever higher levels of moral and spiritual perfection. In a book entitled *Germany and the Next War* (1912), he argued that 'the law of the strongest' is a general principle of nature and that it governs the behaviour of both animals and humans, individually and in groups. War is a central phenomenon in nature and in history. Indeed:

> War is a biological necessity of the first importance, a regulative element in the life of mankind which cannot be dispensed with, since without it an unhealthy development will follow, which excludes every advancement of race, and therefore all real civilization. 'War is the father of all things.' The sages of antiquity long before Darwin recognized this. (Bernhardi 1912, p. 18)

Von Bernhardi did not fear the coming war. He welcomed it. A good world war would once and for all reveal the weak and cowardly nature of the peace-loving and corrupt Anglo-Saxons and finally demonstrate the spiritual superiority of the German nation, he argued.

Darwinian influences III: Haeckel and Continental nationalism
Von Bernhardi was not the average German academic. But his arguments were not the ravings of a lunatic, either. He had been the chief of the war historical section of Germany's General Staff and commanding general of Germany's Seventh Army Corps. His attitudes were entertained by militaristic and imperialistic circles in Germany. Indeed, they reflected the mood at the imperial court of Wilhelm II. They were entirely in keeping with those of the nationalists in the Pan-German League. And they expressed the sentiments of patriotic German youth movements whose members often portrayed Marxism and liberalism as intertwined faiths, and opposed both of them in the same breath.

The Prussian zoologist Ernest Haeckel (1834–1919) wrote a lengthy essay to rescue Darwinism from the clutches of the revolutionaries. He argued that socialism and liberalism are theories which assume that people are naturally equal; Darwinism, on the contrary, advocates social *in*equality. Darwin's theories corroborate the fact that animals evolve in the direction of ever greater differentiation; the higher or more perfect the animal, the greater the inequality existing. The same principle holds good for the human animal, Haeckel continued. Human society, too, is marked by a great divide between social classes and nations; the more developed a human society is, the more specialized the social division of labour and the stronger and abler are its ruling members.

Darwinism shows that the struggle for survival is not only unavoidable but a law of nature. Indeed, the struggle fuels social evolution. Those members of society who are unfit for competition will perish, whereas those who are best qualified for it will survive. Consequently, the struggle for survival is accompanied by an ever greater perfection of society. This may be lamentable – just as it is lamentable that all must die. However, it is a fact of human existence, which it would be foolish to deny and disastrous to alter. 'Darwinism, or the theory of selection, is thoroughly aristocratic', Haeckel wrote:

> it is based upon the survival of the best. The division of labour brought about by development causes an ever greater variation in character, an ever greater inequality among the individuals, in their activity, education and condition. The higher the advance of human culture, the greater the difference and gulf between the various classes existing. (quoted in Pannekoek 1912, pp. 29f)

Haeckel extended this Darwinian logic to international politics. In his view, states relate to each other in a lawless environment, in a state of nature, where competition is naked and absolute and where only the fittest of states would survive and the unfit would be conquered. Actions of states could therefore not be judged according to legal or moral standards. Each state should act solely according to its own interest.

225

Seen in isolation, Haeckel's arguments did not bring new insights to International Relations theory. Seen in the context of the age, however, this old axiom evolved into a distinct political doctrine. It got caught in the complex, intellectual maelstroms which swept the Continent, such as the Romantic movement, whose influence attained a torrential force in central Europe in the mid-nineteenth century. In Germany Romanticism transcended the narrow boundaries of literature and art; it emerged as an irresistible political force, intimately intertwined with nationalism, Hegelianism and frustrations about the political fragmentation of the German *Volk*.

Early in the nineteenth century, Hegelian dialectics explained that the disunity of Germany would produce the idea of unity, which would, with historical necessity, bring about the creation of a German state. Conservative Hegelians argued that this idea would find its supreme articulation in the Prussian state. However, by mid-century, the Hegelians no longer possessed the only theory of political evolution; they were challenged by the Darwinists, who expressed the same themes in a more concrete, materialist discourse. In 1860, Haeckel began to dress the right-wing Hegelian message in Darwinian terms. At a sports camp in Coburg, he conceived of the idea of a 'single people of brothers', living a healthy life in accordance with the laws of nature. He elaborated this notion in a doctrine of 'monism' – Haeckel used the term to differentiate himself from west European 'dualism', a view which drew a distinction between humanity and nature. To the monist, humans were part of nature, animals who were distinguished from other animals only by a superior degree of development. Darwin had united the natural and the social worlds: humanity was part of nature and had, according to laws of natural selection, evolved from the animal kingdom.

Haeckel used Darwinism as the scientific basis for a new, cosmic philosophy of history and politics. Human history must be re-examined in terms of humanity's biological nature, Haeckel claimed. This will show that human society is ruled by the laws of competition. Nowhere is this more evident than in world politics. Nations are living organisms, which must fight to survive.

In 1862, Haeckel began to present his monist philosophy on lecture tours all over Germany. His ideas were well received in a fragmented nation which was in the throes of an industrializing process of unparalleled scope and pace. Haeckel's theories reverberate with the strong, Romantic chauvinism and the unprecedented socio-economic turbulence of the age; they both reflected the rapid social change of the era and fuelled its growing demands for economic integration and political unification.

The Germans were a superior *Volk*, Haeckel argued. But they could remain so only by ensuring the survival of their distinct Aryan features. They must minimize the influence of alien elements; they must remove foreign doctrines, such as liberalism, which praise equality and harmony, from the German educational system. Such ideas were false, and had a corrupting influence on German youth. The encouragement of reason and free will must also be discouraged, Haeckel argued, because organisms did not triumph by reason but, as Darwin had shown, by struggle and purity. 'The human will has no more freedom than that of the higher animals, from which it differs in degree and not in kind.' Humanity can experience freedom only in the context of an ordered society; and 'the greater the freedom, the stronger must be the order'. Thus, he made liberty a consequence of submission to the authority of the group and the primacy of the group's survival. In the interest of the state, the individual was unimportant. In order for an individual biological organism to survive, 'thousands, indeed millions of cells are sacrificed'. And just as cells die to save the organism, so individuals might be sacrificed for the greater good of the State (Gasman 1971).

Haeckel stirred the imagination of his colleague Friedrich Ratzel (1844–1909), who also applied Darwin's theory to human history and society. Ratzel, whose chief interest lay in the dialectics between people and their physical environment, made important contributions to several social sciences. He made an indelible impression on International Relations theory with his concept of *Lebensraum* (or 'living space'). It elaborated on the territorial nature of the state, explaining that a close relationship exists between a *Volk* and the geographical space in which it has historically evolved. Ratzel viewed the nation-state as an organism, which expanded and contracted its boundaries according to the quality and the capabilities of its inhabitants (Ratzel 1896; Haushofer 1928). Comparable arguments were formulated by several other social theorists – starkly by Ludwig Gumplowicz (1885), more subtly by the young Max Weber (1994, pp. 2, 5, 16, 84, 134).

In 1899, Haeckel published *Das Welträtsel* ('The Riddle of the Universe'). An immediate best-seller, it spread the ideas about an evolutionary process driven by struggle between social groups founded on force and maintained by power. It evoked Germany's pagan past and extolled the virtues of the German nation. In 1906, Haeckel founded the Monist League, a youth movement, dedicated to sports and national virtues. Within five years, the League had become an international movement. In Germany, it became increasingly influenced by the anti-Enlightenment romanticism of Herder and Fichte. In the decade which preceded World War I, the Monist League introduced a generation of German teenagers to an intense German nationalism.[10]

International Relations theory comes of age

The final decades of the nineteenth century were years of change and uncertainty. They were also years in which societies and social relations were portrayed in organic terms. States were commonly depicted as organisms. Societies were generally described as compounds of interconnected organs – units, or 'organizations' – that had evolved distinct functions that helped sustain the larger body. This organicist perspective reflected a late nineteenth-century reality: an evolution which transformed the North Atlantic societies: namely, the advent of new 'organizations' – clubs, unions, parties, voluntary associations, new kinds of commercial firms and new governmental offices. It rendered Western societies increasingly complex, interdependent and modern.

The final quarter of the century was also an international age. It saw a new preoccupation with world events. This is reflected in the literature of the age – for example in the success of authors like Jules Verne, who wrote best-selling books about travel, adventure and technological triumph. The rising interest in the world is also reflected in the renewal and popularity of geography. It is also reflected in the success of l'École libre des sciences politiques in Paris, the establishment of l'Institut de droit international (the International Institute of Law) in Ghent and the rise of modern, secular peace organizations all over the Western world.

Rising interest

These diverse phenomena were outcomes of the education and mobilization of the popular masses. Mass-mobilization had profound effects on the very organization of Western society. It boosted the development of workers' unions and a vast variety of voluntary associations, clubs and circles of all kinds, debating societies, interest groups, organizations and social movements. It increased pressures for electoral reform and stimulated the growth of modern political parties. This increased the importance of parliaments, which required that ministers and politicians defended their policies publicly. This in turn created a need to be better informed on national as well as international affairs. Mass-mobilization and political reform required that governments adapt; to increase the professionalization of public servants and improve their knowledge of economic, political and social affairs. All these changes involved the rise of modern society. And they created pressures to reform higher education.

An increasing interest in foreign events and world affairs was part of this larger cluster of events. The interest was additionally boosted by international events – first by a spate of European wars that began in the mid-1850s, later by Western interventions in Africa and Asia and by colonial wars (Reinsch 1900; Farwell 1985).

The rising interest was also conditioned by social changes at home – for example by a veritable media revolution. Education reform, which had swept the West during the first half of the nineteenth century, had created a literate mass public by the beginning of the second half of the century. This public provided in turn the basis for a mass-market of printed matter. It boosted the production of books about adventure, world travel, spies, wars and colonial issues.[11] It helped turn news into a commodity. It stimulated the rise of new kinds of newspapers – large, regional newspapers (like *The Manchester Guardian*) or papers with a political message (like *The Star* and *The Nation*). It brought forth new forms of journalism – for instance it boosted the rise of the 'foreign correspondent' who travelled to distant regions and provided dramatic eyewitness accounts of faraway events. The increase in popular literacy also opened up a commercial space for magazines – like the *Revue des deux mondes* in France, the *Atlantic Monthly*, *The Forum* and the *North-American Review* in the USA, and the *Review of Reviews* and many more in Britain. Around the turn of the century a steadily increasing number of books discussed international topics – many of them written by authors who had been foreign correspondents a decade or two previously (Stead 1899a, b; Angell 1903; 1910; Morel 1912; Fullerton 1913; Brailsford 1914).

Movements and institutions of international politics

This development of a modern Western society went hand in hand with a prolif-eration of new universities. This rise was particularly evident in the United States, where big, new state universities were built during the so-called 'progressive era'. The rise of modern society was also intimately connected to the rise of the modern social sciences – stimulated by the establishment of organizations like Britain's National Association for the Promotion of Social Science (NAPSS) and the Associ-ation internationale pour le progrès des sciences sociales in France (Collini 1991).

The advent of new sciences like economics and sociology stimulated the scientific study of international politics. However, significant impulses were also provided by more traditional academic fields, in particular history, geography and law. The impetus provided by events outside of the halls of academe should not be underestimated, in particular the incentives provided by the rise of the modern peace movement.

The modern peace movement emerged along the North Atlantic rim during the 1860s and 1870s. It was in important ways a reaction to the new cluster of wars that shook Western nations during the third quarter of the nineteenth century, and tended to front the argument that wars were destructive and that they served neither ordinary people nor their nations. The American Civil War (1861) triggered a wave of anti-war activism in the USA. It also ignited early initiatives to regulate soldiers' conduct during war, such as the so-called Lieber Code (Witt 2012). The outbreak of the Franco-Prussian War (1870) released similar waves of war protests and peace activism, as well as initiatives to regulate warfare (Lange 1919: Ceadel 1987). The British pacifist William Randal Cremer founded the Workman's Peace Association and the International Arbitration and Peace Association (both in 1870). The French economist and free-trade advocate Frédéric Passy helped reorganize the Société française des amis de la paix in 1872 – after the peace treaty of Frank-furt and the lifting of wartime censorship. Peace organizations were founded all over the West – locally and nationally. In 1891 the International Peace Bureau was established to co-ordinate the activities of about five hundred peace societies all over the world (Beales 1931).

The new, secular peace movement boosted the efforts of international legal scholars to renew the discipline of international law. This is evident from the pages of the *Revue de droit international et de legislation comparée* (*RDI*), and in the establishment of the Institute of International Law (in 1873). Its purpose was to make war more humane and develop just norms and rules to prevent war from breaking out among states in the first place. The new international lawyers explored methods of international arbitration – especially after the amicable resolution of a longstanding Anglo–American conflict, the '*Alabama* case', by arbitration in 1872. The *RDI* and the Institute of International Law worked hand in hand with the expanding peace movement. Some peace associations worked to establish arbitra-tion panels or to found a permanent international court of arbitration.[12] Frédéric Passy's Société française des amis de la paix changed its name to Société d'arbi-trage entre les Nations in 1878. A decade later Passy and Cremer founded the

Inter-Parliamentary Union (IPU), an association composed of members of national assemblies around the world. The IPU had an important influence on the development of the arbitration movement.

Industrialists and people in business, who were easily persuaded by the free-traders' argument that war is bad for commerce, were drawn towards peace work and international law. Towards the end of the century some of them established trusts and foundations to fund various types of peace work. In the 1890s, the Swedish industrialist Alfred Nobel set aside some part of his considerable fortune to reward individuals who had made exceptional contributions to brotherhood and peace.[13] A few years later, the industrialist Edwin Ginn founded a peace organization of his own. The US steel magnate Andrew Carnegie established a generous Endowment for International Peace to fund scholarly work on the causes of war and the preconditions for peace.[14] The British industrialist Sir Richard Garton set up a foundation to sponsor Norman Angell's investigations into the causes of war (Knutsen 2013).

Private initiatives were also important in the evolution of the new scholarly institutions. The École libre des sciences politiques in Paris is a case in point. It was founded in 1872 by Émile Boutmy as a result of the French defeat in the Franco-Prussian War. Boutmy was convinced that the German victory reflected superior knowledge and organizational skills. He raised private money to build a professional school which would form an elite of French economic and political leaders.[15] The school offered no exams or certificates, but it evolved classes in political economy, comparative government, international law and international relations. The 'Sciences Po', as it was popularly called, quickly became a centre where aspirants for the French civil services could prepare for entry examinations.

Boutmy's school became an inspiration to others. In 1880, John Burgess established a 'School of Political Science' at Columbia University in New York – with the model of Sciences Po in mind. When Sidney and Beatrice Webb established the London School of Economics and Political Science (LSE) in 1895, they were similarly inspired by the purpose and curriculum of the Sciences Po.

Academia and international-relations scholarship
If the early decades of the nineteenth century were marked by reforms in elementary education, then the final decades were marked by changes in higher education. This involved a proliferation of big, new universities and the development of the modern social sciences. The growing interest in international affairs benefited from this development.

The impact of modern economics is readily apparent. Most economists noted how their countries continued to increase productivity and industrial output. Some of them also noted that the rate of this increase in industrial production was higher than the increase in exports and trade; this caused them to wonder whether industrialized nations of the West were accumulating capital faster than they could consume it. The financial panic of 1873 made some economists ask whether the industrialized West was choking on its own excess capital.

A most significant contribution to this discussion was provided by the French economist Paul Leroy-Beaulieu. He claimed that Western states were struggling to export their excess capital and that this effort was the real motor behind the neo-colonial expansion of his day. Leroy-Beaulieu made a convincing case in his thick and influential book, *De la colonialisation chez des peuples modernes* [1874]. A similar argument was voiced in the USA – by financiers like J. P. Morgan and politicians like Brooks Adams, Henry Cabot Lodge and Theodore Roosevelt. The radical US economist Charles Conant (1898) streamlined Leroy-Beaulieu's argument into a simple claim: capitalism was threatened by an accumulation of finance capital, which would result in a glut and another stagnation and crisis, unless the surplus was removed through foreign investment.

Sociologists had less direct effect on international relations debates. They tended to focus on the internal dynamics of countries and not on international relations – although many of them sought to extend their ideas about social conflict to relations in the international society and to questions of war, peace and international order (Ramel 2006: Mazower 2013, pp. 94ff). One of them was Herbert Spencer; and, although his discussions were abstract and general, he left a deep mark on international debates – especially with his concept of 'the survival of the fittest' (Hobson 2012). A more directly relevant sociologist was Jacques Novicow, who brought sociological analysis directly to bear on international society and questions of war, peace and interstate order.

Novicow's *Politique internationale* [1886] was an original and pioneering effort to address interstate relations from an evolutionary perspective. The book emphasized the solidaric and co-operative aspects of Darwin's theories and was deeply sceptical of those who only saw the conflictual aspects of Darwin's argument. Novicow criticized the so-called social-Darwinists for having misunderstood evolutionary theory and bent Darwin's theories entirely out of shape. When Spencer (1864, pp. 444ff) wrote about 'the survival of the fittest', he did not mean survival of the strongest or the biggest. He did not mean 'fit' to be a synonym for strong, noted Novicow. Rather, it was a synonym for flexible or an ability to *adapt*. It is the ability to adapt which is the key to human progress, noted Novicow. He agreed with Spencer (1882, §561–2) that that human societies have evolved through history: they have evolved from primitive social formations based on force and militarism to modern, industrial societies that are based on co-operation and interdependence.

This idea that humankind naturally evolved from a primitive condition of war to a civilized condition of lasting peace was immensely popular. It defined the outlook of the progressive evolutionists. Its basic vision was similar to that of liberal historians who considered reason and organization to be decisive driving forces in history. If the ultimate task of the historian is to observe historical change and understand the mechanisms behind it, they ought to observe the immediate past, they argued. Never had society changed as fast as now. Never has historical progress been so rapid. By following near-contemporary events systematically with a historian's gaze, it should be possible to observe how human beings, through technological and political innovation, moulded their age and drove history.

This was the view of the Cambridge historian John Seeley, who advocated the value of studying contemporary events as history. Seeley was supported in his views by his colleague at Oxford, Professor Edward Freeman, whose sentiment is expressed in his famous claim that 'history is past politics and politics is future history'. Since Seeley and Freeman argued that history should be studied scientifically and also have some practical value, it would be hard to separate the study of contemporary history from that of political science.

German historians, too, were preoccupied with progress and evolution. But they were less concerned with individual reason adaptation, and more with political struggle. Germany was, after all, unified through a series of late wars. This experience affected the German discipline of *Staatswissenschaft* which developed during this period. Working in the shadow of a newly established state, Germany's political scientists were self-absorbed. They discussed the origins, the nature and the purpose of the state in general terms – although it was often their own experiences which echoed through their analyses.

One of the greatest of the German historians was Leopold von Ranke. He had coined the concept of 'Great Power' (Ranke 1925 [1833]). It was a useful innovation which had greatly simplified the analysis of modern state relations and had made it easier to conceive of Europe as a system of states. The most prominent of Ranke's successors was Heinrich von Treitschke. For many years, Treitschke taught an annual course in Politics at the University of Berlin. It focused on the state. It was immensely popular and was followed by civil servants and students alike. It shaped the self-perception of an entire generation of Germans.

Treitschke's course was in many ways about state building, taught to a nation which had just got itself a proper state and wondered what it could do. His lecture series began with the idea of the state. It continued with its social foundation, its internal development, design, constitution and administration. It concluded with Treitschke's musings on the international relationships of states. There existed two approaches to the study of such relationships, he explained. On the one hand was the 'naturalistic' approach, informed by concerns of power and represented by statesmen like Otto von Bismarck. On the other was the 'moralistic' approach, informed by concerns of trade and represented by liberal rationalists and free-traders like Richard Cobden:

> The first, the naturalistic, whose chief champion we already know to be Machiavelli, starts from the principle that the State is absolute power, and may do anything which serves its ends, consequently it can bind itself by no law in relations with other States ... [The other is] the moralizing doctrine of the Liberal theorists. Here we find the State regarded as if it were a good little boy, who should be washed, and brushed, and sent to school, who should have his ears pulled to keep him obedient. (von Treitschke 1963 [1916], pp. 294f)

Treitschke was, needless to say, a spokesman for the naturalist approach. His lectures reflected the political uncertainties and the evolutionary doctrines of the age. He portrayed international relations as a battlefield and history as a relentless struggle among nations. His arguments were steeped in *Realpolitik* – that is, the view that 'the law of power governs the world of states just as the law of gravity governs the physical world'. This view, introduced by Ludwig von Rochau (1853), entrenched itself later in the century – especially after Kaiser Wilhelm II came to power in 1888. German society grew more autocratic under his rule. Political discussions became more restricted. Academic freedoms were constrained as institutions grew more authoritarian. Liberal perspectives retreated as power politics advanced – and was increasingly informed by biological theories.

German historians and political scientists tended to turn their attention towards the structure and the inner workings of the new German state. Theories about interstate relations were not much discussed in German political science. They were, however, all the more discussed among German geographers. One of the most influential of them was Friedrich Ratzel. He defined the territorial state as an organism which may flourish and evolve – if conditions are right. If it evolves, it grows in size as well as complexity. It develops sustaining organs in the form agriculture and industry; it develops distributory systems in the form of networks of communication and transportation. Also, a healthy state will require more land and more resources in order to evolve further. Ratzel was inspired by *Realpolitik* and by the biological theories of Alexander von Humboldt, Karl Ritter, Ernst Haeckel and others.

Ratzel (1901) imported into his analysis the concept of *Lebensraum* – the habitat or living space into which a healthy organism would need to expand if it were going to evolve. Ratzel's line of reasoning was pursued by his talented Swedish student, Rudolf Kjellén. In an innovative study of Sweden, Kjellén first announced his debt to Humboldt, Ritter and Ratzel. He then accounted for his own approach – which he called 'geopolitik' (Kjellén 1900, p. 17) – and presented the evolution of Sweden through history, as if it were a living organism which struggled for space (pp. 31ff). A few years later, Kjellén presented his geopolitical approach more closely. In the more theoretical study *Der Staat als Lebensform* (1917) Kjellén accounted for the function of the many organs or sub-systems of a state. The state, he argued, was an organic composite of territory and *Volk*. The territory must be cultivated so as to maintain self-sufficiency, argued Kjellén (who thereby gainsaid the advocates of interdependence theory). The *Volk* must be educated and unified into a proper nation. It would be presided over by a government – a centralized bureaucracy supported by a strong military – which would advance the interests of the state vis-à-vis other, rivalling states.

Few geographers leaned so heavily on evolutionary biology as Ratzel and Kjellén. Yet, their basic concerns were not unique. Problems connected to resource scarcity, space limitation and a deficient national character were raised by other authors as well. In the USA Henry Jackson Turner (1893) and Brooks Adams (1896) were concerned that North America had reached the limits of its territorial expansion. Turner formulated his famous thesis that the American frontier had formed the most characteristic and unique features of the American character. The inability to expand any further would therefore mean the end of the frontier as a formative force on the American nation. The limits of expansion would, in fact, represent a threat to the unique qualities of the American character.

A major influence on this geographical approach to international politics was the American naval officer and historian Alfred T. Mahan. He was a prolific contributor to American magazines and to the public debate about US foreign policy. His major work was a historical study of naval power from the perspective of *Realpolitik*. The book, *The Influence of Sea Power upon History* [1890], was an ambitious effort to view the interaction of the Great Powers in a worldwide or planetary context. Mahan argued that sea power was of paramount importance for the development of any Great Power who sought economic and military supremacy.

In Britain the young Halford J. Mackinder (1904) developed a similar, planetary view of interstate relations. He agreed with Mahan that sea power was important for any state with Great-Power ambitions. In Mackinder's view, however, Mahan exaggerated the importance of sea power. First, sea power was entirely dependent on command over landed territories – it needed material resources that were found only on land; it needed personnel, secure harbours, command over safe straits and strategic choke points. Second, there was an area in the world that no sea power could reach: the inner regions of Russia were invulnerable to sea power. Mackinder called this area 'the Heartland' of Eurasia.

Mackinder explained that, since the age of Columbus, Western explorers had travelled the earth, observed, catalogued and mapped the land. In recent times, however, explorers like Scott and Nansen had charted the planet's last, unknown lands. They had closed the age of discovery and led humanity into a new, post-Columbian age. There is nothing more to explore, Mackinder (1904) noted. After decades of technological development and colonial expansion, the Great Powers had conquered most of the world and were confronting limitations in space.

> Whether we think of the physical, economic, military or political interconnection of things on the surface of the globe, we are now for the first time presented with a closed system … Every shock, every disaster or superfluity, is now felt even to the antipodes, and may indeed return from the antipodes … Every deed of humanity will henceforth be echoed and re-echoed in like manner round the world. (Mackinder 1919, p. 40)

The world had become an interdependent whole. The planet must be considered a closed and interconnected system. On the basis of this claim, Mackinder inferred two arguments.

First, that in this new age of high technology and interdependence, 'the Heartland' of Eurasia would become a singularly important region. Because any power that commanded this region could use modern means of transport and extraction to mine its fabulous wealth and develop powerful capabilities. Since the region lay outside the reach of sea power, no one could prevent such a development. In time the Heartland power could expand and command all of Eurasia – if not the entire world (Mackinder 1919; Knutsen 2014).

Second, since 'the exploration of the world was finished' and no more 'fertile, relatively vacant insular regions' were available, the Great Powers faced two options: either expansion must stop or it must take place at the expense of land that already belongs to someone else. The first option was the more sensible. However, since Mackinder did not trust human reason fully, he did not rule out the second. Even though this would be a sure road to rivalries, arms races and warfare.

In an age of industrialism and interdependence, a Great-Power war would be more destructive than any war in history. This was the argument of many peace activists and an increasing number of businessmen and politicians. It drove them to participate in a vast disarmament conference in The Hague at the end of the century. Virtually every sovereign state on earth sent representatives to The Hague in 1899. The conference, which had been called by the Russian Tsar Nicholas II, created high expectations and was closely covered by major news media.

The Hague conference produced several agreements which served to regulate the behaviour of states in war. These agreements were commonly seen as a victory of reason and a result of work done by the international peace movement. Yet, the conference did not succeed in its original purpose: that is, to end the international arms race. To some observers, the conference reflected an international atmosphere increasingly marked by rivalries and suspicion, not by harmony and co-operation.

The international peace movement and the members of the Institute of International Law were driven by liberal ideals – by a faith in human reason and historical progress. Their notion of interdependence was informed by a faith in universal laws. Frederic Seebohm (1871, p. 140) saw interdependence as the outcome of 'an irresistible historical current which seems to be bearing us onward'. As he expanded on his argument, it became clear that this current was driven by human reason. His argument ended up in the vicinity of David Ricardo and Richard Cobden and the claim that the free-market model of international trade would produce increasing wealth as well as a robust peace.[16]

James Lorimer found the solution to conflict and war in science: in the systematic construction of international law and the establishment of institutions which assume functions of jurisdiction and curtail the sovereignty of states. He elaborated this argument in his large *Institutes of the Law of Nations* [1884]. Here he discussed the key problem of international law and international relations. Also, he provided careful definitions of the specialized concepts which allowed him to grasp that key problem.

The book should have been celebrated as an early classic in the science of international politics, because the concepts that Lorimer carefully defined – first and foremost the concepts of 'anarchy', 'balance of power', 'interdependence' and 'international law' – have remained central in the field of International Relations ever since. Yet, although the book was celebrated among international lawyers when it was published in 1884, it did not have an active life. It was quickly relegated to the shelves of the dusty division of special collections in university libraries.

The Institutes of the Law of Nations proceeded from the assumption that Reason is one and indivisible – that all people are endowed with the same kind of reason and that when they think through the same questions, they will arrive at the same answers. The book was written in the tradition of Natural Law and was a monument to the Enlightenment ideals of reason and progress. These ideals, however, were weakened at the time of the book's publication, and the Natural–Law tradition was quickly fading. Lorimer was, in fact, one of its last big defenders.

Modernity and beyond

The nineteenth century opened in an atmosphere of rationalistic optimism which saw in reason the guiding influence in human affairs. This 'age of reason', which was represented by luminaries like Kant, Jefferson and Humboldt, was then replaced by an age of will. When the American historian and diplomat Paul S. Reinsch returned from a visit to Europe in the late 1890s, he commented:

> The serenely quiet and completely harmonious balance of an existence such as Goethe's, reflected in his whole art, has given way to a rush of wild spirits that fight their way through storms of passions where only the strongest will, the most violent energy, can prevail.
>
> This general character of the age is written plainly in the records of contemporary political life. (Reinsch 1900, p. 8)

The optimism of reason was replaced by 'the optimism of force, which sees in triumphant energy the sole condition of happy existence' (Reinsch 1900, p. 8). This change was driven by a turn towards evolutionism. It was foreshadowed by Darwin, who had excluded rational and moral considerations from his theories; his theory of evolution relied on biological and environmental variables alone. This disregard for human reason was then emulated by others. One of them was Karl Marx. Drawing on German methodology, French politics and British political economy, Marx developed a bitter critique of modern society, whose inhuman mode of production alienated individuals. But in the final account, Marx's castigation of the capitalist mode of production was an argument from within the tradition of Western modernity. It was a limited critique in the sense that the Marxists proposed to replace one vision of modernity (capitalism) with another (socialism). Marx's analysis was less of a stinging critique of modern society than was the dismal appraisal of Friedrich Nietzsche.

By Reinsch's account, Nietzsche was, more than anyone else, the main representative of the new, post-humanist age. Nietzsche mocked the core idea of modernity (shared by liberals and radicals alike) that each individual is an infinite reservoir of possibilities and that these possibilities will prevail once society is rearranged. Nietzsche was sceptical of human reason and morality. In fact, he turned the human faculty of reason against rationality itself in order to disclose its flimsy nature. He doubted the human ability to find truth and moral universals, and sought to reveal the contingent nature of human moral standards. He attacked the moral pretensions of liberals and radicals alike. He argued that 'good' and 'bad' are inappropriate terms in historical and social analysis. He doubted the ability of human language to describe any real or true thing, and held moral rhetoric to be just one more political tool in the hands of those hungry for power. He insisted on revealing the power structure which moral discourse concealed and on which the entire social order was built. 'Seek ye a name for this world? A solution for all its puzzles? ... This world is the will to power – and nothing else', he affirmed (Nietzsche 1960, p. 917).

There are strong Darwinist echoes in the social philosophy of Friedrich Nietzsche. He rejected, like Darwin, the facile belief in progress. But Nietzsche's rejection was a frontal attack on the values and assumptions on which modern Western society was based. Some of his themes were taken up by others. For example by Sigmund Freud, who expanded upon Nietzsche's claim that human beings were prey to unconscious drives that operated in hidden and devious ways. Freud sought to identify the principles of those operations in a model of the human mind. Ferdinand de Saussure expanded on Nietzsche's claim that the human language was not a consistent product of human reason. Saussure argued that languages are rather haphazardly constructed and then socially maintained by human individuals who are socialized into their distinct rules of syntax and semantics. A language, he continued, also formats the perceptions of its users; it conditions the way they observe the world and shapes their thoughts and arguments through its vocabulary and its distinct rules of grammar.[17]

Around the turn of the century, then, social theories were developed according to which human behaviour may be driven by concerns other than rational calculation. The effect of these theories was to splinter the modern image of the human being as a coherent individual who responds rationally and intelligently to events. The new theories represented an epistemological rupture with the old, representational reasoning of the West that had held sway since the Renaissance. They indicated the coming of an abstract trend which would soon engulf writing, poetry, music no less than social theory, and which would bring artists and scientists self-consciously to reject old, accepted forms and traditional preoccupations with causality, natural symmetry and three-dimensional space.[18] They sounded early warnings of the dangers which attended the modern quest for wealth and power.

These ideas evolved in Europe in general and in Germany and Russia in particular. They were launched during the first decade of the twentieth century but they detonated much later. They were torpedoes with delayed charges. Their impact was not really felt until after World War I.

Notes

1 As indicated in Chapter 3: Bible translations played a particularly important role in this process. The case of Henry VIII is a famous example. During the 1530s he broke with the pope and established an independent Church of England. In 1539 his 'Great Bible' was printed in English, distributed to every church in England and chained to the pulpit. Similar processes took place in other countries in northwestern Europe. Translations of the Bible allowed a monarch to impose a distinct interpretation of Christianity upon his people. By translating the Bible into a national language, a prince also contributed to the standardization of a distinct vernacular which emphasized the distinctness of his people (Eisenstein 1993, pp. 148ff; Anderson 1983, p. 41).

2   Benedict Anderson (1983) presents nations as 'imagined communities'. He traces the emergence of nations back to the growth of standardized languages, and singles out the printing press as one of the most significant of its encouraging factors. It dissolved ancient allegiances and established new ones.

3   By 1900, the extreme nationalists had often become reactionaries and opponents of democracy. Bismarck introduced democratic reforms solely to draw their sting and to use them for his own, Prussian purposes. In Italy Garibaldi's Red Shirts of the 1870s would evolve into Mussolini's Blackshirts of the 1920s.

4   The first industrial revolution was driven by practical men, by artisans and engineers who improved traditional methods of production. The second was driven by scientists, by men who invented new types of commodities, and by capital. Innovations in smelting, working and rolling improved the quality of metals; new tools for cutting and welding improved large-scale commercial production of rails, plates, castings, tools and engines. The introduction of steel as the basic material for the construction of railroads, ships, buildings, machinery and weapons also introduced new products for the booming mass-consumer market. Goods which previous ages had never conceived of – the telegraph, the telephone, the radio, the gramophone, the electric lamp, the sewing machine, the machine gun, the bicycle, pneumatic tyres, the internal combustion engine, underground trains, the typewriter – appeared during the busy, optimistic 1860s (Barraclough 1976).

5   Britain was a pioneer in such political organization. The Reform Act of 1832 gave voting rights to adult males who rented propertied land of a certain value; which expanded suffrage to about 15 per cent of Britain's male population. The Reform Act of 1867 extended voting rights even more. The Representation of the People Act of 1884 extended the voting rights to 60 per cent of British males – in effect enfranchising a significant part of Britain's urban male working class. After 1885, a suffrage movement emerged which worked to extend the voting right to women – a movement which was stunted by the outbreak of World War in 1914 but which was soon picked up again and led to the Representation of the People Act of 1918 which introduced universal suffrage for men over the age of twenty-one and for women over thirty.

6   In the Americas, the United States industrialized at a rate which exceeded even that of Germany. In Asia, Japan took to electricity, petroleum engines, railways and steel-hulled ships at such a rapid pace that it had, by 1900, emerged as the primary power in the region. In 1850, Britain had possessed half the world's industrial production; by 1870, the figure had sunk to one-third; and by 1910 to one-sixth (Kennedy 1987, pp. 198ff).

7   Waves of religious revival would follow in the wake of modernization. Fundamentalist movements developed hand in hand with modernization in all the three big monotheistic faiths of Christianity, Judaism and Islam.

8   Darwin took part in discussions about other authors who had explored the nature and mechanisms of organic evolution, such as Lamarck and Lyell. Darwin, in short, stood on the shoulders of others. He consulted in particular Jean-Baptiste Lamarck's *Philosophie zoologique* [1809], which saw evolution in terms of a reciprocal action between heredity and adaptation, which provided Darwin with a promising core for his theory of evolution. Darwin formulated his questions within the

framework of Charles Lyell's important *Principles of Geology* [1830], which argued that the thin crust of the earth had been continuously formed through the infinitely long history of the planet. However, neither Lyell nor Lamarck could give Darwin a satisfactory explanation for his own research question. It was Malthus (1982 [1798], p. 207) who provided him with an explanatory mechanism in the form of a principle of selection.

9 The British naturalist Alfred R. Wallace developed an almost identical theory to Darwin's about the same time. The social philosopher Herbert Spencer developed arguments that were similar to both Wallace and Darwin. In *Social Statics* [1851] Spencer described society as a compound or an aggregate whole made up of inter-connected parts; 'an infinitely complex organization'. A particularly important influence on the debate was Robert Chamber's bestseller *Vestiges of the Natural History of Creation* [1844]. Chamber had published the book anonymously. It was a wise move, because it contradicted the theological orthodoxy of creationism and caused quite a stir. Darwin wrote later that *Vestiges* paved the way for the publication of his own *Origin*; that it prepared the public mind for scientific theories of evolution.

10 The political importance of the Monist League lies in the long-term effects that its ideas exerted on the generation of Germans who were born in the 1890s. This generation became soldiers in World War I – during which they suffered a costly defeat. Although the Monist League was dissolved after 1918, other youth organizations were established along the same lines and stressed the same explosive mix of social-Darwinist doctrines and the romantic myths of a pagan past. The 'Thule Gesellschaft', the 'Vril Gesellschaft', the 'Artaman Bund' and other organizations contributed to the rise of bio-political patriotism in the Weimar Republic. They advocated the creation of a racially pure Germanic peasantry through the culti-vation of the nobility inherent in German blood. They argued that Poles should be removed from the territories east of Germany in order to give the expanding German population *Lebensraum*. This land should be resettled by racially accept-able Germans rescued from the alienating slums of the new industrial zones of the Ruhr and the Saar. Among the individuals who received their ideological and politi-cal training in the Artaman Bund were Walter Darre, Rudolf Höss and Heinrich Himmler – all of whom later joined the Nazi movement and became officers and leaders of Hitler's SS (Gasman 1971, pp. 152f).

11 New print technologies and cheaper paper lowered the price of books – and helped ensure that Henry M. Stanley's book *How I Found Livingstone* (1872) was a best-seller through the 1870s. During the 1880s a new kind of fiction literature developed rapidly in the Western world. In France, this fiction was pioneered by Alexandre Dumas and Ponson de Terrail and developed by Louis Boussenard, Jules Verne and a host of imitators. In Italy it was associated with Emilio Salgari, in Germany with Karl May and in the USA with Thomas M. Reid. In Britain it was popularized by Robert Louis Stevenson, H. Rider Haggard and others. *Treasure Island* (1883) and *King Solomon's Mines* (1886) were big best-sellers. These years also saw a rapid diversification of popular fiction into new literary genres – westerns, spy novels, mystery, science fiction and other new genres.

12 The Permanent Court of Arbitration (PCA) was established in 1899 by an act made at the first Hague Peace Conference (1899).

13 To be more precise: In his final will, Alfred Nobel specified that four prizes were to be awarded by the Swedish Academy of Sciences (in Physics, Chemistry, Medicine and Literature). Then he added a fifth prize which were to be awarded by the Norwegian national assembly: a reward for the most significant contribution to the cause of brotherhood of humanity, to disarmament and to peace congresses. A prize for advances in the field of Economics was later added – and funded by the Swedish National Bank.

14 Similar endowments would be part of the early twentieth-century philanthropic activities of men like John D. Rockefeller and Henry Ford.

15 Boutmy was surrounded by a group of French intellectuals which included Hippolyte Taine, Ernest Renan, Albert Sorel, Paul Leroy-Beaulieu and François Guizot. All feared that France's international stature was waning due to inadequate teaching of its political and diplomatic corps. In order to reform the training of French politicians, the school developed a humanistic and pragmatic teaching programme: instructors included academics as well as ministers, high civil servants and business people.

16 These free-marked models had been long attacked by economists who were historically bent. Richard Jones, for example, had criticized the free-trade argument for being ahistorical and opening up a dangerous, deductivist path that would remove economic analysis from useful, empirical work. Friedrich List [1841] had opened up a different angle of criticism: in an international free-market competition the strongest industrial states would always win and the weaker nations would slide into dependency, he argued. The free-market argument of Ricardo and his liberal friends was nothing more than a justification of practices which benefited the wealthy. In his words, free-market models were 'pure ideology'. They simply justified the extant practices of a powerful Britain. While free trade was the sensible policy for an industrially dominant nation like Britain, it would not serve weaker nations well. Rather, a policy of protectionism would be preferable for weaker nations because it would enable them break the British stranglehold.

It may be added that German scholars had long pursued such points. They had tended to associate *laissez-faire* and interdependence with inequality, class struggle and exploitation. Fichte (1979b [1800]) had touched on it. Hegel (1980 [1821], p. 150) had elaborated on it and argued that, as industrialism progressed, countries would divide into two major classes: a wealthy elite on the one hand, and a 'rabble of paupers' on the other. Statesmen could delay or diminish this division by resorting to colonialism, Hegel had argued. Foreign expansion could, in other words, soften the domestic class struggle and mitigate the inequality between the poor and the rich. However, just as the poor are exploited and alienated as a class at home, they will continue to be exploited when they settle abroad as colonists. This argument, which was curiously overlooked by Marx, was elaborated by Engels, Bebel, Kautsky and other German socialists in the final years of the nineteenth century.

17 Saussure's point about how a language is socially maintained by human individuals who are born into it and socialized by it is derived for example from Jean-Jacques Rousseau. The point about how language formats the perceptions of its users is an elaboration of arguments made by Johann Gottfried Herder.

18 These tendencies began to emerge as features of consequence in intellectual life

during the first decades of the twentieth century. They were most immediately perceived in the abstract art of Klee (1879–1940), the atonal music of Schoenberg (1875–1951) and the poetry of Eliot (1888–1965). But the same sentiments are apparent in scientists' rejection of causality – they are most famously noticeable in Einstein's 'theory of relativity'.

8

The Great War, the big League and the twenty years' crisis

The Great War was a catastrophe. Its effects were momentous. It exhausted Europe. It reshuffled the Western system and dealt the cards for a new game of international politics. It destroyed four Western empires – the German, the Russian, the Ottoman and the Austrian-Hungarian – and shaped the social formations that emerged from the ruins. From the German and the Russian empires emerged new, totalitarian systems that would add new contests and tensions to the twentieth-century world. From the Ottoman and the Austrian-Hungarian empires emerged new subsystems that attached themselves to the established Great-Power system of old: from the ruins of one emerged the modern Middle East; from the other grew a new central and eastern Europe.

Also, the warfare in Europe greatly strengthened the Americas. It made Argentina and the USA into wealthy countries. It especially enriched the USA, which was converted from a debtor nation to a wealthy creditor nation within a handful of lucrative years. It also pulled the Americas into the main arena of world politics. By making the USA a decisive player in world politics, the Great War not only altered the international system. It also altered the way in which statesmen and scholars thought and theorized about world affairs. In a word, it created what Edward H. Carr (2001 [1939]) would refer to as the 'science of international relations'.

By Carr's analysis this new science was at first hardly a science at all, but a utopian movement devoted to ending war and establishing a lasting peace. In Carr's view, this utopian approach was subsequently challenged by a more scholarly realist school. As the international situation grew increasingly grim, these two schools locked in a 'great debate'. This is, in a nutshell, Carr's view of the birth of International Relations. It is a simple, streamlined and deeply influential story. It is, however, far too simple – as the subsequent pages will show.

This chapter will first discuss the Great War. It will note the main characteristics of the war and the highlights of war diplomacy and discuss the turbulent atmosphere that marked world affairs at war's end. It will pay particular attention to the 1919 peace conference in Paris – to the preparations for the conference because they shaped the idea of a new liberal world order, and to the Paris conference itself because it had a formative effect on the establishment of International Relations as a new academic field. Also, the war and the peace conference that followed paved the way for the interwar emergence of communism and fascism, two mass-movements which challenged liberal democracy and the international system that it sustained in the postwar years.

The Great War

The war began when a Serb nationalist, Gavrilo Princip, assassinated the Austrian Crown Prince Franz Ferdinand on 28 June 1914 in the remote Balkan town of Sarajevo. The Austrian emperor was enraged by the assassination of his son and resolved to punish the nationalist Serbs. First he secured Germany's support to repress nationalism in the Balkans. Then he began to bomb the Serb capital of Belgrade.

The Serbs were allied with Russia. Russia's short-sighted politicians sided with Balkan nationalists because it caused turmoil in the Ottoman Empire and served Russian aims of gaining control over the Bosporus and access to the Mediterranean. This policy fuelled a fateful chain of events: when the Austrian emperor began to bomb Belgrade – and when Germany's Kaiser Wilhelm II supported the move – Russia's Tsar Nicholas II felt compelled to honour his obligations to the Serbs; and, fearing war, he ordered military mobilization. As soon as Russia's mighty, military machine began to stir, the German Kaiser feared for the security of his empire and felt a need to mobilize as well.

Tragically, the Germans had not prepared for war in the Balkans. They had only prepared for war against Russia and France, and had only one mobilization plan.[1] This provided the background for another fateful chain of events: When the German Kaiser faced a grave crisis in the Balkans and gave the order to mobilize, the German military machine executed the only response it had been designed to deliver: to quickly dispatch two million men in the opposite direction and invade Belgium.

Waging the war

When German troops began to flood into Belgium, it triggered all-out war among Europe's Great Powers. The petty nationalist issues which were at the heart of the Balkan crisis were immediately overwhelmed by more momentous concerns.

The war put all plans and expectations to shame. The military men expected a short war; they got one that lasted four long years. The Germans had expected that a quick invasion of Belgium would be followed by a flashingly fast conquest of France and then a quick campaign against Russia. Nothing of the sort happened. The German invasion of Belgium was halted immediately by Belgian, French and British forces on the flat fields of Flanders. Here both sides dug deep trenches for shelter. These, in turn, became permanent installations. Instead of the quick war of movement that German strategists had planned for, the war congealed into a bitter war of position.

Bogged down on its western front, Germany was never free to concentrate its forces into a full offensive against the east. Instead, in autumn and winter of 1914, the German leaders saw the emergence of their worst fear: a two-front war. By 1915 they were fighting a trench war in the west and facing the Russians in a drawn-out, exhaustive slog in the east.

This would continue for four years. Soldiers from the Triple Entente and the Triple Alliance would shell each other unceasingly in an unprecedented exercise of mutual exhaustion. At the fronts, there would be a bloodbath which had scarcely seen its equal. It would cost nearly ten million soldiers their lives (Strachan 2011).[2]

The trench warfare of the western front provided the most potent image of the war: machine guns and automatic rifles would shoot at everything that moved above ground. This made the spade a defensive tool, because it allowed the soldiers to save their lives by digging shelters below ground. As these shelters interconnected and expanded, growing mazes of trenches would emerge, one trench system on the German side, another at the Allied side. The two sides would shell each other incessantly, turning the fertile fields of Flanders into a pock-marked moon landscape. When it rained, the trenches would be filled with water and rats and become a nightmare of mud, illness and death. A steady stream of young men would be sent to the trenches to dig deeper and further. Between the trenches they would establish a no-man's-land that separated the two enemy fronts and was marked by impenetrable webs of barbed wire.

The Entente was dominated by Great Britain who struggled to co-ordinate the merchant fleets of the alliance and establish an Allied Maritime Transport Executive (AMTE), a powerful organization designed to regulate world shipping. It supplied the Entente powers with resources necessary to conduct the war, while denying such resources to the Triple Alliance. Behind the scenes, wartime diplomacy was a complex tangle of secret agreements and double deals. The Great Powers worked desperately to maintain the unity of their alliance, and to gain new members to it. The Triple Alliance was dominated by Germany, which steadily sought to broaden its war aims – by conquering new territory in both the east and the west, Germany's leaders hoped to destroy the encirclement that had confined its freedom of action in the past. Its ventures were not met with success. Austria-Hungary was rent with internal conflict and was not an efficient ally. Italy changed sides and joined the Triple Entente in the spring of 1915.[3]

Germany did, however, convince Ottoman Turkey to join the Triple Alliance. This was a terrible blow to the Triple Entente. Turkey's defection intimidated Russia, which now feared Germany's influence along its vulnerable south-western border. Also, the Ottoman declaration of *jihad* threatened Britain, which had long used Ottoman power to contain Russian ambitions around the Black Sea and the Adriatic. In a stunning reversal of traditional policy, Britain and France promised Russia influence over the Bosporus. Also, Britain's Sir Mark Sykes and France's Georges Picot agreed to divide Ottoman territories. Britain would assume control over Iraq and Palestine, whereas France would control Syria and Lebanon. On top of it all, British Foreign Minister Balfour secretly promised to support the

Zionist demand for a Jewish homeland in Palestine, if the Zionists would support the Allied war effort. Diplomatic deals made during the war would reconfigure the region. The deals were often contradictory, if not mutually exclusive. They contributed to the entanglements and conflicts that would riddle the new international sub-system, the 'Middle East', for the remainder of the century.

Wilson's war and his vision of peace

While Europe's Great Powers were engaged in a complex diplomacy of war, others worked to establish peace. The international socialist movement busily pressured the labour parties and governments to begin peace negotiations, but to little avail. Pope Benedict XV pushed the French and Italian governments to consider peace negotiations, but without success. Across the Atlantic, the American president Woodrow Wilson, too, had peacemaking ambitions. His impact on the war, on postwar affairs and on the development of International Relations would prove momentous.

Wilson initially believed that America's national interest was best served by staying out of the Great War. By remaining aloof, he imagined that he could play the role of a neutral broker. However, when his first efforts to mediate were rebuffed, Wilson faced a dilemma. If Germany won, it would mean the triumph of German militarism on the Continent and a blow to democracy and free trade. However, if the Allies won, autocratic Russia would exploit the victory to expand into eastern and central Europe.

Wilson was torn between his belief that only as a neutral actor could he mediate a just peace and his fear that only as a belligerent could he obtain a seat at the peace conference which would define the postwar order. During his re-election campaign in 1916, Wilson publicly repeated his pledge to keep the United States out of the war. But in private he began to consider his options more carefully.

His dilemma ran through a speech he made to Congress on 22 January 1917. Here the American President urged the European belligerents to accept a 'peace without victory'. He told them to simply end the war and bring neither victory nor defeat upon Germany. He added that the old, European balance-of-power games had failed to prevent the war and criticized the Europeans for now relying upon power-politics to secure the peace. 'There must be, not a balance of power, but a community of power', he warned; 'not organized rivalries, but an organized common peace'. Such a peace could be founded only on peoples' full freedom to travel and trade. 'The freedom of the seas is the *sine qua non* of peace, equality and cooperation', Wilson said. 'The free, constant, unthreatened intercourse of nations is an essential part of the process of peace and development.' 'I am proposing', he concluded, 'that the nations should with one accord adopt the doctrine of President Monroe as the doctrine of the world' (Smith 1966, pp. 165, 167).

This reference to the Monroe Doctrine was a huge *faux pas*. It enraged European statesmen who saw Wilson as provincial and chauvinistic. 'The man is the quintessence of a prig'; he dares to come after three years of terrible war to ask us to put down our arms and meekly agree to American principles, commented a

British observer. A French writer called Wilson's comments 'fetid, ignominious, obscene, fistulous and haemorrhoidal' (Link 1967, pp. 273f). The most significant reaction came from the German Kaiser, who struck straight at the heart of Wilson's proposal: on 28 January 1917, six days after the President's speech, the Kaiser initiated a policy of total submarine warfare against neutral or enemy vessels.

The German response was compounded by dramatic events in Russia. In February Tsar Alexander II was unseated and his absolutist regime replaced by a provisional government led by the reform-willing Alexandr Kerensky. The German submarine war and the Russian revolution forced Wilson to make up his mind. As German U-boats began to sink American merchant ships, Wilson reasoned that, if he wanted to protect the freedom of the seas, he could do so only by becoming a full belligerent against Germany.

Wilhelm, Wilson, Lenin and Locke

On 2 April 1918, President Wilson declared war on Kaiser Wilhelm II – and it was important for Wilson to make clear that his declaration of war was addressed to the Kaiser and not the German people.

German submarines were destroying American property and American lives, Wilson angrily argued before Congress. Yet, he did not insist on revenge. Rather, he appealed to universal principles of decency and to arguments of natural law: the German attacks were not only acts of war against the United States, they violated the very rules by which civilized humanity lives, argued Wilson. Germany was an aggressor who declared war on the reason and law which maintained the order of humankind. Thus, America must rise to defend reason and law. In the name of all humankind.

Wilson's close adviser Edward House feared the consequences of Wilson's sweeping logic: if his notion of war on behalf of humankind were to be taken literally, it would involve an invitation to unlimited military engagement across the globe. The US Secretary of State Robert Lansing had similar reservations. He was particularly concerned with the upheavals in Russia. He feared what would happen if Kerensky lost control of the Russian revolution and the vast tsarist empire was plunged into a 'hideous state of disorder'. It might totally undermine the Allied war effort on the eastern front (Lansing 1935, p. 337).

On 7 November 1917, Lansing's worst fears materialized. Kerensky lost control. Vladimir I. Lenin and his revolutionary Bolsheviks seized power in Petrograd and announced to the world that they would pull Russia out of the war. Worse, they called upon all belligerent peoples to follow the Bolshevik example and 'start negotiations for a just, democratic peace'. On 9 November Lenin announced a 'Decree of Peace':

> The [new Soviet] government considers it the greatest of crimes against humanity to continue this war over the issue of how to divide among the strong and rich the weak nationalities they have conquered, and solemnly announces its determination immediately to sign terms of peace to stop this war ...

The government abolishes secret diplomacy, and, for its part, announces its firm intention to conduct all negotiations quite openly in the full view of the whole people. It will proceed immediately with the full publication of the secret treaties endorsed or concluded by [Kerensky's] government of landowners and capitalists from February to October 25, 1917. (Tucker 1975, p. 541)

Lenin's initiative put Wilson in a diplomatic squeeze, and set the tone for seventy-five subsequent years of hostile international discourse. First, Lenin largely repeated the same argument as Wilson: that the common people of the world are inherently peaceful but that their leaders are a dictatorial clique of self-serving, militant oppressors.

Then he opened the archives of the Russian Foreign Office and made public all the duplicitous deals that European governments had secretly made during the war. These documents made it obvious that Britain and France had no intention of supporting Wilson's war aims, and lent credence to Lenin's charge that European capitalism was fighting a costly war to consolidate its overseas possessions and pursue policies of imperialist expansionism.

Finally, Lenin offered a radical alternative to Wilson's liberal theories of a new world order. He not only withdrew Russia from the Allied war effort, he incited workers and soldiers of all countries to turn their weapons on their domestic capitalists and imperialist oppressors and begin a revolution. Only revolution, Lenin argued, could end the war and bring self-determination for all nations.

In late December 1917 Lenin's, government began separate peace negotiations with Germany in the city of Brest-Litovsk. Negotiations proceeded slowly. The Russian government exploited the peace negotiations as a propaganda platform. Lenin's charismatic foreign minister, Leon Trotsky, directed revolutionary arguments against the workers in Europe; his agents spread propaganda in leaflets in the trenches for the benefit of French and British soldiers. The Germans, too, exploited the negotiations: they afforded an armistice which allowed them to transfer thousands of troops from the eastern to the western front. This added more disillusion to the cold and war-tired troops of Britain and France. Discipline was unravelling. Trenches were seething with signs of mutiny.

Wilson immediately called for a 'very grave scrutiny' of America's war aims. He worried that the Bolsheviks used populist rhetoric – 'no annexations, no contributions, no punitive indemnities' – to lead the people of Russia astray (Walworth 1969, p. 144). Besides, Lenin had become Wilson's chief competitor for conceptual leadership in the postwar world. He had 'absconded with the biggest piece of liberal theory: the principle of self-determination' (Gardner 1984).[4]

The Fourteen Points
Wilson met the double challenge of Bolshevik propaganda and the crisis in Allied morale by a major address on the American war aims and the postwar order. This address was destined to be 'democracy's answer in its first full-dress debate with international communism' (Link 1971, p. 108). On 8 January 1918, Wilson outlined his peace programme. He began by carefully discussing the situation in Russia.

Commending Lenin's insistence on open negotiations, 'in the true spirit of modern democracy', Wilson then adopted this principle as his own. He denounced the secret deals of old diplomatic practices. He called for 'open covenants of peace, openly arrived at, after which there shall be no private international understandings of any kind but diplomacy shall proceed always frankly and in public view' (Walworth 1969: 148). This became the first of Wilson's 14 Points for Peace.

Next, Wilson reiterated his old *sine qua non* of peace: 'absolute freedom of navigation upon the seas, outside territorial waters, alike in peace and war' (Point II). He called for 'the removal, so far as possible, of all economic barriers and the establishment of an equality of trade conditions among all the nations consenting to the peace ...' (Point III). He insisted on 'a free, open-minded, and absolutely impartial adjustment of all colonial claims' (Point IV). After several specific proposals for redrawing contested boundaries in Europe, Wilson finally presented a draft charter – or Covenant, as the biblically inspired President called it – for a League of Nations: 'A general association of nations must be formed under specific covenants for the purpose of affording mutual guarantees of political independence and territorial integrity to great and small states alike' (Walworth 1969, p. 148).

Ending the war

The Fourteen Points got mixed reviews in Europe. On the one hand, the bereaved and war-tired masses leapt at Wilson's promise of a lasting peace; they eagerly embraced his idea of an international organization designed to guarantee open diplomacy and arbitration of international disputes.[5] On the other, the European statesmen were sceptical. Even Wilson's greatest European supporter, Britain's Prime Minister David Lloyd George, was lukewarm. France's Prime Minister Georges Clemenceau, always sceptical of Wilson and his liberal philosophy of world affairs, was not enthusiastic. 'Fourteen?' he is supposed to have said when he heard about Wilson's points; 'the good Lord contended himself with only ten'. Yet, Lloyd George and Clemenceau both recognized Wilson's popularity and did not publicly reject his proposals.

Wilson was their last hope. On 3 March 1918, Lenin's Bolshevik government signed a draconian separate peace with Germany at Brest-Litovsk.[6] Germany seemed to have won the war on the east front, and was free to transfer troops to the west front and launch new offensives in the spring of 1918. Lloyd George and Clemenceau desperately needed US reinforcements. And when the American troops began to arrive in Europe a few weeks later, they made all the difference. They blunted the German offensives. They beat the Germans back and greatly encouraged French and British soldiers.

By midsummer it was clear that Austria-Hungary was quietly dissolving under the impact of nationalist uprisings. Germany was being pushed beyond exhaustion and its armies grinding to a halt. The summer offensives killed over a million German men and drained the Reich of its final reserves. In early August a costly defeat at the Battle of the Somme broke the German spirit. In September general Erich Ludendorff, the German chief of staff, informed the Kaiser that his army was finished. On 3 October the Germans accepted Wilson's Fourteen Points and requested an armistice.

On 11 November 1918, after four years of war, the carnage finally ended. The most direct costs of the war were 9,800,000 dead young men and over 21,000,000 wounded. The indirect costs are impossible to assess. First there are the direct economic losses – the capital destroyed and the resources expended in the service of destruction. Then there are the political and social costs associated with the collapse of order. The political costs associated with the collapse of four empires – the German Reich, Austria-Hungary, Tsarist Russia and the Ottoman Empire – were enormous.[7]

The great peace: the League, Wilson and Versailles

The Great War had first brought four years of stalemate slaughter to the Continent. In early 1917 this stalemate was broken by events beyond the traditional cockpit of European politics: by the Russian revolution in March and by America's entry in April. At that time, President Wilson's calls for a League of Nations ensured him a large popular following. When he arrived in Paris in January 1919 to participate at the peace conference, he was greeted as a new Messiah. There is no doubt about it, Wilson made an absolutely crucial contribution to that conference. Without his dogged insistence, the League would never have been established.

Two things need to be clear. First, that Wilson was not the first caller for an international organization where states could meet to end war and build a better world. Second, that he did not have a clear plan for how it should actually be organized – until very late in the game. So, where did the plan for a League of Nations come from?

Thinking about the League

The basic idea for a congregation or a league of nations goes far back. Dante had suggested something like it as early as 1300. During the eighteenth century the idea was often repeated in the century's many plans for perpetual peace. The idea was then elaborated by members of the nineteenth-century peace movement. As soon as the war broke out in the autumn of 1914, activists and scholars spontaneously picked up the idea and began to develop new schemes to end war and enforce peace. The most consequential new discussions took place in two scholarly groups in Britain.

One of these groups was organized by the Cambridge historian Goldsworthy Lowes Dickinson to discuss the causes of war and the preconditions for peace. An idea that quickly emerged from the group was that the most fundamental reason for the outbreak of war lay in the anarchic nature of the international system. Dickinson presented this argument in *The European Anarchy* (1916), a slim volume that discussed the international events leading up to 1914. Another idea that emerged from Dickinson's group was that, to establish a lasting peace after the war, it was not enough to beat Germany and eradicate Prussian militarism;

it would also be necessary to establish an international organization designed to counteract the anarchic nature of international relations. John Hobson set out the argument in *Towards International Government* (1915). The book advocated a concert or a league of nations to be established after the war. The term was snappy. In the spring of 1915 a group of influential and well-known men got together – the most prominent among them was the highly respected member of the Foreign Office, James Bryce – and established 'The League of Nations Society' (Marriott 1939, p. 172).

The other scholarly group that emerged in Britain sprang out of the Fabian Society, a left-wing group of academics associated with the Labour Party. Early in 1915, Fabian editor Sidney Webb invited the publisher and independent writer Leonard Woolf to explore the idea of an international peace organization. Woolf threw himself into the project, read vociferously and quickly submitted a report. It was published as a special section of *The New Statesman*, and soon after as a book (Woolf 1916).

Other groups also emerged to discuss questions of war and peace.[8] Yet, none of them were as influential as the Fabian Society and the League of Nations Society. One reason for this was that the diplomat and scholar James Bryce had friends in both groups. And when the British Foreign Office in 1916 established a committee to study the prospects for a peaceful postwar world, Bryce was appointed to chair it. He filled the committee with learned intellectuals from both groups. During the spring of 1916, the members of the Bryce committee investigated classical peace plans from Saint-Pierre and Rousseau through Bentham and Cobden. They called upon international lawyers and leading members of British peace organizations to testify at their meetings.[9]

Britain's Undersecretary of Foreign Affairs, Robert Cecil, sat in on some of the meetings. He drew on its work to write memorandums to Cabinet meetings that discussed the postwar order. In order to establish a stable and peaceful postwar world, Cecil wrote, it was necessary to establish a League of Nations. Cecil's memos received stinging critique from some and high praise from others. One of his sternest critics was the senior diplomat Sir Eyre Crowe. One of his defenders was Jan Smuts, the South African foreign minister and a member of the British War Cabinet. Soon after a Cabinet that had discussed Robert Cecil's memorandum, Smuts took the time to read through Wilson's many pronouncements on a League. He had found Wilson vague and imprecise. With the Cabinet discussion freshly in mind, Smuts tried to sharpen Wilson's key ideas and give them coherent form. The result was a memo which Smuts entitled 'A Practical Suggestion' and sent to his government. The Prime Minister Lloyd George quickly sent a copy to President Wilson (MacMillan 2001, pp. 96ff; Mazower 2013).

In September 1917 Wilson established his own study group, 'the Inquiry'. It was intended to help him prepare for the peace negotiations which would inevitably follow the war.[10] The French Foreign office, too, established a study group about this time, the Comité d'études; in fact, it established two.[11]

Establishing the League

The picture is often painted of a messianic Wilson who sailed across the Atlantic to present the idea of the League to European statesmen. Most of this is false. True, Wilson was messianic. And he did sail across the Atlantic. However, when he boarded the *USS George Washington* in New York on 4 December 1918 to sail for France, his idea of the League was far from clear. His plan was to work out the practical details on the voyage across the Atlantic. Among the papers he brought on the trip was Jan Smuts's memo, 'A Practical Suggestion'. He was deeply impressed by it. As he worked out the details of a League, he borrowed heavily from Smuts's memo.

When President Wilson arrived in Paris in January 1919, he was received by David Lloyd George and Georges Clemenceau who, together with the Italian Prime Minister Vittorio Orlando, would go to work immediately and preside over the Versailles Peace Conference as the almighty 'Council of Four'. The four powerful men of the council invited few others to join them. They met a storm of complaints from lesser powers who were left out of the procedures.[12] The Four, however, waved off all criticism, arguing that openness would steal time and produce nothing but chaos. If anything were to be done at all, it must be done fast and by a small group, they argued.

They had a point. Events were moving quickly in the wake of the war. Collapsing empires and revolutionary insurrections constantly threatened to undo their diplomatic dispositions. The Council of Four also dealt with collapsing empires, with failing states and with a refugee problem of staggering proportions. Millions of people needed aid and opportunities for repatriation in the wake of the war. They debated the thorny issues of colonialism.[13] They presided over committees and special commissions. They received representatives and hosted delegations. And they met once or twice – or sometime three times – every day for most of the spring of 1919.

The Council defined the framework for the League of Nations. It was a milestone both in international diplomacy and in discussions about war and peace. President Wilson's primary goal in Paris was to establish the League. He was willing to haggle and bargain to reach it. Indeed, many delegates were surprised at Wilson's insistence. Members of his own delegation were deeply frustrated by Wilson's willingness to compromise on other issues in order to get his way on the League.[14]

President Wilson has been given the credit for establishing the League. It is often forgotten that his work was supported and encouraged by British, French, Italian and American civil servants who had worked together during the war in the Allied war effort against Germany. They had built huge administrative structures together and drawn unique lessons from their wartime co-operation; after the war they relied on their common experience to design an organization which could keep the peace.

Among the most important supporters of the League were the three leaders of the old Allied Maritime Transport Executive (AMTE) – Arthur Salter, Jean Monnet and Bernardo Attolico. These individuals were the most powerful men in the world during the Great War, because they headed the organization that controlled and co-ordinated all Allied shipping – which is to say 90 per cent of all the shipping in the world. These men, who commanded the hub of the Allied war machine, would also prepare the instruments of peace that were established in war's wake. For the organizations which secured the wartime co-operation of the Atlantic powers also provided the practical joists upon which the League of Nations would be built. Thus, the three men who ran the AMTE during the war – Salter, Monnet and Attolico – would form the Secretariat of the League of Nations after it.[15]

IR: In the shadow of the League

The victorious states had prepared well for the Paris Peace Conference. On both sides of the Atlantic, ministers and diplomats had taken up ideas and arguments that the peace movement had argued for decades. The arguments of the prewar peace movement were, however, updated during the Great War – by Hobson (1915), Lowes Dickinson (1916), Woolf (1916; 1917) and others. This updating involved a moving away from the old theories of the prewar free-traders and their concept of interdependence; instead a new argument emerged, fuelled by inter-Allied co-operation. It advocated the need for an international organization – a League of Nations – and elaborated on the concept of collective security.

These new ideas impressed the diplomatic circles in London and Washington, where ministers and diplomats supported the idea of a League. The establishment of the League was, in turn, influential in establishing the academic field of International Relations, whose members would in turn elaborate on the importance of the League and on the concept of collective security.

The supporters of the League and the members of the emerging field of International Relations all agreed that a well-functioning League would depend on an enlightened public. And they considered the dissemination of knowledge about the causes of war and the preconditions for peace to be an important task for peace activists. But they also agreed that such knowledge must not only be disseminated, it must also be scholarly refined and systematically expanded. And that required more than writers.

There had been plenty of writers in past. It was now necessary to add institutions and co-ordinated activities. The writers needed journals. The journals needed readers. The writers would be co-ordinated in institutes and the readers educated in new schools. All would be interconnected in conferences and networks. All these institutions were added in the wake of the Great War. Many of them were initiated during the Paris Peace Conference in 1919, and sponsored by the League in the subsequent years. They provided the institutional underpinnings of what would soon become the 'science of international politics'.

The first International Relations institutions
It all began at the Paris Peace Conference. This was unique in many respects. It was unique in its result – in the creation of the League; for although many thinkers in the past had discussed the formation of such an organization, no one had actually taken the initiative to make one. It was also unique in its process – for never before

had so many academics attended a peace conference. In addition to over a thousand delegates from twenty-seven different states, the conference included hundreds of lawyers, historians, economists and political scientists whom the delegates had brought to serve as experts and consultants. *They* were the true pioneers, the unsung heroes of the scholarly field of International Relations.

For the important institutions, which would ground International Relations nationally and internationally, were not made by conference delegates; they were initiated and pursued by the experts and consultants whom the delegates had brought with them.

Institutes and journals

The experts enjoyed Paris. And they enjoyed each other's company. When the delegates negotiated, expert consultants often gathered and talked shop. On one particular occasion – on 30 May 1919 – about twenty of them gathered at the Hôtel Majestic to talk about a first draft produced by the delegates for a peace treaty with Germany. The British and the American experts agreed that the draft was unsatisfactory; that Lloyd George and Wilson had compromised excessively with the Continental powers.

One of the experts at the Hôtel meeting was Robert Cecil, who three years earlier had sat in on the meetings of the Bryce committee and had written memos about the League to the British Cabinet. He pronounced the draft a big disappointment. But, he added, the disappointment must not lead to pessimism and passivity; it must be an inspiration for action. Lionel Curtis agreed. He was a central member of the British Round Table group, a friend of Philip Kerr and close to the British Prime Minister David Lloyd George. However the Conference turned out, argued Curtis, there would be a need for an institute devoted to examine and distribute information about international affairs. Such an institute would be a venue where academic experts, diplomats and political leaders could meet and discuss international relations.

Why establish only one institute? Why not establish two – one in Britain and another in the United States? The two could establish a close relationship and open up a new era of co-operation as well as a new scholarly field. The question sparked organizational initiatives on both sides of the Atlantic (Shotwell 1937, p. 346). In 1920 the British Institute of International Affairs opened in London – at the prestigious address of 10 St James Square: Chatham House.[16] The first director of the Institute was Robert Cecil. Its first secretary was Lionel Curtis. They established a journal, *International Affairs*.[17] In 1921 the American Council of Foreign Relations was established in New York, founded by seventy-five members of the America delegation to Paris – many of them members of Wilson's 'Inquiry' team. In 1922 it launched its own journal, *Foreign Affairs*.

The two institutes were big successes. They constituted models for other institutes which were established in other countries – Germany, Poland, Denmark, Canada and Hungary among them. They all sought to inform the public on current international events. But they also did research – most particularly on the causes of war and the preconditions for peace. They all tended to focus on the processes of the Paris Peace Conference and the documents and institutions that it produced.

Schools and associations

For Wilson, the main task of the League was to build a world order of democratic states in free and open interaction. He had in mind a *world* order; he spoke for humanity as a whole, and was pleased to note that twenty-six of its original forty-two members came from outside Europe. The most immediate tasks of the League, however, were associated with Europe, the scene of destruction and misery of unprecedented scale. The war had created millions of homeless people who had to be fed and cared for. The League established vast refugee camps and organizations for humanitarian aid and repatriation on an unprecedented scale.

The League also sought to settle conflicts. For fighting did not end in Europe just because Germany surrendered; the violence continued, especially in the central and eastern regions of the continent.

In addition, the League worked to establish institutes for research and education. For that purpose, it set up international organizations like the International Committee on Intellectual Co-operation (ICIC) and the International Institute of Intellectual Co-operation (IIIC). These institutions would identify schools and institutes that taught international subjects and encourage them to co-operate and co-ordinate. This was not an easy task, for a steady stream of new courses in International Relations were added to the curriculum of schools and universities in the wake of the war. The world's first chair in International Politics was established at the University of Wales, Aberystwyth, in 1919; other chairs followed in other British institutions.[18] About half a dozen schools devoted to International Relations were established in the USA in the wake of the Great War, to say nothing of the many new departments and institutes that also saw the light of day.[19] Outside of the English-speaking world, the most significant new school was the Graduate Institute of International Studies, which was established in Geneva, close to the League headquarters, in 1927.

The IIIC tried to establish contact between the schools, co-ordinate them and help develop standardized curriculums, and establish an international network of experts and scholars in the growing field. This was the specific purpose of the International Studies Conference (ISC), which was set up in 1928. The ISC helped develop international scholarship in important ways – generously assisted by the American Rockefeller Foundation, which now added international understanding and conflict resolution to its many sponsorship activities. Clearly, by the end of the 1920s, International Relations was institutionalized as an academic field. What was its content? What was its theoretical orientation?

Woodrow Wilson and the American approach to International Relations[20]

Most of the early students of International Relations saw the Versailles Treaty as a watershed and the postwar period as an era of reason and progress. They saw each new international agreement as a new step away from past problems of conflict and war.[21]

They tended to be religious men. The British pioneers in International Relations entertained an optimistic, Christian evolutionism which informed their perspectives of war and peace (Studdert-Kennedy 1995). The Americans, too, tended to be religious men, President Wilson very famously so; he was a Presbyterian elder and a member of the Social Gospel movement. There always remained an element of Protestant millenarianism in his visions of war and peace.[22]

But Wilson's vision also had another, more secular taproot. His arguments were deeply influenced by the social-contract tradition that received an early expression in the arguments that were formulated by John Locke and elaborated by Émeric Vattel. The political logic of Locke is clearly visible for instance in Wilson's declaration of war against Germany. The war, Wilson emphasized, was directed against the aggressive militarism of the Prussian regime, not against the people of Germany.

> We have no quarrel with the German people. We have no feeling towards them but one of sympathy and friendship. It was not upon their impulse that their government acted in entering this war. It was not with their previous knowledge or approval. It was a war determined upon as wars used to be determined upon in the old, unhappy days when peoples were nowhere consulted by their rulers and wars were provoked and waged in the interest of dynasties or of little groups of ambitious men who were accustomed to use their fellow men as pawns and tools ... Such designs can be successfully worked out only under cover and where no one has the right to ask questions ... They are happily impossible where public opinion commands and insists upon full information concerning all the nation's affairs. (Smith 1966, pp. 194ff)

This brief declaration is grafted on to Locke's liberal, social-contract philosophy. In Wilson's mind, the German Kaiser had knowingly violated the Law of Nature. This Law, which is based on Reason, would apply to the German Kaiser as it would apply to all other 'Rulers of Independent Governments all through the World, [who] are in a State of Nature' (Locke 1960, p. 317). Kaiser Wilhelm II had shown by his aggressive acts that he had chosen to live by other rules than those inherent in the Law of Nature. By violating those rules, the Kaiser had declared war on all law-abiding rulers. He had thus placed himself outside the Law of Reason, and could no longer claim to be protected by it (Locke 1960, p. 320). Thus, anyone had the right to pursue and punish him – not for their own sake, but for the sake of the Law itself. The German Kaiser had violated the very rules by which civilized humanity lives, argued Wilson. His violations amounted to a declaration of war on all humankind, and America must punish Germany in the name of Reason, order and the rights of all humankind.

Wilson, then, declared war on Germany, motivated not by 'revenge or the victorious assertion of the physical might of the nation, but only the vindication of right, of human right, of which we are only a single champion' (Smith 1966, p. 191). America should fight for 'the ultimate peace of the world and for the liberation of its peoples, the German people included: for the rights of nations great and small and the privilege of men everywhere to choose their way of life'. The United States sought no selfish ends, Wilson insisted. 'We desire no conquest, no domination. We seek no indemnities for ourselves, no material compensation for the sacrifices we shall freely make'. America's war aim was only to defeat 'autocratic governments backed by organized force which is controlled wholly by [the autocrats'] will, not by the will of the people'. All peoples naturally want democracy. If the autocrats were destroyed, then the peoples of the world could create the democratic, peaceful governments they naturally sought, join the 'partnership of democratic nations' and help cement a 'steadfast concert for peace' (Smith 1966, pp. 194ff).

When Wilson arrived in Paris to negotiate with the European leaders, he met politicians steeped in a very different tradition. He saw them as cynics. They, however, saw him as a strange and out-of-touch utopian. They were weary of his universalism and his moralistic pronouncements. John Maynard Keynes (1920, p. 38) noted after a meeting that Wilson's 'thought and temperament were essentially theological, not intellectual'. Clemenceau commented in his memoirs that he had looked forward to meeting Wilson and hoped to meet a fellow statesman, but that he had met a theologian.

The Paris negotiations involved more than clashes of strong personalities; they also involved a clash of political cultures. On the one side were Wilson and his advisers – young and clever Americans who invested their trust in institutions that would enable rational actors to co-operate in peaceful ways. On the other were the old statesmen of Europe. Clemenceau in particular, but also Orlando and Lloyd George, were jaded men, raised in the old school of interstate diplomacy. The Americans were liberal internationalists who wanted to establish participatory institutions in order to harness the self-interest of states and replace the ancient mechanisms of power with institutions of collective security. The Europeans saw international politics in terms of self-interested states and they negotiated in order to strike diplomatic deals which would satisfy their state's interest for security and power. The rancorous debates at Versailles between Americans and Europeans testified to a clash between two very different approaches to international affairs.

The difference could readily be seen in the contrasting attitudes to the League that emerged during the discussions at the Paris Peace Conference. Whereas Wilson would hold a generally optimistic view of human beings as rational and human nature as good, the Continental statesmen would hold a pessimistic view of human nature as self-serving. Where Wilson would tend to see the people as rational and reasonable and prone to make rules and institutions to ensure orderly conduct in society, Continental statesmen would tend to see political actors as guided by efforts to secure and protect their interests – by the use of force if necessary. Where Wilson would tend to see international politics in terms of people, his Continental interlocutors would tend to view international politics in terms of interaction of territorial states.

The political philosophy of John Locke is quite apparent in Wilson's arguments. Also, Émeric Vattel's elaborations of Locke into a doctrine of collective security reverberates through Wilson's advocacy for a the League of Nations. Wilson saw the League as an outcome of reason and believed that it could sustain itself simply on openness and freedom of information. Georges Clemenceau, by contrast, consistently brought up realist concerns. How would the League enforce its decisions, he wanted to know. How would it stop aggressors? How would it intervene into conflicts, separate quarrelling parties and make them obey? Surely, the League needed some means of military enforcement? Clemenceau consistently worked to provide the League with sharp teeth and proposed a military force under League command. And Wilson consistently rejected it. Clemenceau proposed that the League at least got its own general staff. Wilson refused. His League should have no military component! The entire French delegation threw up their collective hands in the end (MacMillan 2001).

Interwar approaches to international politics

French diplomats may have thrown up their hands at Wilson, but Western academics did not. During its first, formative years, the study of International Relations was deeply influenced by Wilson and the liberal tradition he represented. During the war, peace groups had revived the central idea of the perpetual-peace tradition, the idea that a lasting, just peace could be guaranteed by international law and a body of international arbitration.[23] After the war the inheritance of the liberal tradition was evident in the very titles of the books that were put on reading lists of early International Relations courses – books like *The Law of Nations*, *International Government*, *The Function of Law in International Community*, *The League of Nations and the Rule of Law* and *International Law*.[24] James L. Brierly equipped his most influential book, *The Law of Nations* [1928], with the telling subtitle *An Introduction to the International Law of Peace*.

Other perspectives existed. They were, however, rarely represented on early International Relations reading lists. The most conspicuous exclusion from these early International Relations courses was the old approach of *Realpolitik*. This approach was usually expressed by conservative statesmen, like Clemenceau in France or Churchill in England. They found Wilson's Fourteen Points dangerously naive – but, as statesmen, they were too busy to engage in scholarly debate; and, as conservatives, they were not inclined to theorize.

Two additional approaches emerged during the course of the 1920s. Neither one was included in early International Relations syllabuses. The first of these was the radical approach of the revolutionary socialist movement. Although their basic doctrines could be traced back to social theorists of the Enlightenment and in spite of their having a great impact on political events after World War I, the theories of revolutionary socialism did not influence the early International Relations scholars. The internationalist doctrines which were seductively refined by the cosmopolitan intellectuals of Russia's Bolshevik revolution remained oddly quarantined by members of the academic international-studies community.

The second approach which emerged during the interwar period was fascism. But this was largely an anti-intellectual movement, and exerted only slight influence on International Relations.

At least four perspectives of world politics, then, existed side by side in the interwar period: (1) the liberal legalism of President Wilson; (2) the old tradition of power politics; (3) the new communist approach; (4) fascism. The last three were largely excluded from International Relations reading lists. If mentioned at all, they were regularly rejected as unhelpful, if not inimical. However, when the world was hit by a deep and lasting depression in the 1930s, the dominant liberal approach found itself seriously challenged from three sides.

Idealism and Woodrow Wilson

President Wilson's approach dominated International Relations after the Great War. Academics in schools and institutes tended to draw heavily on a liberal social-contract tradition, and to formulate their arguments in a tight, legislative form which strongly echoed those which Émeric Vattel and Jeremy Bentham had formulated over a century before.

Vattel, Bentham and Wilson emphasized the role of human reason, individual liberty, public opinion and social openness. Their faith in reason and public opinion dominated social thought in both England and America after Waterloo. After 1850, however, it was increasingly criticized in Europe. At the turn of the century, the belief that human reason alone was sufficient to promote right conduct was challenged by psychologists; the identification of virtue with enlightened self-interest was refuted resoundingly by political economists.

After 1900, it would have been difficult to find any serious European thinker who accepted the Benthamite assumptions without qualification. In the United States, by contrast, the early nineteenth-century assumptions survived the critique of the 1860s and the economic upheavals of the 1870s. Indeed, Bentham's utilitarian argument was fortified by the tonic of American social-Darwinism around the turn of the century, and re-emerged in American politics in the 1910s. It was launched into the debate about international politics during World War I, and became a formative force in the new science of international relations. International Relations, commented Edward Carr (2001 [1939], p. 26), can be seen as a reflection, in an American mirror, of early European liberal thought.

The influence of social thinkers like Locke, Vattel and Bentham was apparent in the idea of a League of Nations. The League was portrayed as an organization which could sustain itself on openness and the free circulation of information, without resort to force. The liberal logic was also conspicuously present in the introductory texts in the emerging field of international politics – in texts by Satow (1917), Cooley (1918), Heatley (1919) and Allen (1920). Pitman Potter (1922) stands out as a notably comprehensive presentation of the history of interstate relations and the diplomatic procedures of international relations – including a definition of the key concept of sovereignty, an introduction to the nature and role of conferences, arbitration and treaties, and a lengthy explanation of the League of Nations. Such themes also mark the texts by Lawrence (1919), Muir (1918), Brown (1923), Brierly (1928), Mitrany (1933) and Zimmern (1936).

Clyde Eagleton formulated a tight, time-typical argument in his admirable little book *Analysis of the Problem of War* (1937). Eagleton rejects the assumption held by many Realists 'that war results from the innate desire of human beings to fight'. Instead he extols the Enlightenment assumption that people are endowed with desires and with reason, and will strive to satisfy their desires in rational ways:

> Force has always been called upon because it is the ultimate method by which peoples, whether individually or in rational groups, have been able to achieve their desires. It is not war which is desired, but other things, good or bad, which it is hoped can be attained through the use of war. It is logical to believe that, if a more effective method could be discovered for accomplishing these ends, that method would be employed rather than war. (Eagleton 1937, p. 117)

The Idealist approach to international politics was preoccupied with finding reason-based substitutes for war. It claimed that if there had been a chance to bring grievances out in the open before the Balkan conflict erupted into war in 1914, if there had existed a forum in which national leaders could talk things out, the escalation towards war might have been avoided. The alternative to balance of power and war, argued the postwar idealists, was international organization.

Realism, Mackinder and Winston Churchill

Woodrow Wilson's worldview reflected the social philosophy of the Enlightenment. It was anchored in contract theory and a religiously inspired natural-law philosophy. Wilsonism, which dominated the infant discipline on International Relations, had its opponents. The most well-known opponents were Western statesmen and diplomats – such as Georges Clemenceau and André Tardieu who had compared Wilsonism to Leninism already in 1918 and brushed off both as 'pure ideology' (Tardieu 1921; Clemenceau 1930, p. 140).

But there were academic opponents as well. One of them had once been very close to President Wilson: the talented, young Walter Lippmann. He had been the first director of Wilson's 'Inquiry' and one of the President's advisers at the Paris Peace Conference. Lippmann grew disillusioned with the conference proceedings and left Paris in a huff in 1919, sharply criticizing the League for being an instrument for an unjust peace. This dissatisfaction was echoed by Lippmann's successor at the 'Inquiry', the geographer Isaiah Bowman. He too had accompanied Wilson to Paris. His *New World, Problems in Political Geography* [1922] drew upon first-hand experiences from the Paris negotiations and reflected a disillusion with the course of events. 'From a state of high idealism maintained during much of the war, men have passed into a state of realism', commented Bowman as early as 1922 (p. 8).

One of the most consequential of the early realist critics of the League was the British geographer Halford J. Mackinder. He published *Democratic Ideals and Reality* in the spring of 1919, intending it to be a warning to the delegates at the Paris Peace Conference. 'Our memories are still full of the vivid detail of an all-absorbing warfare', Mackinder (1919, p. 1) began. Under the impact of those memories, the language of diplomats is a language of détente. But these memories will fade, he continued. Attitudes will alter, language will change and interstate conflict will soon re-emerge – though slowly at first. If the diplomats in Paris will only lift the gaze from their legal briefs and consult the larger lines of international history, they will observe that revulsion for war is always a temporary condition. And that different states will evolve at different paces, develop different interests and create tensions and conflicts between them.

Lippmann, Bowman and Mackinder were not opponents of the League of Nations. On the contrary, they all argued that a league was the best hope for a stable world order. What they warned against was not the League as such but establishing the League on the principles of international law alone. Mackinder was crystal-clear on this point: It is, he insisted, necessary to also base the League on the 'realities of power'.

What realities are these? Mackinder addresses the question indirectly. He begins by distinguishing between two approaches to politics: On the one hand, there is the approach of the Idealist; on the other that of the Organizer. Idealists work to improve society; they are visionaries, preoccupied with the ends of politics. Organizers work to maintain society; they are practical men, concerned with the means of politics. They work to uphold the system – to keep the machinery humming and spinning and to sustain 'the complicated interactions of myriads of men'. Idealists want to improve society; they want to change it. Organizers want society to run smoothly; they see change as a threat.

Mackinder's point was not to argue that one approach is right and the other wrong. His point was that both are necessary. In practical politics, Idealists and Organizers complement each other. In political analysis, there is a tension between them that produce thoughtful examinations. Idealists, says Mackinder are 'the salt of the earth; without them to move us, society would soon stagnate and civilization fade' (Mackinder 1919, p. 7). Organizers, however, work out the practical preconditions for politics; without them, little would be done and even less would be sustained over time. The Organizers are concerned with rules and resources; with proper procedure, with costs and with staying within budgets. 'The great organizer is the great realist' (Mackinder 1919, pp. 13f).

Mackinder's fear, then, was that the League would be dominated by Idealists, who would produce an unworkable organization founded on the principles of international law but be oblivious to the larger system that sustained order and gave substance to the law. He feared that they would be carried away by the appealing nature of the goals and forget about the necessities of ways and means; that they would overemphasize the importance of reason and good intentions and overlook the pressures and dynamics of the larger, international system.

Mackinder was not the only one with such worries. Other authors entertained similar notions. They expressed them publicly and participated in discussions about international affairs all during the 1920s. They were, however, hardly included on scholarly reading lists on International Relations. It is an odd omission. Anyone interested in international affairs could hardly miss Winston S. Churchill's arguments in the British Parliament or the views presented in his six-volume work on the Great War, *The World Crisis* [1923–31]. Both speeches and texts were thoroughly realist in tone. Churchill was never impressed by the optimism and promises of the Paris Peace Conference. He was experienced in the art of politics and had the eye of Mackinder's 'Organizer'.

Churchill's *The World Crisis* is rich and erudite. It is informed by a deep knowledge of history and guided by a sceptical anthropology. It doubts the claim that human action is led by reason. It portrays human interaction in terms of conflict rather than harmony. It depicts international relations as a contest in which war is a frequent occurrence. The actors on Churchill's international state are selfish nation-states. The *dramatis personae* of the works are 'the great States and Empires and its theme is their world-wide balance and combinations' (Churchill 1923, p. 19). The states are seen as unitary actors.[25] Following the example of historians since Thucydides, Churchill describes them in anthropomorphic terms. His text abounds with expressions like 'Italy saw ...', 'Russia thought ...' and 'Austria decided ...'. He portrays Germany as 'obstinate', 'reckless' and 'ambitious'; he describes France as 'brooding' and England as 'entirely unconscious of the approaching danger'. Thus, Churchill discusses the interaction between states in terms of interaction between egotistical individuals of different psychological dispositions. All states seek to maximize their own security. Each state does so according to its own situation and sentiment – each analyses international events in the light of its own distinctive interests and acts according to its own cultural predisposition and its own assessment of its relative military strength.

When Churchill began the first volume of his work, Realist approaches were largely absent from scholarly reading lists on international relations. When he completed his final volume, things were changing. Charles Hodges (1931), for example, encouraged his students to transcend the orthodoxy of legal idealism, study the realities of power and observe international events in the historical light of actual interstate relations. David Davies (1932) showed that international politics has always been rife with conflict and the use of power. Reinhold Niebuhr (1932) warned that the study of international affairs was dominated by naive idealists who approached the relations among states through a misplaced moralism based on individual-rights philosophy. These idealists have occasioned 'considerable moral and political confusion' because they have 'completely disregarded the political necessities' in their naive struggle for justice, argued Niebuhr (1932, p. xii). Hersh Lauterpacht (1933) reminded the advocates of the League that, although law is essential for a peaceful world, it is no panacea. There are limits to the authority of law, he argued. And in his *Function of Law in the International Community* (1933) he sought to identify these limits.

A growing number of authors also voiced concern about the increasing disorder that emerged in contemporary international relations during the 1930s (Schmitt 1932; Schuman 1933; Simonds and Emeny 1935; Shotwell 1937; Mantoux et al. 1938). One of them was Edward Mead Earle at the Institute for Advanced Studies at Princeton. Trained as a historian, he organized a cross-disciplinary seminar on issues of foreign policy, security affairs and international relations. This seminar, which started up in 1938, had developed a realist thrust. It brought together an impressive roster of historians, political scientists, policy-makers and strategists – among them were Bernard Brodie, William T. R. Fox, Harold and Margaret Sprout, John von Neumann and many others. Earle's ambition was to create 'a new regime of inquiry' that would draw on different approaches and disciplines and develop a systematic approach to 'national strategy' thinking in American academia. By the assessment of observers like Ekbladh (2011), Earle's seminar prepared the foundation for a field of security studies.

Communism, Marx and Lenin

The third interwar approach to international politics was informed by the writings of Karl Marx and Friedrich Engels. The most forceful representatives of this approach were the intellectuals in the Russian Bolshevik Party, especially Vladimir I. Lenin. This tradition, too, had roots in the social philosophy of the Enlightenment. Lenin, like Wilson, subscribed to the precepts of rationality, equality, liberty and human power over nature. However, Lenin followed the radical interpretation of the Enlightenment *philosophes*. He embraced a nineteenth-century, Continental reaction to liberalism; notably to Marx and Engels's vision of a historical *Stufengang*. Lenin based his theories on the claim that people interact dialectically with nature and propel human history from one evolutionary stage, or 'mode of production', to another – from the 'Asian mode of production', through slavery, feudalism and capitalism to socialism.

Marx had argued that each mode of production is characterized by distinct economic relationships. Engels had added that each such mode is also characterized by a distinct mode of warfare. The Austrian economist Rudolf Hilferding had pursued this argument. In *Das Finanzkapital* (1955 [1910]), Hilferding saw militarism as part of the capitalist mode of production. He saw that, in the final years of the nineteenth century, a tendency for capital to centralize and concentrate transformed capitalism from its old mode of free competition to a new mode in which a few gigantic financial institutions exercised tight control over industry. Relying on Marx and on the liberal economist John A. Hobson (1902), Hilferding claimed that capitalism had entered a new stage of 'finance-capitalism' which forced Western states on to a course of imperial expansion and war. In this latest phase of capitalist development, finance-capital – 'capital controlled by banks and employed by industrialists' – needs new markets and new supplies of raw materials to expand (Hilferding 1955).

Other Marxists (Luxemburg 1951 [1913]; Kautsky 1970 [1914]) elaborated on the connection between capitalism and militarism. Werner Sombart showed, in *Krieg und Kapitalismus* [1913] how the military was one of the major customers of capitalist commodities and how colonial wars served to internationalize the capitalist system. A most significant contribution was made by Nikolai Bukharin, who, in *Imperialism and World Economy* (1973 [1915]), anchors Hilferding solidly in Marx's axiom that capitalism naturally tends to concentrate and centralize. Eventually, capitalist competition will concentrate production into vast, monopolistic combines and centralize financial power in the hands of a narrow oligarchy of industrialists and financiers. To ensure their own survival, the combines will be forced to expand beyond the boundaries of their nation for continued supplies of raw materials and new markets. The combines of different countries will then begin to compete. Again, capital will concentrate and centralize; only this time on a global scale, and with governments backing the economic interests of the financial oligarchs with military might. The world will divide along class lines between wealthy industrial regions and poor colonies. Gigantic combines will form, divide the poorer regions of the world among themselves and incorporate them into a gigantic, global division of labour. In the end, the combines will reach the limits of further expansion. At that point, when no nation can expand except at the expense of another, begins a phase of violent competition for world markets and natural resources. 'Capitalist society is unthinkable without armaments, as it is unthinkable without wars,' concluded Bukharin (1973, pp. 139f).

Bukharin's book on imperialism may be the most theoretically interesting of these Marxist arguments, but Lenin's has been the most influential – indeed, Lenin's *Imperialism: The Highest Stage of Capitalism* (1975b [1917]) may be the single most influential book on international politics of the century. Lenin gave Hilferding's and Bukharin's arguments a popular, accessible form and an empirical base. According to Lenin, World War I must be understood as a 'territorial division of the whole world among the greatest capitalist powers'. The war, he insisted, was 'an annexationist, predatory war of plunder', fuelled by the imperialist powers' need for markets and raw materials. As the Great Powers expand and take control of more and more land, there are steadily fewer parts of the world left to conquer. International competition grows more intense and erupts in war 'for the division of the world, for the partition and repartition of colonies and spheres of influence' (Lenin 1975b, p. 206).

For Lenin, war is the weapon that the capitalist classes apply against a double enemy: against the capitalist classes of other territorial states and against the proletariat of their own country.

Fascism, Mussolini and Hitler
Fascism, like conservatism, is rooted in a reaction to the optimistic values of the Enlightenment project. Both reject the doctrines of liberalism and socialism. They share a pessimistic view of human nature and maintain that humans are passionate and vain rather than rational creatures. Both emphasize that human society is marked by struggle and war.

In the 1920s it was not easy to distinguish the doctrinaire conservatives from the emerging fascists. But a clue to the difference between them lies in their origins. For whereas conservatism was a creation of the ailing, landowning nobility of the eighteenth century, fascism was a function of the crisis-ridden, illiberal, industrial mass-societies of the twentieth. Thus, fascism parted ways with conservatism on two important points. First, whereas conservatives preferred the popular masses to be passive, even docile, fascists envisioned a mobilized, dynamic population which actively supports an omnipotent state. 'The fascist conception of the state is all-embracing,' argued Mussolini, 'outside of it no human or spiritual values can exist, much less have value. Thus understood the fascist state is totalitarian' (Mussolini 1933, p. 3).

Second, whereas the conservatives merely sees conflict as inevitable, the fascists attribute positive values to struggle and argue there are ennobling qualities to war. This vision of struggle justified a fascist foreign policy of imperial expansion. Benito Mussolini argued that Italy should conquer North Africa and make the Mediterranean 'an Italian lake'. Adolf Hitler (1943 [1925]) insisted that Germany needed *Lebensraum*.

One of the problems when discussing fascism is that it tends to have a strong anti-intellectual tendency; fascists tend to be actors rather than analysts. They prefer doing to thinking. There are important exceptions to this, of course.[26] Three German exceptions will be discussed here – one geographer and two professors of law – Karl Haushofer, Heinrich Triepel and Carl Schmitt.

Haushofer was inspired by the holistic and organic tradition of German social thought; in particular by the political geography of Karl Ritter, Friedrich Ratzel and his Swedish student Rudolf Kjellén, and by Halford Mackinder. They all conceived of states as organisms. Ritter had developed the notion that states evolved through successive phases of evolution and, like any other organism, a state needed provisions to sustain itself. Ratzel and Kjellén emphasized that the state was a spatial organism; it was a territorial entity whose provisions relied on the amount of natural resources and the quality of its soil. Such claims are central to Haushofer's notion of *Geopolitik*, that is, as the study of geography as it relates to expansion and war. The state, he argued, had 'a duty to safeguard the right to the soil, to the land in the widest sense'. And as the population of the state increased, the healthy state depended on its ability to acquire more resources and more good spoil. The pursuit of *Lebensraum* is the basic law of all politics, argued Haushofer (1928).

Heinrich Triepel, too, depicted the state as a social organism and explored its power and influence. Other scholars had long argued that order among states were established either by *empire* or by *balance of power*.[27] Triepel (1938) argued that there is a third principle of order as well, namely, that of *hegemony*, and wrote a detailed study of the hegemonic order. He began by distinguishing hegemony from 'domination' (*Herrschaft*) in that it is not based on force or compulsion (*Zwang*). Rather, it is based on the influence which a leader exerts on the will of its followers. A hegemon, explains Triepel, is a sovereign state which leads other sovereign states because it enjoys their trust. The hegemon is a *primus inter pares*, or first among equals. The hegemon enjoys pre-eminence in the system because other states consider it a legitimate leader and allow it to define basic rules of behaviour because they know that these rules will benefit them all. A hegemonic system, then, consists of sovereign states (just like the balance-of-power system). But it is a system where the usual balance-of-power mechanism is suspended. Triepel uses a variety of historical examples to illustrate his point, but he emphasizes ancient Athens and its leadership role in the Delian League (founded in 478 BC) as a classic case of hegemonic leadership. He also discusses the process of German unification as an example of hegemony. And he intimates that Germany could play a role in the contemporary world that was comparable to that played by Athens in antiquity.

What Triepel developed in *Die Hegemonie* was an international variant of the fascist leadership principle (*Führerprinzip*) – as is suggested by the book's subtitle: *Ein Buch von führenden Staaten*. Triepel sees hegemony as leadership by consent. He sees hegemony as resting on an active and self-conscious consensus among all parties involved. Triepel does not attribute any positive values to conflict or war. In fact, hegemony is pretty much the opposite of coercion and violence; it is leadership by moral force. Thus, there may be more conservatism in Triepel's argument than genuine fascism – in spite of the author's reverential genuflection, on the last page, to Hitler and Goering. On this point Triepel's argument differs from that of Schmitt, who placed enmity and conflict at the centre of his argument. There is another telling difference between the two jurists as well: Schmitt was a member of the Nazi Party whereas Triepel was not.

Carl Schmitt wrote several theoretical works on power and social order, and his argument tended to emphasize the role of conflict and strife. In *The Concept of the Political* (1927), Schmitt made three points which also blaze through many of his subsequent works. First, he cultivated the notion that politics is always and inevitably confrontational. This connects up with Schmitt's second point, that is, that at the core of politics lies a distinction between friend and enemy – not any distinction, but the existential distinction. A dispute can arise in any area, but it becomes political when one side refuses to barter, compromise or back down and instead begins to treat its opponents as deadly enemies. The, 'enemy', then, is different 'in a particularly intense way, existentially something different and alien, so that in the extreme case conflicts with him are possible' (Schmitt 1932, p. 27). Schmitt's third point is that order and peace depend on a strong state. Because the truly political cannot be settled through deliberation, negotiation or conferences. At moments of acute confrontation one man must decide who is friend and (more important) who is enemy. That man, for Schmitt, is 'the sovereign'. *He* decides. And his decision is not driven by discussion but by political will and by power. Ideally his will is backed by the united will of the people and his power legitimised by this backing.

Schmitt's approach to politics reflected a deeply pessimistic anthropology. Influenced by Hobbes and traditional Catholicism, Schmitt (1938) saw human nature as sinful, if not downright evil. From this pessimistic anthropology flowed his defence of a powerful state – for, since human nature is evil, man is in need of *dominion*. From this core definition of politics, it follows that such dominion can only be established by reference to an 'other'. Thus, every state will by necessity involve a separation from other men or other groups. This idea ran through Schmitt's discussions of international relations, which are strongly informed by the idea of politics as a struggle for power. In book after book Schmitt did not only seek to justify *dominion* in the form of strong, centralized state, he also criticized alternative approaches which advocated the necessity of limiting state power in the name of human liberty.

Schmitt (1930; 1938) elaborated his argument into scathing condemnations of parliamentary democracy. He criticised the liberal tradition which upheld the Anglo-American systems of parliamentary democracy. This system had reduced politics to mere legality. It pacified the population, denied real politics and deprived its citizens of identity and dignity. Liberal democracy, in fact, put people to sleep and was not democratic at all. The only true democracy, Schmitt implied, is a dictatorship in which a strong 'sovereign' is backed by the united will of an active *Volk*.

One would think that the Nazis were impressed by Schmitt's theories. They were not. Schmitt realized quickly – as did Oswald Spengler, Heidegger and other academics who joined the NSDAP – that the Party leaders had nothing but contempt for intellectuals who offered to do their thinking for them. Leaders of the SS frowned on Schmitt because he did not present the *Volk* as a racial unity. Also, his argument implied that there was a conflict within the *Volk*, and that was impossible.

As SS criticism mounted, Schmitt backed off issues of constitutional theory and developed an interest in international law. He published *Völkerrechtliche Grossraumordnung* ('The Order of Spheres of Influence in International Law') in 1939 – at a time when Hitler expanded Germany's influence in central and eastern Europe. The book discussed the reorganization of the old Westphalian system, the collapse of the British Empire and the emergence of a new world order. The new order would be based on big, continental security blocs, each bloc dominated by a leading power, Schmitt argued. Germany deserves a sphere of influence – a *Grossraum* – in the east just like the USA has established its own sphere of influence in South America, he continued.

Hitler's doctrine of *Lebensraum* in the east was not so different from America's Monroe Doctrine, Schmitt asserted.[28] Schmitt knew, of course, that a *Grossraum* had to be conquered by military force; that German armies first had to invade and seize several small countries that had once been part of Austria-Hungary; then they had to cross the vast plains of Poland and invade Belarus and Ukraine. This would all mean a lengthy, large-scale war. And Schmitt was deeply uncomfortable at the prospect.

Adolf Hitler, too, realized that a German *Lebensraum* could be established only through large-scale war. However, he held that war would strengthen the German will and benefit the German nation. The soil of Europe 'exists for the people which possesses the force to take it', argued Hitler (1943). And if the present possessor objects, 'then the law of self-preservation goes into effect; and what is refused to amicable methods, it is up to the fist to take' (Hitler, 1943, pp. 138f). Germany deserves to expand eastwards, claimed Hitler – into the fragmented lands of the inferior nations of the Slavs and the Jews.

This racial aspect was an important element of Hitler's theory of international relations; one which marks a final difference between conservatism and fascism.[29] German fascism, then, was more than a compound of mobilized masses into a *völkisch* community, serving an omnipotent state guided by a martial code and visions of an imperialist foreign policy; it was also informed by a racist ideology.

Much of this ideology was based on ethnic mythologies. And it is sobering to think back, and realize that this mythological seduction did not occur in a 'primitive' and 'superstitious' region of the world; rather, the spell was cast upon a nation which was generally admired as one of the most technologically developed, spiritually advanced and well-educated nations in the Christian world. By applying the new mass media in propagandistic ways, the Nazi Party transformed ethnic mythology into a political message which spellbound an entire nation. And led it into a new, ruinous world war.

'The old is dying ...'

The Italian communist Antonio Gramsci, who was arrested by the Mussolini regime in 1926, tried to follow world events from his prison cell. His simple assessment of the international situation hit the nail on the head: 'The old is dying and the new cannot be born', he noted in his prison diaries. 'In this interregnum', he continued, 'there arises a great diversity of morbid symptoms' (Gramsci 1974, pp. 275f).

This chapter has noted how the Great War destroyed Europe and ruined the old, Eurocentric world order. It has also noted how the peace conference in Paris in 1919 did not succeed in establishing a new and stable order. The chapter has not surveyed the international situation exhaustively; it has focused rather narrowly on Western events that have been seen as directly relevant to the emergence of the new science of international politics.[30] The four approaches to international politics sketched above capture the diversity of international views, approaches and themes of this unruly period. The sketch has touched some of the morbid variations on these themes, but has not dwelt on them.

It may be useful to close this section by noting a couple of obvious caveats. First, that the four approaches that are sketched here are ideal types. They are not mutually exclusive; they overlap. Among the difficult overlaps are those between conservatism and fascism. Among the more interesting are the overlaps between fascism and radicalism – as when similar theories of hegemony appear both on the radical right and on the radical left. Gramsci (1974 [1947]), for example, also developed an influential theory of hegemony (Knutsen 1999). Stripped from its Marxist garb, Gramsci's theory is quite similar to that of Triepel. Second, these four approaches to international politics are not exhaustive; there are more approaches than these. Some of them may be seen as variants of the ideal types. A most important variation of communism, for example, emerged in Asia during the 1920s and 1930s. The Chinese communists, under the leadership of Mao Zedong, adapted Marx's concept of the 'proletariat' to their own non-Western situation. Where Marx (and Lenin and Stalin) defined the proletariat as urban, industrial workers, Mao saw them as poor peasants. This redefinition gave the old concept of a 'proletarian revolution' an entirely new meaning.[31]

Third, it is tempting to speculate on the connection between the Great War and the totalitarian mass movements which emerged in its wake. The war brought down four land empires – the Austrian-Hungarian, the German, the Ottoman and the Russian. From the turbulence and chaos that ensued, there quickly emerged various kinds of radical mass movements. In Russia emerged a radical communist movement which seized power in 1917. In other regions there emerged fascist movements during the 1920s. In Germany, there emerged the virulent and racist version of the Nazi Party, which seized power in Germany in 1933. In the Ottoman Empire, a political movement emerged with Islam as its base in the Muslim Brotherhood. All three movements were anti-liberal and informed by a deep resentment against the imperial practices of Europe's colonial powers. All three expressed regional or even universal ambitions.

A science of international politics

World War I broke out in August 1914 and was long and complex. So is this chapter. The war destroyed the old regimes of Europe. The Versailles conference that formally ended the war failed to establish a lasting and stable peace. Instead, new and unpredictable actors emerged from the ruins of the old order.

This chapter has outlined the process of change and suggested the contours of the new actors – two new international sub-systems (one which emerged from the ruins of the Austrian-Hungarian Empire and drew the contours of a new central and eastern Europe; another which emerged from the ruins of the Ottoman Empire and became the new 'Middle East'); and two new, totalitarian states with imperial ambitions. Towards the end of the 1930s, these two totalitarian states challenged Western liberalism in a formidable way. Each represented a new ideology – communism on the left and fascism on the right. Each mobilized the popular masses on an international scale. And each evolved its own, characteristic theories of international politics.

The institutions of International Relations

This chapter has also sought to outline how a new science of international politics emerged from the Great War of 1914. This emergence of International Relations was reflected in the growth of scholarly institutions of education and research. The first chair of International Politics was established at the University of Wales, Aberystwyth, in 1919. The decades that followed saw several more chairs emerging in Britain, Switzerland and other countries – the London School of Economics developed a department of International Relations in the early 1920s; the Graduate Institute of International Studies was founded in Geneva in 1927.[32]

The Americans were particularly productive. Several hundred new courses in international-relations themes were added during the 1920s (Symons 1931).[33] About half a dozen schools devoted to International Relations emerged in the wake of the Great War, to say nothing of the departments and institutes that were established at Georgetown, the University of Chicago, Johns Hopkins University, Yale and other places. In 1934, James T. Shotwell explained in a report to the League of Nations that the USA in less than a generation had adjusted 'to a world of nations, from which throughout its previous history it held itself singularly apart. The change in outlook which this involves has been little short of revolutionary' (Shotwell 1934, p. 3).

Shotwell addressed his comments to the League of Nations – the most influential of all the new institutions. More specifically, Shotwell addressed the ICIC (the League's International Committee for Intellectual Co-operation). This was a most significant driver in the postwar establishment of schools and research institutes. The ICIC founded international associations and sponsored conferences, like the International Studies Conference (ISC), which regularly brought scholars together for professional meetings.

There were other institutions as well. Endowments and philanthropic organizations played increasingly important roles as sponsors of international scholarship. Among the most significant sponsors were the Carnegie and the Rockefeller Foundations. The Carnegie Endowment had supported studies on the causes of war and the preconditions for peace since before World War I. In the late 1920s the Rockefeller Foundation, too, began to allocate some of its substantial social-science research funds to studies of international relations. The ISC benefited greatly from its support. From 1932 the ISC could afford to arrange conferences devoted to broad, predetermined topics – such as 'the State and Economic Life' (topic in 1932 and 1933), 'Collective Security' (in 1934–35), or 'Peaceful Change' (in 1936–37). The members' list of the ISC read like a veritable Who's Who of the rapidly maturing discipline.[34]

These ISC meetings were dominated by a liberal orientation. They reflected the liberal outlook which dominated the International Relations scholarship of the age. Although the outlook was liberal, it differed from the liberalism of the pre-War era. It did not claim that international peace and order should be based on the theories of free-market trade alone. Rather, it argued that international order and peace relied on international co-operation and that this was best consolidated by a framework of international institutions – such as the League. Critics labelled this new outlook Idealism or Utopianism. But it would have been better served by the label 'liberal institutionalism'.

The substance of International Relations – the legacy of Mackinder and Carr

Just after World War I, Halford J. Mackinder (1919) drew a distinction between Realists and Idealists. It took many years before the labels stuck. It was Edward H. Carr who managed this, just before World War II.

Edward Hallett Carr was appointed to the Woodrow Wilson Chair of International Politics at the University College of Wales, Aberystwyth, in 1936. He had spent some twenty years at the Foreign Office, and resigned from the civil service to become an academic. In 1937 he published *International Relations since the Peace Treaty*, a fine history of the postwar diplomacy of the Great Powers. Two years later came *The Twenty-Years' Crisis, 1919–1939*, which also contained discussions of theory. Carr's appointment was surrounded by controversy, for it was apparent from the start that the new occupant of the Woodrow Wilson Chair was not among Wilson's most ardent fans. His books, too, were controversial – especially *The Twenty-Years' Crisis*, whose opening pages claimed that the new science of international politics was not a science at all. It was a dream. It began as a utopian wish.

The new field emerged from World War I as a protest against secret treaties and a wish to end the war. Thus,

> the overwhelming purpose which dominated and inspired the pioneers of the new science was to obviate a recurrence of this disease of the international body politics. The passionate desire to prevent war determined the whole initial course and direction of the study. Like other infant sciences, the science of international politics has been markedly and frankly utopian. It has been in the initial stage in which wishing prevails over thinking ... In this stage, attention is concentrated almost exclusively on the end to be achieved. (Carr [1939] 2001, p. 8)

The Twenty-Years' Crisis was one of the first works to call for an unsentimental and systematic analysis of international politics. It approached its subject in a systematic and scientific way and was deeply influential. The book may in fact have been the most influential introductory textbook to International Relations ever written. It was used for decades. It taught several generations of students. However, its authority may not have been entirely beneficial for the new discipline. It is worth spending a few comments on Carr's book and its legacy before concluding this chapter.

First, Carr discusses twenty years of interwar diplomacy in the light of two different worldviews or approaches: Realism and Utopianism. His presentation of these two approaches is hardly original; they strongly echo the distinction that Mackinder (1919) had made twenty years earlier between Idealists and Organizers. When Mackinder wrote, however, his critical views of the League were seriously out of fashion and rebuffed. When Carr wrote, twenty years later, the League had not performed according to expectations and his critical arguments fell on a more fertile ground. Carr's portrayal of the League supporters as naive utopians struck home.[35]

Second, *The Twenty-Years' Crisis* was one of the first works to call for an unsentimental and systematic analysis of the facts of international relations; as such it has often been regarded as belonging to the realist tradition. However, there are so many non-realist elements in Carr's book that it is difficult to place it in the realist category without reservations. It is not, for example, informed by a conservative social philosophy. Rather, its basic philosophy of science draws heavily on Hegel, Marx and Mannheim. For example, Carr treats Utopianism and Realism as thesis and antithesis, respectively, in a larger dialectic. Carr's ambition was to develop a synthetic approach from the two. But he failed, because his criticism of Utopianism was entirely destructive whereas the criticism of Realism was weak. Thus, no synthesis is obtained.

Third, *The Twenty-Years' Crisis* presented the origins of International Relations. It laid the premises for a distinct history of the new discipline – a very seductive and deeply influential history. Carr famously argued that International Relations began as a wish to end all war and establish a durable peace by judicial means. This naive wish informed the early, Utopian, years of International Relations. However, this wish was soon challenged by a more critical, Realist school. As the interwar period progressed, the two schools engaged in a 'great debate' during which the Utopian school was pushed increasingly on the defensive.

This is Carr's argument in a nutshell. It is elegantly formulated. It is a simple, streamlined and pedagogically dialectical account. And it remained the standard account of the origins of International Relations for several decades. Its basic points are not wrong. The 'science of international politics' *did* emerge from wartime discussions to end war and to establish a durable peace. In the wake of the Great War, courses were taught, chairs were endowed, departments and institutes were established, and International Relations scholarship thrived. Yet, Carr's version is too simple.

On the background of information presented in this chapter, several critical points can be raised against Carr's influential account. First, he neglects the long prehistory of International Relations scholarship – especially the formative forays that evolved during the decades leading up to the Great War; these forays make it hard to see the clean, scholarly break with the past that Carr implies.

Second, it is difficult to see that a distinct 'Utopian' school emerged from the Great War; it is hard to find obvious commonalities in the many liberal arguments that emerged from the War and unite them by a single label as a distinct and particularly novel school.

Third, even if a distinct 'Utopianism' can be identified in the wake of the Great War, it is too simple to argue that Realism then emerged as a reaction to it. The origins of Realism, like those of liberalism, go further back.

Fourth, if a 'great debate' took place between Utopianism and Realism, it has left very few traces in the printed record of journals and books.

Fifth, Carr's account is parochial: it focuses narrowly on the English literature of international politics and overlooks Continental and American forays into the field.

Sixth, Carr neglects the institutional underpinnings of International Relations; the co-operative institutions that emerged from the Allied war effort and the co-ordinating role played by the League, the social networks created by the professional associations (especially by the ISC) are not part of Carr's account.

In sum, Carr's account of the origins of International Relations is simple, streamlined and pedagogical. However, it is simple, parochial and incomplete. Carr has not provided the history of International Relations as much as its founding myth. As a *founding* myth it has important pedagogical value. Yet, as a *myth*, it cannot be taken literally. One of the tasks of this long chapter has been to suggest a more empirically grounded account.

Notes

1 Germany had one, big fear: to be caught in a two-front war between Russia and France. The German generals under General von Schlieffen, had in 1905 laid a plan in response to such a war: to first invade Belgium, circumvent the French defences, turn Germany's massive military force southwards and, quick as lightning, attack Paris. With Paris captured, the German army would quickly itstroops eastwards, across Poland, to face the advancing Russians. Germany's vast military capabilities were organized for that one, detailed, inflexible purpose alone.

2 This would translate roughly into the death of 250,000 young men every month, about 50,000 a week, 7,200 every day or about 300 every average hour.
   About 12 per cent of of all British soldiers who took part in the war were killed. The loss was spread unevenly. For peers the share was higher – approaching 20 per cent. Of all men who graduated from Oxford in 1913, 31 per cent were killed. The losses were heavier in other countries. In Germany, more than 35 per cent of all men who were between the ages of nineteen and twenty-two when the war broke out were killed during the next four and a half years. For France, the losses were proportionately higher still: 50 per cent of all Frenchmen who were between twenty and thirty-two at war's outbreak, were dead by the time the war was over (Hochschild 2011, pp. xiv, 348).

3 Italians feared that Germany's ambitions would land them in trouble. Besides, Italy engaged in a veritable bidding war for its services, in which the Triple Entente gave the better offer: Britain and France promised to give Italy colonial gains as a compensation for its wartime co-operation. (Since the two Great Powers planned to reward Italy with territories from faraway Austria-Hungary, it was an easy promise to make.) The deal was closed in the secret treaty of London of April 1915.

4 For the next seventy-five years, American and European statesmen would be constantly harassed by the Leninist charges of imperialism and oppression, and challenged by the Leninist doctrine of national liberation. Little wonder Wilson sweated blood over Russia (Fromkin 1995, pp. 150–64).

5 When Wilson arrived in Europe in January 1919, adoring populations in several European capitals greeted him as the sole visionary statesman of the age. It is a measure of his popularity that he was awarded the Nobel Peace Prize for 1919.

6 'Draconian' is an apt term. The collapse of the Russian state during wartime was an unimaginable catastrophe. It allowed Germany to advance unopposed and conquer a third of Russia's farmland, a third of its population and over half of its industrial plant. In addition to these enormous material gains, the Germans gained peace in the east.

7 When the Ottoman Empire collapsed, modern Turkey emerged from the wreck-age as a major actor; the remaining provinces in the old empire would provide the building blocks for the modern Middle East and quickly constituted a new, regional interstate system. The remains of the Austrian-Hungarian Empire would reconstitute themselves into another, regional, central European system. Austria and Hungary would emerge as its two major actors, but half a dozen other sovereign states would also emerge – some of them stable, others not. Russia and Germany collapsed, yet both managed to reconstitute themselves – not as unitary states but

as empires. Both would oppose the liberal democratic standards imposed by the victors of the Great War, and would present themselves as alternative social formations, whose unity was provided by ideology imposed by one-party rule.

8 There was the patriotic Round Table Group. There was the liberal League of Free Nations Association. There was a circle of more radical academics, lead by writers like Henry N. Brailsford and H. G. Wells who argued that nothing less than world government was needed to abolish conflicts and rivalries among states. A most influential group was the Garton Foundation, which sponsored Norman Angell and the monthly magazine *War and Peace* (Knutsen 2007).

9 It might be added that in spring of 1917 the British Foreign Office established a more traditional committee to consider the geographical, economic and legal aspects of the peace negotiations, under the direction of the historian and publicist George W. Prothero.

10 The group, composed of about 150 academics, was directed by Wilson's primary adviser Edward House. Its first head of research was the writer, reporter and public intellectual Walter Lippmann. He was quickly replaced by the geographer Isaiah Bowman. 'The Inquiry' helped write the Fourteen Points speech that Wilson made in January 1918, in which he advocated the establishment of a League of Nations.

11 The French Foreign Office asked the historian Ernest Lavisse to head a preparatory *Comité d'études* for territorial questions, and invited senator Jean Morel to direct a special committee on economic affairs.

12 None of them missed the opportunity to remind the Americans about Wilson's maxim of 'open covenants openly arrived at'.

13 Notably the fate of the German colonies. As soon as the four statesmen began to discuss the fate of Germany itself, disagreements and conflicts broke out. Wilson wanted to replace Germany's old autocratic regime with a new liberal democracy. Clemenceau and Lloyd George wanted to punish Germany. When the Council began to discuss the fate of Germany's colonies, members of the US delegation noted immediately that the European delegations thought about the peace settlement in terms of spoils of war: Britain, France and Italy all volunteered to govern Germany's colonies, because they hoped to include them in their own overseas empires. And, to the great dismay of many members of the American delegation, Wilson let them get away with it

In the end, the French got Togoland and Cameroon; the Italians got parts of Somalia, whereas Britain took the lion's share of German East Africa. When it became obvious that the British had made a secret deal with the French to divide up the Ottoman Empire, several American delegates were upset and created bitter dissension in the American delegation. The situation grew worse when Wilson chose not to involve himself, thus allowing the Allies to get away with their dirty deals.

14 Some members of the American delegation – like Walter Lippmann – left Paris in protest; other frustrated members (among them the Dulles brothers, Allan and John Foster) chose to stay. British delegates were also frustrated – among them Edward H. Carr, a junior member of the British delegation who witnessed the statesmen's bargaining and who was left with impressions which paved the way for his subsequent harsh criticism of Wilson and his 'utopian' ways (Carr 2001, pp. 3–8).

15 The story of the inter-Allied war effort is told e.g. by Salter (1961) and Monnet (1976, pp. 92ff) – the latter would continue his activism for peace-through-integration in Europe during and after World War II.

16 Three former British Prime Ministers had lived at that address, one of whom was the elder William Pitt. Since he was created the First Earl of Chatham, the house was named after him. The Institute received a Royal Charter in 1926, and has since been the Royal Institute of International Affairs (RIIS).

17 They hired a young historian as research direction, Arnold J. Toynbee. He was extraordinarily well read and a prolific writer. Every year he edited a comprehensive assessment of international events – the annual *Survey of International Affairs*. He also edited the Institute's new journal, *International Affairs*. Toynbee, in turn, found a young research assistant in the talented young pacifist Martin Wight.

18 The Sir Ernest Cassel Professorship of International Relations was established at the University of London in 1919. The industrialist Sir Montague Maurice Burton endowed chairs of International Relations at the universities of Jerusalem (1929), Oxford (1930), LSE (1936) and Edinburgh (1948).

19 Georgetown University established its Edmund A. Walsh School of Foreign Service already in 1919. The Committee on International Relations at the University of Chicago offered a graduate degree in International Relations in 1928. Johns Hopkins University opened its Walter Hines Page School of International Relations in 1930; the same year that Princeton University founded its School of Public and International Affairs. The Fletcher School of Law and Diplomacy opened at Tufts University in the autumn of 1933. Yale University established America's first department of International Relations in 1934. By then it was possible to get a doctorate in International Relations at several US universities. In addition to schools, the USA saw the rise of research institutes, such as the Council on Foreign Relations, the Foreign Policy Association, the Brookings Institution and the Bureau of Economic Research among them.

20 The curriculum tended to focus on the historical roots and diplomatic implications of international events. In the USA, the early courses in International Relations became quickly popular. In British universities, the very first courses tended to discuss the historical roots and the diplomatic implications of international events. In the United States, the curricula focused on current events and were preoccupied with international law. The heavy American legal emphasis tended to stress discrepancies between the formal obligations and the actual conduct of states – which, on occasion, lent support to chauvinist myths of US isolationism and exceptionalism. Emerging from these initial foci, the infant discipline did not beat any new paths. However, it did promote some appreciation of the geography and some understanding of the diversity of the world. It did not rely as much on social science methodology as on historical investigations and on jurisprudence.

21 Their hopes increased with every major treaty signed – thus, they celebrated the establishment of the Permanent Court of International Justice in The Hague (in 1921), encouraged the expansion of the Geneva Protocols (1924), lauded the Locarno treaties (1925) and praised the Paris Pact on the Banning of War (the so-called Kellogg–Briand Pact of 1928). They warmly welcomed every new member that was included in the League of Nations – some twenty new members in all during

the 1920s, including the former enemy states Austria and Bulgaria (1920), Hungary (1922) and Germany (1926); the Soviet Union was admitted in 1934. They hailed every country that adopted democratic institutions, and counted the establishment of seventeen new democracies between 1915 and 1931.

22 It has often been observed that America's notions of exceptionalism and liberal internationalism have Christian roots. The idea may well be expanded: that liberal internationalism in general hinges on claims about eternal principles and individual rights that reach back into the universalist ethic of the Christian faith, observed Hans Morgenthau (1946, p. 52) a few years later. That Morgenthau had a point is suggested by Wilson's speeches, for example his address to the US Senate in the summer of 1919, where he portrayed the pre-1914 world order in eschatological terms as the reign of Satan. The Paris peace, he announced, would bind 'the monster that resorted to arms ... in chains that could not be broken' (Wilson 1919). This idea, that Wilson's liberal internationalism was a secular expression of the biblical programme of salvation, gives a deeper meaning to the label 'utopianism'.

23 In 1917, Jacob ter Meulen published the first volume of an encyclopaedic trilogy which traced the idea of a league of nations from the High Middle Ages to modern history. Ter Meulen discussed twenty-nine peace projects in detail, and concluded by supporting Kant's argument that peace is a natural condition in a world of democratic states. In the years which followed, several such works were published (York 1919; Marriott 1937). When President Wilson proposed the establishment of a League of Nations, public opinion cheered him as the man who would forgive a corrupt Continent its past sins and lead civilization out of its wasteland.

24 Respectively written by Brierly (1928), Eagleton (1932), Lauterpact (1933), Zimmern (1936) and Oppenheim (1937).

25 This is a point worth repeating, for, when Churchill discusses the perceptions and actions of states, he initially neglects complicating domestic dynamics. In his account 'the Government', 'the Cabinet' or, quite often, a single statesman tend to speak on behalf of the entire state and to express the national interest. The states, then, are unitary actors, speaking with one voice in foreign affairs. Churchill's portrayal is replete with imagery from the Absolutist age, when interstate relations were largely the business of kings and their close advisers. Under such circumstances, the personality of the monarch was often reflected in the policies of the nation. It is the image of absolutist politics, then, which is reflected in Churchill's view of world affairs. A similar comment could be made about Morgenthau's (1948b) view.

26 Romantic views may be traced in fascist thinkers who tend to elaborate on the ills of modern industrial societies. Three Italians contributed to this discussion: Wilfredo Pareto, Gaetano Mosca and Benito Mussolini. There was also the brilliant young Russian émigré sociologist Pitrim Sorokin, who, after the Russian Revolution, feared that Western civilization was descending into chaos – a theme pursued by Oswald Spengler's massive study *The Decline of the West* of 1918–22.

27 An imperial order was created by conquest; one powerful state would occupy the territory of other states, seize their sovereignty and assume pre-eminence – as Rome did in the ancient world. An order based on balance of power would consist of several sovereign states; they would maintain order by entering and leaving alliances in a conscious effort to sustain equilibrium among themselves. One Great Power

might be able to play the role of a balancer and would then emerge pre-eminent in the system – as in the case of Britain after the Napoleonic Wars.

28 In April 1939, after US President Roosevelt had protested against Germany's invasion of Czechoslovakia, Hitler responded that the USA had no business meddling in European affairs, and that Germany was simply implementing a doctrine which would guarantee the Germans a sphere of influence in Europe just like the one the USA had long enjoyed in South America. In March 1940, the US Deputy Secretary of State Sumner Wells visited Germany to meet with representatives of the German government. He was taken aback when the German Foreign Minister Ribbentrop referred to the Monroe Doctrine and claimed that the division of Poland was an affair between Germany and the USSR and none of America's business.

29 These racist elements had first been developed by some of Darwin's Continental followers. In the 1870s, the German historian Heinrich von Treitschke glorified the Prussian state and proclaimed war the highest expression of humanity. In the 1880s, Ernest Haeckel reformulated Treitschke's basic visions in atheistic, racial terms. In the 1890s, Houston S. Chamberlain – British by birth but Prussian by choice – rewrote Western history as a struggle between the 'two pure races', the Germans and the Jews.

30 It is with great regret that extra-Western events are not included in this discussion. However, the space is simply not available in a chapter that is already uncomfortably long. There are many texts that discuss non-Western events of the period alongside themes that have been raised in this chapter. See Barraclough (1976) for the general picture and Hobson (2012) for an elaboration of the racist theme.

31 Many Asians had been in Europe during the Great War – some had been students, others workers and still others had been drafted as soldiers in Western armies. Ho Chi Minh, Zhu De, Li Lisan, Zhou Enlai and Deng Xiaoping were among these Asian immigrants who experienced wartime or postwar Europe. All of them joined the Communist Party while in Europe. And when they returned to Asia, they were ardent anti-imperialists who participated in the building of communist parties in their homelands. Ho Chi Minh founded Vietnam's Communist Party; Zhu De, Li Lisan, Zhou Enlai and Deng Xiaoping became collaborators of Mao Zedong, possibly the most influential non-European political theorist of the twentieth century.

32 The department of International Relations at the LSE was founded at the behest of the Nobel Peace Prize winner Philip Noël-Baker, and was the first institute to offer a wide range of degrees in the field. The Graduate Institute of International Studies in Geneva was established to educate diplomats for the League of Nations, whose headquarters was located there.

33 In 1931 Farrel Symons gleaned the course catalogues for 465 American colleges and universities in search of course offerings in international affairs. He found 573 courses in all – 234 courses on International Law, 75 on International Organization and 264 on International Relations more broadly defined (see Symons 1931; also Ware 1934).

34 Among the names found on the ISC lists are Stanley H. Bailey, Charles A. Beard, Edward H. Carr, John F. Dulles, Ernest Haas, Hans Kelsen, Christian L. Lange, Hersch Lauterpacht, Charles A. W. Manning, Paul Mantoux, David Mitrany, Philip

J. Noël-Baker, Pitman Potter, Georg Schwarzenberger, James Shotwell, Nicholas J. Spykman, Arnold Toynbee, Arnold Wolfers, Quincy Wright, Alfred Zimmern …

35 The way that Carr presented this distinction spelled a Kantian revolution in International Relations: it drew attention away from the empirical world, and it focused scholarly attention on the existence of the contending approaches, the traditions, the worldviews or the ontologies of the field (Wilson 2013).

9

World War II, the UN and the postwar order

Twenty-five years after the Great War erupted in Europe in 1914, a second, even greater war broke out in Europe. It merged with a big war in Asia and became truly world-wide in its compass. The immediate cause of the European was Germany's invasion of Poland. But there were deeper grounds behind it: some of the most important causes of the Second World War are found in the aftermath of the First. Most significant, perhaps, was its effect on six vast empires.

The victors of World War I were Britain and France, both of whom commanded formidable colonial empires overseas. But the war had seriously weakened their empires. They had won a pyrrhic victory. Britain encountered demands of increasing self-determination from India; France confronted revolts in Indochina.

Four empires had collapsed as a result of the First World War – the Ottoman, the Austrian-Hungarian, the Russian and the German empires. From the ruins of the first two emerged two entirely new regional sub-systems – one in Central Europe, the other in the Middle East. From the ruins of the last two arose new empires, but of a novel, ideology-based and dictatorially mass-mobilizing kind. From the ruins of Tsarist Russia emerged a communist empire; from the wreck of Germany emerged a new *Reich* based on racist doctrines of National Socialism. Both empires rose to Great-Power status. Both were anti-liberal powers who perceived international relations in terms of struggle. Their ambitions and rivalries deeply affected the international scene.[1]

The stock-market crash in October 1929 was a turning point. It triggered a steep economic downturn which initiated a decade of economic crisis, political rivalries and a rapid descent into pessimism. The crisis first hit the capitalist countries of the West. But it soon affected the East as well and pulled Asian powers into the international turmoil. The Chinese empire, already traumatized by internal strife, was badly shaken by World War I, and broke into civil war.

Japan, by contrast, was strengthened by wars in Europe and China – war in Europe stimulated Japan's industries because Western demand for war materiel expanded Japanese trade and made Japan a wealthier and stronger nation; war in Asia stimulated Japan's imperial ambitions. But the Great Depression hit Japan hard, destroyed its primary export markets and shattered its trade-based economy. Japan's exports quickly fell by two-thirds. By 1931, half of Japan's factories were idle. Unemployment was skyrocketing. Millions of peasants and workers were thrown into destitution. Export outlets on the Asian mainland became crucial. At a time when Europe's colonial powers were weakening and China was rent with internal strife, Japan exploited colonial unrest and the misfortunes of the crumbling Chinese empire to expand its control over new lands.

These Asian affairs are important, for they involved frictions and conflict that led to large-scale war in the late 1930s. The war affected all of Asia – at a time when the League of Nations had deteriorated into a mere arena for diplomatic posturing and large-scale conflict was brewing in Europe. The war would eventually pull in the United States as well – first against Japan in Asia and, a few days later, against Germany, Japan's ally, in Europe. World War II, then, was not *one* war; it was *two* wars that merged into one. The two were united in December 1941, as the result of Japan attacking the US naval base at Pearl Harbor and Nazi Germany declaring war on Washington.

The Asian war will be only cursorily treated in this chapter. Its main focus is on Europe – on the preparations for war, on the diplomacy of the war and on the consequences which the war wrought on the international system. The chapter will begin with an outline of Germany's war aims, because the racist theories that drove them and the single-minded effort to destroy all that stood in their way rank among the major horrors of international history. Adolf Hitler is a central figure in the story and his Nazi Party was an important force in twentieth-century politics. First, and most obviously, because it caused suffering and misery for untold millions of people, brought all of Europe to its knees and created the preconditions for the bipolar constellation that appeared after the war. But also because the Nazi Party expressed a noxious ideology and engineered a political programme that actors of the civilized world have wanted to distance themselves from. Hitler has, since the end of World War II, personified political evil. The atrocities of his war machine have represented an image of naked power politics. The Nazi ideology, with its mix of biology and politics and its lack of any universal notions of ethics, has become a representation of ideas and theories that are barbaric and beyond the pale of acceptable political discourse.

After World War II the study of International Relations has been affected by two fearful memories from World War II: one is the Nazi death camps; the other is the atomic bombs over Hiroshima and Nagasaki. Both have left deep imprints on political theory in the postwar area. They have affected the processes of European integration and peace, the robustness of Western co-operation, the development of international law and the authority of postwar institutions of order. All have been affected by the long shadows cast over world events by holocausts past and future.

This chapter will begin with an outline of Germany's war aims – with the first set of memories which include racist theories, the Nazi objectives and the single-minded effort to destroy all that stood in their way – including the extermination of entire ethnic groups. The chapter will then present the allied efforts to contain and destroy Hitler and his Nazi war machine. The 'Big Three' – Stalin, Churchill and Roosevelt – play important roles in this chapter. Their ideas and their wartime diplomacy to co-ordinate the anti-Nazi alliance left an immediate impact on the scholarly field of International Relations. The same can be said of the tensions which marked this wartime alliance – especially the tensions between communist Russia on the one hand and the liberal Atlantic states, Britain and the USA, on the other. This tension deeply affected postwar International Relations theorizing, which quickly came to be dominated by Realist approaches.

Hitler's plans for war

Unfinished business from the First World War shaped many of the conflicts which led to the Second. Both Europe and Asia suffered from the world economic crisis that hit with full force in 1929. The Great Depression, with its collapse of markets for both goods and labour, turned the attention of political leaders inwards. On both continents there was a rise in egotistical and national concerns. This made economic co-operation and trade more difficult.

The situation grew tenser when some leaders got the idea that imperial expansion might help solve their political and economic problems of the nation. In the early 1920s Italy saw the rise of a fascist party which advocated expansion into North Africa. Japan expanded into China, took control over Manchuria and set up its own government, Manchukuo, in 1931. In Germany a nationalist party emerged which advocated expansion into Eastern Europe and which nourished – as noted at the end of Chapter 8 – a particularly vitriolic version of fascism: National Socialism or Nazism.

Diplomacy was powerless. The Western democracies did little or nothing to address the mounting tensions. They were weakened by the Great Depression, torn by class cleavages and split by ideological disputes that made foreign-policy co-ordination almost impossible. The USA, which had emerged as a leading international actor, rejected its rising status as a Great Power. Instead of engaging in international diplomacy, the USA retreated into a policy of isolationism and paid little attention to the worsening world situation.

The institutions that had been set up at the Paris Peace Conference in 1919 were losing legitimacy and authority fast. The peace treaty had saddled Germany with a draconian peace treaty, which not only gave the Germans the responsibility for the outbreak of war in 1914, but also decided that Germany had to pay enormous reparations to the victorious powers. This treaty, which was signed in Versailles in 1919, fuelled deep German resentments that gnawed away at the Weimar regime. Also, the League of Nations was floundering and proved too weak to solve the conflicts that followed Italy's invasion of Ethiopia, Japan's seizure of Manchuria and Germany's bids for Central and Eastern Europe.

Finally, there is the role that ideas and theories played in the preparations for war in Asia and Europe. This chapter will begin by highlighting these ideas. First the ideas that informed Adolf Hitler and his National Socialist Workers' Party

(Nationalsozialistische Deutsche Arbeiterpartei or NSDAP) and provided the German leaders with its expansionist plans in Eastern Europe. Then it will relate how the Great Powers of the West responded to Hitler's challenge and discuss the Western views that emerged from the War.

Hitler's ideas and political programme
Adolf Hitler began his political career as a vitriolic agitator in the NSDAP in the southern region of Bavaria. His rise to national fame began in November 1923 when he incited a violent crowd to call for the overthrow of the Bavarian government and was sentenced to five years in prison for treason. He was quickly pardoned by a sympathetic court and released in December 1924. He had used his prison time well. He had written a thick manuscript which catapulted him to power. Its original title is suggestive of its shrill tone and rambling content: *Four and a Half Years of Struggle against Lies, Stupidity and Cowardice*. It contained his political ideas and was published in two volumes in 1925 and 1926 under the pithier title *Mein Kampf* ('My Struggle').

When Hitler was released from prison, it was too late to participate in the parliamentary elections, which gave the NSDAP 3 per cent of the votes. His book, however, boosted the party profile. It railed against what Hitler saw as the liars and idiots who ran German and European politics. It argued that the Versailles Treaty had been the outcome of a vast conspiracy. That the victors of the war had unjustly saddled Germany with the responsibility for starting it. Their treaty demanded that Germany pay huge war reparations – money transfers so absurdly big that the German nation staggered under their weight. The whole purpose of the treaty was to cripple the German economy and to emasculate the German nation, Hitler maintained.

Mein Kampf also explained Germany's ills by invoking the forces of international capitalism, Marxist movements and the Jews – especially the Jews (whom Hitler portrayed as both capitalists and Marxists). It was necessary to combat these three forces, which kept Germany weak and emasculated, he continued. In the final chapters of the book Hitler presents a political programme which would not only rebuild Germany to its former glory, but establish a new German *Reich* – an empire which would include large parts of Continental Europe. First, it would be necessary to seize the fragmented and inferior 'Slavic lands' on Germany's eastern border; then to occupy Poland and finally conquer large parts of Bolshevik Russia (Hitler 1943 [1925], p. 654).

Hitler streamlined the NSDAP. He designed symbols and uniforms – including those for the party militia, the SA (*Sturmabteilungen*). When his speaking ban was lifted in 1927, Hitler threw himself into public speaking tours. In 1929, when the economic crash hit Germany with full force, the party's luck changed. The SA grew. The sales figures of *Mein Kampf* picked up.[2] The NSDAP rose in the polls. In the 1930 elections the NSDAP received 18 per cent of the votes and received 107 seats (out of a total of 491) in the German parliament.

As the economic crisis deepened, the NSDAP became more popular. In 1933 Hitler was offered the post of *Reichskanzler*, the head of the German government. In the November elections the Nazi Party received 44 per cent of the votes and

Hitler formed his own government. He was granted emergency powers in order to manage the rampant crisis, and he used these powers to appoint himself supreme leader of the German state and nation – *Führer des Deutschen Reiches und Volkes*. That was the end of the German democracy and a fatal turning point in German history – indeed, in the history of the twentieth century.[3]

One of Hitler's most important moves was to integrate the NSDAP's own, vast militia, the SA, into Germany's small defence forces. This move created a new organization, *die Wehrmacht*, which was controlled by the Nazi Party and its leader, or *Führer*, Adolf Hitler. This move violated the Versailles Treaty which had put a strict limit on the size of Germany's armed forces.

Hitler's move was only the first of several moves which violated the Versailles Treaty. He also expanded Germany's production of weapons. He ordered the *Wehrmacht* to enter the demilitarized zone of the Rhineland. He supported Italy's and Japan's invasions in Ethiopia and Manchuria, respectively (1935). He assisted Franco and the fascist side in the Spanish civil war (1936–39). All these moves were in violation of the Versailles Treaty. No one, however, tried to prevent them. The Soviets encouraged European anti-fascists to volunteer and fight on the Republican side in the Spanish civil war. But no single power threatened Hitler with punishment or reprisals as a consequence of these events. The League of Nations debated Germany's reoccupation of the Rhineland – as it debated Italy's invasion of Ethiopia and Japan's occupation of Manchuria. The actions were generally condemned. But the League was unable to muster any force behind the condemnations.

The road to war

Hitler first formulated his ideas in *Mein Kampf* [1925–26]. Later he expanded upon his foreign-policy goals in an unpublished sequel (Hitler 2006 [1928]). In 1937 Hitler did this at a secret meeting with a narrow elite of ministers and military leaders. He repeated that the aim of German foreign policy was to secure, preserve and enlarge the racial community (Hossbach 1998 [1937]). It was all a question of space, he continued. The fundamental question of German foreign policy was about how to acquire *Lebensraum* in the east – about conquering territory at the expense of Germany's eastern neighbours.

At this meeting Hitler announced a schedule consisting of three geopolitical moves. First, it was necessary to conquer Austria and Czechoslovakia. This would be easy, in Hitler's view. It would probably occasion some protests from England and France, but both countries were weak – in terms of military strength as well as political will. They did nothing to prevent the German conquest.

Second, it was necessary to conquer Poland. This would be more difficult; it would be necessary to use substantial military force to conquer and hold the territory. Also, England and France would protest more loudly, continued Hitler. But, again, the popular will in both countries was divided and the leaders would fear that military action on their part would unleash a great war.

The third move in Hitler's ambitious plan was the boldest and most difficult of all: a massive German invasion of the USSR across the plains of Belarus and

Ukraine. Germany was bound to emerge victorious, argued Hitler. First, because these territories were inhabited by inferior peoples like Slavs and Jews. Second, because all of Western Europe, including England and France, would ultimately come to their senses and support the German invasion. For when the nations of the West were faced with the choice of supporting either the Aryan cause or siding with the Jewish communists of Russia, their choice would be easy: They would rally to the German side.

Hitler made his first move in 1938. He ordered the invasion of Austria in the spring, and annexed Sudetenland, the eastern province of Czechoslovakia, in the autumn. It all went according to plan. Britain and France protested. Hitler heeded the protest, met with the British Prime Minister Chamberlain in Munich, explained his reasons and emphasized his desire for peace. Chamberlain was satisfied and signed an agreement which in effect transferred the sovereignty of Sudetenland to Nazi Germany.[4]

British leaders, who recalled World War I with horror, drew a sigh of relief when Chamberlain returned to London, waved the signed document and proudly proclaimed that Germany and Britain would never go to war again. But Chamberlain was also criticized. No one was more critical than Winston Churchill. Whereas Chamberlain praised the Munich Agreement as 'a peace with honour', Churchill condemned it in Parliament as 'a disaster of the first magnitude'. Munich, Churchill continued, was 'only the first sip, the first foretaste of a bitter cup which will be proffered to us year by year' (Churchill 1989a, p. 143). It represented the first step on a slippery slope that would ultimately undo the system of alliances upon which Britain and France had relied for safety, he averred.

In the spring of 1939 Hitler unexpectedly approached Stalin, his arch-enemy in the east, and offered him a treaty of friendship. Stalin considered his options. Then, in early May he removed Foreign Minister Maxim Litvinov, who was of Jewish ancestry, and replaced him with Vyacheslav Molotov, whom he sent off to Berlin to negotiate with his Nazi counterpart, Joachim von Ribbentrop. After many weeks of tough negotiations Molotov and Ribbentrop signed an agreement on 23 August 1939.

Some observers greeted the Molotov–Ribbentrop Pact as good news. They did not realize that the pact in reality was Hitler's second step towards *Lebensraum* in the east. Its purpose was to pacify Russia so that Germany could invade Poland unhindered.[5] To sweeten the deal, the pact included a secret annexe in which Hitler shared Poland with Stalin and also allowed Stalin to occupy the three small Baltic states of Estonia, Latvia and Lithuania. Hitler was in a hurry. Only a week after the pact was signed, German troops invaded Poland: on the morning of 1 September 1939.

The British and the French were taken by complete surprise. The British Prime Minister Chamberlain quickly issued an ultimatum, demanding that Germany withdraw its forces immediately. The German leaders did not even bother to respond. Instead they drove their troops deeper into Poland and occupied the western half of the country. Two weeks later the Soviet army invaded and occupied Poland's eastern half, together with Estonia, Latvia and Lithuania. Nazi Germany and communist Russia then began to implement their political programmes. On the heels of the German *Wehrmacht* came troops from the *Schutzstaffel* (or SS), a Nazi 'protection squadron', which began to separate the Jews from the rest of the Polish population and kill them. On the heels of the Red Army came Stalin's political commissars and troops from the Soviet secret police (the NKVD). First, they rounded up Poland's leading figures – leaders of key organizations in civil society as well as higher military officers. Then they killed them.

Thus, in early September 1939 another Great War broke out in Europe. Yet, for several weeks there were no military clashes in the West. This period of tense inaction was termed 'the phony war'. In November, however, the USSR invaded Finland. The Soviet army encountered unexpectedly strong resistance and was driven back with high losses. Only a second Soviet assault ended with victory in March 1940. A few weeks later Germany invaded Denmark and Norway (9 April 1940). One month later Germany launched a massive invasion of the Netherlands, Belgium and France.[6]

Pinnacle of Nazi power

Hitler was never as self-confident as he was during the spring and summer of 1940. In the east he had an alliance with Stalin – who not only provided security to Germany's eastern frontier, but who also provided Germany with vital supplies like oil, ore and wheat. In the west, Germany controlled Europe's entire North Atlantic coastline – from Norway in the north, via Denmark, to the Netherlands and France in the south. Spain and Portugal were neutral countries, but they were both (like Italy) governed by fascist regimes whose leaders leaned towards Germany (Franco in Spain, Salazar in Portugal and Mussolini in Italy).

Britain alone withstood Germany's military power. Hitler was confident that Britain's surrender was only a question of time and that his war in the west could be brought to a close. When all of Western Europe was secured, he would launch the third stage of his plan and attack the USSR.

The day Germany invaded France, Neville Chamberlain resigned as British Prime Minister. He was replaced by Winston Churchill, who had long urged Britain to prepare for war. The British had developed a strong air force, but they had very little else. Churchill was gravely concerned.

His concerns deepened when Germany suddenly launched a major air offensive against London and other cities in the south of England. This began the so-called 'Battle of Britain'. The German leaders were surprised by the ability of British pilots to outwit German air defences, bomb German cities and challenge the Luftwaffe's claim to mastery of the European air space. Churchill realized, however, that Britain could not survive the German onslaught in the long run. So, while organizing the nation's defences and maximizing the production of aeroplanes, Churchill worked hard to convince the Americans of the necessity to join Britain in a war against Germany.

US leaders followed the European development with increasing alarm. The Roosevelt administration began measures to prepare for war. A corner was turned in September 1940, when the US sold destroyers to Britain and accepted payment in the form of basing rights in British territories. Then, in May 1941, the US Congress accepted Roosevelt's request to sell, lend and lease war equipment to countries which were strategically important for US security. This so-called Lend-Lease Act enabled Roosevelt to transfer weapons and other war materiel to Britain. About the same time the USA began the construction of a large naval air station at Keflavik, Iceland.

Hitler, too, was concerned. He had planned to invade the USSR in early May 1941 but was falling behind schedule, partly because diplomacy with the suspicious Soviets was painfully slow and partly because of unexpectedly though resistance from Britain. When summer came, he decided that he could not afford to postpone his plans any longer. He ceased the air war on Britain, transferred all his attention eastwards, and prepared all of Germany's military might for a gigantic assault on Russia.

Hitler launched the attack during the early hours of 22 June 1941. Some 4,300,000 soldiers – Germans assisted by forces from Hungary, Slovakia, Romania, Italy and Finland – crossed the Soviet border along a three-thousand-kilometre broad front. It was the largest military offensive in history. It took Stalin and Western leaders by surprise.

Reversal of fortune

The German assault on Russia changed the dynamics of the war. Churchill immediately offered Stalin aid through an anti-German alliance. Stalin leapt at the offer and concluded a defence pact with Britain within a matter of days.

While German troops were advanced across the plains of Poland and Belarus, Churchill secretly sailed across the Atlantic to meet with President Roosevelt off the New England coast. Churchill implored the USA to join the new Anglo-Soviet alliance. But Roosevelt drove a hard bargain. He agreed to nothing until Churchill signed a joint Anglo-American declaration that specified the goals of the war. This document, the so-called Atlantic Charter, bore the unmistakable marks of Roosevelt's vision of war and peace. It asserted that the war should be fought to protect the sovereignty of all nations, and to maintain the freedom of the seas. It promised to establish a 'general security' system and an open and fair world economy which would guarantee equal access to the world's wealth for 'all states, great or small, victor or vanquished'. Churchill had little choice but to sign the Charter if he were to obtain American support for his war effort.

The dynamics of the war changed once more half a year afterwards. On 7 December Japan attacked the US naval base on Pearl Harbor, Hawaii, and destroyed the US Pacific Fleet. This pulled the USA into war. In fact, it pulled the USA into *two* wars. One in Asia as a direct result of Japan's surprise attack on Pearl Harbor. Another in Europe four days later when Germany, Japan's ally, declared war on the USA.

In less than half a year, then, Hitler's actions had turned both the USSR and the USA into enemies of Germany. He had also driven the two powers into an alliance with Britain. It was a fatal mistake. For the USSR had personnel reserves that far exceeded those of Germany. And the USA had far greater economic capabilities. Britain had neither. And as the war progressed, Britain's significance would fade and the war effort would be increasingly shaped by Soviet personnel and America's industrial might.

Great-Power goals

The immediate goal of Nazi Germany was to occupy new territory in the east, consolidate it, colonize it and establish a new 'thousand-year *Reich*'. First, the *Wehrmacht* tore through Poland, Belarus and Ukraine. Then came troops from the SS who began to clear the region of its original inhabitants so that Aryan immigrants could come and settle the region and transform it to a productive part of Hitler's vast *Kontinentalimperium*. The SS rounded up the civilian population, separated out the Jews and the Slavs and killed them.

The SS first executed people by asphyxiating them in specially built vans. The casualties counted tens of thousands of people. SS leaders nevertheless found the process to be too cumbersome and the tempo too slow. In 1942 Nazi Party leaders devised a more efficient method: they would build extermination camps equipped with gas chambers which could kill thousands of unwanted people every day and with incinerators which would burn the dead bodies.[7] During the subsequent months the Germans began the construction of veritable extermination machines at places like Auschwitz-Birkenau, Belzec, Chelmno, Majdanek, Sobibor and Treblinka. Millions of people were killed in these camps. The precise number is surrounded by controversy, but the number of people exterminated with industrial efficiency in the horror known as the Holocaust easily exceeds ten million people. The number of Jews killed was around six million. In addition came over three million Soviet prisoners of war, nearly two million Poles, a quarter of a million Romanies (or gypsies), plus disabled people, homosexuals and Jehovah's Witnesses.

The immediate goals of Britain, the USSR and the USA were to stop Germany; to destroy the Nazi war machine and remove the Hitler regime with its imperial ambitions. The 'United Nations alliance' (as Roosevelt called it) presented a united face of solidarity to the world. The Soviets dismantled the Communist International (the Comintern) as a symbol of good faith. Stalin put aside his Marxist–Leninist rhetoric and refrained from his previous calls for revolution. Roosevelt, on his side, began to refer to Stalin as 'Uncle Joe'.

Behind the scenes, however, there were conflicts and high tension among the Allies. The Americans and the British largely spoke the same language – both in a literal and an ideological sense. They were separated from Stalin by an ideological gulf. Their relationship with the USSR was often tense. Churchill was particularly distrustful of Stalin, whom he perceived as a ruthless thug and a callous opportunist. Stalin, on his side, trusted neither Churchill nor Roosevelt, viewing them both as cynical capitalists.

Stalin's immediate goal was to get Allied help in the war against Germany. This he received from the USA, which shipped thousands of tons of weapons and supplies to the USSR under the Lend-Lease Act. Stalin implored his allies to invade Europe and engage Germany in the west. His Red Army bore the brunt of the war. And an allied attack in the west would force the Germans to transfer military forces from the east and ease the heavy pressure on the Soviet army. Churchill repeatedly told Stalin that the Western powers were too weak; that they had neither soldiers nor weapons enough to open a second front in the west. But Stalin knew full well that Churchill was stalling because he wished to see the Soviet army and the German *Wehrmacht* fight and exhaust each other in battles that were far removed from Western Europe.

Britain's immediate aim was to prevent Hitler from dominating the European Continent – it was to achieve this that Churchill offered to make an alliance with Stalin in July 1941. Another of Britain's goals was to protect and preserve the British Empire and the spheres of influence it represented. It was the Empire that had made Britain a Great Power, he argued. In the longer haul, Churchill also wanted to contain Stalin. The USA provided Lend-Lease, which strengthened the Red Army and enabled it to contain the German advances. However, there was a danger of strengthening the Red Army too much. As the fortunes of war began to change during 1943, Churchill began to warn the Americans against Stalin's expansion in eastern and central Europe. There was the obvious point of military conquest: namely, that the Red Army advanced and consolidated its hold over territory that the German *Wehrmacht* gave up. But there was also the larger geopolitical point: namely, that whoever gained control over the plains of central Europe would also control the gateway to the vast Eurasian land mass – to what Mackinder (1919) had called the 'Heartland of the World Island'.

The American war aims were largely the same as those of the British. The Americans, too, wanted to prevent Hitler from dominating the Continent. The US war plan – the Victory Program, which was designed with Mackinder's (1919; 1943) geopolitical theory in mind – was to prioritize the war effort in Europe and defeat Germany and then launch a full-force offensive against Japan. However, Roosevelt's long-term goals differed from those of Churchill's. Roosevelt wanted to avoid the establishment of spheres of influence in the world. He wanted instead to establish a postwar peace on the principle of free intercourse among open and democratic states.

The basic US war aims were reflected in the Atlantic Charter, which Roosevelt and Churchill had drawn up during their meeting off Newfoundland in August of 1941. The Charter safeguarded the principles of popular sovereignty, so that no state should take advantage of the war to aggrandize their territory, no territorial changes should be made against the wishes of the peoples who inhabited the territory, and self-government should be restored to those people who had been deprived of it. The Charter also advocated the liberal ideals of freedom of trade – it held that all states should enjoy freedom of the seas and free access to raw materials (Welles 1997, pp. 300ff).

The brief text also adumbrated 'the establishment of a wider and permanent system of general security'. On this final point Roosevelt drew on interwar experiences – especially on Wilson's work with the League of Nations and his own experiences with the Great Depression. Roosevelt and his Secretary of State, Cordell Hull, analysed the work of the League before they set up a political organization which would solve conflicts, support cooperation and keep order in the world – a new and more efficient version of the League of Nations. Roosevelt and Hull drew on experiences from the Great Depression when they designed an organizational framework which would guarantee freedom of international trade and help countries develop their industries and economies.

Roosevelt also drew on the considerable rhetorical gifts of his Vice President, Henry Wallace, and made him an early and efficient spokesman for a new postwar world order. In 1942, in a speech which commemorated President Wilson's birth, Wallace celebrated Wilson's visions of a league and presented it as a model for a future architecture of peace – for a new world organization as well as institutions that could stabilize the world economy (Wallace 1944).

Early in the war Roosevelt called on the foreign-policy adviser Sumner Welles to head a committee which would start planning for the postwar world. It addressed the question of why the League of Nations had ultimately failed. One reason, it concluded, was that Wilson had waited too long to establish it; he had waited so long that discussions about the League had become entangled in the diplomatic tug-of-war at the Paris Peace Conference. In order to avoid a similar scenario, Welles argued, it was necessary to establish new institutions for a postwar order during the course of the war. These could then be present as a *fait accompli* when the war ended but before the peace negotiations were to begin (Welles 1997, pp. 324ff).

Another reason for the failure of the League was that Wilson had focused his attention solely on political institutions. Drawing lessons from his work to end the Great Depression, Roosevelt reasoned that a lasting world order would also have to include institutions that could stabilize the world economy. Thus, he proposed to establish an international monetary fund to co-ordinate and stabilize the exchange rates of the world. Also, he proposed a world bank which would lend money to reconstruct countries that had been destroyed by the war. Finally, he wanted to found an international trade organization – a body which would work to reduce international tolls and taxes and thereby encourage international trade.

Roosevelt, in short, proposed a global New Deal. And he connected it up with the Atlantic Charter, which Roosevelt and Churchill had signed on their first meeting in August 1941. As more and more countries joined the United Nations alliance during the course of the war, they all signed this Charter.[8]

The diplomacy of war and peace

Churchill and Roosevelt had a second conference in January 1943, in the Moroccan city of Casablanca. The two leaders did not discuss postwar plans at this conference. They restricted their conversations to the joint conduct of the world war. They agreed to postpone the planned offensive against Germany. Churchill accepted Roosevelt's argument that it was necessary to fight the war towards a clear victory. It was important to deal the Nazi *Reich* such a decisive battlefield defeat that its leaders recognized the loss and surrendered unconditionally, Roosevelt argued. This, he thought, would thwart any future excuses and hinder any future revanchist temptation in Germany.

Roosevelt, on his side, accepted Churchill's proposal to attack Italy. Half a year later Allied forces landed in southern Italy and began an offensive northward, up the Italian boot. The invasion triggered a coup at the end of June which removed Mussolini from power. A new Italian government was formed under Marshal Pietro Badoglio. He negotiated a surrender with the Allies in early September, broke all relations with Nazi Germany and joined the United Nations alliance instead.

Stalin reacted with anger and suspicion to these events. Churchill and Roosevelt had met at Casablanca without him. They had agreed to postpone an invasion of Germany once more. They had invaded Italy without consulting him. In November 1943 Churchill and Roosevelt travelled to Tehran to meet with Stalin. Here, Roosevelt presented his plans for a United Nations Organization (UNO) that would help design a new and peaceful order for the postwar world. Churchill and Stalin agreed to the plan.

Stalin's most pressing demand was once more the opening of a 'second front'. Once more, Churchill stalled, explaining that neither the USA nor Britain had soldiers enough for such a large-scale offensive. Although Stalin was upset, he accepted Roosevelt's request to join America's offensive in Asia three months after the war in Europe was brought to a close.

During the fall of 1943, an allied victory in Europe became more and more certain. The Germans suffered steady defeats on the eastern front and the Red Army pressed the German *Wehrmacht* westwards, re-conquering Ukraine and Belarus. In the early months of 1944, the Soviet army also entered Bulgaria, Romania and Hungary.

In June 1944 Stalin finally got his second front when British and US forces invaded Normandy on the north-western coast of France. During the subsequent months Allied forces advanced into France and the Netherlands and, towards the end of the year, into Germany itself. At this time Stalin drove the Soviet forces hard. He sped up their westward push and drove the retreating *Wehrmacht* through Hungary and Poland.

At the end of July 1944 the Soviet army approached the Polish capital of Warsaw. The Polish resistance movement took this as a sign that help was on its way and organized a large-scale rebellion to finally oust the German occupation forces. However, instead of advancing into Warsaw to lend the Polish resistance a helping hand, the Soviet forces halted outside of the city. They remained there, as passive onlookers, while the German army fought the Polish rebellion into submission and then bombed the city from the air. Only when Warsaw was ruined and the Polish resistance movement destroyed did the Soviet army resume its westward offensive.

Churchill understood that Stalin wanted his army to advance as far as possible westward before Germany surrendered. This worried him. In utmost secrecy, without consulting Roosevelt, Churchill flew to Moscow in October 1944 for a personal meeting with Stalin. The two wartime leaders agreed to divide the Balkans and south-eastern Europe: the USSR would receive 90 per cent influence in Romania and 75 per cent in Bulgaria; Britain would have 90 per cent influence in Greece. They agreed to share influence in Yugoslavia and Hungary 50/50. Poland was not mentioned. These events – the forced offensive of the Soviet forces and the lacking debate about Poland – would create major problems for the final conference of the 'Big Three' in Yalta in February of 1945 and draw the contours of a postwar rivalry between the USSR and the USA.

Roosevelt's preparations for order

The ideational constellation from the Versailles conference echoed through the diplomatic constellations of 1945. European statesmen like Churchill and Stalin approached the politics of war in terms of *Realpolitik*. They discussed war and peace in terms of spheres of influence and balance of power. The American President, by contrast, approached conflict and war in terms of rights, law and international organization.

True, Realist arguments were voiced in the USA as well. One of the most influential of the wartime voices of Realism was that of Nicholas Spykman, an immigrant from the Netherlands. He argued that it was decisively important for the United States to prevent one single Great Power from dominating the European continent, and that it therefore was imperative for the USA to actively support forces which sought to thwart Hitler's plans to found a vast, German *Reich* on the great plains of central Europe. This argument received wide American support. His subsequent warning, however, stirred up much disagreement: The USA needed to calibrate its support carefully so that it neither strengthened the position of the USSR too much in Eastern Europe nor initiated a process of progressive integration in Western Europe. 'A European federation is not a power constellation that the United States should encourage. Balanced power, not integrated power, is in our interest', concluded Spykman (1942, p. 488).

Reinhold Niebuhr disagreed. An international equilibrium is no automatic thing, Niebuhr averred; it relies on perceptive statesmen to observe the international scene and manipulate the balance wisely. Spykman's balance of power would be nothing but a 'potential anarchy and cannot preserve peace' argued Niebuhr (1943, p. 4). Europe, as well as the world at large, 'requires instruments for the manipulation of its social forces. Without them, it is bound to fall into periodic anarchy' (1943).

This was not far from the view of President Roosevelt. For him, European peace would be best secured if politicians on the Continent were made to respect human rights and international law and tied together by institutions of co-operation. Roosevelt's vision, outlined in the Atlantic Charter of August 1941, was expressed in the political and economic institutions that he worked so hard to establish during his wartime diplomacy. He wanted to convert the wartime alliance into an organization which would secure a peaceful post-war order. Also, he worked to set up interlocking institutions that would stimulate Western trade and regulate the international flows of finance and goods.

Planning for the postwar world

Roosevelt's vision of a postwar organization was not novel; it was inspired by Woodrow Wilson and modelled on the League of Nations. Roosevelt's idea of an interacting set of economic organizations, however, was original. Here he drew on experience from the Great Depression and on his own work to revive the US economy. The international organizations he established during the last two years of his life – the United Nations Organization and the Bretton Woods system – remained important for several decades after the war. Indeed, they contributed greatly to shape the twentieth-century world scene.

The UN

The UN was built around the design of the old League, composed of a General Assembly, a Secretariat and a Council. Like the League, the UN rested on two key principles. First, the principle of functional integration – which was most clearly expressed in the establishment of an Economic and Social Council (EcoSoc).[9] This principle hinged on the idea that, if international relations were institutionalized and encouraged in certain key sectors, then co-operation would evolve and spread to other areas as well.

Second, the UN was established around the principle of collective security. In theory this meant that if one state were to attack another, then this would be considered as an attack against all of the UN's members and the aggressor would subsequently suffer massive reprisals from all other states. In practice, this principle was hard to implement. During the time of the League, member states had followed national interests when push came to shove; they had not shown the required amount of international solidarity.[10] In order to strengthen the resolve of the organization, the Council was strengthened. It was charged with maintaining international peace and security. The responsibilities which were reflected in its name, the 'Security Council', and its authority.

The Security Council got the power to suspend and expel members, impose economic sanctions and take military action to maintain or restore order, peace and security. The Council was given a wide mandate in order to strengthen the role of the UN as observer, negotiator, peacekeeper and, ultimately, peace enforcer. The Council had fifteen members. Five of them (the USA, the USSR, Britain, France and China) were permanent members with veto power. The remaining ten members were temporary, non-veto powers; five were elected each year to serve two-year terms.

Detailed plans for the UN were drawn up in October 1944 in a conference at Dumbarton Oaks. In February 1945, at a summit meeting at Yalta, Stalin and Churchill agreed to back the Dumbarton Oaks scheme. The UN received its final form at a big conference in San Francisco two months later.

The Bretton Woods system

The most novel aspect of Roosevelt's postwar plans was his vision of a set of inter-locking economic organizations designed to sustain the new world order. Details were hammered out in July 1944, when delegates from forty-four countries met in the resort town of Bretton Woods in New Hampshire. The delegates drew on historical experiences, discussing both the growth that preceded World War I and the Great Depression which followed in its wake. They agreed that the growth that preceded World War I had been due to three interacting factor: low levels of international tolls and taxes, a high volume of trade and the easy convertibility of the world's major currencies.

Before World War I, the currencies of the world had been convertible to gold. This made the currencies stable; no state could print up more money than the counter-value in gold would support without creating inflation. Also, mooring the currencies in a common gold standard stimulated trade because it made the currencies easily convertible.

After World War II the allied governments faced the common problem that most of them had given up the gold standard during the interwar recession. The delegates to Bretton Woods therefore had to devise some new mechanism which could ensure the convertibility and stability of the world's currencies. Their solution was to establish two new institutions: the International Bank for Reconstruction and Development (IBRD or the 'World Bank') and the International Monetary Fund (IMF). Both were unprecedented organizations.

The purpose of the World Bank was to lend money to governments which worked to rebuild their economies after the destructions of war; the bank's initial capital was a large sum of dollars which the Americans made available.[11] The purpose of the second organization, the IMF, was to ensure convertibility and stable exchange rates for the world's major currencies. Stability was ensured when all IMF members invested a large sum into a common fund, which each member then could draw on if it needed to counteract unforeseen fluctuations in its currency. Again, the USA guaranteed the working of the fund.[12] The Bretton Woods system, in other words, gave the American dollar a key role in the postwar world economy.

ITO (and GATT)

The Bretton Woods delegates agreed that, in order to stimulate world trade, it would be wise to create an International Trade Organization (ITO) which would complement the IMF and the World Bank. The ITO would work to lower tolls and remove protectionist measures that would hinder trade. But the delegates also agreed that their responsibility lay with international finance not with trade. They agreed that it was not within their mandate to establish a body of trade. So they left this task undone, imploring the trade ministries of the capitalist world to send delegates to future conferences to establish an ITO.

Several such conferences were arranged – in 1945, 1946 and 1947. They all ran into snags. The delegates long disagreed on the nature and role of a trade organization. And when agreement was finally reached and the charter of a new ITO was submitted to the US Congress in the spring of 1948, Congress refused to ratify it.

The US government put the ITO on ice. Instead it transferred its attention to another diplomatic effort: namely, to a group of Western countries which had produced a Protocol of Provisional Application of the General Agreement on Tariffs and Trade (or GATT).[13]

Energy regime

Roosevelt's plans for an ITO ran into early difficulties, but its ideals limped along in the form of GATT. His plans for a postwar energy regime, however, died almost as soon as it was presented – although this regime was envisioned to play an important role in the postwar world economy.

Roosevelt had a vision of a postwar world of democratic and open industrial states that engaged in free trade with each other. The World Bank, the IMF and the ITO were institutions designed to rebuild states, encourage industrial production and increase international commerce. But Roosevelt's vision presupposed that each industrial state actually produced goods that other states wanted to buy. And such production, in turn, required a reliable supply of affordable sources of energy.[14]

A smooth flow of cheap oil from countries in the Persian Gulf was, in Roosevelt's mind a vital precondition for a stable postwar world economy. He was deeply disappointed when it proved impossible to broker a deal between British and US oil companies that held concessions in the Gulf and British and US lawmakers. The US Congress was particularly sceptical about Roosevelt's proposal; it would, in their mind, undermine the free-market mechanisms of the energy sector. Roosevelt quickly gave up the idea. Instead he worked out a plan to secure some of the major petroleum fields in the Gulf region for US companies. As Roosevelt prepared for the Yalta conference, he also laid plans for a visit with King Ibn Saud of Saudi Arabia to discuss US concessions for the petroleum resources which had been recently discovered in the country.

Yalta

The 'Big Three' met for a final wartime conference in February 1945 in the Livadia Palace, the splendid seaside resort near Yalta on the Crimean peninsula. The Allied wartime diplomacy reached its highpoint at Yalta. Allied victory was in sight and the three leaders could more confidently draw the contours of the postwar world. The Soviet host was the most confident of the three. He was in an excellent mood, and for good reasons. The military forces of the Soviet Union were driving the German *Wehrmacht* westwards, through Poland, quickly replacing the Germans as the occupying force of the region.

Stalin controlled the situation in Eastern Europe. The other wartime leaders might negotiate and draw lines on their maps, but Stalin's military forces created facts on the ground. The Red Army advanced fast. And in its tracks followed commissars – political organizers who established communist institutions in the occupied territories, including a new Polish government of Communist Party members handpicked by the Soviets. At Yalta Stalin saw no reason to grant Churchill or Roosevelt any influence on the Polish situation. Stalin's self-confident behaviour at this last wartime conference has made 'Yalta', together with 'Munich', into a potent symbol of a turning point in modern international history.

Roosevelt arrived at Yalta exhausted and very ill. He concentrated his attention on Stalin and played psychological games to win his confidence. He flattered the Soviet *Generalissimo*; he joked with him – often at Churchill's expense. He secured Stalin's promise to support the UN and join the Organization as an active member after the war. Also, he got Stalin to confirm that the Soviet forces would join the USA in the war against Japan three months after Germany's surrender in Europe.

Churchill was marginalized during the proceedings. However, he managed to convince the others that it was necessary to occupy Germany after the war and to divide the country in four zones of occupation – one for each of the 'Big Three', in addition to one zone for France. Yalta was the last and the most important of the wartime meetings between the 'Big Three'. The decisions made there drew the contours of the postwar order.

On his long voyage home Roosevelt made a stop in Saudi Arabia. His Presidential yacht anchored up in the Suez Canal and hosted the Saudi Arabian King Ibn Saud. This meeting between the two old men paved the way for a unique, robust and important relationship, whereby Saudi Arabia would provide the USA with access to oil, whereas the USA would guarantee the security of the Saudi kingdom.

The end of the war

President Roosevelt died on 12 April 1945. He was succeeded by Harry S. Truman. Adolf Hitler committed suicide in his Berlin bunker at the end of April. The nation was collapsing around him. US and British forces were advancing from the west; Soviet forces were moving in from the east. The two Allied armies met in Berlin around 1 May 1945. Germany surrendered one week later, on 8 May.

The war in Europe was over. But the transition to peace was hard and slow. In many countries the German retreat also meant loss of authority and order. National economies were destroyed by war. Populations had suffered horrible losses and societies were tense with stress and pent-up anger. The countries received new leaders who were recruited from anti-fascist movements. They often struggled hard to maintain social order at home.[15] Also, relations among European states were marked by the re-emergence of old rivalries.

During the second half of July 1945, the USA, the USSR and Britain met in Potsdam in occupied Germany to decide how to handle the transition from war to peace, to decide the fate of Europe in general and Germany in particular and to establish a stable postwar order. Stalin represented the USSR. The new American president, Harry S. Truman, represented the USA. Britain was first represented by Winston Churchill; after Churchill lost the British elections in the third week of July, Britain's new Prime Minister, Clement Attlee, represented Britain.

The fate of Europe was largely decided by the location of the victorious armies. The USSR occupied and effectively controlled Eastern Europe – from the Baltic states in the north, via Poland, Czechoslovakia, Hungary, and Romania to Bulgaria in the south. The leaders of the West grew concerned about the Soviet consolidation of a communist empire in Eastern Europe, and this common concern drove them more tightly together.

The fate of Germany had been settled at Yalta six months previously. The country was split in four between the USA, the USSR, Britain and France. Each established a zone of occupation. Austria was split in the same way. The capital cities of Berlin and Vienna were similarly split in four. Increasing east–west tension drove the Western states together; the USA, Britain and France began to co-operate closely and to merge their occupation zones. The USSR, by contrast, ruled its own zones without any external involvement.[16]

On 16 July US scientists brought the secret Manhattan project to a successful conclusion and detonated an atomic bomb.[17] One week after the Potsdam conference, the USA dropped nuclear bombs on the Japanese cities of Hiroshima and Nagasaki.

Japan surrendered immediately – only days before Stalin was to fulfil his promise from Yalta and enter the war against Japan. Stalin had expected to gain some influence over occupied Japan, and protested when Truman offered him none.

Ideas and ideologies – in the East and the West

Hitler's successes make it hard to deny him political genius. Yet, the ideas that he entertained and the goals that he pursued have caused innumerable observers to doubt his sanity. The Nazi theories of racial purity were callous in the extreme. Their pseudo-scientific speculations of race (Grant 1916; Hitler 1943) supported the absurd notion that the national organism would improve in strength and spirit through conflict and struggle and legitimized a political programme of expansion into a deserved *Lebensraum* (Schmitt 1939).

Many German officers considered these ideas dysfunctional from a military point of view. They feared that the Nazi leaders' obsession with them would increase the costs of warfare unnecessarily. They were proved right. When the *Wehrmacht* invaded the USSR in June 1941, the German soldiers were in some places greeted as liberators from Stalin's terror. But when Hitler's SA began to systematically round up and execute civilians, the population quickly changed their loyalties and fled into the arms of Stalin.

Soviet approaches

Stalin, too, entertained political theories based on notions of social antagonisms, conflict and struggle. He saw society as divided into two main classes, the capitalists and the proletariat. The capitalist class was the implacable enemy of the proletariat and the two were, in Stalin's mind, engaged in an epic worldwide struggle.

Stalin's view of politics drew heavily upon Lenin. He saw historical evolution as propelled by struggle – not among races but among social classes. Notions about the historical struggle of the proletariat against the capitalist class had a formative influence on Stalin's internal as well as on his external dispositions.

Internally, Stalin sought to eliminate entire social groups if he thought they harboured capitalist tendencies. Where Hitler had sought to exterminate biologically defined races, Stalin sought to eliminate economically defined classes.[18] This notion of class struggle also made a mark on Soviet foreign relations. From Stalin's point of view, the main cause of war lay in the nature of the capitalist world system – in its tendency to centralize capital and concentrate power and in the unceasing need of capitalist states to expand.

These ideological precepts of Marxism–Leninism were apparent in Soviet politics from the start. Throughout the 1930s, Stalin argued that a world composed of capitalist states is a world of conflict and war, because capitalism drives states into an unceasing competition for scarce resources and for international markets. During the course of World War II, as long as he was allied with the world's leading capitalist powers, Stalin never invoked this theory. However, he never put it fully aside. From his point of view Hitler, Churchill and Roosevelt were all capitalist leaders. Consequently, he saw no essential difference between the three of them.

When Germany and Japan had surrendered in 1945, Stalin resumed his orthodox Marxist–Leninist analysis. In February 1946, in a speech which praised the Soviet people for their courage during the Great Patriotic War, Stalin summarized his wartime experiences and explained the causes and the nature of the war. World War II, he argued, was the product of competition among the capitalist powers. It was fuelled by the internal dynamics of the capitalist system. And, he continued, because capitalism survived the war new wars would be expected to break out in the future.

The world was divided into two camps, Stalin explained: a capitalist and a socialist camp. America, Britain and Germany all belonged to the former; the Soviet Union alone belonged to the latter. The USSR must, accordingly, be prepared for new wars and for attacks from the capitalist camp. The Soviets could celebrate, but they could not afford to relax, Stalin concluded. It was necessary to begin preparation for a new war. In order to defend their socialist fatherland, the Soviets had to put shoulders to the wheel, rebuild the nation's heavy industry and get arms production going. They had to start more five-year plans at once, with all the discipline and sacrifice that this would imply (Stalin 1946).

British perspectives
British leaders reacted to Stalin's speech with incredulity. Even Churchill was surprised. He saw in Stalin's speech the final proof of an irreconcilable division of Europe in two competing zones and the world into two competing systems.

The leaders of the Labour Party, who had replaced Churchill's Conservative wartime Cabinet at the end of July 1945, were taken aback. The new Foreign Minister, Ernest Bevin, made a bleak assessment of the international situation. He was painfully aware of how five years of war had altered the international constellation of power. Britain was exhausted, whereas the capabilities of the USA and the USSR were greatly enhanced. 'Instead of a world co-operation we are rapidly drifting into spheres of influence, or what can better be described as three great Monroes', Bevin averred. The first sphere was the Americas and was dominated by the USA. The second sphere covered large parts of Eurasia and was dominated by the USSR. Between these two great 'Monroes' lay an unclear region of exhausted

European states, with Britain as the most powerful among them. Bevin's great fear was that the USA would pull out of the Continent while Europe was still in this weakened condition, in order to concentrate on consolidating its own sphere of influence in the Americas. If this was the case, the USSR might see an opportunity expand westwards. Stalin might capture one war-tired small state after the other, and then draw on the resources of these states for his own postwar reconstruction. Britain did not have the capabilities to contain such a Soviet expansion. The country was weakened by two world wars. It was balancing on the brink of bankruptcy.

On this grim analysis, Bevin made two foreign-policy initiatives. First, he tried to convince the Americans to let their troops remain in Europe. Second, he tried to make Europe's old Great Powers enter into a tighter community of states. Partly to help reconstruct Western Europe after the destructions of war. Partly to contain Soviet influence. Churchill had reasoned along similar lines.

American views

Observers and policy-makers in Washington developed comparable ideas. In February 1946 they listened to Stalin's speech and reacted with disbelief, confusion and fear. Stalin had issued a 'declaration of World War III', remarked the US Supreme Court Justice William O. Douglas to the Secretary of the Navy James Forrestal. He was not alone in this view. Officials in Washington fired off a telegram to the US Embassy in Moscow, asking for a background sketch and an explanation for Stalin's belligerent claims. They received a long response from one of the analysts at the Embassy, a young *chargé d'affaires* by the name of George F. Kennan, who placed Stalin's speech in a historical and geopolitical perspective.

Stalin is no run-of-the-mill Western statesman, Kennan began. He is a product of an autocratic Russian tradition and of a closed Soviet system. His outlook relies on well-known terms from Marxist–Leninist theory. This theory sustains a rather orthodox argument but it also reflects a typical Russian/Soviet distrust of the Western world. This distrust cannot be assuaged, Kennan continues. Stalin and his circle insisted on seeing the world as divided between a capitalist and a communist camp. Capitalism was, according to their view, fraught with internal contradictions and would soon collapse. Socialism would then rise to rule the world. In the meantime, the Soviets would use any opportunity to weaken the West and undermine America's power. In particular, they would use the worldwide network of communist parties to trigger popular protest, create conflict and undermine democratic societies from within.

Under such circumstances only two courses of US action existed, Kennan continued: either to wait for changes within the USSR or to actively resist Soviet attempts to undermine the West. Kennan recommended the second course. He repeated that the Soviet theory of International Relations was the product not of an objective study of world politics but of ideology. And he emphasized that the Soviet way of arguing stemmed from the leaders' need to justify their autocratic rule. They used Marxism–Leninism as the 'fig leaf of their moral and intellectual respectability', Kennan (1946, p. 700) claimed. The Soviets may be bold, but they are not reckless, he continued. Echoing old theories of counterpoise, Kennan wrote:

> [The Soviet Union is] impervious to [the] logic of reason, and it is highly sensitive to [the] logic of force. For this reason it can easily withdraw – and usually does – when strong resistance is encountered at any point. Thus, if the adversary has sufficient force and makes clear his readiness to use it, he rarely has to do so. If situations are properly handled there need be no prestige-engaging showdowns. (p. 707)

Kennan's 'long telegram' created a big stir at the highest political levels in Washington in March 1946. The US Secretary of State, George C. Marshall, read Kennan's telegram and was deeply impressed. He called Kennan home from Moscow and made him one of his closest foreign-policy advisers. Kennan also became the first Deputy for Foreign Affairs of the newly formed National War College.

The USA initiated a new and tougher approach to the Soviet Union. The policy change was reinforced when Winston Churchill made a speech in the United States on 5 March. Stalin had expanded his influence westwards, Churchill began. Stalin was using the Soviet army and local communist parties to seize and control the eastern half of Europe. Then Churchill continued:

> From Stettin in the Baltic to Trieste in the Adriatic an iron curtain has descended across the continent. Behind that line lie all the capitals of the ancient states of Central and Eastern Europe. Warsaw, Berlin, Prague, Vienna, Budapest, Belgrade, Bucharest and Sofia; all these famous cities and the populations around them lie in what I must call the Soviet sphere, and all are subject, in one form or another, not only to Soviet influence but to a very high and in some cases increasing measure of control from Moscow. (Churchill 1989b, pp. 303f)

If the West were to bargain with Stalin, it would only encourage him, Churchill warned. If it tried to use the UN, it would prove ineffective. The only sensible response would be to establish a 'fraternal association of the English-speaking peoples' (p. 301). Half a year later he expanded upon the idea. Stalin cast his shadow over a divided Continent. 'Among the victors there is a babel of jarring voices' and only one remedy can rectify the situation: namely, to unify Europe and 'provide it with a structure under which it can dwell in peace, in safety and in freedom. We must build a kind of United States of Europe', argued Churchill (1989c, p. 311).

Institutions of liberal internationalism
The analyses of Stalin, Kennan and Churchill in February and March 1946 testified to the rapid unraveling of the wartime alliance. Stalin struck confusion and fear in the West. Kennan's 'long telegram' provided the conceptual basis for an active American foreign policy of containing Soviet expansionism in Europe and the Near East. Churchill's 'iron-curtain speech' provided the idea for an alliance between the Atlantic states as a bulwark against the Soviet Union. All three speeches were based on a Realist assessment of the world situation. They reflected

well the approach that dominated the academic study of International Relations just after World War II.

The dominance of Realism, however, was not total. In the USA there was tension between a tough foreign-policy analysis of the overall world situation and more solidaric foreign-policy practice. US relations with the liberal democracies of the Western world were clearly in tune with the ideals of liberal internationalism. Also, these ideals were preserved in the UN and in other institutions which Roosevelt established during his busy wartime diplomacy.

The ideals of liberal internationalism also coloured US attitudes towards Japan and Germany after the war. They were, for example, apparent in the charges which the US chief prosecutors Joseph B. Keenan and Robert H. Jackson formulated in the war trials against Japanese and German leaders in Tokyo and Nuremberg, respectively. When the Nuremberg Trials opened in November 1945, Jackson charged that Germany's Nazi leaders had committed wrongs 'so calculated, so malignant, and so devastating, that civilization cannot tolerate their being ignored, because it cannot survive their being repeated'.

Jackson's claim was thoroughly substantiated during the Nuremberg Trials. Testimonies and proofs revealed to the world the atrocities of the Nazi regime in all their malignant enormity. Detailed accounts were produced of the well-planned invasions, the systematic procedures of ethnic cleansing and the industrial-scale methods applied to mass transport to the huge death camps. The documentation shocked international public opinion.

Under the influence of the Nuremberg Trials the members of the United Nations grew doubly determined to rid humanity of such massive crimes as those committed by the German Nazi Party. This determination weakened the tradition of legal positivism which had long dominated the discipline of International Law and revived the older tradition of natural law. Western jurists were deeply frustrated by Nazi lawyers who had used the legal principle of state sovereignty to cloak a policy of domestic genocide in a mantle of formal legality. They felt a need to establish a higher set of values against which domestic acts and national law could be assessed. In order to do this, it was necessary to establish universal or natural principles of law. They avoided a direct appeal to the natural law of old; instead, they dressed the principle up in the modern language of human rights and moored them in the Charter of the United Nations Organization.

The principles were displayed in the Preamble of the Charter, which defined the purpose of the UNO in four succinct points:

- to save succeeding generations from the scourge of war
- to reaffirm faith in fundamental human rights, in the dignity and worth of the human person, in the equal rights of men and women and of nations large and small
- to establish conditions under which justice and respect for the obligations arising from treaties and other sources of international law can be maintained
- to promote social progress and better standards of life in larger freedom.

The Charter was signed in San Francisco in June 1945 by fifty states. The signatories promised to be bound by the articles of the Charter. In addition they agreed (as specified in Article 103) to let obligations to the UN prevail over all other treaty obligations. As a result, the UN Charter became basis for common norms, rules and laws which regulate the behaviour of states in the international community.

In spite of the cold tension that paralysed diplomatic relations between the USA and the USSR, the UN continued to work. Between 1946 and 1949 UN bodies produced several important legal documents. First – and under the impact of the Nuremberg trials – the UN General Assembly passed the Genocide Convention on 9 December 1948. The very next day, it passed the Universal Declaration of Human Rights. Three months later, in March 1949, the UN made four additions to the Geneva Convention on the International Law of War, further regulating the treatment of prisoners of war and civilians during war.

These UN documents – the Genocide Convention, the Declaration of Human Rights and the additions to the Geneva Convention – complemented the UN Charter and contributed to the establishment of a new basis for International Law. Together they advanced beyond the classical, state-centred understanding and prepared the springboard for a new jurisprudence – an understanding that is not limited to defending the principle of state sovereignty but which also obliges governments to abide by a higher code of human rights and constitutional norms.

War, peace and Hans Morgenthau

The UNO was the result of President Roosevelt's wartime diplomacy. It was based on broadly held American ideals and reflected a liberal approach to world affairs.

American Idealism

A most representative version of this liberal approach was Wendell Willkie's popular book *One World*. Willkie was a Republican Senator and his book was an instant best-seller when it was published in 1943. The book was a fast-paced travelogue in which the senator related his world travels and his meetings with citizens, statesmen and soldiers around the globe and which ended with a discussion of the need for a world government.

The liberal vision was also apparent at a symposium which was organized in 1943 and devoted to the postwar peace. Willkie was one of the participants. Besides him on the podium were influential public figures like former President Herbert Hoover, Vice President Henry Wallace and Assistant Secretary of State Sumner Welles. The symposium (and the popular book that resulted from it) demonstrated how these powerful men, who disagreed deeply on many domestic issues, were of one mind when it came to international affairs.

First, they agreed that that the prewar international system had been deeply flawed and must be abandoned. Second, they found it necessary to build a new world order – and one that must be constructed on the principle of popular sovereignty. 'The people of the world want to be free, not only for their political satisfaction but also for their economic advancement', claimed Vice President Wallace (Willkie 1943, p. 135). Third, they agreed that a new and peaceful world order would depend on the determination of the USA to take part in maintaining it. 'So long as our cooperation is effectively offered, so long can one hope that peace can and will be maintained', wrote Welles (1943, p. 437). Finally, they agreed that a peaceful world order must depend on maintaining close and cordial relations among the members in the United Nations alliance. Willkie (1943, p. 129) put it most succinctly: 'The United Nations must become a common council, not only for the winning of the war but for the future welfare of mankind.' Wallace emphasized that a world peace hinged on co-operation between the two great federations that were likely to dominate the world after Germany was defeated: namely, the USA and the USSR. 'The American and Russian people can and will throw their influence on the side of building a new democracy which will be the hope of all the world', argued Wallace (1943, p. 381).

It was an important symposium, and the book it produced – *Prefaces to Peace* – reflected the liberal institutionalism of its times. It advocated the establishment of institutions which would facilitate orderly interaction among states. Its arguments were thoughtful but not particularly novel. It largely echoed visions that were developed by British and American theorists a generation or so earlier. Arguments based on Locke and Vattel which had been introduced by Woodrow Wilson during the First World War were elaborated by Franklin Roosevelt, Sumner Welles and Cordell Hull during the Second.

Hans Morgenthau and power politics

This absence of novelty was noted by several observers. David Mitrany noted that Wilson's attempt to establish a collective security organization had failed. He argued that the Americans tended to overestimate human reason and the force of federal arrangements, and republished his 1933 book, *A Working Peace System*, to substantiate his criticism (Ashworth 2013). It was, however, a young scholar of Jewish ancestry, Hans J. Morgenthau, who delivered the hardest-hitting critique of the American political tradition and who stole the academic limelight in the wake of the World War.

Morgenthau had come to the USA as a refugee from Nazi Germany in 1937. He was deeply dubious of the attitudes reflected in *Prefaces to Peace* and in the entire American approach to International Relations. He did not pull his punches. He compared Roosevelt's Secretary of State, Cordell Hull, to Neville Chamberlain. Both have been dangerously deluded in their views of international affairs, Morgenthau declared. They suffer from 'a fundamental misconception of what foreign policy is all about' (Morgenthau 1948a, p. 127).

Morgenthau vented his frustrations in *Scientific Man vs. Power Politics*. The book was published in 1946 and delivered a hard critique of what Morgenthau considered America's naive, technical and misinformed approach to world affairs. American diplomats ambled around in two blind alleys. They tended to stress the importance of justice in international affairs. And they tended to think that science and technology offered solutions to political and social problems – they approached foreign conflict as if they were engineers facing a motor that needed repair. These two orientations are contradictory; issues of justice cannot be settled by mechanical arguments. Also, they are analytically useless; a proper analysis of international politics cannot begin with norms and bright wishes, it must begin with assessments of the interests and the capabilities of states!

Politics is first and foremost about power, Morgenthau insisted. And power relations are constantly changing. They cannot be grasped in universal concepts derived from moral philosophy and they cannot be reduced to simple, mechanical models.

Americans are in a habit of confusing politics with law, Morgenthau continued. US policy-makers tend to think that, if they can impose legal norms upon society, then co-operation, order and peace will follow. This assumption may hold for domestic affairs in a liberal society, but it is useless when it comes to interaction among sovereign states that are engaged in non-rational power games, Morgenthau maintained. President Wilson had based his negotiations in Versailles on that flawed assumption, and it had ended in failure. President Roosevelt had based his wartime diplomacy on the same premise. Roosevelt's postwar vision would also meet with failure, Morgenthau implied, unless the norms imposed reflected the hard power realities of the postwar world.

Morgenthau identified the flaws in American foreign policy in a brief diagnosis: it suffered from excessive liberalism. The American approach was not only liberal, but it was built on a simplistic understanding of human nature and an incomplete appreciation of interstate relations. It depicted humans as reasonable beings – as social and gregarious, and endowed with reason and with an awareness of their own true interest. Upon that simple anthropology, Americans tried to establish a science of politics. Morgenthau expressed a deep scepticism towards what he dubbed the 'scientistic' faith of America.

First, he criticized the American approach for treating society as a machine and for assuming that the social world could be investigated through the methods of natural science. This approach will never work, argued Morgenthau. Second, he claimed that Americans do not understand that politics *among* states is a different game from politics *within* states and that the two must be played by different rules. American liberals tend to apply rules from domestic politics when they play international games. The result is confusion, argued Morgenthau – echoing a point that Niebuhr (1932) had made a few years earlier. Morgenthau then presented an alternative approach to politics; a power-centred rather than a reason-centred view of human nature which underpinned a different view of the human condition.

Morgenthau did not deny that humans were endowed with reason but he argued that human reason was regularly guided by non-rational forces – by desires, cravings and temptations. This was a pessimistic view of human nature. It tallied with the view of old-fashioned conservatives. Also, it tallied with that of Christian theologians (like Niebuhr) who captured these non-rational human inclinations in the concept of 'sin'. Morgenthau, however, referred to those non-rational forces as a will or a lust for 'power'.

There are similarities between Morgenthau's political philosophy and that of Niebuhr – and Morgenthau was undoubtedly influenced by Niebuhr (Rice 2008). However, the most formative influences in Morgenthau's thought did not come from US authors. They came from his European past – from his legal studies in Germany, from his political debates with conservatives and racists in the Weimar Republic, from the deterioration of law and the erosion of civil order as the Nazis gained power, from his experience as a Jewish refugee in Spain and France.

The criticisms that Morgenthau levied at American politics and society were thematically close to those expressed by other intellectuals who fled Nazi Germany and struggled to establish a new life in liberal America (Rösch 2014) – from Leo Strauss and Eric Voegelin on the conservative end of the political spectrum to Theodor Adorno and Max Horkheimer on the left. Whereas critics like Adorno and Horkheimer (1944) viewed the USA with scorn and contempt, Morgenthau saw the USA as the major hope for the future of humanity. One the one hand, Morgenthau saw the USA as the predominant power of the postwar world, saddled with the responsibility of establishing an international order which would defend and develop human civilization. On the other he was deeply concerned that the USA was woefully unprepared for the task. To help remedy the situation, Morgenthau invested his energies into completing another book, *Politics among Nations*. He had worked on it off and on for well over a decade. It was going to be a master-piece – it would differ from traditional textbooks in international politics as an automobile differs from a horse and buggy. And it was going to be important. 'The understanding of the forces that mold international politics and the factors that determine its course has become for the United States more than an interesting intellectual occupation. It has become a vital necessity' (Morgenthau 1948b, p. 26).

Scientific man and politics among nations
Morgenthau developed key notions of politics and the centrality of power during the 1930s. These notions are apparent in *Scientific Man vs. Power Politics*, which defines politics as 'a struggle for power over men, and whatever its ultimate aim may be, power is its immediate goal' (Morgenthau 1946, p. 195). This definition applies to domestic politics and international politics alike. But the nature of politics is so much more raw and obvious in international politics. For whereas domestic politics occurs within the legal and ordered framework of a state, international politics takes place in a lawless setting, among sovereign states who all seek to preserve their sovereignty. Their aim is to satisfy basic needs and then protect their wherewithal from the incursion of others. They are prone to counteract any effort to establish a supreme authority which will co-ordinate or affect their behaviour.

Scientific Man vs. Power Politics appeared at a time when US foreign policy was in flux. Its bold claims, its incisive analysis and its clear policy recommenda-tions were written after the University of Chicago offered Morgenthau a job at its prestigious Department of Political Science. Here Morgenthau quickly completed *Politics among Nations*. In a thick tome which was as simple in concept as it was ambitious in execution, Morgenthau set out to examine some four hundred years of diplomacy with an eye to identifying patterns and regularities in Great-Power behaviour.

Although Morgenthau relied on historical material to discover regularities, he did not arrange his argument chronologically; rather *Politics among Nations* is arranged thematically. And the theme that dominates his arrangement is the concept of 'power' and the basic anthropology on which it rests – namely, that 'man is a political animal by nature' (Morgenthau 1946, p. 168). Humans are driven, by biological and psychological needs, to gain 'power' (Morgenthau, 1948b, p. 53). There is no natural limit to this lust for power. It can be satisfied only 'if the last man became an object of his domination, there being nobody above or beside him, that is, if he became God' (1948b p. 193).

The first section of the book lays out the nature of 'politics' – very much along the lines of *Scientific Man vs. Power Politics* as a 'struggle for power'. The most important aspect of power is military capability. But Morgenthau is quick to note that this capability is a complex composite of industrial capacity, wealth, number of citizens who can be converted into soldiers, and so on. He is careful to emphasize that power also has intangible aspects, such as a nation's character, morale and quality of governance. These intangibles of power may be even more significant than simple, material force.

The second section of *Politics among Nations* describes how the 'struggle for power' manifests itself on the international scene. The behaviour of nations can be explained as reflecting various concerns with power – that is, to keep and defend it, to increase it, or to demonstrate it, claims Morgenthau (1946; 1948b).

A third section discusses ways to constrain 'the evil tendencies of human nature within socially tolerable bounds'. This can be done through 'social equilibrium' or balance of power – the discussion of which constitutes a substantial part of the book. It can also be done through international law and by improving the moral climate of the world. Finally, social conflict can be reduced by minimizing the psychological causes that lead to conflict – by reducing fear and enhancing a feeling of security and well-being in the world opinion.

The concluding section of the book discusses problems of establishing order and peace in the wake of World War II. Here, Morgenthau makes the point that international law is an indispensable institution of order. But, he adds, law is an insufficient principle of order on its own. He acknowledges that international law is often written by strong states who seek to further their own interests. But he also defends the law against its extreme critics, by noting that, during the four hundred years of its existence, international law has in most instances been scrupulously observed.

On the one hand, *Politics among Nations* is infused with a pessimistic anthropology. Its argument hinges on two assumptions. First, on a Malthusian assumption that sees society as an environment of scarcity. Second, on a distinct view of human nature that portrays all humans as endowed with a will to power. Given these two assumptions, human relations are marked by tensions, conflict and strife. Such tensions cannot be removed and the tensions cannot be 'solved'.

On the other, Morgenthau notes that tensions can be controlled and conflicts can be managed. International law is presented as a force for order. Diplomacy, economic progress, increasing welfare and an evolving public enlightenment are presented as forces of peace. Human behaviour can, in other words, be restrained by institutions and socialized by norms. Limits can be imposed on the human will to power. It is worth noting that, although Morgenthau was critical of the American legal approach to international affairs, he was not against international law. Quite on the contrary, Morgenthau was a jurist and considered himself an expert on international law.[19] What he wanted to tell the Americans was that legal norms do not create order by themselves. Laws are effective if they properly reflect power relations in international society.

This is a key point in Morgenthau's argument. And it contains a normative core which makes Realism different from the naked power politics of the old, German concept of *Realpolitik*.

The first reviews of *Politics among Nations* were very positive and helped establish the book as an instant classic. It was immediately adopted as a textbook for foreign policy and International Relations at all the American Ivy League universities. By 1950, some ninety US colleges had adopted the book – which was more than all other previous textbooks combined (Frei 2001, p. 73). By 1955 the book had sold around forty thousand copies.

Realist hegemony

When World War II began, there were four broad approaches towards international politics: realism, liberalism, communism and fascism. When the war ended, fascism was branded unwanted, immoral and, in some states, illegal. But realism, liberalism and communism remained. However, only realism and liberalism were considered respectable approaches by the scholarly International Relations community in the West. Communism was generally perceived by scholars as an ideology and a doctrine of state. George F. Kennan (1946, p. 700) saw it as the 'legitimizing fig leaf' of Stalin and the Communist Party of the Soviet Union (CPSU).

The waning of wartime idealism

The liberal outlook exerted a strong influence in the US Department of Commerce and in the US Department of State. Liberal ideals informed US efforts to set up economic organizations like the World Bank and the IMF and encourage the free international flow of commodities. Liberal ideals also informed Western efforts to set up political organizations like the United Nations Organization (UNO) and to improve international law. Furthemore, liberal ideals informed American foreign relations towards its capitalist allies in Western Europe. Increasingly, however, Realism emerged as the more influential approach. International Relations scholars, who searched for a general theory of international relations, would increasingly navigate by Realist stars.

An early indication of this were the influential seminar on foreign policy and security affairs that Edward M. Earle ran at Princeton during the course of the

war and the publication of his popular book on strategic thought (Earle 1943).
It was of course no coincidence that Halford Mackinder's *Democratic Ideals and
Reality* [1919] was re-published in 1942 on Earle's initiative. The Dutch-born
Yale professor Nicholas Spykman wrote two Mackinder-inspired volumes in rapid
sequence before his untimely death: *America's Strategy in World Politics* [1942] and
The Geography of the Peace [1943]. Both books had considerable influence in the
immediate wake of World War II.

In order to emphasize America's rapidly rising status in the world, Spykman
introduced the concept 'superpower'. A 'superpower' is more powerful than the
Great Powers of the past, Spykman explained. It has unique military capabilities,
it enjoys global reach and it plays a special role as an ordering force in the world.
America's development of the nuclear bomb in 1945 served to confirm this claim.
William T. R. Fox embraced the new term and included it in the title of his 1944
book, *The Super-Powers: The United States, Britain and the Soviet Union*. The
three states in the book's title share a responsibility for securing a peaceful international order after the war, Fox argued. The USA has a special responsibility, he
continued. On the strength of its superior military capabilities the USA can project
its power globally and lead other Western powers in the establishment of a new,
liberal postwar world order.

Fox was not a fully fledged Realist. He described a postwar world order which
was competitive but essentially liberal in nature. Such liberal ideals were even more
evident in *One World* [1943], US Senator Wendell Willkie's best-selling book, and
in *Prefaces to Peace* [1943], a book which Willkie edited and which featured a representative bouquet of idealist approaches. Here some of America's most influential public figures argued that the USA must take the lead in establishing a new
and peaceful world order. Their proposals were variations over the basic theme of
liberal internationalism. The authors advocated the establishment of institutions
of law and of moral education. The authors largely condoned the wartime efforts
of the Roosevelt administration to establish political and economic organizations
for postwar order.[20]

The views of Spykman, Fox and Willkie spanned the spectrum of theories,
from Realism to Idealism, during the final war years. They all agreed that the USA
ought to assume an ordering role in the international system after the war, but they
differed in the means they proposed. Willkie argued that institutions, education
and international law would sustain a new world order; Spykman argued that a new
order must be built along balance-of-power lines.

Willkie was an Idealist and expressed opinions that were popular during the war.
These opinions survived the war, but not for long. They flowered around the time
of the German defeat, and were soon extinguished by the postwar chills. The influential columnist Walter Lippmann was one of the early opponents of the Idealist
arguments. If the USA sought to establish a new international order after the war,
he wrote in *U.S. Foreign Policy* [1943], it would be an honourable project but it
might also be a very costly one.

The waxing of postwar Realism

Neither Spykman nor Lippmann managed to shake liberal internationalism as thoroughly as Stalin did with his speech at Moscow's Bolshoi Theatre on 9 February 1946. Stalin explained that the two destructive world wars, which had broken out within the last thirty years, were both 'the inevitable result of the development of world economic and political forces on the basis of present-day monopolistic capitalism'. Since capitalism survived the most recent world war, he continued, another war was inevitable. Therefore the USSR needed to begin preparations at once for a new war with the major capitalist countries of the West. Only by tripling the industrial output of the USSR 'can we be sure that our Motherland will be insured against all contingencies', Stalin concluded.

Western policy-makers reacted with shock and disbelief. George F. Kennan, however, found little new in Stalin's speech. He had long observed Soviet affairs and in his mind the speech reflected what Stalin had long believed and often said. So when the shocked policy-makers in Washington wondered what Stalin meant by his belligerent speech, Kennan described the Soviet political culture to them. It involved a mode of thinking that was alien and 'strange to our form of thought', he wrote in his 'long telegram' to the Department of State on 22 February 1946. Two weeks later, on 5 March 1946, Winston S. Churchill made a similar analysis in his 'iron-curtain speech' before President Truman and a large American audience.

These three events early in 1946 – Stalin's election speech, Kennan's 'long telegram' and Churchill's 'iron-curtain speech' – mark a slide into Cold War. They also mark the transition from an Idealist to a Realist mindset in Western postwar affairs. Influential commentators now began to argue that appeals to law, moral duties and educational efforts were useless. The one-world movement faded quickly – in fact, during the course of 1947, 'one-worlder' became a term of abuse used by the nationalist right to ridicule Idealist writers and liberal statesmen like Cordell Hull, Adlai Stevenson and others. In 1948, the former Vice President Henry Wallace published *Towards World Peace*, a final Idealist argument which criticized the Truman administration's harsh condemnation of the USSR. The USA ought to co-operate with the Soviets and further the common interest of order and peace, argued Wallace. His argument – which had been quite popular three or four years earlier – was now ridiculed and vilified.

Walter Lippmann, always good at adapting to the shifting mood of the times, had the previous year published an influential book which introduced the term 'cold war' to a larger audience. Lippmann (1947) noted that the relationship between the USA and the USSR had deteriorated into a global rivalry. In this situation, a revival of the woolly Utopianism of the 1920s represented a dangerous diversion from the need to contain Soviet expansionism (Lippmann 1947). George F. Kennan agreed, arguing that the new rivalry between the USA and the USSR made it impossible for the USA to return to a foreign policy based on naive legalities and isolationism. Churchill joined in, recalling the Munich Agreement and drawing a parallel between the failure of Western democracies to oppose Nazi Germany in the late 1930s and the Idealist reluctance to contain Soviet Russia after 1945. When

Western leaders accepted Hitler's predatory designs on Czechoslovakia, it had been a disgrace, said Churchill – who had been one of the few outspoken critics at the time. Munich demonstrated that a dictator who is set on conquest can be contained only by the threat of overwhelming military force, he continued. This 'lesson of Munich' was now widely invoked. In fact, it became a central tenet of the Cold War discourse.

A Morgenthauean afterthought

Informed by the advent of the Cold War, the scholarly field of International Relations embraced theories that confirmed Lord Palmerston's old maxim about how states have neither permanent friends nor permanent enemies, only permanent interests. International Relations scholars invoked the agreements reached in Munich in 1939 and at Yalta in 1945 to show that diplomacy was worthless lest they reflected more basic 'realities of power'.

One of the most forceful academic spokesmen of this argument in the wake of World War II was Hans Morgenthau. He rejected out of hand the peace perspectives of Wallace, Welles and Willkie. He read the memoirs of US diplomats like Cordell Hull and James Byrnes and despaired. He concluded that they, like Chamberlain and many other Anglo-American diplomats, suffered from a common disease which made them blind to the realities of the world and produced 'a fundamental misconception of what foreign policy is all about' (Morgenthau 1948a, p. 127). 'That blindness', he continued,

> manifests itself in Neville Chamberlain in the conviction that all men will act like businessmen from Birmingham and that international politics is in its essence a series of business transactions among peoples speaking different tongues. In Cordell Hull that blindness takes the form of an unquestioning faith in the simple virtues which all statesmen ought to practice and whose absence in some of them calls for moral indignation and exhortation. (1948a, p. 128)

Realism came to dominate the academic study of International Relations in the wake of World War II. One of the basic assumptions in this Realist approach was that the sovereign state is the main actor in international politics. Another assumption was that the primary goal of all such states was survival; that all states sought to accumulate power so that they could deter other states from attacking them and, if push came to shove, repel the attack. The Realists also argued that, in a world of sovereign states, no legislator or authority exists above the states; in an international system that is composed of sovereign states, each individual state has no one to rely on for safety and survival but itself.

These Realist theories are often captured by the three concepts of State, Survival and Self-help. However, a fourth concept needs to be added to complete the Realist outlook: Suspicion. For the Realist approach also rests on a suspicious or pessimistic view of human nature. This pessimistic anthropology informs Carr's (1942; 1945) bleak analysis. It sustains his view that history has left the liberal countries of the West behind; that nineteenth-century liberalism has failed and that the future belongs to more socially disciplined and economically planned social formations such as fascism and communism.

The introduction of a pessimistic anthropology also complicated the issue and split the Realist camp. One the one hand were thinkers like Carr who seemed to despair and to argue that liberal democracy is not well equipped to offer the world a new and stable order; fascism and, in particular, communism are, in fact better endowed, Carr (1945) seemed to argue. On the other were thinkers who defended the West and considered its values the best hope for an orderly and peaceful future. These thinkers – Realists like Niebuhr, Morgenthau, Kennan and Thompson – entertained a pessimistic anthropology but they nevertheless expressed hope for the future. Why?

It is tempting to suggest that they were supported by faith. In the case of Niebuhr, there is little doubt; he was a Protestant theologian and a founder of America's Christian Realism. The title of his 1945 book, *The Children of Light and the Children of Darkness* – indicates that political conflicts are more than clashes of material interests; that there is also a transcendental dimension to political strife. Kenneth W. Thompson admired Niebuhr, accepted his Christian Realism and referred to him as 'the father of us all'. Kennan is a more difficult case; there are no analytical arguments in his oeuvre which are obviously founded on religious axioms. Yet, towards the end of his life, in an effort to identify a coherent personal and political philosophy, Kennan (1993) wrote an elegant little book which provides a glimpse of the archaic philosophy of one of America's most influential Realists. In *Around the Cragged Hill* Kennan draws a self-portrait of an American Presbyterian gentleman. He makes a sharp distinction between body and soul and acknowledges the existence of a just and divine presence.

In Morgenthau's case, it is hard to find a clear religious element in his political philosophy. There is, however, a clear element of transcendent morality there. This is apparent in a review which Morgenthau wrote in 1948 of Edward Carr's most recent books. Although Morgenthau had admired Carr's *Twenty-Years' Crisis* and its diagnosis of Utopianism, he disagreed deeply with Carr's illiberal prognosis in *Conditions of Peace* and *Nationalism and After*. These are disillusioned books. They rested on a Machiavellian analysis of naked power, Morgenthau protested that they were totally devoid of moral principles.

> Consequently, Mr. Carr, philosophically so ill-equipped, has no transcendent point of view from which to survey the political scene and to appraise the phenomenon of power. Thus the political moralist transforms himself into a utopian of power. Whoever holds seeming superiority of power becomes of necessity the repository of superior morality as well. Power thus corrupts not only the actor on the political scene, but even the observer, unfortified by a transcendent standard of ethics. Mr Carr might have learned that lesson from the fate of the political romantics of whom the outstanding representatives are Adam Müller and Carl Schmitt. It is a dangerous thing to be a Machiavelli. It is a disastrous thing to be a Machiavelli without *virtù*. (Morgenthau 1948a, p. 134)

Notes

1   When World War I ended in 1918, all empires were exhausted. The end of the Great War was met with a huge sigh of relief. It was followed by a vast peace conference in Paris which sparked a general mood of optimism. Great hopes were attached to the establishment of the League of Nations. The League played an important role during the early 1920s in co-ordinating international rescue operations, economic recovery plans and political conflict resolutions. By 1930, however, Great-Power rivalries were constraining the activities of the League. Also, the mass-mobilizing ideologies of the new empires were adding a new, incendiary element to Europe's traditional power games. The rivalries between Russia, Germany, Britain and France were intensified by international ideologies where Soviet communism and German Nazism were pitted against one another as well as against the traditional liberal-democratic ideals of the Atlantic West.

2   *Mein Kampf* sold increasingly well as Hitler rose through the German political system. By 1934 it had sold 250,000 copies. During the next ten years about ten million copies had been sold and distributed. Royalties from the sales made Hitler a very wealthy man.

3   They brought to an end parliamentary government in Germany and set the nation on a new and active foreign-policy course which was in flagrant violation of the Versailles Treaty. They opened up for Hitler's systematic preparations for war and conquest – which in turn ignited a new world war.

4   The infamous 'Munich Agreement' was brokered by the Italian leader Benito Mussolini, who made Britain accept a German occupation of the Sudetenland. The Czechoslovak government was not invited to the talks, but submitted to compulsion and promised to abide by the agreement.

5   On the face of it, the Molotov–Ribbentrop Pact was a statement of friendship between two states which had previously been enemies – like the Rapallo Treaty (1925). However, the Molotov–Ribbentrop Pact had (just like the Rapallo Treaty before it) a secret annexe involving military collaboration between Germany and the USSR: the two foreign ministers agreed, on behalf of their dictatorial bosses, to invade Poland and divide the country between them. For Hitler the Pact was a way to secure *Lebensraum* in Poland and deal with the reactions from the west while minimizing the chances of war in the east. For Stalin, the Pact was a vehicle for buying time.

6   France was politically split, offered little resistance and the Germans gained control quickly. British troops, who had come to assist the French, were suddenly trapped in the small coastal city of Dunkirk. Thousands of British vessels crossed the Channel and managed to evacuate over three hundred thousand British and French soldiers at the end of May. On 10 June the French government signed an armistice with Germany.

7   The 'final solution to the Jewish question' – *die Endlösung* – was discussed at a conference in Wannsee, a suburb of Berlin, at the end of January 1942. The leader of the Reich's Main Security Office, Reinhard Heydrich, led the conference and presented a plan to round up all 'unwanted people', starve them, subject them to exhausting work and kill them in specially designed extermination camps. Minutes were taken at the Wannsee conference and circulated in the German ministries and the SS. By 'unwanted people' Heydrich would first and foremost mean Jews,

but Slavs, handicapped people, homosexuals, communists, Jehovah's Witnesses and others were also included in the term.

8   The United Nations alliance counted twenty-six member states in the end. On 1 January 1942, a joint declaration was issued by the members of the United Nations alliance, to the effect that all members of the alliance pledged adherence to the principles of the Atlantic Charter.

9   The UN took over from the League a fairly elaborate system of co-operative institutions in sectors as diverse as education, health, culture, trade and work life. The 'EcoSoc', which consists of fifty-four members elected by the General Assembly, was set up to co-ordinate and administer them all. The number of institutions has expanded over the years along functional lines. EcoSoc has come to administer the World Bank and the IMF (and, later, the World Trade Organization) as well as the International Labour Organization (ILO), the World Health Organization (WHO), the United Nations Educational, Scientific and Cultural Organization (UNESCO), the United Nations Children's Fund (UNICEF) and many other programmes, funds and special agencies.

10 The lack of solidarity was demonstrated most clearly in the early 1930s – e.g., in 1931 when Japan invaded Manchuria and in 1935 when Italy invaded Ethiopia.

11 The Americans invested some $7.6 billion in the World Bank, which could then offer long-term loans at commercial but reasonable rates to responsible governments in industrial countries who worked to rebuild their means of production after five years of war.

12 First, by contributing to the fund with a large dollar donation. Second, by tying the dollar to gold. And third by making the dollar convertible into other major currencies – thus also making those other currencies mutually convertible.

13 The GATT agreement was signed in October 1947, by eight states (out of an original twenty-three states who had participated): the USA, Britain, Canada, Australia, France, Belgium, the Netherlands and Luxembourg.

14 Both the USA and Europe were well supplied with coal. The USA was also self-supplied with oil, whereas Europe was not. All European countries were depended on imported oil – primarily from sources in Turkey, Syria and Iraq (Yergin 1991). Also, the USA was so well supplied with oil that it guaranteed to supply its European allies in case usual sources should fail.

15 Order was shaken by waves of revenge and ethnic cleansing months, even years, after the German surrender. The Germans were generally distrusted and regularly mistreated. Persons who had collaborated with German invaders were pursued and punished – in some countries even killed – by popular mobs and angry neighbours. Italy balanced on the brink of collapse. Greece erupted in civil war. Poland, Ukraine and the Baltic republics were rendered unsafe by new resistance movements which emerged to fight the Soviet occupiers (Lowe 2012).

16 The continued aggravation of the Cold War drove the three Western zones more tightly together, until they constituted the quasi-state of 'Trizonia'.

17 Truman was informed about the successful test. He in turn told Stalin that the USA had developed a new weapon. Stalin wished Truman good luck – it is reasonable to assume that Stalin was better informed about the Manhattan project than Truman was.

18 This extermination of class enemies, however, stopped during the war. It was not resumed afterwards.

19 Morgenthau was educated as a jurist and had published books in German and French on the importance of international law in international relations. He wrote a dissertation in Germany on the international administration of justice, and got it published in 1929 – his first book. He then wrote another dissertation in Geneva – with the great jurist Hans Kelsen as his adviser – on the reality of norms in international law.

20 Also, the World Federalist Movement (WFM) was established in 1947 by people concerned that the UNO cleaved too closely to the ideal of the sovereign nation-state – just like the League of Nations. The movement established its headquarters in New York and associate organizations all around the world.

10

Rivals, realists and Cold War

Dean Acheson entitled his memoirs *Present at the Creation*. Acheson argued that a new world order was created during the few, eventful years when he was US Secretary of State, between 1949 and 1953. His memoirs describe the consolidation of the bipolar, Cold War world – the world which is also presented in this chapter. The chapter aims to show how the Western Bloc, presided over by the USA, became pitted against the Eastern Bloc, dominated by the USSR. It records the formation and consolidation of the bipolar rivalry that dominated world affairs for the subsequent forty years or so.

The chapter has a narrow focus; it sketches the nature of the superpower rivalry from the late 1940s and through the 1950s and seeks to show how it affected inter-state relations and shaped international institutions. It presents the rivalry as a composite of ideological, military and geopolitical concerns. It discusses the inter-connections of these concerns, during the first few Cold War years when no regular diplomacy existed between the USA and the USSR.

The USSR was a closed country in those years. The USA had little reliable information about its inner workings. It is one of the claims of this chapter that Western attempts to explore the nature of the Soviet system, to identify its interests and to divine its foreign-policy goals affected the nature of International Relations scholarship; and that such efforts consolidated the approach of *Realpolitik* in the USA and shaped a new branch on the trunk of the scholarly International Relations tree: security studies.

The Cold War finds its form

In the early years of the Cold War the countries of Western Europe looked to the United States for aid and protection. The economies of Western Europe were driven into closer cooperation with the USA by the Marshall Plan. The deliveries of USA aid began in the summer of 1948 and were institutionalized in the Organization for European Economic Co-operation (OEEC).

The countries in Eastern Europe were occupied by the Soviet army and forced to co-operate closely with the USSR. These countries were not allowed to accept the

US aid offered through the Marshall Plan. Instead, Stalin announced an economic plan of his own, the Molotov Plan, with its own economic organization, the Council for Mutual Economic Assistance (CMEA or Comecon).

By the late 1940s, the USA had consolidated itself as the leading power in a Western Bloc – a system of sovereign states which were capitalist in their economies and liberal democratic in their political orientations. The USSR had consolidated itself as the leading power in the Eastern Bloc – a system of states which were tightly controlled by ruling communist parties. Stalin created the Communist Information Bureau (Cominform) in 1947 in order to better co-ordinate the activities of European communist parties to those of the Communist Party of the Soviet Union (the CPSU). The leaders in Moscow used the CMEA to consolidate their political power over the new-won satellites. Party discipline and economic interdependence united the Eastern Bloc, assisted by the Soviet armed forces and an elaborate secret-police system.

The superpower rivalry allowed the USA and the USSR to consolidate their authority and power over Western Europe and Eastern Europe, respectively. The Soviet leaders believed the capitalist states were expansionist and warlike. Soviet activities made Western leaders nervous. The leaders embraced US economic aid and accepted American leadership in political and economic matters. Also, they made self-conscious efforts to consolidate democratic institutions at home and to establish new co-operative institutions among themselves.

The Cold War had three major taproots. The first was ideological. Each superpower felt threatened by the ideology of the other.[1]

The second was geopolitical. The two superpowers competed for territorial influence and strategic positioning; they involved themselves in a race to control the territories of the world and influence their populations.[2]

A third taproot of the Cold War concerned the development of atomic weapons. When the USSR tested its own atomic bomb in December 1949, the two superpowers become engaged in a nuclear arms race. This was to remain a characteristic feature of the superpower rivalry for the duration of the Cold War. During the 1950s, the USA and the USSR built new and more powerful nuclear-based weapons systems. The two rivals had soon outpaced all other powers and entered a category of their own: they became 'Super-Powers', a denotation that distinguished them from the mere 'Great Powers' of the past (Fox 1944). They monitored each other's nuclear capabilities and watched each other's strategic moves. They behaved like 'two scorpions in a bottle', Robert Oppenheimer remarked. It was an apt metaphor for the way in which two deadly antagonists kept each other under control under the threat of mutual destruction.

Ideological conflict
An ideology is a description of how the world works. It also offers a vision of what a better world would look like and an account of how it is possible to move from the flawed world that exists today into the peaceful and harmonious world that ought to be created tomorrow.

The US ideology has its conceptual roots in social contract philosophy of orthodox liberal type, as expressed by thinkers like John Locke and Jeremy Bentham; it sees democratic states in free interaction as the key precondition for a peaceful world order. The Soviet ideology was rooted in the theories of Marx and Lenin; it saw the eradication of private property and the capitalist classes as a precondition for a peaceful world order.

The ideological roots of the Cold War go back to World War I – to the Russian Revolution which replaced the Tsarist monarchy with a communist regime and to the rivalry after Versailles between Lenin and Wilson. At that time, however, this rivalry did not find any institutional expression in a military contest of serious geopolitical competition. The basic ideologies, however, have remained remarkably constant over time.

Stalin perceived the world in term of a struggle among classes. This struggle manifested itself as an irreconcilable contest between socialism and capitalism. During the 1930s he had presented his theory in pamphlets and speeches. He had soft-pedalled his communist analyses during World War II. But he had not altered his basic understanding of world affairs. He had reclaimed his old analysis when the war was over. And in February 1946 he had made a speech so orthodox in its analysis that it had sent shock waves across the world. The world is divided into two camps, Stalin had explained: a capitalist camp that was expansionist and warlike and a socialist camp that was just and peace-loving. America, Britain and Germany all belonged to the former camp; the USSR belonged to the latter. The countries of the capitalist camp were encircling the USSR. Sooner or later they would attack. The socialist camp must build up its military arsenals so that it can be prepared to meet the attack, win the war and finish capitalism once and for all.

Stalin followed up the speech by upgrading research and development into rockets and atomic bombs and by a campaign to 'purify Soviet cultural life' by removing foreign impulses. He put Andrei Zhdanov in charge of this campaign. And when Stalin established Cominform in the early autumn of 1947, he once more relied on Zhdanov, appointing him to lead the new international organization. At the opening congress of Cominform in September, Zhdanov made a keynote speech in which he explained that the world was sharply divided into two irrecon-cilable camps: On the one hand the 'imperialist camp' headed by the USA; on the other the 'democratic' and peaceful camp, headed by the USSR.

Zhdanov essentially repeated the argument that Stalin had revived over a year earlier. Zhdanov expressed an updated version of the official Soviet view. It was a response to the speeches made by Winston Churchill in March 1946 and by Presi-dent Truman in March 1947. It confirmed the two-camp view voiced by Stalin, Churchill and Truman before him.[3]

The two-camp vision of the world entered the political imagination of statesmen, scholars and the public opinion at large during 1946 and 1947. In Western Europe, the uncompromising formulations of the Soviets, the establishment of the CMEA and the Cominform created a perception of an expanding Soviet camp. West European leaders recalled interwar experiences and not only feared a new and expanding totalitarianism; they also recalled how the interwar years were troubled by a revanchist Germany and an isolationist United States and they feared that history would repeat itself. In 1949, however, the Americans assuaged the European fears by establishing the North Atlantic Treaty Organization (NATO). It was a military alliance which provided a double deterrent against both the USSR and Germany. This was reflected in a careless remark that Lord Ismay made when he was Secretary General of NATO in 1952. The purpose of NATO, he quipped, was to keep the Russians out, the Americans in and the Germans down.

One threat, however, was not addressed by military alliances: the internal threat of espionage and of communist preparations for a coup.[4] The coup in Czechoslovakia, the Berlin crisis and the Korean War fuelled a deep sense of insecurity in the West. Many Western governments organized vast surveillance systems to keep an eye on radical individuals (Barnes 1981a, b). The USA was gripped by a Cold War fear that approached hysteria – and which was most memorably reflected in witch-hunts for communists at the hand of Senator Joseph McCarthy (Barnes 1981a, b; Weiner 2007).[5]

Geopolitical rivalries

The basic foreign-policy goal of the USSR was to maintain its great, new empire. Stalin directed his main focus towards the West; especially towards the vast plains of central and eastern Europe. He worked to convert the many countries of the region to a Soviet sphere of influence, which might serve as a buffer in case of new war against the powers of the West. For these were capitalist and, by Stalin's reckoning, expansionist powers. They would inevitably seek to expand eastwards and enter into conflict and war with the Soviet Union.

Having consolidated his hold over Eastern Europe, Stalin's greatest concern was the fate of Germany. The victors of the war had weakened Germany by dividing it into four zones of occupation. The Soviets imposed a pliable puppet government upon their occupation zone. Also, they weakened their zone by removing capital from it, transporting the capital deep into the USSR and rebuilding Soviet industries there. The three Western powers – the USA, Britain and France – did the opposite. They strengthened their occupation zones, partly by co-ordinating and integrating their zones and partly by injecting capital to stimulate the growth of a common capitalist economy – an activity Stalin observed with deep suspicion.

The basic policy of the USA was to contain communism in Europe. The best way to do this was to ensure that the countries there were prosperous. To ensure this, the Americans designed the Marshall Plan – a vast economic aid project to rebuild Western Europe. The US Congress supported the plan as it was thought to also boost America's own prosperity. The democracies of the world were embedded in a web of interdependent transactions. The welfare of the United States depended on prosperous societies abroad. An affluent Europe would provide markets for US products and investment opportunities for US capital. The Marshall Aid programme increased Stalin's suspicion of the West and his old fears of a revived and strong Germany.

In June 1948, the USA, Britain and France introduced a currency reform to their German occupation zones. The Soviet Union responded by totally closing off its own occupation zone in eastern Germany. As a result, all surface communications between the Western occupation zones and Berlin, which was situated inside the Soviet zone, were severed. Stalin apparently believed that his blockade would force the Western powers to abandon the currency reform – and possibly abandon Berlin itself. The USA and its allies instead responded with a massive airlift. A non-stop stream of US and British cargo planes supplied the people of Berlin with foodstuffs, building materials, gasoline, coal and other basic necessities. It denied the Soviet control over Berlin. It was a powerful demonstration of the capabilities of the West – the airlift counted nearly 280,000 flights; at the height of the airlift, an Allied plane landed in Berlin every thirty seconds. Also, the airlift boosted Western morale and dealt the USSR a humiliating propaganda defeat.

In May 1949, Stalin lifted the blockade of Berlin. By that time Germany was irreconcilably divided into an eastern and a western half. The three Western powers had integrated their occupation zones tightly – partly to secure the zones, partly to stimulate the German economy. Eventually, they merged their three zones into the quasi-state of 'Trizonia'. Stalin viewed this merger as an effort to reunify Germany and to strengthen the capitalist West. He resented it deeply. For in his experience a strong and unified Germany would bring with it rearmament and revanchism.

In April 1949 the USA and a dozen Western countries established a common defence alliance, the North Atlantic Treaty Organization (NATO).[6] Stalin grew even more resentful when 'Trizonia' was transformed into a self-governing country: the West German Federal Republic (Bundesrepublik Deutschland or BRD).[7]

At that point events in Asia turned Stalin's attention to the East. Mao Zedong took power in China in the fall of 1949. Stalin greeted the event without enthusiasm. Mao travelled to Moscow; he stayed for several months, trying to persuade the Soviets to assist his revolution and to co-ordinate the foreign policies of the two communist countries.

Stalin could not make up his mind whether he should treat Mao as a colleague or a client. During the spring and summer of 1950 Stalin and Mao encountered their first serious foreign-policy test when the North Korean leader Kim Il-Sung attacked South Korea in an effort to unify the Korean peninsula under a communist government. Stalin and Mao had cleared the invasion with Kim. The communist leaders were prepared for loud Western protests against the invasion, but they were convinced that the Western powers would not intervene.

This was a major miscalculation. US President Truman immediately drew the parallel with Hitler's aggressions in the 1930s. He brought Kim Il-Sung's attack before the UN as a case of aggression and quickly organized a military response as a collective-security UN operation. The operation stopped the attack. During the autumn and winter of 1950 the US-led forces also drove the North Korean attackers far back into North Korean territory – so far that China sent two hundred thousand Chinese troops into North Korea to stop the UN troops and drive them back across the old north–south boundary.

The Korean War brought the superpower rivalry to Asia and brought the Cold War to a new phase. It intensified the US containment policy. It spurred the US Secretary of State John Foster Dulles to give NATO a central command structure, to integrate new members into the NATO alliance to and begin negotiations to create other defence alliances in other parts of the world. He succeeded in making Greece and Turkey new NATO members (in 1952). But when he proposed membership for West Germany, many nations balked at the idea. France and Britain reacted against it and speeded up plans for a European Defence Community (EDC). The proposal triggered one of Stalin's major foreign-policy fears. He launched a propaganda campaign against 'German rearmament' and instructed communist parties all over the West to engage actively in peace work – especially to support campaigns to abolish nuclear weapons.

In Europe the outbreak of the Korean War heightened confusion and fear at first. Then it stimulated unprecedented initiatives of co-operation and solidarity – enthusiastically supported by the USA and quite the opposite of what Stalin had expected with his 'German armament campaign'. In 1951 France, West Germany, Italy, Belgium, the Netherlands and Luxembourg signed the Treaty of Paris. This treaty established the European Coal and Steel Community (ECSC), the first transnational institution in Europe and a first move towards tighter European integration.

In Asia, the USA intensified its efforts to contain communist influence. The USA began to rebuild and rearm Japan. Also, it began to organize new alliance systems in the Pacific and in South East Asia.[8]

Superpower arms race
Not only did the Korean War intensify the geopolitical competition of the superpowers, it also stimulated their arms race – or, more precisely put, it fuelled their race of technology-based prestige. For nuclear weapons, with their delivery vehicles and their navigation and tracking systems required advanced capabilities in science and technology. Such capabilities were symbols of sophistication and high civilization and gave prestige in themselves.

In 1950 the USA and the USRR both intensified their efforts to develop a powerful hydrogen bomb and to build better bombers and rockets. This found its expression in a Soviet–American space race which was justified in the name of science. Both superpowers developed new rockets,[9] whose launchings were presented as feats of science. Space flights were compared to the voyages of great discoverers like Columbus and Vasco da Gama. They caught the popular imagination everywhere. In the West they were fed by a growing entertainment industry that helped coat the superpower space race with a legitimizing varnish of technological triumphalism and national prestige.

The USA tested its first hydrogen bomb in 1952. The USSR followed three years later. In 1957 the USSR scored a triumph when it launched a rocket that placed a small satellite, Sputnik, in orbit around the earth. The Soviet triumph caught Western observers by surprise, and made US leaders acknowledge that they had underestimated the capabilities of the Soviet arms industry. Some observers argued that the Soviets had not merely caught up with the US weapons technology; they were in fact leading the space race. It was argued that a 'missile gap' was quickly developing between the two superpowers and that the USA was falling behind.

This 'missile gap' was a myth. It was fed by US suspicions and fears and by a general ignorance about the USSR caused by the closed nature of the Soviet Union and the lack of accurate information about Soviet politics and industry. In fact, the USA had more rockets, more bombs and more accurate navigations systems than the USSR. Nevertheless, the 'Sputnik-shock' triggered a ferocious debate in the USA and caused, among other things, the Truman administration to refurbish the curriculum for natural-science education in US schools. Also, it caused the administration to greatly speed up the US rocket programme. This lifted the superpower arms race on to a wholly new level. In 1960 both superpowers began to deploy strategic missiles on submarines which could travel the oceans of the world unnoticed with their deadly cargo.

Colonial conflicts and proxy wars

The end of World War II did not mean the emergence of world peace. The transition from war to peace took time. The Europeans were long preoccupied with repairing the enormous destructions caused by the war – not only by reconstructing buildings and roads but also by persecuting and punishing Nazi collaborators. In southern Europe these preoccupations were complicated by political instability; in Eastern Europe by communist bids for power. Greece erupted in civil war; Poland, Ukraine and the Baltic republics were rendered unsafe by anti-communist resistance movements (Lowe 2012).

This was the second time in thirty years that a vast war had destroyed Europe, tarnished its prestige and weakened its role in world affairs. It reduced Europe's capabilities and power. The reduction was noticed in Asia and Africa where it undermined Europe's prestige. Colonial subjects demanded self-rule and independence. And such demands were supported by the superpowers, both of whom had a strong anti-colonial orientation. The demands were also supported by the majority in the United Nations' General Assembly.

Demands for independence were expressed by several non-white leaders who argued that the Great Powers of the West had done little for their colonies in the past. The Western powers had exploited their colonies for centuries. Also, they had pulled the colonies into their own huge wars. But these wars had also weakened the empires; especially in Asia. Here leaders like Ho Chi Minh and Mao Zedong argued that they had nothing to gain from the reestablishment of the old international system. They argued that the poor countries of the world would be better off if they broke out of the colonial empires of the West, declared sovereignty and took charge of their own fate.

Japan had invaded European colonies in Asia at the beginning of World War II and taken control over them. When the Japanese surrendered in August 1945 and retreated from these colonial areas, pro-independence sentiments sprang up in many places. The colonial powers, however, did not want to give up their overseas empires. They struggled to retain them, but found this to be a hard and costly proposition. Britain had been forced to grant India independence in 1947; and France quickly allowed some of its colonial enclaves in the region to be incorporated into the newly independent nation.

The British retreated from Palestine – partly they pulled out because of wartime promises,[10] partly they were pushed out by militant Zionists who used all means to establish a sovereign Jewish state. The Zionist success, in May 1948, triggered a war between the new state of Israel on the one side, and Egypt, Syria, Lebanon, Iraq and Transjordan on the other.

France refused to give up its old colonies in Indochina; when Japan retreated in 1945, France sought to regain Vietnam and Cambodia. Portugal was also determined to keep its colonies. Similarly, the Dutch refused to surrender their Indonesian possessions to nationalist leaders like Sukarno and Mohammad Hatta, who had unilaterally declared independence in 1945. France, Portugal and the Netherlands intervened militarily to retain their colonies. They succeeded in reoccupying most of the colonial territory but could not regain full political control. They were opposed by insurgents who fought with guerrilla tactics.

The Dutch gave up in 1949 and recognized Indonesian independence. The Portuguese, by contrast, continued to fight their colonial wars through the 1940s and 1950s – for instance in the Indian enclaves of Dadra and Nagar. The French did not give up Indochina; they poured a steadily increasing number of soldiers into a war against irregular forces in Vietnam; at the same time, the French were facing resistance in Thailand, Madagascar and Algeria as well.

The British faced insurgencies in Malaya. In 1948 British troops intervened to fight the communist-inspired Malayan National Liberation Army (MNLA). The British also faced independence movements in other colonies; most seriously in Kenya, where an increase in militant nationalism caused them to declare a state of emergency in 1952 and to begin a long military engagement against the Mau-Mau rebels of the Kikuyu tribe.

The USA continued its effort to contain radical influence in world affairs by covert and overt means – a new urgency was added to the effort by the Chinese Revolution (1949) and the Korean War (1950). In 1950 the Americans started to give economic and military support to the Philippine government who fought Maoist rebels in the Hukbalahap movement. In 1953, the Central Intelligence Agency (CIA) engineered a coup against the democratically elected Prime Minister Mohammed Mosaddeq of Iran, and replaced him with the autocratic Shah Reza Pahlavi. The following year, the USA ousted the popularly elected President Jacobo Árbenz from power in Guatemala, and replaced him with a military junta.[11]

Also, the Americans gave increasing support the colonial wars of their European allies. They supported British anti-insurgency efforts against radical rebels in Malaya and Kenya and sponsored the French war against Ho Chi Minh's government in North Vietnam and the communist-supported rebels in South Vietnam.

When France negotiated a quick peace settlement with North Vietnam in 1954 and pulled its forces out of Indochina, the US government refused to accept the terms of the peace treaty. It opted instead to continue the war against Vietnamese communists on its own (US Senate 1984a, b).

Variations on a Realist theme

The end of World War II was followed by a new world order. Europe was in peace; however, it was a tense and precarious peace in the shadow of the superpower rivalry. Outside of the West and the communist East, there existed a third and varied region which was aligned with neither the capitalist nor the communist bloc. It was a region of largely poor countries, which had been largely ignored by both the West and the East, but which would attain more significance as it was pulled into the geopolitical rivalry of the superpowers. During the early 1950s, this non-aligned region quickly became known as 'the Third World'.[12]

Under the impact of the superpower rivalry and Third World conflicts, discussions of international politics lost much of the Idealist orientation that had marked the immediate postwar period. As the world war was drawing to a close in early 1945, scholars and statesmen were discussing the legal and educational prerequisites for a lasting peace. However, as the wartime alliance dissolved, Idealist discussions of a lasting peace gave way to debates on security and national interest. In the West, these discussions were framed in the general terms of the two old contending approaches of Idealism and Realism – with Realism quickly emerging as the dominant approach. In Eastern Europe and the USSR public discussions of politics ceased altogether. Stalin tightened his control of the Soviet federation, integrated the six occupied countries of Eastern Europe into a totalitarian Bloc and imposed a single, tight Marxist–Leninist perspective on his entire empire.

East-Bloc story

The official Soviet approach to all politics was laid down by Stalin and the Communist Party. Its theoretical focus was primarily based on an economic analysis power and class relations. International politics were largely construed as a world-encompassing class struggle, where the capitalist system of the West was pitted against the new, socialist system of the USSR.

Stalin had not flaunted this argument during the World War, but instead emphasized the common struggle against fascism. However, as soon as Germany had surrendered and the war ended, Stalin brought Marxism–Leninism back and made it the general framework for all Soviet social-science discussions. He tightened his ideological grip. He closed the USSR off from the rest of the world. He gave Andrei Zhdanov the task of formulating a communist doctrine, to impose it upon his realm and to 'purify Soviet life'. The result was the so-called *Zhdanovschina*, a campaign which resurrected the orthodox Marxism–Leninism of the mid-1930s and purged all views that were inconsistent with it. Zhdanov's version of world events was imposed upon the Soviet federation. It was also communicated to the countries in Eastern Europe through the Cominform and the Communist Parties.

The Eastern Bloc, then, had an official political view of world events. Did this view amount to a theory? The answer depends on what one means by 'theory'. What is clear, however, is that the view did not amount to a scientific theory. Science cannot exist under conditions where the axioms of social argument are defined by totalitarian dictate, as they were in Stalin's empire. The USSR had no real public sphere, no free political debate and no independent theorizing. The political discussions that took place in the totalitarian East were not like those which took place in the pluralist West; they were more akin to discussions of medieval theology. No social science could exist under such conditions. The social theories of Soviet communism were stale and disingenuous.

The discussions that were conducted throughout the Eastern Bloc in these times were not debates as much as dictates from above. Stalin formulated the basic political ideas. Andrei Zhdanov developed the finer details and selected illustrating examples. All served the interest of political power. All furthered the demands of political control. In terms of political theory, the Eastern Bloc was a dry desert.

West-Bloc story

In the Western world, political discussions were open and public. Although here, too, the postwar years were marked by a tightening of views. The old discussion of the legal, organizational and educational prerequisites for a lasting peace (Eagleton and Wilcox 1945) faded as soon as the war was over. Fascist theories were outlawed in many countries, and thus legally excluded from the public sphere. Also, communist discussions were often restricted, as governments in many Western countries had systems of surveillance to observe and map the activities of communist parties and radical individuals; they would write reports for domestic security analysts – and they might share them with the American CIA (Barnes 1981a, b; Weiner 2007). Such activities tended to constrain and discipline academic debates.

Also, many Western scholars recalled the Idealism which emerged on the heels of World War I and feared that the study of world affairs might again become mired in naive and dangerous utopianism. As the wartime alliance unravelled, good will gave way to suspicion. Common cause yielded to concerns of national interest. Realism quickly emerged as the dominant approach to International Relations. The scientific study of international politics, it was commonly argued, must build not on good intentions but on 'ascertainable facts' (Dunn 1949, p. 67).

At the onset of the Cold War, Russian studies emerged as a distinct academic subject in the West. One reason was that the USSR was a closed country while the West had a growing need to collect reliable knowledge about Soviet affairs. The new subject was an interdisciplinary field, combining history and language studies with social-science skills. The RAND Corporation began to study Soviet affairs in 1947. Harvard University opened a Russian Research Center in 1948. Pioneering scholars from these centres influenced the way American leaders perceived the Soviet Union during the early years of the Cold War.

One influential Soviet scholar was Nathan Leites at RAND. He developed a method for understanding Soviet leaders – the so-called operational-code analysis.[13] Another early contributor was Merle Feinsod at the Harvard's Russian Research Center. His book on *How Russia Is Ruled* defined the field of Soviet studies and was standard reading in many American International Relations courses for over twenty-five years.[14] However, no other scholar had the influence of George F. Kennan. While *chargé d'affaires* at the US embassy in Moscow, Kennan had written a long telegram and analysed Soviet behaviour. He had subsequently rewritten his analysis and published it in the July 1947 issue of *Foreign Affairs*. 'The Sources of Soviet Conduct' was published anonymously and signed by 'X'. The article made a Realist analysis of Soviet policy. The mysterious Mr 'X' warned against overemphasizing ideology as a driving force in Soviet affairs. Instead, he directed attention to other driving forces, such as the quest for power and security. In order to understand Soviet foreign policy it is important to appreciate the interests of the leading Soviet elite as well as the character of the Russian nation and the historical and cultural factors which have shaped those interests and character.

American International Relations

The United States emerged as a dominant power and the leader of a Western alliance of states in the wake of the World War. US scholars increasingly influenced the academic study of International Relations. They discussed world affairs in terms of the old division between a Realist and an Idealist approach. On the face of it, this juxtaposition continued the scholarly discussion of the late interwar years. However, a different tenor was introduced after World War II. Whereas prewar scholars like Mackinder (1919) and Carr (2001 [1939]) had presented the relationship between Realism and Idealism as dialectical and dynamic, postwar authors often saw the two as stark oppositions. American scholars in particular tended to draw a clear line between the two. They often treated Idealism as a straw figure which they could easily discredit and then portray the Realist alternative as mature wisdom.

Traditional Realists were unhappy with this development. Niebuhr, for example, saw the emergence of the sharper dichotomy as a dangerous vulgarization. He warned against what he saw as the emergence of dangerous foreign-policy blinders. The artificial distinction between Realism and Idealism confronts us 'with two horns of a dilemma and beg us to choose between them', he argued. For the greater majority the choice would be easy, he continued, for the Idealist position had become impossible to defend. This was evinced for instance by the rapid decline of Henry Wallace and his Progressive Party. People let go of the Idealist horn because they 'could not keep a grip on it', wrote Niebuhr (1950b, p. 338).

> Our realists are convinced that neither world government nor a pragmatic under-
> standing with the Russians is an attainable goal. They are therefore tempted to
> grasp the second horn of the dilemma. They accept the fact of an inevitable war.
> From the idea of an inevitable war it is only a short logical step to the concept of
> a preventive war. For if we must inevitably fight the Russians, why should we not
> have the right to choose the most opportune time for joining the issue? (1950a)

John H. Herz agreed with Niebuhr. In *Political Realism and Political Idealism* [1951] he juxtaposed Realism and Idealism and carried out an even-handed and dialectical discussion of the two approaches. The selfish pursuit of egotistical interests is irresponsible in the age of nuclear weapons, Herz argued. It is necessary to temper Realism with considerations of responsible social action, he continued. Herz arrived at a synthetic approach in the end and called it 'realist liberalism'.

When Hans Morgenthau in 1954 published a new edition of his best-selling *Politics among Nations*, he explicitly favoured Realism. He added a new introductory chapter, entitled 'Six Principles of Realism'. It defined Realism and presented *Politics among Nations* as a Realist text. First, Morgenthau argued, Realism is based on the same principle that underlies all modern social science, namely, that the world is governed by objective laws. Second, Morgenthau continued, Realism pays little attention to what politicians say about their own motives and avoids speculation about the motives and ideologies of statesmen. Instead, Realism focuses on the interest of states and defines interest in terms of power.

'Interest', however, is a slippery term. A 'national interest' cannot be fixed once and for all. Beliefs, ideologies, motives and policy goals differ between statesmen, political cultures and historical periods. Neither of them will provide a robust basis for a general theory of international politics. Human nature, by contrast, is constant, Morgenthau claimed. This assumption lies at the core of Morgenthau's third principle of Realism: that all statesmen at all times are concerned with securing their own position and that of their state. All states can be assumed to be rational actors who seek to minimize risks and maximize benefits.

Morgenthau's first three principles of Realism were concerned with the object of Realist analysis; with the behaviour of states. The final three principles were concerned with the observing subject – with the Realist scholar – and warned against the seductive force of universal principles. Thus, the fourth principle cautioned against the tension between moral principles and the requirements of successful political action. The fifth explained that moral principles are always anchored in particular societies and that they must be seen as products of a particular time and place. From this Morgenthau inferred his sixth and final principle of Realism: namely, that any Realist must be attuned to the moral principles involved in political behaviour. But they must also acknowledge that such principles are products of concrete circumstances of time and place. Consequently, these principles can never be applied to the actions of states in their abstract universal formulation; and they can never be assumed to coincide with the interest of their country of origin. Morgenthau put this point sharply: the mark of the Realist scholar is the refusal to identify the moral aspirations of a particular nation with the moral laws that govern the universe. Morgenthau warned against the seductive powers of political rhetoric. Language is power, Morgenthau seemed to say. Do not consider only what statesmen say, he warned; observe also what they do.

The chapter on the 'Six Principles of Realism' marked a difference between the first and the second edition of *Politics among Nations*. First, because the chapter framed the second edition by explicitly – and for the first time – identifying the book as a Realist text. Second, because he no longer included a critical discussion of the American social science tradition – a discussion which was so palpable in the first edition of *Politics among Nations* (and which had been so obviously present in his *Scientific Man vs. Power Politics*). Instead, the second edition simply asserted that the world works according to objective laws, and claims that the purpose of scholarly International Relations is to discover those laws.

The basic message of the second edition of *Politics among Nations* remained the same as that of the first.[15] But the message was now framed differently. Also, the second edition of the book met with more substantial criticism than the first. It seemed that an evolution in scholarly self-awareness had occurred in American International Relations during the few years that separated Morgenthau's two editions. Reviewers of the second edition noted that Morgenthau's basic definitions were vague and some of his basic assumptions abstract and philosophical. They noted that the concept of 'power' was unclear. They saw the concept of 'interest' as doubly unclear – first, because it could not really be determined once and for all and, second, because it was defined in terms of (the already unclear) concept of power. They also noted that Morgenthau's entire argument hinged on a particular vision of human nature – that is, on a contested philosophical claim rather than on a firm, more scientifically robust axiom.

Morgenthau defended his views. He reiterated that 'power' is a complex phenomenon and, essentially mental in nature. He presented power as a product of both material and spiritual factors – mitigated by perception, 'moral conviction' and 'will'. He assured that a balance of power is never an automatic outcome of military force alone. It is not a function of material capabilities alone, but also of actors' perceptions of those capabilities. A balance of power is more than a simple balance of forces. In order for the international balance of power to work properly, it must be sustained by an underlying perceptual consensus – or 'silent compact' (Morgenthau 1978, p. 226).

However, Morgenthau's arguments were often brushed aside by a new generation of analysts. They disagreed with his views of power as essentially a psychological relationship between human beings; they preferred to see power in terms of material capabilities – especially military might. Whereas Morgenthau saw the balance of power as a complex product of statesmen's perceptions and diplomatic co-operation, they saw the balance of power as a simple equilibrium of force. Under their impact, the old classical Realism was pushed on the defensive. The new analysts criticized the historical similes and the philosophical arguments of the old realists. They insisted on sharper definitions and on tighter and more logical analyses. They invoked systemic reasoning. They defined their systems in terms of co-related variables and used economic models to probe the interrelations.

John Herz had adumbrated such a systems approach in his *Political Realism and Political Idealism* [1951]. He had begun with the Realist claim that states are ultimately dependent on themselves and the perceptions of their statesmen for survival. But he had then added that 'reality' was not an easily observable entity, and that statesmen's perceptions are always affected by factors of human psychology.

Statesmen who fear for the security of their state (let's call it A), will tend to strengthen their military defences. The statesmen in question may see this as a purely defensive measure. However, the leaders of a neighbouring state (let's call it B), may nevertheless perceive the act as threatening – even despite (or perhaps precisely because of) proclamations to the contrary. The leaders of B know that weapons systems that are procured for defensive purposes may also be used offensively. Fearful that their own security is threatened, they may decide to strengthen their own military capabilities. The statesmen in A may in turn perceive B's move as legitimizing their original concerns – and also to consider whether they need to strengthen their defences further. This relationship, where states A and B both seek to enhance their own security, will easily produce an arms race that threatens the security of both. The result is a spiral of insecurity, or what Herz called a 'security dilemma'.

The significance of Herz's contribution, does not lie exclusively in his description of the dilemma – other scholars had pointed it out before.[16] Rather, the larger significance was that Herz portrayed the dilemma as a structural attribute of the anarchic system of sovereign states. The 'security dilemma', wrote Herz (1950, p. 157) is a 'structural notion in which the self-help attempts of states to look after their security needs tend, regardless of intention, to lead to rising insecurity for others as each interprets its own measures as defensive and measures of others as potentially threatening'. Another contribution of Herz's was the insight it is not possible to escape this dilemma from within the confines of the Realist approach. That in order to break out of the spiral of insecurity it is necessary to complement the Realist approach with a reasonable amount of socially responsible arguments culled from Idealist theory.

From Realism to security studies

There is in Herz's simple abstraction an indication of a new, technocratic brand of Realism which was emerging among analysts and policy-makers in the wake of World War II. Its adherents would cleave to the notions that states were the dominant actors of the international system and that state behaviour was driven by interests and power. However, they would define power in more material and concrete terms. Also, they would put little store in lessons from history. They would tend to argue that the introduction of nuclear weapons had launched a new age with an entirely new kind of warfare. Lessons from history could contribute little to the strategic constellation of the nuclear world (Brodie 1946).

One of the main roots of the new technocratic approach lay in the activities of the US strategic bombing surveys conducted during World War II. These surveys were based on photographic analysis of wartime bombing raids – on measurement of damages done and numerical assessment of effects. The survey results were in turn used to plan new raids. Such plans for massive campaigns of destructive bombing during the hot war provided a basis for discussions of devastating attacks by nuclear weapons during the Cold War.

George F. Kennan had little taste for these calculated procedures. He was historically and philosophically inclined. He read Gibbon's account of the decline and fall of the Roman Empire to improve his understanding of Soviet and American behaviour. He distrusted the new behavioural approaches (Gaddis 2011, p. 410). When he resigned as director of the Policy Planning Staff for the US State Department at the end of 1949, he was replaced by Paul Nitze, who had been an analyst for the US strategic bomber surveys during World War II. Nitze used economic models and was much at home with the pragmatic arguments of the administrator (Talbott 1988). He did not read ancient history to improve his understanding of world affairs but studied production figures for wheat and steel.

In 1949, after the Soviet nuclear tests and the Chinese revolution, the Policy Planning Staff began work on a new strategic study. It was completed the following spring under Nitze's leadership and presented as a policy directive to the US National Security Council (NSC) in April 1950. This document, simply named *NSC-68*, began with a short discussion of what it was that the USA needed to defend. Invoking the Declaration of Independence and the US Constitution, the *NSC-68* claimed that the USA must defend individual liberty, free institutions, representative government and the federal structure – in short the American way of life. The study then identified the threat: Soviet communism, a global movement directed from Moscow and set on world domination. In order to fend off the Soviet threat, the *NSC-68* recommended a massive military buildup designed to create a favourable balance of forces between the USA and the USSR. Its purpose would be to deter the USSR from making aggressive initiatives. Also, the *NSC-68* recommended the USA to buy time and allow for changes to take place in the Soviet system through means other than all-out war.

NSC-68 did not recommend that the USA should engage the USSR in diplomatic negotiations. Rather, it mandated three other courses of action. First, to develop a hydrogen bomb in order to counter the Soviet nuclear threat. Second, to build up the conventional forces of both the United States and its allies. Third, to forge strong alliances worldwide under US leadership. The directive recognized that these recommendations would be very expensive, but concluded that they were necessary in order to defend the USA against the Soviet threat. The US government could easily pay for all by increasing the federal tax rate, it concluded.

President Truman did not like the *NSC-68*. He did not like its gloomy scenario and he recoiled before the prospect of a big defence-driven tax increase. The *NSC-68* triggered an intense, internal debate which rippled through the US national security establishment in the spring of 1950. In June discussion was cut short when North Korea attacked South Korea as a bolt from the blue. President Truman acted quickly. Within a week he had not only dispatched US troops to Korea, he had also approved *NSC-68*, lock, stock and barrel. As Dean Acheson (1969, p. 420) recalled it, with one stroke Korea 'removed the recommendations of *NSC-68* from the realm of theory and made them immediate budget issues'.

The reforms were expensive – as Nitze had said. The cost is indicated by Table 10.1. It reveals a jump in the US defence expenditures from about $13 billion before the outbreak of the Korean War to over $40 billion after its outbreak.

Table 10.1 US national security expenditures, 1945–55 ($ billion)

Fiscal year	Defence expenditures	% of govt expenditures allocated to defense	GNP allocated to defence	% of GNP
1945	81.6	85.7	211.9	38.5
1946	44.7	72.4	208.5	21.4
1947	13.1	35.5	231.3	5.7
1948	13.0	35.6	257.6	5.0
1949	13.1	32.2	256.5	5.1
1950	13.1	30.4	284.8	4.6
1951	22.5	49.1	328.4	6.9
1952	44.4	64.7	345.5	12.7
1953	50.4	65.6	364.6	13.8
1954	46.6	65.7	364.8	12.8
1955	40.2	58.7	398.0	10.1

Source: US Bureau of the Census (1975, pp. 224, 1116)

In the wake of the Korean War, the USA accelerated its programme to develop a hydrogen bomb and make it small enough to fit into the nose cone of an intercontinental ballistic missile (ICBM). The USA also began to build up its own conventional forces to assist its allies in building up theirs. Finally, the US Secretary of State, John Foster Dulles, began to negotiate with governments all over the world to establish new pacts and alliances. During the early 1950s, the USA would organize alliances like the Pacific ANZUS and the East Asian SEATO – involving some forty different states and protecting US interests in several different regions.

During the 1950s, the Americans increased their nuclear capabilities at a rapid rate. They built the offensive Thor and the Jupiter rockets, which were introduced in 1958. The bigger Atlas and Titan models followed in 1959. The Americans also developed big defensive systems. One of them consisted of a chain of radar stations stretched all along North America's Arctic border from east to west. A combination of advanced communication technology, logistical planning and successful negotiations with the Canadians led to the building of the DEW-line during the late 1950s. Its purpose was to detect Soviet planes and rockets before they reached American air space and shoot them down before they caused a 'nuclear Pearl Harbor'.

Another development took place at sea – or rather under it. During the 1950s the USA developed new classes of nuclear-powered submarines that could stay submerged for weeks, even months, without having to surface and refuel. In 1960 the first submarines were fitted with nuclear-tipped missiles that could be launched from a submerged position. The Americans argued that these submarine-launched ballistic missiles (or SLBMs) represented a defensive weapons system. Because they were hidden at sea they would survive any attack that the USSR might launch on the American mainland. They could respond with an all-destructive counter-attack from their submerged locations. The American SLBMs could, in other words, guarantee the USA a 'second-strike capability'. This capability would deter the Soviets from making a surprise attack in the first place. In this sense it would represent a defene weapons system. And it would stabilize the nuclear balance of terror.

The logic behind this system was developed by strategists at RAND, one of the new think tanks that contracted by government agencies or firms to investigate social issues. Scholars at RAND, which specialized in security issues and produced many reports for the US Department of Defense, made important contributions to game theory and applied it to strategic analysis. Among them were the mathematician John von Neumann and the economist Oscar Morgenstern who had laid the foundation for game theory during World War II (Neumann and Morgenstern 1944). After the war they studied the works of Carl Clausewitz and discussed his works with RAND colleagues like Herman Kahn and Albert Wohlstetter. They probed his definitions of 'war' and 'strategy' and found that Clausewitz's concept of 'absolute war' was a useful term for discussions of strategy in the nuclear world. Bernard Brodie, author of the influential book *The Absolute Weapon* [1947], joined RAND. His book *Strategy in the Missile Age* [1959] drew on Clausewitz as well as game theory to analyse the security situation of the USA. It introduced the modern concept of 'deterrence' and reflected very well the attitude of the strategic theorists at RAND during the late 1950s.

In the nuclear age, Brodie begins, all wars are more dangerous than before. Even small and limited wars are more dangerous, for, if a nuclear power got involved in a limited war, there was always a chance of an escalation which in turn could lead to absolute war. To reduce the possibilities of nuclear war, the superpowers must do two things. First they must realize that war is now a dangerous means to obtain foreign-policy goals. Second, and less obvious, they must abandon the idea of a first strike. They must not build nuclear weapons in order to strengthen their first-strike capability because that will only trigger an arms race. Instead, the super-powers must build weapons which will ensure a second-strike capability. They must construct a large number of 'hard' missile silos on their territories and ensure their survivability. Also, they must place nuclear missiles on submarines which can cruise undetected below the surface of the world's oceans. A great number of hard silos and a vast fleet of nuclear submarines would ensure that a great number of retaliatory missiles survived any surprise attack. These missiles would in turn provide a solid deterrent against a first-strike threat and thus enhance the national security of both superpowers.

Other RAND scholars wrote similar analyses on nuclear war and deterrence (Kaplan 1957; Wohlstetter 1959; Kahn 1960). However, few of them were as influential a Brodie. His argument was tight and lean. Also, his theory of deterrence is based on two assumptions that tallied with the military realities of the age. First, that each side in a nuclear rivalry has enough weapons to destroy the other. Second, that each side nevertheless has protected or hidden away enough missiles to be able to retaliate immediately, massively and without fail. Under these conditions each state would be deterred from launching a nuclear surprise attack, for any such first strike would trigger an immediate and totally destructive response. This mutual-hostage logic was game-theoretically based and elegantly modelled by John von Neumann who, in a fit of black humour, referred to it as a situation of mutually assured destruction (or MAD).

Game theory was a new analytic tool in International Relations and it helped shape the new field of security studies. There was another new tool that also exerted great influence: namely, systems analysis. The concept of a system was not new to the social sciences.[17] Security studies, however, looked to biology and engineering for working definitions (Bertalanffy 1950). During the mid-1950s general systems theory was introduced to business administration, foreign-policy analysis and security studies.[18] Academics in these fields mapped out social interaction as flowcharts that looked like wiring diagrams and circuit boards from electrical engineering. Social groups were said to have adaptive properties and were compared to self-equilibrating models of thermostat systems. Terms like 'input', 'output' and 'feedback' were introduced to represent various stages in economic and political processes. States were depicted as 'blackboxes' and assumed to be rational actors whose behaviour could be analysed as so many utility-maximizing moves in political games.

Game theory and systems analysis were largely developed by scholars in think tanks. But university professors would also draw on these theories to analyse processes of political decision-making and of social behaviour more generally. Many of them were economists – Oscar Morgenstern, Thomas Schelling and Kenneth Boulding among them. Others were mathematicians – like John von Neumann, Lewis Richardson and Anatol Rapoport. During the late 1940s, Schelling and Boulding wrote books on economic issues; during the late 1950s they shifted attention to issues of war and peace.

The nature of the US–Soviet rivalry

During the late 1940s there emerged a new, bipolar world order – a 'tight bipolar system', to use one of Morton Kaplan's terms. A Western Bloc was presided over by the USA and became pitted against an Eastern Bloc, which was dominated by the USSR. The rivalry between the two bloc leaders grew in intensity and expanded geographically. The outbreak of the Korean War (1950) would make it more intense and expand it towards a near-global rivalry – and it would give it features that would characterize it for the next forty years.

Of scorpions and tarantulas

By that time, the economic activities of Western Europe were being organized under the American Marshall Plan, under the co-ordinating auspices of the Organization for European Economic Co-operation (OEEC); the economic activities of the Eastern Bloc were being organized by the Molotov Plan under the Council for

Mutual Economic Assistance (CMEA or Comecon). The military forces of the Western Bloc were being boosted by the USA and organized around the NATO alliance; those of the Eastern Bloc were controlled by the USSR and the arrangement would soon be organized under the Warsaw Pact.

There was a certain symmetry to this bipolar constellation of powers. Europe was divided between the superpowers like 'two halves of a walnut', noted Walter LaFeber (1987). Robert Oppenheimer likened the superpower rivalry to 'two scorpions in a bottle'. Louis Halle (1967) begged to disagree. Oppenheimer's image exaggerated the symmetry of the bipolar constellation, he argued. True, the Cold War was a rivalry between two deadly creatures. Yet, the two main actors were dissimilar in essential respects. Halle suggested that the essence of the Cold War was better captured by the image of 'a scorpion and a tarantula in a bottle' – both of them deadly but each in its particular way.

Halle made an important point. The USA and the USSR represented very different ways of life; their societies were organized differently, their inhabitants were shaped by very different historical experiences and informed by different outlooks (Westad 2005). Also, they related differently to other states. Both had invaded smaller countries and sought to shape them in their own image. But whereas the USA worked to establish a government based on popular sovereignty and then withdraw, the USSR had worked to integrate the occupied countries into its own administrative system on a permanent basis. Where the USA had given more than $15 billion worth of economic and technical assistance to the countries of Western Europe during the late 1940s, the USSR had removed a comparable amount from the countries of Eastern Europe.

Also, the conditions of scholarship were different. If we speak in ideal types, the Western Bloc consisted of liberal democracies, each with a public sphere where members of society could organize freely and engage in open political discussion. The Eastern Bloc, by contrast, comprised so many dictatorial regimes, all connected up to the Soviet Union and its Communist Party (the CPSU). Political discussions were monopolized by the Communist parties and coordinated by Cominform. A vast secret police force prevented the emergence of a proper public sphere. This made political discussions and social theorizing difficult – if not downright dangerous.

Of empires and hegemons

To capture the essential difference between the two Cold War blocs, it is useful to recall the interwar contributions of Antonio Gramsci (1974) and Heinrich Triepel (1938). Both authors discussed variations of social order and political control. They presented remarkably similar arguments, although Gramsci was a left-wing Italian communist and Triepel was a right-wing German conservative. Gramsci explored the concept of 'hegemony'. So did Triepel, only he compared the concept of 'hegemony' to those of 'empire' and 'balance of power'.

'Balance of power' refers to an orderly constellation of several sovereign states which maintain order by a conscious and sustained effort to sustain equilibrium among themselves. Before World War II, the European order was based on a balance-of-power principle. After World War II, Europe was divided in an Eastern and a Western half – one dominated by the USSR, the other by the USA. Whether this bipolar constellation constituted a bipolar balance of power will not be discussed here.[19] The point here is different: it is that the two superpower blocs can be distinguished and understood in terms of empire and hegemony.

'Empire', by Triepel's account, is created by conquest. An empire is built by one powerful state which invades and occupies the territories of others, assumes pre-eminence over them, seizes their sovereignty and rules them from its own metropolitian centre. Ancient Rome is a classic case of empire. The Soviet Union, too, fits the definition. During the endgame of World War II, the armed forces of the USSR occupied countries in eastern and central Europe, organized political institutions, assumed pre-eminence over all political processes in the region and ruled the nations from Moscow – the imperial metropolis monopolized all political power and allowed no satellite to act as a sovereign state. It is useful to think of the USSR as an empire. This way of thinking opens up new ways to understand the foreign-policy behaviour of the USSR in general and Soviet relations to its East European allies in particular.

'Hegemony', according to Triepel, is based on a community of sovereign states. However, in contrast to a balance-of-power system, a hegemonic order is an alliance or a league that is dominated by one, pre-eminent state which influences the outlook and the will of its allies. A hegemon, explains Triepel, is a sovereign state which leads other sovereign states because it enjoys their trust.

The hegemon is a *primus inter pares*, or first among equals. The hegemon enjoys pre-eminence in the system. Other states consider this leading state a legitimate leader and allow it to define basic rules of behaviour; they trust that these rules will benefit them all. A hegemonic system, then, consists of sovereign states (just like the balance-of-power system). But it is a system where the usual balance-of-power mechanism is suspended. Triepel uses the example of ancient Athens and its leadership in the Delian League (founded in 478 BC) as a classic case of hegemony. The relationship between the USA and Western Europe after World War II fits the definition. It is useful to think of the USA as a hegemon. This way of thinking opens up for new ways to understand the foreign-policy behaviour of the USA in general and of American relations to its West European allies in particular.

Also, following up on Louis Halle's image of the Cold War as a scorpion and a tarantula caught in a bottle, it is useful to think of the Cold War as an asymmetric rivalry. As a contest between a Soviet empire and an American hegemony. This approach invites new ways of understanding the relations that shaped international relations during the Cold War and of appreciating the International Relations theories that emerged under its impact.

Notes

1 Leaders of the West feared the ideology of Soviet communism because they associated it with expansion and totalitarian repression. Many Western leaders likened the Soviet brand of totalitarian repression to that of the Nazi regime, which they had recently experienced (see e.g. Friedrich 1954).

2 Geopolitical rivalries were present already at the wartime summit meetings of Yalta and Potsdam. They were at first expressed in quarrels over the fate of Poland and Berlin – as explained in the previous chapter. And, as this chapter will show, the geopolitical rivalry then quickly expanded to steadily larger segments of the globe – first to the oil-rich regions of Iran, then to Asia where Mao's victory in 1949 affected conflicts in Malaya, Indochina and Korea.

3 In March 1946, Churchill had been very clear about how Europe was divided in two by an 'iron curtain'. In March 1947, Truman had been clear about how the entire world was divided into two irreconcilable camps, 'one free' and 'the other enslaved' (Truman 1985 [1947]). One camp 'is based upon the will of the majority, and is distinguished by free institutions, representative government, free elections, guarantees of individual liberty, freedom of speech and religion, and freedom from political oppression'. The other 'is based upon the will of a minority forcibly imposed upon the majority. It relies upon terror and oppression, a controlled press and radio; fixed elections, and the suppression of personal freedoms' (Truman 1985 [1947]).

4 The fears were exaggerated but not empty. Communist Parties in the West were affiliated with the CPSU to varying degrees and were regularly charged with passing information to Moscow. Espionage was an integral element in the Cold War. Western leaders suspected that the USSR had acquired nuclear technology through industrial espionage in the USA and Britain. Soviet spies in the USA delivered important information which helped speed up Soviet nuclear weapons programmes. Soviet agents in Britain gave Moscow the names of anti-Nazi and anti-communist activists in East Germany, in the Baltic states and in other countries. And Soviet agents liquidated thousands of them.

5 The new US atmosphere of insecurity was also reflected in skyrocketing budgets for the CIA's covert activities – from $4.7 million in 1949 (before the Korean War) to some $200 million in 1953.

6 NATO was formally established in Washington DC on 4 April 1949 when the foreign ministers of twelve Western countries – Belgium, Canada, Denmark, France, Iceland, Italy, Luxembourg, the Netherlands, Norway, Portugal, the United Kingdom and the USA – signed the North Atlantic Treaty. The treaty was ratified by the parliaments of these countries within five months.

7 In 1955, the USSR responded in kind. The Soviets transformed their occupation zone into the German Democratic Republic (Deutsche Demokratische Republik or DDR). Later they organized the countries in Eastern Europe in a military alliance, the Warsaw Pact (WP).

8 ANZUS (the Australia, New Zealand, United States Security Treaty) was established in September 1951 as a defence treaty for the Pacific Ocean. SEATO (the South East Asia Treaty Organization) was established in 1954 as a defence treaty for

South East Asia and included countries like Pakistan, the Philippines and Thailand; but it also included Australia, France and Britain in addition to the USA.

9 Both superpowers were assisted in their efforts by German scientists whom they had imported from their respective occupation zones. The USSR developed their R-7 Semyorka rocket with the assistance of German scientists. The USA developed their Redstone and Jupiter-C rockets on the basis of German designs.

10 Some of the promises stretched back to World War I – such as the Balfour Declaration (of 1917) which confirmed Britain's support for a Jewish homeland in Palestine.

11 These two coups, both engineered by the CIA, removed leaders whom the Americans considered inimical to their political as well as their economic interests. Mosaddeq tried to nationalize the Iranian oil industry. Arbenz worked to push through a substantial land reform. See e.g. Weiner (2008, chs 9 and 10).

12 The term 'Third World' was coined in 1952 by the French anthropologist and historian Alfred Sauvy, who referred to those countries which were aligned neither with the capitalist nor with the communist bloc in world affairs. Sauvy (1952) had the upheavals of the French Revolution in mind when he coined the term, arguing that the superpowers played a role in world affairs that were akin to the roles played by the nobles and the clergy – the First Estate and the Second Estate, respectively – during the French Revolution. The poor majority of countries constituted a 'Third World' – ignored, exploited, despised like the third estate, but also with the ambition of improving their own lot, argued Sauvy.

13 Leites's approach was greatly influential among scholars as well as diplomats and was applied to Stalin and other members of the Soviet Politburo. Leites was preoccupied with how Soviet decision-makers reasoned – with the analytical concepts they used, their mental categories and their ways of reasoning. On the basis of these preoccupations, Leites developed the very useful concept of 'the Operational Code' (Walker 1990).

14 *How Russia Is Ruled* was published a few months after Stalin's death in 1953. It was later revised and updated and finally republished under the title *How the Soviet Union Is Governed*.

15 Both editions open with the claim that politics among states is different from politics within states: because interstate relations are more obviously a 'struggle for power'. Both editions see 'power' essentially as a psychological relationship between human beings. Both books claim that the quest for power is deeply engrained in human nature. Both books echo a European philosophy of science – Morgenthau's emphasis on 'power' and on 'objective laws' should not be understood in an American, positivist sense; it should be understood along Nietzschean lines. Also, the basic design of the two editions remains the same: a first section lays out the nature of international politics as a struggle for power; a second shows how this struggle manifests itself on the international scene; a third discusses different ways to constrain the struggle for power (through a policy of equilibrium, through international law or through improving the world opinion). A fourth section seeks to employ the definitions and the general propositions to an analysis of the contemporary world.

16 This dynamic, which Herz (1950; 1951) referred to as the 'security dilemma' was also discussed by the British historian Herbert Butterfield, in his *History and Human*

Relations [1951] in very similar terms. The basic concept had been adumbrated e.g. by Rousseau (1964a).

17 Thomas Hobbes had used the term in chapter 22 of his *Leviathan* [1651]. 'By Systems I understand any numbers of men joined in one interest or one business of which some are regular and some irregular', wrote Hobbes (1951, p. 146).

18 An important early contributor to systems analysis was the Austrian academic Ludwig von Bertalanffy, who extended the holistic models of general systems theory into new fields like cybernetics, taught in England, Canada and California after World War II.

19 The theoretical debate was always whether a bipolar system was a proper balance-of-power system or whether a lacking balance required more than two states. Traditional Realists have tended to argue that the Cold War did not constitute a proper balance-of-power system because it lacked flexibility. A classic balance-of-power system consists of a flexible constellation of five or seven sovereign states, it was argued. Territorial states, sovereignty and flexibility are key terms here, because in a proper balance-of-power system sovereign states maintain order by entering and leaving alliances in a conscious effort to sustain equilibrium among themselves (Triepel 1938; Gulick 1967). Theorists who were influenced by systems analysis tended to disagree. For them, two equally powerful actors could well constitute a stable balance-of-power order (Waltz 1979).

11

The thaw and the Third World: the Cold War after Stalin

On the morning of 1 March 1953, after an all-night dinner with close associates and ministers, Stalin did not emerge from his bedroom. His guards were under strict orders not to disturb him. Only late in the evening did one of the guards collect enough courage to check on his boss. He found Stalin lying on the floor in his pyjamas, paralysed and unable to speak. His eyes, however, fixed angrily on the frightened guard, who rushed to the bedroom telephone to call officials of the Communist Party. A little past midnight Lavrenti Beria came, chief of the Soviet security and secret police apparatus (NKVD). Soon after came other members of Stalin's inner circle – Georgij Malenkov, Nikolai Bulganin and Nikita Khrushchev. After that, doctors came.

Stalin died four days later, on 5 March 1953, at the age of seventy-four. The members of the Soviet Politburo did not know what to do at first. After a period of indecision, the leading members of the Politburo collected their wits and executed the most powerful member of their circle: Stalin's chief of police, Lavrenti Beria. The remaining members then agreed to break with Stalin's ruthless one-man rule and establish a collective leadership. This marked a new phase in Soviet politics: the stakes of politics were lowered and government positions were no longer held at the risk of arrest, trial and execution.

The death of Stalin also marked a new phase in the Cold War. This chapter discusses the main features of this new phase. It focuses on the new Soviet leaders and the changes they made. First, it presents the careful rapprochement which took place between the two Cold War blocs in the wake of Stalin's death. Then it notes some of the changes that occurred within each of the blocs – within the Communist bloc frictions were visible on the 1955 Bandung Conference; within the West frictions broke out as a result of the 1956 Suez Crisis. The chapter also notes how the two superpowers busily build atomic weapons and accumulate huge nuclear arsenals. Finally, the chapter notes how the overseas empires of European powers begin to unravel.

These two processes – the nuclear arms race and decolonization – affected the superpower rivalry so deeply that they became defining elements of the Cold War.

They also affected the academic study of International Relations. The nuclear arms race would spur two new additions to International Relations – strategic studies on the one hand and peace research on the other. Decolonization would broaden the academic focus of International Relations – to the traditional focus on Western relations would be added new topics pertaining to questions of economic development, political evolution and social-science procedures. The chapter ends with a review of Martin Wight's three scholarly traditions and Kenneth N. Waltz's three levels of analysis.

Changes in world affairs

In the late 1940s the USSR installed communist governments in several countries in Eastern and Central Europe. This frightened the West. The common fear of Soviet expansionism came to override individual state interest and to drive the Western states together in a more tightly knit community. First, it drove the Atlantic states together in a common defence organization, NATO. Then it drove several Continental states together into a more tightly integrated co-operation in political and economic matters.

A first initiative towards the closer integration of the West was made by Winston Churchill, who argued, as early as 1946, that it was necessity to safeguard the long European tradition of liberty, democracy and human rights in the face of totalitarian threats. Churchill's diagnosis was followed up in 1949 when ten European states met in London and established the Council of Europe. Another initiative was taken by the US Secretary of State George C. Marshall who announced a large US aid package to Europe in 1947. Marshall envisioned that infusions of capital, encouragement of free trade, and a joint organisation of common effort would spur a process of economic and political integration in Europe. His generous vision also has a strategic side. A rebuilt and tightly integrated Europe, with a reconstructed West Germany as an important member, would help contain Soviet expansionism.

First World initiatives
Such early initiatives were, however, blocked by state interests and balance-of-power dynamics. The Europeans welcomed American aid. But they were uncomfortable with the US visions of a United States of Europe. The British were particularly dubious. They had a zone of free trade and organizations to sustain it in their Empire. They did not concede that the days of empire were numbered. On the contrary, they had fought a war and rescued the Empire. It was the foundation of their economic system and the source of their international power. They had beaten Germany and saved France. The thought of now co-operating with Germany and France in an all-European structure appalled them. They found the American idea of European integration odd and misinformed. Britain had, in their view, a special relationship to the USA. The British expected to participate in the Marshall Plan, but on the same bilateral terms in which they had participated in Lend-Lease – and with the same degree of priority. They could not accept being reduced to a power

on the level of Germany and France – both of them defeated and exhausted nations.

The French, too, were sceptical of European integration. They distrusted the US free-market argument; it was incompatible with French ambitions of holding on to their old colonies. Also, they were deeply dubious of the American plans to give West Germany an important role in an integrated Europe; they considered the plans naïve and dangerous. Germany had attacked France in 1871, 1914, and 1940 and inflicted enormous destruction. The French were not at all interested in German recovery. They wanted French recovery. And they wanted it fast. The French government understood that, if the postwar poverty was not alleviated quickly, the communists (already a powerful party in France) would increase in number and might take over the government. The French badly needed the Marshall Plan. And if Europe were to defend itself against the Soviet Union, it needed military guarantees from the USA. It also needed an industrially revived West Germany. These were American arguments. The French could not find any flaws in the logic. But they did not like them one little bit.

In May 1950 the French government conceded. The Foreign Minister Robert Schumann proposed the integration of Europe's coal and steel industries – the German industries included. Schumann presented his proposal in a speech which was written by Jean Monnet, who had long argued that a federation of states was the only sensible solution to Europe's problem of recurrent wars. His argument was reflected in Schumann's proposition to establish a European Coal and Steel Community (ECSC). The ECSC would, first, bring under collective control the two key industries in the production of modern weapons systems – coal and steel. Second, integration of these important industries would be followed by integrative spinoffs in other industries and initiate a Continental development towards greater interdependence.[1]

Schumann was also supported by Charles de Gaulle, a powerful influence in French politics. He, too, saw that Europe could not resist the Soviet Union without American support. Also, de Gaulle understood that West Germany would have to be resurrected if Europe were to develop quickly and if NATO were to be effective. He recognized that France sooner rather than later would have to co-operate with West Germany in a mutual project of postwar reconstruction.

However, de Gaulle did not share Monnet's vision of a peaceful European federation. He thought that Monnet underestimated the power of the nation-state. The bonds that held a people together were forged in history. Once formed, they could not easily be changed; they could certainly not be quickly altered or transcended by political decree. New bonds could not be ordered at will. De Gaulle countered Monnet's vision of a federation with the vision of a con-federation consisting of sovereign states; but a con-federation which France could dominate and use for its own ends. When Britain opted out of integration, France was free to play the leading power in postwar Europe. In de Gaulle's mind, it was better to play the leader of the process than to be a follower (Calleo 1965). If France could actively shape an increasingly integrated Europe, this would help contain the Soviet threat – which would please the USA who would, perhaps, help France contain common enemies in other settings. At the same time, French leadership of a European coalition of states could also counterbalance US influence in Europe.

The common fear of Soviet communism, then, drove Western states together in a more tightly knit community. This was first apparent in the wake of the communist coup in Czechoslovakia early in 1948. Western co-operation was stimulated further after June 1950 when war broke out in Korea.[2] As a response to the Korean War, the USA streamlined NATO and called for rearmament of West Germany.[3]

Second World Changes

Stalin's death triggered a brief struggle for positions and power in the Soviet leadership. Within a year Nikita Khrushchev was appointed First Secretary of the CPSU and emerged as the leading man in the USSR. He changed Soviet politics. In domestic affairs, Khrushchev discontinued Stalin's habit of purging political opponents; as soon as he attained power, Khrushchev eased Stalin's dictatorial methods and announced a new government based upon a principle of collective leadership.

In foreign affairs, Khrushchev replaced Stalin's belligerent diplomacy of struggle and conflict with a new rhetoric of peace. Stalin had argued that it was in the Soviet interest to prolong the war in Korea and to keep the Americans busy in an increasingly unpopular war against the Chinese. The new Soviet leadership, however, feared that war in Korea might instead spark a larger war which the USSR was not prepared to fight. As soon as he saw a chance, Khrushchev took the initiative to negotiate an armistice between the two Koreas in June 1953.

In the Eastern Bloc, Khrushchev worked to reduce tensions, initiating an epoch that received its name after Ilja Ehrenburgh's 1954 novel *The Thaw*. At the twentieth CPSU Congress, in February 1956, Khrushchev made a secret speech where he listed some of Stalin's excesses and referred to them as crimes.[4] He dissolved the Cominform, which Stalin had established to co-ordinate the policies of the East Bloc countries.

Khrushchev's de-Stalinization was greeted with a sigh of collective relief in the Soviet Bloc. People began to take to the streets to demonstrate their collective opinion. This, however, threatened the Communist elites. Khrushchev improvised to regain control, but with mixed results. By October, Poland and Hungary were in deep political crises. Khrushchev flew to Warsaw, employed a mix of threats and promises and managed to defuse the conflict. In Hungary, however, the situation was getting out of hand.

Soviet leaders were discussing their options in late October when a crisis erupted in the Middle East. Egypt's strongman, Gamal Abdel Nasser, had nationalized the Suez Canal and had upset Britain and France. The Suez Crisis was a godsend to the Soviet leaders, whose network of spies had informed them that Britain and France plotted with Israel to attack Egypt. The Soviets decided to use the Middle East crisis as a diplomatic smokescreen and laid detailed plans to invade Hungary. Israel invaded Egypt on 29 October and moved quickly across the Sinai Peninsula. Britain and France quickly issued a prearranged ultimatum to both Egypt and

Israel, pretending to offer mediation in the conflict. When Egypt refused to comply, the two European powers bombed Cairo and seized the Suez Canal.

The Soviet foreign minister Bulganin went on the diplomatic offensive immediately. He asserted that the Israeli aggression was part of a larger conspiracy cooked up by the old imperialist powers of Europe. He condemned their clumsy collusion to regain imperial control of the Middle East. He threatened to intervene on the Egyptian side and to launch rocket attacks on Britain, France and Israel. The Soviet threats frightened and angered the Americans. They feared that the conflict might spin out of hand and trigger a major war in the region.

While Bulganin fanned the fires of crisis in the Middle East, defence minister Zhukov built up the Soviet military presence in Hungary. On 4 November the Soviet air force bombed Budapest and the Red Army poured into the city is a massive dawn offensive. The Soviet army encountered unexpectedly hard resistance, but the poorly armed Hungarians were no match for Soviet tanks and heavy guns. The USSR quickly re-established order in the country – although strikes and civilian resistance continued far into 1957.

The Soviet tactic worked beautifully – mainly because its charges turned out to be true. US President Eisenhower condemned the Suez operation. He pressured the French and British forces to withdraw their forces. Atlantic relations were cold and depressed for years thereafter. The Soviet invasion of Hungary, together with Khrushchev's 'secret speech', created a crisis in international communism. The invasion was a bad blemish on Khrushchev's effort to present the USSR is a new, post-Stalinist light. It created a wave of refugees – some two hundred thousand Hungarians fled their country across the Austrian frontier to the West. In Eastern Europe, hopes of further liberalization were crushed. In Western Europe, radicals were shocked; tens of thousands of people cancelled their membership in the Communist Party in protest – and the party suffered a sharp decline in the polls. This disillusion swelled the ranks of rootless radicals who scanned the world for alternative causes. A number of them turned their attention towards anti-colonial wars in Africa and Asia and to Mao and his vast social experiment in China.

Khrushchev continued his charm offensive in spite of these adversities. First, he initiated an ambitious fence-mending campaign in the Soviet neighbourhood; he toured the 'near abroad' with his rotund and affable foreign minister, Nicolai Bulganin – with mixed results. Second, he introduced a foreign policy towards the rest of the world that was more in tune with the norms of classic diplomacy. He softened Stalin's irreconcilable Cold War rhetoric, putting aside the old communist axiom that an international class struggle existed between capitalist and social countries.

Khrushchev made a strong effort to demonstrate his commitment to peace. He sponsored the World Peace Council and attended international peace conferences. He supported the peace movement and protests against atomic weapons. He invited President Eisenhower to normalize the US–Soviet relationship. In 1961 he met with America's newly elected President John F. Kennedy in Vienna. Superpower relations cannot be based on enmity, he said; they must instead be based on 'peaceful coexistence'.

All the time Khrushchev argued that imperialism was a cause of war and that anti-colonial struggle was active peace work. Whereas Stalin had largely neglected the conflicts that erupted in the Western colonies in wake of World War II, Khrushchev observed these conflicts with very different eyes. And here lies a final point of importance in Khrushchev's foreign policy: He began to support anti-colonial movements and thus change Soviet relations with nations in Asia and Africa. When non-Western countries called for an African–Asian Conference in the Indonesian city of Bandung in 1956, Khrushchev recalled Lenin's Congress of the People of the East in Baku in 1920 and sent Soviet observers.

On the Third World and radical International Relations theory
Khrushchev was happy to contribute to the Bandung discussions on the nature of Western imperialism. He was elated to note that the conference condemned the colonial practices of the West. He was, however, deeply disturbed when conference delegates began to discuss whether Soviet policies in Eastern Europe should also count as colonialism. When the African–Asian Conference finally reached a consensus in which 'colonialism in all of its manifestations' should be condemned, it implicitly reprimanded the Soviet Union as well as the West. Khrushchev fumed with anger.

Khrushchev was particularly perturbed when the Chinese representatives at Bandung did not come to the defence of the USSR. He had never liked Mao. Now the Chinese behaviour at Bandung drove a wedge through the Sino-Soviet relationship. The Soviet leaders began to view China as a rival in the Third World – a view that was strengthened when Albania's communist leader, Enver Hoxa, broke with the USSR in 1960 and took China's side in a sharp Sino-Soviet polemic.

Khrushchev engaged more actively in the Third World and supported the cause of anti-colonial rebels. He cultivated relations with Cuba's revolutionary leader Fidel Castro among others. The USSR established diplomatic relations with Cuba in 1960 – to the great frustration of the USA. Khrushchev's Third World orientation opened up a new dimension in the geopolitical competition of the superpowers. It created huge problems for American foreign-policy-makers, thereby strengthening the Soviet hand in the superpower competition for Third World allies. Khrushchev's rhetoric of peace appealed to many idealists in the West. His support of anti-colonial rebels strengthened the position of the USSR in the Sino-Soviet rivalry for influence in the Third World.

In January 1961 Premier Khrushchev made a speech at the Soviet Academy of the Social Sciences. Here he emphasized the peaceful intentions of socialist states and contrasted them with the expansionist and conflict-prone properties of the capitalist system. These was little new in his analysis. He echoed the basic arguments of Lenin and Stalin when he maintained that the capitalist system had an inherent tendency to expand and that expansion means conflict and war. The context, however, was new. Among politicians and statesmen of the world there was a growing recognition that colonialism was a thing of the past. Among scholars there was a growing effort to develop social-science theories based on notions of systems and structures. Khrushchev reflected both tendencies. His speech served to remind the scholarly community of some of the analytical promises that were contained in the Marxist tradition of social analysis.

The primary questions of Soviet social research, Khrushchev (1961, p. 54) said, was 'how to prevent a world thermonuclear war and attain lasting peace on earth and friendship among all peoples, and how to insure peaceful coexistence of states with different social systems'. These goals, he explained, would best be attained by supporting all progressive forces in the world and expand the Soviet sphere of influence.

He brought up Soviet relations with the Third World and quoted Lenin to the effect that one of the most overlooked forces of progress in the twentieth century was found in colonies and countries oppressed by imperialism:

> Stressing that this struggle is aimed primarily at national liberation, Lenin said: It is quite clear that in the future decisive battles of the world revolution, the movement of the majority of the population of the globe at first aimed at national liberation will turn against capitalism and imperialism and may play a much greater revolutionary part than we expect. (Khrushchev 1961)

The USSR, Khrushchev continued, would support 'without reservation' all wars of liberation which began as 'uprisings of colonial peoples against their oppressors' and developed into 'guerrilla wars'.

Khrushchev's speech made a big impression on the Western left; gaining support from the international peace movement as well as the anti-colonial movement. The speech also made a big impression on Western governments. Especially on the newly elected US President John F. Kennedy, who read it time and again. He sent copies to his top aides and urged them to comment and analyse Khrushchev's speech. He saw that Khrushchev's support for Third World rebels created huge problems for the USA. First, if the USSR began to sponsor radical rebels around the world, the US policy of containment might deteriorate into several purely reactive actions, pulling the USA into one colonial conflict after the other all over Asia and Africa. Second, it would place US foreign policy on the horns of a horrible dilemma: the USA had traditionally been an anti-colonial power; but if the Soviets were to sponsor anti-colonial rebels around the world, the USA would be pulled into wars on the side of the old colonial powers. Partly because the USA was driven by a policy of containment to counter Soviet expansion; partly because the USA was committed to assist close European allies – which also happened to be old colonial powers. As a result America's traditional liberal, democratic and anti-colonial foreign-policy rhetoric would be belied by US foreign-policy practice. The Soviets had found a way to make America betray its traditional foreign-policy ideals; they would make the USA praise liberty and freedom on the one hand, while invading small countries on the other. It would make the USA appear to the world as a big hypocrite.

New typologies, new beginnings

Khrushchev's relationship to Kennedy resembled Lenin's relationship with Wilson half a century earlier; Khrushchev's socialist argument challenged the liberal-democratic order of the USA and the West. However, the presence of nuclear weapons and the unravelling of colonialism introduced important differences in the US–Soviet rivalry.

The colonial wars were changing world politics in ways that the established approaches of Rationalism and Realism could not fully explain. Khrushchev's argument – which drew on the analyses of Lenin (1975b [1917]), Ho Chi Minh (Neuberg 2008 [1930]), Zhdanov (1947) and liberation theories of radical insurgent groups – challenged the established approaches of Western International Relations. But Khrushchev was a controversial figure. He contributed to dissent among communists, socialists and other radical groups in the West. From such dissent and discussion came new arguments and new approaches and theories.

Radical challenges to Realism

The dissent on the left increased during the late 1950s – stimulated by the Sino-Soviet tiff in Bandung, the Soviet invasion of Hungary and Khrushchev's secret speech. These events created protests and political crises in Western communist parties. They fuelled the flight from the old communist parties. But they also encouraged establishment of alternative organizations. Passionate debates sprang up among Western leftists over the finer points in Marxist theory. New journals emerged to carry radical commentaries on world affairs to a waiting audience. In France, intellectuals quit the Communist Party and carried on their radical analyses in journals like *Les temps modernes*. Its editor, the philosopher Jean-Paul Sartre, defied his own government by arguing the cause of Revolutionary enemies in Indochina and Algeria. In the USA, *Monthly Review* published analyses by left-wing academics like Paul Baran, Paul Sweezy, Leo Huberman and others. In Britain, the late 1950s saw the advent of a 'new left' and journals like *The New Left Review*.

The 'new left' also left traces in international organizations. In the UN political economists wrote radical analyses on questions of poverty and postwar reconstruction. Among the influential examples were members of the UN Commission of Latin America (ECLA), which housed radical economists like Hans Singer, Raul Prebish and Celso Furtado. They studied the causes of poverty and the precondition for economic development, and described the Americas as an economic system in which the USA was so dominant that it affected the development of all other states.

The Argentinian economist Raul Prebish (1950) argued that North America played the role of an independent metropole to the dependent satellites of the countries of South America. Prebish broke with the tradition of liberal economics, which saw economics as separate from politics; instead, Prebish saw economics and politics are interwoven. He imported terms from the history of imperial Rome in his analysis of the relations between metropoles and satellites. He resurrected old concepts like 'moral philosophy' and 'political economy'.

Such left-wing analyses provided different explanations for the causes of war from those of Realism. The radical argument offered an alternative account of war and had considerable explanatory power. Whereas Realism dealt in territorial states, national interests and power, radical arguments offered a holistic view that explained world events in light of the capitalist world system. They presented the behaviour of states as driven by economic concerns. They saw the world as a relationship between wealthy metropoles in the North and exploited and impoverished satellites in the South.

Radicalism represented a challenge to the Realist approach because it did not really discuss world affairs in political terms; it depicted the world as an economic system. It did not explain the behaviour of states in terms of political interest as much as responses to the internal economic dynamics of capitalist society. It focused less on sovereign states and more on classes and international class relations.

Liberal challenges to Realism I: strategic studies
Realism was challenged not only from the economic approaches of the radical left. It was also challenged by liberal theory and its assumptions of rational individuals. This had long been apparent in the field of security studies.

Security studies was, on the face of it, a variant of classical Realism. It shared many of the assumptions of Realism – it was concerned with the behaviour of territorial states, it discussed issues of war and peace, and it did so in terms of state interests and capabilities of power. However, its key contributors – authors like John von Neumann, Bernhard Brodie, Herman Kahn – supported their analyses on liberal economic theories and premised their arguments on the assumption that states and statesmen were rational actors. They had developed new approaches to conflict and security based on rational-actor theories of games and systems, using carefully defined terms like 'deterrence', 'Mutual Assured Destruction' (MAD), 'first strike' and 'second strike'. They had exerted an increasing influence on strategic planners in the US Department of Defense.

These approaches provided the backdrop for a speech that the US Secretary of Defence Robert McNamara made in June 1962. McNamara explained to the American public that development of nuclear technology had brought forth entirely new weapons systems and that it was necessary to develop new approaches to war and military planning to handle them. In wars of the past, states had levied their armed against other in vast contests of military strength. Each state had sought to destroy the military forces of its opponent, McNamara argued in terms that echoed those of Clausewitz. No state had sought to destroy the opponent's population, because, as long as the opponent's forces remained intact, there was not anything decisive that a state could do to the enemy nation. However, this situation began to change with the advent of air power, continued McNamara.

During World War I, strategists developed theories of air-war to target and affect the enemy nation. During World War II, Hitler bombed London and other cities in order to break the will of the English nation. He did not succeed. The bombing rather seemed to unite the population and to steel the British in a more determined opposition. Besides, the Royal Air Force paid Germany back in kind, taking the war straight to the interior of Hitler's *Reich* and destroying cities like Hamburg and Dresden. The bombing technology of World War II was limited, and the belligerents attacked military targets as well as populations. They could no defeat an enemy by only destroying population centres. The advent of nuclear weapons changed this. It opened up for the possibility of bypassing troops and going exclusively for massive destruction of enemy populations. But to do this, McNamara continued, would also open up for a destructive fury of Biblical proportions.

Was it possible to prevent modern wars from escalating into an all-destructive Armageddon? asked McNamara. The only solution, he answered, was to return to the logic of the past: to limit the wars and ensure that they remained contests between military forces. It is necessary to return to traditional ideals of war and cultivate a common recognition that mass destruction of enemy populations and cities would serve no military purpose. However, limited wars were only one side of the coin. To ensure that all nuclear powers abided by the traditional ideals of war, each must be assured that the other had the capability to launch a massive attack on people and cities, should they choose to do so. Thus, the massive destruction of civil populations would serve no military purpose but the continued *threat* of such destruction might serve a political purpose: that threat would depend on their not being destroyed yet. Thus conceived, 'deterrence' might not only prevent war, it might also operate during war itself and limit its scope, because belligerents might, out of self-interest, work to limit the use and destructiveness of nuclear weapons.

As a consequence, the fury of nuclear attacks might mainly fall on the belligerents' weapons and military forces. 'The United States have come to the conclusion', said McNamara,

> that to the extent feasible, basic military strategy in a possible general war should be approached in much the same way that more conventional military operations have been regarded in the past. That is to say, principal military objectives ... should be the destruction of the enemy's forces, not of his civilian population ... giving the possible opponent the strongest imaginable incentive to refrain from striking our own cities. (Schelling 1966, p. 25)

It may appear odd that McNamara claimed to have created a 'new strategy' and a 'new deterrence' for the USA, when all he did was to restate conventional verities of the past. The novelty, however, lies in the context. McNamara made his claim at a time when nuclear science had made weapons systems all-destructive. Drawing on rational-actor models, he proposed to employ only a small part of America's considerable arsenal. He proposed to limit the war by concentrating the war effort on the enemy's military installations while deliberately holding in reserve a massive capability which could destroy its cities, exterminate its population and eliminate its society – on condition that the enemy observe similar restraint while retaining the capabilities for a similar threat. This was no conventional approach.

Liberal challenges to Realism II: peace research

To fight an all-out military engagement while holding in reserve one's all-destructive capabilities, on condition that the enemy does likewise, was not the way military operations had been approached in the past. It was a new approach to Great Power war, designed to suit a new era. However, the new design was met with protests and intense opposition. Many social scientists were horrified by the streamlined logic of the new nuclear doctrines. They found it cynical and immoral. The doctrines developed by the new field of strategic studies were criticized by scholars in the new field of 'peace studies' or 'peace research'.

The new field of peace research was diverse and varied and it is hard to characterize it by a sweeping generalization – except that it carried the message of the old peace movement. The peace-research community was an academic anchored movement. If strategic studies challenged the Realist concept of war, then peace research challenged the Realist notion of international order and peace.

Its members applied social science methods to study the causes of war and the preconditions of peace. An early case in point was the French sociologist Gaston Bouthoul. In the wake of World War II he founded the new discipline of 'polemology' and, together with Louise Weiss, established an institute to house it – l'Institut français de polémologie. Bouthoul (1951) and Weiss explored statistical covariations between war and a variety of other social variables related to economic, cultural, psychological and, above all, demographic phenomena.

By applying statistical techniques to information about war, violence and mass death, the French polemologists hoped to establish a new and 'scientific pacifism'. This ambition reveals a second feature that characterized peace research in its early years: it was marked by an activist streak. It did not merely discuss conditions for peace, it sought to bring these conditions about. The American psychologist and educator Theodore F. Lenz was a pioneer in this respect. Lenz (1955) proposed to build 'a science of peace' founded on the values of democracy. He, and many peace researchers with him, engaged themselves in popular movements to ban nuclear weapons and to establish a fair and just world through international law or redistribution of global resources.

Members of the Peace research community were abhorred by the cynical logic inherent in the theories of John von Neumann and the arguments of Robert McNamara. Yet, they tended to rely on the same behaviourist methods that had brought forth the field of security studies – that is, mathematical models, statistical studies, game theory and systems analysis. The early proponents of peace research were particularly motivated by Lewis Richardson, a British meteorologist who had been driven by his pacifist leanings during World War II to apply statistical techniques to arms races and interstate conflicts in an effort to identify the causes of war. His two books, *Arms and Insecurity* (1949) and *Statistics of Deadly Quarrels* (1950) are classics in modern peace research.

Richardson inspired other peace advocates, like the American economist Kenneth Boulding. He was an active member in the Religious Society of Friends, influenced by the Quaker pacifist William Penn and much attuned to the dynamics of co-operation and peace (Boulding 1962). Like Richardson, Boulding relied on statistics; but also on economic models. The Russian-born mathematician Anatol Rapoport applied systems theory to questions of conflict and war (Rapoport 1960). Memories of Soviet and Nazi persecutions in the late 1930s increasingly steered him into research in conditions for peace (Rapoport 1964).

The new theories of games and systems were not only embraced by mathematicians and economics professors; political scientists, sociologists and other social scientists embraced them as well. One of them was Thomas Schelling. An economist, like Boulding, he relied on rational-actor models to discuss issues of peace, war and arms races. His analyses of foreign and security affairs contributed greatly to the study of conflict behaviour and war studies (Schelling 1960; 1966).

Another important professor was Morton Kaplan (1957). Inspired by general systems theory, he deduced six distinct types of international systems – or, rather, six versions of interstate equilibrium. In addition to the well-known 'balance of power system', Kaplan introduced two bipolar systems – one 'loose' and one 'tight' – together with a 'universal system', a 'hierarchical system' and a 'unit veto system'. Kaplan's book, *System and Process in International Politics*, was a major innovation in International Relations. Other authors quickly engaged with his argument, among them Charles McClelland, George Modelski and Richard Rosecrance. Kaplan's book sparked a scholarly effort which would quickly lift International Relations up to new, abstract systemic levels.

Sociological challenges to Realism
Realism was also challenged by more sociological approaches. One of these was expressed by the British Committee on the Theory of International Politics. This group was created in 1959 by the Cambridge historian Herbert Butterfield. It was supported by a generous grant from the Rockefeller Foundation – an important sponsor of academic International Relations during the 1950s.[5] The British Committee would meet about three times a year. Its aim was to define a basic conception of the very phenomenon 'international politics'.

Its members would start out from the assumption that the world was composed of sovereign, self-interested states and that the interaction of these states constituted an international system which was anarchic in nature. Since the international system is anarchic but not chaotic, it must possess some mechanism that provides order to international interaction. What mechanisms are those? How do they operate?

Similar questions had been asked by international lawyers – from Hugo Grotius (1853 [1625]) via James Lorimer (1877) to Hans Morgenthau (1933; 1948b). And, to be honest, the British Committee did not really develop answers that were very different from theirs. However, its members pursued the notion of states as social actors, conceived of state interaction in social terms and came up with sophisticated answers which laid the rafters of the so-called 'English School of International Relations'.[6] It was more informed by social theory than by classical Realism and less informed by economics than security studies.

The main difference between Realism and the English School is apparent in a volume edited by Herbert Butterfield and Martin Wight in the mid-1960s, *Diplomatic Investigations*. Where US Realists discussed the 'international *system*', members of the English School explored the 'international *society*'. The concept of an 'international society' was old and much bandied about. Members of the English School sought to give it a precise content. Charles A. W. Manning contributed greatly to this effort. And his much-neglected book deserves an in-depth comment.

Manning was a founding member of the British Committee on the Theory of international Relations and a veteran teacher of International Relations at the London School of Economics (LSE). He had for many years taught an introductory course on 'The Structure of International Society'. The international society consists largely of sovereign states, Manning began. In their interaction these states produce more than a system of states, he continued; they constitute a society of states because their interrelations add a normative and rule-based character to their interaction. This society is, however, different from other societies – largely because its members are sovereign states. It is a society *sui generis*. As such it is a definable object which can be systematically studied.

This was Manning's premise. He ruminated over its implications for the thirty years or so that he taught at LSE. He influenced several generations of students. But he published little. Only upon his retirement in 1962 did he publish a book, *The Nature of International Society*. It was philosophical and abstract, rife with neologisms and wordplay and hard to read – and consequently no best-seller. However, it expressed well its key point: namely, that the main object of International Relations is the international society. An understanding of the unique character of its members and of the society they constitute – in particular the special 'rules of the game' that result from their interaction and lend order to that society – make up the basic substance of International Relations as a scholarly field. International Relations is a complex subject. And it is best studied by a multidisciplinary kind of sociology, argued Manning.

Manning's views affected the members of Butterfield's Committee. They worked from the assumption that the world is made up of sovereign states and that the interstate relations constitute an anarchical society. But they also observed that states tend to negotiate, make agreements and alliances and develop rules for proper conduct. States develop rules to protect their own interests. And they tend to punish those who break the rules.

Rise of an international sociology
The members of the English School did not assume at the outset that states were rational actors; rather, they assumed that they were social actors. They did not assume that states acted irrationally; they simply toned down the assumption of rationality and emphasized the assumption of sociability. They found little attraction in the engineer-inspired international systems developed by their America colleagues. Instead, they entertained the notion of an international society, whose order was provided by the workings of diplomacy, international law, the balance of

power, and Great Power concerts. This, at least, was the claim of Martin Wight, one of the members of Butterfield's group.

There were other authors, too, who viewed international interaction in terms of social rather than rational interaction. Among them were David Mitrany and Karl W. Deutsch. Both of them were Europeans who had fled from Nazism before World War II. They imported sociological terms and theories into their studies of international interaction. They relied in particular on social theories of communicative interaction and arrived at a fairly simple but important observation: namely that a steadily denser pattern of interconnection and integration emerged among Western states after World War II.

The Romanian-born David Mitrany (1965 [1943]) had made a similar argument as early as the 1930s. During World War II he had observed that when several Europeans states co-operated in order to obtain a specific goal they engaged in activities which fuelled international integration. Such integration created ties and trust among the nations and disposed them for peaceful relations, he argued.

The Czech-born Karl W. Deutsch (1957) made a similar argument – and demonstrated it statistically. He collected information about international mail, telephone conversations and other kinds of transactions. His data demonstrated empirically the growing interconnectedness within Europe as well as between Europe and North America. From this, he inferred that the North Atlantic community was being tied together, through a steadily denser web of interaction, into what he called 'a security community'. Increasing transactions among Atlantic states developed a steadily growing common sense of community and trust, argued Deutsch. This sense developed to such a degree that members could be assured that all disputes would be resolved peacefully. The possibility of conflict and war falls as interconnectedness increases, Deutsch concluded.

The core argument was not that different from that of, for example, Norman Angell's (1910) and other early theorists of interdependence. However, Deutsch's argument was formulated in the clean and tight language of variable analysis. As interconnectedness reaches a high level, this will give rise to security communities, which are characterized by dependable expectations of peaceful change.

Reformulating the canon

In the immediate wake of World War II, the study of International Relations was dominated by Realism. During the late 1950s, Realism was challenged by new approaches. Observers of European politics noted that states drifted away from the old balance-of-power policies and began to co-operate more extensively. They noted in particular that Europeans established international organizations that were explicitly designed to co-ordinate interstate behaviour. The European Coal and Steel Community (ECSC) attracted particular attention (Mitrany 1965; Deutsch et al. 1957; Haas 1961; 1964).

Realists were also challenged by the colonial conflicts and the wars that erupted in the Third World. Wars in Asia (like Indochina) and Africa (Kenya and Algeria) were not convincingly explained as mere by-products of Great Power rivalry. Radical authors, however, portrayed them as wars of liberation – fought by native actors who sought political independence and economic development. Many observers found this to be a more convincing explanation.

Also, the rise of Radicalism was affecting the Rationalist approach. Radical theories were gaining adherents among opponents of colonialism As a result, a split was emerging within Rationalism between the moderate political reformers on the one hand and the more radical anti-nuclear protesters, peace activists and Third World revolutionaries on the other. Rationalism was pulled towards the political left by the Revolutionary approach which was gaining ground under the impact of colonial warfare. At the same time new methodological approaches were tugging in Realism and pulling many adherents towards the new field of security studies. The traditional field of International Relations was, in short, fragmenting. Among the several efforts to make sense of it all, two contributions will be discussed here: Martin Wight from London's LSE and Kenneth N. Waltz from New York's Columbia University.

Martin Wight and three traditions
Martin Wight was educated at Oxford. He was a historian by training and had worked with Arnold Toynbee at the Royal Institute of International Affairs He was a Christian and a pacifist who, in 1949, came to the London School of Economics to teach an introductory course in International Relations. Here he sought to transcend the preoccupations of his own postwar times and approach International Relations from a broader perspective.

Introductory courses to politics are often presented as a long, sustained tradition of ideas; introductory courses to International Relations, however, have no comparable tradition, Wight (1966) observed. Why is there no International Relations theory? Drawing on diplomatic history and the history of Western thought, Wight formulated three intertwining answers. First, the Renaissance discovery of ancient classics – from Plato and Aristotle on – presented the state as the proper form of political organization, Wight argued. Second, from the fourteenth century onwards this privileging of the state was reinforced, as European thinkers tended to see their main political task as building states that would provide order within a demarcated territory and security from foreign enemies. Finally, during the wars of religion, churchmen as well as humanists developed arguments that supported state sovereignty and autonomy – arguments which were seized by monarchs who were interested in justifying the absolute status of their own power.

Against this background, political philosophy in the West has largely been preoccupied with the nature of state power and how to harness and control this power, that is with issues internal to states. Theories of relations among states have, accordingly, been sparse and scattered. However, when examined more closely, Wight continued, three sources of International Relations theory may be identified. First, discussions of international law, such as Vitoria and Grotius. Second, some political philosophers who have discussed issues of war and peace – such as the plans for perpetual peace like those of Kant and Bentham. Third, some diplomats and practising politicians – like Machiavelli, Bismarck, Woodrow Wilson and Churchill – have sought to draw lessons from their experiences or presented their thoughts on war and peace and balance of power in histories, memoirs, speeches and other texts. Wight drew on sources like these to conduct 'an experiment in classification, in typology' with an aim to locate recurrent themes, thoughts and theories of international politics. During the course of his lectures at the LSE in the 1950s, Wight (1991) elaborated on three approaches which he cultivated in ideal type and referred to as the Realist, Rationalist and Revolutionary approaches to international relations.

Each of the three approaches hinged on a distinct ontology, argued Wight – on a particular view of the world. Realism sees the world in terms of states, state interests and power. Rationalism perceives the world as inhabited by rational humans driven towards cooperation. Revolutionism observes the world through moral-tinted glasses of right and wrong and dreams of a peaceful and unified world. Each approach sustained a distinct tradition and could be represented by a famous political thinker – by Machiavelli, Grotius and Kant, respectively.

The Realists, or Machiavellians, emphasize the anarchical elements of international politics; they see a world composed of 'sovereign states acknowledging no political superior, whose relationships are ultimately regulated by warfare' (Wight 1991, p. 7). The Rationalists, or Grotians, stress the importance of 'diplomacy and commerce'; they are preoccupied by institutions that sustain a 'continuous and organized intercourse' (Wight 1991) in the international society. The Revolutionists, or Kantians, underscore the 'concept of a society of states, or family of nations'; they pursue the realization of an imperative vision of the moral unity of humankind (Wight 1991, p. 8).

Realist ideas have been pursued by philosophers like Hobbes and policy-makers like Frederick the Great. They have tended to deny the existence of international moral and legal obligations based on natural law. They have instead appealed – implicitly, if not explicitly – to principles of expediency.

Rationalists have been closely associated with the Western traditions of liberalism and constitutional government. Philosophers such as John Locke and politicians such as Gladstone and Lincoln have usually taken Rationalist positions, often arguing that moral obligations are rooted in natural law (which in turn is discernible by reason). Rationalists have also emphasized the moral tensions and difficulties involved in limiting power and in identifying the lesser evil in specific situations.

Revolutionist thinkers are rooted in a Christian tradition which asserts the rights and duties to intervene in other states to promote order and peace. They also include the intellectual forefathers of the French Revolution, such as Rousseau, as well as the leaders of the revolution – such as the Jacobins. Also, they include the champions of 'ideological uniformity' as a path to international order and security, such as Kant, Mazzini and Woodrow Wilson. The totalitarian ideologues, both communists and fascists who have tried to impose their conceptions through conquest and coercion, have affected Revolutionist thought, argued Wight. Revolutionists have tended to argue that the end justifies the means, or that political ethics must be identical to those of private life, he continues.

The Realists and the Rationalists have drawn on coherent bodies of thought; both are self-conscious and continuous intellectual streams or traditions. The Revolutionist tradition, by comparison, 'is ambiguous and uncertain. The Revolutionist tradition is less a stream than a series of waves ... [or] disconnected illustrations of the same politico-philosophical truths' (Wight 1991, p. 12). It is a characteristic feature of Revolutionism to deny its past, to try to start from scratch, to jump out of history and begin again. Table 11.1 summarizes some of the main points of Wight's three traditions.

Table 11.1 Wight's three traditions

	Realism	*Rationalism*	*Revolutionism*
Chief actor	sovereign states	rational humans	all humanity
Main focus	conflict and war	co-operation/norms	justice
Key explanatory principle	state interest	enlightened self-interest	human solidarity
Main variable	power	diplomacy, commerce	fairness
Ideological leanings	conservatism	liberalism	radicalism
Important contributors	Machiavelli, Hobbes, Frederick the Great	Grotius, Locke, Gladstone	Rousseau, Kant, Wilson

Wight did not publish much. Nevertheless he had a great influence. First, because he developed his ideas during the lectures he made in the 1950s to a generation of LSE students. Also, Wight became an influential member of the British Committee on the Theory of International Politics in 1959. Wight's three traditions were discussed in the early meetings of the Committee and influenced its members – among them Charles A. W. Manning at the LSE, and Adam Watson and the young Australian scholar Hedley Bull from Oxford.

Kenneth Waltz and three levels of analysis
While Wight taught in London and developed his three traditions, a young scholar was struggling with an ambitious Ph.D. thesis in New York City: Kenneth Neal Waltz. He, like Martin Wight, tried to lift his gaze above the din of contemporary issues and sought to capture some basic lines of international arguments. His Ph.D. thesis, which he pursued at Columbia University, addressed two impossibly broad core International Relations questions: what are the causes of war; what are the preconditions for peace? Waltz delved into political philosophy, diplomatic history and statesmen's memoires to search for answers – and his thesis adviser, William T. R. Fox, feared that he would never finish. Waltz himself suffered the same doubts, until he came upon the idea of organizing his vast number of findings according to three different 'images' or levels of analysis.

Waltz finished his dissertation in 1954 and later turned it into a classic book, *Man, the State and War* [1959]. Its main organizing idea was plainly visible in the title. The book maintained that questions of war and peace can be addressed on three levels of analysis: the level of the individual human being, the level of society and the level of the international system. Answers as to the causes of war and preconditions for peace will differ according to the level of analysis on which the discussion is situated.

Answers that are pursued at the individual level will tend to rely on images of human nature or on psychological theories. *First-image theories* will tend to see the causes of war in human nature. Reinhold Niebuhr and Hans Morgenthau are influential representatives of one kind of first-image theory. They are pessimistic about the prospects of peace, for they consider human nature to be constant. In their view conflict and war will consequently remain a permanent condition for humankind. For Niebuhr and Morgenthau, international conflict cannot be resolved; conflict is the normal state of human affairs. International conflict can, however, be managed; order can be maintained by gifted statesmen who engage in wise balance-of-power politics (Morgenthau 1948).

However there is also another, more optimistic type of first-image theory. It is represented by thinkers like Jean-Jacques Rousseau and Norman Angell who argue that human nature is *not* constant but that human beings are malleable creatures whose basic attitudes are reflections of the culture they inhabit. Human beings can learn. They can draw on experience and they can analyse; they can identify the causes of war and they can learn to behave differently. For thinkers like Rousseau and Angell research and education are important aspects of peace-building. However, even in the most peace-loving of societies, conflict and war may always be occasioned by the troubled psychology of powerful individuals. In order to avoid war, it is important to prevent unstable characters – like Adolf Hitler or Joseph Stalin – from attaining positions of political leadership.

Waltz's *second-image theories* are located at the level of social analysis. It draws on theories which tend to find the causes of conflict and war in the properties of distinct social formations. There are many variations of such theories. One particularly influential kind was formulated by Vladimir Lenin, who argued that capitalist societies cause war. There is an inherent expansionist dynamic in the capitalist mode of production, argued Lenin. Capitalist societies are driven into expansionist (or imperialistic) behaviour on the world scene. The only way to create peace goes through a socialist revolution because this will destroy capitalism and remove the cause of war. However, revolution in one single country would not be sufficient; a worldwide revolution was necessary to destroy the global capitalist system and establish a peaceful world on socialist premises. This second-image argument, then, was universal in ambition. And it was embraced not only by Lenin but also by Stalin, by Khrushchev and by the entire Soviet leadership, argued Waltz.

Clearly, the members of the American Eisenhower administration disagreed with the Revolutionist argument. However, their approach to the question of conflict and war was also a second-image theory. Only that they found the main cause for war in totalitarianism – in its communist as well as in its fascist versions. For any absolute form of government which destroy individual liberties and which brainwashes its people into hatred and blood-thirst foments conflict and war. The basic preconditions for peace are open societies with limited governments whose main task is to guarantee the natural rights of its citizens – including their freedom of faith, speech and organization. In other words, liberal democracy is the solution to the problem of war. This was the claim that President Woodrow Wilson presented on the Paris Peace Conference in 1919. However, it is not sufficient that one or two or a few countries establish liberal democracy; *all* countries in the world must become liberal democracies if a robust peace is to be instituted in the world. Wilson invested an enormous effort into establishing a League of Nations which would sponsor research into the causes of war, co-ordinate education about the preconditions for peace and spread institutions of human rights, law and democracy all around the globe.

Waltz's *third-image theories* are situated at the level of the international system, and find the causes of war in the peculiar characteristics of systemic politics. The international system, explains Waltz, is constituted by sovereign states. And whereas politics *within* a state is regulated by a sovereign government, politics *among* states is not. This lack of regulation is, according to third-image theories, the main cause of war. The international system consists of sovereign states, and their very sovereignty disposes them all to reject any outside effort to impose authority over them. The international system is, in short, 'anarchic'. And in an anarchic system each sovereign actor is concerned with his own, individual interest.

One of the first thinkers to probe this deeply was Jean-Jacques Rousseau, argued Waltz. In his discussion of a primitive deer hunt, Rousseau placed primitive but rational actors in a situation where their behaviour was governed by two principles: well-being and self-preservation. Under such conditions it is hard for humans to associate, let alone co-operate. As humans develop reason, co-operation becomes more possible, but only in the most dire and peculiar of circumstances; they may be driven into cooperation by a common threat or common need.

Rousseau imagines a situation in which a handful of natural men are driven into co-operation by starvation. They all know that each man knows that he can satisfy his hunger by trapping a hare, a catch which will provide a small meal for one hungry man. They also know that several men can get many good meals if they co-operate in hunting down a deer. However, as Rousseau demonstrates, co-operation among sovereign individuals is much more difficult than most people assume, argued Waltz. Through his parable of primitive men Rousseau has captured the core principle of state behaviour in an anarchic international system.

In more recent years, Waltz continued, this kind of behaviour had been explored more precisely by John von Neumann and Oskar Morgenstern in their *Theory of Games and Economic Behavior* [1944]. The development of formal theories of rational action offered promising ways of improving upon International Relations analysis and furthering the science of international politics, he argued. Such theories might help develop the academic promise of third-image approaches. First-level and second-level approaches are not unimportant, wrote Waltz; they contain basic theories and are part and parcel of the study of International Relations. However, it was the third-level theories that offered the greatest promise of developing International Relations into a real social science. Theories developed by game theorists and economists would be of great help in developing new systemic theories of International Relations, Waltz concluded.[7]

Table 11.2 summarizes a few of the basic points in Waltz's approach.

Table 11.2 Waltz's three images/levels of analysis

	First image *(man)*	*Second image* *(the state)*	*Third image* *(international system)*
Level of analysis	Individual level	Social level	Level of the international system
Auxiliary disciplines	Psychology Philosophy	Sociology Political science Political economy	Systems theory Game theory Strategic analysis Micro-economics Strategy/game theory

Changes in International Relations and the Second Great Debate

In the late 1940s, the old dichotomy of Realism and Idealism constituted the main approaches to International Relations. A decade later, the theoretical landscape was vastly expanded. First, by an additional approach, Revolutionism. Then by new methodologies. Authors like Martin Wight and Kenneth Waltz discussed these changes and sought to make sense out of them in philosophical terms. Wight discussed the origins and the properties of Realism, Rationalism and Revolutionism. Waltz introduced the notion of levels of analysis. Together, the two thinkers opened up new theoretical outlooks.

Wight and Waltz were primarily concerned with the ontological aspects of International Relations theories; they did not elaborate on the methodological changes that took place. They did not address the new research techniques that had affected the discipline since before World War II. Scholars like Quincy Wright (1942) used statistical techniques and encouraged students of International Relations to think in terms of co-relations between variables and to use this to focus discussions of causalities. Wiring diagrams from electrical engineering inspired International Relations theorists to think of social relations in terms of complex interconnections. Such innovations introduced new, behaviourist approaches to the study of International Relations. They quickly clashed with traditionalist orientations that relied on historic, legal and interpretationist approaches. This would trigger controversy and new debates that rattled and shaped the discipline during the 1960s.

Innovations of the postwar age

One factor which deeply affected this debate was a rapid advent of electronic computing machines. This development was driven by innovations in electromagnetic communications technologies made during World War II. Large computers were installed at universities during the postwar years. This revolutionized research in all social sciences. It enabled scholars to use quantitative methods and variable analysis on a vast, new scale (Eulau 1961). Statistical analyses of war and peace, which Quincy Wright (1942) had performed largely by hand in the late 1930s, could now be made by big computers installed in major universities.

Another factor which affected the debate was a new methodology which swept the social sciences during the 1950s. A new philosophy of science was introduced. It was spearheaded by thinkers like Karl R. Popper and Carl G. Hempel. Popper was Austrian by birth but had emigrated to Britain during the 1930s as Nazism gained influence in his homeland. He criticized the old argument that science evolves as scholars steadily prove the truth of more and more claims about the world. He argued instead that no general claim can really be proved true. What *can* be proved, however, is that particular claims are *false*. Consequently, science does not evolve through a process of verification whereby scholars prove claims to be true and add them to humanity's growing store of verified knowledge; rather, science evolves through a systematic process of *falsification*, whereby scholars prove claims to be false and thus eliminate erroneous propositions from the ranks of human knowledge.

Also, Popper continued, theories are attempts to simplify and streamline the world; they are mental constructs and must not be confused with descriptions of the real world. Theories must not be assessed by empirical criteria. Since theories are figments of the human imagination, scientists should not ask of them whether they are true or false; rather, they should ask whether they have more or less explanatory power.

Carl Gustav Hempel largely agreed with Popper's philosophy of science. He agreed that scientists should not ask whether a theory is true or false; rather, they should ask whether it can engender a good hypothesis. Such a hypothesis can be operationalized and converted into a concrete claim about the world and then tested – that is, it can be confronted by empirical evidence in an attempt to falsify it. Of hypotheses one can ask whether they are true or false – and the answer can be determined by an empirical test. Popper and Hempel revolutionized philosophy of science. They gave the postwar social sciences a new methodological foundation (Moses and Knutsen 2012, pp. 38ff).

Two sets of innovations then – the Popper–Hempel innovation in methodology and the invention of electronic computing machines – ushered in postwar social sciences. Together they paved the way for techniques of hypothesis-testing. This in turn increased demands for new skills in research techniques and in standard social-science procedures. They opened up new avenues for empirical research. Reams of information were collected, converted into vast, new data sets and subjected to statistical analysis. The new techniques were applied to all kinds of international phenomena (Singer 1968), a practice which triggered ridicule in hostile circles. Traditional scholars doubted the utility of diagramming voting patterns in the UN and the exchange of letters among countries. These were exercises of meaningless mapping, argued traditionalists who feared that formal technique might replace analysis and drive out substantial knowledge.

The 'positivist debate'

Hostility grew as adherents of the new techniques drew on disciplines like economics (which had formalized models that could be mathematically expressed) or engineering (which could depict any process in terms of flow-charts or wiring diagrams).

The new techniques were most strongly defended in the USA, where the new scientific attitude was particularly pronounced. This attitude was often referred to as 'positivism' or 'behaviourism' – as it was based on the assumption that the science should restrict itself to examine phenomena that were positively given and thus directly observable (such as the observable behaviour of social actors). It should leave out unobservable phenomena (such as ideas or intentions that occur in people's minds). Behaviourism affected all social sciences in the West in the 1950s.

The new techniques met with a particular scepticism in Germany. They triggered a methodological debate which was commonly referred to as 'the Positivist Debate' – *der Positivismusstreit* – during the early 1960s. The debate was intensified by the particular subtext shaped by Germany's painful experience with Nazism and stirred deep, political antagonisms in a turbulent, post-fascist society. The debate pitted the new, rationalist philosophy of science against the anti-fascist arguments of the political left.

Karl Popper, one of the main proponents of the new scientific approach, became a target of the left. He was a refugee from Nazism and a defender of an open, liberal democracy of the Anglo-American type (Popper 1945). He was deeply sceptical of German social philosophy and criticized the German tradition of idealism with an argument of critical rationalism – whose vision of science included variable analysis and the systematic testing of hypotheses. Among his sternest opponents were members of the Frankfurt school, especially Theodor Adorno. He, too, had been a refugee from Nazism. Adorno had spent several war years in the USA and had hated every minute of it. He had no admiration for America. On the contrary, Adorno had, together with fellow-refugee and colleague Max Horkheimer, written a scathing condemnation of American society (Adorno and Horkheimer 1979 [1944]). After the war, Adorno could not return to Germany quickly enough. Back in Frankfurt, he became an influential thinker in the tradition of critical theory.

The German positivism debate took place in a peculiar political climate of postwar traumas and Cold War tensions. The debate was caught in a deeply politicized antagonism between the 'leftist', 'liberationist' and anti-capitalist arguments of Adorno and the critical theorists on the one hand, and the 'rightist', 'bourgeois' and liberal-democracy arguments of Popper and the reformist rationalists on the other. Cold War sentiments quickly transmitted those antagonisms to other countries. Controversies about Western imperialism and warfare in the Third World poisoned the debate about scientific methods with political passions. The debate began in the 1950s and grew sharper during the 1960s. It paved the way for the so-called 'Second Great Debate' in International Relations.

The 'Second Great Debate'

The Second Great Debate is so named through a tacit reference to the 'First Great Debate' – which took place during the 1930s between the advocates of Realism and Idealism. The Second Great Debate was a clash which took place a generation later between advocates of the traditional approaches to International Relations and the proponents of the new scientific approach.

On the one side in the debate were the 'behaviourists' or 'positivists', championed by social scientists in the USA where the development of computers had come furthest and where the scientific attitude was particularly pronounced. Their outlook was based on the assumption that the sciences should restrict themselves to examining phenomena that were positively given (such as the observable behaviour of social actors); it should leave unobservable phenomena (such as ideas or intentions) out of social-science analysis. Behaviourism affected all social sciences in the late 1950s. It instructed scientists to observe social actors objectively and then describe their behaviour in precise, measurable terms. Such descriptions would be standardized and codified and included in a catalogue or database of systematic records. Scientists would then rely on statistical techniques to analyse the data in order to extract general statements and patterns.

J. David Singer was an early proponent of behaviourism in International Relations. Aided by the mainframe computer at the University of Michigan, he studied the causes of war with quantitative methods. He developed a legendary data set – of 'Correlates of War' (or COW) fame. Singer would rely on COW data, on formal procedural design and on computer techniques to test carefully crafted hypotheses related to the outbreak, intensity, size and longevity of war (Singer 1966; 1969).

The traditionalists criticized this kind of approach. They argued that there is a qualitative difference between the natural sciences and the social sciences and insisted that social relationships could not be fully grasped with methods imported from the natural sciences. This argument was expressed by Hedley Bull, an Australian student of strategy and arms control. When Bull became a professor at Oxford University and a member of the British Committee on the Theory of International Relations, he turned his attention to the historical study of international order.

On the face of it, the Second Great Debate was a discussion about appropriate methods of International Relations research. But this debate also expressed deeper philosophy-of-science issues. Its contours had been visible already in the 1930s – for example in Edward H. Carr's argument that the science of international relations cannot rely on methods drawn from the natural sciences. They were also apparent in the harsh criticism that Hans J. Morgenthau (1946) had levied against 'American rationalism' in the mid-1940s. When Hedley Bull opposed Singer's behaviourist approach in the 1960s, there were philosophical echoes of both Carr and Morgenthau in his arguments.

On the threshold to the 1960s

Events of the late 1940s defined the fronts of the Cold War. The consolidation of Soviet power in Eastern Europe (1945–48), the Berlin blockade (1948–49), the Soviet atomic-bomb test (1949) produced increasing fear of communism in the Atlantic world. The Chinese Revolution (1949) and the outbreak of war in Korea (1950) released a 'red scare' in the USA. Spy hunts and spy trials whipped up an anti-Soviet hysteria, reflected in the meteoric rise to prominence of the anti-communist senator Joseph McCarthy in American politics.

At that very point Stalin died (1953). McCarthy's communist witch-hunt was working its way towards its climax and blinded US politicians to the implications of Stalin's death. The Americans overlooked efforts on the part of the new Soviet leadership to break with the Stalinist past. They ignored the widening Sino-Soviet split that followed the death of the great generalissimo – disregarding the manifestation of that split in a heated debate between Soviet and Chinese representatives at the Bandung conference in 1955. The brawl at Bandung clearly showed that the USSR's post-Stalin leadership was losing Mao's allegiance and that of the Chinese Communist Party.

The Americans were, however, painfully aware of similar antagonisms within the Western Bloc. A split appeared with the outbreak of the Suez Crisis in 1956. US President Eisenhower was furious at the way that Britain and France conspired with Israel to retrieve control over the Suez Canal. Anglo-American relations were severely dented by the crisis. Franco-American relations never recovered from it. If the USSR had problems keeping China and Mao within the communist camp, then the USA had difficulties keeping France and de Gaulle within the Western alliance.

The Suez Crisis also triggered reactions within the British and the French empires. It sharpened the colonies' accusations of Western imperialism and played into the hands of rebels who worked to break out of colonial relations. The crisis hastened decolonization.

The crisis caught the USA on the horns of an unenviable dilemma. The Americans were pressured to make a difficult choice: either to continue their traditional opposition to European colonialism or to break with tradition and help European powers defend their empires against Soviet incursions. When push came to shove, America's ancient ideals lost out to pressing Cold War concerns. The Americans chose to support the wars that Europe's colonial powers fought against rebels and independence movements in the Third World. They argued that, if colonies obtained independence, they might fall under the influence of Soviet power.

This American perception was deeply informed by bitter US experiences with Fidel Castro and the Cuban revolution. The Americans had initially perceived Castro, who had toppled the dictator Fulgencio Batista in an armed revolution in 1959, with curiosity – even with sympathy. However, Cuban–American relations quickly deteriorated. American leaders balked when Castro's government quickly announced progressive land reforms. When he followed up by nationalizing US oil refineries, the American government became actively hostile to the Castro government and cancelled US imports of Cuban sugar. The situation went from bad to worse when Castro accepted a Soviet offer to buy all the sugar that Cuba could sell. The Americans were shocked when Castro declared that his revolution had always been Marxist–Leninist. In 1961 they tried to start a counter-revolution by landing a motley crew of US-trained anti-Castro forces in the Bay of Pigs. The operation was a military failure and a political disaster for the USA.

Plagued by fear of a US invasion, economic sanctions and CIA plots (Weiner 2007), Castro asked the USSR for protection – preferably in the form of nuclear missiles to deter the Americans. Khrushchev agreed. During the summer of 1962 the USSR began to secretly ship medium-range missiles to Cuba. US spy planes discovered the missiles in mid-October. This triggered a serious diplomatic crisis between the two superpowers. The Kennedy administration quickly implemented a naval blockade of Cuba. Tensions increased as Soviet cargo ships approached the Caribbean island. The situation was all the more serious because there were no standard diplomatic relations between the two superpowers. No direct channels of communication existed between the White House and the Kremlin. Contact was improvised and unsystematic and added uncertainty to the tense and dangerous situation. During the third week of October 1962 the two superpowers 'stared into the abyss'. At the eleventh hour Khrushchev ordered the Soviet cargo ships to stop and missiles to be withdrawn. The USA promised never to invade Cuba again.

The Cuban revolution and the subsequent Missile Crisis represent turning points in the Cold War. The events made the United States suspicious of anti-colonial rebellions. They steeled US resistance to Third World radicalism. They deepened US support of Europe's old colonial powers and caught the Americans in a difficult and often embarrassing dilemma. But the Americans argued that, if colonies obtained independence, they would become victims of Soviet influence and perhaps become members of an expanding Soviet empire.

The Cuban Missile Crisis gave a new dynamic to the superpower relations. It introduced a new phase to the Cold War – a phase in which Khrushchev no longer played any role. Khrushchev was removed in a coup by Soviet leaders who had seen enough of his policy initiatives – now often referred to as 'harebrained schemes'. Khrushchev was replaced by the more stolid and predictable Leonid Brezhnev. A Stalinist by disposition, Brezhnev tightened political controls at home. He also initiated new Soviet armament programmes. He accelerated the build-up of the USSR's atomic arsenal. And he began a long-term naval programme to make the USSR a first-rate sea power.

The Cuban Missile Crisis also had implications for International Relations theory. It lent itself beautifully to game-theoretical analysis. It became a favourite case study which International Relations students could examine to capture the tit-for-tat logic of the Cold War rivalry. During the 1960s, International Relations students modelled the crisis in an innumerable variations of chicken and prisoners'-dilemma games.

Graham Allison at Harvard University was sceptical about game-theoretic and strategic analysis and unconvinced by the rational-actor assumptions which provided the premises for them. It was in his mind hard to know whether the USSR in fact *was* a rational actor. US policy-makers knew little about the workings of the Soviet system and next to nothing about the decision-making procedures of its government. The Americans did not know whether Soviet foreign policy-making was rational or not. They simply assumed that it was.

But what if it was not? After all, the USSR was different from the USA in many crucial respects – its political system, its economic orientation, its entire social philosophy was pretty much the precise opposite of everything that the USA stood for. So was it reasonable to expect that Soviet decision-makers obeyed a rationality that was built on the assumptions of free-market economics? In fact, was it reasonable to assume that *American* decision-makers obeyed such a rationality? For when US political practice was more carefully examined, this ideal-typical rationality was trumped by standard procedures of bureaucratic structures and by the narrow self-interest of political actors. Allison demonstrated convincingly how the decision-makers of the Kennedy administration were affected by the standard operational procedures (SOPs) laid down in the state bureaucracies and offices and coloured by traditional log-rolling and political compromise. And if such non-rational procedures were at work in the USA, would they not also be at work in the USSR as well? If the Kennedy cabinet was affected by concerns of political prestige, would not the Khrushchev cabinet be affected by similar concerns?

Allison (1971) made a detailed study of US decision-making during the Cuban Missile Crisis. First, he carefully applied the rational-actor model (RAM) – the dominant strategic model of the time – and raised several questions about the rational nature of certain actions. Then he reviewed the crisis in the light of two alternative models – a bureaucratic procedures model and a political bargaining model – and showed that each of them provided satisfactory accounts of the actors' decisions. Allison's study was an instant classic. He had contrasted three different models of foreign-policy decision making, two of them good alternatives to the rational-actor model.

Allison's critique was as devastating as it was subtle. The rational-actor model was easy and seductive. It relied on just a few assumptions. It required little or no empirical evidence. Anybody could use it. You could sit down, close your eyes and imagine how statesmen would behave. You could simply ask yourself how *you* would behave if you had your rational wits about you. And you get, 'free of charge, a lot of vicarious, empirical behavior' (Allison 1971, p. 19).

Allison did not draw the obvious implications of his critique. But they should be frightfully clear: namely, that during the first phases of the Cold War – during the years when US politicians knew little about the structures of the Soviet government and next to nothing about its decision-making processes – American analysts simply assumed that the Soviets were rational actors bent on conquest. In the late 1940s, the Americans did not know their enemy. So they invented an enemy they could know, because they invented it as their own mirror image. Against this imaginary enemy they began to play a dangerous game of nuclear chicken.

Notes

1 The ECSC was a new phenomenon in European politics. It was based on the principles of super-nationalism and run by four institutions: a High Authority composed of independent appointees, a Common Assembly composed of national parliamentarians, a Special Council composed of ministers from the member states, and a Court of Justice. These institutions would ultimately form the blueprint for the EU – with the European Commission, the European Parliament, the Council of the European Union and the European Court of Justice, respectively. International Relations scholars were quick to see the significance of the ECSC and to see it as an unprecedented and hopeful innovation. The ECSC was followed by the establishment of another super-national organization in 1957, the European Atomic Energy Community (or Euratom) and the Treaty of Rome, which was a declaration to establish a European Common Market.

2 The USA encouraged European integration and saw it as an important contribution to containment. The US Foreign Secretary John Foster Dulles worked to streamline and strengthen NATO and to make Germany a full member. Also, Dulles travelled the world and established new pacts and alliances as part of a strategy to encircle the USSR and contain what he referred to as 'Godless Communism'. Dulles was instrumental in forming both ANZUS and SEATO. Also, the Americans initiated a military build-up which included new more rockets and other new weapons systems. They redesigned their Strategic Air Command (SAC) for use in Asia. Here, the USA was slowly taking over France's war in Indochina.

    These initiatives carried a high price tag. Table 10.1, in the previous chapter, shows how the US defence budget makes a big jump after the outbreak of the Korean War: whereas the US defence amounts to about 5 per cent of GNP in the late 1940s, it more than doubles in the early 1950s to well over 10 per cent of GNP – a percentage which remains the norm until the 1970s. This American militarization occurred just as Stalin was dying and a new Soviet leadership resolved that the old aggressive foreign-policy stance was counter-productive.

3 France reacted at first by proposing to organize a European Defence Community (EDC); this was a clear balance-of-power reaction on the part of the French Prime Minister René Pleven, designed to contain Germany. The proposal, however, was never implemented. The European fear of a rearmed Germany was overtaken by the growing alarm of Soviet expansionism, and this broke the balance-of-power dynamics which had marked European relations for hundreds of years. In fact, the old balancing game was replaced with a project for co-operation and common defence. And it can well be argued that Stalin was an unwitting mover behind this unprecedented process of co-operation and integration among the states of the North Atlantic rim.

4 In his speech, Khrushchev accused Stalin of creating a regime based on 'suspicion, fear, and terror'. Khrushchev added that he wanted to break the cult of Stalin, who had died three years before. He condemned the mass repressions that took place between 1936 and 1938, lashed out at Stalin's foreign policy during World War II, and accused him of nationalism and anti-Semitism.

5 The Rockefeller Foundation was an important patron of academic International

Relations. From the early 1950s, International Relations was promoted by the Legal and Political Philosophy Program of the Foundation. The head of that generous programme was Kenneth W. Thompson. In May 1954 Thompson presided over a planning meeting which decided to promote the development of 'international relations theory'. The meeting set a course which was to influence the evolution of International Relations in general and of Realism in particular. The story is elaborated in Guilhot (2011). It is worth noting that Thompson received his Ph.D. in 1950 from the University of Chicago, where he was the research assistant of Hans J. Morgenthau. Thompson was influenced by Morgenthau and represented what he called 'Christian Realism'. When Morgenthau died in 1980, Thompson was asked to revise *Politics among Nations* – whose most recent edition is referred to as Morgenthau and Thompson (1985).

6 The label 'English School' appeared in 1981 in an article by Roy Jones (1981).

7 Waltz pursued this conclusion for twenty years and published a refined and streamlined version in his 1979 *Theory of International Politics* – another of the most important International Relations books written, and one which laid the basis for what would later be called Neorealism.

12

Arms races and revolutions: systems and structures in an age of upheaval

The Cuban Missile Crisis introduced a new phase to the Cold War. Shaken by the sudden risk of nuclear war, the two superpowers developed new diplomatic institutions – conferences, summit meetings and new treaties and obligations – designed to harness the competition for international power and influence. The Cold War was marked by growing aspects of co-operation as well as of conflict.

The transition to a new phase in the Cold War was accentuated by a shift in superpower leadership. In the USA the aged and formal President Dwight D. Eisenhower was replaced by the young, charismatic John F. Kennedy. His presidency symbolized the advent of a new generation with new political ideals. The USA was deeply shaken when Kennedy was assassinated in Texas in October 1963 and replaced by the Texan Senator Lyndon B. Johnson (1963–69). In the USSR, the Soviet Premier Nikita Khrushchev was toppled in a palace coup in 1964 and replaced by Leonid Brezhnev.

One of the most significant issues that marked international relations during these years was that of decolonization. Nations in Asia and Africa demanded self-rule and independence. In many cases demands were backed by armed rebellion. These pulled Britain, France and other colonial powers into irregular wars in the Third World. Another important issue concerned energy. Questions were increasingly raised of whether the wealth-engendering industries of the West could continue to count on a smooth supply of cheap oil from extra-Western sources. The issues of decolonization and energy were linked. And they were discussed in the shadow of the third and dominant issue of the age: the continuing nuclear rivalry of the two superpowers.

This chapter will first outline the most important international events of the 1960s and 1970s. It will then consider how the major issues of the age were addressed by International Relations scholars who developed new concepts and approaches to grasp and understand them. Authors like Keohane, Nye, Krasner and North expanded on liberal approaches to co-operation and order. Authors like Baran, Sweezy, Gunder Frank and other radical authors elaborated on Marxist theories of exploitation, conflict and revolution. The turbulence and changes that marked the diplomatic relations of these years, then, also shook established analytical approaches in the field of International Relations. One of the major changes of the age was that Revolutionism evolved into maturity and established itself firmly as a new tradition or paradigm in International Relations scholarship, alongside Realism and Rationalism. The evolution stimulated the development of a new, structuralist social philosophy. It encouraged scholars as different as Wallerstein, Waltz and Bull to develop new grand theories of world politics.

In the wake of the Missile Crisis

The Cuban Missile Crisis affected the superpowers and their relationship deeply. It affected US foreign policy because American leaders considered the Soviet pull-out a victory for their doctrine of containment and a vindication of rational-actor approaches. It affected the USSR in other ways: members of the Politburo drew the lesson that that they had seen enough of Khrushchev's independent initiatives – now increasingly referred to as 'harebrained schemes' – and that he had to go. In November 1964 he was removed from power in a palace coup and replaced by Leonid Brezhnev. Brezhnev was a hard-liner who learned from the Missile Crisis that the USSR should never again be caught in a situation of embarrassing inferiority. As soon as he attained political power, he began to build up the missile forces and strengthen the Soviet navy.

The Cuban Missile Crisis also affected the scholarly study of International Relations. It encouraged the use of rational-actor approaches and of game theory. In the wake of the missile crisis superpower relations were modelled and remodelled as games of chicken and prisoners' dilemma. On the abstract level, these were approaches which gave a simple and streamlined understanding of the superpower relationship. Clearly, the superpower behaviour could be understood in terms of the mutual suspicion and fear of the security dilemma. Yet, rational-actor models rested on the premise that the two superpowers were comparable and equal actors. But were they really equal enough for game theories to be apply? The two superpowers differed in political cultures and political outlooks. They also differed in strength: during the Cuban Missile Crises, the USA possessed nearly ten times more nuclear weapons than the USSR.[1]

When the USSR removed its missiles from Cuba, several Kremlin leaders argued that the USSR needed to accelerate its nuclear-missiles programme and catch up with the US lead. In 1964, when Leonid Brezhnev replaced Nikita Khrushchev as the leader of the USSR, the Soviets still had fewer than five hundred nuclear missiles, whereas the USA possessed well over three thousand. Brezhnev increased the pace of the Soviet arms build-up. By 1970, the Soviets had more than quadrupled their number to over two thousand missiles. The USA had increased its number to nearly five thousand (SIPRI 1991, p. 25 and Table 12.2, below). The Americans still had more missiles than the USSR, but gap was closing.

The more missiles the two superpowers had, the less the gap mattered. By 1970 both of them possessed enough atomic weapons to destroy each other several times over. For all practical purposes, a rough strategic equivalence of capabilities now existed between them. The constellation of power between them approached 'parity'. The world could be described as 'bipolar' in a technical as well as an ideological sense.

This rough equivalence of capabilities marked a new phase in the Cold War. The transition was aided by an advent of more regular diplomatic intercourse and by a change in the international climate. This was expressed, for example, in the Vienna Convention of Diplomatic Relations, negotiated under the auspices of the UN during the early 1960s and which led to a landmark agreement on rules of diplomacy and treaty-making. Other treaties were also negotiated and signed in the wake of the Cuban Missile Crisis. Among them were treaties which sought to limit the spread of nuclear weapons and harness the arms race. Most important among them was the Nuclear Test Ban Treaty (of July 1963).

These were signs that superpower tensions were lessening. A new phase opened up where the two superpowers engaged in bilateral negotiations to control and co-ordinate the arms race and even reduce the stockpiles of nuclear weapons. This phase of increased co-operation and reduced tension is commonly referred to as a phase of détente.

Third-World wars

The USSR continued to support anti-colonial liberation movements in the Third World. The USA, guided by its doctrine of containment, found itself opposing these movements. US leaders tended to see them as sponsored by the USSR and as tools of Soviet expansionism. Increasingly, the USA found itself driven to the side of the old colonial powers.

Soviet leaders observed this tendency with glee. They exploited it for all it was worth and caught the USA in a dilemma. The Americans had traditionally seen themselves as enemies of colonialism. Their foreign-policy rhetoric was democratic and anti-colonial. However, this traditional rhetoric was increasingly belied by their foreign-policy practice. The Americans assisted first Britain and then France in wars against anti-colonial insurgents in Third-World conflicts. Then they began to intervene on their own in countries like Iran, Congo, the Dominican Republic and Cuba (Takeyh 2014; Weissman 2014).

Such interventions placed the USA in embarrassing situations. In the interest of anti-communism, the USA not only supported old colonial powers, it also found itself shoulder to shoulder with new, anti-communist, all-white, racist minority regimes – as in Rhodesia and South Africa. A most painful predicament developed in Indochina. When France pulled out of Vietnam in 1954, the USA continued the anti-communist struggle there on its own. Victory was elusive, and the USA steadily escalated its presence – from about five hundred advisers in 1960 to ten thousand soldiers in 1962. After the assassination of President Kennedy, Lyndon B. Johnson increased the number of US soldiers to two hundred thousand in 1966 and then to five hundred thousand in 1968. At that time the USA also began secret bombing campaigns in Laos and Cambodia – to be followed by secret ground operations two years later to destroy Viet Cong sanctuaries there. All in the name of containment.

American warfare in Indochina met with strong protests at home. The protests affected America's political climate deeply. It split Johnson's Democratic Party and helped Richard Nixon get elected President on a Republican ticket in 1968. American warfare also triggered protests abroad – even among America's own NATO allies. But the strongest protests came from the USSR and China – especially from China, the leaders of which recalled the US intervention in Korea and who sought to keep the Americans mired in an exhausting war.

In spite of Third World wars and a sharpening of ideological rhetoric, détente continued. In January 1967 the superpowers signed a treaty to ban nuclear missiles from outer space. In July 1968 they signed the Nuclear Non-proliferation Treaty.

Détente

When Richard Nixon became US President in 1969, he expanded the dialogue with the USSR. He engaged the Soviet leaders in talks to reduce the number of strategic nuclear weapons – the Strategic Arms Limitations Talks (or SALT). Détente between the superpowers also led to relaxation of political tension in other regions.

In Eastern Europe, relaxation encouraged nations to test the limits of Soviet tolerance. Czechoslovakia, for example, elected a reformist leader in the spring of 1968, Alexander Dubcek. He initiated economic reorganizations and political reforms. This worried the Soviet leaders, who feared that, if they tolerated the reforms of the so-called Prague Spring, similar reforms would quickly appear in other Eastern Bloc countries. In August 1968, the Soviet leaders removed the problem by military means: Soviet forces invaded Czechoslovakia. Soviet Premier Brezhnev argued that this was necessary in order to 'help a brother in need' and rescue the Czech people from capitalist corruption. Dubcek was deposed. The Soviet army kept order in the country until a more orthodox regime, led by Gustav Husak, replaced him.

In Western Europe political groups organized protests against American interventionism. They opposed US bombing raids in Vietnam and criticized the US internment of the Vietnamese population in camps, or 'strategic hamlets'. When the United States was charged with encouraging a military coup in Greece in April 1967, some West European governments protested against the US behaviour.

West Germany developed its own form of détente in the so-called *Ostpolitik*. It was launched by Chancellor Willy Brandt in the autumn of 1969 and its purpose was to reduce tensions between West Germany and the Eastern Bloc.[2] Brandt's *Ostpolitik* made US President Nixon deeply unhappy. His mood did not improve when several European countries accepted an invitation from the USSR in the autumn of 1972 to gather in Helsinki for a Conference on Security and Co-operation in Europe (or CSCE).

The Soviet aim was partly to sow dissention in the Atlantic community, and partly to reduce tensions on the Continent – to stabilize the European borders and gain acceptance for the gains that Stalin had secured after World War II. The aim of European diplomats was also to reduce tensions. In addition they wanted to further economic co-operation and obtain humanitarian improvements for the nations of the Eastern Bloc. Nixon thought the Europeans were naive. They might buy stability, but at a dangerously high cost, he fumed. However, after a few years it turned out that it was the USSR who found the costs to be dangerously high. For the CSCE led to the 1975 signing of the Helsinki Act, which included a general acceptance of human rights and freedom of the press. This greatly encouraged dissidents and human-rights organizations in all countries of the Eastern Bloc. The Soviet negotiators had apparently not understood the appeal of human rights. The idea that the CSCE's mentioning of rights and freedoms would fire the political ambitions of the Soviet public and help bring the Soviet empire to its knees was a possibility far beyond their wildest imagination.

Blows to the US hegemony
The Vietnam War proved to be very costly for the USA. It was a burden on the US economy and a drain on its foreign reserves. Also, it undermined America's prestige. The war made the USA look militaristic and mean, and exhausted the enormous goodwill that the Americans built up during World War II. Also, it fuelled a new kind of anti-Americanism, an animosity that was different from the old, right-wing and elitist charges of the USA as a vulgar and uncultured nation.

The new anti-Americanism was left-wing and radical and rooted in Marxist economic theory and in charges of imperialist expansionism. It painted America's political economy in hues of dark suspicion. US military forces were increasingly portrayed as tools of capitalistic avarice, exploitation and repression. Chinese and Soviet leaders had long launched charges of imperialism against the USA. During the late 1950s radical Third World leaders had added their voices to the choir. Ho Chi Minh, Fidel Castro and Ernesto 'Che' Guevara had been at the receiving end of US imperialism and testified to its repressive and extortionist character. During the 1960s such Third World testimonies wielded a significant influence on a new generation of young people in the Western world. Young radicals, discouraged by the grey conformity of Khrushchev's USSR and disillusioned by Soviet invasions of Hungary (1956) and Czechoslovakia (1968), embraced the slogans of Mao Zedong's 'Hundred Flowers Movement' and the ideals of his Cultural Revolution.[3] Thousands of young Westerners visited China to experience the Chinese miracle for themselves. They returned with Mao's Little Red Book in their luggage. A good many of them also returned with red stars in their eyes.

In February 1972 Richard Nixon, too, visited Beijing and met with the ageing Mao Zedong. Nixon's errand was motivated by Henry Kissinger's Realist analysis: China supported the Vietnamese rebels. To make China stop this support, it was first necessary to open up diplomatic relations with the Chinese; this was a first step on a long road towards ending the Vietnam War.[4] Besides, an alliance with China would strengthen the American hand in negotiations with the USSR. Some analysts feared that Nixon's visit to China would make the Soviets angry and undermine the Soviet–American détente. Their fears were groundless. Superpower arms talks continued. Indeed, in May 1972 the two superpowers signed an important treaty that limited missile technology – the first Strategic Arms Limitation Treaty (or SALT I).

Many young radicals who had their political imagination fired up by the Vietnam War were further affected by a wave of revolutions during the mid-1970s. It began in the Iberias – with a coup in Portugal (1974) and the death of General Franco (1975) in Spain – and rippled across Latin America and Africa. As the new Portuguese government pulled out of their African colonies, new and radical regimes took power there. They condemned the colonial practices of the West and developed close ties with the USSR and Cuba.

Soon power struggles erupted in these countries. The two superpowers intervened and backed different factions. This nourished the flames of conflict and kept colonial wars going for decades – contributing to the death of millions of Africans. Similar developments soon took place in other countries with a colonial past. To the wars in Vietnam, Cambodia, Laos, Angola and Mozambique were added wars in Somalia, Ethiopia and Afghanistan.

The increase in international conflict is suggested by Table 12.1, which presents the number of wars in the world by type and decades.

Table 12.1 Number and type of wars in the first half of the Cold War, by decade

	Interstate	Extrastate	Intrastate	Total	Estimated war deaths
1950s	3	6	11	20	1,083,956
1960s	6	3	16	25	2,090,581
1970s	7	3	25	35	2,707,155

Source: Sarkees (2000)

The table shows the increase in violent conflict and war across three decades. The 1950s saw three interstate wars, six extrastate wars, and eleven intrastate (or civil) wars – which makes twenty wars in total. The 1960s had twenty-five wars in total. The 1970s had thirty-five. This increase in number of wars was matched by a comparable increase in the number of war dead – a number which increased from about 1.1 million in the 1950s, via 2.1 million in the 1960s to 2.7 million war dead in the 1970s.

This simple table suggests that the 1970s was a conflictual decade. Soviet analysts noticed this increase in wars and argued that the world was being divided more clearly along Cold War lines. Soviet leaders observed the advent of radical regimes in the Third World with optimism. Greatly encouraged by the establishment of new client states in Africa and Asia, they were led to think that their orthodox theories of socialist revolution might be confirmed at last. The flurry of Third World revolutions in the late 1970s confirmed their Marxist–Leninist theory: the capitalist West was in deep trouble, and the world revolution was just around the corner.

In the West, several statesmen and scholars were of a similar opinion. They observed the spate of Third World revolutions with deep forebodings. Their pessimistic predictions were strengthened by financial downturns that shook the capitalist world economy and weakened the pre-eminence of the United States.

A first indication of this US decline came in 1972, when President Nixon removed the US dollar from the gold standard. This caused the value of the dollar to plummet. The entire Bretton Woods system, which was founded on the premise that all member currencies could be exchanged into gold by way of the dollar, suffered as a result.

A second indication of a capitalist crisis came in the autumn of 1973, when the Organization of Oil Producing Countries (OPEC) halted petroleum exports to countries that had taken Israel's side in the Yom Kippur War (of October 1973). The immediate result of the OPEC blockade was a severe oil shortage in several Western countries. This pulled rationings, riots and skyrocketing oil prices in its wake. The price for a barrel of oil nearly quadrupled within weeks from about $3 to over $11 per barrel.

The economic consequences were immediate. On the one hand, OPEC members grew richer. Oil-exporting countries, like Saudi Arabia, experienced a steep rise in national income, which they invested in modernization projects at home, in education and missionary projects in the Muslim region, and in Western financial markets. On the other hand, oil-importing countries saw their oil bills increase. This was more than some of the more fragile economies of the world could take; some of them began to take up large international loans in order to secure their oil supplies and meet their industrializing ambitions. Industrialized countries in the West introduced measures of energy conservation. Also, they began to think more systematically about oil supplies and about alternative sources of energy.

The oil crisis of 1973 introduced a range of new policy issues. Some of them were reflected in a growing concern of environmental protection. Others were reflected in new concerns with 'energy security'. The US geoscientist M. King Hubbert had argued many years earlier that domestic US oil production would peak around 1965–70 (Yergin 2011, p. 235ff). US analysts increasingly came to think that he was right. They noted that domestic oil production had stagnated at a time when America's demand for oil was growing more steeply than ever. The USA could no longer supply its allies with fossil fuels in a crisis. In fact, the USA might not even cover its own oil consumption by domestic sources alone.

This development worried President Nixon, who saw in it an emerging threat to national security. The USA had a way of life that was predicated on a huge consumption of fossil fuels, which might no longer be supplied by domestic sources alone. The USSR, by contrast, seemed to increase its oils production and emerge as a major exporter of fossil fuels. Increases in Soviet oil production as well as petroleum price hikes boosted Soviet earnings of hard currency, which in turn could be used to support radical regimes in the Third World.

Nixon's fears lingered over the presidency of his successor, Jimmy Carter (1977–81). Carter put the US energy crisis on the national security agenda by referring to it as the 'moral equivalent of war'. He was reminded of the security aspects of the energy issue when a new oil crisis erupted in the wake of revolution in Iran in 1979 – after which the spot price of oil nearly tripled to more than $40 per barrel. US security analysts steadily criticized Carter for fully seeing the connection between oil and a new Soviet effort to expand its influence in the Third World. The Soviets were 'jumping over the fence of containment', as one observer put it (Knutsen 1992). When the Soviets invaded Afghanistan at the end of 1979, Carter finally reacted and gave a clear warning to the Soviet leaders: the USA would not allow any other power to gain control of the oil-rich region around the Persian Gulf. The announcement was quickly known as the Carter Doctrine.

Years of upheaval?

The times were marked by a sentiment of crisis. Several popular books reflected this. Among them were *Future Shock* (1970) by Alvin Toffler, *Limits to Growth* (1972) by the Club of Rome and *Crisis of Democracy* (1975) by Crozier, Huntington and Watanuki. But was there a crisis? Wasn't this also an age of improving Soviet–American relations?

Yes, this was an age in which the superpower rivalry was brought into more orderly forms through arms control and détente. However, the superpower rivalry was hard to harness. The arms race, for example, was not just a question of quantity; it had a qualitative side as well. The USSR caught up with the USA in number of missiles, but the missiles were also steadily improved. Especially in the USA, which was ahead of the Soviets in miniaturization, computer technology and navigation systems. US engineers developed smaller bombs and built rockets which could carry several warheads at once. US rockets could leave the earth's atmosphere, travel in a ballistic orbit through space and then re-enter the atmosphere to release their deadly cargo of multiple warheads – each warhead programmed separately to follow its own, individual trajectory towards a particular target. The Americans did not increase their number of rockets, yet the development of multiple independent re-entry vehicles (or MIRVs) gave them an edge in the strategic race. While the USSR built more and bigger missiles, the USA built smaller and more accurate warheads. As a result, the nuclear balance was not as equal as it appeared from the mere counting of launchers or carriers.

Table 12.2 indicates this imbalance. First, it shows that at the time of the Cuban Missile Crisis in 1962, the USA enjoyed a substantial superiority in nuclear weapons – with about seven times as many launchers (that is, silos, submarines and strategic bombers) and warheads. Second, the table suggests how the USA developed its MIRV technology during the 1970s – as the number of warheads increased whereas the number of US launchers remained fairly constant. Third, the table shows how the USSR caught up with the US number of launchers in the late 1960s, and that parity was reached between 1968 and 1970. The numbers also show that the USSR remained behind the USA in number of warheads, suggesting that the USSR was slower to MIRV its missiles. Also, there were frictions and conflicts within the blocs. The bloc members grew more independent in relation to the bloc leader. In the West there were increasing protests against US warfare in the Third World. In

Table 12.2 Numbers of US and Soviet nuclear launchers and warheads, 1962–80

	USA		USSR	
	Launchers	*Warheads*	*Launchers*	*Warheads*
1962	1,653	3,267	235	481
1964	2,021	4,180	425	771
1966	2,139	4,607	570	954
1968	2,191	4,839	1,206	1,605
1970	2,100	4,960	1,835	2,216
1972	2,167	7,601	2,207	2,573
1974	2,106	9,324	2,423	2,795
1976	2,092	10,436	2,545	3,477
1978	2,086	10,832	2,557	5,516
1980	2,022	10,608	2,545	7,480

Source: SIPRI (1991, p. 25)

particular, the relationship between the USA and France deteriorated. The French President Charles de Gaulle pulled France out of the NATO command in a huff in September 1966. In the Far East the Soviet relationship with China deteriorated rapidly, ending with Sino-Soviet border clashes along the Ussuri during spring and summer 1969.

The increase in international conflict on a general, worldwide level is indicated in Table 12.1, above. It can be added that these decades also saw an increase in *coups d'état* and terrorist acts.[5] Terrorism was not unknown previously, but it had largely been confined to national conflicts and had been a negligible phenomenon in international politics. During the 1970s, however, local tensions increasingly flared up in acts of terrorism – including acts in Germany, Italy and the Americas. In addition, terrorist groups might now organize and plan their activities in one country but commit terrorist acts in another. The development of this 'international terrorism' was pioneered by groups which wanted to draw attention to the Israeli–Palestinian conflict.[6]

By these simple indicators, the 1960s and 1970s were years of political crisis. Economic figures convey a similar message. Inflation picked up during the late 1960s and was higher in the 1970s than in the previous two decades.[7] The economic situation was exacerbated by a simultaneous increase in unemployment. This combination of inflation and unemployment was unprecedented. It indicated that something was seriously amiss in the economic system, and a new term was coined to describe it: stagflation. It brought the postwar boom to a sudden halt in the early 1970s.[8]

Economic booms and busts put an end to the sustained economic growth of the postwar era and caused waves of unemployment. This came at an unfortunate time. The many children who were born during the baby-boom years that followed World War II were coming of age just when economic conditions became more uncertain. A pronounced expansion of higher education took place during the 1960s; it received an

extra stimulus when young people who wanted to enhance their chances of employment in a more uncertain job market entered high schools and universities. This
happened at a time when student politics became rapidly radicalized and violent
riots shook several big cities – the most notorious of them was the week-long race
riots that largely destroyed the Watts neighbourhood of Los Angeles in August 1965.

What could explain these changes? Demographers pointed to the sharp increase
in fertility rates some eighteen to twenty years earlier, in the wake of World War II.
They also noted the equally sharp drop of fertility rates that occurred in the 1960s,
after the introduction of the oral contraceptive pill. 'The Pill' made it possible to
regulate the human reproductive cycle. It revolutionized female freedom because
it gave women a new control over their bodies. This in turn paved the way for a
sexual and feminist revolution. It also altered the traditional family. In the developed nations of the secular or Protestant West, women had fewer children. The
population growth rate fell noticeably. Families became smaller. Some sociologists
added that the traditional family structure was undermined; they defended their
claims with statistics that showed how marriage rates declined, whereas divorce
rates increased – as did the number of children born out of wedlock. Breakdown of
traditional values affected the very fibre of society, they argued – and showed how
crime rates were increasing in several countries of the West (Fukuyama 1999, pp.
32ff, reproduces some telling statistics).

Conservative statesmen noted the changes and did not like them. President
Nixon said that the changes in the USA reminded him of Rome during the last
days of the Republic. His German-born national security adviser, Henry Kissinger,
detected on the unruly campuses the sinister scent of the Weimar Republic.
Orthodox radicals, however, were encouraged by the changes; Soviet leaders saw
them as omens of the imminent collapse of capitalism and the transition to a
better society. Radicals in the West were not so sure. These ideological claims were
countered by scholarly arguments that did not conform to orthodox forecasts. It
was clear for example that neither capitalist nor socialist states seemed to handle
the environmental threats particularly well. And when the issue was pressed, it was
reasonably clear that the socialist states were in worse ecological shape than the
capitalist West. In the USSR, for example, huge engineering projects were causing
the entire Aral Sea to dry up.

Transcending Realism

Around the time of the Cuban Missile Crisis (1962), International Relations had
been a simple and tidy field, commonly framed in terms of the concepts of Realism
and Idealism or Rationalism. The next ten years brought big changes to the field
of International Relations. By the time of the first oil crisis (1973), International
Relations scholars had embraced several new issues and developed new international approaches. Some of the new issues concerned the nuclear arms race.
Others were connected to colonial wars, decolonization and the emergence of new,
independent states in the Third World.

Under the impact of such new concerns, International Relations evolved new questions, new theories and new approaches. Decolonization, for example, directed attention to the situation of the new states in the tropical regions of the world. Since these states tended to be poor, populous and wooed by both superpowers, scholars asked questions about the preconditions for their economic growth as well as their political independence. Such questions encouraged approaches of political economy and stimulated the growth of a new, Revolutionist approach in International Relations.

The impact of economics

Scholars who studied the superpower arms race moved away from the Realist approach. True, they retained a view of the world as a multiplicity of interacting states; also, they saw international interaction in terms of military power and national interest. Yet, they tended to shy away from the historical and diplomatic methodologies of classical Realists like Hans Morgenthau and George F. Kennan. They gravitated instead towards approaches that were more formal and more closely aligned with the ideal of the natural sciences than did the old Realists. Students of the arms race – contributors to security studies, like John von Neumann, Herman Kahn and Thomas Schelling – had more in common with Martin Wight's Rationalist approach than with Realism.

John von Neumann was a mathematician and Thomas Schelling an economist. Both pioneered game theory and relied on it for their studies of bargaining and strategic behaviour. Schelling had an enormous influence in security studies in the USA and the West during the 1960s. Especially after the Cuban Missile Crisis, when models of rational choice received a boost. After the tense days of October 1962, US–Soviet interaction were commonly depicted as analogous to games of 'chicken', 'prisoners' 'dilemma' or other two-actor games.

These formal approaches were also embraced by the new community of peace studies. This was a field that had been pioneered by Anglo-American economists and mathematicians like Lewis Richardson, Anatol Rapoport, Kenneth Boulding and others. And while European scholars were hesitant before the new field of strategic studies, they were often inspired by Rapaport and Boulding and more eager to embrace the new field of 'peace research'.[9]

The influence of sociology

In Britain there was also a drift away from old-fashioned Realism, as evinced by the work of the so-called English School. Its members retained key assumptions of traditional Realism but also included sociological arguments – as advocated for instance by Charles A. W. Manning (1962). Similar ideas were expressed by American International Relations scholars. Inis L. Claude was one of them; his celebrated book *Power and International Relations* [1962] was more readable – and also more read – than Manning's. Claude too discussed the ways in which states try to establish a mutually acceptable order through institutions of co-operation and co-ordination. Claude discussed the interstate balance of power, but he also seriously probed the possibilities of world government. He acknowledged a predisposition to the view 'with special favour and sympathy' the system of collective security (p. 10) which he placed between the two other possible systems – that of balance of power on the one hand and that of world government on the other.

The French social philosopher Raymond Aron (1966) advocated 'a sociology of International Relations'. He was thoroughly familiar with the traditions of social theory when he published his seminal overview: *Paix et guerre entre les nations*. This thick tome was an ambitious effort to cover the scholarly substance of International Relations. It had a Realist vantage point, but it transcended the Realist approach by covering International Relations from four interrelated angles or 'four levels of conceptualization'. Aron gave each angle or level – that of History, Sociology, Theory and Praxeology – an in-depth discussion.

Aron, like Manning and Claude, argued that the international society consists of sovereign states. However, these states do not merely compose an interstate system. They constitute an international society. An analysis of it would require a more elaborate and sociological approach than traditional Realism would allow.

A similar argument had been suggested by Karl W. Deutsch and David Mitrany in the late 1950s; both of them relied on theories of communicative interaction in their discussions of international affairs. Deutsch (1954; 1957) had observed the interaction of North Atlantic states and argued that their steadily denser web of interaction was producing a peaceful 'security community'. Mitrany (1933; 1965) had analysed the co-operation in organizations like the European Coal and Steel Community (ECSC) and argued that their goal-directed activities fuelled international integration. In the early 1960s the German-born Ernst B. Haas made essentially the same observation. Western Europe is experiencing an increasing degree of integration, he argued in his book *Beyond the Nation-State* (1964).

The analyses of Deutsch, Mitrany and Haas contributed importantly to the study of European integration. The theoretical core of their argument was simple; they had, in fact, revived the old, half-forgotten theory of interdependence (Seebohm 1871; Angell 1910). But they had also expanded upon it and refined it. Mitrany and Haas had, for example, used their observations to criticize federalist theory and pave the way for alternative theories of integration. Mitrany argued that co-operation works best when states focus on specific activities (functions) that can be performed more effectively through collective action than through unitary efforts by individual states. Besides, Mitrany continued, states which co-operate to reach specific goals will also find it natural to establish institutional arrangements (forms) to facilitate the co-operation. Mitrany (1965) expressed his argument in a snappy maxim: 'form follows function'.

Mitrany's claim, that fruitful co-operation begins over specific transnational issues and then develops into a wider process, furnished the core of his 'functional' theory of integration. This argument did not convince Haas. Mitrany was too optimistic. Integration at the regional level might produce the kind of results Mitrany had predicted; but his forecasts about integration at the global level were unrealistic, argued Haas. Besides, Mitrany was too idealistic if he thought that states would willingly delegate influence and power, Haas continued – arguing the Realist point that international co-operation is much more difficult than often assumed. Delegation of power is so untypical that if it occurs at all it must have a very specific cause, Haas maintained. In the European case he found this cause in powerful transnational constituencies. Powerful political elites and influential advocacy groups – such as Jean Monnet's European Movement – have been important forces behind European integration, Haas postulated in *The Uniting of Europe* [1968]. Organizations and institutions are important international actors in the theory that Ernest Haas termed 'neo-functionalism'.

This emphasis on powerful elites and social institutions was also pursued by Samuel Huntington. His *Political Order in Changing Societies* (1968) was an ambitious effort to write a general theory of political development. He criticized previous efforts for having followed the lead of nineteenth-century European thinkers (like Maine, Marx, Tönnies and Weber) who focused exclusively on the development of Europe. From European examples, theories of modernization assumed that there exists one, true path of political, economic and social development. And that late-coming, Third World states must follow that one path if they want to attain order, wealth and freedom. This was all dangerously wrong, Huntington warned. Modernization is not the outcome of one, single process pioneered by the West. Rather, modernization involves many different processes. They are related, but they are not part of one, big package. Therefore one cannot expect that a newly independent country which experiences economic development will also evolve liberal democracy or freedom for the masses. In fact, efforts to mobilize the population may destabilize society; premature elections may result in violence and conflict – and destroy productive capital, paralyse economic productivity and disrupt trade. The most important goal for newly independent countries is *order*, Huntington insisted. And order, he continued, was not the outcome of modernization, it was the *precondition* for modernization. For without order, no social interaction of any systematic kind could take place. There could be 'no culture of the earth, no navigation nor use of the commodities that may be imported by sea, no commodious building, no instruments of moving and removing such things as require much force' (Hobbes 1951 [1651], p. 186).

Political Order in Changing Societies destroyed the theories of modernization which dominated Western scholarship during the 1950s and 1960s. It left in tatters the naive notion that all good things go together. It opened up for an alternative perspective that emphasized variation, context and the important role that institutions played in the establishment of order. Institutions, Huntington wrote, are 'stable, valued, recurring patterns of behaviour'. Their purpose is to facilitate collective action. The problem is, continued Huntington, that a transition from colonial to postcolonial status is perilous and slippery. It involves a change in institutions. And there is no guarantee that the old institutions can be peacefully removed and new ones created. If the old institutions remain, it may mean that a repressing and exploiting colonial elite is simply replaced by an equally repressing elite of natives. If new institutions cannot be created, the result will be disorder and power struggles. If new institutions are created there is no guarantee that they will sustain a progressive political order.

Western economists, sobered by many failed Third World development programmes, had come to share some of Huntington's concerns. Many of them were critical both of liberal market-based models and of anti-capitalist protectionists and idealist self-sufficiency advocates. The economic historian Charles P. Kindleberger argued that the USA had shirked its responsibility as a victor after World War I. Instead of taking political charge of the postwar world order that had emerged from the Versailles Peace Conference, the USA withdrew into isolationism. And in America's absence, there was no one to take the leadership of the world economy. As a consequence the international economy slid into disorder. The international market economy did not adjust itself automatically, Kindleberger (1973, pp. 291ff) pointed out. If the international economy were to adjust itself, it would need an adjusting agent – it would need a hegemon.

Kindleberger's point, that a well-functioning market economy is dependent on political action, was noted by other economic historians as well. Among them were Douglass C. North and Robert P. Thomas who probed the old question of how Europe got rich. Their aim was traditional – it was to identify general conditions for economic growth (a worthy quest in an age when poverty plagued many newly independent nations). Their conclusions were original. As they studied the rise of European states, they discovered that several of the most important preconditions for growth were political and that were formed several centuries ago. North and Thomas (1973) delved into early modern history and compared the relatively rapid development of the United Provinces and England with the more sluggish economies of Spain and France. Two things characterized the fast-growing Dutch and English societies. First, their economies grew faster than their populations. Second, activities of individuals shaped collective habits and norms that benefited society as a whole. Thomas Malthus (1982) had touched upon the first observation; Adam Smith (1976) upon the second – and Smith had invoked the principles of a social division of labour and a 'hidden hand' to account for the beneficial behaviour that resulted. North and Thomas provided a different explanation. They argued that Dutch and English entrepreneurs were affected by distinct incentives which were formed by sustained human interaction. These incentives were often informal, expressed in collective habits, customs and social norms; however, sometimes they were made explicit as rules or laws of the land. North and Thomas called them 'institutions'.

Institutions, explained North (1990), are 'humanly devised constraints' that provide the structures of everyday life. Institutions constrain human behaviour. They provide codes and rules for human conduct. Social actors who violate such rules suffer punishment or costs. Nations that developed quickly had distinctive institutions which allowed individual entrepreneurs to get rich. In addition, their economic growth lifted all boats. The creation of individual fortunes did not remain on family hands; they were not enjoyed only by a narrow social elite but benefited society as a whole.

The ideas that carried the arguments of Huntington and of North and Thomas were not entirely new. A variety of older concepts had captured the basic notion that human beings are born into a world shaped by previous generations and that the habits and norms of those forbears shape their thoughts and behaviour.[10] During the 1970s yet another variation of this argument saw the light of day and rippled through Anglo-American social sciences: the concept of 'institutions'. It made immediate marks on International Relations. Among the first authors to import the idea of institutions to International Relations were a circle of young scholars at Harvard University. They edited the journal *International Organization*, which they lifted to prominence. In 1972 two of them, Robert O. Keohane and Joseph S. Nye, edited a special issue of the journal on transnational relations. Its articles explored the weaknesses of Realism and sought to develop an alternative approach which could better explain the events of the contemporary world. When the special issue was completed, the two authors continued to pursue this task. In 1977 they published the influential book *Power and Interdependence*. Here they argued that the Realist paradigm is of limited use in today's world and that international affairs are better understood through an approach of 'complex interdependence'.

Keohane and Nye echoed the old, near-forgotten concept of Norman Angell (1910) and other pre-World War I theorists. But they were also informed by North and Thomas (1973) and the 'new institutionalism'. Stephen Krasner and others pursued these ideas to address the question of why international economic co-operation had remained stable in spite of an uneven distribution of power in the world – a stability which was all the more remarkable given the volatile nature of international relations in the 1970s. As they applied arguments from 'new institutionalism' to International Relations, they also developed the related concept of 'international regimes'. Regimes are 'social institutions around which actor expectations converge in a given area of international relations', explained Krasner (1983). Regimes are governing arrangements constructed by states. Regimes are constructed by states which seek to pursue shared goals in specific issue areas. GATT (General Agreement of Tariffs and Trade) is one example. The European Coal and Steel Community (ECSC) is another. Both are established in order to further a particular goal which is shared by its members – increasing international trade and controlling armaments industries, respectively. Both are governed by norms and rules which specify the rights and obligations of its members. These norms are expressed in and sustained by a formal structure, a secretariat, which manages the discussions and defines the decision-making procedures of the members. Discussions like these paved the way for the later development of regime theory (Krasner 1983).

Radical approaches

Institutionalists see interdependence as a good thing. For Keohane and Nye (1977) interdependence meant wealth and peace – as it had done for liberal social theorists since Smith and Ricardo. Others saw interdependence as a bad thing. Jean-Jacques Rousseau (1964a, p. 568), for example, saw interdependence as the dependence of everyone upon everyone else – in other words, a universal loss of independence and liberty for all. It meant an increasing social division of labour, isolation, exploitation, increased alienation and social anomie. In Rousseau's mind, then, an increasing division of labour was connected to a steady loss of liberty, to growing alienation, increasing exploitation and to rising repression. Interdependence was, in short, tied in with the ills of modern society. In his mind, human beings were enslaved by the social division of labour. They could break the chains that bound and alienated them only through a liberating act of revolution.

Rousseau was a major contributor to the radical tradition, and Martin Wight invoked Rousseau when he introduced Revolutionism as a third tradition in International Relations during the 1950s. This was a prescient initiative on Wight's part. During the 1960s the new tradition reflected the tenor of the times increasingly well. As decolonization picked up speed and the Third World saw the emergence of anti-colonial liberation movements, advocacies of revolution made deep marks in the scholarly study of International Relations. The argument, however, had an analytical problem. Wight had identified Rousseau as a major inspiration for the Revolutionist approach and he had followed its development through the writings of Immanuel Kant. However, the revolutionary ideas that emerged during the 1960s were not influenced by Kant as much as by Marx. It was not Kantian but Marxist ideas that were embraced in the Third World.

These ideas tended to draw on Marx and on anti-imperialist ideas of liberation developed by Lenin (1975b), Ho Chi Minh (Neuberg 2008 [1930]), Mao (1965a) and 'Che' Guevara (1961). These Third World ideas were then important by radical theorists in the West. European theorists tended to pull in communist classics as well as modern social theorists (Lenin as well as Adorno, Horkheimer, Sartre and others). Anglo-American radicals tended to be less orthodox and more inventive. In Britain a new radicalism developed in the early 1960s around the journal *New Left Review*, under the editorship of Stuart Hall and Perry Anderson. In the USA, radicalism had deep roots in the variegated academic world of urban immigrants. All of them found a decisive inspiration in the writings of Marx (more than Kant).

The Anglo-American elaborations affected International Relations theory deeply. The elaborations that took place in New York are especially worth a second look. First, because radical approaches were vibrantly present in the universities of Manhattan – in uptown Columbia as well as downtown City University (CUNY). Also, the influential Marxist magazine *Monthly Review* had its editorial offices in New York and was frequented by left-wing academics like Paul Baran, Paul Sweezy, Leo Huberman and others. Finally, New York hosted the UN. Its many committees and commissions housed some radical scholars. The most important among them were associated with the Economic Commission of Latin American (ECLA).

ECLA housed several radical economists who studied issues of poverty, postwar reconstruction and development. Among them were Hans Singer, Raul Prebish and Celso Furtado. They described the Americas as an economic system in which the USA was dominant and affected the development of all the other states in the hemisphere. Prebish (1950), for example, wrote that the USA was an independent metropole and the countries of South America were dependent satellites. This claim broke with the tradition of liberal economics, which saw economics as separate from politics; instead, Prebish saw economics and politics as interwoven. His work opened up for a more holistic approach to the analysis of finance and trade relations and helped develop the new field of International Political Economy (IPE) during the 1960s.

An important contributor to the field of IPE was André Gunder Frank. He was a German-American economic historian and sociologist who had taught in Latin America and written articles for *Monthly Review*. In the second half of the 1960s he published several influential books on Latin-American development; among them *The Development of Underdevelopment* [1966] and *Capitalism and Underdevelopment in Latin America* [1967]. Another important contribution to the fledgling field of IPE was *Monopoly Capital* [1966], written by Paul Baran and Paul Sweezy. It presented international relations as driven by economic concerns in a global capitalist system and was a landmark contribution to the Revolutionist tradition.

From two to three approaches

The new, Marx-derived arguments addressed issues like decolonization, liberation struggles, state-building and economic development in the Third World. They broadened the scope of International Relations theory. They were collected in the approach of Revolutionism and accepted as a new approach to International Relations. Revolutionism was added alongside the two traditional perspectives of Realism and Rationalism which had dominated International Relations for half a century or more. During the 1970s, introductory textbooks would increasingly portray International Relations as a field that was torn between *three* different traditions – or paradigms as was now the fashionable term. These texts offered a parsimonious first overview of the field. The image of three contending approaches imposed a simple and sensible order on an increasingly complex body of literature.

The Realist tradition would, according to this image, treat the state as the primary actor in world politics. It would describe the state as a sovereign, territorial unit which surrounds itself by a hard, impenetrable shell (Herz 1957). Realism did not concern itself with the processes and properties that occurred within the hard shell of the state; it portrayed the state as a closed and unitary actor. It presented international relations in terms of rivalries among self-absorbed, sovereign states. The interaction among these states constituted a system of egotistical actors marked by anarchy. Realist theories were primarily interested in the way state interaction maintains order and stability in the international system. Maintaining order and solving disputes in an anarchic system of states dominate the Realist agenda.

The Realist tradition has traditionally hinged on philosophical assumptions which were informed by old social contract theorists like Thomas Hobbes and Benedict de Spinoza. Also, the Realist approach has traditionally been associated with a conservative ideology. As traditional conservatism was generally on the wane during the 1960s, squeezed out by arguments rooted in the social philosophy of really old-fashioned liberalism, Realism lost much of its philosophical appeal. Realist arguments were, however, increasingly sustained by arguments drawn from systems theory and micro-economics (Kahn 1960; Schelling 1960; Waltz 1975).

As a consequence Realism shed some of its classic features, and approached the Rationalist tradition and strategic studies in some respects.

The Rationalist tradition was also preoccupied with the territorial state. However, it did not portray the state as a unitary actor, but was deeply interested in the social processes that were internal to the nation. The state is, from the Rationalist perspective, composed of a myriad of smaller parts – departments, groups, teams, offices, companies, organizations, directors, secretaries … These parts, including the decision-makers and managers of the state, can be analytically disaggregated, their complex interaction traced and their different motivations scrutinized.

Rationalism, then, viewed the state as one of several actors in international politics. It tended argue that all political actors behave rationally in their attempt to pursue their own interests. Thus, one of the key concepts which help bring these diverse interactions under a common perspective is the notion of bargaining. In a complex web of interdependence, each actor seeks to further its interest or maximize its gain through bargaining, which involves a mixture of both conflict and co-operation. Rationalists often argue that, as the scope and pace of human interaction increase, the web of interdependence grows ever more intricate. Interdependence will in turn stimulate co-operation and lower levels of international conflict. This argument draws on a long line of liberal economic and legal philosophers, such as Grotius, Montesquieu, Locke, Smith and Vatell.

Although the Rationalist tradition recognizes that states are important actors in world politics, it contends that the dominance of states has diminished and that other actors have become steadily more important. International politics, then, is an infinitely complex process, which involves both public and private actors of a wide variety, incessantly interacting on local, national and transnational levels (Deutsch 1957; Mitrany 1965; Haas 1968). Various types of international organizations have gained an important, independent impact on world politics – international governmental organizations (IGOs) and non-governmental international organizations (INGOs). Such organizations have gained considerable influence in an increasingly interdependent world, the Rationalists would tend to argue.

The third and most recent approach to International Relations – that of *Revolutionism* – did not view the territorial state as the basic unit of international analysis. Instead, it focused on economic actors – on capitalists and firms, such as the multinational corporations (MNCs) which gained an increasing influence during the 1960s and 1970s. The Revolutionists would tend to discuss state relations in a worldwide economic context. Drawing on radical social philosophy (Rousseau 1950a, 1950c), theories of classical economics (Marx 1977; Ricardo 1984) and theories of imperialism (Hobson 1902; Bukharin 1973; Lenin 1975b; Hilferding 1955), the Revolutionists would depict the world as a class-divided, modern capitalist world system. This world system is, by their theories, composed of two major classes or regions or zones: the centre and the periphery. These two zones are separated by a gap in wealth. The states which inhabit the centre zone of the world system are wealthy, whereas those which inhabit the periphery are poor (Frank 1966; Baran and Sweezy 1966, Wallerstein 1974).

The relationship between the centre and the periphery is governed by a global division of labour which works to enrich the capitalist states in the centre to impoverish the periphery. An essential feature of the world system, then, is its exploitative nature. The rich states in the centre are rich (and the poor states in the periphery are poor) because value and wealth are unceasingly transferred from the peripheral to the central zone. In the Revolutionist view, this unjust distribution of global wealth is a characteristic feature of the world system. The ultimate preoccupation of the Revolutionist approach is to destroy the exploitative world economy and thereby liberate the impoverished and exploited masses of the world. Since the exploitative dynamics are built into the global division of labour, the system cannot be amended or reformed. In the interest of global freedom and justice, the entire system must be torn down and replaced.

The interparadigm debate

The three approaches of Realism, Rationalism and Revolutionism dominated the study of International Relations during the 1970s. Each approach highlighted specific properties in world affairs. Realism highlighted the competitive relations of an anarchic interstate system. The approach was sometimes illustrated by the image of a pool-table where billiard balls, representing the unitary states, would knock each other about.

Rationalism emphasized the co-operative aspects of international relations. Some authors likened international relations to a wiring diagram of interconnected parts or a global web of interdependence.

Revolutionism highlighted the wide gap between the rich and the poor nations in the world economy. They tended to emphasize the mechanisms by which the wealthy North would exploit and repress the impoverished South. An apt illustration would be that of a giant octopus which would hold the globe in its tentacle embrace while extracting wealth and values from the South. The main points of this brief discussion of the three different paradigms of International Relations are summarized in Table 12.3. The table indicates the main features of the three approaches of Realism, Rationalism and Revolutionism. It is a snapshot of International Relations around the middle of the 1970s.[11] It suggests the main lines of a theory discussion which was once referred to as the 'inter-paradigm debate' – and which sought to clarify the relative merits of these three traditions in International Relations theory. But two caveats need to be appended to this figure. First, that its illustrative value is limited in time – that it represents International Relations during the 1970s reasonably well. During the 1980s, however, it became increasingly out of date – as the next chapter will suggest. Second, this simple snapshot does not provide a complete picture of the 1970s. Other approaches were also evolving at the time. Often in the wake of the steadily evolving structuralist methodology.

Table 12.3 The three main traditions of International Relations, *c.* 1975

	Primary unit of analysis	*Primary level of analysis*	*(Key) explanatory concepts*	*(Main) topic or focus*	*Image*
Realism	the state	group/state level	might/ power, state interest balance	conflict, order in anarchy	pool-table
Rationalism	rational actors	individual level	bargaining, compromise, interests	mutually beneficial co-operation	wiring diagram, global web
Revolutionism	the capitalist world economy	world systems level	structural power, repression, exploitation	economic development, political independence	octopus

Systemic approaches

During the 1960s and 1970s International Relations scholars struggled to keep up with the changes that took place in world affairs. They developed theories that grasped the new realities. But they tended to cling on to the old, distinguishing precept that International Relations was a discipline of contending traditions – or 'paradigms'.[12] But whereas the 1950s had presented International Relations as torn between *two* traditions (Realism and Rationalism), the 1960s introduced a third, Revolutionist, tradition.

The notion of three contending traditions represented a simple and tidy image. It was parsimonious. It imposed an intuitively sensible order on an increasingly complex body of literature. Also, it performed a didactical function – it was easy to introduce International Relations as an academic field by invoking three contending traditions. But there were factors which complicated the tidy picture. The most disturbing factor was that theories were constantly evolving. During the 1960s and 1970s a most significant evolution took place in what Kenneth Waltz (1959) had referred to as 'third-image' theories. Three contributors in particular contributed to this evolution: Immanuel Wallerstein (1974), Kenneth Waltz (1975) and Hedley Bull (1977).

These three authors discussed different subjects – Wallerstein wrote a rich, macro–historical study of the world economy; Waltz developed a simple model of the Great-Power interaction; Bull tried to capture the most important ordering forces of international society. Yet, they all share some salient characteristics which reflect the theoretical preoccupations of their day. Most obviously, they are all grand theories. In addition, they argue on the system level of analysis and are concerned with interaction in structural terms. Finally, they tend to argue that states do not act as much as they *react*. All three authors argue, each in his own way, that states are subject to systemic pressures and demands and that these systemic impulses condition their behaviour in decisive ways.

Immanuel Wallerstein and The Modern World System

Immanuel Wallerstein published *The Modern World-System* in 1974, as the first volume in a larger four-volume work. It is an ambitious discussion of a historical subject: it analyses 'the long sixteenth century' and seeks to explain the birth of the capitalist modern world economy. The book is a major contribution to the Revolutionist paradigm. It represents a radical tradition of international political economy.

Theories of imperialism play an important role in the work – not so much the orthodox Marxist theories of Bukharin and Lenin who emphasized the capitalist mode of production; instead, Wallerstein drew on authors like John A. Hobson (1902), who stressed the role of international commerce and trade.

Another source is the French *Annales* school of history – thus labelled because its members edited the cross-disciplinary journal *Annales d'histoire economique et sociale*. Wallerstein was especially inspired by the historian Fernand Braudel, who had devoted a multi-volume work to the analysis the advent of the modern capitalist system in sixteenth-century Europe. During the century, Braudel explained, the rivalling Great Powers of Europe expanded their commerce and influence across the globe. The world was consequently divided into three segments or successive zones. First, there is the *core*, the central, wealthy pivot of the capitalist world economy. Then comes the intermediate zone, encompassing the poorer, struggling nations of the *semi-periphery*. Finally, there are the wide areas of *periphery*, which are marked by poverty and which, in the division of labour characteristic of the world economy, are subordinates rather than participants.

All the three zones of the world economy are capitalist, argues Wallerstein. However, each zone displays a different kind of capitalism and plays a distinct role in the operation of the overall system. It is only in the core, for example that capitalism works on the liberal principles of the free market. The core develops highly skilled workers, sophisticated techniques of agriculture and, later, industries; all controlled by an indigenous bourgeoisie. In the periphery, the economy is primarily agrarian; as capitalism develops, peripheral countries tend to develop mono-economies geared towards the export of raw materials – such as sugar, wood and foodstuffs – to the industries in the core.

Each zone shapes the agents and the institutions that inhabit it according to the role it plays in the overall system. Consequently, different parts of the world have different kinds of ordering institutions because these are formed by the distinct properties of the zone that they inhabit. In the core, for example, the institutions of economic order are based on a free labour market. In the semi-periphery, economic institutions are fewer and transactions are affected by different degrees of corruption. In the peripheral zones capitalism is marked by strict forms of labour control.

Also, political institutions differ from one zone to the next. In the core of the world economy, where labour is free, the political system is based on individual freedom and has, over time, developed into the distinct form of liberal democracy. In the semi-periphery, where people are poorer and less free, the political institutions are marked by authoritarian rule. In the periphery, where people are poor and repressed, social order rest on force. The political processes tend to serve those who are in power and they use tyranny and repression to remain in power. Here 'life often resembles purgatory or even hell' (Braudel 1977, p. 82).

The *Modern World-System* lays the rafters for a truly grand theory designed to capture some five hundred years of world history in a streamlined, sociological model. Other volumes followed – in 1980, 1989 and 2011 – each applying the basic argument to steadily more recent phases of global history.

Kenneth Waltz: Theory of International Politics

The basic methodology of Kenneth Waltz was not so different from that of Immanuel Wallerstein. Both presented the states of the world as units in a larger system and saw their behaviour as the outcome of larger, systemic forces. Both interpreted the actions of states as responses to pressures and demands presented by the larger system of which they are parts. Also, both divided this larger system into different strata or classes defined in terms of capabilities of wealth or power. Both argued that states which belong to a particular stratum or class behave in ways which are characteristic of this stratum.

For Wallerstein, all core states tend to behave in the free-market capitalist ways which characterize the core. For Waltz, all Great Powers tend to behave in typical Great-Power ways, just as all small states tend to behave in typical small-state ways – regardless of the properties of their internal system of government. Waltz observed that although the USA was a capitalist democracy and the USSR a communist dictatorship, both tended to behave in similar ways on the international scene. Both were superpowers and competed for strategic advantage. The question that preoc-cupied Waltz was why their behaviour was so similar when their domestic systems were so different. He found the answer in the nature of the international system – or, more precisely in the peculiar, anarchic nature of the system of sovereign states.

Waltz had adumbrated this argument as early as the 1950s. For example, in the concluding chapter of *Man, the State and War* [1959], Waltz argues that the best way to approach international relations is to begin at the systemic level. During the 1960s, he probed the argument more carefully. And when, in the early 1970s, he was invited to contribute a chapter on the science of 'International Relations' for a new handbook of Political Science, he began to work more systematically on his grand theory.

The result would transform the Realist paradigm. For when Waltz's 'Theory of International Relationss' was printed as a ninety-page chapter in *Handbook of Political Science* in 1975, it did not really represent the field of International Relations; it demolished it. First, Waltz subjected classical Realism to a devastating critique. Realism rests on vague philosophical suppositions about human nature, Waltz claimed. A scientific theory of International Relations cannot be built on such nebulous assumptions. Second, it is not possible to understand world politics by only inspecting the insides of states. It is absolutely necessary to develop a system approach.

Waltz followed up his critique of classical Realism with a presentation of a methodological alternative. His 1975 chapter introduced nothing less than a new philosophy of science, tailor-made for a new kind of Realism which approached International Relations from a systemic vantage point.

What is an international system? Waltz asked. His answer is hard to summarize in a couple of paragraphs. But the best place to begin is with the two principles which define the system. First, its *ordering principle*: namely, the principle of anarchy. Here Waltz makes the same point that for example James Lorimer (1877) had made a century previously – and which has been repeated by many International Relations theorists since (for instance, by Dickinson 1916): namely, that the international system is anarchic because its constituent units are sovereign states. And because they are sovereign, they want to maintain their independent status. Each state looks after its own security and manages its specific security problems by itself – to the greatest degree possible. No state can count on anyone else helping out in times of trouble. The international system is, in effect, 'a self-help system'.

The second defining principle of the international system, continued Waltz, concerns the *distribution of capabilities* among the major units (the states) in the system. The biggest or most capable states shape the system. They pose the issues that all the units have to deal with. This is a hugely simplifying move – and pretty much the same that Leopold von Ranke (1925 [1833]) made nearly 150 years earlier: namely, that, in political practice, a few Great Powers dominate the international system and define its major issues. Great Powers have a formative impact on international relations. The international system is, in effect, shaped by the interaction of a few, big and powerful states.

It is important to note the essential difference between Waltz's two defining principles. The first, anarchy, is constant. International politics is by definition an anarchic realm. Here lays the key to understand the nature of international politics in general. The second defining principle, that of distribution of capabilities, varies over historical time. Different epochs in history have had different numbers of Great Powers – which is another way of saying that they have represented different distributions of capabilities. Up until World War I, for example, there were usually about half a dozen Great Powers in the international system. After World War II the number was reduced to two – the USA and the USSR. The distribution of capabilities before World War I produced a different system than after World War II, and states acting in those two different systems faced different kinds of challenges or impulses. After World War II states like France and Britain, had to come to terms with the fact that they were no longer Great Powers. And as they did so, their concerns changed. Britain and France came to realize that they could no longer provide for their own security vis-à-vis the USSR. They were concerned about wars no longer with each other or with Germany but with the Soviet Union. This concern drove them into co-operation – with each other and with the USA. Since the distribution of capabilities had shifted so much, neither Britain nor France would make much of a difference for the outcome if a Great-Power war were to break out. Great-Power war was now the concern of the USA and the USSR – both of whom realized this and adapted to the new international structure. They assumed new, international responsibilities. As a result, the international system was marked by the rivalry between these two powers. The interrelationship between the two superpowers defined the main agenda of world affairs.

Waltz's vantage point was a systems analysis of international relations. It presented the international system in terms of two analytic levels: on one level, interacting units, or the states; on another, the structure. It is a common mistake to think that the states compose the structure. They do not. In fact, the states are, in a sense, shaped by the structure. The states are incessantly impinged upon by the international system. States are subject to systemic impulses and their behaviour is shaped by those impulses.

'A system', writes Waltz, is

> defined as a set of interacting units. At one level, a system consists of a structure, and the structure is the systems level component that makes it possible to think of the units as forming a set as distinct from a mere collection. At another level, the system consists of interacting units. The aim of the systems theory is to show how the two levels operate and interact, and that requires marking them off from each other. (Waltz 1975, p. 45)

To put it simply: in order to explain the behaviour of a particular state, the most important thing to know is whether that state is a Great Power or a small state. For all Great Powers are subject to the same kind of systemic pushes and pressures; they tend to respond to them in similar ways and therefore to behave similarly. Small states are also subject to impulses from the system. But they behave differently from Great Powers.

Waltz's chapter was hotly debated among International Relations scholars. The many criticisms he received made him clarify, expand and apply his argument. In 1979 he published *Theory of International Politics* (affectionately known as *TIP* by its many adherents). It is one of the most important books to have been published in the scholarly field of International Relations. It made at least three important contributions. First, it demolished the old Realist tradition of International Relations. Second, it built a parsimonious new paradigm on the ruins of the old – that is, the paradigm of 'structural Realism'. Third, it provided a crisp and convincing new methodological foundation for the scientific study of International Relations.

Hedley Bull

Hedley Bull, like Waltz, accepted the vantage point of traditional Realism: that is, that sovereign states are the basic actors of international politics and that their interaction constitutes an anarchical system. Bull largely agreed with Morgenthau's claim that states strive for security and influence. But Bull also stressed the importance of social interaction, arguing that, during the course of international history, interacting diplomats have evolved organizations and norms which serve to maintain order in interstate relations.

How do diplomats behave when they do this? And what kind of organizations and norms do they evolve? In his book *The Anarchical Society* [1977] Bull argues that the most important ordering institutions are diplomacy, international law and balance of power – pretty much as Morgenthau (1948b) argued thirty years earlier. Bull, however, had a different vantage point. Where Morgenthau anchored his argument in a pessimistic philosophy of a constant human nature, Bull assumed a more plastic and pliable anthropology. Also, where Morgenthau focused on sovereign states that each pursued its own interest and ended up in conflict, Bull added that, during the course of their interaction, states develop certain common interests, and that these may serve as a basis for international co-operation. Where Morgenthau relied on a pessimistic view of human nature, Bull relied on discussions in the British Committee on the Theory of International Politics. He included social theories from anthropology and sociology, law and political science. *The Anarchical Society* is often referred to as the central expression of 'the English School'.

Bull accepted Martin Wight's claim that there exist three main traditions of International Relations. He also relied on Manning's argument that sovereign states, through their interaction, constitute an international society. Bull argued that 'a group of states, conscious of their common interests and common values, forms a society in the sense that they conceive themselves as bound by a set of rules in their relations to one another, and share in the workings of common institutions' (Bull 1977, p. 13). Where Realists argued that the international order is produced by a settled balance of power, Bull saw order as something more intrinsic. He saw it not as a product only of an international anarchy but as an outcome also of common interests, rules, norms, values and institutions. Through their interactions, states form something more than an interstate system: they constitute an international *society*.

This is a key point for Bull – and it is where he and Waltz part ways. For a society is different from a system. A society assumes a system but refines its interactions into something more and qualitatively different. A society is formed by a process of communicative interaction; it exists when a group of actors conceive themselves to be bound by a common set of norms and rules. In the case of an international society, member states develop such norms and rules in order to obtain certain common goals, argued Bull. Among the most important goals are, first, to preserve of the system of states and the international society that is built upon it. Second, to protect and maintain the independence of individual states. And, third, to maintain peace – that is, to prevent war from being the normal condition among sovereign states.

Where do these goals – and the norms and rules established to reach them – come from? Ultimately they come from the states themselves. They are constituted through social interaction. Also, they are maintained by a distinct set of international institutions. States that respect these basic norms and engage with these institutions to achieve common goals form the international society. Such a society exists when

> a group of states, conscious of certain common interests and common values, form a society in the sense that they conceive themselves to be bound by a common set of rules in their relations with one another, and share in the working of common institutions. (Bull 1977, p. 13)

Which institutions are these? The three most obvious institutions of international order are 'diplomatic interaction', 'international law' and the principles of 'balance of power'. These are constituted and maintained by interacting states. Since the international system or society is formed by interactive states who seek to preserve their sovereignty, it lacks a supreme, overarching political authority. It is, in effect, an anarchy. In such an anarchy the rules of interaction are made, administered, interpreted, enforced, adapted and protected by the sovereign states themselves. On this logic Bull adds two more ordering institutions to the three that he has already identified. First, he adds the 'Great Powers', for in political practice the ordering functions of the international society are carried out by the most powerful member states. Then he adds 'war', for disagreements about international rules of conduct are in political practice settled by war and usually defined by the peace conference that follow.

Of systems and structures in international relations

The 1960s and 1970s were years of turbulence and transformation. The nuclear arms race accelerated – and fuelled radical anti-nuclear campaigns of a new peace movement. The process of decolonization reached a climax. Revolutionary rebellions proliferated in the South and radical sympathy movements sprang up in the North. The economic development of the West reached its zenith and moved into a phase of stagnation. These were years in which the statesmen and scholars of the West discovered a new awareness of limits and sought to understand the constraints under which they worked.

Politicians tried to break out of these constraints. They worked to alter traditions and change the extant system. Sometimes they succeeded. US and Soviet diplomats, for example, succeeded in establishing new institutions of co-operation that harnessed the arms race – a situation captured by the term détente. However, oftentimes the politicians did not succeed; they only made the situation more complex. As when the Nixon administration tried to improve upon the US economic situation by taking the dollar off the gold standard and caused the value of the dollar to fall steeply. This undermined the Bretton Woods system and motivated America's European allies to develop their own set of financial norms and rules to stabilize their economies. It served to increase the pace of European integration, to define new, higher ambitions for the European Community. It also lessened America's influence over Europe in financial matters. However, although the states of Europe built new institutions for economic co-operation and financial control, they were still dependent on steady supplies of cheap oil to keep their economies going. This made them vulnerable to political changes in the volatile Middle East. Also, it made them dependent on the USA for stabilizing the Middle East and securing the steady oil supply – a task which was complicated by America's more vocal guarantees to support the security of Israel.

These were years in which the concept of 'interdependence' was reintroduced in International Relations theory (Keohane and Nye 1977). Discussions that surrounded this concept confirmed Karl Deutsch's (1957) characterization of interdependent communities as robust and peaceful regions in the international order. At the same time, the concept of interdependence also introduced new notions of vulnerability. Although interdependence brought increasing wealth (as argued by Adam Smith) it also brought increasing complexity to international action and greater vulnerability to each participant actor (as pointed out by Jean-Jacques Rousseau). During the 1970s the world situation resembled the predicament which Mackinder (1904), Angell (1910) and others had described over half a century earlier. They had described the world as a 'single organism' or a 'closed system' where 'every shock, every disaster or superfluity, is now felt even to the antipodes, and may indeed return from the antipodes ... Every deed of humanity will henceforth be echoed and re-echoed in like manner around the world' (Mackinder 1919, pp. 389f).

Systems and structures
The systemic perspective represented an effort to capture this new complexity. It was an attempt to provide a holistic approach and explain the behaviour of individual actors in light of the workings of an overarching international system. When this effort began in the 1940s and 1950s, it was informed by biology and progress in electrical engineering; during the 1960s the effort was enriched by the social philosophy of structuralism.

The structuralist approach is predicated on the premise that the whole is more than (and different from) the simple sum of its constituent parts. It first evolved in the field of linguistics, where it proceeded from the claim that a language is more than the simple sum of its words. The relations among words are governed by grammar – by rules that determine the words' order, declination and composition into clauses and meaningful phrases. This notion of governing rules spread to the social sciences where it was conceived of as basic principles which govern human thought and action. Human action is always *inter*-action, it was argued. Human behaviour is intelligible only as part of a web of social interrelations, argued the structuralists.

One of their pioneers was the French anthropologist Claude Lévi-Strauss. During the 1950s and 1960s he wrote innovative studies that earned him the title of 'the father of modern anthropology'. For him structuralism was 'the search for the underlying patterns of thought in all forms of human activity'. His works had an immediate impact on sociology, political studies and other social sciences (cf. Moses and Knutsen 2012, ch. 8).

Lévi-Strauss assumed human equality. He began with the premise that human beings are the same everywhere. He studied tribal societies on the premise that the 'savage' mind has the same structures as the 'civilized' mind. If human beings behave differently, this is due to differences in the societies they inhabit, not to differences in human nature. This assumption dovetailed with the basic premise of progressive political movements. The structuralist approach brought new arguments to their cause and affected their political activism. It informed the American civil-rights movement, which gained force during the 1960s. Leaders like Martin Luther King worked to end racial segregation and discrimination and to secure legal recognition of citizenship rights for all black Americans. But there were also leaders who, influenced by the structural perspective, argued that legal recognition was not enough; that that the removal of deep-seated norms and racist practices were necessary components of a strategy of black liberation.

The proposition of the fundamental equality of human beings also sustained the feminist movement. Since the late nineteenth century, women activists and female scholars had documented that women occupy subordinated roles in society. They had explained this subordination in terms of social norms and legal rules and argued that by reforming society and removing legal obstacles it was possible to overcome women's subordination. During the 1960s, structuralist approaches shone a different light on relations of subordination. A new generation of feminists began explain it in terms of social structures – and to develop new strategies for women's liberation. They argued that women's subordination was conditioned by unequal distributions of wealth and of political and cultural power. Subordination was, in effect, an outcome of sexist power practices anchored in deep structures of patriarchy, which could not be overcome by legal remedies alone. It was most particularly rooted in the social division of labour, which offers greater rewards and prestige for paid work in the public sphere than for unpaid work in the private sphere of the household. Men are highly valued for their role as labourers in the economic system of production; women are not appreciated for the role they play in the social system of re-production. Encouraged by structuralist arguments – and by 'the Pill', which gave women the power to govern their reproductive function – women organized politically and set out to change not only legal rules but also the very dynamics that govern sexual action and thought about gender.

During the 1960s and 1970s, structuralist theory altered discussions about civil rights for women and minorities. It made deep impacts on the fields of sociology and political science – including the study of International Relations. The first discussions to be affected concerned the process of decolonization and development of the Third World – discussions which were encased in radical theories of political economy. Soon, however, structuralist arguments also began to affect questions of war, peace, security and order in the international system.

Agents and structures – and the return of Rousseau
Structuralist theory provided a new approach to some of the oldest questions in social philosophy. For example, it shone new light on the old question of why social actors behave in ways that are counter to reason, defy the actors' own will and undermine their interests.

These questions, which are among the oldest puzzles in political theory, find a classic formulation in the words of Paul: 'I have the desire to do what is good, but I cannot carry it out. For I do not do the good I want to do, but the evil I do not want to do – this I keep on doing' (Romans 7:18–20). Christian theologians had traditionally explained this gap between knowledge and behaviour by invoking the concept of 'sin'. This was, for example, the argument of Reinhold Niebuhr (1932; 1949).

Secular thinkers argued differently. They claimed that humans are not fully rational but are driven by whim, passions and short-term goals. This was the argument of conservative thinkers (Burke 1988). It was also the answer of classical Realists (Morgenthau 1948b; 1978).

Structuralist authors developed another secular argument. To explain the human tendency to behave in ways that defy reason and which are counter to the actors' own interest, they claimed that human deliberations are shaped not so much by internal reason as by the external environment. Humans who live under different natural conditions develop different manners of living and different patterns of social behaviour, they argued.

Jean-Jacques Rousseau had provided a first cut of this argument. He had explained how differences in context and circumstance gave rise to difference in human skills and, with time, to a division of labour and in turn to an evolving society. Adam Smith, Georg W. F. Hegel and other social philosophers were inspired by Rousseau's argument. Many of them developed it further. Some of them applied their elaborations to the study of international politics. Kenneth Waltz is an influential case from the 1970s.

When Waltz described the ways in which sovereign states interact, he often invoked Rousseau. In particular he referred to Rousseau's (1950c, p. 238) description of how primitive men might have been driven together by hunger to co-operate in a hunt for food. If they were to catch a deer for dinner, they needed to co-operate. However, in the absence of social norms, rules, institutions and agencies of enforcement, co-operation is difficult. If a hare were to come within the reach of any one of the natural men, that man would abandon his post to pursue it. Preoccupied with the possibility of his own dinner, natural man would give no thought to how his defection would ruin the hunt for his companions and cause them to go hungry.

Waltz's point was, that relations among sovereign states in the international system were similar to relations among natural men. Both live in a context of anarchy. Both have their own, short-term goals foremost in mind. The anarchical context matters. The absence of norms and rules affects behaviour of self-centred actors. It makes co-operation extremely difficult. Waltz's main point, that the context of anarchy matters decisively became the subject of a huge debate – which reintroduced arguments from eighteenth-century social-contract theory. Especially, perhaps, arguments from Rousseau. Some of these arguments will be touched on in the next chapter.

Notes

1 During the presidential election in 1960, John F. Kennedy had claimed that a 'missile gap' had developed between the two superpowers, and that the USA was falling behind the USSR in the number of nuclear weapons. This was an enormous exaggeration. It helped Kennedy win a narrow victory in the presidential election. But it also increased the American fear of the USSR.

2 Brandt signed agreements with the USSR, recognizing Germany's borders towards the east. He thereby also recognized the East Germany (GDR). On a trip to Poland Brandt visited Warsaw and, in a symbolically charged gesture, fell on his knees before the Warsaw Ghetto monument. In 1971 Willy Brandt received the Nobel Peace Prize for his *Ostpolitik*.

3 In 1956, Mao granted the Chinese population greater freedoms under the slogan 'let 100 flowers bloom'. Western radicals did not seem to appreciate that this was Mao's cynical opening move in a domestic power struggle. The Cultural Revolution was another such move. It was initiated by Mao in 1966 and marked his return to power after the disastrous failure of the Great Leap Forward.

4 The strategy was developed by Nixon's National Security Adviser Henry Kissinger, who argued that 'the road to Saigon goes through Peking' (see Kissinger 2014, p. 295). The policy, however, had a price. First, the US rapprochement to China undermined America's traditional ties with its long-term anti-communist ally, the island republic of Taiwan. Also, while the Americans prepared their 'China card' which they could use in their diplomatic game with the USSR, they also allowed China to create a 'US card', which the Chinese could use in their deteriorating relationship with the USSR.

5 For *coups d'état*, see the data set available from the Center for Systemic Peace. It suggests an increase from 119 coups around the world in the 1960s to 135 in the 1970s.

6 Domestic terrorist groups worked in Ireland (IRA) and in Spain (ETA). During the 1960s groups also emerged in the Americas (Tupamaros in Uruguay and the Weather Underground in the USA) and in Europe (like the red Brigades in Italy and the Baader-Meinhof gang in Germany). International terrorist groups emerged in the wake of the Arab–Israeli War (1967) and attacked Israeli airliners at the Munich (February 1970) and Uganda airports (Entebbe, June 1976) and killed Israeli athletes at the Munich Olympics (September 1972).

7 In the UK, consumer price inflation rose from less than 4 per cent during the 1960s to nearly 13 per cent during the 1970s – hitting a stunning high of 27 per cent in August 1975. The United States, too, experienced a high rate of inflation during the 1970s – expressed in two-digit interest rates which earned President Jimmy Carter much criticism. This criticism was sharpened by the simultaneous increase in US unemployment figures – from 4.6 per cent in October 1973 to 9 per cent in May 1975.

8 The Atlantic economy suffered two waves of recession: the first lasted from December 1969 to November 1970; the second from November 1973 to March 1975 – initiated by the greatest stock market crashes in British history, which saw the Financial Times All Share Index fall by more than half. The timing of the

    crash suggests that OPEC's oil embargo in October triggered a crisis in November, in which increased oil prices and energy shortages shook the economies of many oil-importing countries.

9   Scandinavian scholars were particularly inspired. Institutes devoted to Peace Research were established in Norway (1959) and Sweden (1966).

10 This basic idea has been a mainstay in theories of customary law for centuries. David Hume had argued that human beings are creatures of habit and that societies are constructed on the basis of the daily routines of citizens. This concept was followed up by Halford Mackinder (1919), who saw society as 'a Going Concern'. Social theorists on the political left have often repeated Karl Marx's famous quip that 'human beings make their own history, but not in circumstances of their choosing' (Moses and Knutsen 2012, p. 189). Theorists on the political right find similar ideas in the writings of conservatives like Edmund Burke or libertarians like Friedrich Hayek. A fertile line of relevant theorizing was initiated by members of the French *Annales* school during the interwar period and expressed in concepts like *mentalités*, *longue durée* and 'everyday life'. 'I think man is more than waist-deep in daily routine', Fernand Braudel (1977, p. 191) once noted. 'Countless inherited acts, accumulated pell-mell and repeated time after time to this very day become habits that help us live, imprison us, and make decisions for us throughout our lives ...'

11 The inter-paradigm debate is often counted as the third 'great debate' in International Relations – the first being the debate between Realists and Idealists between the World Wars, and the second being the debate between the 'scientists' and the 'historians' in the early 1960s. The inter-paradigm debate refers to the debate took place during the 1970s between proponents of Realism, Rationalism and Revolutionism as approaches to International Relations.

12 As a testimony to the increasing awareness of a scientific methodology, notions like 'tradition' or 'approach' were phased out and replaced by the concept of 'paradigm' – a term taken from Thomas Kuhn's influential contribution to the philosophy of science, *The Structure of Scientific Revolutions* (1962).

13

The turn: the coming of the neo-liberal world

When the British Prime Minister James Callaghan stepped down in May 1979, he said in his farewell speech that his handing over the keys of 10 Downing Street to Margaret Thatcher was more than just a change of PMs, it was a 'sea change' in British politics. In fact, it was more than that. The year 1979 marked a turn in Western, if not in world, affairs.

The turn came with big debates. The events resurrected old controversies about interstate relations and fuelled new discussions about international economics. It whirled up ideas, old and new, that challenged engrained perspectives and brought forth new views – which were critiqued in turn. Materialist theories were questioned by ideational arguments. Structural theories were challenged by post-structural approaches. Big controversies surrounded Margaret Thatcher, the new leader of the British Conservative Party. Many observers assumed that she represented a conservative reaction to the radical 1960s. This, however, was not entirely on target. For, although she represented a turn which involved restorations of traditional views and values, the thrust of her arguments was not conservative in the traditional, philosophical sense; it was liberal or libertarian.

The election of Ronald Reagan as US President in November 1980 signalled a similar sea change in American politics; only with a more immediate and fundamental international importance. The election of Reagan boosted the significance of the liberal turn, commented Thatcher, 'because it demonstrated that the United States, the greatest force for liberty that the world has known, was about to reassert a self-confident leadership in world-affairs'. Britain and the USA would make sure that the West would no longer 'retreat before the axis of convenience between the Soviet Union and the Third World' (Thatcher 1993, pp. 156f). To counter the East and the South, the West now resurrected old-fashioned liberal or libertarian ideas. It reasserted liberal core values like individual rights to life, liberty and property. It argued that free, self-interested interaction of rational individuals would yield a better world.

This chapter addresses this revival of liberal ideas which affected the political climate of the 1980s. It discusses some of the liberal reforms that began in the West and brought with them adjustments in the political economy of the world at large. It argues that these changes were associated with new international concerns – among them the availability and the price of oil – the all-important source of energy for the industrial world. And it notes how these events ushered in a new political climate in the Middle East – the most oil-rich region in the world.

In its final section the chapter discusses changes in the ideas and approaches of International Relations scholars. It argues that the scholarly study of International Relations distanced itself from the structural approaches of the past and instead embraced the core ideas of rejuvenated liberalism. This is evident for example in the so-called Neorealist approach which gained an enormous influence in the International Relations community during the 1980s. Although it retained the holistic view that marked structuralism, its basic logic rested on the individualistic rationalism of liberal economic theories. Neorealism was a child of its times. And it embodied tensions which fuelled theoretical debates all through the 1980s.

New faces, new issues

In the late 1970s the old generation, which was shaped by World War II, was leaving political office. A new generation of leaders was emerging. They brought with them new ideas – or, in many cases, old ideas in new wrapping. The reintroduction of orthodox economic liberalism is a case in point.

The West and the changing Middle East

Margaret Thatcher was an important carrier of the ideas of the new liberalism. Their international significance was boosted by the November 1980 election of Ronald Reagan as US President. Reagan, too, was an old-fashioned liberal. He ran, like Thatcher, on a platform which promised economic deregulation, dismantlement of federal bureaucracies, fewer taxes and more individual freedoms. His election campaign combined orthodox liberal doctrines with an optimistic patriotic fervour. It transformed the Republican Party. And it transformed American politics.

Once installed as the fortieth President of the United States in January 1981, Reagan forged a solid ideological rapport with Britain's Margaret Thatcher, confirming the notion of a 'special relationship' between the USA and Britain. He contrasted the Anglo-American tradition of liberty with the drab repression of the Eastern Bloc. Reagan was an anti-communist. Eager to combat the USSR and its 'evil empire', Reagan observed that the old generation of communist leaders was approaching an average age of eighty and that the Soviet economy was stagnating. The USSR was facing a political as well an economic crisis. Also, the USSR had many client regimes – the result of expansionist foreign policies in the 1970s – which were in need of Soviet attention and aid. The Soviet Union was, in short, suffering from a serious case of imperial overstretch: A stagnating economy at home could no longer sustain increasing commitments abroad. Reagan argued that Communism was rotting from within and that the simple idea of individual freedom would hasten its demise. In 1979 yet another, more subtle, challenge was added to the Soviet difficulties: the new pope, Cardinal Karol Jósef Wojtyla, visited his native Poland. The visit had an electric effect on the nation. It stimulated a human-rights movement and sparked the establishment, in 1980, of an independent labour union, Solidarity. Its success encouraged similar organizations and anti-communist movements in other East Bloc countries as well. The enormous popularity of Pope John Paul II was a huge challenge to the Soviet empire, which was committed to an increasingly unpopular atheism.

The rising importance of religion was apparent in other parts of the world as well. Not the least in the Middle East. In 1979 the secular Shah Reza Pahlavi of Iran was overthrown and the fundamentalist Muslim cleric Ayatollah Khomeini installed as new leader. The Ayatollah represented a new and radical brand of Shia Islam, tinged with nationalist colours, a pronounced anti-Western sentiment and an increasing criticism of Sunni Islam. The rise of Saddam Hussein to dictatorial power in neighbouring Iraq later that year increased the tensions between the two countries.

An Islamist rebellion in the holy Saudi city of Mecca added oil to the religious fires in the region. So did the Soviet invasion of Afghanistan in December 1979. In fact, the invasion pulled Afghanistan into the vortex of the Cold War, enhanced its role in the region and radicalized its religion. New and more politicized brands of Islam evolved in Iran, Saudi Arabia and Egypt. Doctrinaire versions of Sunni Islam followed in the wake of the Soviet invasion and Western and Arab efforts to punish the Soviets for their occupation, adding to the overall change of the Middle East in world affairs.

The Afghan war increased the domestic difficulties of the USSR. Because the USA exploited it to add more weight to the Soviet burden, the war quickly became far more costly, in money and in men than the Soviets had bargained for. The war quickly undermined the economy and the prestige of the USSR.

Over the longer haul, the Afghan war burdened the USA as well. The new brands of Islamism that affected the Muslim world had deleterious effects on the USA and other Western countries. The Soviet invasion, in short, was an important ingredient in a larger turn of world events in 1979. Together with the civil war in Lebanon and the increasing Sunni–Shia tension, it constituted the backdrop to increasing conflicts that would mark Middle Eastern politics throughout the 1980s. These conflicts would, in turn, create nervousness in the Western world as it was growing increasingly dependent upon oil from the region. Middle Eastern conflicts and concern for the stable prices and the smooth delivery of oil were constant preoccupations of Western politicians. These preoccupations also marked the new questions that emerged in international relations scholarship during the 1980s – an increasing preoccupation with the connection between politics and religion, with international political economy and with the expansion of the concept of security to accommodate energy security.

Economics, energy and religion
In the early 1970s, President Nixon had noted that America's domestic oil production had tapered off whereas US oil consumption continued to increase. The growing

gap between production and consumption had to be filled by imported oil, most of which came from the Middle East. Nixon introduced a new question to US foreign and security policy: how should the USA tackle its increasing dependence on fossil energy which was imported from a region that was as unstable as the Middle East?

The question became acute during the 1970s as the Americans pledged to guarantee the security of Israel at the same time as their dependence on oil from Israel's Arab enemies increased. It drove President Carter to launch several foreign-policy initiatives. First, he encouraged Americans to conserve energy and lessen the need for imported oil. Second, he introduced incentives to stimulate the development of alternative sources of energy – among them new technologies to convert solar rays, wind and tidal changes into electrical power. Third, he searched for more countries that could supply oil and reduce US dependence on the conflict-ridden Arab world. Fourth, he set in motion diplomatic processes to solve conflicts and stabilize the Middle East. In particular he tried to solve what he considered to be its most important dispute: the Arab–Israeli conflict.

In the spring of 1978, Carter proudly announced that he had brokered a peace treaty between Egypt and Israel. Western countries hailed this treaty as a great step towards stability and peace – the Israeli Prime Minister Begin and Egypt's President Sadat shared the Nobel Peace Prize that year. Large segments of the Muslim world, by contrast, rallied against the treaty. They denounced Sadat as a traitor and condemned his deal with Israel as a cowardly act. Anti-Egyptian demonstrations erupted throughout the Arab world and Islamist groups hatched plots to kill the Egyptian leader. One of these groups, el-Jihad, succeeded in killing Sadat during a military parade in October 1981.

President Carter's peace initiatives were stunted by these Arab reactions. His policies were further derailed by the overthrow of the US-friendly Shah Reza Pahlavi of Iran. This not only robbed the USA of a traditional ally in the Middle East, it also established a hostile Islamic republic whose religious leaders angrily denounced the USA as a 'great Satan'.

The Iranian revolution added to the turmoil in the Middle East. It also triggered a substantial price hike on oil – from about \$16 to \$40 a barrel.[1] The result was a new energy crisis. On top of it all, an Islamist rebellion broke out in Saudi Arabia, the world's greatest oil producer and the most reliable supplier to the West. Radical members of the Muslim Brotherhood seized the Grand Mosque in the holy city of Mecca in November of 1979 and held pilgrims hostage for several days before the rebels were removed by military force (Hegghammer and Lacroix 2011). Ayatollah Khomeini pronounced that the occupation was engineered by American imperialists and international Zionists. Anti-American demonstrations followed in Bangladesh, Pakistan, the Philippines, Turkey and other countries.

These events made Western leaders deeply pessimistic about the situation in the Middle East. Their outlook grew even darker when the policies of Iran's theocratic regime came to loggerheads with the secular dictatorship of neighbouring Iraq. The tumultuous relationship between Iraq's Saddam Hussein and Iran's revolutionary Ayatollah led to war in the autumn of 1980. It lasted eight years and brought ruin on both countries and suffering to millions of people.² Also, it contributed to a further poisoning of the relationship between Sunni and Shia branches of Islam, fuelling schisms and religious conflicts in many Muslim countries.

Such events altered the political dynamic in Middle East. Also, they made the USA and the West realize how brittle many Middle Eastern regimes were – and how vulnerable their economies were to changes in the price and supply of Middle Eastern oil.

The second Cold War

The Soviet invasion of Afghanistan in December 1979 happened on the heels of radical Third World revolutions and a bout of Soviet expansionism. The US government feared for the oilfields in the Middle East. In January 1980, President Carter pronounced the Middle East to be of great strategic interest to the West and promised quick US reaction against anyone who sought to increase their influence over the region at America's expense. The pronouncement was a clear warning to the USSR to stay away from the Middle East. The warning was quickly dubbed 'the Carter doctrine'.

Also, Carter allied with Pakistan and Saudi Arabia to supply anti-communist groups in Afghanistan with weapons to fight the Soviet occupiers. President Reagan expanded the effort. Not only did Reagan greatly increase the military aid to the Afghan *mujahideen*, he also furnished comparable aid to anti-Soviet groups in several other countries as well. These actions marked a self-conscious rupture with the old US Cold War doctrine of containment. Reagan had never believed in containment. He had always considered it a passive and foolish doctrine: it was purely reactive and left the political initiative to the USSR. Reagan preferred a proactive policy according to which the USA should confront Soviet client regimes in the Third World and undermine their influence. Reagan, in short, replaced half a century of containment policy with a new policy of roll-back.

Reagan did this because the US intelligence services informed him about the double crises in the Soviet Union. After the death of Leonid Brezhnev, Reagan began to escalate US support to anti-communist movements in Soviet client states all over the world – in Angola, in Indochina, on the Horn of Africa and in Central America.³ US military aid to the Afghan *mujahideen* increased particularly fast. It was secretly channelled through Pakistan's military intelligence services (ISI). The leaders of the ISI received enormous quantities of weapons which they, in turn, distributed to Afghan rebel groups – prioritizing those groups which were loyal to Pakistan. Saudi Arabia supplied Afghan rebels with just as much arms and money as the USA. In addition they supplied aid in the form of theologians and radical organizers.

This aid strengthened anti-communist groups in Afghanistan and the surrounding area and created troubles for the USSR. For nearly a decade the Soviets would be engaged in a costly war that would burden its economy and demoralize its military forces. The war would also have long-term consequences for the USA. The Americans would soon be haunted by one of the most tenacious of the Saudi organizers, Osama bin Laden, and his international brigade of radical Islamists, al-Qaida.

Economic concerns and neo-liberal reforms

The 1970s had seen the end of the long, sustained boom that had marked the capitalist economies of the West since World War II. The 1980s began with economic crises and uncertainties. The oil crises of 1973 and 1979 had been major factors behind these uncertainties, causing concerns about oil stable and sufficient oil deliveries to the industrial economies of the West. An unprecedented combination of high inflation and economic stagnation ('stagflation') had caused economists and politicians to look for solutions in increased trade. Measures designed to liberalize world trade and international finance, agreed upon by members of GATT during the 1970s, paved the way for a decisive round of international negotiations in Uruguay in the 1980s.[4]

These reforms reflected a revival of liberal economic theories, expounded by people like Keith Joseph, Lewis Powell, Friedrich von Hayek and Milton Friedman.[5]

American changes

This is not the place to discuss why British and American political economies went through such profound political changes during the 1970s and 1980s. Suffice it to say that American politics was affected by the rise of a patriotic movement that advocated traditional American ideals of free-market fundamentalism.[6] Its message of individual liberty was substantially fuelled by a popular reaction to the anti-war radicalism of the 1960s.

The message was boosted by a rapid development in technologies of communication which triggered a veritable media revolution – a proliferation of local broadcasters,[7] and transition from text to image and from paper to screen. The revolution began by the development of toys and electronic arcade games produced by firms like Atari. It continued with the production of the personal computer (PC) – the Commodore 64 home computer revolutionized the US consumer market when it was introduced in 1982.

The PC changed the world. But it changed it in very particular ways. The new technologies were not value free. The communications revolution that they launched carried the stamp of the society that produced it. In some ways, the new technologies were an outcome of the Cold War, as they were regularly pioneered by corporations which worked for the US Department of Defense. The first programmable computer, for example, was built by the IBM Corporation on contracts from the Defense Department during the Korean War. During the 1950s and 1960s, important innovations in technology and design were made by tinkering amateurs as well as professional university engineers. However, the main sponsor behind a rapid succession of computer generations was the US military budget.

The dynamic centre of its evolution was concentrated in the Santa Clara Valley around the shallow bay of San Francisco. During the 1970s, its high-tech computer industries boomed – buoying the micro-chip industry and lifting firms like Hewlett-Packard and Apple – and the region came to be known as 'Silicon Valley'. This region had a long tradition of radical individualism – from the bohemian lifestyles of artist communities via the counter-cultural movement of the hippies to the ambitious members of the Objectivist movement. They stressed the importance of self-sufficiency as the way to independence and individual freedom. They wanted to replace big government with grass-roots networks of free and informed individuals. They were sceptical of big industrial centres. Some of them favoured local ecological communes. Others imagined that their new technologies might make knowledge instantly available to everyone and spread reason, harmony and peace as a result. In the early 1970s, their ideas were embodied for example in *The Whole Earth Catalog*. In the 1980s they were expressed in the Whole Earth 'Lectronic Link ('the Well').[8]

First World initiatives

In 1984, Apple introduced the Macintosh, the first commercially successful PC to employ graphical user interface and mouse. As other produces emulated the innovation, the PC quickly evolved into a new mass medium. The values of the new counterculture were apparent in the famous TV advertisement which announced Apple's new Mackintosh computer. The ad was seen by millions because it was broadcast during the US Superbowl. It began with scenes from George Orwell's dystopian novel *1984*, depicting a drab and mesmerized mass audience staring blankly at the face of Big Brother on a giant screen. Suddenly a lone, athletic women bursts upon the scene, dressed in bright colours she runs towards the big screen. She is pursued by the riot police and carries a sledge hammer in her hands. She hurls the hammer at Big Brother's face. From the exploding screen comes the message: 'On January 24 Apple Computer will introduce Macintosh. And you will see why 1984 won't be like "1984"'.

Big government could be destroyed! That was the message of the times. New technologies could bring enlightenment and freedom. Individual liberties would release initiative and bring a new social order. These had been central ideas in the political platform of the two-term California governor Ronald Wilson Reagan. They remained central to the presidential campaign that he launched in 1979. Reagan promised to reduce taxes, explaining that lowering taxes would leave each individual worker with more income, more money to spend and, thus, more freedom in the marketplace. An increase in consumer spending would stimulate the market – it would boost production and sales and create a more vibrant economy. And as the economy grew, so would the nation's tax base, which in turn would yield more revenue for the government.

These were controversial theories. Reagan's opponents often ridiculed them. It was absurd to think that lowering the rates of taxation would in fact increase the fiscal income of government, they argued. Reduction of taxes would only reduce government income. This would in turn lead either to reduction in government services or to growing budget deficits – or to both. President Reagan, however, paid little attention to such criticism. Tax reduction was for him about something more than the balancing of books. It was a worthy political goal in its own right. It would force reductions in government size, and roll-back in state activities and, in turn, increase in individual freedoms.

As soon as he was installed as president in January 1981, he began to implement liberal reforms. He broke up unions. He dismantled regimes of regulation
and control that President Franklin D. Roosevelt had established during the early
1930s to combat the Great Depression. Big government was not the solution to
anything; it was always part of the problem, Reagan argued as he weakened the old
institutions of America's political economy in the name of liberty, patriotism and
traditional values.

Reagan triggered a cultural revolution. His slogans and ideas changed the
political debate. His reforms altered US political practices. He implemented
a neo-liberal vision, fuelled controversies and deepened ideological cleavages
in American politics. Reagan's years in the White House saw the growth of two
contesting sets of cultural values in American life. The clash between them would
soon be referred to as the American 'culture wars' (Hunter 1991).

Similar development took place in other countries. The governments of Malcolm
Fraser in Australia and Brian Mulroney in Canada introduced neo-liberal policies.
A wave of liberalization washed across Western Europe as well. In Germany it
was helped along by a conservative coalition, led by Helmut Kohl. In France, the
socialist President François Mitterrand bucked the liberal trend at first, but quickly
made a political U-turn. His economics and finance minister, Jacques Delors,
introduced liberal reforms to France. And when Delors was appointed President
of the European Commission in 1985, he favoured monetary stability over traditional left-wing spending priorities. In 1986, the European Community revised
the Treaty of Rome, adopting the Single European Act (SEA). It developed plans
for a single European market and formulated ambitious goals of creating a single
European currency.[9]

Oil shocks, development and the Washington consensus

Neo-liberal reforms had originally been developed by countries in the capitalist
West to address the economic difficulties that had shaken their countries in the
1970s. These difficulties were associated with the rising prices of energy that
followed the oil crises of 1973 and 1979.

These fluctuations are indicated in Figure 13.1. It shows the price for one barrel
of crude oil during the 1970s and 1980s in constant 2010 US dollars. The figure
shows that the oil price jumped from about $14 to around $45 per barrel around
1973, and then jumped from about $34 to well over $70 in 1979/80. The figure also
shows how the oil price tapered off throughout the 1980s, and ended up around
$22 at the end of the 1980s. These fluctuations are tied in with important political
events of the 1980s, and the connections between oil and politics will be briefly
explored in this section.

Oil is indispensable for modern industrial societies. Changes in supply and price
have serious ripple effects throughout the world society. Oil also illustrates the
interdependence of the modern world and the intimate interconnections of power
and money. Was it an economic or a political initiative that led some of the world's
primary oil producers to establish the Organization for Petroleum Exporting

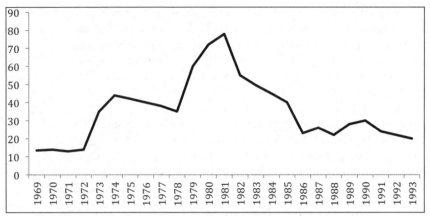

Figure 13.1 The price of crude oil during the 1970s and 1980s
(in constant 2010 US $)

Countries (OPEC) in 1960? The question is purely academic; for in practice the political and economic aspects cannot be usefully separated.

This is evident from the 1973 agreement among OPEC's members to reduce production. The decision was political – Egypt and Syria had launched a surprise attack on Israel during the Yom Kippur holidays in October 1973; because the USA supported Israel, Arab members of OPEC announced an oil embargo against the USA and its NATO allies. The immediate effect was to create a deep rift within NATO. In the longer term, the embargo triggered ripple effects that ushered in new political and economic concerns.

Most obviously, the price hikes increased the fuel bills of oil-importing nations. It caused them to tighten their budgets and rearrange their political priorities. The industrial countries of the West were shaken by the rising prices; however, they quickly found ways to save on oil consumption. The result was a quick evolution of new policies – campaigns of energy conservation tied in with environmental arguments, boosting the popularity of green parties and initiatives to explore alternative sources of energy. The newly independent industrializing countries of the Third World, however, were badly hurt. They suffered balance-of-payment deficits which wiped out years of economic progress.

Oil-exporting countries, on the other hand, increased their incomes immensely. The oil-producing countries around the Persian Gulf hardly knew what to do with all the new money. They built roads and infrastructure. They built modern schools and universities and triggered a revolution in education at home.[10] Also, they sponsored education abroad. Saudi Arabia, for example, began to fund Islamic schools in Pakistan and other countries. The Saudis built thousands of new *madrasas* to spread the strict Saudi doctrines of Wahhabi Islam.

Finally, oil-exporting countries invested their new-found wealth in the First World. They bought Western real estate – in New York and London. And they placed enormous sums in Western banks. A flood of big deposits caused a glut in the financial markets of the West, driving interest rates down. In their efforts to move their capital, Western banks offered cheap loans to countries in dire need of capital. Many poor countries (whose increasing fuel bills had just caused large deficits in their budgets) took up cheap loans. Only to find that when the interest rates increased again during the early 1980s, they were saddled with a rapidly growing debt.

Power, faith and money affected international relations in the early 1980s. The First World suffered economic fluctuations and unemployment.[11] Countries in the Third World were saddled with a steadily increasingly debt. The problem exploded in August 1982 as Mexico declared inability to service its debt. Other countries in Latin America, among them large countries such as Brazil and Argentina, quickly followed suit with similar declarations. The West responded with diplomatic efforts to adjust the debt burden – even to cancel the debt in some cases. But on the condition that countries which had relied on policies of import substitution had to switch to strategies of export-oriented industrialization. During the 1980s the IMF, the World Bank and the US Treasury worked out strategies to alleviate the debt problem of poor nations. They devised policy prescriptions to reform the crisis-racked nations and put their economies on a new footing. They demanded 'structural adjustment' along liberal lines. They introduced policies of liberalization and privatization in order to expand the domestic market and stimulated foreign investment to increase international trade. By 1989 the primary economic institutions of the West had agreed on a 'standard' package of liberal reforms. It became known as 'the Washington consensus'.

The Second World and the kiss of debt
The Third-World debt was much debated in International Relations journals and books during the 1980s. One aspect of the world economic crisis, however, was seriously underreported at the time: namely, its effect on the Second World. For the fact of the matter was that countries in the communist East Bloc had also been pulled into the more free-floating capitalist world economy. When that economy was shaken by crises in the early 1980s, communist countries would also suffer from its consequences.

The USSR had become a part of the world capitalist system during the 1970s through increasing exports of fossil fuels.[12] Increasing energy prices during the 1970s had encouraged the USSR to expand its production and export of fossil fuels to First World markets – steadily more gas to Europe and more oil to Japan. In return, the USSR had received technology and hard currency. American policymakers observed this development with increasing apprehension. President Reagan forbade the use of US technology in Soviet energy projects. He was annoyed when the Europeans in 1982 agreed to finance a new Soviet gas pipeline which would supply Europe with Siberian gas. First, Reagan feared that Europeans were becoming increasingly dependent on Soviet fossil fuel – a situation which he saw as a threat to the unity and the security of the Western alliance. Second, because the Europeans paid for Soviet fuel with hard currency which the USSR in turn used to subsidize its client states in Eastern Europe and the Third World. In Reagan's view, America's allies in Western Europe helped keep the Soviet empire afloat.

Soviet allies in Eastern Europe noted these transactions. And they asked the USSR to support their economies, which were sluggish and slow. The Soviets sold oil and gas to their allies at reduced prices, but refused to do much more. Communist leaders like East Germany's Walter Ulbricht had asked the USSR for financial assistance. Their plea, however, had fallen on deaf ears in Moscow. In the early 1970s Ulbricht was replaced by Erich Honecker. He developed a clever economic plan to pull East Germany out of the economic doldrums. East Germany would take up cheap loans in the glutted financial market of the capitalist West, invest in modern means of production, boost production and develop new, sophisticated products. The East Germans would then sell these products on the international market and earn enough money to pay back the capitalist loans. Leaders in other East Bloc countries developed similar schemes. They all made the same mistake. They assumed that the capitalist economies of the West were as stagnant as their own. They overlooked the fact that the capitalist economy was steadily transforming.[13]

When interest rates began to increase again, several East Bloc countries faced a serious debt problem. East Germany saw its Western debt increase from about $1 billion in the early 1970s via $12 billion in 1980 to over $25 billion in 1989 – at which time the annual cost of debt services alone amounted to $4.5 billion, or nearly 60 per cent of East Germany's hard-currency export earnings (Kotkin 2010, p. 84). Poland and Hungary ended up in a similar fix. The two countries had accumulated hard-currency debts to the tune of about $20 billion and $18 billion, respectively. In contrast to the capitalist countries in the Third World, the socialist countries in the Second World did not enter into debt-reducing negotiations.[14]

Putting pressure on the Soviets
The Reagan administration observed the East Bloc crisis. Reagan noted that Soviet sales of oil and gas provided foreign earning that kept the USSR afloat. Also, energy sales financed Soviet expansion into the Third World; most conspicuously in Afghanistan, Angola, Ethiopia and Indochina. Reagan also argued that Soviet influence was increasing in Latin America; that Cuba and the radical Sandinista regime in Nicaragua were exporting revolution to unstable countries like El Salvador.

In order to reduce the USSR's income of Western currency, Reagan pressured European statesmen to stop buying Soviet gas and cancel the building of the Siberian pipeline. He had no success; the Europeans were too dependent on Soviet gas to comply. Some of Reagan's economic advisers suggested a new US strategy. They had traced the foreign trade flows of the USSR and found that the sums that the Soviets earned from their energy exports were not so large. They had also found that the Soviets used nearly all of their hard-currency earnings to subsidize client regimes.[15] The Soviet economy, in other words, was vulnerable to price fluctuations. If oil prices were to drop, the Soviet books would no longer balance. If prices dropped badly, the USSR would soon be forced to either cut subsidies to its client regimes abroad or face the risk of insolvency at home.

It was a simplistic argument and it was based on uncertain economic data. But Reagan was convinced by it. Around 1985 he leaned heavily on Saudi-Arabia and convinced its leaders to increase their oil production considerably. This caused an international oil glut and made oil prices fall steeply – from a peak of about $40 in 1980 to below $10 in 1986. The price fall was of great benefit to the USA and the capitalist countries of the West; it enabled them to re-inflate their economies with cheaper fuel. But it was a disaster for the USSR, because the price fall cut the Soviet export earnings by more than half.

A severe economic crisis hit the USSR in the mid-1980s – at the very time when the Soviet succession crisis was becoming acute.[16] During this moment of a double Soviet crisis – economic as well as political – President Reagan announced his plans for modernizing America's armed forces. In March 1983, he promised the US army a new tank, the US air force new planes, and the US navy new ships. Also, he announced the development of a new Strategic Defense Initiative (SDI), which would place an array of sensors and sophisticated weapons systems in orbit around the earth and constitute a protective shield of missiles in space. Reagan's opponents quickly dubbed it the 'Star Wars' project. It was enormously expensive, for it was partly designed to challenge the USSR to a costly arms race that Reagan knew the Soviets could ill afford.

Two years later Reagan added yet another initiative: he announced his intention to support anti-communist insurgents – 'freedom fighters' as he called them – in Angola, Nicaragua and other countries he considered Soviet satellites. This support, undertaken as an effort to roll back Soviet influence in the Third World, was hailed as the 'Reagan doctrine'. The idea was to challenge the USSR to a strategic competition, increase the military expenditures of the USSR and add greater burdens to an already faltering Soviet economy.[17]

Rivalry, diplomacy and economic competition

Soon after Reagan announced his initiatives, the Communist Party of the Soviet Union (CPSU) elected a new and younger Secretary General – a spry youth of fifty-five by the name of Mikhail Gorbachev. His domestic policies were driven by an acute awareness of the difficulties of the Soviet economy. He quickly initiated domestic reforms, first a policy of *glasnost* (openness), then one of *perestroika* (restructuring). His foreign policy was dominated by mounting problems in client regimes in Europe and in the Third World. In Eastern Europe there was a growing dissatisfaction with both local regimes and Soviet leadership. In the Third World, where client regimes depended on Soviet aid and support, war and conflict put increasing demands on the troubled Soviet economy. These demands were additionally increased by the military build-up and the roll-back initiatives of the Reagan administration.

Gorbachev knew that the Soviet political economy was in no shape to compete with the USA. So instead of accepting Reagan's challenge to a new arms race, Gorbachev responded with a peace proposal: he offered a plan to reduce the world's stockpiles of nuclear weapons by 50 per cent. Reagan was surprised. But he took Gorbachev's proposal seriously and met with the Soviet leader in November 1985 to discuss the plan. They met in Geneva, Switzerland, where they quickly gained each other's confidence and launched an unprecedented diplomacy of disarmament.

Reagan and Gorbachev met for a second time, in October 1986, in the Icelandic capital of Reykjavik. Here the two leaders came close to an agreement that would have destroyed nearly all superpower missiles. The deal fell through at the very last minute, when Reagan refused to give up his Strategic Defense Initiative. This meeting did result, however, in a treaty which eliminated all medium-range, ground-launched nuclear missiles from the superpowers' arsenals. In December 1987, Gorbachev travelled to Washington to sign the Intermediate-Range Nuclear Forces (INF) Treaty. In May 1988, Reagan paid a visit to Moscow. The two leaders finalized the INF treaty and signed several agreements on lesser issues and discussed bilateral issues concerning Central America, southern Africa and the Middle East; including the Soviet withdrawal from Afghanistan.

This was a remarkable turn of events. A decade previously détente had collapsed, a new arms race was under way, and the USSR was expanding its influence in the Third World. The late 1980s saw major diplomatic initiatives, big arms reductions and Soviet pull-outs from Third World wars. However, this visible turn was connected to a more invisible web of global events. Behind the scenes of diplomatic progress, the USSR was struggling to make ends meet. US analysts knew this, and worked to make the Soviet predicament even worse. In 1985 the Reagan administration doubled America's military assistance to the Afghan *mujahideen*; Saudi Arabia matched the US generosity. The result was an escalation of *mujahideen* activities, which forced the new Soviet leaders to send more soldiers to Afghanistan and more aid to Najibullah's regime in Kabul.

In 1986, the Americans doubled its Afghan aid once more. In addition, they gave the *mujahideen* sophisticated Stinger missiles to shoot down Soviet battle helicopters. Saudi Arabia helped by greatly increasing its oil production in order to depress the world's energy prices. The USSR's oil earnings fell so much that the Soviets had to dip into their financial reserves to keep their economy afloat. When the reserves were depleted, the Soviets began to sell off their gold reserves. By May 1988, when Reagan visited Moscow, the Soviets had drained their treasury and were running on empty. Now they had to cut costs – including the costs of empire. These were the circumstances under which Reagan and Gorbachev signed the many agreements on nuclear disarmament and discussed issues concerning superpower activities in Central America, southern Africa and the Middle East. Behind the diplomatic smiles and the surface cordiality, then, there was still the superpower struggle for power and dominance. Only this time, the USSR was close to exhaustion and on the deep defensive.

Expansion and transformation

The 1980s began in the tense atmosphere of the 'second Cold War'. Its concerns with national security were reflected in more assertive foreign policies in the West – in Thatcher's Falklands War against Argentina in 1982 and in Reagan's replacing the old doctrine of Containment with a new, confrontational policy of roll-back. Soviet leaders were surprised by the change; some of them were gripped by fear of a surprise attack by NATO.[18]

During the mid-1980s, superpower relations changed. The USSR descended into crisis, whereas the USA was buoyed by economic recovery and a new, national optimism. A new generation of Soviet leaders addressed the crisis by introducing reforms at home and initiating a new, more accommodating stance abroad. The USA responded to the Soviet accommodation with accommodations of its own. Reagan's second term saw a new rapprochement between the two superpowers. This was reflected in new and wide-reaching agreements on nuclear disarmament and arms control. ·

Discussing events; assessing Neorealism

IR scholars observed these changes and discussed them. Several of them noted that the world was changing before their eyes. Superpower relations were improving. A new Soviet–American rapprochement was reflected in more congenial relations in the UN. Delegates from both countries began to agree in UN debates. The Cold War deadlock was removed from discussions in the UN Security Council, which was suddenly able to make substantial decisions. It initiated new peacekeeping operations – after a decade-long hiatus – in Afghanistan, Angola, Iraq, Iran and Central America. This improvement in the international climate could not be captured by Neorealist terms.

First, Neorealism disregarded dynamics within states. American politics was transformed by Ronald Reagan; the West by liberal reform, technological innovation and economic dynamism. The USSR suffered political paralysis under an unfortunate succession of dying leaders; the Eastern Bloc was altered by economic dissatisfaction and ideological disillusion. These were domestic events. They altered the political climate in entire regions. They had international consequences. Neorealism had no room for popular uprisings or other domestic changes.

Friedrich Kratochwil (1981) made the point that change always comes from below. Structural theories, which restrict themselves to discussing the international system, are static. They cannot explain change – and they have special difficulties with change in ideas and popular moods. Change always comes from some transformation within individual states.[19] Kratochwil's point became starkly obvious during the mid-1980s with the unexpected emergence of the new and dynamic Soviet leader, Mikhail Gorbachev, with whom the West 'could do business'. He adjusted the communist ideology which altered the policies of the Communist Party which changed everything.

Second, as was noted by observers like Robert Cox (1981), Waltz's theory excluded social relations. Consequently, Neorealism was a static theory, Cox continued. It could not account for change. The point was elegantly expanded upon by John G. Ruggie (1986). He argued that Waltz's Neorealism was, in essence, a mechanical model. It shows how the international system reproduces itself, but it cannot explain how it changes. The theory could, for example, not explain how the international system emerged in the first place, noted Ruggie. He then proceeded to demonstrate how Waltz's theory lacked terms that are necessary to grasp the most important transformation in world politics over the last thousand years, namely, the transformation from late medieval feudalism to the early modern international system.

In order to add dynamism to Waltz's mechanical model, Ruggie (1986) introduced a concept from Émile Durkheim's sociology: namely, 'dynamic density'. The concept adds social relations and dynamism to the model as it indicates 'the quantity, velocity, and diversity of transactions that go on within society'. Members of the English School made a similar critique and proposed that Neorealism would gain a vital social dimension if it added the concept of 'interaction capacity' – by which they meant means of communication which allowed for social interaction.

Barry Buzan (1991) pursued this critique and proposed to refine Waltz's basic concept of 'anarchy'. There are more mature and less mature types of anarchy, he proposed. A 'mature anarchy' would have a higher degree of communicative interaction and would represent a more integrated and more orderly and stable kind of international system. Technology is the decisive factor here, Buzan continued. Technologies of transportation and communication change the character of what might be called 'the interaction environment' of the international system. These technologies are dynamic; they evolve and change continually. Also, they are international in their deployment and they have system-wide effects. States are sovereign actors; but in theory only. In practice they are embedded in a technology-based web of communicative interaction. The evolution of technology continually raises the interaction capacity in the system.

Stephen Krasner, Robert O. Keohane and Joseph S. Nye made similar points – but they anchored it in economic rather than sociological terms. All of them praised Waltz's structural approach and accepted his main claims. They accepted that states are the major actors in International Relations and that states are rational and egotistical – an acceptance which was a major concession on their part; it distanced them from the famous argument they had made a few years previously in *Power and Interdependence* (1977). However, Krasner disagreed with Waltz's view of sovereignty. Although states in principle are independent masters of their own domain, in practice they are hemmed in by webs of interdependencies (Krasner 1999).

Keohane and Nye disagreed with Waltz's claim that interstate co-operation under anarchy is difficult. Co-operation can very well occur among rational egotists, they claimed – even under conditions of anarchy. This is evident from empirical observations, they continued. Norms and rules do in fact exist in the world and they regulate state behaviour. Conventions, institutions and regimes exist and facilitate interstate co-operation, they argued – agreeing with Buzan and Krasner.

Spontaneous development of conventions and institutions could be experimentally demonstrated, argued Robert Axelrod (1984). He used computers to run variations of classical game-theory in long, repeated games, and showed that when such games are played more than once – when they are endlessly repeated by the same actors – they produce conventions and rules of co-operation. This is what states in fact do, argued Axelrod; states do not relate once, they exist in an interstate society where they interrelate continuously. Waltz presented international events as so many snapshots of interstate constellations. He presented them as history-less single games. But international events are never single games. Each event is an outcome of past interactions. If an international event were to be discussed as a game, it had to be seen as one instance in a very long and organic chain of iterated games. And such iterated games produced norms, rules and ordering institutions.

Also, the existence of such institutions is intuitively obvious, Keohane continued. They are, in fact, necessary preconditions for the system. An anarchic system without ordering institutions would not be a system at all; it would be chaos. Neorealism needs to add an institutional component, concluded Keohane (1984; 1989).

In human relations some norms and conventions will always exist. In relations among states, norms and rules will always evolve. Institutions will always develop in some form or other and to some degree. Institutions are made by states through their rational interaction. States use them politically. But to do that, norms and rules have to be generally obeyed. Neorealism represents a huge advance in academic International Relations; but it is underspecified, Keohane (1989, p. 9) concluded. It overlooks the fact that institutions exist as an important part of the international system. States have made them. And they obey them – most of the time. Institutions condition state behaviour. They facilitate co-operation and contribute to order. The higher degree of institutionalization that exists in an international system, the more cooperation and order there is in it, argued Keohane.

A third and final point made by international observers during the 1980s was that the changes that occurred in the world were fuelled by economic activities – economic stagnation was a major source of the Soviet crisis; technological innovation and reforms in finance and trade were factors which stimulated the new dynamism in Britain, America and the West. Susan Strange expressed this point pithily. In order to understand modern International Relations, it is necessary to rely on economic as well as on political approaches. Students of International Relations have traditionally had a poor understanding of economics; they have relied excessively on arguments based on power and institutions, argued Strange. Students of economics, on the other hand, have had a poor understanding of power; they have tended to rely excessively on abstract, market models. It was necessary to command both perspectives, she insisted. Other International Relations authors agreed; among then was Robert Gilpin, who published *Political Economy of International Relations* in 1987. It was one of the most popular introductions to its subject.

Susan Strange was a driving force behind the rise of international political economy (IPE) as a sub-field of International Relations. She designed new courses in the subject. She taught a generation of students at LSE and at the European University Institute in Florence. She pioneered IPE arguments with books like *States and Markets* (1988). Her book focused on the 'market–authority nexus'; that is, the balance of power between the international market on the one hand and political authority on the other. It argued that, since the 1970s, the global market had gained significant power relative to that of the state and that a 'dangerous gap' was emerging between the two.

To capture the point, Strange began by discussing four aspects of power – four channels through which powerful actors can exert influence on the world: protection, production, finance and knowledge. Power is the ability to provide protection, make things, obtain access to credit, and develop and control authoritative modes of interpreting the world, argued Strange (1988, pp. 23ff). The first aspect – the ability to provide protection and security – was at the core of traditional International Relations thinking and defined in military terms. Production has also been an important of traditional International Relations because it concerns the economic/industrial base for military power. Financial access has, by Strange's account, been the most overlooked of all the channels of power. It is impossible to comprehend contemporary international relations without a good understanding of international financial markets, she insists.

She pursued the point and probed the 'market–authority nexus' in *Rival States, Rival Firms* (Stopford and Strange 1991). In *The Retreat of the State* (1996) she argued that governments are not fully in charge of the world economy. They have stiff competition from big businesses, accountants, insurers, drug barons, international bureaucrats and other actors who all encroach on the sovereignty of the state.

Expanding the concept of security
Susan Strange honed in on a new sense of uncertainty that had emerged in the 1970s. Her political-economic themes spilled over into debates about national security and were seized upon by authors like Barry Buzan. His *People, States and Fear* (1991 [1983]) broadened the traditional concept of security and exceeded traditional International Relations discussions in which the state was the main referent.

Buzan criticized Neorealism for presenting a mechanic model; he proposed that adding technology and innovation would transform it to a dynamic theory. He noted how innovations in transportation technology and communication technology altered the interaction capacity of the international system; how it made the international anarchy more mature and stimulated cooperation, order and peace. But technology and innovation are also key components in international rivalry and decisive factors in war – as superior technology is a precondition for making superior weapons systems. Technology, then, is Janus-faced. It may contribute to progress, wealth and comfort. But it may also fuel change, insecurity and fear.

Only people can experience insecurity and fear. People have, at all times, created states or other social formations in order to safeguard themselves. In the modern, interdependent world, however, the traditional, state-centred concept of security is too narrow. Today, security takes on many forms. Security organizations are built on different levels of analysis – on the individual and the systems level, as well as that of states. Individual security involves measures to protect 'life, health, status, wealth and freedom' among other things. State security involves measures to protect three basic and interlinked elements: the idea of the state, its physical base and its institutional expression. Also, since security is a relational phenomenon, one cannot understand the security of any given state without understanding the international context of interdependence in which the state is embedded – both regional and global.

Buzan (1991 [1983]) conjured up a many-levelled concept of security. And he added complexity to the security debate by adding *sectors* of security – primary among them were the political, military, economic, societal, and environmental sectors. The last created much controversy, because Buzan did not only discuss earthquakes and hurricanes and other aspects of the 'struggle humans have with nature'; he also discussed human-generated environmental threats, such as resource depletion, pollution of the oceans and the changing composition of the earth's atmosphere, to name a few.

The rise of new concerns
The expanded definition of 'security' provided a new analytic context for concerns about the health of the global environment. These concerns had long been growing due to the increasing consumption of the earth's finite resources and the pollution of the oceans and the atmosphere.

They had been addressed during the 1970s by social scientists like Paul Ehrlich (1968) and Schumacher (1973) and by associations like the Club of Rome (1972). During the 1980s the concerns were broadened and discussed by several governments around the world. Politicians, who had become concerned with links between environmental problems and population-health issues, finally challenged the claim that there was no proven causal link between tobacco smoke and lung cancer. They asked whether acid rain and the depletion of the earth's protective ozone layer caused diseases. They provided funding to researchers who had identified a new disease which had originated in west-central Africa and spread to the West. In early 1980s the US Center for Disease Control and Prevention (CDC) found that the disease was spread by a virus and could cause an acquired immune deficiency syndrome (AIDS) in humans. Concerns about epidemics and pandemics were enhanced by environmental catastrophes, such as the chemical plant disaster in Bhopal, India, in 1984 and by the nuclear accident in Chernobyl, Ukraine, which spread radioactive fallout over large parts of north-western Europe in 1986.

Issues about the global environment and international health were increasingly brought up by the UN. In 1983, for example, the UN took ambitious initiatives in the area of environmental politics by establishing a World Commission on Environment and Development (WCED) and appointing Norway's former Prime Minister Gro Harlem Brundtland as chair. The WCED issued *Our Common Future* in 1987, a report which discussed the global threats from industrial pollution, climate change and new pandemics. The report thoroughly demonstrated the extent to which the natural environment of the planet was deteriorating. It argued that future human needs must be met within the carrying capacity of the natural systems of the planet. One of the first initiatives of the WCED was to explore the depletion of the world's protective ozone layer and to work out a convention to protect the world's atmosphere from damaging effect of CFC gases. A treaty text was opened for signature in 1987. The treaty entered into force on 1 January 1989.

The WCED popularized the notion of 'sustainable development', and paved the way for the establishment of the International Panel on Climate Change (IPCC) in 1988 and the Conference on Environment and Development in 1992 (UNCED or the 'Earth Summit'). Discussions drew on insights from medicine, biology and other life sciences. A closer understanding of ecological issues would depend on so many other concerns than power and production. It needed theories that could describe the planet as a living organism; theories that could draw on insights from biology and chemistry. Most basically, it would need solid knowledge about the biosphere's carbon cycle. Social theories, in other words, would have to include material and institutional preconditions for political processes and economic transactions; factors that are part of any production process but which economists usually take for granted, exclude from their models and consider as external to their calculations. A fuller understanding of the issues involved in an environmentalist approach to International Relations would have to include these so-called 'externalities'.

Such an approach was boosted by developments in the life sciences, such as the so-called Greenland Ice Core Project (GICP). Its participants drilled down through 3000 metres of Greenland's ice sheet and detected in the ice traces of some 250,000 years of natural history. When they analysed samples of ice from around 500 BC, they observed that the earth's atmosphere contained increasing quantities of lead, silver and copper. This observation documented traces of early human metallurgy – thus confirming archaeological records of early human mining. The GICP scientists also documented that, beginning in the final decades of the eighteenth century, the earth's atmosphere was rapidly being filled by increasing amounts of carbon dioxide. This coincided precisely with the beginning of the Industrial Revolution.

Greenland's vast sheet of inland ice, in other words, contained a unique record of ways in which human activities had altered the composition of the earth's biosphere. Furthermore, changes in the biosphere correlated with atmospheric temperatures, erratic weather patterns and tendencies towards regional climate changes. These discoveries confirmed a connection between human pollution and climate change. They raised new concerns about the conditions for life on earth and lifted discussions of the global climate to a new level. And they relied on theories and models which were based in the natural sciences.

Although these discussions relied on evidence from organic chemistry, biology and other natural sciences, they were quickly embraced by International Relations scholars. Harold and Margaret Sprout (1965) had imported environmental problems to International Relations during the 1960s; with mixed success. The US ecologist Garrett Hardin (1968) made a more successful move when he used the rational-actor perspective to discuss ecological questions. He discussed the historical decline of the British commons to demonstrate that Western societies are essentially unsustainable. 'A finite world can support only a finite population', he claimed. Growth cannot continue at the present rate; it 'must eventually equal zero' (p. 1243).

Others began to echo the argument. Ernst Schumacher (1973), for example, argued that most of his fellow economists were misguided because they treated all resources as expendable income. Wouldn't it make more sense to treat natural resources as non-renewable inputs (fossil fuels being a case in point) and treat them as capital? he asked. Economists treat waste and pollution as external factors in their analyses; wouldn't it give a more realistic view of the costs of industrial production if these externalities were included in the analyses? Also, since the earth is a closed system, nature's resistance to pollution is limited – as everything else is. The cost of externalities is bound to increase more than industrial production itself.

Such arguments were also embraced by International Relations scholars. The basic concept was already familiar: It concerned the natural preconditions for human societies and echoed the logic of the systems theories of the 1950s and the structuralism of the 1960s. However, the environmental arguments also relied on theories and evidence from organic chemistry, biology and other natural sciences. They portrayed the earth as a closed biological system. Thus, they added to International Relations an organic, natural-science aspect which had been absent from the social-science-based approaches of Realism, Rationalism and Revolutionism.[20]

The view of the earth as a closed biological system was hammered home by James Lovelock, a British environmentalist who worked for the National Aeronautics and Space Administration (NASA) during the 1960s. What is the largest living thing on earth, Lovelock asked rhetorically? His answer, elaborated in his book *Gaia* (1979), was: the earth itself. The living and non-living parts of the earth form a complex interacting system that can be thought of as a single organism, argued Lovelock. The earth is covered by a thin biosphere which has a regulatory effect on the earth's environment that acts to sustain life.

Lovelock's book has been reissued in several editions. On the cover of some of them is a famous photo taken by an astronaut on board Apollo 8 on Christmas Eve 1968. It shows the earth as a small blue planet rising above the horizon of the moon against the black backdrop of empty space. This photo, entitled 'Earthrise', communicates very effectively the view of the earth as a small, limited, lonely self-maintaining system, suspended in empty space (Poole 2008).

The coming of the neo-liberal world

This chapter has argued that the late 1970s saw a change in the climate of international politics. It has suggested that a transition took place around 1979 and that it was marked by the election of Margaret Thatcher as British Prime Minister and Ronald Reagan as President of the United States. If the 1960s and early 1970s had been years of radical politics and radical thought, 1979 inaugurated an age marked by liberal – or rather, neo-liberal – ideas.

Thatcher and Reagan presented themselves as champions of a new form of conservatism. The policies of Thatcher and Reagan are easily seen as reactions to the radical excesses of the 1960s – they were reactions to the radical rejection of the capitalist economy, to the criticism of Western democracy and to the protests of the antiwar movement. Both Thatcher and Reagan saw it as their task to reintroduce traditional values into societies that had been ravaged by radical reform. In a sense, theirs was a conservative reaction. However, the values they worked to introduce were hardly conservative – certainly not in the sense that Edmund Burke used the term. Rather, they were the ideas of orthodox liberalism.[21]

These ideas swept the globe and steered social and economic policies during the 1980s. It began in the Anglo–American world where the governments of Thatcher and Reagan implemented liberal reforms. Britain began the practice of 'privatizing' big state-run businesses – dividing up, converting and selling to private owners. Other countries quickly followed suit. In one Western country after the other, state-owned companies were dismantled and sold off to be run as private enter- prises – especially in the field of mass transport and communications (national railways were privatized together with airlines, telephone and telegraph companies, electrical companies, water works … and so on). Then the rest of the world followed (Yergin and Stanislaw 1998).

The waning of the old radicals
While orthodox liberalism was on the rise, orthodox radicalism was on the wane. Revolutionist approaches remained influential for a while. During the 1980s, left-wing scholars observed the rising impact of neo-liberal theories with dismay. Some of them argued that the world economy was evolving into new phase of 'late capitalism' (Mandel 1982). They tended to accept the Marxist claim that capital had a natural tendency to centralize and concentrate and forecast the growth of steadily larger and more influential firms with a steadily broader global reach – thus foreshadowing later studies in 'globalization'. Also, they expected to see capitalist exploitation increase on the world scale. They saw evidence of such a develop- ment in the rising indebtedness of the Third World. Immanuel Wallerstein argued along these lines, as he published two more volumes of his influential *Modern World System* (in 1980 and 1989). Nevertheless, the Revolutionist approach declined during the course of the decade.

Old-fashioned materialist Marxism, which explained how changing relations of production altered social structures, faded in importance. New theories, which discussed social and cultural phenomena as outcomes of social interaction, prolifer- ated. Radical theorists who adapted to the trend and developed theories of social interaction, continued to make a mark in International Relations.

One of them was the Canadian political economist Robert Cox, who presented a Marxist argument which defied materialist orthodoxy. Cox (1981) was inspired by the Italian communist Antonio Gramsci and he used Gramsci's concept of 'hegemony' to explain the international power and impact of the USA. His *Produc- tion, Power and World Order* (1987) sets out the social forces of modern capitalism in a theoretically and historically rich account of America's rise in the international system from a peripheral and exploited nation at the beginning of the nineteenth century to the leader of a hegemonic world system at the end of the twentieth. The American hegemony is sustained by a set of generally accepted liberal values with long historical roots and with a distinct appeal to other nations in the system, argued Cox.

This kind of argument, together with the advent of new types of electronic media, opened up new fields of analysis. Social scientists asked new questions – for example about the nature and social impact of cable network news stations, satellite-distributed TV channels, film/video and other electronic media. They developed new fields of research – such as culture studies and media and communication studies. They asked questions about how a particular medium related to ideology, social class, nationality, ethnicity, gender and/or sexuality. Their aim was to show how meaning is generated, disseminated and produced within a given culture.

The rising of the new liberals

Economics had long been an auxiliary discipline in International Relations. During the 1950s and 1960s it had provided a toolkit for systems theory. It had been a rich reservoir for building rational-choice theories, offering concepts that could portray decision-making as rational games, cost-benefit calculations and strategic analyses. During the 1970s and 1980s several authors applied economic theory to questions of conflict and war.

Robert Axelrod (1984) is a good example. His brilliant little book *The Evolution of Cooperation* showed how iterated games among rational actors could produce rules of cooperation.[22] Another example is Bruce Bueno de Mesquita. In *The War Trap* (1981) he explored the decision calculus that leads nations into war. Microeconomic models allowed him to calculate the expected utility for state leaders who faced international conflicts. Using elements from theories of marginal utility, Bueno de Mesquita deduced hypotheses and tested them against empirical evidence. A third example is George Modelski. He had long used economic approaches to explore the nature of multinational corporations, principles of world order and the evolution of the international system (Modelski 1972; 1987).

George Modelski and William R. Thompson broadened economic analyses to chart the shifts and cycles of political leadership through international history. Their effort produced theories for the rise and decline of world powers (Modelski and Thompson 1988). Robert Gilpin (1981) made a similar approach. Like Waltz, he developed a structural approach to International Relations. Like Modelski and Thompson he argued that war is an important force for change in the international system. His *War and Change in World Politics* (1981) is a carefully argued, historically rich study of the long cycles of war and peace.

Axelrod, Bueno de Mesquita, Gilpin and Modelski and Thompson relied on economic models to make important theoretical contributions to International Relations. However, the singly most influential author through the 1980s was, without a doubt, Kenneth N. Waltz. His *Theory of International Politics* [1979] continued to create controversy and dominate International Relations debates throughout the decade. In fact, it provided the vantage point for the so-called 'third great debate' in International Relations (Lapid 1989).[23]

Children of the times?

It could be said, in line with Whitehead's famous comment on Western philosophy being a string of footnotes to Plato, that International Relations debates during the 1980s were a string of footnotes to Waltz. His *Theory of International Politics* (1979) was a towering presence in International Relations throughout the decade. It was a forceful criticism of traditional Realism. Also, it provided an alternative Realism; a powerful, new Realism that relied on a structuralist methodology. But did this new theory represent an improvement over previous theories? Did it rest on a sound methodological footing? What kind of structuralism was this? Such questions were asked and hotly debated during the course of the 1980s – and well into the 1990s.

Waltz's ambition was to provide a simple, yet powerful new theory about the nature and the workings of the international system. A *system*, Waltz explained, is made up of two elements: units and relationships among units. An *international* system, he maintained, is made up of states and of relationships among states. Such relationships, he continued, are characterized by two defining properties. First, by anarchy. Second, by polarity – by the distribution of capabilities among the actors. Both were defined in micro-economic terms. When Waltz explained them, he invoked concepts from liberal market economics.

The first defining principle, anarchy, is explained by way of an analogy to the free-market model of liberal economics. It shows how order is spontaneously formed from the self-interested interactions by rational, sovereign and self-regarding units. 'International-political systems, like economic markets, are individualist in origin, spontaneously generated, and unintended,' noted Waltz (1979, p. 91). 'International politics is structurally similar to a market economy insofar as the self-help principle is allowed to operate in the latter', he continued (p. 91). The order which emerge from the interaction of such units is based on a self-help principle. Which means that it relies on the balance of power as its primary ordering principle.

The second defining principle of interstate relations, the distribution of capabilities among the actors, is also fashioned on the analogy of the free-market model. In this case, however, Waltz does not invoke the standard model of a purely competitive market as described in mainstream liberal theories; rather, he invokes the more restricted kind of competition found in the oligopolistic sectors of capitalist economies. In these sectors the larger, more capable units set the scene and define the market rules that all units must abide by. Here Waltz drew on William Fellner's *Competition among the Few* (1949). Fellner's analysis of market competition among a handful of major firms was a direct inspiration for Waltz's analysis of an international system marked by competition among a handful of major states. Although they are competitors, Waltz's Great Powers (like Fellner's big firms) reach agreement on some basic norms and rules of behaviour. These norms serve to harness the inherent anarchy of the system. They furnish the rational basis for the balance of power that maintains order in the system.[24]

It could be said of Waltz that he was a child of his times. He was inspired by the liberal market theories which dominated the age – and it is tempting to speculate whether his argument would have been as successful and controversial if it had been introduced into another academic atmosphere. Several critics quickly pointed out how Waltz's theoretical assumptions dovetailed nicely with the liberal sentiment of the age. One of them was Richard Ashley (1984), who criticized Waltz's methodological approach and argued that Waltz's theory had little to do with structuralism; there was not a trace of the usual terms and theories of structuralism in it – classic authors like Claude Lévi-Strauss were wholly absent from his book. Waltz's theory was, in Ashley's mind, was a worthless example of positivist atomism.

Robert Cox (1981) made a similar point. He echoed the critical comment which Rousseau had levied against Hobbes and turned it against Waltz: Waltz made the mistake of assuming that the institutions and power relations of his own age were permanent properties of international politics. Waltz's theory was not a general theory of International Relations, Cox averred, it was in fact a child of its own, liberal age. In Cox's mind, Waltz had greatly impoverished the rich tradition of Realism. He had reduced it to a mere 'problem-solving' theory – of what Cox (1981) called 'a form of neorealism'.

Waltz did not only make a clear break with traditional Realism; he also made a big theoretical step in the direction of the Rationalist tradition. Several of his critics celebrated his effort. Two of the celebrants are particularly important and a brief presentation of them will close this chapter. The first important critic is Robert Keohane. He lauded Waltz's structural theory as a crucial addition to International Relations theory. He convinced by Waltz's premise that, for purposes of theory, sovereign states are the primary actors in international politics, that states must be seen as rational actors and that sovereign states together constitute an anarchic system. However, he was troubled by the static nature of Waltz's structuralism. Drawing on Axelrod (1984) and on institutional economists (Coase 1937; North 1981), Keohane proposed that rational human interaction will always produce norms, rules, conventions and social institutions. Adding an institutional element to Waltz's model would make it a dynamic theory, Keohane (1984; 1989) claimed.

Keohane's importance does not lie in his amendment of Waltz's theory; rather it lies in his acceptance of Waltz's premises. For if Waltz's embrace of liberal micro-economics brought him a long step closer to Rationalism, then Keohane's acceptance of Waltz's state-centred premises moved *him* a long step away from Rationalism and in the direction of Realism. Together, Waltz's and Keohane's operations bridged the gap that had traditionally existed between the two main International Relations paradigms, Realism and Rationalism. Waltz's Neorealism and Keohane's Neoliberal Institutionalism met in a neo-neo-synthesis (Waever 1996). And International Relations theory would never be quite the same afterwards .

The final important critic to be introduced here is Barry Buzan. He was also deeply impressed by Waltz's structural theory. But he recognized, like Keohane and several other critics, that Waltz had produced a static theory and that this presented a practical problem. How could it be made more dynamic? Drawing on the English School and its concept of international society, Buzan resolved that Waltz had not distinguished carefully enough between system and structure. To make the distinction clearer, Buzan amended Waltz's definition of a social 'system'. To Waltz's two key elements of a system – units and relations among units – Buzan added a third element: structure. This structure, Buzan continued, exists on many levels. However, it may be convenient to distinguish between a 'deep structure', which remains fairly constant over the centuries, and a 'distributional structure', which concerns the distribution of capabilities among the units *and* which changes over time.

For Buzan, one of the major forces of change is technological innovation; especially innovation in technologies of transportation and communication. Such innovation directly affects the capacity of the units to interact and communicate. This affects the relations among them and, ultimately, the whole technology-based web of communicative interaction. The evolution of technology continually raises the interaction capacity in the system. Buzan's addition is important. Not solely because he improved upon Waltz's system, but because he redefined the system in a way that allowed Waltz's structural model to be combined with theories of communicative interaction. Such theories, foreshadowed by Rousseau (1997) and adumbrated by Bull (1977), would make an important mark on International Relations theory in subsequent years.

Notes

1 For details, see Figure 13.1 which depicts the price hikes in 1973 and in 1979.
2 Firm numbers are hard to come by. But at least five hundred thousand Iraqi and Iranian soldiers are believed to have died in the Iran–Iraq War (1980–88). A similar number of civilians are likely to have been killed and many more injured.
3 The Reagan administration supported opposition groups that fought a Soviet-supported regime – as in Angola, where it supported Jonas Sawimbi's UNITA movement. In Nicaragua, the Reagan administration created its own opposition group, 'the contras', and funded its guerrilla operations against the Nicaraguan Sandinista regime.
4 The Uruguay round began in September 1986 and extended the free-market principle of trade to several new areas, including trade in services and intellectual property. It also introduced reforms to trade in the two sensitive sectors of agriculture and textiles. The Uruguay round also established the World Trade Organization (WTO), which was finally signed in April 1994.
5 Joseph and Powell were policy advocates. Joseph was a member of the British Institute of Economic Affairs, a liberal think tank in London. His criticism of John Maynard Keynes and the idea of a mixed economy made a deep impression on Prime Minister Thatcher. Lewis Powell was an American business lawyer and a nominee for the US Supreme Court. Deeply concerned with what he saw as a mounting influence of left-wing groups in US politics, he wrote a memorandum presenting a strategy designed to contain and combat it. Powell's strategy had an enormous influence on the US business community, on the Republican Party and on the administration of Ronald Reagan.

   Hayek and Friedman were economic theorists. They were members of an international network of scholars which advocated a free-market message. Hayek had argued for well over half a century that any economic system was so infinitely complex that no single office could ever fully understand its operation. Any effort at central planning would not only result in economic failure, it would also bring with it needs to regulate and control and thus cause autocratic rule to be imposed on the political system. The only way to ensure human liberty, Hayek continued, was to trust the free market. Its price system, reflecting the activities of myriads of individual business calculations, provided a mechanism for communicating that there was a need for materials and products, and moving them in the right direction – without the issuance of any kind of central command.

Friedman agreed. He was a member of the Chicago School, which, in contrast to Keynesianism, argued that markets left alone produced the best outcomes. Friedman argued, like Hayek, that prices were the best allocators of resources. These ideas, whose roots go far back in the history of social thought, experienced a revival when the Western economies reached an impasse in the 1970s.

6 Lewis Powell's memorandum was very influential. His anti-left strategy rippled through the US business community. It inspired wealthy industrialists to sponsor libertarian or patriotic projects. Such sponsorship transformed old organizations like the American Enterprise Institute (AEI), and created new think tanks like the Heritage Foundation and the Cato Institute. Powell's big-business initiative was only the tip of the iceberg. American politics saw a groundswell of responses that emphasized patriotism, pride and a return to traditional American values, among them religious freedom and individual liberties.

7 The increasingly popular talk radio, which featured a seductive host and an element of listener participation, evolved as a platform for political messages in several states. During the 1990s, business-sponsored TV channels would provide platforms for commercial and ideological messages. The prime example of an ideological channel is Rupert Murdoch's Fox News Channel.

8 *The Whole Earth Catalog* was a thick, user-generated book that listed all kinds of things and notions. A rich source of knowledge about everything under the sun, it pushed the basic idea of self-reliance and grass-roots power. The objects depicted in the catalogue were seen as tools of independence and self-sufficiency – the definition of 'tool' influenced by the philosopher and engineer Buckminster Fuller and his theories about 'whole systems' and by E. F. Schumacher and his 'Buddhist economics'. 'The Well' was an electronic gateway to counter-cultural knowledge; a dial-up bulletin board which was designed by Steward Brand and Larry Brilliant in 1985 to form a virtual knowledge community.

9 The USA had introduced liberal economic models to several Asian countries in the wake of World War II – the Americans had encouraged a model of export-led growth in Japan and given Japanese products access to America's own, vast market; they had overseen similar development in South Korea. The results were amazing. During the 1950s and 1960s, the growth of Japan's GDP per capita averaged around 8 per cent annually. Several other South East Asian nations adopted Japan's model of export-led growth and delivered equally remarkable results. The GNP per capita of the so-called 'Asian dragons' (Hong Kong, Singapore, South Korea and Taiwan) grew by 5–7 per cent annually during the 1970s and 1980s. This was a much higher rate of economic growth than in other regions of the world.

The World Bank explained the high Asian growth rate as a result of neo-liberal reforms. The claim was met by a howl of protests by economists who pointed out that the fastest-growing 'dragons' were rarely liberal democracies; rather, they were authoritarian states whose governments regularly intervened into the economy to shape its course according to long-term plans. The economists began to distinguish between the 'liberal market economies' of the West and the 'co-ordinated market economies' of the Asian tigers which depended heavily on non-market arrangements. They needed a third economic model to account for the remarkable example of communist China: that of 'state capitalism'. Following the death of Mao (in 1976), Deng Xiaoping selectively introduced capitalist principles and created a mixed economy within a totalitarian one-party system. During the 1980s, China's GDP expanded by about 10 per cent a year. The world's most populous country was also one of the world's fastest-growing economies. And it had an enormous impact on Asia – and on the world.

10 This rapid expansion in education was not always attended by a comparable expansion in the overall economy and in employment opportunities. As a result, several oil-exporting countries developed a cohort of highly educated young people who had no jobs to go to. The result was growing frustration among groups of young academics. These groups would supply tinder for a new wave of Islamic radicals – especially on the Arabian peninsula (Hegghammer and Lacroix 2011).

11 The United States would be hit severely, boosting inflation to an annual rate of more than 12 per cent and increasing unemployment figures to around 7.5 per cent.

12 In 1960 the USSR had produced less than 3 million barrels a day (BD). The output had more doubled by 1970, and doubled again by 1980 – exceeding 12 million BD by 1980.

13 The ghosts of Marx and Lenin ought to have warned them. However, East Bloc leaders understood too late that borrowing on the capitalist market was a primrose part to perdition. They discovered too late that the export-led economies in Asia were more dynamic than their own and that hi-tech products from Eastern Europe were inferior to those from Japan and South Korea in terms of price as well as quality. The only option left to the East Bloc countries was to sell their products to each other within their own, politically regulated economic sphere. In the end it was the USSR that ended up with the brunt of these Eastern European products. However, the USSR could not pay for the products in hard currency which was needed to pay off the Western debts.

14 Only Romania saw the danger. The country had increased its foreign debt from about $1 billion in 1970 to nearly $10 billion in 1980. In 1981 President Ceauşescu saw the writing on the wall and initiated a draconian austerity programme to pay off the debt. Food, electricity, medicine and other basic necessities were rationed; infrastructure maintenance ceased. By 1989, the Romanian debt had been reduced to a little over $1 billion. But at a high human and political cost. Capital had decayed. The standard of life had fallen steeply. The Ceauşescu regime had seriously undermined its own legitimacy.

15 To put the sums in perspective: during the early 1980s the USSR had an annual foreign currency income of $30–5 billion. That was not a big sum in the larger picture – the largest US multinationals Exxon and General Motors represented

sales that approached $100 billion, or three times the amount of the Soviet foreign currency income. Economists in the Reagan administration reasoned that $30 billion a year is not a big sum for a superpower which was running a vast empire that stretched from Hanoi to Havana. They made some rough estimates of the annual cost of the running of the Soviet empire, and the results surprised them: the equivalent of about $30 billion. The Soviets were, in effect, running their empire on a shoestring. Also, it was, in a manner of speaking, the Western countries that kept the Soviet empire afloat with their purchases of fossil fuels, their technology transfers and their cheap loans. This analysis provided an important element in Reagan's strategy to bring the USSR to its knees: weaken the shoestring budget.

16 Soviet President Brezhnev, stolid, ill and slowly fading into senility, appeared as a symbol of the state of Soviet affairs. When he finally died in 1982, he was succeeded by two other creaky old men – first by Juri Andropov, who died in 1984, after a little more than a year in office; then by Konstantin Chernenko, who died even sooner (in 1985).

17 Congress rejected Reagan's proposal to support anti-communist rebels in Angola and Nicaragua, so he concentrated his attention on supplying the Afghan rebels. The USA transferred enormous resources to Pakistan's ISI and the so-called *mujahideen* – around $500 million in 1986 and 1986 – and Saudi Arabia matched the amount.

18 The fear flared into panic in September 1983, when the Soviet early warning systems malfunctioned during a NATO exercise and erroneously reported that the USA had launched nuclear ICBMs against the USSR.

19 One famous case is the rebellions which erupted in Paris at the end of the 1780s. They sparked the French Revolution (1789), which altered France, created rivalries within other European societies, ignited wars among Western states and changed the world. The Bolshevik Revolution of 1917 is another case in point; it established the Soviet Union and affected interstate relations for decades to come. Political history provides many more examples.

20 This organic approach may well be considered a new, fourth approach to International Relations – an 'ecological paradigm'. It can easily be presented in the same terms that were used in the previous chapter to discuss Realism, Rationalism and Revolutionism (cf. Table 12.3, above). First, the primary unit of analysis of 'Ecologism' is 'Gaia' – the earth as a self-regulating, complex system. Second, its level of analysis is the eco-system – situated in the thin layer of water and gases (the biosphere) which covers the earth. Third, its key explanatory concepts are bio-diversity, adaptability, sustainability and biospheric structures and functions – with a particular attention to the biochemical cycles of carbon, nitrogen and water. Finally, the main focus or topic of discussion of 'Ecologism' is the effect of human behaviour on the eco-system – especially the effect of demographic change, resource consumption, pollution and climate change on the resilience of the system.

21 The ideas of orthodox liberalism emerged during the late eighteenth century, under the influence of moral philosophers like Adam Smith. It is, however, important to note that Smith was not an economist (in the modern sense of the term) but a 'moral philosopher'; his self-equilibrating marketplace was encased in a larger 'moral economy'. His free market was predicated upon the existence of 'moral sentiments'

which provided norms of conduct and common values which all economic actors obeyed (Smith 1982b).

Later authors, like John Stuart Mill, argued that, in the absence of a common moral sentiment, the free market would produce inequalities in society. To prevent the production of a widening gap between rich and poor – and to stave off rebellion and revolution – he argued that the government must assume a redistributive role, for example by transferring goods and values from the rich to the poor. Neo-liberals like Thatcher and Reagan wanted to reduce the redistributive role of government and increase that of the market. They often used Smith's *Wealth of Nations* [1776] to justify their argument; but they tended to forget Smith's *Theory of Moral Sentiments* [1759] which set out the social preconditions necessary for a market economy to work. The neo-liberals advocate a free-market theory that is long on reason but short on social theory and moral sentiment.

22 Also, Axelrod's results threw new light on old questions in economic theory as well as in political philosophy about the origins of rules and the functions of norms in a society of egotistical actors. In iterated games, co-operation turns out to be evolutionary advantageous, argued Axelrod – thereby triggering controversy by using Darwinian themes and drawing on arguments from evolutionary biology.

23 Or the 'fourth great debate' if we include the 'inter-paradigm debate' of the 1970s and count it as the 'third debate'.

24 In the light of theories of oligopolistic competition, Waltz argues that the smaller the number of Great Powers, the more easy it is to arrive at common norms. Consequently, an interstate system that has very few Great Powers will tend to be more stable than a system that has many. Thus, Waltz infers that bipolar systems are more stable than multipolar systems. This argument flies in the face of most classical Realists, for whom the most stable international system consists of about half a dozen fairly equal Great Powers

Waltz elaborates this point and develops a theory of polarity, which will not be repeated here. Suffice it to say that Waltz acknowledges only two interesting power constellations: bipolarity and multipolarity. Waltz is not interested in international systems with only *one* Great Power, because he holds it as inherently unstable. Other powers will form an alliance, counterbalance this sole power of pre-eminence and contain its influence. A system of *two* Great Powers will easily negotiate a common understanding between themselves on norms and rules of behaviour. They will constitute a simple balance-of-power system – and will be stable because it is simple and transparent. A multipolar system, consisting of *three* or more powers, is a system whose order is also maintained by balance-of-power politics, but the balance is more complex etc.

Part IV

A future history
of International Relations

14

Unipolar world?

In the early afternoon on Saturday 19 August 1989, a crowd of about a hundred people collected near the Hungarian border town of Sopron. Suddenly, they began to move towards the Austro–Hungarian border post. They walked up to the chief officer on guard, Lt Col. Arpád Bella, who was handed a leaflet by a passing man. They did not slow their pace but walked towards the old wooden gate that marked the border, forced it open and walked into Austria.

The border had been closed for forty years. It was heavily guarded but its alarm systems had fallen into disrepair. Lt Col. Bella had only a few seconds to react. The leaflet announced a picnic at the other side of the barrier. He recalled the telegram which the Sopron station had received the previous day from the border patrol agency's headquarter in Budapest, informing them about the arrival of a 'large number of East German citizens'. Bella had expected an official delegation, not a crowd of family picnickers. He also remembered the standing order to shoot anyone who tried to cross the border but was reluctant to fire into the crowd of men, women and children who rushed past him. His reluctance grew when he noticed another group approaching. He was not going to be a mass murderer. It was his wedding anniversary. He ordered his team of four border guards to check the papers of everyone who tried to enter Hungary but pay no attention to people leaving for Austria.

This irregular border crossing opened up the floodgates of events which unravelled the Soviet empire. This unravelling is well worth a closer scrutiny, because scholars and statesmen and stateswomen observed the events and drew lessons from them – lessons which in turn would affect national policies and international theories for many years afterwards. One of these lessons was that the Soviet empire had eroded from within through popular, democratic processes that originated within the civil society of individual states. Systemic theories did not explain such events very well. They may provide nice accounts of repeated behaviour but they do not explain change.

The international system changed because the Soviet Union unravelled. The simplest way to explain this unravelling was to look for causes within the USSR –

in the faulty performance of the Soviet economy or in the increasing tensions in Soviet society and in the emergence of strong, charismatic leaders.

The collapse of the USSR triggered many events and many discussions. They cannot all be captured in a single chapter. Only the most basic events and the most central discussions will be covered here. The chapter will first discuss the two superpowers – the unravelling of the Soviet empire and the reactions of the USA. It will then focus on the way American statesmen and scholars perceived the post-Cold War world – and pay particular attention to the discussion which surrounded the theory of 'the democratic peace' which emerged during the post-Cold War euphoria. Finally, the chapter will indicate some of the themes that were discussed in the wake of the Soviet demise, debates about the nature of the world order that followed and of America's role in it.

The unravelling of the Soviet empire

Hundreds of people crossed the Sopron checkpoint by the end of that day in August. They were soon followed by thousands of others (Oplatka 1989). In September, when Hungary opened the borders towards *all* its neighbouring countries, the trickle swelled to a flood. People travelled to Hungary from Romania and Bulgaria in the south, Russia and Ukraine in the east and Czechoslovakia and East Germany in the north in order to travel through and cross the border into Austria and the West.

Protests and elections in the satellites
The Soviet President Mikhail Gorbachev was immediately informed about the irregular border crossing that took place in the outer empire in August 1989. He had his attention focused on bigger problems; he brushed it aside as a minor irritant. This was a short-sighted move. His failure to respond was interpreted as indecision by members of the inner empire. First, the Baltic states interpreted Gorbachev's non-response as an opportunity to make a bid for independence.[1] Then other Soviet republics followed suit. Mass demonstrations in Armenia, Azerbaijan, Belarus, Georgia, Moldova and Ukraine first supported the Baltic demand; then they began to voice their own claims of independence and multi-party elections. Outside of the Soviet empire, claims for multi-party elections emerged in Slovenia, Croatia and other members of the Socialist Federated Republic of Yugoslavia (SFRY).

Events came to critical head in Poland, where a popular wave of demands overwhelmed the Communist Party, which lost control of the situation. Mass strikes pressured the government of General Wojciech Jaruzelski into negotiations with the independent labour union Solidarity. Pressed on the defensive, the general promised new elections.

The Polish elections were a turning point. The returns showed victory for Solidarity. This victory, and the fact that the leaders of Solidarity quickly formed a new, non-communist government, sent shock-waves throughout the Soviet empire. Popular demonstrations for free elections erupted in Hungary, East

Germany, Bulgaria, Czechoslovakia and Romania as well. During the course of a few astounding months during the autumn of 1989, the empire that Stalin had built nearly half a century before unravelled.

The events of that fall are worth an extra inspection, because they indicate how top-level diplomacy works and provide glimpses into the national characters of the participants.

The special case of Germany

In East Germany the government of the veteran communist Erich Honecker resigned in October 1989. The country could neither handle the economic crisis nor prevent several thousand people from leaving the country every week – most of them young and well-educated and the most valuable workers of the land. A new communist government was appointed, but it did not know what to do with the demonstrators who marched through the streets of Berlin and chanted 'Wir sind das Volk' (We are the people). They could not count on help from the USSR – Soviet President Gorbachev had revoked the old 'Brezhnev Doctrine' in his comments on the elections in Poland. The communist leaders of East Germany watched incredulously as crowds of people attacked the Berlin Wall with sledge-hammers and pickaxes. They broke through on 9 October 1989.

The 'fall of the wall' was another indication of the turn in international affairs. It was marked by celebration and optimism – the American conductor Leonard Bernstein travelled to Berlin to conduct Beethoven's 'Ode to Joy' from the wall; Pink Floyd performed 'The Wall' at Potsdamer Platz. Some observers noted yet another turn of events; how the mass chant 'Wir sind das Volk' changed to 'Wir sind *ein* Volk' (we are *one* people). They understood this as a popular mood in favour of German reunification and associated it with contours of old and too-familiar configurations – a strong Germany at the centre of Europe, surrounded by several smaller states, tottering and nervous because they might want to leave the influence of the USSR but were apprehensive about the embrace of a united and strong Germany.

The West German Chancellor Helmut Kohl observed the international concern and understood that he needed to play his cards carefully. He considered an East German collapse likely, studied the two German constitutions carefully and drafted a ten-point plan of rescue and reunification. On 28 November Kohl made a speech where he went public with his points (Kohl 2005). The speech was well received domestically, but it met with misgivings abroad. The Soviet President Gorbachev was dead set against a German reunification. The British Prime Minister Margaret Thatcher, who had always reviled communism and despised the Soviet hold over the Eastern Bloc, agreed with Gorbachev. In a meeting with the French President François Mitterrand, Thatcher pulled a map out of her handbag, stabbed her finger at Germany and noted that the country had never found its true frontiers. A unified Germany would undoubtedly dominate Hungary, Poland and Czechoslovakia, she averred (Thatcher 1993, p. 796).

French President Mitterrand told Thatcher that he shared her worry about Germany. But he also warned the Germans about Thatcher. The US President

George Bush was concerned about the German events for different reasons. Kohl's government had assured him that Germany sought only security and wanted to avoid annoying the USSR. Kohl and Bush shared the same fear: namely, that, in order to achieve unification, Germany might have to leave NATO and assume a neutral foreign policy. If this happened, NATO might collapse. Bush did not want this to happen; if NATO collapsed, the USA would lose its ability to co-ordinate the military activities of European states. Kohl wanted it even less; without NATO, the USA might pull out of Europe, and nuclear powers like Britain and France might form a tighter alliance. Bush decided to support the loyal Kohl. He supported Kohl's plans to reunify Germany provided Germany remained in NATO.

British diplomats were surprised. East Germany was a member of the Warsaw Pact and 350,000 Soviet troops were stationed in the country. They believed that reunification was politically improbable because Gorbachev would never accept German reunification *and* NATO membership. However, the diplomats did not realize the depth of the Soviet economic crisis. Gorbachev had no economic resources left at home; he was forced to sell off Soviet gold reserves just to keep the USSR afloat.

As 1989 gave way to 1990, the European situation was tense. The two halves of Germany were being pulled together by strong internal forces. The USA supported German reunification. Britain, France and Russia did not. However, there was little they could do to prevent it. One of the problems was that no formal peace agreement had officially ended World War II. This presented two main options. The first was to call for a peace conference to settle the old 'German question'. This would mean a cumbersome conference (of fifty-three countries) and an embarrassment for Germany; some countries might demand reparations for the atrocities committed by Hitler's Nazi regime.

The second option was to call in a meeting of the four Great Powers who had occupied Germany in 1945 and divided the country into occupation zones – Britain, France, the USA and the USSR – and then invite East and West Germany to join them in negotiations to renegotiate the division. This was another embarrassment for Germany. The Foreign Minister Hans-Dietrich Genscher preferred to present the negotiating parties as the 'two–plus–four countries' – thus placing the two Germanys at the core of the conference and at an equal standing with the four Great Powers.

The negotiations began in March 1990. Britain, France and the USSR were unhappy at the prospects of a reunified Germany – 'We've beaten the Germans twice, and now she's back', Margaret Thatcher snarled at the opening meeting (Kohl 2005, p. 1013). The French delegates may have harboured similar sentiments, but were too polite to express them in public. However, Britain and France also wanted to keep NATO – Britain in order to keep the USA in Europe; France in order to tie Germany to European institutions. The Soviets did not want to see a reunified Germany – and certainly not one that was a member of NATO. However, they had other and more immediate concerns as well. The USSR was rapidly approaching bankruptcy. It needed big loans in a hurry. West Germany stepped up and was willing to give big loans – provided the USSR would accept a German reunification. It was a painful choice, but the Soviets accepted the deal in the end.

The dissolution of the Soviet metropolis

By the time the 'two-plus-four conference' had cleared the way for German reunification, the Soviets were wrestling with more serious political problems. Elections were prepared in all the fifteen constituent republics of the USSR, and in one republic after the other the CPSU lost its seventy-year monopoly of political power. Non-communist parties won the elections in six of the Soviet republics – in Armenia, Moldova, Georgia and the three Baltic republics (Lithuania, Estonia and Latvia). All of them quickly demanded independence from the USSR.

Communist parties won the elections in the nine remaining republics. Among them was Russia, the largest and most important of the constituent republics of the USSR. Russia played a unique role in the Soviet federation. Like every other republic it possessed a full set of institutions for self-government; but in addition it hosted the political headquarters of the Union of Soviet Socialist Republics (the USSR). The 1989 elections in Russia made Boris Nikolayevich Yeltsin President of Russia. He was a controversial but charismatic figure and an important delegate to the CPSU. During 1990, the interests of the Russian republic became pitted against those of Soviet federation. Yeltsin and Gorbachev became rivals in a high-stakes political game.[2]

The rivalry between the two came to a head in the summer of 1990, when Russia followed the example of the six republics which demanded independence from the Soviet federation. In June the Russian Congress of People's Deputies elected Boris Yeltsin President of Russia. Soon thereafter Yeltsin met as a delegate to the twenty-eighth Congress of the CPSU. In a speech to the other delegates he repeated the Russian demand for sovereignty. He added drama to his speech by declaring his own resignation from the Communist Party, whereupon he marched out of the hall of deputies – his every step followed by thousands of shocked eyes, including those of Mikhail Gorbachev who presided over the CPSU meeting.

This was the beginning of the end. For when an exhausted Gorbachev left for summer vacation on the Black Sea, hardliners in his own cabinet launched a *coup d'état* in his absence. Early in the morning on 19 August 1991 the coup-makers ordered the Soviet armed forces to secure order in Moscow and began to issue decrees on Soviet radio and TV. They had made sure that Premier Gorbachev was isolated on his Black Sea resort, but they had failed to silence Russian President Boris Yeltsin. When soldiers and Soviet battle tanks drove up in front of the Russian Parliament just before noon, the Russian President was on the street to receive them. Yeltsin greeted the soldiers. He climbed up on the first tank and shook hands with the soldiers who drove it. Then he stood up and made an impromptu speech from the top of the tank. He denounced the coup and told his fellow Russians to disobey the coup-makers and resist their decrees.

The Soviet soldiers listened to his appeals. They watched as his words were picked up by microphones and TV cameras and broadcast to an audience who recognized an act of great courage when they saw it. The audience also understood that one man could make all the difference. Thousands of people dropped what they were doing. They converged on the Parliament building, which soon became a symbol of resistance.

Yeltsin's quick reaction turned the popular momentum against the coup before it really got going. The coup collapsed. And people's fear of the Communist Party collapsed with it. When Gorbachev returned to Moscow, the coup-makers had been arrested and Russian president Yeltsin was the hero of the hour. The CPSU was badly shaken. Soviet President Gorbachev lost authority and power. Russian President Yeltsin emerged as a new leader. On Christmas Day 1991, Gorbachev appeared on TV to announce his departure as Soviet leader and, even more dramatically, the dissolution of the Soviet Union. The Federation that had been born out of World War I in 1917 died with a whimper, seventy-four years old.[3]

Post-imperial fears and Neo-idealist hopes

When the USSR collapsed, the US president George Bush greeted the new Russia as friendly and peaceful successor to the USSR and assured Russia's President Yeltsin of his intent to establish a new world order of stability and peace.

George Bush, Sr, was a pragmatic statesman of long foreign-policy experience. He was an old-fashioned Realist. He was well aware of America's new dominance in the world. With the USSR gone, the USA was the only remaining superpower. The world was, in the words of the columnist Charles Krauthammer (1991), a unipolar system dominated by the USA. Bush saw how change opened up great opportunities for shaping a new world order. But he also saw the dangers in transformation and rapid change.

Dark fears
The early 1990s were, as Dickens wrote of the French Revolution, the best of times and the worst of times. The collapse of the Soviet Union involved popular mobilization on a vast scale. It included the establishment of new political parties in many countries, multi-party elections and the appointment of elected governments all across Eastern Europe.

This was, in the main, a remarkably peaceful process. However, in the Socialist Federal Republic of Yugoslavia (SFRY) it got out of hand. When communism collapsed, nationalism soared. Popular mobilization, nationalist rhetoric and ethnic slurs ignited chauvinistic rivalries. In 1990 and 1991 ethnic conflicts erupted in several places in the region. European politicians called upon the USA to intervene, but President Bush refused. This was, in Bush's mind, a European problem. His Secretary of State, James Baker, put it succinctly, 'We have no dog in that fight'.

Events were also getting out of hand in Russia, where President Yeltsin had initiated a transition to capitalism.[4] The rouble collapsed immediately. Industry stopped. Workers lost their jobs. Unemployment soared. Runaway inflation wiped out people's life savings and reduced state salaries and pensions to a meaningless pittance.[5] The collapsing economy and rampant corruption tore the state apparatus apart. The government sold off state property and converted the profits to so-called privatization vouchers. No sooner had it distributed the vouchers among Russia's citizens than they were bought up cheaply by speculators. Enormous values were transferred to private hands – often on a corrupt and favoured basis. The Russian state became impoverished. But a super-rich elite emerged from Russian society – the so-called 'oligarchs'. They did not do the bidding of the Kremlin. They rigged the political game in their own favour.[6] The transition to democratic politics derailed.

On the top of it all, conflicts erupted along Russia's new, southern border. Yeltsin ordered the Russian army to invade the rebellious republic of Chechnya in 1994. This triggered a bitter and brutal war in which rebels used terrorist tactics that brought violence and bloodshed to some of Russia's major cities (Burleigh 2009).

US President Bush supported Yeltsin politically and economically. He worked to ensure nuclear safety and played a careful and delicate game in Russia and Eastern Europe. In the Middle East, by contrast, he was direct and decisive. When the Iraqi strongman Saddam Hussein fatally misjudged the new international situation and invaded the small, neighbouring state of Kuwait, President Bush reacted forcefully. He condemned Hussein's invasion and presented him with a clear ultimatum: withdraw all Iraqi forces from Kuwait or be driven out by military force. Having secured Russian agreement in the UN Security Council, Bush quickly dressed up his ultimatum as a collective-security operation under the UN.

During the autumn of 1990, the Americans built up a vast military force around the Persian Gulf. In January 1991 they led a massive invasion of Iraq. The Iraqi forces were quickly swept away. Bush – always the Realist – let Hussein remain in power. He feared that Iraq might break up if he pursued the war to full military victory and destroyed Hussein's regime. This, he reasoned, would ignite a struggle for power in the region and destabilize its complex equilibrium. This might suit Iran but it would imperil US interest in the region (Bush and Scowcroft 1998, pp. 357ff).

The USA led an international coalition which would prevent a dictator from altering the balance of forces in the region. Yet, the US-led invasion unleashed unpredictable forces. It destabilized Iraq and strengthened Iran. It allowed anti-American Shiites to gain influence in the region, which in turn created a strong reaction among radical, Sunnis. Neo-fundamentalist Sunni groups rose up in Saudi Arabia, Pakistan and other countries. The secular Palestine Liberation Organisation (PLO) was brushed aside by events which cleared the way for radical, religious organizations – such as the Hezbollah on the radical Shia side and al-Qaida on the radical Sunni side.

Western intelligence agencies began to fear that these groups would commit acts of terrorism. Their fear intensified when it became known that no one had full control over the military forces of the USSR – including the old arsenals of atomic, bacteriological and chemical weapons. US intelligence services feared that the old Soviet weapons of mass destruction (WMDs) might fall into the hands of radical terrorist groups. This fear was enhanced by the fact that several states had long tried to make their own atomic weapons – Libya, Pakistan and North Korea foremost among them. These states might now see a chance to buy uranium and nuclear scientists on the black market. And if states could do this, was there any reason why wealthy terrorist organizations couldn't do the same? During the course of the 1990s, the USA and its NATO allies became increasingly concerned with the proliferation of technologies, and materials of dangerous weapons to 'rogue states' and 'terrorist groups'.

In early March 1992 an assessment of the new international situation was completed under the leadership of Assistant Secretary of Defense, Paul Wolfowitz. The secret *Defense Planning Guidance, FY 1994–1999* defined a new course for US foreign and security policy and triggered debates on America's role in the post-Cold War world.

The report first identified three changes that had fundamentally altered the international situation: the collapse of the Soviet Union, the US victory over Iraq, and the integration of the world's leading democracies into a US-led system of collective security (White House 1992, p. 1). These changes strengthened America's international position. Yet, times of change were also times of uncertainty. The report insisted that the USA must remain vigilant. It asserted that the most important objective of US policy after the fall of the USSR was 'to prevent the re-emergence of a new rival'. In order to do this, the USA would have to maintain unquestioned military superiority. Anti-Soviet alliances had played important strategic roles during the Cold War. In the post-Cold War world, their importance was reduced. The USA would have to employ force unilaterally if necessary.

Allies, in other words, would be nice. But in the post-Cold War situation the United States should no longer consider them necessary.[7]

Bright hopes

It was a time of hope and it was a time of despair. On the one hand, the Bush administration was preoccupied with the new security risks that emerged from the Soviet collapse and the Gulf War. When the USSR collapsed, the USA reacted quickly and worked to convince the new nuclear powers in the east – Russia, Ukraine and Kazakhstan in particular – to give up or destroy their newly acquired nuclear arsenals. NATO members offered to help secure the submarines of the inactive Soviet fleet and to clean up the dangerously polluted Arctic waters north of Murmansk.

Also, members of the Bush administration noted that the fall of communist regimes conformed to a larger pattern: that autocratic rulers had collapsed in many countries and been replaced by more democratic regimes. The point was forcefully made by Samuel Huntington in his influential book *The Third Wave* [1991]. It showed how a wave of democratization had begun in the mid-1970s; first with the ouster of military rulers in Greece and the Iberias, then with the fall of autocratic regimes in Latin-America, Asia and Africa, followed by some form of democratic transition during the 1980s. This wave of democratization during the 1970s and 1980s involved some fifty countries. When communism collapsed in the early

1990s, it was tempting to see this as part of a larger, democratizing trend.

A similar idea was noted in the secret US *Defense Planning Guidance, FY 1994–1999*. Its first pages elaborated on the changes that had altered the international situation. First, the collapse of the Soviet Union – 'the internal as well as the external empire'. Second, 'the victory of the United States and its Coalition allies over Iraqi aggression'. And thirdly, the 'less visible … integration of the leading democracies into a U.S.-led system of collective security and the creation of a democratic "zone of peace"' (White House 1992, p. 1).

The foundation of this democratic zone had been laid in the wake of World War II by initiatives like the Marshall Plan, the report continued. The zone of peace had then evolved during the course of the Cold War as the result of Atlantic solidarity and interaction, it noted – echoing the argument that Karl Deutsch (1954) had formulated more than a generation earlier. Relations within this zone were marked by order and peace.

The world outside the zone, however, was characterized by flux. It harboured threats and dangers and the USA needed to convey strength and resolve. In particular, the USA needed 'to prevent the re-emergence of a new rival' and deter 'potential competitors from even aspiring to a larger regional or global role'. Here the report specified Europe, East Asia, the Middle East/Persian Gulf and Latin America as regions of specific American interest.

The report also noted that it was a US goal 'to reduce sources of regional instability, by encouraging the spread and consolidation of democratic government and open economic systems' (White House 1992, p. 2). 'At the end of World War I, and again to a lesser extent at the end of World War II, the United States made the mistake of believing that we had achieved a kind of permanent security' (Deutsch 1954, p. 3) and that international order could be maintained without American leadership. The USA must not make the same mistake again, the report continued. Instead, the USA must

> show the leadership necessary to encourage sustained cooperation among major democratic powers … We must also encourage and assist Russia, Ukraine, and the other new republics of the former Soviet union in establishing democratic political systems and free markets so they too can join the democratic 'zone of peace'. (White House 1992, p. 3)

Clinton follows suit

This idea that democracies are peaceful was in tune with a long perception in US foreign-policy analysis. It had been expressed by several US presidents in the past (Wilson 1919), but never had the connection between democracy and peace been so specifically defined.

The Bush administration was enamoured by the idea that democratic states enjoy peaceful relationships among themselves. The President, however, was an experienced diplomat and a pragmatic and prudent practitioner of *Realpolitik*. He found the democratic peace thesis a useful foreign-policy concept but he did not commit firmly to its optimistic vision. His successor, however, did.

During his presidential campaign in 1992, William 'Bill' Jefferson Clinton had repeated the idea that democracy and peace go hand in hand. In 1993, after Clinton was installed as America's forty-second President, his national security adviser, Anthony Lake, arranged policy talks around the proposition that democracies don't tend to go to war with one another. In his 1994 State-of-the-Union address, Clinton argued that 'the best strategy to ensure our security and to build a durable peace is to support the advance of democracy elsewhere. Democracies don't attack each other.' Clinton then explained that his security policy rested on three central components: (1) maintain strong defence forces, (2) promote alliances and co-operative security measures, and (3) open foreign markets and promote democracy abroad. The third point was reflected in the very title of Clinton's strategic document: *A National Security Strategy of Engagement and Enlargement*. It announced a more active policy of building democracies and thereby enlarging the zone of order and peace (Clinton 1994).

One aspect of this policy was apparent in the concept of 'humanitarian intervention'. The first case of such intervention took place under President Bush in the autumn of 1991, just after the end of the Gulf War, in the form of another military operation in Iraq. This operation had a purely humanitarian purpose, Bush explained. It was made in order to protect the Kurds against the aggressive forces of Saddam Hussein. Bush's message was broadly supported. The term 'humanitarian intervention' stuck and the Clinton administration used it to justify a handful of subsequent interventions – in Somalia, in Haiti and in the Balkans (in Bosnia and in Kosovo). US troops intervened in Somalia in 1992 in order to protect shipments of emergency aid and ensure that supplies of food and medicine would reach the civilian population. Troops then intervened in Haiti (1994), Bosnia (1995) and Kosovo (1999) in efforts to secure civil order and assist in the build-up of new democratic government. After the Balkan interventions, however, the term slowly disappeared from use.[8]

Another aspect of America's new foreign policy was the effort to transform NATO – from the military alliance of the Cold War into a new, collective-security organization for a new post-Cold War world. This involved changes in the military structures of all member countries – force structures that were designed for territorial defence were phased out and new, expeditionary structures were phased in. It also involved a shift in mission – from an organization whose activities were tailored to Europe and the Atlantic area to an organization that might send forces all over the globe.

A third aspect of Clinton's policy of engagement and enlargement was America's new attitude towards the ex-communist countries in central and eastern Europe. Several of the new governments feared a renewed Russian dominance and were eager to join NATO. Bush had been reluctant to accommodate the wishes of these new, post-communist governments; he knew that the Russians would be upset if their old client states were admitted to NATO and he was concerned about giving NATO new responsibilities in an unstable region. Clinton, however, had no such reservations. He welcomed new NATO members. However, applicants would be

seriously considered only if they could demonstrate that they were stable democracies. The EU adopted a comparable policy – it would consider new membership
applications but only from democratic states. In 1995, Austria, Finland and Sweden
were admitted, boosting EU's membership to fifteen countries. At the same time, a
long list of new applicants from the former Eastern Bloc was being vetted.

The democratic peace and its critics

The collapse of the Soviet Union and the end of the Cold War changed the international correlation of forces and altered the dynamics of world affairs. It also made
a deep impression on the study of International Relations.

The end of the Cold War was, like the end of World War I, followed by the
idealist notion that an expanding democratic order would eventually lead the
greater part of humanity to liberal democracy and peace. Or, as Francis Fukuyama
so pointedly put it in his Hegelian terminology, that history had in fact come to an
end (Fukuyama 1989; 1992).

The democratic peace

The argument that democracies are peaceful has deep roots in the liberal outlook
and in America's political philosophy. It flows from a social-contract logic which
emphasizes rational interaction among free and equal actors. The idea had been
adumbrated in several Enlightenment projects of 'Perpetual Peace'. It was expressed
in the *Federalist Papers*. It informed President William McKinley's explanation for
invading Cuba (1898) and was echoed by American presidents and academics –
perhaps most explicitly by President Woodrow Wilson who was an academic before
he became President and a dominant figure at the Versailles conference.[9]

During the 1980s, the thesis was expressed by scholars like Michael Doyle
(1983) and Francis Fukuyama (1989). It was also explored by quantitative scholars
who monitored international conflicts and wars and who observed a marked fall
in the number of wars in the world (Russett 1990; 1993). Their key observations
are captured in Figure 14.1. The figure depicts the amount of war in the world
at five-year intervals between 1950 and 2005. The numbers on the left scale are
index values that indicate the number and magnitude of war. The three curves
give different depictions of the amount of war in the system. The topmost curve
indicates the full amount of war in the system. According to this curve, 1955, with
an index score of about 20, marks the most peaceful year after World War II. Since
then, the number and intensity of wars has steadily increased, reaching a maximum
index score of around 180 around 1985.

The lower curve indicates the amount of 'interstate wars' in the international
system. It shows that such wars have been few in number and varied little over time.
The major message of the curve is that the number of 'interstate wars' increased
around 1980 – from a low-point index number of fewer than 10 in 1975 to a high-
point of around 40 in 1985. The figure indicates that the late 1970s saw an upswing
in international conflict.

Figure 14.1 Trends of war in the world system, 1950–2005

Source: Center for Systemic Peace: www.systemicpeace.org

The most striking message of Figure 14.1 is the steadily increasing amount of 'societal war' in the international system between 1955 and 1990. The reason is easy to find. After World War II the overseas empires of European states unravelled in a lengthy and violent process of decolonization. This process, marked by insurgencies or 'wars of liberation', meant that many colonies attained independence and established themselves as new, sovereign states. These states were generally poor and unsteady. Their independence often led to internal struggles for influence and power. Thus, what was commonly lauded as 'wars of liberation' or 'revolutionary wars' would often deteriorate into 'civil wars' or 'separatist wars'. Regardless of label, such 'societal wars' were difficult to end. They often got caught up in the superpower rivalry for power and control. If one superpower picked sides and began to supply its postcolonial clients with moneys and guns, the other superpower would often begin to support the other side in the conflict. External supplies could fuel local, societal wars for decades.[10]

Figure 14.1 shows that the 1980s marked a high-point in the number/intensity of societal wars. This is the time of the Reagan doctrine, when the USA supported anti-Soviet forces in Cambodia, on Africa's Horn, in Angola and in Afghanistan – especially Afghanistan, which was 'turned into a Soviet Vietnam'. The USSR sent a steady stream of soldiers and weapons to support the communist government in Kabul, whereas the USA and its allies escalated their support of the anti-Soviet *mujahideen* (Knutsen 1992).

The figure also shows that when the Cold War ended around 1989-91, hot wars were drained from the system. The number of wars dropped steeply from an index value of around 185 in 1990 to about 120 in 1995 and to a little less than 100 in year 2000.

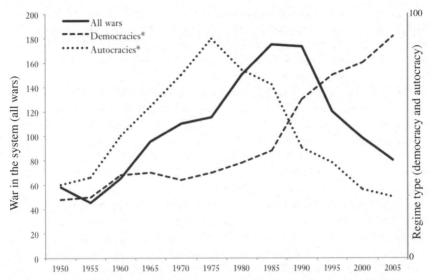

Figure 14.2 Trends of war and regime type in the world system, 1950–2005

*Values for Democracies and Autocracies have been doubled
Source: Center for Systemic Peace: www.systemicpeace.org

This declining curve after 1990 reflects the economic crisis in the USSR. This crisis forced Mikhail Gorbachev to end Soviet sponsorship of Third World wars. When the USSR collapsed in 1991, allies of the former USSR were left without any support. Their resources ran out and the wars wound down. The USA, seeing no reason to support anti-Soviet forces after the USSR had collapsed, ended its own engagements in Third World wars. Without superpower sponsorship, one Third-World war after the other 'burnt out', so to speak.

Figure 14.1 is based in numbers gathered by scholars who rely on quantitative methods to monitor conflicts and wars in the world. They noted the stagnation and decline in number and severity of war that began during the late 1980s. And although they did not disagree with the explanations set out above, they also elaborated on another argument. They noted that the decline in warfare coincided with another striking trend: namely, the growing number of democracies in the world. There was a connection, they claimed, between these two trends – the decline of wars on the one hand and the growth of democracy on the other.

These trends are depicted in Figure 14.2. The left-hand scale shows index values which indicate the number and magnitude of wars. The right-hand scale shows the number of democratic (and autocratic) states in the world. The figure shows how the number of democratic states rose only slowly between 1950 and 1980; the number of autocracies increased steeply during the same period. Together, these two curves show how the number of sovereign states in the international system increases after World War II, under the impact of decolonization. The curves also indicate that the greater number of new states by far were autocratic states rather than democracies.

Then these trends change. The number of autocratic states falls during the mid-1970s and the number of democracies begin to increase – slowly during the early 1980s and then more steeply. The two curves intersect in 1985. At that time the number of democracies exceeded the number of autocracies, and the number of democratic states is climbing steeply.

US peace researchers noted another trend as well. They observed that, as the number of democracies began to rise more steeply, the number of wars in the system began to fall – from a peak index number of 185 in 1985 to fewer than 100 in year 2000. The beginning of the new millennium, then, marked a period of peace. And as the war numbers continued to fall and scholars began to compare wars at different periods, they observed that the new millennium marked a uniquely peaceful period in human history (Pinker 2011).

When the British PM Margaret Thatcher visited newly independent Czechoslovakia in 1990, she referred to the democratic peace thesis: she praised the country's transition to democracy as a contribution to world peace. 'If we can create a great area of democracy stretching from the west coast of the United States ... to the Far East, that would give us the best guarantee of all for security – because democracies don't go to war with one another' (Thatcher 1990). Economists in the World Bank followed suit; they argued that the 'Washington consensus' would bring prosperity and peace to the poorer countries of the world.

Quantitative scholars backed up such claims with persuasive figures. Democracies have rarely fought one another, argued Bruce Russett (1990; 1993). He showed that, from 1816 until 1980, there had been 416 wars between states; only twelve of them were even arguably wars between democracies – and most of those had broken out under extenuating circumstances.[11]

By 1992 the democratic peace thesis was lifted high by the self-congratulatory triumphalism that washed across the Western world in the wake of the collapse of the USSR. Francis Fukuyama's book *The End of History* is often seen as the very embodiment of that triumphalism. Democracy had emerged victorious from the Cold War, he argued. Liberal values have brushed aside all autocratic and totalitarian alternatives, and are now the only ideological game in town. In most of the world 'there is now no ideology with pretentions to universality that is in position to challenge liberal democracy, and no universal principle of legitimacy other than the sovereignty of the people' (Fukuyama 1992, p. 45).

Critics

Not everyone subscribed to this thesis. Radical critics held the democratic peace thesis to be pure ideology. The thesis implied that major problems like war could be solved by increasing liberal values like individual freedom – and that wealth could be created at the same time. The democratic peace thesis 'is merely an adjunct of American foreign policy ... and is just another tool in the hands of Western powers to challenge the sovereignty of the states in the era of globalisation' (Bharadwaj 2008, p. 305).

Traditional realists, agreed with the main thrust of the radical critique. The democratic peace theory was suspiciously convenient. It suited the pro-liberal mood of the post-Cold War situation like a glove (Smith 2007). For the idealist academic it made all good things go together. For the pragmatic statesman and stateswoman it offered a 'vision' with which he could ennoble an otherwise disorganized set of foreign-policy reactions in turbulent times. For if democracy is really the best bulwark against war, then many seemingly hard political choices can be simplified. Idealism and *Realpolitik* could be made to go hand in hand.

Neorealists, who focused on system dynamics, brushed the democracy-peace thesis aside. Some Realists argued that the quantitative approach was inappropriate – that statistical methods were unsuitable for historical phenomena or that the data sets were faulty (Spiro 1994). Others accepted the correlation but noted that although the Peace Researchers had successfully demonstrated a statistical correlation, they had failed to develop a convincing theory that could explain it (Layne 1994). For John Mearsheimer (1990), the democratic peace thesis was simply at odds with international events. He claimed that the post-Cold War world was not as peaceful as the Neo-idealists argued; it was conflictual – and as conflicts grew and the future became more fractured and rivalrous, we would soon come to miss the Cold War. Robert D. Kaplan (1994) agreed. He had travelled around the post-Cold War world and could report an increase in civilizational conflicts. He, too, feared that the international situation was descending into anarchy.

The most original and complex alternative to the democratic peace thesis was provided by Samuel Huntington. First, Huntington agreed that a wave of democracy was sweeping the world (Huntington 1991, pp. 77f). His analysis was hailed as brilliant. Few readers seemed to notice that Huntington also observed that the sweep was largely limited to Catholic countries and that he wondered whether this was due to pro-democratic pronouncements of the Second Vatican Council rather than the spread of Reason and free markets. Also, few readers drew the implication from his observation that democratization tends to occur in waves – that democratic gains in one period are regularly followed by losses and retreats a few years later. The implication was that the democratic peace was not permanent but an unstable condition, vulnerable to backlash.

Democratic peace theory
The democratic peace thesis represented a direct challenge to Neorealism. Structure mattered most, argued the Neorealists; domestic politics cannot explain international interaction. No, responded advocates of the democratic peace thesis. It is domestic government that matters most – at least in questions of war and peace. Whether a country is democratic or not makes a big difference. Democracies may not be more peaceful than states with other regime types. However, it can be empirically demonstrated that democracies do not go to war against each other – and it can be logically inferred that the proliferation of democratic states should reduce the likelihood of war.

For a long time the advocates had a hard time explaining why. They scrutinized and re-examined their data sets and controlled for every conceivable variable. They demonstrated repeatedly that the correlation between democracy and peacefulness was robust and significant (Bremer 1992; Maoz and Russett 1993). After nearly a decade of such investigations, Bruce Russett and John Oneal presented a fully fledged theory. In *Triangulating Peace* (2001) they explained the democratic zone of peace in terms of the virtuous interaction of three factors: democratic government, interdependence and international organizations. Democratic government, they argued, constrains decision-makers. Interdependence will limit the likelihood that one state uses force against its commercial and financial partners. International organizations provide arenas for co-operation and may lower tension, solve conflict and prevent war. All individual points had been made by previous authors – among them Madison (1987), Angell (1910) and Hobson (1915), respectively. But Russett and Oneal tied them together, and mustered much empirical evidence and delivered a convincing case for the democratic peace thesis.

Unipolar world?

Liberal idealists seemed to think that the democratic peace was a natural condition. Radicals and realists both saw it as an outcome of American pre-eminence. For clearly, after the dissolution of the Soviet empire, the USA was the only superpower left standing. The world was now a unipolar system, some observers argued. But what, precisely, did unipolarity mean?

The term was introduced by systems theorists of the 1950s (compare Kaplan 1957). The term had been put aside during the Cold War when attention was focused on the bipolar rivalry of the two superpowers. However, after the end of the Soviet collapse the concept fell into fashion again. A new discussion proceeded from the definition given by Kenneth Waltz (1979). Polarity, Waltz, wrote, expressed the distribution of capabilities in the international system. He then listed half-a-dozen dimensions which characterized such capabilities. Among them were size (of population and territory), military strength, resource endowment, economic capability, political stability and competence. Any actor who scored high on these six elements, must be reckoned as a pole of the international system.

The US newspaper columnist Charles Krauthammer claimed that the USA in fact was the *only* pole. The USA scored so much higher on all these dimensions of power than any other single actor in the system that the world could be seen as a unipolar system with the USA as its unchallenged leader. The USA needed to use its 'unipolar moment' wisely, Krauthammer cautioned (1991).

Military strength

The USA was a vast and varied country with a big population – about 250 million people lived on its huge, resource-rich territory. In 1992, the US military might was second to none. Its military budget was vastly larger than that of any other state. Table 14.1 suggests the relative size of the US military when defence budgets is used as operational indicator. The many reasons why the values presented here should be taken with a pinch of salt are too numerous to list. Yet, the table shows very clearly the enormous lead of the USA – the size of the US defence budget is well above the remaining nine budgets put together.

Table 14.1 The ten largest defence budgets in the world, 1993
(in millions of current [1993] US$)

1	United States	297.6
2	France	42.6
3	Japan	39.5
4	Germany	37.2
5	United Kingdom	34.1
6	Italy	20.6
7	Saudi Arabia	16.5
8	China	12.7
9	Taiwan	11.6
10	Russia	7.8

Source: SIPRI Military Expenditure Database

The table indicates a couple of additional noteworthy points. First, when we know that the Soviet Union sustained a military establishment with the rouble equivalent of about $100 million in 1988 and 1989, the table indicates the steepness and the vastness of the Soviet collapse. By 1993, Russia's military budget was $7.8 million – less than 10 per cent of that of the old USSR, by SIPRI's best estimates. Russia's huge military machine slowly ground to a halt because there was no money for necessary repairs. Soldiers and officers received no pay. Russia lost its old strategic buffer zone towards the West – where its old arch enemy, Germany, was reuniting.

Second, the table indicates the staggering difference between the US and the Russian military capabilities. Not only because the difference in defence expenditures is so huge, but also because most of the other powerful countries in the world are allied with the USA – through NATO or some other military alliance. USA's political influence, in other words, was more substantial than the mere numbers in the table would suggest.

The US budget sustained a vast arsenal of conventional forces. The US army and the US air force were numerous and well equipped. Also, they were deployed on military bases in about sixty of the world's nearly two hundred countries. The vast vessels of the US navy were sailing the Seven Seas. And underneath the oceans, US submarines were hiding with their payloads of nuclear missiles, guaranteeing America's second-strike capability.

The USA, in short, was second to none in the quantity as well as the quality of its military might. The USA controlled bases all over the globe and enjoyed a strategic sea power that was unique. World history may never before have seen an international configuration in which a single entity was as powerful and pre-eminent as the USA in the early 1990s. Not since the end of World War II. Perhaps not since the glory days of ancient Rome (Bender 2004).

Economic capabilities

America's military and political capabilities were an expression of a rich resource base and an advanced industrial economy. The USA was the largest economic entity in the world. Table 14.2 shows that the US economy had an annual GDP of well over $8 trillion, over twice as much as the second largest economy on the list (Japan) and about four times as big as number three (Germany).

Also, with the fall of the USSR there no longer existed a worldwide alternative to the US-led capitalist world economy. Although China was ruled by a communist party, its economy worked on capitalist principles. It was modernizing according to an export- and trade-based strategy of development – and was doing very well for itself. The USA was the most important member of institutions which regulated the world economy – such as the IMF and the World Bank. Also, the US dollar was the most important currency in the world, dominating international markets of banking and finance.

Finally, America's large industrial base was innovative and dynamic. During the 1980s, the USA had pioneered new technologies in several fields – electro-magnetic processing, super-conductors, miniaturization, digital communications systems. During the 1990s the American industries transformed the big calculating machines of the past into smaller, cheaper and more powerful personal computers. This created a worldwide communications revolution. It boosted the availability of information and created a new knowledge economy. The new computer technology altered media. It changed the global structures of finance.

The new technology was predicated on social openness. Closed societies like the USSR had to adapt or fall hopelessly behind. Open societies, like the USA, were leading actors in the new knowledge economy. Table 14.2, which lists the thirty largest economies in the post–Cold War world, offers some indications of America's dominance by the mid-1990s. Most obviously, it shows that the USA was the world's single largest economy – greater than the next five economies put together.

The ten largest economic shown in Table 14.2 were run on capitalist premises. Nine of them were 'Western countries' with market economies and democratic constitutions. Eight of them were allies of the USA. The next batch of ten economic entities – from Mexico (no. 11) to Sweden (no. 20) – is a mixed lot. Some are large economies because they are large countries – like Mexico, which was approaching 100 million people in the mid-1990s, and India (no. 12) which was pushing one billion people in 1995. Other are relatively small countries but with big economies because their productivity is high – like Belgium (no. 19) and Sweden (no. 20). These smaller countries have long-established democratic regimes. Some of the more populous countries were also developing productive economies and were growing fast – such as South Korea (no. 13) whose economy had long been growing at a pace of 10 per cent per year. Most of these fast-growing countries had long ties with the USA – and access to the US market might be one of the reasons for their rapid growth. Then there was Russia. A large economy because it is a very large and populous country. But it was a country in crisis. It had not managed the transition from communism to capitalism at all well. Its GNP and its population were

Table 14.2 The thirty largest economic entities in the world, in the mid-1990s ($ million)

1	United States	8,708,870.00
2	Japan	4,395,083.00
3	Germany	2,081,202.00
4	France	1,410,262.00
5	United Kingdom	1,373,612.00
6	Italy	1,149,958.00
7	China	1,149,814.00
8	Brazil	760,345.00
9	Canada	612,049.00
10	Spain	562,245.00
11	Mexico	474,951.00
12	India	459,765.00
13	South Korea	406,940.00
14	Australia	389,691.00
15	Netherlands	384,766.00
16	Russian Federation	375,345.00
17	Argentina	281,942.00
18	Switzerland	260,299.00
19	Belgium	245,706.00
20	Sweden	226,388.00
21	Austria	208,949.00
22	Turkey	188,374.00
23	General Motors	176,558.00
24	Denmark	174,363.00
25	Wal-Mart	166,809.00
26	Exxon Mobil	163,881.00
27	Ford Motor	162,558.00
28	DaimlerChrysler	159,985.70
29	Poland	154,146.00
30	Norway	145,449.00

Sources: Fortune (31 July 2000); World Bank (2000)

both falling (Maddison 2001).[12] In other words, the list's second batch of entities is very diverse. They develop at different paces and the internal ranking order is continually changing.

The third batch of economic entities – from Austria to Norway – contains some small but very wealthy democracies, like Denmark and Norway. It also includes newly democratic Poland – which indicates that the Poles managed the transition from communism reasonably well. Finally, this batch indicates the influence of the USA. First, because all its entities have ties with the USA. Second, because some of the entities are not states but corporations, such as General Motor, Ford, and DaimlerChrysler, the retail company Wal-Mart and the oil company Exxon Mobil. All of them have larger economies than Poland and Norway. All of them are American.

Soft power

Kenneth Waltz defined power as a composite of size, strength, resource endowment, economic capability, political stability and competence. The USA scores high on all of them. No other state has a higher score.

Many of Waltz's critics noted that this definition of power relied almost exclusively on material factors – especially on military might and economic wealth. They criticized Waltz for his materialist focus and introduced other, more ideational definitions of power. Joseph Nye (1990) for example, argued that, although 'hard power' might have marked the Great Powers of the past, politics in the modern world also depended on 'soft power'.

Hard power relies on the ability to punish/coerce or to reward/pay. Soft power, however, involves neither coercion nor payment but is, in its simplest form, the power to make others like you and wish to emulate you. If a state's culture and ideology are attractive, others will be more likely to follow its lead, wrote Nye (1990, p. 32). 'If a state can make its power legitimate in the eyes of others, it will encounter less resistance to its wishes', he continued – with a nod to Robert Cox (1987) and his concept of hegemony. Soft power rests on three main sources, Nye (2011) argued: 'its culture (in places where it is attractive to others), its political values (when it lives up to them at home and abroad), and its foreign policies (when others see them as legitimate and having moral authority)'.

Globalization

A comparable idea informed the concept of 'globalization'. This was the dominant, new buzzword of the social sciences in the 1990s. Most of the early discussions linked the term to technological innovation, expanding trade and increasing interdependence (Levitt 1983). Anthony Giddens (1990, p. 64) defined globalisation as 'the intensification of worldwide social relations which link distant localities in such a way that local happenings are shaped by events occurring many miles away and vice-versa'. Globalization meant the 'widening, deepening and speeding up of worldwide interconnectedness' (Held et al., 1999, p. 5).

Its basic elements had been prepared by progress in new technologies of transport and communications – in particular technologies of electromagnetism and digitalization which spurred a revolution in communications systems. How rapid this development had been is suggested by the evolution of the telephone and the falling prices of intercontinental phone-calls. In 1930, a three-minute call from London to New York cost $250; by 1990 it the cost was reduced to less than a dollar and by 2000 a few cents. The introduction of the Internet made the transfer of text, images and vast amounts of digitalized information virtually free. Digital communication is nearly instantaneous and free. Transport of goods and people is not. Yet, technological innovation has lowered transport costs as well.

One of the symbols of globalization is the intermodal container. It was introduced in the 1950s, and its use grew quickly. The container is essentially a reusable standardized steel box, about 8 feet wide, 8 feet high and 20 feet long. It is sealable and stackable. It can be loaded and sealed at its point of departure – for example at a toy factory in Hong Kong. It can then be easily transported across boundaries without inspection, unloading and reloading; it can be moved from one mode of transport to another (from truck to ship to rail to truck), and then opened and unloaded at its final point of destination – for example at a shopping mall in Madison, Wisconsin. The smooth transport of intermodal containers requires specially designed cars and ships, specially built docks with standardized equipment for lifting and stacking (Levinson 2008). The intermodal container is a central element in globalization. It requires a complex international infrastructure – including a complex web of international agreements to guarantee fast transport and respect for containers' certificates and seals.

Intermodal container technology has been an agent of change. Has it been a change to the better? The protagonists of globalization believe so. They see globalization as a process of integration on a global scale. Informed by theories of interdependence and by their own interpretation of authors like Adam Smith (1976 [1776]), they see globalization as the opening up of national economies which are then integrated into an enriching world market. They envision a world in which neither national borders nor distance impede economic transactions; a world in which costs of communications and transport are tending towards zero and the barriers created by national jurisdictions are vanishing.

The critics of globalization beg to differ. The weakening of international barriers and of national control would enhance international competition; it would lead to the collapse of some industries and to the concentration of wealth and power in others. The global spread of container traffic may have simplified international trade and lowered the prices of consumer goods, but it has also meant the ruin of many established ports, the collapse of manufactures in many nations and the growth of such industries in nations with low-salaried workers. Besides, globalization also enhances vulnerability and insecurity, argued the critics. On this point they echoed Rousseau. On a level playing field, interdependence means that each actor is dependent upon all the others and that no one is sovereign, self-sufficient or free. In an unequal game, it makes the weak vulnerable to the power plays of those who are strong.

America in the new world order

The new technology which drove globalization was overwhelmingly American. In many regions of the world, 'globalization' became another word for 'Americanization' – and the new term carried with it old, anti-American associations.

Democratizer?

American statesmen, by contrast, insisted that the USA was a benign power. Bush and Clinton regularly presented the USA as a force for good. A *democratizer* who spreads liberal ideals and builds a peaceful world order. This view reflected the long tradition of American exceptionalism. It implied that the USA was not like other states. That the USA has a particular historical role to play; a civilizing role of expanding individual rights and material gain. That American ideals enjoy the support of common people – not only at home, not only in the West, but all over the world. Because all people really wants liberty and freedom if given a choice.

Empire?

Charles Krauthammer and his Republican cohorts worked along the same individualist logic of American liberalism as Clinton. But they were less concerned with material gain and more concerned with values, norms, rights and political principle. For them, the USA represents a particular set of civilizational values. In the wake of the Soviet collapse the USA had the opportunity to mould the world in its image. Suddenly it was fashionable to write books on ancient Rome and compare the might and the civilizing role of the ancient Roman republic to that of the modern USA (Bender 2004; Cullen 2007; Malamud 2008; Smil 2010).

Niall Ferguson (2005) argued the civilizing point with great force and a twist. He argued that the USA had all the trappings of an *empire* – overwhelming military capabilities, wealth and high culture. The USA, like ancient Rome, saw itself as responsible for order and for civilizing the world by moulding others it its image. Yet, the Americans did not perceive their state as an empire; they perceived it as a republic – and an anti-imperial republic at that. By misperceiving itself in republican terms, the Americans were reluctant to play an active and ordering role in the world. The USA, concluded Ferguson, *was* an empire; but it was in fact 'an empire in denial'. It had a confused identity which could at times produce a weak and confused foreign policy.

Imperialist?

At the opposite end from the conservative Republicans were the left-wing radicals, who maintained that the USA was neither a champion of democracy nor an empire but an *imperialist*: a capitalist power with an expansionist economy that, driven by its inner dynamics, was led to expand and exploit other nations (Chomsky 2008).[13]

Those on the traditional left invoked materialist, often Marxist, theories to support their view. They saw the USA as the leading member of a vast, world-encompassing economic system. They tuned down the importance of states and tuned up the importance of the capitalist system. And they saw politics as shaped by material interests which were in turn rooted in economic systems dynamics.

Hegemon?

For still others, the USA was a hegemon – a stabilizer of the world. This perspective portrayed the USA as a member in a larger international system. However, this system could not be reduced to economic variables. The system hinged on political interaction and was essentially social in nature. And America's behaviour could not be reduced to self-interested reason. Rather, the USA was portrayed as a leading actor that expressed and enforced norms and rules which stabilized the system and which was obeyed by others because they saw them as in harmony with their own interests. A hegemon does not seek to further its own interests; it furthers the order of the system. Other states will perceive this. Many of them will see that the system benefits them. They will support the hegemon because they consider it a legitimate leader. They will embrace its norms and rules.

This was the argument of Robert Cox. He presented a Marxist argument bud did not invoke materialist orthodoxy. He was less concerned with the operations of the society's economic base and more with its cultural superstructure. In his 1987 book *Production, Power and World Order*, Cox relied on Gramsci's analysis to present a rich, three-hundred-year background for how the USA emerged as a hegemonic state in the international system after World War II.

The American hegemony, argued Cox, was sustained by a set of generally accepted liberal values with long historical roots. Examining US foreign policy during the late 1940s, Cox (1981, p. 145) argued that the US Secretary of State 'Cordell Hull's conviction that an open trading world was a necessary condition for peace, could be taken as its ideological text, supplemented by confidence in economic growth and ever-rising productivity'. Other Western states embraced these American arguments which served to justify America's international pre-eminence and make the USA the hegemon of the postwar world system.

Critical theories
Orthodox liberal theories, which had re-emerged during the 1980s, gathered force during the 1990s – in the wake of the Soviet collapse. Among academics there was also a resurgence of critical theory. On the political left, scholars tried to show how the spread of democratic ideals were, in fact, an expansion of the political power of the West. The spread of democracy carried with it liberal political ideas and advanced the interests of the USA and other liberal nations. Robert Cox argued along similar lines. The ideals of liberal democracy were temporal ideas formulated in universal terms; they were in effect an expression of American hegemony.

Such arguments did not exist only on the radical left. They had long been a component of traditional Realism as well. Reinhold Niebuhr, Hans Morgenthau, George F. Kennan and others had all emphasized the political importance of language and ideas. They insisted that analysts must go beyond the rhetoric of politicians – analysts are fooled if they apply 'universal moral principles ... to the actions of states in their abstract, universal formulation', argued Morgenthau (1978, p. 10). The analyst must search for the realities of power behind the words. Realists had noted that values, norms and principles play important roles in the exercise of political power. And they had argued that a stable international order will ultimately rest on an underlying consensus or a 'silent compact' about basic values (Morgenthau (1978, p. 226).

Samuel Huntington (1993) drew on such Realist teachings when he intimated that the world consists of about seven or eight basic civilizations with tensions and conflicts among them. Among two of them in particular there is a steadily growing conflict: namely, between the civilization of the West and that of Islam.

Huntington did not believe that the USA represented Reason and universal moral principles. On the contrary, he considered this belief to be dangerous hyperbole. George F. Kennan tended to agree. However, whereas Huntington warned the Americans about how their arrogant universalism was likely to stir animosity in the Muslim world, Kennan was deeply concerned by the effect of US moralism on Russia. At the time of his ninety-third birthday, in February 1997, Kennan published a piece in the *New York Times* where he argued that Clinton's foreign policy was moralistic and that it was likely to erode the silent consensus between the USA and Russia. The result would be new conflicts between the two.

Kennan did not pull his punches. Clinton's policy of NATO expansion was a dangerous mistake, Kennan warned:

> [E]xpanding NATO would be the most fateful error of American policy in the entire post-cold-war era.
>
> Such a decision may be expected to inflame the nationalistic, anti-Western and militaristic tendencies in Russian opinion; to have an adverse effect on the development of Russian democracy; to restore the atmosphere of the cold war to East-West relations, and to impel Russian foreign policy in the direction decidedly not to our liking ...
>
> It is, of course, unfortunate that Russia should be confronted with such a challenge at a time when its executive power is in a state of highly uncertainty and near-paralysis.
>
> And it is doubly unfortunate considering the total lack of any necessity for this move. (Kennan 1997)

Hubris and nemesis

Kennan criticized the Clinton administration for being blinded by its own Neo-idealist rhetoric. The Americans were unable to observe how their well-meaning actions inflamed 'nationalistic, anti-Western and militaristic tendencies in Russian opinion'. Kennan's observation was restricted to Russia; but his larger point applied to other nations and other regions as well. The West's well-intentioned re-emphasis on human rights triggered reactions in the Far East, where several states claimed that Asia had other values and identities than the West – that Asia had a tradition based on collective goods rather than on the Western principle of individual rights (see for instance Bary 1998). In the Middle East the Organisation of the Islamic Conference (OIC) produced a 'Declaration on Human Rights in Islam' which stressed that Islamic *sharia* is the sole source of human rights.

Samuel Huntington (1996), like Kennan, warned against an excessive faith in soft power. He reminded his readers that there are many reasons behind the expansion of the West and its world-encompassing power. Competition among

European states is one reason. A sense of national consciousness among Western peoples is another. The development of efficient state bureaucracies is a third. 'The most immediate source of Western expansion, however, was technological', argued Huntington. Simply put, the development of guns, ships and superiority in organization. 'The West won the world not by the superiority of its ideas or values or religion (to which few members of other civilizations were converted) but rather by its superiority in applying organized violence. Westerners often forget this fact; non-Westerners never do' (Huntington 1996, p. 51).

In the age of globalization, this main source of Western power – state of the art technologies – is no longer considered a state secret and protected by the government. Any government can acquire it. It is developed in international research institutions; much of it is for sale on the open world market, still more is available on the black market. International pre-eminence was never a lasting proposition. In the globalized age it is more transitory than ever before. The international system may have been unipolar in the immediate wake of the Soviet collapse. But as time has passed – and as the global markets have been rocked by recessions and crises – the international hierarchy of power has changed. India and Brazil, for example, have developed at a quicker rate than most European powers and moved up the hierarchy. China has developed more quickly than anybody. It has bypassed all the European economies as well as that of Japan in size. By 2011 it was the second largest economy in the world. With an annual growth rate of around 10 per cent, China was rapidly catching up with the USA. Two Chinese energy companies – Sinopec Group and China National Petroleum – were breathing down the neck of the biggest US corporations.

Table 14.3 shows an estimate of the ten largest economic entities in the world in 2014. When wealth is measured in a simple GDP, the USA is still the world largest economy; China is in second place, and Japan is a distant third. However, if the GDP is adjusted for purchasing power, which takes into consideration the relative value of the currencies, the ranking list is very different. Now China is the largest economy in the world, with the USA in second place. India occupies third place, separated by a significant gap from Japan and Germany, Russia, Brazil, and France.

Table 14.3 also includes estimates of the defence budgets of these ten largest economic entities. It indicates that the USA still has the largest defence budget in the world. But it also shows that China is in second place – and that a substantial gap separates the Chinese military budget from those further down the list, such as Russia (no. 4).[14] China, in other words, has increased both its wealth and its military power enormously over the last twenty years – as a quick comparison between Tables 14.3, 14.2 and 14.1 will show.

Many observers have noted China's rapid growth in productivity and military capabilities and argued that China represents the main challenge to the unipolar constellation and to American pre-eminence (Zakaria 2011). Some have added that the interstate ranking order is not merely an outcome of the material capabilities of states; it is also a product of others' perception of those capabilities. They note that the currency of international politics is not so much 'power' as 'prestige' (Gilpin

Table 14.3 The ten largest economic entities in the world, 2014
Gross Domestic Product (GDPs), Purchasing Power Parity (PPP)
and defence expenditures ($ million)

World rank		GDP	GDP/ PPP	World rank	Defence budget	World rank
1	United States	17,416	17,632	1	581.0	1
2	China	10,355	17,416	2	129.4	2
3	Japan	4,770	4,788	4	47.7	7
4	Germany	3,821	3,621	5	43.9	9
5	France	2,902	2,587	8	53.1	6
6	United Kingdom	2,847	2,435	10	61.8	5
7	Brazil	2,244	3,073	7	31.9	11
8	Italy	2,129	2,066	12	24.3	12
9	Russia	2,057	3,557	6	70.0	4
10	India	2,047	7,277	3	45.2	8

Sources: IMF (2014); IISS (2014)

1981, pp. 30f; Knutsen 1999, pp. 80ff). From this perspective, which emphasizes perception, the incremental increase of China's material capabilities over the last few decades may have done less to shake US leadership and the unipolar world than Russia's decisive reconquest of Crimea in 2014.

Fewer observers have noted that the growth of non-Western powers in general represents a challenge to the West as a whole. Fewer still have proposed that this development may challenge the world order that was established long ago. A five-hundred-year epoch of Western dominance may, in other words (Mackinder 1919), be nearing its end. And judged by the speed with which some of the non-Western economies are evolving, that end may come surprisingly soon.[15]

Notes

1 Latvia, Lithuania and Estonia had been included in the Soviet empire by the secret agreement between Stalin and Hitler in August 1939, and had long wanted independence. But whenever the issue had been raised, the USSR had reacted with refusal and threats. When the Soviet leaders appeared irresolute in the autumn of 1989, the Baltic states pressed their demands once more.

2 The Russian elections in March 1990 triggered a political process that was as important as it was complicated. An appreciation of the complicated situation hinges on a good understanding of the difference between (and the complex interaction of) Soviet Union on the one hand and Russia on the other. The Soviet Union (or the USSR) was a federation made up of fifteen republics of varying size. Russia was the largest and most important of these constituent republics; so large, in fact, that it was itself a federation – officially named the Russian Soviet Federative Socialist Republic (or RSFSR). Mikhail Gorbachev was the President of the Soviet Union and the leader (the first secretary) of the Communist Party (CPSU) which had the

monopoly of power in the USSR. The Russian elections of March 1990 brought Boris Yeltsin into the mainstream of Russian as well as Soviet politics. The March elections won Yeltsin a seat in the Russian Congress of People's Deputies, which elected him to Russia's most important political office in May: that is, chairman of Russia's Presidium of the Supreme Soviet. As the leading politician in Russia, the largest single republic in the USSR, Yeltsin emerged as the main rival of Mikhail Gorbachev – a rivalry which was exacerbated by the chaotic political situation of the times.

3 At the time of the Soviet collapse, Russia's President Boris Yeltsin had already prepared a successor to the Soviet empire: a new confederation led by Russia. Yeltsin quickly secured agreement from eleven of the fifteen former Soviet republics to join him in the new Commonwealth of Independent States (CIS). At the beginning of 1992, the CIS included Armenia, Azerbaijan, Belarus, Kazakhstan, Kyrgyzstan, Moldova, Russia, Tajikistan, Turkmenistan, Ukraine and Uzbekistan. Georgia joined in 1993, bringing the number of members to twelve. The three Baltic states did not join – and are the only ex-Soviet republics which have remained outside the CIS.

4 Institutional economists had warned against the sudden transition. Douglass North had noted that Russia had a meagre civil society with few ordering institutions. A rapid dismantlement of the existing command economy will not trigger a free market economy; it will produce chaos. North was right.

5 The extent to which Russia plunged into misery during this transition into market capitalism is reflected in Russian health statistics: between 1990 and 2000 the life expectancy for Russian males plunged by an average of five years – to below sixty years.

6 Less than a decade after the collapse of communism, millions of Russians began to wonder whether the Marxist–Leninist analysis might have a point after all. 'Free-market capitalism' tended to concentrate capital and centralize power. 'Democracy' legitimized the law of the jungle.

7 The report (here referred to as White House 1992) remains secret. However, unclassified parts of its draft have been released and are available at www.archives.gov/declassification/iscap/pdf/2008-003-docs1-12.pdf. The secret report was leaked to the *New York Times* and its thrust was criticized for being militarist and unilateralist. The report was also criticized in internal debates by members of the Bush administration – for example by Colin Powell, Chairman of the Joint Chiefs of Staff. The report was quickly revised and a gentler version released to the public. (See Armstrong 2002.)

8 It is worth noting that, although the term 'humanitarian intervention' has been used for a long time (Bass 2008), it is not a concept in international law. However, many progressive observers hoped that the stated aim of 'humanitarian interventions' – that is, to protect innocent civilians from the aggression of their own governments – would become part of international law. They were disappointed. The term faded from use. But the sentiment was preserved in the concept of 'Responsibility to Protect' ('R2P'), which was accepted by the UN in 2005.

9 The first arguments about a connection between war and regime type were indicated by Enlightenment *philosophes* during the mid-1700s. Baron Montesquieu, for

example, had argued that monarchic regimes are war-prone whereas popular-based regimes were not (Montesquieu [1748], part III). William Godwin had argued that adjacent republics compose a zone of peace in the world. And similar arguments were developed by authors like Thomas Paine and Immanuel Kant. The idea existed in various versions within the republican tradition of political thought during the nineteenth century. It was expressed with great conviction by the US President Woodrow Wilson during World War I, and was an important element in the vision that drove him to establish the League of Nations in 1919. It was, however, only in the 1960s that the point was convincingly demonstrated by statistical techniques (for example by Babst 1964). In 1983, Michael Doyle drew much scholarly attention when he formulated a comparative-historical explanation for why democratic states were unlikely to fight among themselves. At that time the argument was lifted to considerable attention when quantitative peace researchers used statistical analyses to demonstrate that democracies do not fight among themselves (Maoz and Abdolali 1989).

10 The most famous example here is the Vietnam War. It steadily increased in intensity during the 1960s as the USA sent more and more soldiers to South Vietnam to support the government in Saigon, whereas China and the USSR sent more and more resources and arms to the communist regime in North Vietnam and to insurgent forces in the south. This war was not settled militarily. It ended politically. And the actor which played the most important role in ending it was the US Congress which, in the early 1970s, refused to give the executive branch more resources to fight the war with. US military involvement in Vietnam ended in August 1973. Its client regime in South Vietnam ran steadily lower on military resources and collapsed when North Vietnam launched a major offensive in spring of 1975.

11 Finland's declaration of war on the anti-Hitler alliance, for example, could be explained by a unique opportunity to fight the USSR. Further back, Wilhelmine Germany and the Boer republic were hardly full democracies.

12 Mexico (no. 11) with about 94 million inhabitants had a GDP per capita of about $6,500 in 1995. India (no. 12) with a population of 930 million had a GDP per capita of $1,538 in 1995. Belgium (no. 19) with a population of 10 million had a GDP per capita of nearly $19,000 in 1995. Sweden (no. 20) was in a similar situation: a population of about 7 million and a GDP per capita of about $18,000. South Korea (no. 13) had a population of 45 million and a GDP per capita of nearly $10,000 – and growing at a rate of around 10 per cent per year. Russia (no. 16) with a population of about 147 million (and shrinking) had a GDP per capita of about $6,000 (roughly the same as Mexico but rapidly falling).

13 The distinction between empire and imperialism is a basic one: empire is a political term and refers to a vast political community. Imperialism is an economic term and refers to a rapacious economic system. Traditional left-wing radicals, who built their views on an ontology which portrayed the USA as a capitalist power, tended to portray America as an expansionist imperialist (see e.g., Baran and Sweezy 1966).

14 The IISS (2014) lists Saudi Arabia's defence budget as the third largest in the world, with an estimated value of around $80 billion. This estimate is suspect. And it is unreasonable to infer from this budget figure that Saudi Arabia is the third greatest military power in the world – behind China but in front of Russia.

Saudi Arabia, however, has a significant economic influence due to its enormous oil reserves. Also, if the Saudi military capabilities may be easily overestimated, the country's ideological or religious influence over the last few decades cannot be underestimated.

15 By some estimates, the Chinese GDP will catch up with the USA in 2020 and push the American economy to second place. Since India's working-age population is likely to increase by more than 40 per cent in the next four decades, India's economy may expand at an even greater rate than China's, and become the world's largest economy by 2050 – pushing China to second place and the USA to a distant third.

15

Global politics:
the end of International Relations?

When a huge passenger plane from United Airlines crashed into the southern tower of the World Trade Center in Manhattan and exploded in a fireball in the morning of 11 September 2001, it was immediately perceived as a catastrophic accident. When shocked bystanders seventeen minutes later witnessed a second passenger place head towards the northern tower, slice into it and explode, it was generally understood that this was a large-scale terrorist attack. All civilian air traffic was stopped. US warplanes took to the wings within minutes and began to patrol the skies. Too late, it turned out, to prevent a third passenger plane from crashing into the Pentagon forty-five minutes later.

It is often said that '9/11' changed international politics. This is an exaggeration. The fact of the matter is that international politics had already changed. It had been changed dramatically a decade earlier by the unravelling of the Soviet empire. This had marked a transition from a bipolar to a unipolar system. It had also involved a normative shift; a rapid fading of the communist ideology and a strengthening – to the point of pre-eminence – of liberal outlooks. After the fall of the USSR, international relations were no longer marked by bipolarity and super-power rivalry. A new age opened up, marked by unipolarity and harmony under USA's liberal leadership.

The 1991 disintegration of the USSR changed the structure of the world. The 2001 terrorist attacks on Manhattan and Washington DC changed the perception of the world. The disintegration of the USSR altered the basic configuration of the international system and inaugurated an age of liberal optimism. The terrorist attacks shook that optimism and revealed that the US-led world was neither as harmonious nor as liberal as previously assumed.

Similarly, it was the 1991 disintegration of the USSR that changed the field of International Relations (from this point I will use the abbreviation 'IR' by which the discipline was by now universally known). The collapse of the USSR was as much a surprise to IR scholars as to everyone else. It shook the academic confidence of the field and stirred waves of criticism. If IR was a science, its scholars should have predicted the collapse of the Soviet empire. The failure to do so ushered in huge debates about the nature and the purpose of IR. Also, it opened up discussions that brought forth new arguments and theories.

Terrorist attacks were not new – terrorism had long been a well-known phenomenon. Also, radical Islamists had struck against the USA before – an Islamic conspiracy had tried to destroy the WTC as early as 1993, but only succeeded in blowing an enormous crater in the building's subterranean parking garage. The nature of the Islamic threat became clear only around 2000, when the USA finally rolled up the terrorist conspiracy which had struck against the US embassies in Dar-es-Salaam and Nairobi two years earlier. Only then did the US intelligence community become fully aware of the anti-American resentment which drove the shadowy figures of Osama bin Laden and Ayman al-Zawahiri and their cabal of radical Islamists organized in al-Qaida al-Sulba ('the firm base' or 'foundation').

This discovery, together with the 2001 terrorist attacks, were bolts from the blue. It confirmed IR's inability to predict. Also it lifted up new issues and subjected them to the heated debates. Primary among them were issues of international security, democratization and political culture. Extra intensity was added to the discussion when newly elected President George W. Bush declared a 'war on terror', the initial phases of which involved US-led invasions of Afghanistan (2001) and Iraq (2003).

The USA had been stung by wasps. President Bush found the wasps' nest and insisted on beating it with a stick. American soldiers who were sent abroad to combat the threatening swarms tried to shoot their way out. Rather than improving upon the security of the USA and world, these invasions released more threats, instability and disorder. By 2006, the Bush administration was badly stung and in deep trouble. The US invasions in Afghanistan and Iraq had triggered Islamic reactions and made the terror threat infinitely worse.

This chapter will pay little attention to the Bush administration's 'global war on terror'. Although this so-called 'war' dominated world news for the first dozen years of the new millennium, this chapter will not focus on news headlines but instead seek to identify longer trend lines. Most of all, it will search for ideational trends. Whereas the previous chapter discussed the post-Cold War world with an emphasis on traditional issues of material interests and capabilities of power, this chapter will focus on the ideational changes that followed the unexpected end of the Cold War.

The chapter will begin by exploring the consequences of the Soviet collapse. It will first note its impact on neighbouring countries and also trace some of its effects on regions farther afield.[1] The chapter will then discuss some of the new concerns that sprang up in the post-Cold War world and note the ways in which in which these concerns affected the political debates. The chapter will finally discuss how the collapse of the USSR caught International Relations scholars by surprise and pushed the international community of IR scholars into a deep crisis of academic identity.

Tenuous transitions

The 1991 collapse of the USSR changed the political map of the region. New, independent states emerged from the ruins of the old Soviet empire and produced a new regional system. The system was dominated by Russia – much like the old. However, the new system, expressed in the Commonwealth of Independent States (CIS), was not an empire like the USSR had been but a looser formation.[2] It was not guided by a single ideology but it was ideationally diverse. It was no longer maintained by a totalitarian apparatus of surveillance and control. Stripped by the disciplining force of the CPSU, Russia was, once more, torn between groups who wanted to emulate the West and those who wanted to preserve the Slavic inheritance.

In 1992, the Westernizers dominated Russian politics. The government of Boris Yeltsin launched optimistic reform programmes to ensure a quick transition from Soviet-style socialism to Western-style capitalist democracy. It could hardly be called a success. Economic reforms triggered a fast inflation which pushed millions of ordinary Russians into financial ruin. Political reforms tore down old institutions of governance, but could not establish a new order. Too many political parties were created. Elections produced a fragmented parliament, too diverse to make effective decisions.

By the end of Yeltsin's second term in office, a generation of Russians had become deeply disillusioned with market reforms and democracy. First, the old political system unravelled. The disappearance of one-party rule was celebrated. But the loss of the socialist system of medical care and social services was increasingly mourned – especially as the economy collapsed and threw millions of people into destitution. The political system quickly slid under the control of a new elite of wealthy speculators and corrupt state officials – the so-called oligarchs (Hoffman 2001).[3]

Implications for the near abroad

Yeltsin's government faced rebellion from several members which wanted to leave the Russian federation. The old satellites of the Soviet empire – the countries of Eastern Europe – wanted to escape Russian dominance. They had been occupied by the Soviet army during the endgame of World War II and joined to Moscow by Stalin through organizations like Cominform and Comecon. Now they wanted to break out of Russia's sphere of influence and tie their fortunes to the West. Most of them had established non-communist governments after free, multi-party elections. They suffered serious economic setbacks when the USSR collapsed. But the collapse also offered political opportunities. Several governments approached NATO and the EU, whose leaders assured them that new applications for membership were always welcome. But the Western leaders also made it clear that NATO and EU were liberal organizations which had liberal democracies as members.

The new governments of Eastern Europe got the message. They bent over backwards to make the transition from socialism to liberal democracy. Poland, Hungary, Czechoslovakia and other countries introduced free-market economies and multi-party politics in record time. There is no doubt that these countries' efforts to conform to liberal criteria defined by the Western world hastened the process of democratization in central and eastern Europe.

The fifteen republics which had composed the old USSR had a harder time. Russia, the largest of the old Soviet republics, descended into political and economic chaos. The Russian government faced rebellion from several of its constituent republics. The most serious challenge occurred on the northern slopes of the Caucasus, where rebellion in the autonomous republic of Chechnya developed into a national insurgency. The Chechen population was predominantly Muslim, and the insurgency was justified by Islamic rhetoric. The Yeltsin government struck at them with massive force in December 1994. The ensuing war reduced Grozny, the Chechen capital, to ruins and the countryside to starvation. Chechen groups retaliated by organizing terrorist attacks in Russian cities.

On the southern slopes of the Caucasus conflicts erupted between the newly sovereign republics of Azerbaijan, Armenia and Georgia. All had problems establishing an orderly government at home and agreeing on stable borders with neighbouring countries.

Further east, beyond the Caspian Sea, the new sovereign republics of Kyrgyzstan, Tajikistan, Uzbekistan and Turkmenistan were also making transitions from Soviet-style communism. They were, however, not introducing liberal democracy; instead they were establishing various kinds of autocratic rule. In Turkmenistan, for example, Saparmurat Niyazov, a former bureaucrat of the CPSU, made himself president for life and based his rule on a nationalistic personality cult and political purges.

The unequal record of other socialist countries

The old allies of the USSR were shaken by the Soviet collapse. Cuba, for example, was taken for a bumpy economic ride during the entire 1900s. The Caribbean island had relied heavily on exports to the Soviet market; when the USSR dissolved, Cuba lost some 80 per cent of its foreign trade and slid into a deep economic crisis.

The Socialist Republic of Vietnam stood out as a happy exception in this sad tale of socialist woes. The country had got a new leadership in 1986. The new party secretary, Nguyen Van Linh, had begun to liberalize the Vietnamese economy and been quickly rewarded by a spurt of economic growth. By the time of the Soviet collapse, Vietnam was well on its way to making a remarkable transformation into a vibrant, market-driven, capitalist system.

The catastrophic development of North Korea marked a sharp contrast to Vietnam's success. North Korea suffered calamitous consequences from the dissolution of the USSR. The population suffered horrible hardships as the economy of that insular republic collapsed and triggered serious famines. Full catastrophe was averted by massive aid from China.

China is a story all its own. The country had brushed aside Maoism and opened up to market capitalism in the late 1970s. The Chinese Communist Party (CCP) kept its monopoly of political power, while the country's economy began to expand. Production increased, incomes rose, the availability of food, housing and other consumer goods improved. Mao had emphasized an economic policy based on national self-sufficiency; he restricted foreign trade – which rarely exceeded 10 per cent of the national income of a very poor China. Deng Xiaoping regarded foreign trade a source of investment capital and modern technology. He encouraged foreign trade, which doubled during the first half of the 1980s – from 15 per cent of national income in 1980 to around 30 per cent in 1985.

This rapid economic development introduced change, tensions and political conflicts. Many Chinese wanted economic freedoms to be followed by political liberties. The aspiration was expressed in several Chinese cities in early spring of 1989. Students had staged demonstrations, encouraged by a visit in mid-May by Soviet premier Gorbachev. His presence had reminded them of Gorbachev's political reforms, and triggered a wave of demonstrations. This so alarmed senior Chinese leaders that they introduced martial law.

Events in China showed that ideals of liberal democracy were not received with equal enthusiasm everywhere. First, the CCP made it quite clear that China had its own tradition of popular sovereignty and its own code of rights. Second, the point was repeated by several Asian states – among them Indonesia, Malaysia and Singapore – in the 1993 'Bangkok Declaration' which argued that the Far East was not tempted by any liberal code because it had its own tradition of 'Asian values'. Third, the Organization of Islamic Conference (OIC) made a similar point during its meeting in Cairo where it produced a 'Declaration on Human Rights in Islam'. It stressed that Islamic *sharia* is the sole source of human rights. Finally, the war in Afghanistan indicated clearly that democratic rule in that poor and fractured country was a utopian dream. When the USSR collapsed and the communist regime of Afghanistan's President Najibullah fell, this did not open up any democratic doors; rather, it opened the floodgates of more civil war. During the mid-1990s, a Pakistan-supported Islamic movement, the Taliban, expanded its influence and established a semblance of order upon that poor country – a *sharia*-based, totalitarian dictatorship based on repression and force. Yet many Afghans found the draconian rule of the Taliban preferable to the constant warfare that had ruined the nation over the previous generation.

Catastrophe also awaited the Socialist Federal Republic of Yugoslavia (SFRY). It had been cobbled together during the endgame of World War II by Josip Broz Tito, who also kept it out of the orbit of Soviet influence – to Stalin's great annoyance. The SFRY had always been rent by frictions and rivalries, but it had been kept together by Tito's shrewd balancing and by the external threat of the USSR. When Tito died (in 1980), ethnic rivalries fuelled deeper conflicts. When the USSR dissolved a decade or two later, conflicts burst into demands for independence and secession. During the autumn of 1991, Tito's SFRY fell apart, descending into a brutal and complex civil war.

A new Middle East

Several regimes in the Middle East were affected by the Soviet collapse. The Syrian strongman Hafez al-Assad was economically hurt by the termination of

Soviet subsidies and trade agreements. The Libyan dictator Muammar Gadhafi, who had long exploited East–West tensions for political profit, could no longer count on Soviet support for his anti-Western antics. In neighbouring Algeria legis-lative elections were interrupted when the first electoral rounds suggested victory for the fundamentalist Islamic Salvation Front (FIS). Fearing the election of an Islamic government, the government intervened in January 1992. It banned FIS and cancelled the elections. This triggered an armed insurgency between Algeria's security forces and the armed wing of FIS (the Armed Islamic Group or AIG). The insurgency quickly spread and caused much international concern.

The Palestine Liberation Organization (PLO) was weakened by the dissolution of the USSR. Deprived of its Soviet subsidies, the PLO leader Yasser Arafat was driven into secret negotiations with Israel. His position was made even worse by the Gulf War, in which he supported Saddam Hussein in the hope of receiving rich rewards with an Iraqi victory. When the Iraqi forces were trounced, Arafat was widely condemned.

Arafat enjoyed a final moment of triumph when he signed an agreement with Israel – the so-called Oslo accord, which had been secretly brokered by Norwegian diplomats and publically signed on the White House lawn in September 1993. The Oslo accord was met with optimistic accolades in the West. But many nations in the Middle East considered Arafat a traitor to the Arab cause and condemned the agreement. Bereft of funds, the PLO faded into political insignificance. It left a political vacuum which was quickly filled by other actors; several of them of a radical Islamist persuasion. Hamas and Hezbollah were local organizations formed to resist Israel.

Then there was al-Qaida, an international organization which had been formed in Afghanistan by Sunni volunteers from many countries. Many members were radicalized by the Gulf War. The leaders vowed to assist Muslims wherever they fought against Jews and Christians. They sent al-Qaida members to Bosnia-Herzegovina to assist the Muslim side in the Balkan wars. They also supported the anti-Russian rebels in the Caucasus. When Afghanistan descended into civil war in the early 1990s, al-Qaida veterans left the country and returned to their original homelands. Here they opposed Western influence by paramilitary sabotage acts and tactics of terror. Their activities increased the level of conflict in several Arab countries in the early 1990s – among them Saudi Arabia and Yemen, but especially in Algeria. Afghanistan veterans strengthened the radical Islamists around Algeria's violent FIS movement. Conflicts flared up that killed more than a hundred thousand people. During the mid-1990s the Algerian situation became a point of international concern.

Coda

The decline of the USSR had many causes. Its collapse had dramatic consequences. It marked the end of the Cold War. It also marked the demise of communism – which had long been the core of traditional radicalism. It gave rise to a dozen new, independent states – some of which hosted Soviet military nuclear installations

(Russia, Ukraine, Belarus and Kazakhstan) and became atomic powers overnight – and altered the distribution of power in the world. Also, the collapse of the USSR deprived old Soviet allies of resources and pushed radical leaders into deep trouble. Cuba found itself in dire economic straits. North Korea was pushed to the cusp of disaster. Soviet clients in the Middle East were starved for funds. The regimes in Libya and Syria found themselves economically constrained. So did the PLO, whose role faded into insignificance and whose organizational role was taken over by radical Islamic groups.

Many academic observers noted that history mattered – that in order to understand the events and the world it produced, it was necessary to understand patterns of the past. The events which brought about the beginning of the Cold War in 1945 and 1946 also framed its end. The four powers which had divided Germany in 1945 reassembled to negotiate Germany's unification forty-five years later. During the unification negotiations they brought up old concerns of national interest, security and relative power – Margaret Thatcher being a particularly outspoken example. When the negotiations were over, they all praised the result in well-known idealist terms – they celebrated the principle of popular sovereignty, toasted a new age marked by democracy and prosperity, and they all praised peace.

Academic observers also noted that people mattered. They recalled how the interaction of the 'Big Three' had shaped diplomacy during World War II and also paved the way for the Cold War which followed. They observed how individual statesmen and stateswomen similarly formed events that ended the Cold War. Clearly, the inflexible political structure of the USSR and its stagnant economy were long-term causes of the Soviet decline. Yet, individual leaders acted within this structure and altered it by their actions. One of these leaders was Mikhail Gorbachev whose policies of *glasnost* and *perestroika* introduced major changes to the Soviet system. Another was Boris Yeltsin, who helped bring the communist structure down. Both of them were influenced by new ideas and theories – by what Gorbachev referred to as 'the new thinking'. Also, they were pressured by other people who also had ideas about the course of events and preferences about its direction. Among them were dedicated activists and organizers who mobilized millions of people behind their various visions of change.[4]

Finally, observers noted that the collapse of the USSR had been extraordinary peaceful. In the West, at least, the unravelling of the USSR produced an atmosphere of optimism and idealism. The end of the Cold War was, in fact, attended by a political outlook very similar to that utopian sentiment which followed the end of the world wars in 1919 and 1945.

Global concerns

Earlier authors had noted how interaction and interdependence would connect the nations of the world and make the globe 'a single organism' (Mackinder 1919). This idea returned in the final years of the twentieth century. But it returned in a new international context.

Global politics

Material progress was one important aspect of that new context. New technologies of production and transport had ushered in a more finely tuned international division of labour that enhanced the interconnectedness among industrial states. New technologies of destruction made war a greater threat and industrial nations steadily more afraid of war. New technologies of communication integrated people into worldwide nets of common knowledge and global awareness. International activities were more co-ordinated and institutionalized than ever. International interaction no longer took place in a 'brute' or an 'immature anarchy' but in a 'mature anarchy' (Buzan 1991 [1983], pp. 122–3); it took place not in a lawless international system but in an international society marked by rules, regimes and other ordering institutions.

Ideational shifts were another aspect of the new international context. The collapse of the Soviet Union and the end of the Cold War were followed by a wave of Neo-idealism which washed across world affairs. It was reflected in the idea that peace, wealth, liberty and other good things go hand in hand with democracy. One of its manifestations was a rejuvenated and more active UN – whose General Secretary proposed rules for international conduct based on the concept of human rights, whose General Assembly discussed ways of expanding international law and whose Security Council approved 'humanitarian interventions' into trouble spots like northern Iraq (1991), Bosnia (1992), Somalia (1992) and Haiti (1994).

The rise of Neo-idealism involved a rapid shift in ideological sentiments. On the one hand, the collapse of the USSR meant a precipitous fall of communist and socialist ideals. On the other hand, the unravelling of Radicalism opened up for the sudden expansion of liberal ideals based on reason, rights and individual liberty. The fall of communism meant the renaissance of free-market models as the proper road to development, wealth and freedom and to liberal democracy as the natural order of government.

The ideal of the centrally planned economy fell into disrepute, whereas the ideal of the free-market economy rose to prominence. Huge state-owned companies of infrastructure and communications were quickly dismantled. Electrical plants, broadcasting corporations, telephone and telegraph companies, railways and airlines were divided up and sold on the market. A huge wave of privatisation washed across the world during the early 1990s. It was the largest real-estate sale in world history (Yergin and Stanislaw 1998).

This neo-liberal groundswell emboldened the liberal democracies of the Western world and placed autocratic regimes – on the left as well as on the right – under great pressure to reform. [5] The assistance programmes of the World Bank and the IMF were reformed along new, free-market lines. Communism was abandoned in Albania, Yugoslavia, Ethiopia, South Yemen, Mongolia and Cambodia. The anti-communist strongman Ferdinand Marcos was ousted from the Philippines in 1989. General Augusto Pinochet stepped down as Chile's dictator in 1990. A symbolically significant change took place in South Africa, where the white apartheid regime unravelled. Democratic elections were held there in 1994 and brought to power Nelson Mandela – a most remarkable man who, after having served twenty-seven years in prison on charges of sedition, high treason, and terrorism, emerged as one of the great African leaders and a powerful symbol of a new and hopeful age.

In the wake of the Cold War, a wave of neo-liberal values washed across the world and brought with it a new emphasis on human reason and individual rights – especially the rights to life, liberty and property.

Neo-idealism

Some of the neo-liberal optimists argued that the steady expansion of the market implied the retreat of the state and the advance of individual freedom. National boundaries were about to become irrelevant, argued Kenichi Ohmae in his best-selling book *The Borderless World* (1990). Free movement of capital, goods and labour would reduce governments' ability to control economies and societies, argued Ohmae (1990).

Walter Wriston (1992) heralded the coming of the information age as the coming of an era of global convergence, rendering national borders obsolete. Ohmae (1995) agreed. Continued globalisation would undermine the interstate system and produce an international society with freedom and justice for all, he predicted. Also, continued migration would make the countries of the world culturally diverse. This point was also noted for instance by the social philosopher Jean-François Lyotard (1979). The old nation-states – product of the modern phase of Western history – were cracking up, he observed. Technological evolution, social change and new modes of knowledge were prising modern society apart, giving rise to a postmodern world. The free movement of goods and people was producing an increasingly multicultural society, where one

> listens to reggae, watches a western, eats McDonald's food for lunch and local cuisine for dinner, wears Paris perfume in Tokyo and 'retro' clothes in Hong Kong; knowledge is a matter for TV games. It is easy to find a public for eclectic works. By becoming kitsch, art panders to the confusion which reigns in the 'taste' of the patrons. Artists, gallery owners, critics, and the public wallow together in the 'anything goes' (Lyotard 1983, p. 75)

Neo-liberal economists noted that this increased freedom of choice and increased everybody's liberty. Some humanist philosophers added that this involved a greater ethnic diversity and cultural freedom. They argued that old norms of integration, citizenship and nationality had to adapt. The old idea of the melting pot, where minority cultures were expected to adapt to the dominant culture, had to go; it must be replaced by new ideas of multiculturalism. Immigrants should not have to trade in their old, native culture for a new, national identity; they should instead keep their values and habits; each individual could have one or more identities or 'complementary ethnicities'. These different identities should all be preserved within the same society and contribute to a diverse and colourful community – a new 'rainbow nation' in the words of the South African Bishop Desmond Tutu.

Critics – migration and multiculturalism
'Globalization' emerged as the new buzzword of the age. It was popularized by Theodore Levitt (1983), who saw it as a techno-economic process of integration which gave rise to a global market on a previously unimagined scale. This process would drive enterprises and companies to compete globally, argued Levitt; in fact, companies would have no choice but to transform themselves to global corporations, he averred. Those which did not would stagnate and wither; some of those which did would grow enormously and contribute to a steadily more pronounced global division of labour.

Levitt's argument was deeply influential. So was that of David Harvey (1989), a radical anthropologist and geographer. His elaboration of the notion that the world was 'rapidly shrinking' deftly introduced notions of subjectively experienced compression of 'time' and 'space' to the debate. Harvey argued that perceptions of a shrinking world were produced by new technologies of transport and communication.

Authors agreed that this development improved the human condition in several respects. New ways of carrying goods and people – in larger numbers, more cheaply and over greater distances than before – and new technologies for disseminating texts and images globally. However, the development also had some considerable downsides. Anthony Giddens, for example, pointed out that a freer global market filled with mass-produced commodities would not necessarily lead to diversity; he argued that it might lead to standardization and increased similarity. Also, a global marketplace was unlikely to bring about universal increase in individual liberty. A free market brings about increased liberty and wealth for some social groups while leaving others worse off. The net result is a loss of equality and an increasing gap between rich and poor. Such a gap would fuel resentment among the poor and – as classical political economists from Marx to Mill have pointed out – move the state to intervene to restore order. Either by redistributing wealth more equitably and securing the rights of the poor or by increasing control and repression.

The state, then, is unlikely to wither away as the market gets freer; rather the state is likely to acquire new roles and responsibilities. So, although the free market might erode state power in some aspects – for example, releasing its grip on the commanding heights of the economy and leaving more distributive functions to the market – it would grow stronger in other aspects (Strange 1988). French authors had long argued that postmodern states were driven to actively cultivate particular kinds of knowledge over others. François Lyotard and Jean Baudrillard both intimated that, in the new global marketplace, states would boost education in technical subjects and business administration while letting the liberal arts starve. Giddens (1990) speculated on how a freer market might bring about in fact not more individual freedom but rather new forms of central planning, surveillance and control.

These sceptics argued that globalization was not merely a process of economic and political interdependence; it was not just a material process of 'widening, deepening and speeding up of worldwide interconnectedness'. There were also

465

social and cultural sides to the process. Globalisation would have profound social, cultural and political implications (Appadurai 1990).

New means of communication and transport permitted capitalists to move production to poor, populous countries where labour was cheap. This boosted industrial growth in poor countries in the South where wages were low. But it also meant that labour-intensive industries were disappearing from rich countries in the North where wages were high. The net effect was a vast reallocation of the productive capabilities in the world – resulting in an enormous loss of industrial employment opportunities in the North, the waning of the traditional labouring classes, and the weakening of working-class institutions such as labour unions and labour parties. This transformed the political landscape in many countries.

At the same time new means of travel provided millions of poor people with opportunities to leave poor regions and travel to countries with greater opportunities for work and wealth. A growing numbers of people migrated from the South, reversing traditional migratory trends. For nearly five hundred years, nations of the North had sent their people to countries in the South; after World War II, an increasing number of people travelled the other way. During the 1990s this migratory flow was increasing so fast that demographers began to talk about a 'new Great Migration'. As a result of it, hundreds of thousands of immigrants from the South accumulated in the cities in Western Europe and the USA. The result was not only Lyotard's 'postmodern condition' of multicultural choice; the mass migration also triggered new social tensions.

Critics of immigration and of the multicultural idea transformed the social debate and altered the political landscape in many Western countries. At a time when the old conservative parties were dying and the socialist parties were no longer rooted in the labouring classes, political spaces opened up for neo-liberal parties and for populist and nationalist movements. Neo-nationalism was fuelled by strong anti-immigration sentiments and by the growth of right-wing populist parties. In Western Europe this was most pronounced in France, where Jean-Marie Le Pen founded the National Front and built it up to a significant political force. In Austria, Jörg Haider boosted the popularity of the Freedom Party. In Hungary Gergely Pongrátz founded Jobbik.

The growth of right-wing parties was fuelled by new wars in the Arab world, by increase in Islamic terrorism and by new waves of Muslim refugees from North Africa and the Middle East. Greece saw the advent of the right-wing Golden Dawn. Italy saw the resurgence of neo-fascist movements like the MSI and protest parties like the Five Star Movement. Virtually every country in Europe saw the rise of neo-nationalist parties. If their growth was fuelled by migration, their protests were sharpened by fear of Islamic terrorism and, later, by economic crises.

New wars and new insecurities
The terrorist attacks on 9/11 introduced new discussions about security and the changing character of war. Mary Kaldor (1999) explored the nature of these new wars. She argued that wars of liberation and of revolution had changed in recent

years. New kinds of war had emerged on the international scene. Affected by the advent of globalization, warfare had developed a handful of distinct characteristics. First, wars were fuelled no longer by ideology but by ethnic concerns. Second, these wars were fought by new kinds of actors – sometimes by states but often by non-state actors. Third, they were not financed over state budgets but through other, often criminal, ways. Finally, the leaders of these 'new wars' did not seek to achieve physical control of a territory but rather political control of populations – often through the use of fear and terror.

Kaldor's book, *New and Old Wars*, written on the experience of the Balkan wars, stirred a big debate. Several other observers had also noted the shifting character of war, but they disagreed on the nature of the shift. Many of them recognized the blur between state and non-state actors. Robert Shaw (2003) noted that warfare had degenerated toward the destruction of populations. John Mueller (2004) argued that the new wars tended to be hard to separate from piracy, banditry and other predatory activities. It is sometimes hard to distinguish between collective violence which is organized to reach political ends on behalf of a considerable constituency and violence organized to enrich a small band of predatory thugs, argued Mueller. Frank Hoffman (2007) characterized modern wars as 'hybrid' in character.

The French polemologist Gérard Chailand (2008), informed by the wars in Afghanistan and Iraq, observed that, when the world was experiencing a steadily declining number of wars of liberation, this had a simple reason: such wars were in effect armed resistance to colonial rule. Wars of liberation had been common enough during four centuries of colonialism; however, as colonial empires were dismantled during the second half of the twentieth century, wars of liberation faded and became a phenomenon of the past. Chailand made a similar argument about wars of revolution: such wars were in effect a creation of modern, revolutionary states like China and the USSR. These wars were a distinct phenomenon during the course of the Cold War – especially during the phase of decolonization when the Soviets sponsored radical movements to take power in Third World countries. However, after the collapse of communism in the USSR and China, revolutionary wars largely disappeared. This has left only one major kind of irregular war: secessionist war. A form of war that is fought to acquire control over a distinct population and is often fuelled by cultural concerns – by language, religion and ethnic identity. However, although secessionist wars are driven by demands for identity, they are usually also tied to a distinct territory. Either because the territory represents 'ancient land' and is symbol of an ancient identity or because the territory contains resources – precious stones or rare minerals – which can be used to finance the war.

'Wars of terror' was presented as a new type of irregular war. Observers noted that Islamist terrorism are often justified by reactionary rhetoric – by arguments that emphasise old, communal values and simple, traditional, male-dominated, rural ways of life. These wars, it is argued, are desperate attempts by traditionalist groups to hold back the march of modernity. In this sense they look like struggles of resistance, driven by frustration, that turn against the perceived main source of modernity: the West, led by the USA. There is often a pronounced, anti-Western

– and in particular an anti-American – element in this rhetoric. It is no coincidence that wars of terror flared up in the age of globalization.

Samuel Huntington saw a simpler pattern at work. He argued that a new dimension of conflict was emerging in IR. He framed it, controversially, as a religiously rooted clash of civilizations. The world was divided into eight or nine basic civilizations, argued Huntington (1993). And far from being drawn together by liberal values – as argued by Wriston (1992) and Fukuyama (1992) – these different cultures were instead being drawn into conflict. The post-Cold War world was in fact experiencing a global culture war. The 'clash of civilizations' was in fact remaking the international order along cultural lines (Huntington 1993; 1996).

Huntington put his argument in a macro-historical perspective. In the sixteenth century, international politics was marked by struggles between princes, he began. In the seventeenth century the major conflicts were among monarchs. In the eighteenth century among states. In the nineteenth century, international relations was a struggle among nations. The twentieth century, Huntington continued, was an age of ideology. Its major struggles were first associated with the mass-mobilizing ideologies of liberalism, communism and fascism; then, after the destruction of fascism, by a rivalry between liberalism and communism. The collapse of the USSR and the end of communism did not mean that liberalism had emerged victorious and dominant, Huntington averred. Rather, it meant that ideology had lost significance. Also, it meant the revival of religion.[6] World politics had now reverted to a normal condition of religiously based conflicts among civilizations.

> It is my hypothesis [wrote Huntington] that the fundamental source of conflict in this new world will not be primarily ideological or primarily economic. The great divisions among humankind and the dominating source of conflict will be cultural. Nation states will remain the most powerful actors in world affairs, but the principal conflicts of global politics will occur between nations and groups of different civilizations. The clash of civilizations will dominate global politics. The fault lines between civilizations will be the battle lines of the future. (Huntington 1993, p. 32)

These battle lines were particularly pronounced between the Islamic and the Christian civilizations, claimed Huntington. His diagnosis drew sharp criticism. When he sought to support his claims by statistics on violence and wars, he provoked howls of protest. Huntington argued that the present clash between Islam and the West represents a reawakening of a longstanding rivalry. His critics claimed that, if there is a rivalry, it is contingent; it is the result of short-sighted politicians on both sides having cultivated egotistical interests. A major taproot of Islamic terrorism lies in a complex interaction between self-serving Saudi rulers, short-sighted US politicians and desperate Soviet ideologues during the final phase of the Cold War.

The wars of terror owe much to the 1979 Soviet invasion of Afghanistan which triggered an Afghan civil war which quickly attracted the attention of external powers. The US government initiated an anti-communist alliance between the USA, Saudi Arabia and Pakistan. The USA gave moneys and weapons to Pakistan's dictator Zia ul-Haq. Zia in turn sponsored Pushtun leaders in Afghanistan to fight the Soviet invaders. Saudi Arabia, too, supported native Afghan leaders. But the Saudis did more: they also emphasized the religious duty of all Muslims to fight enemies of Islam and funded campaigns to organize brigades of international volunteers. Zia admitted these international volunteers to Pakistan and built training camps for them. Saudi Arabia sent instructors to the camps to teach the international volunteers techniques of irregular warfare and sabotage. In addition the Saudis sent theologians who preached a radical *jihadi* version of Wahhabi Islam.

One of the most consequential of the Saudi organizers was Osama bin Laden. Together with the Palestinian leader Abdallah Azzam he developed al-Qaida al-Sulba, an international non-governmental organization designed to fight Western enemies of Islam. When Azzam was killed by a car bomb in 1989, Osama bin Laden took over al-Qaida and transformed it to an elite organization with global reach. He built camps to receive Muslim volunteers from all over the world and train them in techniques of sabotage and terror and instil in them a radical Islamist theology that justified *jihad* against Jews and Crusaders (Wright 2007). On 11 September 2001 bin Laden's organization launched its most ambitious terrorist attack ever: members of a *jihadi* cell in Hamburg hijacked US passenger planes and crashed them into the twin towers of the World Trade Center in New York and the Pentagon.

Changing perceptions

The 9/11 terrorist attack sparked a chain of events that shattered the optimism of the post-Cold War world. The immediate reaction of the US President George W. Bush was to declare a 'war on terror'. Since terror was global, the war on terror must be global also, Bush reasoned. The theory was sound; the practice disastrous.

Massive misadventures

President Bush responded, first, by invading Afghanistan and conspiring to unseat the Taliban government there – an Islamist regime which had unified the clan-based country but under a repressive, Islamist regime that hosted bin Laden and his al-Qaida organization.

Second, Bush upgraded the USA's global intelligence network in order to discover and monitor the several secret terrorist cells that bin Laden had reportedly established around the world. America's allies quickly followed suit. Authorities all over the world introduced checkpoints at airports and at the entrance of public buildings. Legislators passed 'terror laws' which expanded the domestic activities of intelligence services and permitted the use of new interrogation techniques of terrorist suspects.

Third, in March 2003, the Bush administration expanded the military operations in its war on terror. American troops invaded Iraq, unseated its dictator Saddam Hussein, appointed a new government and worked hard to create a new and friendly government based on the principle of popular sovereignty. The USA had beaten another wasps' nest and prompted angry reactions that threatened to destabilize an entire region.

In Afghanistan the US invasion destroyed the Islamist regime of the Taliban. It established a new, constitutional government in Kabul. But the new government was unable to project its authority into the country's many provinces where clan leaders and warlords had returned to power.

In Iraq the US invaders destroyed Saddam Hussein's Baath party and his army – the two main institutions of social order. This destroyed the livelihood of up to half a million able-bodied government employees. These men, suddenly barred from government employment and denied pensions, were angry. They were also armed and they swarmed across Iraq and fought the American effort to establish an order which had no place for them. Many of them were experienced officers with special skills in intelligence and strategic planning. Some of them organized resistance movements. Others joined existing movements. These men quickly advanced to leading positions in anti-Western groups. They constituted a major force behind the expansion of al-Qaida and the rise of other radical Sunni movements in Iraq and Syria, such as the Islamic State of Iraq and the Levant (ISIL). In sum, the 2003 invasion in Iraq paved the way for the chaotic, frontless war in Iraq and Syria; the greatest humanitarian disaster of the new millennium.[7]

The American war on terror fuelled the fires of complex conflicts in a region where tinder had been gathered for decades – a vast geographical belt stretching from the Sahara in the west and eastwards through Egypt and the Middle East, across the fertile crescent and the post-imperial remnants of the Soviet empire, and further along the foothills of the Hindu Kush through Afghanistan, Pakistan and northern India. In this vast region the US war on terror ignited flammable mixes of oil, religion, anti-Western rancour and post-imperial rivalries.

Military forces from the USA and its Western allies got stuck in irregular wars in Afghanistan and Iraq. The operations were condemned in the Arab world – in many places in radical, *jihadist* terms. Condemnations and threats fuelled Western concerns of national security. Authorities appointed commissions to assess the vulnerability of their nations. Governments established agencies for homeland security. Legislators passed 'terror laws' which widened the scope of national surveillance and intelligence services and allowed new interrogation techniques for terrorist suspects. Sudden concerns with national security and public safety washed across the Western world. The concerns were whipped to a pitch by spectacular terrorist acts – for instance in Madrid (March 2004), London (July 2005) and Paris (November 2015) – and by reports that national intelligence services had arrested Muslims who planned acts of terror.

This concern for security altered the tone in Western migration debates. Leaders of the populist right tended to conjure up images of immigrants not only as destroyers of national cultures but also as threats to public safety. Some groups argued that all of Western civilization was threatened by alien enemies who were settling in the West in increasing numbers; that catastrophe might still be averted but that time was getting dangerously short.

Each country addressed the immigrant question in its own terms. Yet, there were some common themes. In all countries right-wing parties tended to single out immigrant groups that were non-Western and to portray them as determined, monolithic, close and increasing in number. And although these arguments echo the fascist myths of the 1930s, they do not invoke support from the biological theories of old. Rather, they are cast in cultural terms. It is not the European race which is threatened but European culture or civilization. The main threat is coming not from the Jews but from Islam. Samuel Huntington had formulated such claims in his controversial book *Clash of Civilizations*. Huntington's observations have since been twisted and elaborated by writers from within the anti-immigration movement. Some of them have, for example, introduced the term 'Eurabia' to indicate that Europe has slid under Muslim influence (Marján and Sapir 2010).

Islamists invoked a medieval discourse that vilified the Christian crusades. Anti-Islamists, too, summoned medieval Christian symbols. But they hailed the Crusaders – in fact, they hailed all historical leaders who fought the Moors, among them the Castilian soldier El Cid (Rodrigo Dìaz) and Polish King Jan Sobieksi who helped defeat the Ottoman Turks outside the gates of Vienna. Islamists and anti-Islamists, then, evolved similar understandings of the post-Cold War world. They phrased the international situation in civilizational or religious concepts and perceived the essential issues in remarkably similar terms.

From headlines to trend lines

Judged by newspaper headlines and TV news, the twenty-first-century world is in a terrible fix. Western governments are portrayed as fragile. Airlines, subways, railway stations and shopping malls are seen as vulnerable to terrorist attacks. The world seemed suddenly filled with violence and war.

'Seemed' is the operative word here. For if we lift our gaze, look behind the newspaper headlines and follow the larger trend lines, the world does not appear more violent and warlike than before but less. Much less.

Steven Pinker goes so far as to claim that

> violence has declined over the long stretches of time, and today we may be living in the most peaceable era in our species' existence … Though it may be hard for news readers to believe, since the end of the Cold War in 1989, organizing conflicts of all kinds – civil wars, genocides, repression by autocratic governments, and terrorist attacks – have declined throughout the world. (Pinker 2011, pp. xxi, xxiv)

The fact of the matter is that after the end of the Cold War violence had fallen. The numbers of wars has declined steeply – as indicated by Figures 14.1 and 14.2 in the previous chapter. The number of people who have been killed in war has fallen steadily over many decades – from an annual number of about five hundred thousand just after World War II to fewer than one hundred thousand after the end of the Cold War.[8] Flare-ups of civil war in Iraq, Libya and Syria in the wake of the 'Arab spring' have increased the numbers again.

If Pinker (2011) is right, and we are 'living in the most peaceable era in our species' existence', why do we generally perceive the world to be more violent than ever? The most immediate answer is 'because of the communications- and information revolution made possible by digital technology'. The electronic news media, in other words, must take much of the blame for why we feel more insecure in a world where war and violence are declining.

Both structure and content of the media were transformed by the digital technologies that were introduced during the 1980s and 1990s. The first cable news channels and the digital media, which were introduced precisely at the time when the Cold War ended, affected public opinion. TV news anchors' quest for the dramatic and the picturesque helped create a misleading image of the world as a more conflictual and violent place. They were able to do this because digital technologies have made the world more transparent.

Transparent world

Transparency is a double-edged sword. On the one hand it makes it possible to record acts of violence and oppression all over the world. The new information technologies have made it difficult for dictators to conceal their acts of discrimination, repression and injustice. The new media have blunted the main, old resource of totalitarian dictatorships: namely, a monopoly of information, through which they could indoctrinate their populations. In this sense, the new communications technologies have altered the conditions of politics in favour of systems of popular sovereignty. When Ridley Scott's 1984 Apple commercial echoed the libertarian sentiment of the times and presented computer manufacturers as liberators of humankind – as the enemies of 'Big Brother' – he was right. However, some twenty years later companies like Apple had become Big Brother.

On the other hand: because the net is transparent, people who possess the right technical skills can tap it for messages, monitor millions of electronic transactions, mine them for information and put them to profitable use. Private advertisers use such net-based information all the time. Advertising 'is like a radar sweep, constantly hunting new prospects as they come into the market. Get a good radar and keep it sweeping', wrote David Ogilvy, the father of Madison Avenue, in his classic 1963 business book *Confessions of an Advertising Man*. Half a century later, computer technology opened up unprecedented opportunities for Ogilvy's strategy. Techniques of behavioural profiling and extreme personalization can identify the location, gender, marital status, shopping habits, travel plans, interests, and browsing history of users and target them for specific messages. Gathering information about Internet users and grouping them into 'segments' have become big business. Thousands of specialist firms have grown up across the Web. They insert cookies, Web beacons, e-tags and a variety of other tools into millions of private PCs to extract information about the users.[9]

Questions have been raised whether the users' right to privacy is violated by such practices – especially when advertisers follow users from site to site. Questions have also been raised about the implications for society. As advertisers adopt techniques of behavioural profiling through the Internet, they reduce advertisement in traditional print media. Since most newspapers get most of their income from ads, their main source of income dries up. What happens to public opinion when citizens' information sources change from paper to screens? What happens to citizens' knowledge of current events and to democratic participation when print media wither and die? Or when influential newspapers are bought up by billionaires and conglomerates?

Private firms exploit the net. So do states. Government agencies distribute information – just like advertisement agencies. 'Sputnik International' – established by the Russian government in October 2014 – may serve as one example among many. It broadcasts news – which other governments would call propaganda – in some twenty-five languages. Its aim is to advertise the official views of the Russian government and to influence the international public opinion.

Also, government agencies block information streams. China, for example, has built Internet filters known as the 'great firewall' – a vast mechanism designed to ensure 'digital sovereignty' (which is 'censorship' by another name). The intention is to prevent Chinese citizens from using Facebook, Google, YouTube and Twitter.

Finally, government agencies collect information – about their own citizens as well as those of other countries. All Great Powers – and a good many not-so-great powers – have expanded their capacity to siphon off electronic signals from world-wide communications networks. Immediately after 9/11, the USA established a tight, top-secret worldwide surveillance system. It was run by the US National Security Agency (NSA) in close co-operation with the security services of America's allies – among them Australia (ASD), Britain (GCHQ) and Canada (CSEC). The system tapped directly into the world's main communications arteries and siphoned off information streams from Apple, Facebook, Google, Skype, Yahoo and other Internet actors (Greenwald 2014). It collects, stores and analyses e-mails, telephone conversations, browser activities and social-media traffic.[10]

Digital information systems have not only been opened up to surveillance and cyber espionage; they have made possible the stealthy hacking into other countries' software, computers or networks. The USA is constantly being attacked by foreign hackers who seek access to the Pentagon and to US defence contractors.[11] It is believed that Chinese hackers in 2015 broke into the files of the US Office of Personnel Management and stole information on over twenty million federal employees – including millions of security clearance applications. But the USA is also doing its share of hacking – it has for example spied on Iran. Also, the Americans have developed novel types of covert action – not merely acts of cyber espionage but of digital infiltration. The Americans have reportedly used techniques of cyber sabotage to compromise Iran's secret nuclear programme.[12] Britain is supposed to have infiltrated an al-Qaida website and replaced the recipe for making pipe bombs with the recipe for making cupcakes. In 2008, after it reported on China's repression on Tibet, CNN was attacked by Chinese hackers. In August that year, when Russian tanks rolled into South Ossetia, the invasion was attended by cyber-attacks designed to paralyse Georgian government websites.

It's a self-reinforcing dynamic. New technologies open up new opportunities for espionage and sabotage which in turn create greater need for surveillance and cyber security. The USA established a Cyber Command in 2009 to assist the traditional commands of the army, the navy and the air force. Several other countries followed suit. They built central command centres to co-ordinate cyber resources and organize defences of their digital networks – including those of big banks and financial institutions. Some observers question the very concept of cyber-war. Others believe it represents the major threat of our age. In 2013, several US intelligence officials considered cyber-war a larger threat to national security than al-Qaida or terrorism.

Methodological shake-ups

When the Cold War ended, a hopeful atmosphere of co-operation and solidarity descended on international diplomacy. This hopeful sentiment was subjected to a test in August 1990 when Iraqi strongman Saddam Hussein ordered a massive invasion of neighbouring Kuwait. The US President George H. W. Bush initiated a vast collective-security operation under UN auspices – much like President Truman had reacted to Kim Il-Sung's invasion of South Korea forty years earlier. During the final months of 1990, the USA organized a coalition of thirty-four states against Hussein and co-ordinated an enormous build-up of troops along the Iraqi border.

In January 1991, as the USA was making its final preparations for a massive invasion of Iraq, a curious essay appeared in the radical French paper *Libération* under the headline 'The Gulf War will not take place'. A couple of weeks later, when the USA invaded Iraq, its author, Jean Baudrillard, published a second essay, 'The Gulf War is not taking place'. In March, as the American-led coalition celebrated their victory, *Libération* printed Baudrillard's final word on the matter: 'The Gulf War did not take place'. Baudrillard's essays were received with incredulity, if not with irritation. They were largely brushed off as nonsense. He did, however, have one or two important points to make. One of them was that in the postmodern age, there are limits to our political knowledge.

Baudrillard raised doubts about the official US version of the Gulf War because he wanted to draw attention to the difficulties in obtaining firm and secure knowledge about politics in the postmodern era. He wanted to discuss the nature of the information which flows through electronic media. He wanted to discuss the contingent and ephemeral nature of the knowledge that resulted from it. He wanted to explore the value of some types of knowledge over other types. More than anything, he wanted to problematize the relationship between knowledge and political power.

One of Baudrillard's points was that there is no *one* true version of the Gulf War. That there is no *one* social reality. There are many realities. Each of them highly subjective and dependent on the identity of the observer – which is shaped and coloured by a variety of interacting factors. Another point was that knowledge yields power and that the evolution of the 'information society' opens up for new ways of wielding power.

These were hardly novel points. And Baudrillard was not alone in making them. Several authors had long criticized modern knowledge for being limiting, autocratic, oppressive, disciplining, and for being the indoctrinating tools of the powers that be. Some of the bolder claims were formulated by social philosophers in France, among them Roland Barthes, Michel Foucault, Jacques Derrida, Jean-François Lyotard, Gilles Deleuze – several of them members of a circle surrounding the radical French journal *Tel-Quel*. They were variously referred to under collective labels like postmodernists or post-structuralists. Their influence soon spread.

During the early 1980s, when IR theory was heavily influenced by structuralist approaches, critics emerged who had been steeped in French post-structuralism. In 1984, for example, Richard Ashley used post-structuralist arguments to write a stinging critique of Kenneth Waltz's structural Realism. Waltz's project is limiting and oppressive, argued Ashley (1984, p. 228). It 'treats the given order as the natural order, limits rather than expands political discourse, negates or trivializes the significance of variety across time and place'. What emerges in the end, Ashley continued, 'is an ideology that anticipates, legitimizes, and orients a totalitarian project of global proportions: the rationalization of global politics'.

Post-structural theories
The end of the Cold War and the collapse of the USSR surprised everybody. IR scholars were no exception. The Soviet collapse triggered huge debates in the IR community. The biggest discussions were not about the causes of the Soviet collapse; they were about why IR scholars hadn't seen it coming.

If IR was a science, why didn't IR scholars observe the weakening of the Soviet empire and debate its precarious nature? Why did no IR journal discuss the possibility of removing the Berlin Wall or reuniting Germany? Had IR scholars no academic imagination at all? The 'science of international politics' had accumulated theories for over a century; it had produced libraries of factual knowledge. Did this not give IR scholars any privileged insights at all into the march of international events? Outsiders poured salt in the wounds. Robert Conquest, the distinguished historian of Soviet affairs, expressed the attitude of many historians when he was asked about the lessons one should draw from the collapse of the USSR. 'If you are a student', he responded, 'switch from political science to history' (quoted in Gaddis 1992, p. 53). The predictive powers of IR have not been particularly impressive, noted Gaddis. 'One might as well have relied upon star-gazers, reading of entrails, and other "pre-scientific" methods' (Gaddis 1992, p. 18).

Questions such as these shook IR. Some of the answers shook even more. The post-structuralists, for example, argued that the basic methodology of IR, uncritically imported from the natural sciences, was misconceived, close-minded and limited. That the knowledge offered by established IR was oppressive and autocratic. That it did not serve the cause of knowledge as much as it served the established order and the powers that be. This critical point, famously argued by Rousseau in the mid-eighteenth century and expanded by for example Nietzsche in the nineteenth, was elaborated by Michel Foucault. His discussions of asylums, prisons, and sexual taboos showed how science has separated deviance from normal behaviour and has helped governments deal with deviance through disciplining and repressive techniques.

Many social scientists found Foucault (1973 [1966]; 1972) helpful in uncovering power structures in society. They were impressed by Foucault's archeological method because it showed them how systems of ideas and schools of social thought were constructed through human interaction. They embraced his discourse analysis because it served as a useful tool to uncover social inequalities and hierarchies of power. They adopted his genealogical approach because it showed them how systems of thought evolve, how they become justifying mechanisms for certain fields of knowledge and how they legitimize and sustain social inequalities and hierarchies (Foucault 1984b).

Students of IR found in post-structural analysis a way to break out of conventions. James Der Derian, for example, one of Hedley Bull's students, maintained that traditional IR has viewed interstate relations in light of Western and modern experiences. As a consequence they had mistakenly portrayed the history of diplomacy as a neat progression of reasonable interaction. He proposed to re-conceptualize diplomacy not as 'the art of negotiation' but as 'mediation of estranged peoples' (Der Derian 1987, p. 42). He took this notion of mediation among strangers from Nietzsche. And it resulted in a very different view of diplomatic history.[13] In fact, Der Derian argued that there is no *one* diplomatic history; there are many – and all of them are dependent upon the identity and the interests of the beholder.

Around 1990, as the USSR was unravelling and IR was shaken by a chain of bewildering events, post-structural approaches hit the discipline with full force. At a time where traditional radicalism was fading fast, post-structuralist approaches formulated radical themes in new ways. Behind the exterior of cynicism and irony were the old, social ideals of critical theory – that social research should unveil the mechanisms of repression, disclose practices of privilege and oppose the abuse of power. Post-structuralist arguments even sharpened the old left-wing diagnosis that the social-science ideal had been subverted by modern, positivist research methods (Adorno and Horkheimer 1979 [1944]). Post-structuralists maintained that positivist science twisted our perceptions and captured social-science research in an alien, technical discourse that did not serve insight and knowledge as much as it served the views of established elites (Rousseau 1950a). Also, post-structuralists were often informed by the same Romantic vision as traditional radicals – who argued that wealth and power corrupts and who therefore invested their hopes in the poor and the powerless masses of society; for, since they are poor, they are also unspoiled and uncorrupted and more authentically human than the wealthy elite (Marx and Engels 1974).[14] Radicals and post-structuralists tended to distrust power – and to see all ugly ducklings as potential swans.

There were differences between post-structuralism and old left-wing radicalism as well. One of them was that the post-structuralists did not rely on analyses of material forces (such as means of production); instead, they based their argument on analyses of ideational structures of society – on communicative interrelations, cultures and perceptions. Another difference was that post-structuralists did not rely on class analysis and did not proclaim solidarity with the working classes of the world; instead, they identified with a wide variety of minority groups which had been oppressed and marginalized by modern elites.

In IR the arrival of post-structuralism was signalled by a special issue of the *International Studies Quarterly* (*ISQ*), the flagship journal of the International Studies Association. The issue, which was entitled 'Voices from exile', castigated the positivist research methods of the hegemonic IR elite; instead it praised the 'sites of struggle' represented by migrants, post-colonial peoples, ethnic factions, religious sub-groups, sexual minorities, single mothers, environmentalists, peace activists and so on (Ashley and Walker 1990, p. 259).

Post-structural practice

The 'voices-of-exile' issue of the *ISQ* revived an old discussion about the relationship between knowledge and power. It relied heavily on the French social philosopher Michel Foucault, who renewed this discussion during the late 1970s with his empirically grounded demonstrations of the tight historical relationship between scientific knowledge, techniques of discipline and social order. It also invoked Edward Said, Palestinian-born professor of English and Comparative Literature, whose theory of 'orientalism' made a deep impression on IR scholarship.

Said studied Western literature. These writings, he found, were steeped in a Western sense of superiority that expressed patronizing perceptions of the people and the societies in the Middle East. Said argued that these Western attitudes of supremacy, which had been shaped during centuries of Western dominance and imperialism, had been continually re-presented by generations of writers – novelists, historians, anthropologists and area specialists – and preserved by academic practices in dominant scholarly communities. All academic communities had in turn been affected by these practices and by the attitudes they carried. One cannot understand the Middle East today without recognizing that the entire region is in some sense produced – politically, sociologically, militarily, ideologically, scientifically, and imaginatively – by the West, argued Said (1978, p. 3; also 1993).

And this was only the beginning of his argument. For when Said wrote that all academic communities were shaped by the discourses of the West, he included academic communities in the Middle East itself. In other words, whenever Middle Eastern intellectuals study their own societies, they do so from perspectives that have been shaped by the dominant Western culture of scholarship. When scholars from the Middle East study their own region, they do so through Western lenses.

Scientific discourse, then, is not neutral. It had disciplined research and shaped knowledge. Research about relations in the Middle East had carried with it constant re-presentations of the superiority of the West – and also quiet reminders of the inferiority of the rest. These re-presentations have in turn shaped the self-image of native scholars. Their identity as academics has affected their national and cultural identities. It has alienated them from their own culture and made them perceive their own region through concepts fashioned in the West. Said's argument was informed by theories from Rousseau, Hegel and Marx.[15] It relied in particular on Foucault's archeological method and explored the connection between power and knowledge.

Said's *Orientalism* [1978] had a big impact. It paved the way for a new academic field, postcolonial studies – a field which addresses identities of decolonized peoples. Postcolonial identities, it is argued, are shaped by cultural interactions and social relations of sex, class and caste; they are affected by the gender and the race of the colonized person but also by the racism inherent in the structures of a colonial society.

In IR, the postcolonial perspective has been expressed for example by John Hobson. His *Eastern Origins of Western Civilization* [2004] and his *Eurocentric Conception of World Politics* [2012] trace the evolution of Western theories of world affairs. The books criticize the study of IR and stress the connection between knowledge and power. This is particularly clear in *The Eurocentric Conception of World Politics*. It argues that IR is encased in a self-congratulatory tradition that stretches back to colonial times. The entire discipline of IR rests on the assumption that the West is sovereign – it has initiated its own evolution – whereas the East and the South have been passive bystanders to modern world history; that the West has possessed agency, whereas the rest has not.

The politics-of-knowledge argument, pioneered by Said and embraced by postcolonial studies, has also affected other fields. The study of sexual orientation and gender identity (SOGI) is one such field. SOGI writers often note how some nations are marked by provisions of sexual tolerance and identity whereas others are marked by persecution and homophobic legislation. They often add that the former tend to be 'modern' or 'Western' societies, whereas the latter tend to be societies that have suffered experiences of colonization (Butler 1997).

The politics-of-knowledge argument has also been imported into more established fields. Women's studies have, for example, been renewed by it. In IR, this emphasis on the politics of knowledge is well represented by Ann Tickner. She expressed the core argument well in an article entitled 'You Just Don't Understand'. First, she blamed mainstream IR for omitting gendered perspectives. Then, she criticized IR for insisting that serious research – including feminist research – should develop scientific, falsifiable theories. This was a fundamental misunderstanding of feminist IR, argued Tickner (1997). Most feminist IR theory does not take an orthodox, scientistic approach to knowledge; it takes a post-structuralist approach. It argues that orthodox theories reflect the gendered positioning of their authors and that these theories obscure the gendered nature of IR theories. Tickner rejected the usual scientific methodologies for being 'top-down' and focusing on masculinist subjects such as men, money and war. Tickner favoured a social, 'bottom-up' methodology that could make the role of women in IR visible. Similar arguments were presented by authors like Cynthia Weber (1994), Christine Sylvester (2002), Cynthia Enloe (2004) and many others.

Philosophy and fragmentation
Post-structuralism opened up new perspectives and cultivated new approaches to IR. The study of international politics had always drawn on other disciplines. From its earliest times it had drawn on theology, philosophy and history. Through the

modern ages it had drawn on law and economics. After World War II IR scholars had included theories from psychology (Fanon 1963), sociology (Aron 1966), and anthropology (Bull 1977); then from evolutionary psychology (Masters 1968; Axelrod 1984) and literary criticism (Said 1978). However, it was Kenneth Waltz (1975; 1979) who opened the doors to a systematic debate on these theoretical inclusions. He asked questions about what kind of field IR really is and wondered about what kind of theories are appropriate for this field, and what kind of philosophy of science could best provide it with a scholarly foundation.

In the first chapter of *Theory of International Politics* [1979] Waltz presented a philosophy of science that he tailor-made for the study of IR. It triggered enormous discussions. IR was never the same again. Many scholars were deeply impressed with Waltz's argument and accepted it. Other scholars were profoundly critical and tried to produce alternative methodological foundations. Steve Smith was one of the most diligent toilers in this regard. He produced, together with Martin Hollis, a most influential alternative to Waltz's philosophy of science (Hollis and Smith 1991). Hayward Alker was another influential contributor. He edited, together with Michael Shapiro, a book which drew on anthropological theories of identity to explore international relations. Alker, always at the cutting edge, had pioneered mathematical approaches to IR during the 1960s (Alker 1965); thirty years later he enriched IR with post-structuralist approaches and humanistic methodologies (Alker 1996; Marlin-Bennett 2011).

The immediate aftermath of the Cold War was an extraordinarily dynamic period in IR theory. Giddens (1990), Appadurai (1990) and others introduced new concepts of globalization. Samuel Huntington (1991) published his analysis of recurrent waves of democracy in global politics. Martin Hollis and Steve Smith (1991) proposed a new philosophy of science for IR. Francis Fukuyama (1992) elaborated his thesis on the 'end of history'. Bruce Russett (1990; 1993) published his influential theory of the democratic peace. A host of critical voices began to re-examine the nature and the history of IR…

These years were, first, marked by the reintroduction of philosophical concerns – by questions pertaining to philosophy of science and by new social theories.

Secondly, the introduction of philosophical concerns and social theories weakened the old notions of levels of analysis. It weakened the old distinction between politics within states and politics among states (Walker 1993). International issues were increasingly discussed in terms that were imported from general social theory and domestic politics. The old image of the interstate system was subtly encroached upon by a new vision of an international society. International politics was increasingly presented in terms of social processes. International relations were seen as affected by mechanisms of socialization, communication and language. International politics was increasingly cast in terms that were previously reserved for domestic affairs. It was affected by notions that society could be shaped and formed by intervention, organization and legislation.

The effect was, third, that the old field of IR was losing some of its old identity. Partly because it was pulled away from its old core questions by increasing competition from new academic fields which discussed international issues – by global political economy, by globalization research and by post-colonial studies – partly because it was pushed in different directions by a variety of special concerns – by ethnic politics, gender studies, women's studies and philosophy of science. During the first decade of the new millennium IR began to resemble a shopping-mall food court. The various outlets had something for every taste. Each student could fill a tray with specialized concerns and join one of the many sub-groups of like-minded academics gathered around one of the several small cafeteria tables – each carrying on its activities in isolation from the rest.

For a century or more the scholarly study of IR had orbited the twin questions concerning causes of war and preconditions of peace. By 2000, direct questions of war retreated in importance. The Western world experienced 'the most peaceable era in our species' existence' (Pinker 2011, p. xxiv). IR lost the gravitational pull of its old preoccupation. It was pursuing all kinds of new questions. But owls fly at dusk. Just as some scholars were leaving the old, disciplinary framework behind, others began to search for its genesis and its true identity.

Disciplinary history
One of the specialized interests that emerged in the dynamic aftermath of the Cold War retained the core concerns of classical IR: the sub-field of disciplinary history, which sought to systematically investigate the nature and the history of 'the science of international politics'. David Campbell (1992) drew on Nietzsche's genealogy to reject conventional notions of security and introduce an alternative concept based on concepts of identity and interaction.[16] Torbjørn Knutsen (1992), motivated by Foucault's archeology of knowledge, wrote a broad overview of the history of IR theory. R. B. J. Walker (1993) used Nietzsche as well as Foucault to 'destabilise seemingly opposed categories by showing how they are at once mutually consti-tutive and yet always in the process of dissolving into each other' (p. 25). The Australian authors Bradley Klein and Jim George argued that the key concepts of IR – such as 'deterrence', 'balance of power', 'alliances', and others – acquire their meaning from concrete political circumstances. Klein (1994) showed how the USA after World War II remade the world order in its own image of Western identity. George (1994) sought to deconstruct modern, mainstream IR theory through post-structural arguments, and then provided a reintroduction to the history of IR theory. Cynthia Weber (1995) relied on Baudrillard to explore the conceptual pair sovereignty/intervention, which, she argued, lies undiscussed at the heart of modern IR theory. Jens Bartlesen (1995) invoked Foucault to challenge existing accounts of international history and reveal 'the unthought foundations of our political knowledge' (p. 4).

David Long and Peter Wilson (1995) placed disciplinary history on a more tradi-tional track by critically rereading the works of a dozen early twentieth-century authors and examining their influence. Their edited book, *Thinkers of the Twenty Years' Crisis*, directed attention towards IR's main point of origin and defined questions which were quickly followed up by others. Edward H. Carr [1939] was a major focus of attention. His simplistic portrayal of the postwar idealists was criti-cally reassessed (Osiander 1998). It was questioned whether his legendary 'First Great Debate' had ever taken place (Ashworth 2002). Under the critical gaze of the new disciplinary historians, Carr's famous narrative of the origins of IR was discounted as a myth (Wilson 1998; Knutsen 2007). Brian Schmidt made a major contribution to the new field of disciplinary history with an empirically grounded early account of IR in America: *Political Discourse of Anarchy* [1998].

The new theoretical landscape – structural Realism and after

The world changed with the collapse of the Soviet Union. The scholarly field of IR had begun to change long before. First, the substance of IR had broadened to include several new issues – such as political economy and finance, the politics of energy, ecology, gender and human rights and so on. Second, the methodology of IR was affected when the publication of Waltz's *Theory of International Politics* [1979] triggered a vigorous debate about the proper philosopy of science of the field. Its waves were felt for a generation. It affected debates on both theory and method. It dominated academic IR during the 1980s. The publication of Waltz's book unleashed another 'Great Debate' (Lapid 1989).

Basic dimensions of social analysis

In order to explain the new orientation, authors like Wendt reintroduced some of the most basic arguments in social philosophy. The final section of this long chapter will follow Wendt's lead. It will first present a couple of the most basic distinctions in social theorizing. It will then illustrate these distinctions with a few examples from political theory. Finally, it will introduce some of the major contributions to IR theory. The purpose of this exercise is to create a conceptual grid which may provide order to the overcrowded contemporary discipline of IR.

One of the most basic distinctions in social philosophy is between individualist and systemic (or holistic) theories. On the one hand are theories which see social events as the outcome of individuals who are driven by private motivations and their own reasoning. On the other are theories which present agents as shaped and coloured by the surrounding society. Individualist explanations are typically presented by neoclassical economists, who explain social events as the outcome of interrelations among individual agents. Systemic explanations, elaborated by theorists like Hegel, Marx and Durkheim, present the whole as more than, and qualitatively different from, the sum of the parts. The debate between these two basic approaches – the so-called 'agent-system' or 'agent-structure' debate – has a long tradition in the social sciences (Crozier and Friedberg 1977; Martinussen 1999).

Another basic distinction in social philosophy is between materialist and idealist approaches. The materialists hold that all things are ultimately composed of physical matter. Idealists do not dispute the material reality of the world, but argue that human activities are not governed by material forces alone. Spiritual concerns propel human action. It is beliefs, values, norms and ideas that define the goals that humans set for themselves. They determine the purpose towards which humans choose to apply their material resources. From the material point of view the world is composed of physical properties; from the ideational point of view, social processes cannot be understood in material terms alone.[17]

A typology of social-science ontologies

Plato is often said to be the prototypical representative of the ideational approach. He explained that, in addition to the material world, there exists an eternal realm of immaterial 'forms', of which material objects are imperfect representations. Georg W. F. Hegel is also taken to represent the ideational outlook in political philosophy. For him 'the state is the actuality of the ethical Idea' (Hegel 1980, p. 155). It is mind objectified.

Thomas Hobbes presented a starkly different view. He reduced all things to material properties. For Hobbes (1951, p. 81) 'life is but a motion of limbs'. What is the human heart, he asked, 'but a "spring"; and the "nerves" but so many "strings"; and the "joints" but so many "wheels", giving motion to the whole body …'? For Thomas Hobbes the individual human being was essentially a complex machine. And society was an aggregation of such human machines. Thus, Hobbes can be placed in cell A, in Figure 15.1. Hobbes represents an ontology which combines a materialist outlook with an individualist orientation.

Karl Marx was also a materialist. However, he was not an individualist. Rather, he developed a holistic social philosophy. For him, the capitalist system shaped human life and the economic foundation of society shaped ideas, religion and laws. Material forces, in short, shaped society's cultural superstructure. Marx's ontology may be placed in cell B, where a material outlook combines with a holistic orientation.

Individualist vs holist/systemic perspectives

		Individualist	*Holist*
Basic social outlook	*Material*	A (Hobbes)	B (Marx)
	Ideational	D (Locke)	C (Rousseau)

Figure 15.1 Four basic types of social theory

Jean-Jacques Rousseau criticized the materialist argument. He argued that Hobbes was a product of his age and that the violent conflicts of that age coloured Hobbes's perception of humanity. When Hobbes imagined a state of nature, he simply removed all laws from England of his own times, Rousseau averred. As a result, Hobbes's natural man was very English and much concerned with satisfying 'a multitude of passions that are the product of [English] society and have made laws necessary' (Rousseau 1950a, p. 222).

Rousseau also held that, when children are born, they are not simply placed in a material world; they are also introduced into a language. As they adopt that language, not as a matter of choice but as a matter of course, they begin to perceive the world through the terms and concepts that are specific to that language. Rousseau's argument can be placed in cell C, where an ideational outlook is combined with a holist orientation. Max Weber's famous criticism of Marx flowed from a similar ontology. Weber rejected the claim that capitalism shaped human ideas and countered it by arguing that it is in fact specific human ideas – most particularly the norms and values, or the 'ethic', of Protestantism – that have paved the way for capitalism. Not the other way around (Weber 1958).

Bishop John Bramhall (1658) protested against Hobbes's materialistic and mechanical philosophy in similar terms. Thomas Hobbes could not, in Bramhall's mind, account for human conduct in society without referring to human knowledge about good and evil. Bishop George Berkeley tended to agree.

Rousseau, Weber, Bramhall and Berkeley opposed the mechanical materialism of authors like Hobbes and Marx. Bramhall, Berkeley and Rousseau agreed that materialist factors alone cannot account for human knowledge of good and evil; it is necessary also to invoke values and norms. Bramhall, in contrast to Rousseau, saw society as a simple aggregate of individuals; his social philosophy may be placed in cell D. Here an ideational outlook combines with an individualist orientation. Here the good society is formed by rational humans who all know the difference between good and evil. Bramhall's basic ontology would later sustain more complex arguments that were famously pursued by social philosophers like John Locke and Jeremy Bentham.

Locke's argument is not so distant from Bramhall's. Locke claimed that human individuals possess Reason, and that Reason enables each individual to identify the Law of Nature. Individual human Reason, in other words, provided a basis for a common moral sentiment – the Law of Nature – which guides human actions in society. The vast majority of people, argued Locke, abide by Reason and follow the Law of Nature. However, a few people do not. As a result, the rational, law-abiding majority establish government in order to protect themselves against the transgressions of the law-breaking few.

Jeremy Bentham did not entirely agree. He had the same individualist orientation as Locke, but he had a more materialist leanings. He elaborated on a notion – which is found in Locke but not emphasized – that humans tend to seek pleasure and avoid pain. Bentham used this human tendency to greatly simplify endless old debates about how to define the two contested terms 'good' and 'bad'. Bentham simply posited that 'good' means pleasure and 'bad' means pain. Thus he could explain the human tendency to seek the good and avoid the bad without resorting to ethical and theological arguments. Also, he could explain human behaviour without having to resort to any abstract notion of natural law. Law, however, remained important to him. And he tended to agree with Locke that following one's desires may bring pleasure, but only following the law can bring happiness.

Early representatives of the Scottish Enlightenment interpreted Locke differently. Francis Hutcheson, for example, agreed that individual humans are endowed with Reason. But he added, rather like Bishops Bramhall and Berkeley, that humans are also endowed with an innate moral sentiment that guides their social actions.

Two of Hutcheson's most gifted students disagreed. David Hume and Adam Smith developed a more complex argument. In their view, human beings were not endowed from infancy either with natural Reason or with an innate moral sense; rather, humans were social beings who developed both faculties – Reason as well as moral sense – through social interaction during the course of their lifetime.

David Hume (1978) lived in France for a few years, read Continental philosophers and developed this view. He wrote essays in exile, in which he expounded on how social interaction gives rise to habit, custom, convention and shared norms. Individuals obey these norms. And through their obedience they recreate and maintain them, Hume argued.

Adam Smith (1982a) agreed. He accepted Hume's view that individualist and holist perspectives are insufficient by themselves. *Both* perspectives are necessary to understand human interaction and social order fully. Smith, like Hume, relied on elements from both cells C and D.[18] This view – which is highly ideational and attentive to how individual reason and social forces interact to construct both individual identities and social norms – has come to dominate the social sciences since the 1990s. In IR this perspective is commonly referred to as 'constructivism'. It is often juxtaposed to Realism and liberalism and presented as a third approach, or 'paradigm' in contemporary IR theory. However, constructivism is not so much an IR theory as it is a general perspective, a basic ontology, in social philosophy.

In sum, the classics of political philosophy referred to in Figure 15.1 capture most of the essential arguments in IR theory. Hobbes, Marx, Rousseau and Locke draw the basic arguments. If Hobbes's theories are enriched by the social philosophy of Spinoza; if Marx is expanded by Gramsci; if Rousseau is enriched with Hume; and if Locke is complemented with the political economy of Smith and the legal philosophy of Vattel and Bentham, then there are few arguments in twentieth-century IR that would surprise us.

A typology of post–Cold War IR theories
Theories of International Relations can, like other social theories, be discussed and sorted according to the general perspectives depicted in Figure 15.1. It is, for example, easy to recognize the distinction between individualist and holist perspectives in the figure as the first-image and third-image theories in Kenneth Waltz's 1959 book, *Man, the State and War*. Here Waltz claimed that the classic Realists relied on explanations that involved the properties of individual agents – and which can be placed on the individual level of analysis. Since the classical Realists were concerned with the material capabilities of states, they may be placed in cell A in the figure above – in other words, in the company of Thomas Hobbes.

The orthodox, radical followers of Karl Marx and Vladimir Lenin can be placed, together with their mentors, in cell B. Their material outlook combines with a holistic perspective of social phenomena. Immanuel Wallerstein's world-systems theory, which moves on production and exchanges of material goods, can also be placed near cell B. Robert Cox's (1981) approach cannot. Although he, too, relies on theories of production and exchange, Cox's argument does not fit easily into the materialist holism of traditional Marxism. Cox emphasizes social interaction and the dialectical relationship between economic base and cultural superstructure. When human beings produce and exchange goods and build and arrange their societies, they also produce social norms and cultural values – ideational forces which in turn affect their behaviour. Cox relied on Gramsci's dialectic, but he refined it and adapted his concept of hegemony to an analysis of international order. He ended up near cell C. Cox is no lonely swallow. After the collapse of the USSR, a good many IR scholars have involved ideational arguments, and the post-Cold War debates have tended to gravitate around cell C.

This has long been a busy corner. Members of the English School have long recognized the importance of ideational factors in maintaining order in international society. They discussed international norms and rules during the 1950s and 1960s. They saw such norms as an outcome of human interaction – as is apparent in authors like Charles Manning (1962) and Hedley Bull (1977). They both distinguished between an international *system* and an international *society*; they were more concerned with the latter and portrayed it as infused with norms and rules that emerged from sustained, social interaction. In fact – as the previous section suggests – such holist-ideational approaches go back to late-Enlightenment English thinkers like David Hume (1978). Hume was in turn inspired by Jean-Jacques Rousseau and by legal philosophers who explained the origin of law through the social interaction among human agents.

The Humean arguments were present in Realist authors. Most clearly so in Halford J. Mackinder (1919), who used Hume's terms of habit, custom, convention and shard norms to explain the origins of international order. A similar argument is evident in Hans Morgenthau, who noted how absolute monarchs, through their interaction, gave rise to common norms and rules of international conduct. These notions have returned after the end of the Cold War in the cumbersomely labelled school of neoclassical Realism. Echoes of Hume are also present in the so-called constructivist approaches; this is evident in the writings of, for instance, Friedrich Kratochwil (1981), who based his contribution to the constructivist approach on Hume's analysis of international relations.

These types of social theorizing, depicted in Figure 15.1, reflect some basic dividing lines among the many IR theories that have emerged since the late 1980s. They provide an easy way to summarize the most common positions in the big debate that was sparked by Waltz and his structural Realism and to order the arguments that resulted. The result is indicated in Figure 15.2.

Briefly told, there are arguments which are individualist in orientation and materialist in perspective. Hobbes and the classic Realists belong here together with the game-theorists and rational-actor strategists.

Then, there are arguments that are material in outlook and systemic (or holistic) in perspective. This is the basic ontology of the classic Marxists. It is retained in the early version of world systems theory.

A third type of argument accepts the holistic perspective but rejects materialism and replaces it with an ideational orientation. These types of argument evolved during the late 1980s. They were greatly encouraged by the end of the Cold War and were much debated. The debates have especially concerned the relative import of individual agents versus social structures. During this so-called 'agent-structure' debate, variations evolved on the ideational theme and produced a range of refined arguments; many of which tend to echo arguments from classical political economy – such as that of Adam Smith.

A fourth type of argument evolved among scholars who entertained an individualist ontology but who were weary of the ideational orientation. One could argue that this group include the neo–liberal arguments of the post-Cold War era. Some of them would argue that social order is impossible if values, norms and rules do not in effect regulate individual behaviour (the 'institutionalists'); others would argue that human individuals are rational and that they will take responsibility for their own behaviour when given full freedom ('the market fundamentalists'). In this region of the theoretical map are also found the arguments of the rational-actor strategists and the game theorists.

Individualist vs holist/systemic perspectives

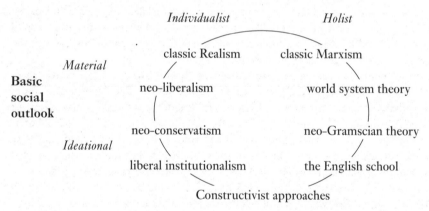

Figure 15.2 A simple wheel of basic IR theories

A world in flux

This chapter has discussed IR theories that have made their mark after the end of the Cold War. It has noted that during the many decades of the Cold War, when international politics was dominated by the superpower rivalry, IR theory was mainly concerned with superpower relations. The collapse of the USSR and the end of the Cold War put an end to this bipolar system and to traditional IR theory. The end of the Cold War was a game-changing event. And, like all big events, it triggered big discussions. These discussions, like similar discussions following big events in the past, produced variations on old arguments, adjusted perspectives and brought forth new IR theories.

Discussions of the past

This book has noted how the Italian wars (1494–*c*.1529) sparked discussions that were recorded by Machiavelli, Guicciardini and other Renaissance authors. It has noted how discussions stirred up by the Thirty Years War (1618–48) motivated Grotius, Crucé, Hobbes and others to probe the causes of war and peace. It has suggested that the turbulence that marked the Enlightenment age – from the wars of Spanish Succession (1701–14), through upheavals and revolutions to the Napoleonic Wars (1791–1814) – produced discussions about the causes of war (Rousseau 1964c; Hume 1985b; Paine 1986) and the preconditions for international order – both theories of balance of power (Hume 1985c; Robertson 1896) and proposals for perpetual peace (Rousseau 1964a, b; Madison et al. 1987; Kant 1979; Bentham 1843a; see also York 1919).

The book has shown how the crises and wars that broke out in the wake of the Industrial Revolution did not only trigger discussions; they also stimulated the rise of an international community of scholars. Around the middle of the nineteenth century, these scholars began to treat earlier discussions in more systematic ways. They reviewed earlier arguments on the causes of war and the preconditions for peace; they mapped these arguments and sorted them into approaches or schools. They established analytic traditions. By the end of the century they also affected a growing peace movement and established institutions of international research and education. With the outbreak of World War I, diplomats and statesmen joined the effort to strengthen such institutions and establish a new *science* of international politics.

Since then, scholarly discussions about war and peace have taken place within such institutions. Academics and politicians have drawn on traditions which have been formalized within these institutions – traditions that emphasize contributions made by Machiavelli, Grotius, Hobbes, Rousseau, Hume, Kant and other past authors (see for example Earle 1943; Forsyth et al. 1949; Hinsley 1967). Scholars have assessed the arguments of Thucydides, Machiavelli and Hobbes – whose concept of a 'state of nature' provided a systemic view on the causes of war and whose notion of 'social contract' provided arguments for the preconditions of peace. They have compared and contrasted them with arguments formulated by Grotius, Bentham and Kant. When G. Lowes Dickinson (1916) wondered, in the autumn of 1914, why the Great War had broken out, he found his answer in Thucydides and Hobbes. When Hobson (1915) and Woolf (1916) wondered how a robust peace could be established after the war, they used as their vantage point the notion of a 'contract' among states.

Hobbes relied on Thucydides. Dickinson relied on Thucydides and Hobbes. IR scholars have, like them, stood on each other's shoulders. Arguments and perspectives of past authors have informed the academic debates of the present. Past efforts to identify patterns and regularities in the macro-politics of their times are essential contributions to the knowledge base of International Relations. Diplomatic history and scholarly debates of the past provide the academic IR community with its distinct identity.

Events of the present

The collapse of the USSR meant that the USA was left as the world's only super-power. It involved the deflation of the Soviet ideals of the one-party state and the centrally planned economy, and it meant the rise to pre-eminence of American ideals. The bipolar system of the Cold War was replaced by a unipolar configuration.

Unipolarity is a rare condition in world affairs. It is so rare, in fact, that IR authors have tended to brush it off as a temporary condition – Waltz (1979 saw it as short-lived because one state's rise to pre-eminence will set off a balance-of-power dynamic that will challenge it. Rather than exploring the concept of unipolarity, IR authors have tended to resort to terms like 'imperialism', 'empire' or 'hegemony'. When these terms were reintroduced during the 1990s, it was to make the point that the USA was more than the strong actor; the USA was also exerting an extraordinary influence on world affairs. Also, the big discussions on the nature of the post-Cold War world were deeply informed by American ideals of democratic politics and of free-market economics.

The discussants often formulated optimistic arguments that hinged on old, liberal concepts like 'rights', 'interdependence' and 'norms'. Rarely has Lord Keynes's famous quip from the 1930s been more appropriate than during these post-Cold War discussions. 'Practical men' Keynes (1936) had averred, 'who believe themselves to be quite exempt from any intellectual influence, are usually the slaves of some defunct economist.' This is particularly apparent in the discussion of 'globalization' – the most fashionable term of the 1990s. At the outset, the main participants revived arguments that surrounded older discussions of interdependence. On the one hand were those who echoed the liberal claims of for example Adam Smith and who claimed that globalization would lead to diversity, productivity and peace. On the other were those who echoed the radical views of Jean-Jacques Rousseau and who claimed that globalization involved a social division of labour which produced alienation, anomie, tensions and conflict.

A main topic in the post-Cold War discussion concerned the position of the USA. Was globalization simply another term for 'Americanization'? Could the USA maintain its pre-eminence over the longer haul? The USA could maintain its pre-eminence a long time, argued William Wohlforth (1999) – who elaborated on the concept of unipolarity and argued that it was a stable form of order in its own right. Other authors disagreed. They argued that the unipolar constellation was being undermined by the rapid economic development of big countries like China and India. Several countries in the East were growing faster than countries in the West and altering the world economy's centre of gravity. China was likely to catch up with the USA sooner or later, claimed Zakaria (2011), who pointed out that this did not mean that the USA is declining in absolute terms. The USA is growing but others are growing faster. This difference in growth rates would, over time, undermine the unipolar nature of the system and produce a multipolar world.

Zakaria's argument builds on a simple systems view, spun around an old-fashioned billiard-ball model of world politics. It excludes the idea that the internal development of states makes a difference. Domestic economic growth is in many countries restricted to a small elite; consequently, it is possible for a country to demonstrate growth in its economy while at the same time an increasing number of people live in poverty. Thus, economic growth is best converted into international power in countries where the wealth produced is distributed by domestic institutions in ways that increase the well-being of the population at large.

Also, Zakaria's simple systems view overlooks the importance of geography. States are territorial units; they are fixed in a distinct geographical space. In addition, states have inhabitants whose societies have been formed through time by historical events. And when these societies grow, they affect their entire neighbourhood. These are arguments made by Katzenstein (2005), Kissinger (2014) and others. They draw on authors as diverse as Mackinder (1900; 1919), Braudel (1982) and Huntington (1993; 1996). They see the emergence not so much of a multipolar world as of a multi*regional* world. They present a view of the world as consisting of several regions, each of which has been shaped by unique geographic conditions and historical experiences, which are guided by its own norms and values and which work according to its own dynamics.

The European region is highly institutionalized. Katzenstein and Kissinger agree that European states obey common norms defined by interacting international organizations. The Americas, too, are reasonably institutionalized. The region has seen a recent growth of regional organizations. And although Brazil is evolving into a powerful state, regional order is, ultimately, monitored and maintained by the United States. East Asia is marked by weak institutions. Here, regional order is maintained by a steadily stronger China. It's a unique property of the region that the rise of Chinese dominance has not produced balancing reactions – East-Asian politics does not seem to conform to predictions derived from Western balance-of-power theory. Rather than opposing China's pre-eminence, most states in the region seem to follow Chinese leadership. They seem to bandwagon rather than balance, and to become willing participants in a tributary system or, perhaps, a neo-imperial order.

Some regions are neither institutionalized nor dominated by an ordering state. Africa has some institutions but they are few and weak; and no single, pre-eminent state is monitoring and maintaining interstate order in the region. The same can be said for the Middle East. It is a politically diverse region. 'Here every form of domestic and international order has existed, and has been rejected, at one time or another' notes Kissinger (2014, p. 96). Charles Glass, ABC's Middle Eastern correspondent, goes further. There are social formations in the Middle East that does not deserve to be called states; they should be seen as clusters of clans or 'tribes with flags' (Glass 1991). After the end of the Cold War tribal conflicts are destroying some of these formations. Millions of people flee these disorderly regions. An increasing number of African and Middle Eastern refugees cross the Mediterranean or gather at strategic transit points to enter EU or other regions marked by stability and order. Everyone is troubled not only with the external threats of a rising Russia but also with internal burdens added by millions of political refugees.

The end of the Cold War inaugurated a period of great change in world affairs. It cannot be taken for granted that all the world's regions are subject to the same forces of change or that they will change in the same ways. Recent events have ignited new discussions and debates about how best to understand these changes and the world that they have produced. These discussions have been eager to explore arguments based on theories of social interaction. Military tensions and armed conflicts will produce new events, trigger other debates and reintroduce arguments about territorial security and power politics. The world is in flux. So is IR theory.

Notes

1 This discussion will no longer use the term 'the Third World'. The term was originally invented in the 1950s to carve out a political sphere which belonged neither to the First World nor the Second (Sauvy 1952). However, when the Second World collapsed, the notion of a 'Third World' lost its analytic meaning.

2 The old USSR was a union of fifteen republics. After the collapse of the USSR, eleven of them joined together and formed the CIS. The remaining four claimed independence.

3 By 2000 Yeltsin had resigned from power and arranged for the unknown and reasonably young Vladimir Putin to succeed him. Russia had not succeeded in establishing any robust institutions after the collapse of communism and the economy was collapsing. Putin represented one of the few still-functioning forces of order: the secret police. He used draconian means to break the wealthy oligarchs and bring the economy under government control. He strengthened the power of the executive and imposed a new, autocratic order on Russian society. He also restored the orthodox Church, stressed the traditional values of age-old Russia and created a new, nationalist sentiment. By 2004 a majority of Russians considered him the saviour of the country and re-elected him as president by a landslide.

4 Some Americans like to think that the ideas of Ronald Reagan also had some influence on the Soviet collapse – that his neo-liberal ideals and his firm anti-communism motivated the Soviet population and that his actions pushed the USSR into insolvency (Kristol and Kagan 1996). They exaggerate. They overestimate the effects of Reagan's early confrontational policy, and they underestimate the effects of the conciliatory policies towards the USSR during his second term – a policy which offered Gorbachev a chance to implement the 'new thinking' which stimulated the unravelling of the USSR (see e.g. Njølstad 2004). In addition they tend to forget that Reagan's confrontational policies created panic in the Kremlin and greatly increased the danger of nuclear conflict.

5 June 1989 was an important month. China was shaken by massive protests in Beijing's Tienanmen Square. Free elections in Poland triggered events which undermined the East European regimes – and ultimately the USSR itself.

6 This revival of religion was most conspicuously apparent in the Middle East, where new and radical versions of political Islam emerged in Shia as well as in Sunni communities and where tension increased between the two. But religion was also on the rise in the West, which experienced a resurgence of Christian faiths.

The collapse of the secular Soviet empire opened up possibilities for a remarkable revival of Orthodox Christianity in Russia. It also triggered a rejuvenation of Catholicism in post-communist countries all across Eastern Europe. The Americas, too, experienced a religious surge. Evangelical brands of Christianity, based on a personal relationship with Jesus Christ, expanded their influence. In South America Evangelical Christianity made substantial inroads into the Catholic culture. In North America, a surge in born-again theology was harnessed by the Republican Party, co-ordinated for political purposes and placed in the service of a neo-liberal (but social-conservative) political agenda. In the USA – as in Russia – the resurgence of religion brought with it 'traditional values' that were entwined with patriotic values and national myths. The rise of religion, in other words, tended to reinforce the resurgence of nationalism in many parts of the world.

7 It is tempting to ask the counterfactual question of how the new millennium would have begun if the Bush administration had not acted unilaterally but instead declared the 9/11 terrorist attack a crime against humanity and invited all nations to participate in a collective-security operation under the UN, rather than unilaterally beating wasps' nests – real and imaginary – around the world.

8 To be more exact: during the first few years after World War II, between three hundred thousand and six hundred thousand people were killed in battle; the numbers were driven up by the Chinese civil war (which ended in 1949) and by the Korean War (which began in 1950). The number of battle deaths then dropped like a brick following the death of Stalin. The number then increased steadily during the 1960s and early 1970s (reflecting the expanding process of decolonization). A new fall in the number of battle deaths took place during the late 1970s, only to be followed by a new increase during the 1980s (reflecting new conflicts in the Arab world, where civil wars in Afghanistan and the Iran–Iraq War contributed heavily to the increasing numbers of global battle deaths). For details, see discussions in Pinker (2011) and statistics produced by the Peace Research Institute of Oslo (PRIO) and Uppsala University.

9 The data brokers in eXelate, to take one example, 'educate and empower marketers at a time when customer data fluency is the most important competitive advantage'. One of the products they sell is 'men in trouble'; men who are presumed to have relationship problems because they are shopping online for flowers and chocolate. Another firm, IXI Services – which 'helps the nation's leading financial services and consumer marketing forms optimize marketing efforts' – sells a segment called 'burdened by debt: small-town singles'.

10 The vastness of these monitoring activities, first exposed by Edward Snowden through *The Guardian* in 2013, is discussed in Greenwald (2014).

11 The USA has been the victim of several co-ordinated waves of hacker attacks, which have tried to break into NASA and defence contractors like Lockheed Martin, Redstone Arsenal and Sandia National Laboratories. The attacks began in 2003. The USA has seen them as serious cases of cyber espionage, referred to them as 'Titan Rain' and suspected them to be of Chinese origin. The US suspicion has been a persistent cause of friction in Sino-American relations (Weimann 2014).

12 The USA has reportedly used a computer worm, 'Stuxnet', to infect programmable logic controllers (PLCs) which controlled the centrifuges that separated Iranian

nuclear material. The worm apparently caused the centrifuges to spin too fast, tearing themselves apart. It is supposed to have ruined almost one-fifth of Iran's nuclear centrifuges.

13 On another occasion, Der Derian (1992, p. 1) plays off Will Rogers's definition of diplomacy as 'the art of saying "Nice doggie" until you can find a rock'. This is a far cry from the definitions used by traditional diplomatic historians like Nicolson (1954, p. 2) or Hamilton and Langhorne (1995, p. 1).

14 Old-fashioned, materialist radicals distinguished between economic base of society and the ideational superstructure – where the second was determined by (and a mere reflection of) the first (Marx 1975b). The post-structuralists turned the old historical materialism on its head, emphasizing the formative importance of the ideational superstructure. Thus, they could also be labelled '*super*-structuralists' – a term which may be more telling than the ambiguous and unhelpful label '*post*-structuralists'.

15 It was noted in Chapter 5, above, how Rousseau was an early contributor to the basic logic of this argument. Hegel expanded upon this logic in his profoundly influential philosophy of knowledge and identity; they are famously present in his discussions of the social relationship between master and slave (Hegel 1980; but see also Fukuyama 1992).

16 Campbell's notion of security is tightly bound up with the notion of identity. And identity is in turn constructed in nations during the course of interaction through time and through differentiation between a 'self' and an 'other'. Security and identity, then, are intimately intertwined. The interconnection is reflected in the foreign policies of states, argued Campbell, who proceeded to examine US security policy as a national project designed to guard and preserve a national self.

17 The Russian-American sociologist Pitrim Sorokin wanted to avoid the terms 'ideal' and 'idealism', so he used the term 'ideational' instead to denote an antithesis to materialism. In order to avoid any confusion with the oft-mentioned 'Idealist' approach to IR, we will here follow Sorokin's example.

18 To be clear on this: it is widely recognized that David Hume (1978, part III; 1985a, b) emphasized the role of habit, custom and convention in developing a society of states with shared norms and rules. It is often forgotten that Adam Smith held a comparable view. In his first book on political economy, *The Theory of Moral Sentiments*, Smith presented an argument along the same lines as his good friend David Hume – an argument which relies on a sophisticated combination of elements from both cells C and D. There has, however, been a tendency for Smith's second volume, *The Wealth of Nations*, to attract more attention and also to be read in isolation from the first. This has been the unfortunate habit of large congregations of market fundamentalists who have succeeded in creating the erroneous impression that Smith's argument lies somewhere between cells D and A.

Bibliography

Acheson, D. (1969) *Present at the Creation*. New York: W. W. Norton

Adorno, T. and M. Horkheimer (1979) *Dialectic of Enlightenment*. London: Verso [1944]

Airas, P. (1978) *Die geschichtlichen Wertungen Krieg und Friede von Friedrich dem Grossen bis Engels*. Rovaniemi: Pohjois-Suomen Historiallinen Yhdistys

Alker, H. (1965) *Mathematics and Politics*. New York: Macmillan

Alker, H. (1992) 'The Humanist Moment in International Relations', *International Studies Quarterly* 36(4): 347–73

Alker, H. (1996) *Rediscoveries and Reformulations: Humanistic Methodologies for International Studies*. Cambridge: Cambridge University Press

Allen, S. H. (1920) *International Relations*. Princeton: Princeton University Press

Allison, G. (1971) *Essence of Decision*. Boston: Little, Brown & Co.

Anderson, B. (1983) *Imagined Communities*. London: NLB

Anderson, M. S. (1988) *War and Society in Europe of the Old Regime, 1618–1789*. London: Fontana Press

Anderson, P. (1979) *Lineages of the Absolutist State*. London: NLB

Angell, N. (1903) *Patriotism under Three Flags*. London: Unwin

Angell, N. (1910) *The Great Illusion*. London: Heinemann

Appadurai, A. (1990) 'Disjunction and Difference in the Global Cultural Economy', *Theory, Culture & Society* 7(2): 295–310

Appleby, J. O. (1978) *Economic Thought and Ideology in Seventeenth Century England*. Princeton: Princeton University Press

Aquinas, T. (1947) *Summa Theologica*. New York: Benziger Brothers

Ardant, G. (1975) 'Financial Policy and Economic Infrastructure of Modern States and Nations', in Tilly, C., ed., *The Formation of Nation States in Western Europe*, pp. 164–242. Princeton: Princeton University Press

Arendt, H. (1951) *The Origins of Totalitarianism*. New York: Harcourt, Brace

Armstrong, D. (2002) 'Dick Cheney's Song of America', *Harper's* (October), pp. 76–83

Aron, R. (1966) *Peace and War*. New York: Doubleday

Aron, R. (1986) *Clausewitz: Philosopher of War*. New York: Simon & Schuster

Artz, F. B. (1967) *The Mind of the Middle Ages*. Chicago: University of Chicago Press

Ashley, R. K. (1984) 'The Poverty of Neorealism', *International Organization* 38(2): 225–86

Ashley, R. K. and Walker, R. B. J. (1990), 'Speaking the Language of Exile', *International Studies Quarterly* 34(3): 259–68.

Ashworth, L. M. (2002) 'Did the Realist-Idealist Debate Really Happen?', *International Relations* 16(1): 35–51

Ashworth, L. M. (2013) 'A New Politics for a Global Age', in Bliddal, H. C., C. Sylvest and P. Wilson, eds, *Classics of International Relations*, pp. 59–68. London: Routledge

Augustine of Hippo (1954) *The City of God*. New York: Fathers of the Church, Inc., Vol. VIII

Axelrod, R. (1984) *The Evolution of Cooperation*. New York: Basic Books

Babst, D. V. (1964) 'Elective Governments – a Force for Peace', *The Wisconsin Sociologist* 3(1): 9–14

Bacon, F. (1852) 'Notes of a Speech Concerning a War with Spain', in *Works of Francis Bacon*, Vol. II, pp. 199–201. Philadelphia: Hart, Casey & Hart [1624]

Bagehot, W. (1889) 'Physics and Politics', in *Works*, Vol. IV. Hartford, CT: The Travelers Insurance Co. [1872]

Bairoch, P. (1975) *The Economic Development of the Third World since 1900*. Berkeley and Los Angeles: University of California Press

Baran, P. and P. M. Sweezy (1966) *Monopoly Capital*. New York: Monthly Review Press

Barnes, T. (1981a, b) 'The Secret Cold War. The CIA and American Foreign Policy, 1946–1956', *Historical Journal* 24(2 and 3): 399–415; 649–70

Baron, H. (1952) 'Die Politische Entwicklung der Italienischen Renaissance', *Historische Zeitschrift* 174: 31–56

Barraclough, G. (1976) *An Introduction to Contemporary History*. Harmondsworth: Penguin

Bartelson, J. (1995) *A Genealogy of Sovereignty*. Cambridge: Cambridge University Press

Bary, W. T. de (1998) *Asian Values and Human Rights*. Cambridge, MA: Harvard University Press

Bass, G. J. (2008) *Freedom's Battle*. New York: Knopf Doubleday

Batscha, Z. and R. Saage, eds (1979) *Friedensutopien*. Frankfuhrt am Main: Suhrkamp

Baudrillard, J. (1995) *The Gulf War Did Not Take Place*. Bloomington: Indiana University Press

Beales, A. C. F. (1931) *A History of Peace*. New York: Dial

Bebel, A. (1893) *Die Frau und der Sozialismus*. Stuttgart: Dietz

Becker, K. L. (1932) *The Heavenly City of the Eighteenth-Century Philosophers*. New Haven: Yale University Press

Belli, P. (1936) *A Treatise on Military Matters and Warfare*. Oxford: Clarendon Press [1563]

Bender, P. (2004) *Weltmacht Amerika*. Berlin: Klett-Cotta

Bentham, J. (1843a) 'A Plan for an Universal and Perpetual Peace', in *Works*, Vol. 2, pp. 546–61. Edinburgh: William Tait [c.1794]

Bentham, J. (1843b) 'Emancipate your Colonies', in *Works*, Vol. 4, pp. 408–19. Edinburgh: William Tait

Bentham, J. (1843c) 'Principles of International Law', in *Works*, Vol. 2, pp. 531–61. Edinburgh: William Tait

Bentham, J. (1948) *The Principles of Morals and Legislation*. New York: Lafner [1789]

Berges, W. (1938) *Die Fürstenspiegei des hohen und späten Mittelalters.* Stuttgart: Hiersman Verlag

Bernhardi, F. von (1912) *Germany and the Next War.* New York: Longman, Green & Co.

Bertalanffy, L. von (1950) 'An Outline for General Systems Theory', *British Journal for the Philosophy of Science* 1(2): 134–65

Bertalanffy, L. von (1956) 'General Systems Theory', reprinted in Singer, J. D., ed. (1965) *Human Behavior in International Politics.* Chicago: Rand McNally and Co.

Bevin, E. (1945) 'On the Foreign Situation', memo by the Secretary of State for Foreign Affairs, 8 Nov. 1945, Foreign Office document (FO) 800.478 *MIS/45/14;* Public Records Office, London

Bharadwaj, A. (2008) 'Man, State and the Myth of Democratic Peace', *Strategic Analysis* 26(2): 305–15

Biersteker, T. and C. Weber, eds (1996) *State Sovereignty as Social Construct.* Cambridge: Cambridge University Press

Bismarck, O. von (1898) *Bismarck, the Man and the Statesman.* London: Smith, Elder & Co

Blainey, G. (1973) *The Causes of War.* New York: The Free Press

Bliddal, H., C. Sylvest and P. Wilson, eds (2013) *Classics of International Relations.* London: Routledge

Bloch, M. (1961) *Les rois thaumaturges.* Paris: Colin

Bodin, J. (1945) *Method for the Easy Comprehension of History.* New York: Columbia University Press [1566]

Bodin, J. (1967) *Six Books of the Commonwealth.* Oxford: Basil Blackwell [1576]

Bondanella, P. E. (1973) *Machiavelli and the Art of Renaissance Italy.* Detroit: Wayne State University Press

Bossuet, J.-B. (1824) *Politique tire des propres paroles de l'Écriture Sainte* Turin: Alliana [1679]

Botero, G. (1956) *The Reason of State and the Greatness of Cities.* New Haven: Yale University Press [1598]

Boulding, K. (1945) *The Economics of Peace.* New York: Prentice Hall

Boulding, K. (1962) *Conflict and Defence: A General Theory.* New York: Harper & Bros.

Bouthoul, G. (1951) *Les guerres, éléments de polémologie.* Paris : Payot

Bowman, I. (1922) *The New World. Problems in Political Geography.* New York: Yonkers-on-Hudson

Bozeman, A. B. (1960) *Politics and Culture in International History.* Princeton: Princeton University Press

Brailsford, H. N. (1914) *War of Steel and Gold.* London: Bell

Brailsford, H. N. (1917) *A League of Nations.* New York: Macmillan

Bramhall, J. (1658) *Castigations of Mr. Hobbes his last animadversions in the case concerning liberty, and universal necessity. With an appendix concerning the Catching of Leviathan.* London: J. Crook

Braudel, F. (1972) *The Mediterranean.* New York: Harper & Row

Braudel, F. (1977) *Afterthoughts on Material Civilization and Capitalism.* Baltimore: Johns Hopkins University Press

Braudel, F. (1982) *The Wheels of Commerce.* New York: Harper & Row

Bremer, S. A. (1992) 'Dangerous Dyads', *Journal of Conflict Resolution* 36(2): 309–41

Brierly, J. L. (1928) *The Law of Nations*. New York: Oxford University Press

Brodie, B., ed. (1946) *The Absolute Weapon: Atomic Power and World Order*. New York: Harcourt

Brodie, B. (1959) *Strategy in the Missile Age*. Princeton: Princeton University Press

Brown, P. M. (1923) *International Society*. New York: Macmillan

Brundtland, G. H. / World Commission On Environment and Development (1987) *Our Common Future*. Oxford: Oxford University Press

Bryce, J. (1888) *American Commonwealth*, Vol. 1. London: Macmillan & Co.

Buckle, H. T. (1862) *History of Civilization in England*. New York: Appleton

Bueno de Mesquita, B. (1981) *The War Trap*. New Haven: Yale University Press

Bukharin, N. (1973) *Imperialism and World Economy*. New York: Monthly Review Press [1915]

Bull, E. (1948) *Arbeiderklassen in norsk historie*. Oslo: Tiden Norsk Forlag

Bull, H. (1977) *The Anarchical Society*. New York: Columbia University Press

Burleigh, M. (2009) *Blood and Rage*. London: HarperCollins

Burleigh, M. (2013) *Small Wars, Far Away Places*. London: Macmillan

Burke, E., ed. (1772) *The Annual Register* (Vol. XV). London: J. Dodsley

Burke, E. (1866) 'Letter to a Member of The National Assembly ...', in *Works*, Vol. IV, pp. 1–57. Boston: Little, Brown & Co. [1791]

Burke, E. (1988) *Reflections on the Revolution in France*. Harmondsworth: Penguin [1790]

Burke, E. (1999) 'Speech ... on Moving His Resolutions for Conciliation with the Colonies', in *Selected Works of Edmund Burke*, vol. 1, pp. 221–84 [1775]. Indianapolis: LibertyFund

Burns, C. D. (1920) *International Politics*. London: Methuen

Burton, J. W. (1972) *World Society*. Cambridge: Cambridge University Press

Bush, G. H. W. and B. Scowcroft (1998) *A World Transformed*. New York: Knopf

Butler, J. (1997) *Excitable Speech*. London: Routledge

Butterfield, H. (1951) *History of Human Relations*. New York: Macmillan

Butterfield, H. and M. Wight, eds (1966) *Diplomatic Investigations*. Cambridge, MA: Harvard University Press

Buzan, B. (1991) *People, States and Fear*. New York: Harvester Wheatsheaf [1983]

Buzan, B. and G. Lawson (2015) *The Global Transformation*. Cambridge: Cambridge University Press

Buzan, B., R. Little and C. Jones (1993) *The Logic of Anarchy*. New York: Columbia University Press

Calleo, D. (1965) *Europe's Future*. New York: Horizon Press

Callières, F. de (1983) *The Art of Diplomacy*. New York: Holmes & Meier [1716]

Campbell, D. (1992) *Writing Security*. Minneapolis: Minnesota University Press

Canard, M. (1966) 'Byzantium and the Muslim World to the Middle of the Eleventh Century', in *Cambridge Medieval History*, Vol. IV part I (ed. J. M. Hussey), pp. 696–735. Cambridge: Cambridge University Press

Cardano, G. (1930) *The Book of My Life*. New York: Dutton [1574]

Carr, E. H. (1937) *International Relations since the Peace Treaties*. London: Macmillan & Co.

Carr, E. H. (1942) *Conditions of Peace*. London: Macmillan

Carr, E. H. (1945) *Nationalism and After*. London: Macmillan

Carr, E. H. (2001) *The Twenty-Years' Crisis, 1919–1939*. London: Palgrave [1939]

Carson, R. (1962) *Silent Spring*. Boston: Houghton Mifflin

Castiglione, B. (1959) *Book of the Courtier*. New York: Doubleday [1528]

Ceadel, M. (1987) *Thinking about Peace and War*. Oxford: Oxford University Press

Cellini, B. (1969) *The Autobiography of Benvenuto Cellini*. New York: Macmillan [1728]

Chailand, G. (2008) 'Stratégie politique et militaire de la guerre révolutionnaire', in *Les guerres irrégulières*, pp. 17–65. Paris: Gallimard

Chamber, R. (1844) *Vestiges of the Natural History of Creation*. London: John Churchill

Chamberlain, H. S. (1899) *Die Grundlagen des neunzehnten Jahrhunderts*. Berlin: Bruckmann

Chanteur, J. (1992) *From War to Peace*. Boulder: Westview

Chartier, R., ed. (1987) *A History of Private Life*. Cambridge, MA: Harvard University Press

Ch'en Po-ta (1953) *Stalin on the Chinese Revolution*. Beijing: Foreign Languages Press

Chomsky, N. (2008) *Hegemony or Survival*. New York: Henry Holt & Co.

Choucri, N. (2012) *Cyberpolitics in International Relations*. Cambridge, MA: MIT Press

Churchill, W. S. (1923) *The World Crisis*. London: Longman, Green

Churchill, W. S. (1989a) 'Munich', in *Blood, Toil, Tears and Sweat: The Great Speeches*, pp. 129–44. London: Penguin [1938]

Churchill, W. S. (1989b) 'The Soviet Danger', in *Blood, Toil, Tears and Sweat*, pp. 295–309. London: Penguin [1946]

Churchill, W. S. (1989c) 'Something that Will Astonish You', in *Blood, Toil, Tears and Sweat*, pp. 310–15. London: Penguin [1946]

Claude, I. (1962) *Power and International Relations*. New York: Random House

Clausewitz, C. von (1922) 'Die Deutschen und die Franzosen', in Rothfels, H., ed., *Carl von Clausewitz: Politische Schriften und Briefe*, pp. 35–51. Munich: Drei Masken Verlag

Clausewitz, C. von (1962) 'I Believe and Profess', in *War, Politics and Power*, pp. 301–4. Chicago: Henry Regnery

Clausewitz, C. von (1976) *On War*. Princeton: Princeton University Press [1832]

Clemenceau, G. (1930) *Grandeurs et misères d'une victoire*. Paris: Pion

Clinton, D. (1993) 'Tocqueville on Democracy, Obligation and the International System', *Review of International Studies* 19(3): 227–45

Clinton, W. J. (1993) 'State-of-the-Union Address', The American Presidency Project, www.presidency.ucsb.edu/ws/?pid=47232

Clinton, W. J. (1994) *A National Security Strategy of Engagement and Enlargement*. Washington DC: US Government Printing Office

Club of Rome (1972) *Limts to Growth*. New York: Signet

Coase, R. (1937) 'The Nature of the Firm', *Economica* 4(16): 386–405

Cobden, R. (1973) *The Political Writings of Richard Cobden*, 2 vols. New York: Garland Publishing

Cockburn, P. (2015) *The Rise of the Islamic State*. London: Verso

Cole, G. D. H., ed. (1950) *The Social Contract and Discourses*. London: Dutton

Collini, S. (1991) *Public Moralists*. Oxford: Oxford University Press

Conant, C. A. (1898) 'The Economic Basis of "Imperialism"', *The North American Review* 167 (502): 326–40

Condorcet, J.-A.-N. de (1788) *Reflexions sur l'esclavage des nègres.* Neufchatel: Societé typographique [1781]

Condorcet, J.-A.-N. de (1970) *Esquisse d'un tableau historique des progrès de l'esprit humain.* Paris: Libraire philosophique J. Vrin [1795]

Connolly, W. E. (1993) *Terms of Political Discourse.* Oxford: Blackwell [1974]

Cooley, C. H. (1918) *Social Process.* New York: Scribner's Sons

Cooper, R. (1968) *The Economics of Interdependence.* New York: McGraw-Hill

Courtilz de Sandras, G. de (1686) *Nouveaux interets des Princes de l'Europe, ou l'on traite des Maximes qu'ils doivent observer pour se maintenir dans leurs Etats, et pour empecher qu'ils ne se forme une Monarchie Universelle.* Cologne [The Hague]: Pierre Marteau

Cox, M. (2001) 'Introduction', in Carr, *The Twenty Years' Crisis, 1919–1939.* London: Palgrave

Cox, R. W. (1981) 'Social Forces, States and World Orders', *Millennium* 10(2): 126–55

Cox, R. W. (1987) *Production. Power and World Order.* New York: Columbia University Press

Cranston, M. (1982) *Jean-Jacques.* Chicago: University of Chicago Press

Cranston, M. (1991) *The Noble Savage.* Chicago: University of Chicago Press

Cranston, M. (1997) *The Solitary Self.* Chicago: University of Chicago Press

Creel, G. (1920) *The War, The World and Wilson.* New York: Harper & Brothers

Crocker, L. G. (1974) *Jean-Jacques Rousseau*, 2 vols. New York: Macmillan

Cronin, V. (1967) *The Florentine Renaissance.* New York: E. P. Dutton & Co.

Crook, P. (1994) *Darwinism, War and History.* Cambridge: Cambridge University Press

Crozier, M. and E. Friedberg (1977) *L'acteur et le système.* Paris: Éditions du Seuil

Crozier, M., S. P. Huntington and J. Watanuki (1975) *The Crisis of Democracy.* New York: New York University Press

Crucé, E. (1972) *The New Cyneas.* New York: Garland Publishing [1623]

Cullen, M. (2007) *Are We Rome?* New York: Mariner

Cumberland, R. (1727) *A Treatise of the Law of Nature.* London: R. Philips [1672]

Darwin, C. (1958) *The Origin of Species.* New York: New American Library [1859]

Darwin, C. (1962) *The Voyage of the Beagle.* New York: Doubleday [1839]

Davenant, C (1701) *Essays upon: I. The ballance of power. II. The right of making war, peace and alliances. III. Universal monarchy.* London: J. Knapton

Davies, D. (1932) *Suicide or Sanity?* London: Williams & Norgate

Defoe, D. (1938) Editorial in *Review of the State of the English Nation* 7(706): 261–3. New York: Columbia University Press

Der Derian, J. (1987) *On Diplomacy.* Oxford: Blackwell

Der Derian, J. (1992) *Antidiplomacy.* Oxford: Blackwell

Der Derian, J. and M. Shapiro, eds (1986) *International/Intertextual Relations.* Lexington, MA: Lexington Books

Deudney, D. (2007) *Bounding Power.* Princeton: Princeton University Press

Deutsch, K. W. (1953) *Nationalism and Social Communication.* New York: John Wiley

Deutsch, K.W. (1954) *Political Community at the International Level.* New York: Doubleday and Company

Deutsch, K.W., S. A. Burrell, R. A. Kann and M. Lee, Jr (1957) *Political Community and the North Atlantic Area.* Princeton: Princeton University Press

Dickinson, G. L. (1916) *The European Anarchy.* London: Allen & Unwin

Dickinson, G. L. (1927) 'Introduction', in Rousseau, J.-J., *A Project of Perpetual Peace.* London: R. Cobden-Sanderson

Diderot, D. (1992) *Political Writings.* Cambridge: Cambridge University Press

Downing, B. M. (1992) *The Military Revolution and Political Change.* Princeton: Princeton University Press

Doyle, M. (1983) 'Kant, Liberal Legacies and Foreign Affairs', *Philosophy and Public Affairs* 12(1 & 2): 205–35; 323–53

Drucker, P. (1939) *The End of Economic Man.* New York: John Day Company

Duby, G. (1968) *Rural Economy and Country Life in the Medieval West.* London: Edward Arnold

Dunn, F. S. (1937) *Peaceful Change.* New York: Council on Foreign Relations

Dunn, F. S. (1949) 'The Scope of International Relations', *World Politics* 1(2): 142–7

Dupuis, C. (1909) *Le principe d'équilibre et le concert européen.* Paris: Perrin & Compagnie

Dyson, K. (1980) *The State Tradition in Western Europe.* Oxford: Martin Robertson

Eagleton, C. (1932) *International Government.* New York: Ronald Press

Eagleton, C. (1937) *Analysis of the Problem of War.* New York: Ronald Press

Eagleton, C. and F. O. Wilcox, eds (1945) 'The United Nations: Peace and Security', *American Political Science Review.* 39(4): 934–92

Earle, E. M. (1943) *Makers of Modern Strategy.* Princeton: Princeton University Press

Ehrlich, P. (1968) *The Population Bomb.* New York: Ballantine

Eisenstein, E. L. (1993) *The Printing Revolution in Early Modern Europe.* Cambridge: Cambridge University Press

Ekbladh, D. (2011) 'Present at the Creation', *International Security* 36(3): 107–41

Ellis, J. (2015) *The Quartet.* New York: Knopf

Elton, G. R. (1981) *Reformation Europe.* Glasgow: Fontana/Collins

Enloe, C. (2004) *The Curious Feminist.* Los Angeles: University of California Press

Erasmus, D. (1964) 'Dulce bellum inexpertis', in H. H. Philips, ed., *The Adages of Erasmus*, pp. 308–54. Cambridge: Cambridge University Press

Eulau, H. (1961) *Recent Developments in the Behavioral Study of Politics.* Stanford: Stanford University, Dept of Political Science

Fanon, F. (1963) *The Wretched of the Earth.* New York: Grove Press [1961]

Fanon, F. (1967) *Black Skin, White Masks.* New York: Grove Press

Farwell, B. (1985) *Queen Victoria's Small Wars.* New York: W. W. Norton

Febvre, L. (1942) *Le problème de l'incroyance au XVIe siècle.* Paris: Michel

Feinsod, M. (1953) *How Russia is Ruled.* Cambridge, MA: Harvard University Press

Fellner, W. (1949) *Competition among the Few.* New York: Knopf

Fénelon, F. de Salignac de la Mothe (1815) 'On the necessity of forming alliances, both offensive and defensive, against a foreign power which manifestly aspires to universal monarchy', in Anon., *A Collection of Scarce and Valuable Tracts on the most Interesting and Entertaining Subjects*, 2 nd ed, Vol. XIII. London: Cadell, Davis, etc. [1700]

Ferguson, Y. H. (1996) *Politics: Authority, Identities and Ideology.* Columbia: University of South Carolina Press

Ferguson, Y. H. and R.W. Mansbach (1988) *The Elusive Quest.* Columbia: University of South Carolina Press

Ferguson, N. (2005) *Colossus.* London: Penguin

Ferguson, N., C. S. Maier, E. Manela and D. Sargent, eds (2011) *The Shock of the Global*. Cambridge, MA: Belknap Press

Ferrari, J. (1860) *Histoire de la raison d'État*. Paris: Michel Levy Frères

Fichte, J. G. (1979a) 'Zum ewigen Frieden', in Batscha, Z. and R. Saage, eds, *Frieden-sutopien*, pp. 83–93. Frankfuhrt am Main: Suhrkamp [1796]

Fichte, J. G. (1979b) *Der geschlossende Handelsstaat*. Hamburg: Felix Meiner Verlag [1800]

Fichterman, H. (1964) *The Carolingian Empire*. New York: Harper & Row

Filmer, R. (1991) 'Patriarcha: A Defence of the Natural Power of Kings against the Unnatural Liberty of the People', in *Patriarcha and Other Writings*. Cambridge: Cambridge University Press [1680]

Finer, S. (1975) 'State- and Nation-building in Europe', in Tilly, C., ed., *The Formation of Nation States in Western Europe*, pp. 84–164. Princeton: Princeton University Press

Fischer, F. (1961) *Griff nach der Weltmacht*, Düsseldorf: Droste

Forsyth, M. G., H. M. A. Keens-Soper and P. Savigear, eds (1949) *The Theory of International Relations: Selected Texts grom Gentili to Treitschke*. New York: Transaction Publishers

Foucault, M. (1972), 'The Discourse on Language', in *The Archaeology of Knowledge & The Discourse on Language*, pp. 215–39. New York: Pantheon

Foucault, M. (1973) *The Order of Things*. New York: Random House [1966]

Foucault, M. (1984a) 'What Is Enlightenment', in Rabinow, P., ed., *The Foucault Reader*, pp. 32–51. New York: Pantheon

Foucault, M. (1984b) 'Nietzsche, Genealogy, History', in Rabinow, P., ed., *The Foucault Reader*, pp. 76–101. New York: Pantheon

Fox, W. R. (1944) *The Super-Powers: The United States, Britain, and the Soviet Union – Their Responsibility for Peace*. New York: Harcourt, Brace and Company

Fox, W. R., ed. (1959) *Theoretical Aspects of International Relations*. Notre Dame: Notre Dame Press

Fraenkel, E. (1941) *The Dual State*. London: Oxford University Press

Frank, A. G. (1966) *The Development of Underdevelopment*. New York: Monthly Review Press

Frank, A. G. (1967) *Capitalism and Underdevelopment in Latin America*. New York: Monthly Review Press

Franke, W. (1968) 'The Italian City-State System as an International System', in Kaplan, M., ed., *New Approaches to International Relations*, pp. 426–59. New York: St Martin's Press

Frederick II (1981) *Anti-Machiœvel*. Athens: Ohio University Press [1740]

Frei, C. (2001) *Hans J. Morgenthau: An Intellectual Biography*. Baton Rouge: LSU Press

Friedrich, C. J., ed. (1949) *The Philosophy of Kant*. New York: The Modern Library

Friedrich, C. J. (1954) *Totalitarianism*. Cambridge, MA: Harvard University Press

Friedrich, C. J. and Z. Brzezinski (1965) *Totalitarian Dictatorship and Autocracy*. Cambridge, MA: Harvard University Press

Fromkin, D. (1995) *In the Time of the Americans*. New York: Knopf

Fukuyama, F. (1989) 'The End of History', *The National Interest* 5(Summer): 3–18

Fukuyama, F. (1992) *The End of History and the Last Man*. New York: Free Press

Fukuyama, F. (1999) *The Great Disruption*. New York: Simon & Schuster

Fullerton, W. M. (1913) *Problems of Power*. London: Constable & Co.

Gaddis, J. L. (1986) 'The Long Peace'. *International Security*, 10(4): 99–142

Gaddis, J. L. (1992) 'International Relations Theory and the End of the Cold War', *International Security* 17(3): 5–58

Gaddis, J. L. (2011) *George F. Kennan: An American Life*. New York: W. W. Norton & Company

Ganshof, F.-L. (1995) 'Le Moyen Age', in P. Renouvin, ed., *Histoire des relations internationales*, Vol. I, pp. 15–243. Paris: Hachette [1953]

Gardner, L. C. (1984) *A Covenant with Power*. New York: Oxford University Press

Gasman, D. (1971) *The Scientific Origins of National Socialism*. London: Macdonald

Gates, S., T. L. Knutsen and J. W. Moses (1996) 'Democracy and Peace: A More Skeptical View', *Journal of Peace Research* 33(1): 1–11

Geiss, I. (1993) *Europa – Vielfalt und Einheit*, Mannheim: B. L. Taschenbuchverlag

Gellner, E. (1983) *Nations and Nationalism*. Oxford: Blackwell

Gentili, A. (1964) *De Jure Belli Libri Tres*. New York: Oceana Publications [1612]

Gentz, F. (1806) *Fragments upon the Present State of the Political Balance of Europe*. London: M. Peltier

Gentz, F. (1953) 'Über den ewigen Frieden', in von Raumer, K.,ed., *Ewiger Friede*. Munich: Verlag Karl Alber Freiburg

George, J. (1994) *Discourses of Global Politics: A Critical (Re)Introduction to International Relations*. Boulder: Lynne Rienner

Gibbon, E. (1994a) *History of the Decline and Fall of the Roman Empire*. London: Penguin (vols 1 and 2)

Gibbon, E. (1994b) *History of the Decline and Fall of the Roman Empire*. London: Penguin (vols 3 and 4)

Giddens, A. (1990) *The Consequences of Modernity*. Cambridge: Polity Press

Gilbert, F. (1965) *Machiavelli and Cuicciardini*. Princeton: Princeton University Press

Gilpin, R. (1981) *War and Change in World Politics*. New York: Cambridge University Press

Gilpin, R. (1987) *The Political Economy of International Relations*. Princeton: Princeton University Press

Glass, C. (1991) *Tribes With Flags: A Dangerous Passage Through the Chaos of the Middle East*. New York: Atlantic Monthly Press

Godwin, W. (1985) *Enquiry Concerning Political Justice*. Harmondsworth: Penguin [1793]

Gordon, D. C. (1991) *Images of the West*. Totowa: Rowman & Littlefield

Gorres, J. (1979) 'Der allgemeine Frieden – Ein Ideal', in Batscha, Z. and R. Saage, eds, *Friedensutopien*, pp. 126–77. Frankfuhrt am Main: Suhrkamp [1798]

Gough, J. W. (1936) *The Social Contract*. Oxford: Clarendon Press

Gramsci, A. (1974) *Selections from the Prison Notebooks*. London: Lawrence & Wishart

Grant, A. J., J. D. I. Hughes, A. Greenwood, P. H. Kerr and F. F. Urquehart (1916) *An Introduction to the Study of International Relations*. London: Macmillan & Co.

Grant, M. (1916) *The Passing of the Great Race*. New York: Charles Scribner's Sons

Grant, R. and K. Newland, eds (1991) *Gender and International Relations*. Buckingham and Milton Keynes: Open University Press

Greenwald, G. (2014) *No Place to Hide*. London: Hamish Hamilton

Gregory of Tours (1974) *The History of the Franks*. Harmondsworth: Penguin [593?]

Grey, E. (1925) *Twenty-Five Years*, Vol. 2. New York: Frederick A. Stokes

Grimm, H. (1928) *Volk ohne Raum*. Munich: Albert Langen

Grotius, H. (1853) *De Jure Belli ac Pacis*. Cambridge: Cambridge University Press [1625]

Guevara, E. (1961) *On Guerrilla Warfare*. New York: Praeger

Guicciardini, F. (1969) *The History of Italy*. London: Collier-Macmillan [1561]

Guicciardini, F. (1970) *Maxims and Reflections of a Renaissance Statesman*. Gloucester, MA: Peter Smith [1857]

Guicciardini, F. (1994) *Dialogue on the Government of Florence*. Cambridge: Cambridge University Press [1527]

Guilhot, Nicolas (2011) *The Invention of International Relations Theory*. New York: Columbia University Press

Gulick, E. V. (1967) *Europe's Classical Balance of Power*. New York: W. W. Norton

Gumplowicz, L. (1909) *Der Rassenkampf*. Innsbruck: Wagner'sche Universitätsbuch-handlung [1885]

Gunn, J. A. W. (1969) *Politics and the Public Interest in the Seventeenth Century*. London: Routledge & Kegan Paul

Gunnell, J. G. (1978) 'The Myth of the Tradition', *American Political Science Review* 72(1): 122–35

Gunnell, J.G. (1989) *The Orders of Discourse*. Lanham: Rowman and Littlefield

Haas, E. B. (1961) 'International Integration', *International Organization* 15(3): 366–92

Haas, E.B. (1964) *Beyond the Nation State*. Stanford: Stanford University Press

Haas, E.B. (1968) *The Uniting of Europe*. Stanford: Stanford University Press

Haas, P., ed. (1992) *International Organization* (Special Issue on Epistemic Communities) 46(1)

Habermas, J. (1991) *Communication and the Evolution of Society*. Cambridge: Polity Press

Haeckel, E. (1896) *The Evolution of Man*. New York: Appleton

Hackel, E. (1900) *The Riddle of the Universe*. New York: Harper & Brothers

Hale, J. R. (1960) *Machiavelli and Renaissance Italy*. New York: Macmillan

Hale, J. R. (1981) 'International relations in the West', in Hay, D., ed., *The Renaissance 1493–1520*, 2nd ed., pp. 259–92. Cambridge: Cambridge University Press [1957]

Hall, J. A. (1986) *Powers and Liberties*. Harmondsworth: Penguin

Halle, L. (1967) *The Cold War as History*. New York: Harper & Row

Halliday, F. (1983) *The Making of the Second Cold War*. London: Verso

Halliday, F. (1994) *Rethinking International Relations*. London: Macmillan

Hamilton, A. (1928) 'Report on the Subject of Manufactures', in Cole, Arthur H., ed., *Industrial and Commercial Correspondence of Alexander Hamilton*. Chicago: A. W. Shaw Co. [1791]

Hamilton, A. (1987) 'Concerning Dangers from War between the States' in Madison, J., A. Hamilton and J. Jay, eds, *The Federalist*. London, Penguin, pp. 104–9 [1788]

Hamilton, K. and R. Langhorne (1995) *The Practice of Diplomacy*. London: Routledge

Hampson, N. (1968) *The Enlightenment*. Harmondsworth: Penguin

Hanke, L. (1974) *All Mankind Is One*. De Kalb: Northern Illinois University Press

Harbutt, F. (1988) *The Iron Curtain*. Oxford: Oxford University Press

Hardin, G. (1968) 'The Tragedy of the Commons', *Science*, 13 December, pp. 1243–8

Harvey, D. (1989) *The Condition of Postmodernity*. Oxford: Blackwell

Haselby, S. (2015) *The Origins of American Religious Nationalism*. Oxford: Oxford University Press

Haushofer, K. (1928) *Bausteine zur Geopolitik*. Berlin-Grunewald: Vowinkel

Hawtrey, R. G. (1952) *Economic Aspects of Sovereignty*. London: Longman Green

Hayek, F. A. (1944) *The Road to Serfdom*. Chicago: University of Chicago Press

Heatley, D. P. (1919) *Diplomacy and the Study of International Relations*. Oxford: Clarendon Press

Heckscher, E. (1935) *Mercantilism*. London: Allen & Unwin

Hegel, G. W. F. (1980) *Philosophy of Right*. London: Oxford University Press [1821]

Hegghammer, T. and S. Lacroix (2011) *The Meccan Rebellion*. London: Amal Press

Heilbroner, R. L. (1986) *The Nature and Logic of Capitalism*. New York: W. W. Norton

Held, D., A. G. McGrew, D. Goldblatt and J. Perraton (1999) *Global Transformations*. Cambridge: Polity Press

Herder, J. G. (1800) *Ideen zur Philosophie der Geschichte der Menschheit*. Riga: J. F. Hartknoch [1784–91]

Herder, J. G. (1829) *Briefe zur Beforderungen der Humanität*. Stuttgart: Cotta

Herz, J. (1942) 'Power Politics and World Organization', *American Political Science Review* 36(6): 1039–52

Herz, J. (1950) 'Idealist Internationalism and the Security Dilemma', *World Politics* 2(2): 171–201

Herz, J. (1951) *Political Realism and Political Idealism*. Chicago: University of Chicago Press

Herz, J. (1957) 'The Rise and Demise of the Territorial State', *World Politics* 9(4): 473–93

Hilferding, R. (1955) *Das Finanzkapital*. Berlin: Dietz Verlag [1910]

Hinsley, F. H. (1963) *Power and the Pursuit of Peace*. Cambridge: Cambridge University Press

Hirschman, A. O. (1981) *The Passions and the Interests*. Princeton: Princeton University Press [1977]

Hitler, A. (1943) *Mein Kampf*. Boston: Houghton Mifflin [1925]

Hitler, A. (2006) *Hitler's Second Book*. New York: Enigma Books

Hobbes, T. (1951) *Leviathan*. Harmondsworth: Penguin [1651]

Hobsbawm, E. (1962) *The Age of Revolution: 1789–1848*. New York: New American Library

Hobsbawm, E. (1969) *Industry and Empire*. Harmondsworth: Penguin

Hobsbawm, E. (1991) *Nations and Nationalism since 1780*. Cambridge: Cambridge University Press

Hobson, J. (2004) *The Eastern Origins of Western Civilization*. Cambridge: Cambridge University Press

Hobson, J. (2011) *The Eurocentric Conception of World Politics*. Cambridge: Cambridge University Press

Hobson, J. A. (1902) *Imperialism*. London: J. Pott

Hobson, J. A. (1915) *Towards International Government*. New York: Macmillan

Hochschild, A. (2011) *To End All Wars*. London: Pan Books

Hodges, C. (1931) *Background of International Relations*. New York: Wiley

Hoffman, F. (2007) *The Rise of Hybrid Wars*. Arlington: Potomac Institute for Policy Studies

Hoffmann, D. E. (2001) *The Oligarchs*. New York: Public Affairs

Hoffmann, S. (1987) 'An American Social Science', in *Janus and Minerva*, pp. 3–24. Boulder: Westview [1977]

Hoffmann, S. and D. P. Fidler, eds (1991) *Rousseau on International Relations*. Oxford: Clarendon Press

d'Holbach, P. H. T., baron (1773) *Système social*. London: Marc-Michel Rey

Holland, T. (2008) *Millennium*. London: Little, Brown & Co.

Hollis, M. and S. Smith (1991) *Explaining and Understanding International Relations*. Oxford: Clarendon

Holsti, K. (1967) *International Politics*. Englewood Cliffs: Prentice-Hall

Holsti, K. (1987) *The Dividing Discipline*. London: Allen & Unwin

Holsti, K. (1996) *The State, War, and the State of War*. Cambridge: Cambridge University Press

Holsti, O. (1972) *Crisis, Escalation, War*. Montreal: McGill-Queen's University Press

Hossbach, F. (1998) 'Hossbach Memorandum', in Louis L. Snyder, *Encyclopedia of the Third Reich*, pp. 172–6. Ware: Wordsworth Editions

Hovelaque, E. (1915) *Les causes profondes de la Guerre*. Paris: Félix Alcan

Howard, M. (1978) *War and the Liberal Conscience*. New Brunswick: Rutgers University Press

Howard, M. (1984) *War in European History*. London: Oxford University Press

Hughes, B. B. (1991) *Continuity and Change in World Politics*. Englewood Cliffs: Prentice-Hall

Hull, C. (1948) *Memoirs*, Vol. 1. New York: Macmillan

Hume, D. (1955) *An Inquiry Concerning Human Understanding*. Indianapolis: Bobbs-Merrill [1748]

Hume, D. (1978) *Treatise of Human Nature*. Oxford: Clarendon Press [1740]

Hume, D. (1985) *Essays. Moral, Political and Literary*. Indianapolis: Liberty Classics [1741]

Hume, D. (1985a) 'Of the First Principles of Government, in *Essays*, pp. 32–7. Indianapolis: Liberty Classics

Hume, D. (1985b) 'Of the Origin of Government', in *Essays*, pp. 37–42. Indianapolis: Liberty Classics

Hume, D. (1985c) 'Of the Balance of Power', in *Essays*, pp. 332–42. Indianapolis: Liberty Classics

Hume, D. (1985d) 'Of the Original Contract', in *Essays*, pp. 464–87. Indianapolis: Liberty Classics

Hume, D. (1998) *Enquiry Concerning the Principles of Morals*. Oxford, Oxford University Press [1748]

Hunter, J. D. (1991) *Culture Wars: The Struggle to Define America*. New York: Basic Books

Huntington, S. P. (1968) *Political Order in Changing Societies*. New Haven: Yale University Press

Huntington, S. P. (1991) *The Third Wave.* Norman: University of Oklahoma Press

Huntington, S. P. (1993) 'The Clash of Civilizations?' *Foreign Affairs* 72(3): 22–49

Huntington, S. P. (1996) *The Clash of Civilizations and the Remaking of World Order.* New York: Simon & Schuster

Hussey, J. M. (1966) *The Byzantine Empire.* Cambridge: Cambridge University Press

Hutcheson, F. (1755) *A System of Moral Philosophy.* Glasgow: R. & A. Foulis

IISS (2014) *The Military Balance.* www.iiss.org/en/publications/military-s-balance

IMF (2014) *World Economic Outlook.* www.imf.org/external/

Janet, P. (1887) *Histoire de la science politique: Ses rapports avec la morale,* Vol. 1. Paris: Alcan

Janis, I. (1972) *Groupthink.* Boston: Houghton Mifflin

Jervis, R. (1976) *Perception and Misperception in International Politics.* Princeton: Princeton University Press

Jian, C. (1994) *China's Road to the Korean War.* New York: Columbia University Press

Jones, R. (1981) 'The English School of International Relations: A Case for Closure', *Review of International Studies* 7(1): 1–13

Jones, W. S. (1991) *The Logic of International Relations.* New York: Harper Collins

Kahn, H. (1960) *Thinking about the Unthinkable.* Princeton: Princeton University Press

Kaldor, M. (1999) *New and Old Wars.* Stanford: Stanford University Press

Kalijarvi, T. V., ed. (1942) *Modern World Politics.* New York: Thomas Cromwell

Kant, I. (1949a) 'What Is Enlightenment?' in Friedrich, K., ed., *The Philosophy of Kant,* pp. 132–40. New York: The Modern Library [1784]

Kant, I. (1949b) 'Idea for a Universal History with Cosmopolitan Intent', in Friedrich, K., ed., *The Philosophy of Kant,* pp. 116–31. New York: The Modern Library [1784]

Kant, I. (1970a) 'On the Commonplace', in Forsyth, M. G., H. M. A. Keens-Soper and P. Savigear, eds, *The Theory of International Relations,* pp. 192–200. New York: Transaction Publishers [1793]

Kant, I. (1970b) 'Perpetual Peace', in Forsyth, M. G., H. M. A. Keens-Soper and P. Savigear, eds *The Theory of International Relations,* pp. 200–45. New York: Transaction Publishers [1795]

Kant, I. (1991) 'A Renewed Attempt to Answer the Question: "Is the Human Race Continually Improving?"' in Reiss, H. (ed.), *Kant: Political Writings,* pp. 177–91. Cambridge: Cambridge University Press [1798]

Kaplan, M. (1957) *System and Process in International Politics.* New York: John Wiley

Kaplan, M. (1966) 'The New Great Debate', *World Politics* 19(1): 1–20

Kaplan, R. (1994) 'The Coming Anarchy', *Atlantic Monthly* 275(2): 44ff

Katzenstein, P. J. (2005) *A World of Regions.* New York: Cornell University Press

Kautsky, K. (1970) 'Ultra-imperialism', *New Left Review* 59(1): 41–7 [1914]

Keane, J. (1996) *Tom Paine.* London: Bloomsbury

Keen, M. H. (1963) *The Laws of War in the Late Middle Ages.* London: Routledge & Kegan Paul

Kennan, G. F. (1946) 'The Charge in the Soviet Union (Kennan) to the Secretary of State', in *Foreign Relations of the United States, 19-16,* GPO, Washington DC, 1969, VI, Telegram 861.00/2-2246 [Moscow, 22 February 1946], pp. 700–7

Kennan, G. F. (1947) 'The Sources of Soviet Conduct', *Foreign Affairs,* 25(4): 566–82

Kennan, G. F. (1950) *American Diplomacy.* Chicago: University of Chicago Press

Kennan, G. F. (1993) *Around the Cragged Hill.* New York: W. W. Norton
Kennan, G. F. (1997) 'A Fateful Error', *New York Times*, 5 February
Kennedy, P. (1987) *The Rise and Fall of the Great Powers.* New York: Random House
Kennedy, P. (1993) *Preparing for the Twenty-First Century.* London: HarperCollins
Keohane, R. O. (1984) *After Hegemony.* Princeton: Princeton University Press
Keohane, R. O., ed. (1986) *Neo-Realism and Its Critics.* New York: Columbia University Press
Keohane, R. O. (1988) 'International Institutions: Two Approaches', *International Studies Quarterly* 32(4): 379–96
Keohane, R. O. (1989) *International Institutions and State Power.* Boulder: Westview
Keohane, R. O. and J. S. Nye (1977) *Power and Interdependence.* New York: Little, Brown & Co.
Keynes, J.M. (1920) *The Economic Consequences of the Peace.* London: Macmillan & Co.
Keynes, J.M. (1936) *A General Theory of Employment, Interest and Money.* London: Macmillan & Co.
Khadduri, M. (1966) *The Islamic Law of Nations: Shabani's Siyar.* Baltimore: The Johns Hopkins University Press
Khrushchev, N. (1961) 'For New Victories of the World Communist Movement', in US Senate, *Hearing before the Subcommittee to Investigate the Administration of the Internal Security Act and Internal Security Laws*, June 16, 1961. Washington, DC: Government Printing Office, pp. 52–78.
Kidd, B. (1894) *Social Evolution.* London: Macmillan & Co.
Kindleberger, C. (1973) *The World in Depression.* Berkeley: University of California Press
Kirk, G. (1949) 'Materials for the Study of International Relations', *World Politics* 1(4): 426–31
Kissinger, H. A. (1954) *A World Restored.* Boston: Houghton Mifflin
Kissinger, H. A. (1968) 'The White Revolutionary: Reflections on Bismarck', *Daedalus* 97(3): 888–924
Kissinger, H. A. (1979) *White House Years.* Boston: Little, Brown & Co.
Kissinger. H. A. (1994) *Diplomacy.* New York: Simon & Schuster
Kissinger, H. A. (2014) *World Order.* London: Penguin Press
Kjellén, R. (1900) *Inledning till Sveriges Geografi.* Göteborg: Wettergren & Kerber
Kjellén, R. (1917) *Der Staat als Lebensform.* Leipzig: S. Hirzel
Klee, H. (1946) *Hugo Grotius und Johannes Selden.* Berne: Verla Paul Haupt
Klein, B. S. (1994) *Strategic Studies and World Order.* Cambridge: Cambridge University Press
Kluckhohn, C. (1949) 'Russian Research at Harvard', *World Politics* 1(2): 266–71
Knutsen, T. L. (1992) 'The Reagan Doctrine and the Lesson of the Afghan War', *Australian Journal of Politics and History* 38(2): 193–205
Knutsen, T. L. (1994) 'Re-Reading Rousseau in the Post-Cold War World', *Journal of Peace Research* 31(3): 247–63
Knutsen, T. L. (1999) *The Rise and Fall of World Orders.* Manchester: Manchester University Press
Knutsen, T. L. (2007) 'A Lost Generation? IR Scholarship before World War I', *International Politics* 45(6): 650–74
Knutsen, T. L. (2012) 'En Machiavelli for vår tid', *Internasjonal politikk* 71(4): 611–25

Knutsen, T. L. (2013) 'A Pillar of Air? Norman Angell and *The Great Illusion*', in Bliddal, H., C. Sylvest and P. Wilson, eds, *Classics of International Relations*, pp. 13–24. London: Routledge

Knutsen, T. L. (2014) 'Halford Mackinder, Geopolitics and the Heartland Thesis', *The International History Review* 36(5): 835–57

Kohl, H. (2005) *Erinnerungen, 1982–1990*. Munich: Dörmer Verlag

Kotkin, S. (2010) 'The Kiss of Debt: The East Bloc Goes Borrowing', in Ferguson, N., C. S. Maier, E. Manela and D. Sargent, eds, *The Shock of the Global*, pp. 80–96. Cambridge, MA: Belknap Press

Krasner, S. D. (1983) *International Regimes*. Ithaca: Cornell University Press

Krasner, S. D. (1999) *Sovereignty*. Princeton: Princeton University Press

Kratochwil, F. (1981) *The Humean Conception of International Relations*. Princeton: Center of International Studies, Princeton University

Kratochwil, F. (1989) *Rules. Norms and Decisions.* Cambridge: Cambridge University Press

Krauthammer, C. (1991) 'The Unipolar Moment', *Foreign Affairs* 70(1): 23–33

Kristol, W. and R. Kagan (1996) 'Towards a Neo-Reaganite Foreign Policy', *Foreign Affairs*. July/August

Kuhn, T. (1962) *The Structure of Scientific Revolutions*. Chicago: University of Chicago Press

LaFeber, W. (1987) *America, Russia and the Cold War*. New York: McGraw-Hill

LaFeber, W. (1989) *The American Age*. New York: W. W. Norton

Lange, C. (1919) *Histoire de l'internationalisme*. Kristiania: Publications de l'Institute Nobel Norvègien, tome IV

Lansing, R. (1935) *War Memoires of Robert Lansing. Secretary of State.* Indianapolis: Bobbs-Merrill

Lapid, Y. (1989) 'The Third Debate', *International Relations Quarterly* 33(3): 235–55

Laslett, P. (1960) 'Introduction', in Locke, J., *Two Treatises of Government*, pp. 15–136. Cambridge: Cambridge University Press

Laue, T. von (1987) *The World Revolution of Westernization*. Oxford: Oxford University Press

Lauterpacht, H. (1933) *The Function of Law in International Community*. New York: Oxford University Press

Lawrence, T. J. (1919) *The Society of Nations*. New York: Oxford University Press

Layne, C. (1994) 'Kant or Cant: The Myth of the Democratic Peace', *International Security* 19(2): 5–49

Leibniz, G. von (1963) 'Entretien de Philarète et d'Eugene sur la question du temps', in *Politische Schriften*, Vol. II, pp. 278–339. Berlin: Akademie-Verlag [1677]

Leira, H. (2008) 'Justus Lipsius, Political Humanism and the Disciplining of 17th Century Statecraft', *Review of International Studies*, 34(4): 669—92

Lenin, V. I. (1975a) 'Decree on Peace', in Tucker, R. C., *The Lenin Anthology*, pp. 540–2. New York: W. W. Norton

Lenin, V. I. (1975b) 'Imperialism, the Highest Stage of Capitalism', in Tucker, R. C., *The Lenin Anthology*, pp. 204–75. New York: W. W. Norton

Lenz, T. (1955) *Towards a Science of Peace*. New York: Bookman Associates

Leonard, I. A. (1949) *Books of the Brave*. Cambridge, MA: Harvard University Press

Leroy-Beaulieu, P. (1874) *De la colonization chez les peuples modernes*. Paris: Guillaumin

Levinson, M. (2008) *The Box*. Princeton: Princeton University Press

Levitt, T. (1983) 'The Globalization of Markets', *Harvard Business Review* (May): 92–102

Link, A. S., ed. (1967) *The Public Papers of Woodrow Wilson*, Vol. V. Princeton: Princeton University Press

Link, A. S. (1971) *The Higher Realism of Woodrow Wilson*. Nashville: Vanderbilt University Press

Lippmann, W. (1943) *U.S. Foreign Polity: Shield of the Republic*. Boston: Little, Brown & Co.

Lippmann, W. (1947) *The Cold War*. New York: Harper

List, F. (1927) 'Das Natürliche System der Politischen Ökonomie', in *Werke*, Vol. IV, pp, 154–550. Berlin: Reimar Hobbing [1837]

List, F. (1930) 'Das Nationale System der Politischen Ökonomie', in *Werke*, Vol. VI, pp. 1–433. Berlin: Reimar Hobbing [1841]

Locke, J. (1960) *Two Treatises of Government*. Cambridge: Cambridge University Press [1689]

Long, D. and P. Wilson, eds (1995) *Thinkers of the Twenty Years' Crisis*. Oxford: Clarendon

Lorimer, J. (1877) 'Le problème final du droit international', *Revue de droit international et de législation comparée* 9(2): 161–205

Lorimer, J. (1884) *The Institutes of the Law of Nations: A Treatise on the Jural Relations of Separate Political Communities*. Edinburgh and London: William Blackwood and Sons

Lottman, H. R. (1997*) Jules Verne*. New York: St Martin's Press

Lovelock, J. (1979) *Gaia: A New Look at Life on Earth*. Oxford: Oxford University Press

Lowe, K. (2012) *Savage Continent: Europe in the Aftermath of World War II*. New York: St Martin's Press

Luard, E. (1992) *Basic Texts in International Relations*. New York: St Martin's Press

Luhmann, N. (1995) *Social Systems*. Stanford: Stanford University Press

Luxemburg, R. (1951) *Accumulation of Capital*. New Haven: Yale University Press [1913]

Lyotard, J.-F. (1979) *La condition postmoderne*. Paris: Minuit

Lyotard, J.-F. (1983) 'Answering the Question: What Is Postmodernism', in Hassan, I. and S. Hassan, eds, *Innovation/Renovation*, pp. 71–82. Madison: University of Wisconsin Press Machiavelli, N. (1961) *The Prince*. Harmondsworth: Penguin

Machiavelli, N. (1997) *Discourses on Livy*. Oxford: Oxford University Press

Mackinder, H. J. (1900) 'The Great Trade Routes', *Journal of the Institute of Bankers* 21: 267–36

Mackinder, H. J. (1904) 'On the Geographical Pivot of History', *Geographical Journal* 23(4): 421–44

Mackinder, H. J. (1919) *Democratic Ideals and Reality*. New York: Holt

Mackinder, H. J. (1943) 'The Round World and the Winning of the Peace', *Foreign Affairs* 21(4): 595–605

MacMillan, M. (2001) *Peacemakers*. London: John Murray

McNeill, J. R. (2010) 'The Environment, Environmentalism, and International Society in the Long 1970s', in Ferguson, N., C. S. Maier, E. Manela and D. Sargent, eds, *The Shock of the Global*, pp. 263–80. Cambridge, MA: Belknap Press

Maddison, A. (2001) *The World Economy*. Paris: Development Centre, OECD

Madison, J. (1906) 'Universal Peace', in *The Writings of James Madison*, Vol. 6, pp. 88–92. New York: G. P. Putnam's Sons

Madison, J. (1953) 'Is Universal Peace Possible', in *The Complete Madison*, pp. 260–2. New York: Harper & Brothers [1792]

Madison, J. (1987) 'The Structure of the Government Must Furnish the Proper Checks and Balances between the Different Departments', *The Federalist* 51: 318–22

Madison, J., A. Hamilton and J. Jay (1987) *The Federalist*. London: Penguin [1788]

Mahan, A. T. (1889) *The Influence of Sea Power through History, 1660–1783*. Boston: Little, Brown & Co.

Mahan, A. T. (1897) *The Interest of America in Sea Power*. London: Sampson Low & Co.

Mahan, A. T. (1912) 'The Great Illusion', *The North American Review* 195 (March): 319–33

Maier, C. (2010) 'Malaise: The Crisis of Capitalism in the 1970s', in Ferguson, N., C. S. Maier, E. Manela and D. Sargent, eds, *The Shock of the Global*, pp. 25–48. Cambridge, MA: Belknap Press

Malamud, M. (2008) *Ancient Rome and Modern America*. New York: Wiley-Blackwell

Malthus, T. (1982) *An Essay on the Principle of Population*. Harmondsworth: Penguin [1798]

Mandel, E. (1982) *La crise 1974–1982: les faits, leur interprétation marxiste*. Paris: Flammarion

Mandeville, B. de (1924) *Fable of the Bees: or Private Vices, Publick: Benefits*. Oxford: Clarendon Press [1714]

Mandrou, R. (1978) *From Humanism to Science, '480–'700*. Harmondsworth: Penguin

Mannheim, K. (1936) *Ideology and Utopia*. New York: Harcourt, Brace

Manning, C. A. W. (1962) *The Nature of International Society*. New York: John Wiley

Mantoux, P., ed. (1938) *The World Crisis*. New York: Longman, Green

Mao Zedong (1965a) 'The Role of the Chinese Communist Party in the National War', in *Selected Works*, Vol. II, pp. 195–212. Beijing: Foreign Languages Press [1938]

Mao Zedong (1965b) 'On Protracted War', in *Selected Works*, Vol. II, pp. 113–94. Beijing: Foreign Languages Press [1937]

Mao Zedong (1965c) 'Talks at the Yenan Forum on Literature and Art', in *Selected Works*, Vol. III, pp. 69–99. Beijing: Foreign Languages Press [1942]

Maoz, Z. and N. Abdolali (1989) 'Regime Types and International Conflict, 1816–1976', *Journal of Conflict Resolution* 33(1): 3–35

Maoz, Z. and B. Russett (1993) 'Normative and Structural Causes of Democratic Peace, 1946–1986', *American Political Science Review* 87(4): 624–38

Marján, A. and A. Sapir (2010). *Europe's Destiny*. Baltimore: Johns Hopkins University Press

Marlin-Bennett, R. (2011) *Alker and IR*. London: Routledge

Marriott, J. A. (1937) *Commonwealth or Anarchy?* London: P. Allan

Marsiglio of Padua (1993) *Writings on the Empire. Defensor minor and De translations Imperii*. Cambridge: Cambridge University Press [1324]

Martinussen, W. (1999) *Sosiologiske forklaringer.* Oslo: Fagbokforlaget

Marx, K. (1964a) 'Marx and Engels in Manchester', in *Werke*, Vol. 30, pp. 130–1. Berlin: Dietz Verlag

Marx, K. (1964b) 'Marx and Ferdinand Lassalle in Berlin', in *Werke*, Vol. 30, pp. 577–9. Berlin: Dietz Verlag

Marx, K. (1964c) 'Der 18. Brumaire des Louis Bonaparte', in *Werke*, Vol. 8, pp. 111–207. Berlin: Dietz Verlag [1852]

Marx, K. (1972) 'The Future Results of the British Rule in India', in *On Colonialism*, pp. 81–8. New York: International Publishers [1853]

Marx, K. (1975a) 'Critique of Hegel's Dialectic and General Philosophy', in Hoare, Q., ed., *Karl Marx: Early Writings*, pp. 379–400. New York: Random House [1843–44]

Marx, K. (1975b) 'Preface to A Contribution to the Critique of Political Economy', in Hoare, Q., ed., *Karl Marx: Early Writings*, pp. 424–9. New York: Random House [1859]

Marx, K. (1977) *Capital*, Vol. I. New York: Vintage Books [1867]

Marx, K. and F. Engels (1974) 'Manifesto of the Communist Party', in Fernback, D., ed., *Karl Marx: Political Writings*, Vol. I, pp. 67–99. New York: Random House [1848]

Masters, R. D. (1964) 'World Politics as a Primitive Political System', *World Politics* 16(4): 595–619

Masters, R. D. (1968) *The Political Philosophy of Rousseau.* Princeton: Princeton University Press

Masters, R. D (1996) *Machiavelli, Leonardo and the Science of Power.* Notre Dame: University of Notre Dame Press

May, E. L. (1975) *Lessons of the Past.* Oxford: Oxford University Press

Mazower, M. (1998) *Dark Continent.* London: Penguin

Mazower, M. (2012) *Governing the World.* London: Allen Lane

Mazzini, G. (1945) *Selected Writings.* London: Lindsay Drummond

Mearsheimer, J. (1990) 'Why We Will Soon Miss the Cold War', *The Atlantic*, August

Meinecke, F. (1957) *Machiavellism.* New Haven: Yale University Press [1924]

Mészáros, I. (1970) *Marx' Theory of Alienation.* New York: Harper & Row

Mill, J. S. (1866) *Principles of Political Economy*, 2 vols, London: Longman, Green, Reader and Dyer

Mitrany, D. (1933) *The Progress of International Government.* New Haven: Yale University Press

Mitrany, D. (1966) *A Working Peace System.* Chicago: Quadrangle [1943]

Modelski, G. (1972) *Multinational Corporations and World Order.* Los Angeles: Sage

Modelski, G. (1987) *Long Cycles in World Politics.* Seattle: University of Washington Press

Modelski, G. and W. R. Thompson (1988) *Sea-power in Global Politics.* Seattle: University of Washington Press

Molnar, M. (1975) *Marx, Engels et le politique international.* Paris: Gallimard

Momigliano, A., ed. (1963) *The Conflict between Paganism and Christianity in the 4th Century.* Oxford: Clarendon Press

Monnet, J. (1976) *Mémoires.* Paris: Fayard

Montaigne, M. de (1935) *The Essays of Michel de Montaigne*, Vol. I. New York: Knopf

Montesquieu, C. L. de Secondat, baron de (1990) *The Spirit of the Laws.* Chicago: Encyclopaedia Britannica [1748]

Morefield, J. (2013) 'A Democratic Critique of the State', in Bliddal, H., C. Sylvest and P. Wilson, eds, *Classics of International Relations*, pp. 24–36. London: Routledge

Morel, E. D. (1912) *Ten Years of Secret Diplomacy.* New York: Huebsch

Morgenthau, H. J. (1933) *La Notion du 'politique' et la theorie des différences internationaux.* Paris: Librairie du Recueil Siray

Morgenthau, H. J. (1946) *Scientific Man vs. Power Politics.* Chicago: University of Chicago Press

Morgenthau, H. J. (1948a) 'The Political Science of E. H. Carr', *World Politics* 1(1): 127–34

Morgenthau, H. J. (1948b) *Politics among Nations.* New York: Alfred A. Knopf

Morgenthau, H. J. (1967a) 'We Are Deluding Ourselves in Viet-Nam', *New York Times Magazine*, 18 April, reprinted in Raskin, M. and B. Fall, eds, *The Viet-Nam Reader*, pp. 37–45. New York: Vintage Books

Morgenthau, H. J. (1967b) 'To Intervene or Not to Intervene', *Foreign Affairs* 45(3): 424–36

Morgenthau, H. J. (1978) *Politics among Nations.* New York: Knopf

Morley, J. (1881) *The Life of Richard Cobden.* Boston: Robert Brothers

Morris, H. C. (1900) *The History of Colonization.* New York: Macmillan

Moses, J. and T. L. Knutsen (2012) *Ways of Knowing.* London: Palgrave

Mueller, J. (1989) *Retreat from Doomsday.* New York: Basic Books

Mueller, J. (2004) *Remnants of War.* New York: Cornell University Press

Muir, R. (1918) *National Self-Government, Its Growth and Principles, The Culmination of Modern History.* London: Constable & Co.

Muir, R. (1933) *The Interdependent World and Its Problems.* London: Constable & Co.

Müller, J.-W. (2003) *A Dangerous Mind: Carl Schmitt in Post-War European Thought.* New Haven: Yale University Press

Mussolini, B. (1933) *The Political and Social Doctrine of Fascism.* London: Hogarth Press

Nedham, M. (1659) *Interest will not Lie, or a View of England's True Interest.* London: n.p.

Needham, J. (1969) *The Grand Titration.* London: Allen & Unwin

Neuberg A. (2008) 'Le travail militaire du parti parmi les paysans', in G. Chailand, *Les guerres irrégulières XXe–XXI siècle*, pp. 583–612. Paris: Gallimard [1930]

Neumann, F. L. (1944) *Behemoth.* New York: Octagon Books

Neumann, J. von and O. Morgenstern (1944) *A Theory of Games and Economic Behavior.* Princeton: Princeton University Press

Ngugi wa Thiong'o (1986) *Decolonizing the Mind.* London: James Currey

Nicolson, H. G. (1954) *Evolution of the Diplomatic Method.* London: Constable & Co.

Nicolson, H. G. (1988) *Diplomacy.* Washington DC: Georgetown University, School of Foreign Service [1939]

Niebuhr, R. (1932) *Moral Man and Immoral Society.* New York: Scribner's Sons

Niebuhr, R. (1942) 'Plans for World Reorganization', *Christianity and Crisis*, 1(2): 2–4

Niebuhr, R. (1943) 'American Power and World Responsibility', *Christianity and Crisis* 3(2): 2–4

Niebuhr, R. (1945) *The Children of Light and the Children of Darkness*. New York: Scribner's Sons

Niebuhr, R. (1949) *Faith and History*. New York: Scribner's Sons

Niebuhr, R. (1950a) 'American Conservatism and the World Crisis', *Yale Review* 40(3): 385–97

Niebuhr, R. (1950b) 'A Protest against a Dilemma's Two Horns', *World Politics* 2(3): 338–45

Niebuhr, R. (1959) *The Structure of Nations and Empires*. New York: Scribner's Sons

Nietzsche, F. (1960) 'Aus dem Nachlass der Achtzigerjahre', in *Werke*, Vol. III, p. 917. Munich: Carl Hansen Verlag [188?]

Nietzsche, F. (1994) *On the Genealogy of Morality*. Cambridge: Cambridge University Press [1887]

Njølstad, O., ed. (2004) *The Last Decade of the Cold War*. London: Frank Cass

North, D. (1981) *Structure and Change in Economic History*. New York: W. W. Norton

North, D. (1990) *Institutions, Institutional Change and Economic Performance*. Cambridge: Cambridge University Press

North, D. and R. P. Thomas (1973) *The Rise of the Western World*. Cambridge: Cambridge University Press

Novicow, I. A. (1886) *La politique internationale*, Paris: n.p.

Nye, J. (1990) *Bound to Lead*. New York: Basic Books

Nye, J. (2011) *The Future of Power*. New York: Public Affairs

Ogilvy, D. (2004) *Confessions of an Advertising Man*. London: Southbank Publishing [1963]

Ohmae, K. (1990) *The Borderless World*. New York: Harper Business

Ohmae, K. (1995) *The End of the Nation State*. New York: Free Press

Olson, W. C. and A. J. R. Groom (1991) *International Relations Then and Now*. London: Routledge

Oplatka, A. (1989) *Der erste Riss in der Mauer*. Vienna: Paul Zsolnay Verlag

Oppenheim, L. F. L (1937) *International Law*. London: Longman, Green

Organski, A. F. K. and J. Kugler (1980) *The War Ledger*. Chicago: University of Chicago Press

Osiander, A. (1998) 'Rereading Early Twentieth-Century IR Theory', *International Studies Quarterly* 42(3): 409–32

Oye, K. A., ed. (1986) *Cooperation under Anarchy*. Princeton: Princeton University Press

Paine, T. (1908a) 'The Crisis', in Wheeler, D. E., ed., *Life and Writings of Thomas Paine*, Vol. 3. New York: Vincent Park [1777]

Paine, T. (1908b) 'Letter to the Abbé Raynal, on the Affairs of North America', in Wheeler, D. E., ed., *Life and Writings of Thomas Paine*, vol. 8, pp. 187–287. New York: Vincent Park [1782]

Paine, T. (1969), *Rights of Man*. London: Penguin [1791/92]

Paine, T. (1986) *Common Sense*. London: Penguin: London [1776]

Palmer, R. R. (1951) *A History of the Modern World*. New York: Knopf

Pannekoek, A. (1912) *Marxism and Darwinism*. Chicago: Charles H. Kerr & Company Co-operative

Parker, G., ed. (1978) *The General Crisis of the Seventeenth Century*. London: Routledge & Kegan Paul

Parkinson, F. (1977) *The Philosophy of International Relations.* Los Angeles: Sage
Paul the Deacon (1974) *History of the Lombards.* Philadelphia: University of Pennsylvania Press [797?]
Pecquet, A. (1757) *L'esprit des maximes politiques.* Paris: Chez Prault père
Penn, W. (1986) *Essai d'un Projet pour rendre la Paix de l'Europe solide et durable.* York: William Sessions [1693?]
Perkins, H. L. (1959) *The Moral and Political Philosophy of the Abbé de Saint-Pierre.* Geneva: Librairie E. Droc
Peterson, V. S. (1993) *Global Gender Issues.* Boulder: Westview Press
Pico della Mirandola, G. (1965) *On the Dignity of Man.* Indianapolis: Bobbs-Merrill [1486]
Pinker, S. (2011) *The Better Angels of Our Nature: Why Violence Has Declined.* New York: Viking
Pirenne, H. (1937) *Economic and Social History of Medieval Europe.* New York: Harcourt, Brace
Pitkin, H. F. (1984) *Fortune Is a Woman.* Berkeley: University of California Press
Poggi, G. (1978) *The Development of the Modern State.* Stanford: Stanford University Press
Poole, R. (2008) *Earthrise.* New Haven: Yale University Press
Popper, K. (1945) *The Open Society and Its Enemies.* London: Routledge and Sons
Popper, K. (1959) *The Logic of Scientific Discovery.* London: Hutchinson [1930]
Popper, K. (1963) *Conjectures and Refutations.* London: Routledge & Kegan Paul
Popper, K. (1979) *Objective Knowledge: An Evolutionary Approach.* Oxford: Clarendon Press
Porter, R. (1999) *The Enlightenment.* New York: W. W. Norton
Postan, M.M., E.E. Rich and E. Miller, eds (1965) *Cambridge Economic History of Europe*, Vol. III. Cambridge: Cambridge University Press
Potter, P. B. (1922) *An Introduction to the Study of International Organization.* New York: Appleton-Century
Prebish, R. (1950) *The Economic Development of Latin America and Its Principal Problems.* New York: United Nations
Pufendorf, S. (1991) *On the Duty of Man and Citizen.* Cambridge: Cambridge University Press [1673]
Pye, L. W., ed. (1963) *Communications and Political Development.* Princeton: Princeton University Press
Quatela, A. (1991) *Invito alia lettura di Guicciardini.* Milan: Mursia
Raab, F. (1964) *The English Face of Machiavelli.* London: Routledge
Rabinow, P., ed. (1984) *The Foucault Reader.* New York: Pantheon
Ramel, F. (2006) *Les fondateurs oubliés – Durkheim, Simmel, Weber, Mauss et les Relations Internationales.* Paris: PUF
Ranke, L. von (1925) 'Die grossen Mächte', in *Savonarola; Die Grossen Mächte; Politisches Gesprach*, pp. 153–97. Berlin: Wegweiser Verlag [1833]
Rapoport, A. (1960) *Fights, Games, and Debates.* Ann Arbor: University of Michigan Press
Rapoport, A. (1964) *Strategy and Conscience.* New York: Shocken Books
Ratzel, F. (1896) 'Die Gesetze des raumlichen Wachstums der Staaten', *Petermanns Mitteilungen* 42 : 101ff

Ratzel, F. (1901) 'Der Lebensraum', in Bücher, K., K. V. Fricker, F. X. von Funk, G. von Mandry, and F. Ratzel, eds, *Festgaben für Albert Schäffle*, pp. 104–89. Tübingen: Laupp

Ratzel, F. (1903) *Politische Geographie*. Munich: R. Oldenbourg

Raynal, G. T. (1804) *Philosofisk og Politisk Historie om Europeernes Handel og Besiddelser i Ost- og Vest-Indien*. Copenhagen: Sebastian Popp [1770]

Reinsch, P. S. (1900) *World Politics*. New York: Macmillan

Reiss, H., ed. (1991) *Kant: Political Writings*. Cambridge: Cambridge University Press

Renan, E. (n.d.) *Qu'est-ce qu'une nation?* www.rutebeuf.com/textes/renan01.html [1882]

Renouvin, P., ed. (1994) *Histoire des relations internationales*, Vol. I. Paris: Hachette [1953]

Ricardo, D. (1984) *The Principles of Political Economy and Taxation*. London: Everyman's Library [1817]

Rice, D. (2008) 'Reinhold Niebuhr and Hans Morgenthau: A Friendship with Contrasting Shades of Realism', *Journal of American Studies* 42(2): 255–91

Richardson, L. (1960a) *Arms and Insecurity*. Pacific Grove: Boxwood Press [1949]

Richardson, L. (1960b) *Statistics of Deadly Quarrels*. Pacific Grove: Boxwood Press [1950]

Robertson, W. (1896) *History of the Reign of Charles V.* London: George Routledge & Co [1769]

Rochau, L. (1853) *Grundsätze der Realpolitik*. Stuttgart: Verlag von Karl Göpel

Rohan, H., duc de (1673) *Interns et maximes des Princes et des Estates souverains*. Cologne: n.p. [1638]

Roosen, W. (1986) *Daniel Defoe and Diplomacy*. Selinsgrove: Susquehanna University Press

Roover, R. de (1965) 'The Organization of Trade', in Postan, M. M., E. E. Rich and E. Miller, eds, *Cambridge Economic History of Europe*, Vol. III, pp. 42–118. Cambridge: Cambridge University Press

Rösch, F. (2014) *Émigré scholars and the Genesis of International Relations*. London: Palgrave

Rosecrance, R. (1963) *Action and Reaction in World Politics*. Boston: Little, Brown & Co.

Rosenau, J. N. and K. Knorr, eds (1969) *Contending Approaches to International Politics*. Princeton: Princeton University Press

Ross, E. (1969) *Social Control: A Survey of the Foundations of Order*. Cleveland: Press of Case Western Reserve University [1901]

Ross, M. (1984) *Leibniz*. Oxford: Oxford University Press

Rousseau, J.-J. (1950a) 'Discourse on the Origin and Basis of Inequality among Men', in Cole, G. D. H., ed., *The Social Contract and Discourses*, pp. 175–282. London: Dutton [1755]

Rousseau, J.-J- (1950b) 'Social Contract', in Cole, G. D. H., ed., *The Social Contract and Discourses*, pp. 1–142. London: Dutton [1762]

Rousseau, J.-J. (1950c) 'Discourse on Political Economy', in Cole, G. D. H., ed., *The Social Contract and Discourses*, pp. 283–330. London: Dutton [1755]

Rousseau, J.-J. (1964a) 'Extrait du projet de paix perpetuelle', in *Oeuvres Complètes*, Vol. III, pp. 563–90. Paris: Bibliothèque de la Pleiade [1760]

Rousseau, J.-J. (1964b) 'Jugement sur le projet de paix perpetuelle', in *Oeuvres Complètes*, Vol. III, pp. 591–600. Paris: Bibliothèque de la Pleiade [1782]

Rousseau, J.-J. (1964c) 'Que l'état de guerre nait de l'etat social', in *Oeuvres Complètes*, Vol. III, pp. 601–13. Paris: Bibliothèque de la Pleiade [1786]

Rousseau, J.-J. (1964d) 'Considérations sur le gouvernement de Pologne', in *Oeuvres Complètes*, Vol. III, pp. 953–1044. Paris: Bibliothè–que de la Pleiade [1782]

Rousseau, J.-J. (1978) *The Confessions.* Harmondsworth: Penguin [1782]

Rousseau, J.-J. (1995) *Oeuvres complètes*, Vol. V. Paris: Gallimard

Rousseau, J.-J. (1997) 'Essay on the Origin of Languages', in *The Discourses and Other Early Political Writings*, pp. 247–300. Cambridge: Cambridge University Press

Ruggie, J. G. (1986) 'Continuity and Transformation in the World Polity', in Keohane, R. O., ed., *Neo-Realism and Its Critics*, pp. 131–58. New York: Columbia University Press

Ruggie, J. G., ed. (1993a) *Multilateralism Matters.* New York: Columbia University Press

Ruggie, J. G. (1993b) 'Territoriality and Beyond', *International Organization* 47(1): 139–75

Runciman, S. (1992) *The First Crusade.* Cambridge: Cambridge University Press [1951]

Russell, F. M. (1936) *Theories of International Relations.* New York: D. Appleton-Century Co.

Russett, B. (1990) *Controlling the Sword.* Cambridge, MA: Harvard University Press

Russett, B. (1993) *Grasping the Democratic Peace.* Princeton: Princeton University Press

Russett, B. and J. Oneal (2001) *Triangulating Peace.* New York: W. W. Norton

Said, E. W. (1978) *Orientalism.* London: Routledge & Kegan Paul

Said, E. W. (1993) *Culture and Imperialism.* London: Chatto & Windus

Salter, A. (1961) *Memoirs of a Public Servant.* London: Faber and Faber

Sarkees, M. R. (2000) 'The Correlates of War Data: An Update to 1997, *Conflict Management and Peace Science* 18(1): 123–44

Satow, E. (1917) *A Guide to Diplomatic Practice.* London: Longman, Green & Co.

Sauvy, A. (1952) 'Trois mondes, une planète'. *L'Observateur*, 14 August, p. 118

Schelling, T. (1960) *The Strategy of Conflict.* Cambridge, MA: Harvard University Press

Schelling, T. (1966) *Arms and Influence.* Cambridge. MA: Harvard University Press

Scheuerman, W. E. (2009) *Hans Morgenthau: Realism and Beyond.* Oxford: Polity Press

Schmidt, B. (1998) *The Political Discourse of Anarchy.* Albany: State University of New York Press

Schmitt, C. (1930) *Der Völkerforbund und das politische Problem der Friedenssicherung.* Berlin: Duncker & Humblott

Schmitt, C. (1932) *Das Begriff des politischen.* Berlin: Duncker & Humblott [1927]

Schmitt, C. (1938) *Der Leviathan in der Staatslehre des Thomas Hobbes.* Berlin: Duncker & Humblott

Schmitt, C. (1939) *Völkerrechtliche Großraumordnung und Interventionsverbot für raumfremde Mächte.* Berlin: Duncker & Humblott

Schumacher, E. M. (1973) *Small Is Beautiful.* New York: Harper & Row

Schuman, F. L. (1933) *International Politics.* New York: McGraw-Hill

Schumpeter, J. A. (1954) *A History of Economic Analysis.* New York: Oxford University Press

Schumpeter, J. A. (1976) 'Die Krise der Steuerstaats', in Hickel, R., *Rudolf Goldscheid, Joseph Schumpeter: Die Ökonomie der Staatsfinanzen.* Frankfurt am Main: Suhrkamp [1918]

Schwarzenberger, G. (1951) *Power Politics.* New York: Praeger

Scott, J. B., ed. (1920) *Proceedings of the Hague Peace Conference.* New York: Oxford University Press

Scott, J. B. (1934) *The Spanish Origin of International Law.* Oxford: Clarendon Press

Seebohm, F. (1871) *On International Reform.* London: Longmans, Green, and Co.

Selden, J. (1652) *Mare Clausum: Of the Dominions or Ownership of the Sea.* London: William Du-Gard

Semmel, B., ed. (1981) *Marxism and the Science of War.* London: Oxford University Press

Shaw, R. (2003) *War and Genocide.* Oxford: Polity Press

Shirer, W. L. (1983) *The Rise and Fall of the Third Reich.* New York: Fawcett Crest [1950]

Shotwell, J. T. (1934) 'Introduction' , in E. E. Ware, *The Study of International Relations in the United States*, pp. 3–22. New York: Columbia University Press

Shotwell, J. T. (1937) *On the Rim of the Abyss.* New York: Macmillan

Simonds, F. and F. Emeny (1935) *The Great Powers in World Politics.* New York: American Book Co.

Singer, J. D. (1966) 'The Behavioral Science Approach to International Relations: Payoff and Prospect', *SAIS Review*, 10(2): 12–20

Singer, J. D. (1968) 'Editor's Introduction', in Singer, J. D., ed, *Quantitative International Politics*, pp. 1–15. New York: The Free Press

Singer, J. D. (1969) 'The Incompleat Theorist: Insight Without Evidence', in Knorr, K. and J. Rosenau, eds, *Contending Approaches to International Politics*, pp. 62–86. Princeton: Princeton University Press

SIPRI (1991) *SIPRI Yearbook.* Oxford: Oxford University Press

Skinner, Q. (1981) *Machiavelli.* Oxford: Oxford University Press

Smil, V. (2010) *Why America Is Not the New Rome.* Cambridge, MA: MIT Press

Smith, A. (1976) *The Wealth of Nations.* Oxford: Clarendon Press [1776]

Smith, A. (1982a) *The Theory of Moral Sentiment.* Indianapolis: LibertyClassics [1759]

Smith, A. (1982b) 'The History of Astronomy', in *Essays on Philosophical Subjects*, ed. W. P. D. Wightman and J. C. Bryce, Vol. III of the Glasgow Edition of the *Works and Correspondence of Adam Smith*, pp. 33–106. Indianapolis: Liberty Fund [175?]

Smith, A. D. (1991) *National Identity.* Harmondsworth: Penguin

Smith, D. M., ed. (1966) *American Intervention 1917.* Boston: Houghton Mifflin

Smith, H. (1990) 'The Womb of War', *Review of International Studies*, 16(1):39–58

Smith, S., K. Booth and M. Zalewski (1996) *International Theory: Positivism and Beyond.* Cambridge: Cambridge University Press

Smith, T. (2007) *A Pact with the Devil.* London: Routledge

Snyder, G. (1984) 'The Security Dilemma in Alliance Politics', *World Politics* 36(4): 461–95

Snyder, J. (1991) *Myths of Empire.* Ithaca: Cornell University Press

Sombart, W. (1913) *Krieg und Kapitalismus.* Munich: Duncker & Humblott

Sonnino, P. (1981) 'Introduction', in Frederick II, *Anti-Machiavel*, pp. 1–23. Athens: Ohio University Press

Souleyman, E. V. (1972) *The Vision of World Peace in Seventeenth and Eighteenth-Century France.* New York: Kennekat Press [1941]

Southern, R. W. (1953) *The Making of the Middle Ages*. New Haven: Yale University Press

Spencer, H. (1864) *Principles of Biology. Vol. I*. London: Williams and Norgate

Spencer, H. (1882) *Political Institutions (Being Pt. V of the Principles of Sociology)*. London: Williams and Norgate

Spencer, H. (1897) *Social Statics*. New York: D. Appleton and Co.

Spinoza, B. de (1951a) 'Theologico-political Treatise', in *Works*, Vol. I, pp. 1–265. New York: Dover Publications [1670]

Spinoza, B. de (1951b) 'Ethics', in *Works*, Vol. II, pp. 43–270. New York: Dover Publications [1677]

Spinoza, B. de (1951c) 'A Political Treatise', in *Works*, Vol. I, pp. 279–385. New York: Dover Publications [1677]

Spiro, D. E. (1994) 'The Insignificance of the Liberal Peace', *International Security* 19(2): 50–86

Sprout, H. and M. Sprout (1965) *The Ecological Perspectives on Human Affairs*. Princeton: Princeton University Press

Spruyt, H. (1994) *The Sovereign State and its Competitors*. Princeton: Princeton University Press

Spykman, N. J. (1942) *America's Strategy in World Politics*. New York: Harcourt, Brace and Co.

Spykman, N. J. (1943) *The Geography of the Peace*. New York: Harcourt, Brace and Company

Stahl, W. H. (1977) *Martianus Capella and the Seven Liberal Arts*. New York: Columbia University Press

Stalin, J. V. (1946) *Speech Delivered by J. V. Stalin at a Meeting of Voters of the Stalin Electoral Area of Moscow, February 9, 1946*. Washington DC: Embassy of the Soviet Union

Stalin, J. V. (1953) 'The Twelfth Congress of the R.C.P.(B.)', in *Works*, Vol. V, pp. 191–200. Moscow: Foreign Languages Publishing House [1923]

Stark, W., ed. (1952–54) *Jeremy Bentham's Economic Writings*, Vol. III. London: Allen & Unwin

Starobinski, J. (1988) *Jean-Jacques Rousseau*. Chicago: Chicago University Press

Stavrianos, L. S. (1981) *Global Rift*. New York: William Morrow and Co.

Stead, W. T. (1899a) *La guerre est-il devenu impossible?* London: Mowbray House

Stead, W. T. (1899b) *The United States of Europe*. New York: Doubleday & McClure Co.

Steel, R. (1980) *Walter Lippmann and the American Century*. Boston: Little, Brown & Co.

Steinbruner, J. D. (1974) *The Cybernetic Theory of Decision*. Princeton: Princeton University Press

Stieglitz, A. de (1893) *De l'équilibre politique de légitimisme et du principe de nationalités*. Paris: A. Durand et Pedrone-Lauriel

Stopford, J., S. Strange and J. S. Henley (1992) *Rival States, Rival Firms*. Cambridge: Cambridge University Press

Strachan, H. (2006) *The First World War*. London: Simon & Schuster

Strange, S. (1986) *Casino Capitalism*. Manchester: Manchester University Press

Strange, S. (1988) *States and Markets*. London: Pinter

Strange, S. (1992) 'States, Firms and Diplomacy', *International Affairs* 68(1): 1–15

Strange. S. (1996) *The Retreat of the State*. Cambridge: Cambridge University Press

Strayer, J. R. (1955) *Western Europe in the Middle Ages*. New York: Appleton-Century-Crofts

Strayer, J. R. (1970) *On the Medieval Origins of the Modern State*. Princeton: Princeton University Press

Studdert-Kennedy, G. (1995) 'Christianity, Statecraft and Chatham House', *Diplomacy and Statecraft* 6(2): 470–89

Sumner, W. G. (1954) *What the Social Classes Owe Each Other*. Caldwell: The Caxton Printers, Ltd [1883]

Sumner, W. G. (1965) 'War', in *The Conquest of the United States by Spain and Other Essays*, pp. 200–35. Chicago: Henry Regenry Company [1903]

Suttner, B. von (1891) *Das Machinzeitalter*. Zürich: Verlags-Magazin

Suttner, B. von (1914) *Lay Down Your Arms!* New York: Longman, Green

Sylvester, C. (1994) *Feminist Theory and International Relations in a Postmodern Era*. Cambridge: Cambridge University Press

Sylvester, C. (2002) *Feminist International Relations: An Unfinished Journey*. Cambridge: Cambridge University Press

Symons, F. (1931) *Courses on International Affairs in American Colleges, 1930–31*. Boston: World Peace Foundation

Szücs, J. (1990) *Die drei historischen Regionen Europas*. Frankfurt am Main: Verlag Neue Kritik

Takeyh, R. (2014) 'What Really Happened in Iran', *Foreign Affairs* 93(4): 2–13

Talbott, S. (1988) *Master of the Game*. New York: Knopf

Talmon, J. L. (1952) *The Origins of Totalitarian Democracy*. London: Secker & Warburg

Talmon, J.L. (1960) *Political Messianism*. London: Secker & Warburg

Tardieu, A. (1908) *La France et les alliances*. Paris: F. Alcan

Tardieu, A. (1921) *The Truth about the Treaty*. London: Hodder and Stoughton

Taylor, A. J. P. (1946) *The Course of German History*. London: Hamish Hamilton

ter Meulen, J. (1917) *Internationalen Organisation in seiner Entwicklung*. The Hague: Martinus Nijhoff

Thatcher, M. (1990) 'Speech to the Czechoslovak National Assembly', The Margaret Thatcher Foundation, www.margaretthatcher.org/document/108194

Thatcher, M. (1993) *The Downing Street Years*. London: HarperCollins

Thucydides (1972) *The Peloponnesian War*. Harmondsworth: Penguin [*c*. 402 BC]

Tickner, A. (1997) 'You Just Don't Understand', *International Studies Quarterly* 41(4): 611–32

Tilly, C., ed. (1975) *The Formation of Nation States in Western Europe*. Princeton: Princeton University Press

Tilly, C. (1994) *Coercion, Capital, and European States, AD 990–1992*. Oxford: Blackwell

Tocqueville, A. de (1969) *Democracy in America*. New York: Harper & Row

Todorov, T. (1989) *Nous et les autres*. Paris: Editions du Seuil

Toffler, A. (1970) *Future Shock*. New York: Bantam Books

Treitschke, H. von (1916) *Politics*. London: Macmillan

Triepel, H. (1938) *Die Hegemonie: Ein Buch von führenden Staaten*. Stuttgart: Kohlhammer

Truman, H. S. (1985) 'Recommendations on Greece and Turkey', in US Department of State, ed., *A Decade of American Foreign Policy Basic Documents, 1941–1949*, pp. 530–4. Washington DC: Government Printing Office

Tucker, R. C., ed. (1975) *The Lenin Anthology*. New York: W. W. Norton

UN (1993) *World Investments Report 1992*. New York: United Nations

Unger, M. J. (2011) *Machiavelli. A Biography*. New York: Simon & Schuster

US Bureau of the Census (1975) *Historical Statistics of the United States, Colonial Times to 1970*. Washington DC: Government Printing Office

US Department of State, ed. (1985) *A Decade of American Foreign Policy Basic Documents, 1941–1949*. Washington DC: Government Printing Office

US Senate (1984a) *The US Government and the Vietnam War I*. Washington DC: Government Printing Office

US Senate (1984b) *The US Government and the Vietnam War II*. Washington DC: Government Printing Office

Varg, P. A. (1970) *Foreign Policies of the Founding Fathers*. Baltimore: Penguin Books

Vasquez, J. (1983) *The Power of Power Politics*. New Brunswick: Rutgers University Press

Vattel, É. de (1863) *The Law of Nations or the Principles of Natural Law Applied to the Conduct and to the Affairs of Nations and of Sovereigns*. Philadelphia: T. & J. W. Johnson [1758]

Veblen, T. (1939) *Imperial Germany and the Industrial Revolution*. New York: Viking Press [1915]

Vergé, C. (1858) 'Le droit des gens avant et depuis 1789', pp. i–lv, preface to 2nd ed. of G. E. de Martens, *Précis de droit de gens moderne de l'Europe*. Paris: Guillaumin Librairies

Verne, J. (1991) *Around the World in Eighty Days*. New York: Bantam [1872]

Vincent, A. (1987) *Theories of the State*. Oxford: Blackwell

Vitoria, F. de (1934a) 'On the Indians Recently Discovered', appendix A, in Scott, J. B., *The Spanish Origin of International Law*. Oxford: Clarendon Press [1532]

Vitoria, F. de (1934b) 'On the Law of War Made by the Spaniards on the Barbarians', appendix B, in Scott, J. B., *The Spanish Origin of International Law*. Oxford: Clarendon Press [153?]

Voltaire (1967) 'Guerre', *Dictionnaire Philosophique*, pp. 228–33. Paris: Garnier Frères [1764]

Voltaire (1980) *Letters on England*. Harmondsworth: Penguin [1733]

Waever, O. (1996) 'The Rise and Fall of the Inter-Paradigm Debate', in Smith, S., K. Booth and M. Zalewski, eds, *International Theory: Positivism and Beyond*, pp. 149–85. Cambridge: Cambridge University Press

Walker, R. B. J. (1993) *Inside/Outside*. Cambridge: Cambridge University Press

Walker, S. G. (1990) 'The Evolution of Operational Code Analysis', *Political Psychology* 11(2): 403–18

Walker, T. (2000) 'The Forgotten Prophet: Tom Paine's Cosmopolitanism and International Relations', *International Studies Quarterly* 44(1): 51–73

Wall, I. M. (1983) *French Communism in the Era of Stalin*. Westport: Greenwood Press

Wallace, H. A. (1943) 'The Price of Free World Victory', in Willkie, W., H. Hoover, H. A. Wallace and S. Welles, eds, *Prefaces to Peace*, pp. 363–417. New York: Simon & Schuster

Wallace, H. A. (1944) 'World Organization', in *Democracy Reborn*. New York: Reynal & Hitchcock

Wallace-Hadrill, J. M. (1956) *The Barbarian West, 400–1000*. London: Hutchinson

Wallerstein, I. (1974) *The Modern World-System*, Vol. I. New York: Academic Press

Wallerstein, I. (1980) *The Modern World-System*, Vol. II. New York: Academic Press

Wallerstein, I. (1989) *The Modern World-System*, Vol. III. New York: Academic Press

Wallerstein, I. (2011) *The Modern World-System*, Vol. IV. New York: Academic Press

Waltz, K. N. (1959) *Man, the State and War*. New York: Columbia University Press

Waltz, K. N. (1975) 'Theory of International Relations', in Greenstein, F. and N. Polsby, eds, *The Handbook of Political Science*, Vol. 5, pp. 1–86. Reading, MA: Addison-Wesley

Waltz, K. N. (1979) *Theory of International Politics*. Reading, MA: Addison-Wesley

Walworth, A. C. (1969) *Woodrow Wilson*, Vol. II. Baltimore: Penguin

Ware, E. E. (1934) *The Study of International Relations in the United States*. New York: Columbia University Press

Watson, A. (1992) *The Evolution of International Society*. London: Routledge

Weber, C. (1994) 'Good Girls, Little Girls, and Bad Girls', *Millennium* 23(2): 337–49

Weber, C. (1995) *Simulating Sovereignty*. Cambridge: Cambridge University Press

Weber, M. (1958) *The Protestant Ethic and the Spirit of Capitalism*. New York: Scribner's Sons [1905]

Weber, M. (1994) *Political Writings*. Cambridge: Cambridge University Press

Weikart, R. (1993) 'The Origins of Social Darwinism in Germany, 1859–1995', *Journal of the History of Ideas* 54(3): 469–89

Weimann, G. (2014) *Terrorism in Cyberspace*. New York: Columbia University Press

Weiner, T. (2007) *Legacy of Ashes*. New York: Random House

Weissman, S. R. (2014) 'What Really Happened in Congo', *Foreign Affairs* 93(4): 14–15

Welles, B. (1997) *Sumner Welles: FDR's Global Strategist*. New York: St Martin's Press

Welles, S. (1943) 'Blue-Print for Peace', in Willkie, W., H. Hoover, H. A. Wallace and S. Welles, eds, *Prefaces to Peace*, pp. 419–38. New York: Simon & Schuster

Wendt, A. (1995) 'Constructing International Politics', *International Security* 20(1): 71–81

Wendt, A. (1999) *Social Theory of International Politics*. Cambridge: Cambridge University Press

Westad, O. A. (2005) *The Global Cold War*. Cambridge: Cambridge University Press

Westlake, J. (1888) *A Treatise on Private international Law*. London: William Maxwell [1858]

Wheeler, D. E., ed. (1908) *Life and Writings of Thomas Paine*. New York: Vincent Park, 9 vols.

White, L. (1972) 'The Expansion of Technology 500–1500', in Cipolla, C. M., ed., *The Fontana Economic History of Europe*, Vol. I, pp. 143–74. London: Collins/Fontana

White House (1992) *Defense Planning Guidance, FY 1994–1999*. Washington DC. www.archives.gov/declassification/iscap/pdf/2008-003-docs1-12.pdf

Wight, M. (1966) 'Why Is There No International Theory?' in Butterfield, H. and M. Wight, eds, *Diplomatic Investigations*, pp. 17–35. Cambridge, MA: Harvard University Press

Wight, M. (1987) 'An Anatomy of International Thought', *Review of International Studies* 13(2): 221–7

Wight, M. (1991) *International Theory: The Three Traditions*. Leicester: Leicester University Press

Willkie, W. L. (1943) 'One World', in Willkie, W. L., H. Hoover, H. A. Wallace and S. Welles, eds, *Prefaces to Peace*, pp. 9–143. New York: Simon & Schuster

Wilson, P. (1998) 'The Myth of the First Great Debate', *Review of International Studies* 24 (Special Issue): 1–16

Wilson, P. (2013) 'Power, Morality and the Remaking of International Order: E. H. Carr's *The Twenty Years' Crisis*', in Bliddal, H., C. Sylvest and P. Wilson, eds, *Classics of International Relations*, pp. 36–48. London: Routledge

Wilson, W. (1967) 'Address to the Senate', 10 July; in Link, A. S., ed., *The Public Papers of Woodrow Wilson*, Vol. V. Princeton: Princeton University Press

Wiltse, C. M. (1960) *The Jeffersonian Tradition in American Democracy*. New York: Hill and Wang

Witt, J. F. (2012) *Lincoln's Code*. New York: Simon & Schuster

Wohlforth, W. (1999) 'The Stability of a Unipolar World'. *International Security* 24(1): 5–41

Wohlstetter, A. (1959) 'The Delicate Balance of Terror', *Foreign Affairs* 37(2): 211–34

Wolfers, A. (1951) 'The Pole of Power and the Pole of Indifference', *World Politics* 4(1): 39–53

Wolfers, A. (1959) 'The Actors in International Politics', in Fox, W. R., ed., *Theoretical Aspects of International Relations*, pp. 83–107. Notre Dame: Notre Dame Press

Woolf, L. (1916) *International Government*. New York: Brentano's

Woolf, L. (1917) *The Framework for a Lasting Peace*. London: Allen & Unwin

Wright, L. (2007) *The Looming Tower*. London: Penguin

Wright, Q. (1942) *A Study of War*. Chicago: University of Chicago Press

Wriston, W. (1992) *The Twilight of Sovereignty*. New York: Scribner

Ye'or, B. (2005) *Eurabia*. Cranbury: Fairleigh Dickinson University Press

Yergin, D. (1991) *The Prize*. New York: Simon & Schuster

Yergin, D. (2011) *The Quest*. London: Penguin

Yergin, D. and J. Stanislaw (1998) *The Commanding Heights*. New York: Simon & Schuster

York, E. (1919) *Leagues of Nations*. New York: Swarthmore University Press

Zakaria, F. (2011) *The Post-American World*. New York: W. W. Norton & Company

Zhdanov, A. (1947) 'On the International Situation'; downloaded from: http://zdanov. blogfree.net/?t=4271252

Zimmern, A. E. (1936) *The League of Nations and the Rule of Law 1918–35*. London: Macmillan

Index

'Abbasid dynasty 23
absolutism 105-6, 130
Adorno, Theodor 303, 357, 379
Afghanistan 399, 409, 468-9
alienation 147-8, 150-4, 177-8, 190, 379, 477
   and war 163
   see also Rousseau; Hegel
American Constitution 160
Allison, Graham 360-1
anarchical society *see* Bull; Manning
anarchy 2, 290, 326
   Dickinson and 249-50
   Lorimer and 2, 218, 347
   more or less mature 409
   Waltz and 354, 386-9 *passim*, 417
Angell, Norman 3, 191, 230, 390, 443
Aquinas, Thomas 35-8, 43n18, 79
arbitration 229, 257
Aristotle 11, 35, 51, 87
arms control 408
   see also SALT
arms race 318-19, 326, 337
   see also security dilemma
Aron, Raymond 375
Ashley, Richard 418, 475, 477
Atlantic Charter 285-90 *passim*,
   see also UN
Atlantic rim 103
atomic bomb 279, 295, 314
   see also deterrence; nuclear weapons

Augustine 27, 82, 93
Ayatollah Khomeini 397-8
Axelrod, Robert 409, 416, 418

Bacon, Francis 79, 95, 106, 118-19, 123
balance of power 2, 59-60, 118, 124, 129, 143, 161-4
   Bismarck and 197
   as distinct from hegemony 331-2
   Guicciardini and 59
   Hume and 135
   Machiavelli and 66n8
   Morgenthau and 304, 325
   Robertson and 3, 157
   Rousseau and 151-2
   see also containment; counterbalance; Waltz
balance of terror 329
   see also MAD
balance of trade 106, 134-5
bandwagon 488
Baran, Paul 343, 364
Baudrillard, Jean 465-6, 474-5
behaviourism 355, 358
Bentham, Jeremy 12n3, 122, 174-6, 191, 258
Berlin blockade 317
von Bernhardi, Friedrich 224-5
'Big Three', the 280, 286, 289 (Tehran), 291, 293 (Yalta), 294 (Potsdam)
bin Laden, Osama 399, 457, 461

bipolar rivalry *see* Cold War; polarity
von Bismarck, Otto 197, 200n11, 209, 232
Bodin, Jean 3, 7, 86–92 *passim*, 105
Bossuet, Jacques-Bénigne 106, 119
Botero, Giovanni 80, 83
Boulding, Kenneth 330, 346–7
Bowman, Isaiah 259
Bramhall, John 121, 483–4
Bretton Woods system, the 291–2, 370, 389
    see also GATT; IMF; World Bank
Brezhnev, Leonid 360, 365–8 *passim*, 422n16
British Committee on the Theory of International Politics, the 347, 352, 358, 388
    see also English School
Brodie, Bernard 262, 329, 344
Brundtland, Gro H. 412
Bryce, James 160, 250
Bukharin, Nikolai 262
Bull, Hedley 351, 358, 387–8, 419, 485
Burke, Edmund 144–5, 158–9, 181–4, 191, 415
Bush, George W. (Jr) 457, 469
    see also war on terror
Bush, George H. W. (Sr.) 430–5 *passim*, 448
    see also Gulf War; zone of peace
Butterfield, Herbert 334n16, 347–8
Buzan, Barry 409–11, 418–19
Byzantium 17, 21–2

caliph/Caliphate 22, 41n6–7, 461
Calvin, Jean 75, 93, 160
Campanella, Tomasso 79–80, 95n1
Capella, Martianus 27–8, 43n13, 50
Carnegie Endowment 230, 269
Carr, Edward H. 242, 269–71, 308, 323
    and the 'founding myth of IR' 271
Carter, James ('Jimmy') 370–1
Castro, Fidel 341, 359–60, 368
Chamberlain, Neville 283–4, 308
Charlemagne 17, 25
chartered companies 101–3

checks and balances 144, 160
China 278, 368, 459–60
Christianity/Church 441
    early 31–2, 38, 471
    Idealism and 255, 351
    Realism and 309, 363n5
    shaken by printing 74–5
    used by princes 54, 77–8, 105–6, 457
Churchill, Winston S. 284–90 *passim*,
    'iron curtain speech' 298, 307
    'percentage deal' 289–90
    Realism and 257, 260–1
    see also 'Big Three'
CIS (Commonwealth of Independent States) 453n3, 458
class struggle 179, 296, 315
von Clausewitz, Carl P. G. 185–8, 195, 329
Clemenceau, Georges 248, 256–7, 259
climate 138, 412–14 *passim*
Clinton, William ('Bill') J. 436, 437, 448
CMEA (Council for Mutual Economic Assistance) *see* Comecon
Cobden, Richard 191, 232
Cold War 42n10, 313–427 *passim*
    defined 313–19
    'thaw' 339
collective security 134, 256, 269, 291
    Vattel and 134
    Wilson and 256–7
    see also Gulf War; Korean War
colonialism 72, 100
    active policy of 80–1, 100–3
    liberal critique if 175
    radical critique of 150, 179–80
    see also chartered companies; imperialism
Comecon 314, 330
Cominform 315, 322, 331, 339
Comintern 286
communism 262, 268, 461
    Stalin and 295, 315, 321
    see also Lenin
conservatism
    Burke and 181–5
    Clausewitz and 185–8

defined 181-8
fascism and 263-4, 268
neo-conservatism 414, 420n6
see also neo-liberalism
constructivism 484, 486
containment 298, 316-18, 342, 366
replaced by roll-back 399, 406
contract 91, 141
see also social contract
corruption 77, 147, 153, 177, 189
counterpoise 161, 168n14, 298
covenant 89, 91, 248
see also contract; treaty
Cox, Robert W. 408, 415-16, 418, 446, 449
CPSU (Communist Party of the Soviet Union) 331, 406, 458
Crimean War 216
critical theory 449, 476, 357
see also Adorno
Crucé, Émeric 7, 108-9, 119
crusades 32-4, 47
CSCE (Conference on Security and Co-operation in Europe) 367
Cuban Missile Crisis 359-61, 365
Cumberland, Richard 119, 121-2, 157
Curtis, Lionel 253
cyber/cyber security 473-4

dar al-Harb 23
dar al-Islam 23
Darwin, Charles 8, 191, 217-27 *passim*
see also social Darwinism
Declaration of Independence 159-60
decolonization 334, 359, 364, 374, 380
Defoe, Daniel 134-5
democracy 138, 197, 448
and peace 138-9, 175, 435, 440, 437-42
Neorealism and 441-2
promotion of 247-8
see also Neo-idealism; zone of peace
Deng Xiaoping 421n9, 460
dependency theory 380-5 *passim*
centre/core and periphery 382, 284
metropole and satellite 343-4, 379
see also imperialism; Revolutionism

détente 366-8
deterrence 344-5
Deutsch, Karl W. 349, 375, 390, 435
dialectics 179, 226, 270
Divine Right of Kings 106, 132
Doyle, Michael 437, 454n9
Dubois, Pierre 38, 44n19

Earle, Edward M. 261, 305-6
East Bloc 315, 321-2, 330, 396, 408
debt 404-6, 421n13
Eastern Europe 17, 101, 268, 277n7, 295, 432, 458
'Ecologism' 422n20
empire 332, 455n13
collapse during World War I 249, 251, 267, 272n7, 278
defined 275n27, 332
Engels, Friedrich 178, 191
England/Great Britain 93-103 *passim*
colonial power 103, 129, 158, 215, 273n13, 320
constitutional monarchy 130-1
evolution of modern state 98-9, 237n1
as Great Power 101
see also Industrial Revolution
English School 167n11, 347, 385, 409, 418, 485-6
equilibrium *see* balance of power
Erasmus, Desiderius 77-8, 148
European integration 298, 375
Churchill's proposal of 298, 337
Council of Europe 337
ECSC (European Coal and Steel Community) 318, 338, 349, 362n1
functional theory 376
Monnet and 338
evolution 148, 163-5, 177, 182, 220-7 *passim*

fascism 262-7 *passim*
assumptions of 262-3
rise of 257, 268
unwanted/outlawed 305
federation 143, 338
of Europe 154

feminism 391, 478
Ferguson, Niall 448
feudalism 18–21, 72, 409
Fichte, Johann Gottlieb 195, 207
Filmer, Robert 105–6, 119, 132
fortuna 54, 64
Foucault, Michel 475–7 *passim*
founding myth of IR 271
Fox, William T.R. 262, 306, 352
France
    absolute monarchy 106, 118–19, 130
    colonial power 103, 273n13, 320, 366
    evolution of modern state 53, 98–100
    as Great Power 101, 118
Franco-Prussian War (1871) 171, 230–1
Frederick II ('the Great') of Prussia 139–
    40, 351
free trade 213, 235
free-market fundamentalism 400,
    423n21, 486
free-market model 417, 463, 492n18
Fukuyama, Francis 437, 440–1, 468,
    479

game theory 329–30, 346, 354–5, 360–1,
    374,
GATT (General Agreement on Tariffs
    and Trade) 292–3, 378, 400
Gentili, Alberico 83–5
Gentz, Friedrich 184–5, 191
geography 137, 151, 183, 488
geopolitics 264, 316–8
Germany/Prussia 139–40
    divided 317
    as empire 152, 266
    fragmented 101
    as Great Power 171, 216
    invasions by 243, 282–4
    romantic politics in 206, 225–6
    unified 197, 200n11, 429–30
Giddens, Anthony 464, 479
Gilpin, Robert 410, 416
glasnost 406, 462
globalization 446–7, 451, 464–5, 488
God 28, 46, 61–2, 120, 159
Godwin, William 135–6, 138, 178, 454n9

Gorbachev, Mikhail 406–7, 428–33
    passim, 453n2
Gramsci, Antonio 267, 331, 415, 484, 486
Great Britain *see* England
'great debates' 270
    first 270–1, 481
    second 355, 357–8
    third? 382, 394n11
    fourth? 423n23, 481
Great Depression 280
Great Power 232, 234–5, 386, 417
Grotius, Hugo 7, 111–13, 126n6
Guicciardini, Francesco 45, 56–60 *passim*,
    91, 125, 487
    History of Italy 58
    Ricordi 57, 61–4
Gulf War (1991) 433, 474
Gunder Frank, André 380

Haas, Ernst B. 375
Haeckel, Ernst 225–7
Hague Peace Conference (1899) 239n12
Hamilton, Alexander 143–4, 200n10
Haushofer, Karl 264
Hegel, Georg Wilhelm Friedrich 8, 179,
    188–91 *passim*
    dialectics 188
    Phenomenology of Spirit 189, 191
    Philosophy of Right 189, 191
    and Spirit, *Volk, Geist* 189–90
hegemony 264, 267, 331, 415, 485
    defined 264–5, 332
    US hegemony 368, 442–6, 448–9
Herder, Johann G. 195, 206, 209, 227
Herz, John 324
Hilferding, Rudolf 262
Hiroshima 279, 295
Hitler, Adolf 9
    and Jews 281, 286, 310n7
    political ideas of 264–7 *passim*, 295–6
    war aims of 286, 295
Hitler-Stalin Pact *see* Molotov-Ribben-
    trop Pact
Hobbes, Thomas 3, 7, 91, 107, 113–18
    passim, 127, 146, 351, 482
    compared to Locke 165n1

Leviathan 114–18,
    pacta sunt servanda 118
    state of nature 115–17
    see also Spinoza; Thucydides
Hobson, John 478
Hobson, John A. 262, 442
Holocaust 286, 310n7
Holy Roman Empire 26, 45, 99–104 *passim*, 152, 199n4,
human nature
    fixed 324–5, 385
    malleable 353, 390–1
    optimistic view of 147, 256
    pessimistic view of 114–16, 256, 265, 302–4
human reason 140, 148, 176
    liberalism and 174
    radicalism and 177–8
human rights 255, 299–300, 451, 460
    see also Paine; Rousseau; UN Charter
humanists 50
Hume, David 15, 135, 156, 163–5, 394n10, 484–5, 492n18
Huntington, Samuel P. 376, 434, 441, 457, 468, 479
    Clash of Civilizations 450, 468, 471
    democracy and peace 434, 441
    discusses institutions 376
Hussein, Saddam 397–8, 433, 469–70

Idealism 258, 300–1
    defined (by Mackinder) 260
    see also liberal institutionalism; neo-idealism; Utopianism
imagined communities 238n2
    see also class, nation, Romanticism
IMF (International Monetary Fund, the) 292–3, 305, 404, 463
imperialism 213–16, 341, 379, 382, 448, 455n134, 477
    see also dependency theory
industrial revolution 169–72 *passim*, 215, 411
industrialism 210–13, 235
'Inquiry, the' 250, 253, 259, 273n10
institutions 376–8, 418

interdependence 3, 149, 152, 194, 217–20, 231, 235, 375, 389, 409, 446–7
    Lorimer and 218–20
    see also globalization
'interest' 55, 125, 153, 324–5
international law 90, 176, 183
    see also UN Charter
international society 388, 418, 479, 485
international system 234, 330, 384–92 *passim*
internationalism 217
'invisible hand' 158, 175
IPE (international political economy) 380, 410
'iron curtain' 298, 333n3
ISC (International Studies Conference) 254, 271
ISIL (Islamic State of Iraq and the Levant) 470
Islam 22–5, 268, 433, 490n6
Italian Wars 53–5 *passim*, 161, 487
Italy 47–52 *passim*
    unified 209

Japan 278–9, 319
    invasions by 280
jihad 23, 244, 457, 469
just war 29, 32, 36, 78, 82, 133

Kant, Immanuel 140, 161, 163–5, 166n6, 379
Kaplan, Morton 330, 347
Kennan, George F. 297, 307, 309, 323, 326–7, 449–50,
    see also containment
    'long telegram' 297, 307, 323
Kennedy, John F. 340–1, 364, 392n1
Keohane, Robert O. 378, 389, 409–10, 418
Keynes, John M. 2, 256, 488
Khrushchev, Nikita 336, 339–42 *passim*, 364
    Mao and 340–1
    wars of liberation and 342
Kindleberger, Charles P. 377
Kissinger, Henry A. 368, 373, 393n4, 488

Knutsen, Torbjørn 480, 481
Kohl, Helmut 429-30
Korean War 317, 320, 330, 339
Krasner, Stephen 378, 409
Kratochwil, Friedrich 408, 485

language and politics 237, 483
de Las Casas, Bartolomeo 81
law/laws 30
    canon 31-2, 37
    civil 86-90 *passim*, 110-11
    constitutional 88
    customary 30-1, 37, 43n15
    diplomatic 169
    reason and 110
    see also international law; natural law
League of Nations 249-60 *passim*,
    origins of 109, 249-52
    reasons for failure 287-8
Lebensraum 233, 264, 282, 295
    Hitler and 239n10, 282-3, 295, 353
    Ratzel and 227
    Schmitt and 266
Leibniz, Gottfried Wilhelm 103-5, 119,
    127n9
Lenin, Vladimir I. 9, 246-7, 262, 341
Leroy-Beaulieu, Paul 191, 231
levels of analysis 352-3, 479
liberal institutionalism 249-50, 291-2, 377
liberal internationalism 256, 269, 299
    after World War I 250, 252-3, 269
    after World War II 299-301, 305-6, 486
Liberalism 174-7
    see also neo-liberalism
Lippmann, Walter 259, 306-8
Lipsius, Justus 79-80
List, Friedrich 191, 195-6, 240n16
Locke, John 8, 131-3, 156, 161
    see also Vattel; Wilson
Lorimer, James 2, 191, 235, 347
LSE (London School of Economics)
    230, 348
Luther, Martin 75, 93
Lyotard, François 464-5, 466, 475

Machiavelli, Niccolò 12n2, 53-6, 61-4,

66n8, 79, 125, 232, 309, 487
Mackinder, Halford J. 191, 234, 259, 287,
    306, 323, 390, 485
McNamara Robert 344-5
MAD (mutual assured destruction) 330,
    344
Madison, James 143-4, 442
Mahan, Alfred T. 191
Malthus, Thomas R. 95n2, 377
Mandela, Nelson 463
Manning, Charles A.W. 348, 352
Mao Zedong 267, 276n31, 317-19 *passim*,
    341-2, 393n3
market *see* free-market fundamentalism;
    free trade
Marshall Plan, the 313, 316, 330, 337-8
Marx, Karl H. 178, 191, 240n16, 379,
    482
marxism 415, 486
Marxism-Leninism *see* communism
Mearsheimer, John 441
media 400
    see also PC; printing; propaganda
de' Medici, Lorenzo 53, 58-9, 68
mercantilism 105-7, 130
Metternich, Clément 170, 184-5, 199n7
Middle East 212, 268, 272n7, 340, 370-1,
    397, 402-3, 460-1
migration 16-18, 21, 464-6, 489
Mill, John Stuart 179, 194, 217
'mirror of Princes' 23, 42n9, 54
Mitrany, David 301, 349, 375
Molotov-Ribbentrop Pact, the 283-4, 310
Monnet, Jean 251-2, 338
Monroe Doctrine 245, 266, 276n18
Montesquieu, (Charles Louis de
    Secondat, baron de la Brède et)
    136-8, 454n9
Morgenthau, Hans J. 301-12 *passim*, 449
    critiques Carr 309
    critiques US foreign policy 308
    human nature and 324-5
    Niebuhr and 302, 449
    Politics among Nations 303-5, 324-5
    six principles of Realism 324-5
    Waltz' criticism of 353

mujahideen 399, 407, 438
Mun, Thomas 107, 119
'Munich' 283, 293, 397-8, 307-8, 310n4
Muslim Brotherhood 268, 398

Napoleon Bonaparte 170, 199n4
Napoleonic Wars 171, 487
nation
  as 'imagined community' 238n2
  contractual view of (*Patrie*) 206
  organic view of (*Volk*) 206-8, 226
national socialism, *see* Nazism
nationalism 187, 204-10
NATO (North Atlantic Treaty Organiza-
    tion) 330, 337, 431
  expansion (after Cold War) 436-7, 450
  formation 316-17, 333n6
natural law/law of nature 85, 112-13,
    116, 165n1, 255, 235, 351, 483
  defined 120, 127n7
  revived after World War II 299
natural right 85
  Hobbes and 116-17
  Locke and 132
nature 46, 62, 131
Nazism 280, 295
  see also Hitler; NSDAP
neo-conservatism *see* neo-liberalism;
    Reagan; Thatcher
Neo-idealism 10, 450, 463-4
neo-liberalism 402, 414-15, 463
neo-neo synthesis 418
Neorealism 408, 411, 417
  Cox coins term 418
  see also Waltz
Netherlands/United Provinces 89, 94,
    98, 100-1
von Neumann, John 262, 329-30, 344,
    354, 374
New Left Review 379
Newton, Isaac 8, 131, 156
Niebuhr, Reinhold 290, 309, 323, 449
Nietzsche, Friedrich 236-7, 475-6
9-11 *see* terrorism
Nitze, Paul 327
Nixon, Richard M. 367, 373, 389, 397

Nobel, Alfred 230
norms and rules 378, 392, 418, 484
  see also institutions
North, Douglass C. 377, 418
north Atlantic rim 18, 37, 39, 99-103,
    174, 188, 197
  commerce/trade 49-50, 71
  humanism 50
  liberal culture 192-3
  public sphere 50
  state formation 99-103
Novicow, Jacques 191, 231
NSC-68 327
NSDAP (*Nationalsozialistische Deutsche
    Arbeiterpartei*) 266, 280-1
nuclear weapons 279, 295, 314
  ballistic missiles 328-9
  MIRV'ed 371
  see also deterrence
Nuremberg Trials 299
Nye, Joseph S. Jr. 389, 409, 446

oil 212, 295, 389
oil crisis 370, 372, 397-8, 400, 402
OPEC (Organization for Petroleum Ex-
    porting Countries) 370
orientalism 477-8
Ostpolitik 367

pacta sunt servanda 91
Paine, Thomas 135-9 *passim*, 141-2
Paris Peace Conference (1919), the 252-8
    passim, 280, 288
passion 154, 182
PC (personal computer) 400, 444, 472-3
peace
  Benthan and 175
  of God 31
  Kant and 141, 161
  movements/groups 299-30, 235, 389
peace research 346-7, 441
perestroika 406, 462
perpetual peace 250, 441-2, 487
  Bentham and 175-6
  Kant and 141, 154
  Rousseau and 146-7

Saint-Pierre and 153-5
see also League of Nations
petroleum *see* oil
'Philadelphian system' 168n13
polarity 330, 417, 442
bipolarity 313, 330, 332, 366
multipolarity 423n24
unipolarity 442-52 *passim*, 456, 488
polemology 346
Popper, Karl R. 356-7
popular sovereignty 129, 170
positivism 357-8
see also behaviourism
post-colonial studies 478, 480
post-structuralism 475-81 *passim*, 492n14
power 325
Hobbes and 117-18
knowledge and 147-9, 474-5, 477
language and 237, 483
Morgenthau and 302
soft 446
Strange and 410
see also Foucault; great power; prestige; superpower
Prebish, Raul 343, 379
prestige 367, 452
printing 71, 74, 155, 205, 228
propaganda 149-50, 171, 198, 267, 413
property 115-16, 182-3
liberal understanding 159, 174
radical understanding 149, 177
public sphere 37, 50, 60, 156, 322, 330
publicists 135, 155-6
Putin, Vladimir 490n3

racism 266-7
radicalism
defined 177-81
see also communism; Marx; Rousseau; socialism
raison d'etat see reason of state
von Ranke, Leopold 232, 386
rational actor/choice 345, 365, 371, 416
Rationalism 343, 350-2, 381-2
see also Idealism; liberal internationalism

Ratzel, Friedrich 191, 227, 233
Reagan, Ronald W. 395-408 *passim*, 438, 490n3
doctrine 438
Realism
after World War II 299, 305, 322, 349, 380-2
assumptions 308
classic 308, 324-7, 484, 486
complementing Idealism 260
Machiavelli and 232, 351-2
Mackinder and 259-60
Morgenthau and 309, 324
neoclassical 485
Niebuhr and 261
security studies and 343
vs. Idealism 259-61, 269-70, 323
see also Neorealism; *Realpolitik*
Realpolitik 233-5, 257
reason 36, 63-4, 93, 110, 129, 163, 237, 255, 483
see also human reason; natural law
reason of state 49, 58-9, 65, 93, 122
regimes/regime theory 378
Reinsch, Paul S. 191, 236
religion 21-38 *passim*, 92, 159-61, 490n6
American politics and 159-60, 255, 275n22
law and 30-2
see also Calvin; Christianity/Church; Islam; Luther; Niebuhr; Protestantism; Puritan; Reformation; sin
religious war 92
see also jihad
'republic of letters' 12n1
'Responsibility to Protect' (R2P) 454n8
revolution
in America 142, 159-60
in England 130-1, 170
in France 170-1
in Russia 246-7, 431-2
see also decolonization; Khrushchev; Lenin; Mao
Revolutionism 351-5 *passim*, 381-2, 415
Richardson, Lewis 330, 346-7
rights 129, 141-2, 159

Locke and 132
Paine and 141-2
Rousseau and 145
see also Declaration of Independence;
human rights
Robertson, William 3, 157, 161-2
Rockefeller Foundation 240n14, 255, 269,
362n5
de Rohan, Henri (II) duc 122, 124-5
Romanticism 206-7
Rome 16, 343, 443, 448
sack of 16-17, 28-9
Roosevelt, Franklin D. 285-94 *passim*, 402
war-time diplomacy 288-9
see also 'Big Three'
Rousseau, Jean-Jacques 8, 145-55 *passim*,
163-5, 167n10, 179, 351-4 *passim*,
391-2, 482
alienation 153-4, 177
balance of power 151-2
Discourse on the Arts and Sciences 145
Discourse on Inequality 146-8
division of labour 148
Judgement of Perpetual Peace 147
origins of states 148-9
Project for a Perpetual Peace 147-8,
151
radicalism and 177, 378-8
Saint-Pierre and 146-55 *passim*
Social Contract 146-56
state of nature 148-9
Waltz and 391-2
Russett, Bruce 440, 442, 479
Russia/USSR 101, 212
as empire 316, 332, 340
as Great Power 98, 286-90 *passim*, 295
revolution in 246-7
as superpower 306, 371-2
unravelling 428-32, 334
see also CPSU; Gorbachev; Lenin;
Stalin; Yeltsin; Zhdanov

de Saint-Pierre, Abbé 146, 153, 155
SALT (Strategic Arms Limitation Talks)
367, 369
Schelling, Thomas 330, 347, 374

Schmitt, Carl 264-6, 309
scientific revolution 122-3, 155
security 163, 411-13, 473
security community 349
security dilemma 326, 334n16, 365
security studies 262, 344
Seebohm, Frederic 191, 235
Seeley, John 232
self-interest 55, 122
see also reason of state
al-Shaybani 24, 42n11
sin 28-9, 36, 46, 392
Singer, J. David 358
Smith, Adam 135, 156, 158, 447, 484,
492n18
Smuts, Jan 250
social contract 112, 141, 255, 487
Hume's criticism 163
see also federation; Hobbes; Locke
social Darwinism 224-33 *passim*, 239n10
Sombart, Werner 262
sovereignty 5, 87, 103-4
Bodin and 5, 6, 117, 129
Hobbes and 117
Leibniz and 103-4
Soviet Union *see* Russia
Spain 80-3 *passim*
Spencer, Herbert 194, 221-2, 231, 239n9
Spinoza, Benedict 3, 7, 107, 110-11, 119,
484
conatus 110
Sprout, Harold and Margaret 262, 412
Spykman, Nicholas 290, 306
Sputnik 318-19
stage theories 164, 177, 190, 196
Stalin, Josef 267-337 *passim*, 341
election speech (1945) 296, 307
foreign policy goals 295-6, 316
see also 'Big Three'; communism;
Zhdanov
Ständestaat 43n16, 73, 88
state 44n20, 65, 73, 125, 128, 183, 186
as organism 227-8, 233
see also city state; nation; territorial
state
state of nature 107, 110, 115-16, 487

Bentham and 176
Hobbes and 115-18, 132
Locke and 132-3
Rousseau and 148-51
Spinoza and 110
see also anarchy; social contract
state system 39, 71, 161-2
Strange, Susan 410-11
strategic studies 337
structure/structuralism 390-2 *passim*,
    418
see also post-structuralism; system
struggle 221-30 *passim*
    in fascism 227, 265
    in Marxism 179, 222, 296, 321
Suez 339-40, 359
de Sully, Maximilien de Béthune, duc
    154
Sumner, William 191, 223
'superpower' 306, 314
Sweezy, Paul 343, 364
system 162, 335n17, 386-7, 390-1, 417
    closed 234, 414
    organic 233-4, 413-14
systems approach/theory 325, 330, 346-
    7, 416, 481-6 *passim*

taxation 72, 100, 142
technology/innovation 400, 409, 411, 418
territorial state 42n12, 98-105 *passim*, 134
territoriality 6, 24, 99,
terrorism 216, 393n6, 433
    international 372, 399, 461, 468, 470
    9-11 attack 456-7
Thatcher, Margaret 395-6, 408, 429-30,
    440
theory 322, 356
    defined 3-4
    wheel of IR 486
Third World 321, 334n12, 342-3, 364-70
    passim, 403
Thirty Years' War 97, 487
Thompson, William R. 416
Thucydides 15, 51, 56, 114, 143, 187
de Tocqueville, Alexis 159
tradition 15, 181-2

analytic 15, 487
historical 15-16
treaty/treaties 89
Treaty of Augsburg (1555) 78
Treaty of Utrecht (1715) 135
Treaty of Versailles (1919) 280
    see also Paris Peace Conference
Treaty of (the Congress of) Vienna (1815)
    193, 208
Treaty of Westphalia (1648) 78, 97-9,
    120-1, 125
    as foundation of international system
    152-3
von Treitschke, Heinrich 232-3
Triepel, Heinrich 264-5, 331
Trotsky, Leon 247
Truce of God 31
Truman, Harry S. 294, 315, 317
two-camp theory 23, 296, 315, 333n3

Umayyad dynasty 23
UN (United Nations)
    as a liberal organization 299
    origins of 285-6, 288-94 *passim*, 311n9
    see also collective security
UN Charter 299-300
unipolarity *see* polarity
USA
    founding 141-3
    as hegemon 331-2, 368
    as superpower 306, 371-2
    unipolar moment 447-8
    see also Cold War; federation
USSR *see* Russia
Utopianism 270, 309

de Vattel, Émeric 8, 133, 161, 168n13,
    484
Versailles Peace *see* Paris Peace Confer-
    ence
Vietnam War 320, 368-9, 454n10
virtù 54, 64
de Vitoria, Francisco 81-3, 91, 112
Volk 185, 189-90, 207, 266
Voltaire 138

Wallace, Henry A. 288, 300, 307, 323
Wallace, Wendell 306
Wallerstein, Immanuel 383-4, 415
Waltz, Kenneth N. 350, 385-7, 416-19
        passim, 442, 446, 479
    Man, State and War 352-5, 484
    Theory of International Politics 385-7,
        416-17, 481
war 186
    Augustine and 28-9
    von Bernhardi and 224
    von Clausewitz and 186, 208
    colonial 319-21, 349-50, 369
    communism and 263, 296,
    Dickinson 249-50
    Hegel and 189
    Hobbes and 115-17
    Hume and 163-4
    interstate 437-9
    just 29, 32, 36, 78, 133
    of liberation 342, 359, 365-7 *passim*,
        438, 467
    Locke and 133, 165
    Mao and 319
    revolutionary 341-3, 467,
    Rousseau and 147
    of secession 467
    societal 438
    against terror 457, 467-8
    see also individual wars
warfare 55, 65, 71-7 *passim*, 97, 171
wars of Louis XIV 128-9
Washington, George 142

Washington consensus 402-3
Weber, Max 227
Wendt, Alexander 481
West Bloc 322-3, 330
Western Europe 314
Wight, Martin 274n17, 348-52 *passim*,
        378, 388
will 63, 164, 187
    to power 236, 302
Wilson, Woodrow 9, 245-54 *passim*,
        454n9
    '14 points' 247-8
Wohlforth, William 488
Wolff, Christian 133
Woolf, Leonard 250
World Bank 292-3, 305, 404, 463
world-system theory 234, 486
World War I 243-50 *passim*
    costs 249
    end of 248, 310n1
    unfinished business of 280
World War II 279-91 *passim*
    end of 292, 294
    preparations for 280-3
Wright, Quincy 355

Yalta 291, 293-5, 308
Yeltsin, Boris 431-2, 453n2, 458
Yugoslavia 432

Zhdanov, Andrei 315, 321-2, 343
zone of peace 135-6, 435, 437, 442